U.S. presidents and foreign
policy : from 1789 to the present

FEB 1 1 2014

U.S. Presidents and Foreign Policy

U.S. Presidents and Foreign Policy

From 1789 to the Present

Carl C. Hodge
and
Cathal J. Nolan, Editors

ABC CLIO

Santa Barbara, California   Denver, Colorado   Oxford, England

Library of Congress Cataloging-in-Publication Data
U.S. presidents and foreign policy : from 1789 to the present / Carl C. Hodge and Cathal J. Nolan, editors.
    p. cm.
 Includes bibliographical references and index.
 ISBN-13: 978-1-85109-790-6 (hardcover : alk. paper)
 ISBN-13: 978-1-85109-795-1 (eBook)
 ISBN-10: 1-85109-790-2 (hardcover : alk. paper)
 ISBN-10: 1-85109-795-3 (eBook)
 1. Presidents—United States—History. 2. Presidents—United States—Biography. 3. United States—Foreign relations. 4. United States—Foreign relations—Case studies. I. Hodge, Carl Cavanagh. II. Nolan, Cathal J. III. Title: US presidents and foreign policy.

 E176.1.U16 2007
 973.09'9—dc22

                      2006030285

 11   10   09   08   07   10 9 8 7 6 5 4 3 2

 ISBN-13: 978-1-85109-790-6   (eBook) 978-1-85109-795-1
 ISBN-10: 1-85109-790-2   (eBook) 978-1-85109-790-6

Production Editor: Kristine Swift
Editorial Assistant: Alisha Martinez
Production Manager: Don Schmidt
Media Editor: Karen Koppel
Media Resources Manager: Caroline Price
File Manager: Paula Gerard

This book is also available on the World Wide Web as an eBook.
Visit http://www.abc-clio.com for details.

ABC-CLIO, Inc.
130 Cremona Drive, P.O. Box 1911
Santa Barbara, California 93116-1911

This book is printed on acid-free paper ∞

Manufactured in the United States of America

Contents

Introduction

This book is about the impact of the presidency on the relationship of the United States of America with the wider world. To claim that successes and failures of presidents account for trajectory of American foreign policy would be to overstate the case for presidential primacy. Many other factors in over two centuries of national development—many of them beyond the control of the United States and its political leadership—have exerted a profound influence on American foreign relations. It is equally misleading, however, to neglect the impact of presidential character and human agency in shaping national and international history. The Constitution of the United States of America declares that "executive power shall be vested in a President" and that the holder of this office "shall be the Commander in Chief of the Army and Navy of the United States, and of the Militia of the several states." It states further that, by and with the advice and consent of the Senate, the president shall have the authority to make treaties and appoint ambassadors. The Constitution is otherwise vague on how a president endowed with these powers should responsibly conduct American relations with other nations. The gap between the authority given to a president by virtue of the occupation of the office of the presidency and what a particular president actually accomplishes within his term is bridged by the grey stuff of politics.

It is appropriate, therefore, that in considering foreign policy we think of presidents as politicians. Furthermore, we must recognize that leadership in foreign policy is an inherently political undertaking. Among the politicians who have held presidential office, many have exerted decisive influence on American foreign relations while a select few have made world history. Presidential power over foreign affairs is exercised, in the words of Reinhold Niebuhr in his classic *Moral Man and Immoral Society*, in "that realm where conscience and power meet, where the ethical and coercive factors of human life interpenetrate and work out tentative and uneasy compromises." It involves the application of political authority in pursuit of national goals in the international arena. It balances a leader's interpretation of the "national interest"—itself a malleable concept that must be defined and redefined according to changes in relations between and among states as well as the domestic national mood—with a calculation about the cooperation or opposition of other states according to their own national interests. Inevitably, it demands a mixture of consent,

persuasion, intrigue, manipulation, strategy, and sometimes also force. Most foreign policy most of the time consists of diplomacy, the art of formal and informal negotiation that is the essential activity of all international affairs. But in a world endowed with severely limited institutions of international governance that are incapable of coercing high levels of cooperation among states, negotiation is frequently accompanied by the possibility of war.

The constraints and opportunities encountered by political leadership are determined above all by circumstance—the national and international conditions prevailing at the moment in history when a leader assumes office. This is true even in a dictatorship, but a democracy compels constant and often detailed attention to public sentiment on the part of officeholders who hold public authority by the consent of the governed. Among democracies, moreover, the presidential system of the United States is especially merciless on officeholders seeking reelection. Whereas parliamentary systems afford sitting prime ministers the authority to dissolve the legislature and set an election on a date advantageous to themselves, the requirement that in the United States a presidential election shall be held on the first Tuesday after the first Monday in November every four years deprives the incumbent of any such advantage. The separation of powers and the fact of the wholly separate election of Congress also imposes a democratic circumspection on the president that is foreign to prime ministers sustained by partisan loyalty and a disciplined parliamentary party they control with the usual inducements and threats of high office.

The political choices an American president makes are therefore more conditioned by the vagaries of circumstance than in other democratic systems. To these choices the presidential leadership applies personal qualities such as intellect, knowledge, experience, and moral courage. The best evidence of history is that there is no ideal mixture of personal qualities that equip some presidents to perform better than others even those more mundane exercises of executive power that are not subject to the slings and arrows of international affairs. Private virtue does not guarantee moral success in the global arena. The record reveals that the road to disaster in foreign policy is often charted by the honorable intentions of thoroughly decent leaders or paved by accumulated national experience too easily assumed to be wisdom. It is generally accepted by scholars that the political vocation raises unique moral questions and calls for personal qualities quite different from those celebrated in the private domain. Bluntly stated, private sinners have often made excellent, even heroic, national leaders. Democratic populations, however, have seldom understood or appreciated this fact.

Such is the weight of the executive office in a republic of the durability and success of the United States that presidents often look to precedence and tradition in making foreign policy. Since 1945 in particular, the responsibility for wielding the unparalleled diplomatic, economic, and military capacity of the United States has made the White House the loneliest of crowded residences. It is therefore scarcely surprising that presidents look for guidance from the experience of past presidents, even as they grapple with the legacy of their immediate predecessor. Presidents such as Washington, Jefferson, Jackson, Lincoln, and Wilson have bequeathed traditions to the foreign policy of the United States that resonate through American diplomacy to this day. Because the United States, unlike Rome, became *more*

democratic as it became more powerful, foreign policy traditions are as much the statements of national self-definition of a deeply democratic society as they are signposts for diplomacy. Presidents invoke tradition in order to articulate the spirit of their foreign policies and legitimate their goals through reference to the hallowed principles or cautionary tales of historic experience.

We are so accustomed to thinking of the United States as the subject of its own history that we easily forget that it was conceived as a creature of international relations and remained for some time an object of the rivalries of more powerful nations. Despite the extraordinary success of American foreign policy, the uncertainties of the international arena mean that the forty-third president shoulders foreign policy burdens every bit as daunting in a United States astride the world as they were when George Washington took the oath of office as the first president of a United States huddled on the eastern seaboard of North America.

Carl C. Hodge and Cathal J. Nolan

George Washington (1789–1797)

Early Life and Military Career

George Washington was born in Westmoreland County, Virginia, on February 22, 1732. His father, Augustine Washington, died when George was eleven and left seven children who were born both by his first wife, who died in 1729, and by George's mother, Mary Ball Washington. Although Augustine was not a member of the Virginia aristocracy by any means, he had made himself relatively prosperous, leaving behind an estate of some 10,000 acres. The bulk of this inheritance went to George's older brothers. The younger Washington spent his adolescence in comfortable, but not opulent circumstances, living with his widowed mother outside Fredericksburg, Virginia. He attended school, but never received the classical education with which many of his contemporaries were so formidably endowed. Even as he displayed mastery over men such as John Adams, Thomas Jefferson, or James Madison, Washington would always feel his lack of a more formal education to some extent. The modesty of both his fortune and his education left him with a driving ambition that manifested itself in a determination, at least in his early years, to become wealthy, and an aspiration throughout his life to achieve the highest standards of conduct, which would bring him approbation and fame from his generation and posterity.

Washington thus needed to make his own way in the world, though, of course, he was of a family and a class that gave him useful connections. He developed expertise at surveying and made his first trip to the very edge of European civilization west of the Blue Ridge Mountains in the employ of the great Fairfax family. In addition, upon the death of his elder half-brother Lawrence in 1752 (whose estate included Mount Vernon, which Washington would eventually inherit), Washington was granted a commission as an adjutant general in the Virginia militia, with the rank of major, despite his lack of prior military experience. It was in the latter capacity that he was exposed firsthand to the imperial rivalries over North America that would constitute the international environment of the American colonies, and later the United States, during his lifetime.

In the spring of 1754, Washington, now a lieutenant colonel, commanded a regiment on an expedition against French efforts to secure control of the entire area west of the Alleghenies. A skirmish near Fort Duquesne (present-day

George Washington was a military hero of the American Revolution and the first president. The advice of his farewell address against permanent alliances has often been quoted in defense of isolationist diplomacy. (Library of Congress)

Pittsburgh), in which the French commander was killed, was at least one of the first (and possibly *the* first) incidents of bloodshed in what became known to Americans as the French and Indian War and to Europeans as the Seven Years' War (1756–1763). Unfortunately for Washington, who by this time had been promoted to colonel, this victory was almost immediately followed by a signal defeat of the forces under his command at Fort Necessity, Pennsylvania, with the death of over 100 of his men, due in part to his poor choice of position. Although he escaped censure, when the House of Burgesses declined to support the necessary taxes and the Virginia Regiment was disbanded he faced a demotion in rank, and rather than accept such a setback, he resigned. He did at least take from the experience a recognition of the pivotal role of the Indian tribes in the international politics of these areas, as well as the absolute necessity of obtaining from political authorities the financial means necessary to wage war—if the fiscal resources were not forthcoming, a strategy of indirection and playing for time was called for rather than riskier combat.

Less than a year later, Washington obtained a second chance to pursue what he had become convinced was his chosen career—military service—when the government in London dispatched General Edward Braddock with a large force to capture Fort Duquesne and all the French forts on the Great Lakes, ending any possibility of linkage between French Canada and the Spanish (though formerly French) colony of Louisiana. Being assigned to the commander-in-chief's staff eased Washington's acceptance of the lower rank of captain. Disaster struck again when Braddock's assignment of transporting an immense baggage train long distances through trackless, rugged country filled with Indians allied with the French proved to be impossible, and the British force was cut to pieces in a disastrous engagement in the summer of 1755. With Braddock's death, Washington rallied the remaining troops for an orderly retreat, once again burnishing his reputation by his conduct in a thoroughly unsuccessful campaign. He was given command of the re-created Virginia Regiment and there gained experience in managing the problems of organizing and supplying a force that he hoped would combine the professionalism of the British regulars with the skills of guerrilla warfare dictated by American conditions. In this post, he attempted to master the deference to his British superior officers necessary to further his advancement. At the same time, Washington developed an increasing resentment of what he saw as the British officers' arrogant assumption of superiority over the Americans and their unwillingness to accept advice from those with personal experience in the country being fought over. A second attempt to conquer Fort Duquesne succeeded in 1758, with Washington serving on the staff of an even larger British force than Braddock had commanded, but the Virginian's disputes with his superiors left him with no pleasure from the campaign. Later that year, he resigned his commission to pursue a political career.

The Path to the Presidency

The year 1758 was pivotal, bringing both Washington's engagement to Martha Dandridge Custis and his election (on the second attempt) to the Virginia House of Burgesses. A widow who was seven years older than her second husband, the new Mrs. Washington was probably not a choice of passion—that role, historians speculate, may have been played by Sally Fairfax—but there is evidence that Washington was devoted to her for the rest of his life, and the immense wealth that she brought to their union made him, for the first time, a rich man. The two, along with the two children from Mrs. Washington's first marriage, made their home at Mount Vernon, which Washington inherited;

the couple never had children of their own. Washington entered the first rank of the Virginia hierarchy.

As a member of the Burgesses, Washington developed political convictions. His resentment of British military superciliousness toward colonial officers was reinforced by his suspicions that the London merchants to whom he consigned his tobacco crop were not dealing fairly with him. He was coming to believe that the imperial system for which he had fought offered no recognition to its colonial servants and that it in fact worked to their economic detriment. During the debates over the Stamp Act of 1765, he voiced the hope that this unpopular legislation would open the eyes of others to the need to reduce American economic dependence on the imperial center. He denied the legitimacy of the royal Proclamation of 1763 that closed the land west of the Appalachians to Anglo-American settlement in order to reserve it for the Indians. In 1769, while still hoping for a resolution of differences, and once the Imperial Parliament could be brought to see the error of its ways, he proposed a coordinated campaign of boycott against a list of British manufactured goods as a means of exerting pressure. In 1774, he served as one of Virginia's delegates to the First Continental Congress, where he supported a similar campaign of economic pressure among all the colonies. In 1775, while in Philadelphia as a delegate to the Second Continental Congress, he received news of fighting at Lexington and Concord and concluded that a military struggle had become unavoidable. As the most prominent military figure in all the colonies, and as a Virginian when it was vital to ensure Virginia's support for a contest that was being fought in New England, Washington was the obvious choice to be selected by the Congress as commander-in-chief of all American forces; he was appointed in June of 1775.

Washington's leadership during what eventually became an eight-year war left him with several lessons that he would apply during his presidency as he grappled with issues of foreign policy. One was that some degree of military power was necessary for diplomatic success and that, ultimately, only a professional military force, organized along European lines, even if it mastered New World tactics, could embody that military power. Another was the need for patience and a long view. Washington lost most of the battles he fought as American commander-in-chief, especially in the early stages of the war, because he was too impetuous in seeking combat with a superior foe. On the other hand, he was always respectful in his dealings with the Continental Congress, even when its actions frustrated him, and this attitude reflected a third lesson: the principle of civilian control, and the respect owed by all executives (whether army commanders or presidents) to the peoples' representatives elected to their legislative bodies. A final lesson concerned the need to place local actions in the broader international context. The destruction of British forces at Saratoga in the fall of 1777, by an American army under the command not of Washington, but of Horatio Gates, not only defeated a sensible British strategic aim of cutting off New England from the rest of the Americans, but also stimulated France into forming an alliance with the Americans, once it had become convinced that they had a realistic chance of prevailing. From initial disasters, like the attempt to conquer Quebec or the vain effort to hold New York City, to the eventual triumph of Yorktown, the revolutionary struggle was not a smooth upward trajectory of increasing successes, but American independence was acknowledged by the greatest imperial power then in existence.

And then Washington went home. Squelching a purported plan by some of his officers for a military coup that would replace Congress with a new royal regime headed by Washington himself, he resigned his command and returned to the life of a Virginia squire that he always insisted he preferred. In these years of retirement, during the 1780s, his belief, forged during the war, that effective government demanded the sinews of both economic and military power, was confirmed in his mind by the performance of the government of the United States under the Articles of Confederation, which he became convinced lacked both. When Shays's Rebellion in the fall of 1786 crystallized mounting doubts about the adequacy of the Articles and a Constitutional Convention was called for the following year, Washington allowed himself to be elected as a delegate from Virginia. He was unanimously chosen in Philadelphia to chair the convention, and legitimized it in popular opinion by his presence. He closely followed the state-by-state campaign for ratification of the new Constitution, though he took no public role in calling for its acceptance. When the new office of president of the United States had to be filled, he was selected—once again unanimously—to fill the seat. After a triumphant journey from Virginia to the new seat of government in New York City, and a delay of several weeks while enough members of Congress arrived to form a quorum to count the electoral votes, he took the oath of office on April 30, 1789.

The Legacy of the Articles

By many measures, government under the initial framework adopted by the Continental Congress in 1781 had performed well. The country had experienced a notable revival in prosperity since the days of privation during the Revolutionary War, and the strict limits on the power of the United States accorded well with the suspicions that most Americans held of excessive governmental authority, with its risks of corruption and the loss of individual liberty and local control. To the supporters of the new Constitution, including Washington himself, however, the Articles had proved wholly inadequate. In the very first of the series of pamphlets advocating adoption of the Constitution, later to

become known as the *Federalist Papers,* the anonymous author (who we now know was Alexander Hamilton) declared in the very first sentence that the country had just had "an unequivocal experience of the inefficiency of the subsisting federal government," and several of the most important papers that followed rested their criticism of the Articles on matters of foreign policy. In particular, the proponents of the Constitution argued that the Articles, which failed to grant to the federal government the power to raise its own funds through taxation or the ability to create its own military forces—both forms of power were, under the Articles, to be requested from the states, though little penalty attached if a state failed to supply the requested money or men—made the United States impotent in the eyes of other governments. Given an inherently threatening international environment, and in particular the continuing rivalry of Britain, France, Spain, and the Indian tribes in North America, remedying this lack through efficient government under the Constitution was thought by many, including Washington, to be the major task left to be completed. In particular, the failure on the part of the British government to carry out several of its commitments under the Treaty of Paris that had ended the War of Independence in 1783 was at least in part attributable to the American government's inability to bring either economic or military leverage to bear on London. Washington saw his task as one of disinterestedly organizing the new government, so that its efficient and dignified execution of the business of governing would earn it the popular support that would in the long run ensure its survival.

Foreign Policy: Organization Followed by Crisis

When Washington assumed the presidency, he had been running large organizations for decades. He never lost the taste for closely managing the several farms that together made up his plantation. Even during his eight years in office, he corresponded frequently and in detail with those he left in charge of Mount Vernon and traveled south regularly to see the state of his affairs for himself. His military career had put him in the position of commanding others rather than being commanded by them, and that was certainly his preference. He was familiar with the promise and pitfalls of delegation to subordinates, the conflicting information that results from the delegation of authority, advancement through indirection, and the power of symbolism. On the other hand, despite his role in the French and Indian War and his efforts at combined military operations with the French in the War for Independence, his purely diplomatic experience was far less than those around him, like Adams or Jefferson, who had served in ministerial posts abroad. He and the country were fortunate that comparatively calm waters of his first term gave him the chance (working with many others) to make progress in constructing the ship of state before the stormy international seas of his second term washed over it.

Organizing for Foreign Policy

Most U.S. presidents, including Washington, have complained about being besieged by enormous numbers of persons seeking appointment to a far smaller number of positions. Washington alone, however, entered office with literally no offices at his disposal, for all of them had to be created by statute once the First Congress entered into its business. For months, he and Vice President John Adams comprised the whole of the new executive branch, while legislation was being considered that would establish the "several departments" that the Constitution alluded to without being specific. In the meantime, Washington relied on holdovers from the days of the Articles, so that John Jay, who had been secretary for foreign affairs, and Henry Knox, who had been secretary of war, continued to perform their duties while the new regime was being set up.

In enacting these laws, Congress necessarily encountered issues of policy that went far beyond the existence of an office for the conduct of foreign relations. Could the legislative branch require reports from the heads of these new agencies—that is, could it force them to deal directly with it, without going through the chief executive? Congress decided that its power extended this far under the Constitution and included provisions instructing the holders of the new offices to provide such information when legislators demanded it. Washington did not disagree, and one of the great state papers of the new government, Hamilton's Report on the Public Credit, was the response to such a request. A more divisive issue concerned the control of Congress over removals as well as appointments. A considerable body of opinion held that, while the Constitution was silent on the subject, the necessity of obtaining the advice and consent of the Senate for executive appointments implied that the concurrence of the Senate was likewise required for dismissals. In each of the bills creating an executive department enacted during the summer of 1789 (State, War, and Treasury), the matter was fought, always with the same result and always by the same narrow margin in both Houses. Had the constellation of institutional and political forces been different—had the Senate not contained more members favorable to executive power, while the House was disinclined to grant additional powers to the Senate—executive officials might have been as responsible to the Senate as to the president, and something more like a parliamentary system might have developed.

Once the offices had been set up, it was Washington's task to fill them, and, at least in the upper reaches of the government, few presidents can have had as deep array of talent from which to choose. His selections, all quickly confirmed, displayed some continuity with the days of the Articles and some desire to work with men in whom he had developed confidence in earlier settings. Retaining Henry Knox at the War Department, one of the most loyal officers on Washington's staff throughout the war, furthered both ends. To head the State Department, Washington made a change from Jay, who had angered Southern opinion during his tenure under the Articles. Jay, whose abilities Washington respected, became chief justice of the Supreme Court, to be replaced in the direction of foreign affairs by Jefferson, a fellow Virginian known by Washington for years, who was presently serving as American minister to France. For the Treasury Department, Washington also reached back to the days of the Revolution, selecting his former aide-de-camp (Colonel) Hamilton. Edmund Randolph became attorney general and Samuel Osgood postmaster general, but at the time the attorney general was considered more as a lawyer on retainer, and the postmaster general a high-level civil servant. Washington allowed his senior appointees to select their immediate subordinates; otherwise, in the posts he filled himself, he endeavored to advance his goal of firmly establishing the new government by choosing persons of known ability, retaining persons who had filled corresponding positions under the Articles, and avoiding persons known to have opposed the adoption of the Constitution.

Washington employed an eclectic style of management, sometimes asking all three members of his inner circle for written opinions on matters requiring decision, sometimes consulting them in individual conversations, sometimes directing one secretary to settle the matter on his own or to act as the sole source of advice to the president, sometimes seeking the counsel of Madison, who, although a member of the House, began Washington's presidency as an adviser and supporter who was as close to Washington as anyone in the executive office. One advisory system that was not employed was that of meeting his advisers collectively. The use of Jefferson, Hamilton, and Knox, supplemented by Randolph, as a "cabinet" in this way (and indeed the use of the term *cabinet* in such a sense at all) would await the tenser days of the second term, when the pace of events precluded the more leisurely forms of consultation and a more partisan domestic atmosphere suggested the political desirability of ensuring that all of Washington's increasingly quarrelsome lieutenants were committed to the same policy.

In relations between the executive and legislative branches, Washington deferred to the independence of Congress to such an extent that he left to his subordinates all advocacy of measures proposed by them, and he propounded the doctrine that the veto should be used only in cases of clear unconstitutionality of a bill, not because of policy disagreements with it.

Congress generally reciprocated by not challenging his executive powers. Nevertheless, the field of foreign policy offered at least one instance in which even such mutually respectful branches could be brought into confrontation. Within months of his inauguration, Washington appeared in the Senate chamber seeking the constitutionally pre-scribed "advice and consent" for the negotiating instruc-tions he proposed to issue to a commission intended to arrive at a treaty with the Creek Indians. The experiment was an unhappy one. Senators asked that sections of the proposed treaty be read several times, called for more infor-mation, and finally moved that the documents be referred to committee. Angered by the delay, Washington agreed to a postponement, but declared as he left that he would "be damned if he ever went there again!" He never did, nor has any subsequent president. The operative meaning of the phrase "advise and consent"—providing information to the Senate as it decided whether to ratify international agree-ments after they had been negotiated by executive agents—had been established.

In all such events, Washington was constantly conscious that he was setting precedents. If he moved cautiously in asserting presidential powers, it was because he wished to found a republican chief executive bound by the rule of law rather than a monarch. If he moved decisively in defending presidential powers (as it will be seen that he did in estab-lishing "executive privilege"), it was because he believed that an independent chief executive was compatible with, and indeed necessary to, both the rule of law and the freedom and prosperity of the country.

Indian Relations

In the late eighteenth century, a major concern for what would today be called homeland security was the threat from hostile Indian nations. As long as the Great Powers of Europe remained counterpoised against one another, each might check the others from threatening the weak United States. The Indians, by contrast, were hard by American borders—and indeed it was the very uncertainty of those borders that helped to create domestic insecurity. The Europeans were a danger to the new republic, in part due to their alliances with the Indians and their ability to use Indian hostility against the Americans.

In the early decades of its existence, the government of the United States had to confront the fact that it was unable to exercise control over some of its own territories. In the northwest sector of the large area between the Alleghenies and the Mississippi, there remained the unfinished business of the War for Independence, the string of British forts commanding a region that, under the terms of the Peace of Paris, Britain had recognized as American territory. Having mistakenly ceded assets that they belatedly wished to retain,

the British had gone from initial protestations of the need for more time to evacuate the forts, to a flat refusal to leave based on alleged American violations of the same treaty. With the forts in place, London could protect its local allies among the Indians and carry on a mutually profitable fur trade with them. From the point of view of the Indians, the British, with their desire only to purchase furs and no known wish to introduce European settlements, were a far more desirable partner than the Americans, with their thousands of settlers crossing the mountains and entering the region every year. Likewise, in the area of what is today Alabama and Mississippi in the Southwest, the Creeks and other tribes had a partner in Spain. In one sense, the secu-rity problem in the Southwest was more complicated than in the Northwest, because it rested not on one disputed treaty but on a tangle of treaties arrived at over two cen-turies among Britain, France, Spain, and the United States. Mutually contradictory and often unclear in their delin-eation of the geography that they purported to regulate, they supplied a fertile source of boundary disputes between the Americans and the Spanish for decades. In another sense, the problem of the Southwest was simpler than its northern counterpart because it offered a negotiating part-ner. Like Britain in the Northwest, Spain in the Southwest held the advantage over the United States because it had no population desiring to occupy these lands, but instead wished to trade with the Indian inhabitants. Whereas in the Northwest the Indians were divided into many tribes with no obvious recognized and legitimate leaders who could speak for the whole, in the Southwest, Washington faced the formidable figure of Alexander McGillivray, principle chief of the Creek Indians. This superior chieftain was often untrustworthy and was the constant recipient of bribes from the Spanish to keep him on their side, but he did offer the prospect of a deal that could be made to stick, if it could be arrived at. One of the obstacles to overcome in reaching an agreement was the seemingly unstoppable flow of set-tlers out of the existing American states into the territories; they recognized no right by their government to prevent them from dispossessing the Indians of lands recognized under treaty as belonging to the tribes.

Washington's policy all along the western frontier had certain common elements: efforts to stabilize the Indian populations within certain boundaries that would be guar-anteed to them, military coercion deployed against them to deter them from launching raids against white settle-ments—at least when it was believed that this could be done without risk of involving the Indians' European allies—and attempts to direct the westward movement of Americans into areas less likely to be contested by any number of Indian inhabitants. In the Northwest, this policy led to two sizable military interventions intended to defeat and over-awe multiple Indian foes. In 1790, under Brigadier General

Josiah Harmar, American forces experienced a considerable reverse, and in 1791, under General Arthur St. Clair, they suffered a far worse one that amounted to the complete disintegration of the entire expedition. Negotiations in the Southwest, on the other hand, fared better when McGillivray was persuaded to come to New York along with a number of other chiefs to negotiate several treaties, and then, with the help of a timely offer of a brigadier's commission in the American Army, with a suitable salary attached, to return to the Creeks to persuade them to honor the agreements. Uneasy conditions continued to characterize the frontier throughout Washington's administration, a state of affairs that he ultimately accepted as inevitable as long as a vigorous and numerous European population continued to be drawn to the rich tracts thinly peopled by tribes unwilling to abandon their ancestral customs for a settled agricultural existence.

The Nootka Sound Crisis

The final security concern arising on American frontiers was sparked by the two continental neighbors of the United States. Washington was never especially concerned by the power of Spain. He regarded Spain as a declining power that might even be useful to the United States as a titular but weak holder of sovereignty over the Southwest until the republic had grown strong enough, and the numbers of its citizens who settled in the territory had grown large enough, for the entire area to fall into the American lap. Britain was another matter. This formidable power, with its naval reach, its financial and commercial strength to which the American economy was still largely tied, its Indian allies, and its forts still solidly planted in American territory, was never far from the thoughts of Washington and his counselors. He dispatched Gouverneur Morris as minister to London to seek a compromise of differences, but the discussions seemed to lead nowhere until, in the spring of 1790, an unofficial emissary claiming to be an aide to the Governor of Quebec appeared in New York, suggesting that in the event of conflict between Britain and Spain the United States would find it advantageous to side with London. This communication brought into focus an existing worry that in such an armed conflict, the United States could not remain uninvolved because of its geography. The decay of royal authority within France, evident since the fall of the Bastille in 1789, suggested that in the event of a confrontation between London and Madrid, Paris would be too distracted to stand by its long-standing Bourbon ally. Britain seemed to think so; in the summer of 1790 it set up a fur-trading station in Nootka Sound (present-day Vancouver Island, on the Pacific Coast). Spain defiantly seized the British naval force, and war seemed an imminent possibility; in fact, rumors circulated in New York that war

had already been declared. Washington felt compelled to address the circumstance that worried him more than any other—a scenario in which Britain, preparing an invasion from Quebec to take the Spanish possessions in the Southwest, requested permission for its forces to cross American territory. Every conceivable combination of responses—acceptance, rejection, qualified acceptance, warning, and war—was canvassed by Washington and his advisers; all appeared to involve the danger of either humiliation or involuntary belligerency. No direct answer was given to the British representative, although it seems clear that if the Americans had been pressed, they would have accepted the risk of acquiescing in the passage of British forces rather than the risk of a military confrontation. On the other hand, Jefferson was to instruct the American envoy in Spain to intimate that, should Spain not grant the United States unrestricted navigation down the Mississippi, an Anglo-American alliance might invade the Southwest. To bow to the strong while threatening the weak was the course that Washington felt was necessitated by the precarious security situation in North America.

The European Crisis

As the Nootka Sound crisis subsided, Washington could have believed that he had accomplished much of what he had intended to do during what he hoped would be a single four-year presidential term. He had helped to set up the institutions of the new government. The Indian tribes of the Southwest were pacified to an extent, and he retained hopes of a settlement of differences with Britain that would end British support to the Indians of the Northwest. The economy was prospering and public opinion appeared to be solidifying its willingness to be governed under the new Constitution. Only the importuning of every adviser—arguing that rivalries and policy differences might still pull the United States apart if his unifying influence was removed—persuaded him to accept a second term, which the presidential electors of 1792 granted him unanimously. Ironically, the predictions of disharmony were to be almost immediately fulfilled, making the second term even far more domestically rancorous, internationally dangerous, and personally unpleasant than the first term had been.

The onset of the French Revolution in 1789 had coincided with the beginning of Washington's first term, but the gradual unfolding of its initial stages, during which changing fortunes in Paris continually raised hopes in New York that events had finally reached a point of equipoise, with a constitutional monarchy that would gratify both the friends of liberty and the supporters of order and good government in the United States. Washington could temporize on European politics and instead spend his attention on domestic questions and border security. With the arrival of the news that, just weeks before the president's second inauguration on March 4, 1793, Louis XVI had been guillotined and the Jacobin government in France had declared war on Britain, Russia, and Holland, Washington confronted a major security menace arising not to the West (from the Indians and the European powers ensconced on the North American continent) but to the East, over the Atlantic. So long as control of the North Atlantic had remained uncontested, the United States could regard with some detachment the collisions of the Europeans. When control of the North Atlantic was contested, in the series of wars that broke out between the revolutionary French regime and the series of coalitions that arrayed themselves against it, the United States found itself almost irresistibly drawn into those conflicts, with the danger that it would be crushed between the much larger powers fighting across, and now on, the Atlantic.

The Neutrality Proclamation

Once the existence of a state of war had been confirmed, the president and his four primary advisers (Hamilton, Jefferson, Knox, and Randolph) began consultations on American policy. Their immediate difficulty was the existence of two treaties with France, both dating from 1778, that might be thought to require intervention on the side of France in the current conflict: one, the Treaty of Alliance, committed the United States to aid the French in defending the French West Indies should France request such assistance; the other, the Commercial Treaty, stated that, in accordance with the law of nations at the time, French privateers might bring captured ships into American ports for trial and sale by a prize court established by French authorities, but that other states hostile to France might not fit out privateers on American territory. It was the opinion of Hamilton and Knox in particular that honoring these obligations would carry a mortal danger, in that by departing so far from a neutral stance as between the belligerent powers the United States would find itself at war with Britain as well. They therefore urged the president to state publicly that no such obligations existed, because the circumstances under which the 1778 treaties had been signed had changed enormously since 1778, making it dangerous for the United States now to fulfill obligations than had been undertaken then. Jefferson argued against repudiation of the treaties, contending that, since France had thus far requested nothing, it was premature to make such a decision. Specifically to deny aid would estrange America from a country that was its natural partner in promoting liberty, and might even lead to war between them. Both sides cited international law and considerations of prudence, though they differed on the direction in which the interest of the United States led it—toward London or toward Paris. Inclined to take no step

before it was demanded by events, Washington decided to issue a proclamation calling on all American citizens to act with impartiality between the two powers; in deference to Jefferson, the proclamation left it open to Congress to change the status of the country, and it avoided using the word "neutrality" altogether, as unnecessarily wounding to France.

Citizen Genêt

In deciding whether to issue a proclamation of neutrality, the cabinet felt pressure to act quickly, because its members were aware that a representative of the new French government was on his way across the Atlantic and might land in an American port at any time. During discussions on the proclamation, Washington had raised the collateral issue of the reception to be given the envoy, given the fact that to receive this servant of a revolutionary regime implied diplomatic recognition of it. Hamilton sought a conditional reception, demonstrating, again with reference to writers on international law, that treaties concluded with one government did not necessarily continue in force with its successor, particularly if the chances were high that the new authorities might in their turn be overthrown as well. If nothing too contrary was said at the time of receiving the representative, that very act could be taken as reaffirming the validity of the treaties, with all the consequences for antagonizing Britain that might follow. Jefferson again followed the course of taking one step at a time, denying that receiving a diplomatic envoy implied anything about the attitude to be taken on subsequent questions, such as the treaties; if adhering to the commitments included in them endangered the self-preservation of the United States, then he agreed that the treaties would have to yield. The president sided with his secretary of state; the French representative would be received without expressions of enthusiasm, but no other issues would be raised at the time of his reception.

Against the backdrop of the Terror in Paris, both Hamilton and Jefferson were playing a double game. In addition to the very real issues of the moral and legal obligations involved, and considerations of the external interests of the United States at stake, each man had in view the domestic political implications of his stance. Each tacitly worked on the assumption that, for the moment at any rate, the cause of France was broadly popular with American citizens, and that the freer the new French envoy, the more his presence would confirm that lack of neutrality in public feeling.

Both cabinet officers reckoned without considering the character of the French minister, Edmond Charles Genêt, who arrived in Charleston, South Carolina, on April 8, 1793. Genêt immediately began to demonstrate that he held a generous view of the authority exercised by the representative of a revolutionary regime stationed in a fellow republic. As he made a leisurely and triumphant tour northward from Charleston toward Philadelphia (where the American government had moved temporarily, pending its location in a new federal city, the location of which was yet to be determined), Genêt encouraged the enthusiastic greetings he received everywhere along his route, believing that such support would force the government into a policy supportive of France. On his arrival in Philadelphia, such mass demonstrations against a supposedly Anglophilic government policy continued, leading Hamilton and others to charge that the Constitution was being threatened by mob rule.

Genêt was equally uninhibited in his actions on the highly sensitive matter of captures and prizes. Despite the provision in the Commercial Treaty authorizing French privateers to bring their prizes into American ports, the Neutrality Proclamation had enjoined on all private American citizens the duty of being "friendly and impartial" toward all belligerents, and warned them that anyone "committing, aiding, or abetting hostilities" against any belligerent or carrying contraband to any belligerent would receive no protection from the government of the United States. The Americans were taken aback to learn that in Charleston and elsewhere, Genêt had authorized French prize courts to adjudicate the status of British ships captured by French privateer, that he had commissioned further privateers manned primarily by Americans, and that he was purchasing ammunition for shipment to France. Despite protests from Washington, he continued and extended these actions, adding that the proclamation was invalid because it contravened the treaties. When the Americans allowed the French to retain the vessel the *Little Sarah*, because it had been captured before the proclamation was issued, Genêt increased its arms and recruited American sailors to its crew—both violations of the proclamation, which had since gone into effect—and then sent it to sea in direct contravention of the order from the American government that it not sail. Washington was enraged by Genêt's statement to Jefferson that, should officials continue to obstruct cordial Franco-American relations, Genêt would appeal over the head of the president to the American people.

After an abortive attempt to sidestep the confrontation by asking the Supreme Court to state the acts that were permissible under the proclamation (the Court, in a precedent-setting move of its own, replied that giving advisory opinions to the executive would violate the separation of powers), the cabinet had to come to its own decision, despite its deep divisions. It did so by drawing up rules for interpreting the proclamation, as well as by agreeing that a record of Genêt's actions should be provided to the French government, along with a statement attributing those actions to Genêt personally (rather than holding his government responsible for them), and asking for his recall. Hamilton, who wished to

discredit the followers of Jefferson who had associated themselves with Genêt, who had done so much harm to his own cause, wished to publish the record in the United States, and eventually this was done. In general, Washington held to a more moderate course, wishing to do only what was absolutely required to uphold American sovereignty, while, to the extent possible, avoiding any action that would increase tensions between the two governments. (Finally, Genêt's government, which had moved in an even more radical direction, directed that he return home to be tried for crimes against the Revolution. In the face of this almost certain death sentence, Washington refused to extradite Genêt, who settled and remained in the United States for the rest of his life.)

The Jay Treaty

If the Neutrality Proclamation and the maneuvers over Genêt related primarily to the threats and opportunities presented by France and the need to take account of popular support for France within the United States, the Jay Treaty performed a similar function in relations with the other great power contesting for control of the North Atlantic. Britain held the key to American security in the Northwest through its retention of the Great Lakes forts. Whatever their political sympathies, most Americans demonstrated by their actions that they preferred to purchase British manufactures and trade with British merchants. Britain had a larger fleet than France and could, if it chose, do more damage to American shipping. Always arrogant, in the American view, British policy hardened on each front as the 1790s progressed and the scale of its war against Revolutionary France became evident. Rather than pleading for more time to evacuate the forts, as it had earlier, Britain frankly rebuffed American complaints with the uncompromising statement that it would not leave as long as the United States government failed to carry out its own promises in the treaty. Most prominently, the British held the federal government responsible for the failure to obtain compensation for Loyalists whose property had been seized during the War for Independence, even though the seizures had been conducted by the several states and the federal authorities could only recommend to the states that they provide compensation. To these long-standing grievances on both sides, the war added new tensions, primarily in the form of the British pursuit of economic war against France through: (1) stopping American vessels on the high seas to search them for contraband and applying a very broad definition of goods that could be seized, such as foodstuffs; (2) seizing vessels flying the flag of neutral countries if they were sailing to or from the French possessions in the West Indies; and (3) manning British ships through taking men off American vessels with the charge that those claiming to be American citizens were British deserters. In the face of all these provocations, the fact remained that the power difference between Britain and the United States was immense, so that simply attempting to harm London in retaliation courted the danger of provoking the economic strangulation of America, and, potentially, a ruinous war that would destroy the United States.

Accordingly, Washington accepted congressional proposals authorizing the creation of a navy and the threat of an economic embargo against Britain, but accompanied them with a mission sent to London to settle differences. The president selected as his minister plenipotentiary former secretary for foreign affairs John Jay, now chief justice, and allowed Hamilton to draft Jay's broad instructions. Jay arrived in Britain in June of 1794, to find that one of his objectives had already been accomplished through Britain's unilateral decision to allow American vessels to carry on direct trade between the French West Indies and the United States and, as long as they stopped in an American port along the voyage, between the French West Indies and France itself. Because the vessels of other states were not granted this privilege, American commerce received a boon. Here, however, British openhandedness ceased, and the treaty that Jay was able to negotiate by November of that year reflected the limitations on American bargaining power. The two countries agreed to refer to binding arbitration commissions three issues: pre-Revolutionary debts owed by Americans to British creditors, many of which had been voided by the American states; compensation to Americans for illegal British seizures of their property at sea; and the determination of the boundary between Canada and New England. If debts were ruled valid and state laws still stood in the way of their collection, the federal government would compensate the creditors. On the issue of British treatment of American shipping and seamen, Jay secured no concessions; the treaty reaffirmed the broad British definition of contraband that could be seized, and impressment of Americans was not prohibited. On the other hand, the British promised to evacuate the forts in the Northwest by June of 1796, and American vessels up to seventy tons were allowed to trade with the British West Indies, while American ships of any size might enter the British East Indies.

The text of the treaty arrived back in the United States at the beginning of March, 1795. Washington called the Senate into special session to consider it on June 8, and on June 24 the Senate ratified it with not a single vote to spare beyond the constitutionally required margin of two-thirds. Only then was the treaty made public, for the Senate had conducted its debate in executive session. Once it became known, it aroused a storm of protest among Jefferson's Democratic-Republicans, especially in the South. It was unpopular because it did nothing to compensate slave owners whose slaves had been freed by British forces during the War for Independence, and because many of the debtors whose obligations might be held valid by the debt commission were southerners. Petitions were signed in great numbers, mass protest meetings were held, and Jay was burned in effigy everywhere, but the activity failed to stop Washington from signing the treaty.

The Jay Treaty therefore became part of American law in the summer of 1795, but it had three sequels, all of which testified to the unsettled domestic and international climate in which it had been negotiated and ratified. Edmund Randolph, who had left the attorney generalship to take over the State Department when Jefferson retired at the beginning of 1795, was accused of seeking French bribes at a time when the very stability of the government had seemed to be at risk during the Whiskey Rebellion of 1793. Anger at this alleged betrayal may have helped to persuade Washington to sign the treaty at a time when its opponents were making progress in raising opposition to it. (Randolph was forced to resign.) In early 1796, the House had to consider bills appropriating funds to establish the arbitration commissions created by the treaty, and opponents of the treaty saw one final opportunity to defeat the treaty by indirection. As part of their effort to defeat the appropriation, they sought all confidential papers relevant to Jay's mission. Washington flatly refused the demand and, although the specific ground was the lack of any constitutional role for the House in deciding whether treaties were to become part of the supreme law of the land, the acquiescence of the House in Washington's assertion of secrecy set the precedent for what became known as *executive privilege*. Thus, the first two of the sequels took place in the United States. The third occurred in Spain, where Thomas Pinckney arrived in May of 1795, having been transferred to Madrid from London with Washington's hope that some sort of parallel settlement of differences with Spain might be arrived at. He came at a fortunate moment, when Spanish relations were tense with both Britain (which Madrid believed had betrayed Spain in the war of the First Coalition against France) and France (with which Spain was about to be forced to ally itself, given French military successes). In the Treaty of San Lorenzo (or "Pinckney's Treaty," as it was called in the United States), Spain endeavored to protect itself against American pressure on its possession of Florida, by granting the United States the privilege of navigating the Mississippi, and it gratified the Americans by including in the treaty a purely rhetorical endorsement of the liberal ideas on freedom of the seas that the British had just refused to grant in the Jay Treaty.

Legacy

By the time Washington left office in the spring of 1797, when he was succeeded by his vice president, John Adams, he was discouraged by the growth of partisanship in the United States, which had led, against his will, to his being identified as the head of a party rather than the nonpartisan leader of the country, and the vilification of his policies and his motives. He was doubly wounded because he believed that his two terms had largely succeeded in the foreign-policy aims that he had set. In his first four years, the institutions and practices for conducting foreign policy in a political system of separated institutions sharing powers had begun to take root, setting patterns for every succeeding president, Congress, and executive agency. In the more uncertain second term, when what amounted to a world war seemed bound to suck the United States into military conflicts that had the potential of jeopardizing its independence, he pursued a policy of modest goals that, with the help of skillful though quarrelsome subordinates, allowed the country to keep its differences with the major powers within bounds that preserved both independence and peace. By the end of his presidency, treaties with the European states bordering the United States both to the north and to the south, and a combination of military successes and informal political arrangements with the Indian tribes, gave hope of some degree of security for the American homeland.

Of course, this course of action had its limitations. It did not prevent the foreign policy of the country from being strongly affected by its domestic political struggles. Washington never knew of the full extent to which both of his primary advisers conspired with foreign powers behind his back—Jefferson with his conversations with the minister of France, and Hamilton with his conversations with the representatives of Britain—leaked confidential information and assured their interlocutors that part of what the United States was saying officially it did not actually mean. Nor did Washington finally solve any of the security problems that he sought to manage. Indeed, differences with France would lead to an undeclared naval war in the later 1790s, and those with Britain would result in an outright shooting war in 1812. Weak Spanish government and hostilities with Indians would continue to plague American security for another generation.

Both the accomplishments and the limitations of Washington's policies may be traced to the lessons he had learned in the harsh international politics of the western frontier as a young military officer—lessons that he applied to the conduct of the affairs of a weak state in the 1790s. He sought to gear his objectives to the power available to achieve them, and he was willing to accommodate himself when his country was the weaker party; he trusted to no paper agreement-granting rights that were greater than the power available to uphold them; and he believed that moderate and upright conduct in foreign affairs constituted a power resource by attaching people more firmly to their new system of government. These lessons, which he laid before his contemporaries and posterity in his Farewell Address, constitute his most lasting legacy.

David Clinton

Chronology

1776

July 4: Continental Congress votes 12–0 in favor of a Declaration of Independence of the American colonies from Great Britain.

September 24–26: Congress approves Model Treaty for relations with Europe and appoints Benjamin Franklin, Silas Deane, and Arthur Lee to negotiate treaties with European governments.

December 26: American forces defeat British troops at Trenton.

1777

April 17: Congress establishes Committee of Foreign Affairs.

October 17: American forces victorious at Saratoga.

November 15: Articles of Confederation adopted.

December17: France recognizes American independence.

1778

February 6: Franco-American Treaty of Alliance, ratified May 4.

September 17: British and French navies clash off Brest.

1779

June 21: Spain declares war on Britain, declines alliance with American rebels, but agrees to subsidize independence forces.

September 27: Congress appoints John Adams to negotiate terms of peace with Britain, independence not negotiable.

February 28: Russia declares "armed neutrality" and is later joined by the Netherlands, the Austrian Holy Roman Empire, Prussia, Portugal, and the Kingdom of the Two Sicilies.

May 12: British troops capture Charleston, South Carolina.

May 25: General George Washington's troops mutiny at Morristown, New Jersey.

July 11: Six thousand French troops arrive at Newport, Rhode Island.

1780

December 30: The Netherlands declares war on Britain.

1781

February 3: British forces capture Dutch colony of St. Eustatius.

March 1: Articles of Confederation adopted as first Constitution of the United States.

October 19: Washington defeats Cornwallis at Yorktown; Britain seeks peace.

October 20: Robert Livingston appointed first secretary for foreign affairs.

1782

February 27: British House of Commons votes to make peace with "former colonies."

April 12: Rockingham government begins negotiations.

October 8: The United States of America signs Treaty of Friendship and Commerce with the Netherlands.

November 30: Preliminary peace terms agreed to with Britain.

1783

January 20: Articles of Peace become effective, Congress approves on April 15.

September 3: Treaty of Paris signed by Britain, France, Spain, and the United States.

December 12: Washington resigns command of American armies to Congress.

December 26: Trade with Great Britain revived.

1784

April 23: Congress approves first Northwest Ordinance.

April 30: Congress requests power to regulate trade.

June 26: Spain closes Mississippi to American navigation.

August 30: France restricts U.S. trade in West Indies.

September 21: John Jay appointed secretary for foreign affairs.

1785

February 24: John Adams appointed minister to Great Britain.

March 10: Thomas Jefferson becomes minister to France.

April 8: Britain restricts U.S. trade with Canadian maritime provinces.

May 20: Congress passes second Northwest Ordinance.

July 20: Jay begins negotiations with Spain over Mississippi.

September 20: Commercial Treaty signed with Prussia.

December 8: Adams demands British evacuation of Northwest posts.

1786

July 17: Congress approves treaty with Barbary state of Morocco.

August 29: Jay agreement with Spain in Congress.

1787

February 4: Shays's Rebellion defeated.

May 25: Philadelphia Constitutional Convention convenes.

October 27: First Federalist Papers published.

1788

September 13: Constitution ratified by eleven states.

December 1: Spain grants limited navigation rights on Mississippi.

Washington Presidency

1789

March 4: Senate unanimous in choosing George Washington as first president of the United States; John Adams vice president.

April 30: Washington inaugurated; establishes cabinet with Departments of State, War, and Treasury.

May 5: French Estates General convenes at Versailles.

July 4: Congress passes protective tariff.

July 14: Bastille stormed in Paris.

July 27: Congress creates Department of State.

August 27: French Assembly issues Declaration of the Rights of Man.

1790

April 30: Britain threatens war with Spain over Nootka Sound incident, Spain yields.

1791

June 20–25: Louis XVI attempts to flee France, is apprehended, and forced to accept constitutional monarchy.

November 4: Ohio Indians defeat American forces with help of British arms.

1792

April 20: France declares war on Austria.

August 10: Revolutionary forces storm Tuileries Palace in Paris, King's powers suspended.

September 21: First French Republic proclaimed.

December 5: Washington reelected president.

1793

January 21: Louis XVI executed.

February 1: France declares war on Britain and Netherlands

April 1: Committee of Public Safety suspends French republic's constitution. Maximilien Robespierre institutes dictatorial Reign of Terror.

April 22: Washington declares American neutrality in European conflict.

August 1: The United States demands the recall of Edmund Genêt, French minister to America, for commissioning privateers to operate against Britain.

1794

April 20: American forces defeat Indians in Ohio territory.

November 19: Jay Treaty with Britain signed.

1795

June 24: Jay Treaty with Britain approved by Congress after heated debate.

October 27: Thomas Pinckney concludes Treaty of San Lorenzo resolving Mississippi dispute with Spain.

1796

June 30: United States stops sale of French prizes of war in American ports.

July 2: France announces it will treat American and British ships alike.

August 19: Spain joins French war against Britain.

September 19: Washington's Farewell Address.

November 15: France suspends diplomatic relations with the United States.

References and Further Reading

Bartlett, Ruhl, ed. *The Record of American Diplomacy: Documents and Readings in the History of American Foreign Relations.* New York: Alfred A. Knopf, 1947.

Ellis, Joseph. *His Excellency: George Washington.* New York: Alfred A. Knopf, 2004.

Flexner, James. *George Washington and the New Nation (1783–1793).* Boston: Little, Brown 1969.

Flexner, James. *George Washington: Anguish and Farewell (1793–1799).* Boston: Little, Brown, 1969.

Freeman, Douglas Southall. *George Washington: A Biography,* 7 vols. Vol. 6: *Patriot and President.* New York: Charles Scribner's Sons, 1954.

Gilbert, Felix. *To the Farewell Address: Ideas of Early American Foreign Policy.* Princeton, NJ: Princeton University Press, 1961.

Lang, Daniel. *Foreign Policy in the Early Republic: The Law of Nations and the Balance of Power.* Baton Rouge, LA: Louisiana State University Press, 1985.

McDonald, Forrest. *The Presidency of George Washington.* Lawrence, KS: The University Press of Kansas, 1974.

Varg, Paul. *Foreign Policies of the Founding Fathers.* Baltimore, MD: Penguin, 1970.

John Adams (1797–1801)

Early Life and Political Career

John Adams was born in Braintree, Massachusetts, on October 19, 1735, and was the eldest of three sons of Deacon John Adams and Samantha Boylston. The family lived a Spartan existence typical of eighteenth-century Puritan New England. Adams's father was a shoemaker and farmer who entertained hopes that his eldest son would enter college and study for the ministry. Adams entered Harvard at fifteen on a partial scholarship, and was placed under the tutelage of Joseph Mayhew. At Harvard, Adams discovered his lifelong love of books and learning, studying Greek, Latin, logic, rhetoric, mathematics, and science. An industrious, if not brilliant student, Adams graduated in 1755.

Returning to Braintree, Adams was uncertain about his future. He resisted his father's chosen vocation for him in the ministry and considered entering the legal profession. Becoming a lawyer, however, required that he be apprenticed to a practicing attorney who would charge a fee, which Adams could not afford. Instead, he took the offer of a teaching position in a grammar school in Worcester, sixty miles from Braintree. Adams soon found life as a schoolmaster in Worcester boring and confining. Seeking solace in books, he was absorbed increasingly by questions of history and politics, just as the French and Indian War was breaking out.

In the late summer of 1765, Adams had had his fill of teaching and began a legal apprenticeship with a young Worcester attorney named James Putnam. Completing his studies with Putnam in the fall of 1758, he was admitted to the bar in Boston in November 1759. That same year Adams met Abigail Smith. After a five-year courtship, the couple were married on October 25, 1764. With the enactment of the Stamp Act in 1765, Adams was drawn into the Boston political circle of his older second cousin, Samuel Adams. In the midst of political fomentation in Boston, Adams produced his first contribution to political philosophy, *A Dissertation on the Canon and Feudal Law*. In it, Adams challenged authority in the name of freedom and obedience in the name of just resistance. He argued that the American colonists were made of stern stuff, and their spirit would not be cowed easily. British repression would only fan the flames of resistance. The efforts of Adams and others led

John Adams was a diplomat of the American Revolution, Federalist president, and father of the first U.S. Navy. (Library of Congress)

Parliament to repeal the Stamp Act. It was replaced, however, with the Townshend Acts, passed in 1767, imposing import duties on goods to the colonies. Britain also increased the number of soldiers in America. Adams was once again at the forefront of the protests against taxation without representation, but his decision to defend the British officer and soldiers accused of perpetrating the Boston Massacre led some to question his commitment and loyalty to the cause of American liberty. The controversial but successful defense of the British soldiers resulted in some losses to his legal practice. In the long-run, however, the honesty and integrity Adams demonstrated in discharging his legal responsibilities earned him great respect and raised his public standing.

Adams continued with his philosophical defense of the cause of American freedom. In his "Novanglus" letters, he drew on the classical teachings of Plato, Aristotle, Cicero, and especially John Locke to deny Parliament's right to rule the colonies and to defend the American people's inherent right to revolution. In 1774, Adams was selected by the Massachusetts legislature as one of five delegates to the First Continental Congress meeting in Philadelphia. By the time he returned for the Second Continental Congress in the spring of 1775, the question of American liberty had been transformed from a philosophical disquisition to a trial of martial strength following the battles of Lexington and Concord. In the Congress, Adams quickly became the leading voice for American independence. He was skeptical of the possibility of any reconciliation with Britain and saw independence as the only guarantee for American freedom. When Congress made the fateful decision in favor of independence, Adams was appointed to a five-man committee whose task was to prepare its proclamation to the world. The exact circumstances surrounding the decision to appoint Thomas Jefferson to draft the declaration remain unclear; both Adams and Jefferson left differing accounts. The force and majesty of the Declaration of Independence bears testament to Jefferson's eloquence as a writer, but its substantive core was fully consonant with the political philosophy that Adams had been expounding for more than a decade. Indeed, for his tireless exertions on behalf of American freedom, Adams earned the sobriquet "the Atlas of American Independence."

Adams Abroad

In 1778 Adams was dispatched to Paris to join Benjamin Franklin and Arthur Lee on a diplomatic mission seeking an alliance with, and foreign aid from royalist France. While serving in the Continental Congress, Adams had gained something of a reputation for acumen in foreign affairs. He had been instrumental in preparing the draft of what came to be known as the Model Treaty, and was one of three congressmen who negotiated with British peace commissioners. In Paris, the laconic Adams was a forceful advocate of American interests, much to the chagrin of his French interlocutors. He had started his mission aware of the importance of an alliance with France not only for the immediate objective of winning the war against Britain, but also for the long-term postwar security of America. Adams understood that an alliance served French as well as American interests, and was never naïve enough to believe that those interests would always coincide. In his negotiations with the French foreign minister, Charles Gravier, Comte de Vergennes, Adams noticed that Franco-American interests were in fact already starting to diverge. He suspected that the French were seeking to exploit the war for imperial advantage and reduce his new nation to the status of a client state. Vergennes, for his part, found Adams to be vexingly stubborn on issues of American interest and attempted to have him recalled, preferring to negotiate instead with the more pliable Franklin. Adams

returned from France in the summer of 1779 to report to Congress on the status of negotiations. In the course of this brief visit, he found time to draft a new constitution for Massachusetts that contained provisions for a separation of powers and a bicameral legislature as well as a bill of rights.

On his next trip to Europe Adams held an appointment from Congress as minister plenipotentiary to negotiate a peace treaty. After a brief stay in France he departed for The Hague in October 1780 with instructions to negotiate a treaty of friendship and commerce with the Dutch. He spent the next two years in Holland, presenting the American case and attempting to overcome the reluctance of the Dutch to commit to the rebel colonies. A breakthrough was achieved in November 1781, following the news of the surrender of Lord Cornwallis and the British army at Yorktown. Adams quickly secured Dutch diplomatic recognition of the United States, as well as a commercial treaty and a financial loan, and returned to Paris. At the insistence of the French, however, Congress had revoked his status as sole peacemaker. He was now to be joined in Paris by John Jay, Henry Lauren, Thomas Jefferson, and Benjamin Franklin, to form a commission to negotiate a formal peace settlement with Britain. The French had also insisted that the American commission not negotiate any settlement with the British without the approval of France, and Congress acquiesced in this French veto over American diplomacy. The French, weary of the toll extracted in blood and treasure by the war, were eager to end it and were prepared to compromise with the British on the issue of American independence to facilitate matters. But Adams was not prepared to watch hard-won independence bartered away. In defiance of both Vergennes and Congress, Adams, Jay, and Franklin concluded a peace treaty with Britain separate from the French. In the Treaty of Paris of 1783, Britain recognized the independence of the United States.

Adams's next diplomatic posting was as minister to the Court of St. James. Although the Treaty of Paris had been signed, there remained several important unresolved issues concerning its implementation. In London, Adams had to deal with the perennial issue of American debt, the awkward issue of compensation to slave owners for slaves freed by the British, the postwar treatment of Loyalists, and the continued presence of British soldiers on American soil. Success eluded him. After a humiliating defeat at the hands of the upstart Americans, the British were eager neither for reconciliation nor accommodation. As a consequence, Adams failed to secure British agreement to open ports to American commerce, obtain guarantees respecting American navigation and fishing rights, or the withdrawal of British troops. The enforced diplomatic idleness nonetheless permitted Adams to meditate on important political developments back home.

Prior to the conclusion of the Treaty of Paris, the United States had adopted the Articles of Confederation. Under the

Confederation, the American national government was based on a loose association of sovereign and independent states, with a weak national legislature and lacking entirely in an executive or national court system. Events during the 1780s—the inability of the Congress to address the issue of war debts, border and commercial disputes among the various states, and Shays's Rebellion in 1786—threatened the premature ruination of the American experiment in self-governance and exposed the inadequacies of the Confederation. The movement toward reforming and strengthening the national government culminated in the constitutional convention that met in Philadelphia in 1787, which drafted and adopted the new Constitution. In London Adams set about writing the three-volume, *A Defense of the Constitutions of Government of the United States of America*. It was a treatise on political philosophy written in part as a response to events in the United States and in part as a counterpoint to the criticisms of French philosophes of American state constitutions and the new federal Constitution. In the *Defense*, Adams advocated the creation of a strong executive, a bicameral legislature, an independent judiciary, as well as the separation of the various organs of government. Sensing that there was little left to be accomplished diplomatically in London, he asked to be recalled and returned to America in March 1788.

Elevation to the Presidency

John Adams was fifty-two when he returned to the United States after spending a decade in Europe in devoted service to his country. By one account, Adams had traveled over 29,000 miles by sea and land in the course of his diplomatic assignments, a distance greater than any other leading American statesman of the time. Even as he was being lauded for his diplomatic achievement, speculation was rife as to his political future. There was talk of Adams as governor, senator, chief justice, and vice president—everything except president. The new Constitution had been ratified and the states were selecting members of the Electoral College who would then choose the president and vice president. There was no doubt, however, that George Washington would be chosen as the first president of the United States. Privately, Adams had decided that he would accept only the position of vice president, considering all other roles to be beneath his stature and dignity. He allowed his surrogates to lobby for his candidacy but maintained a public silence and an air of personal disinterestedness in keeping with contemporary political mores that looked unkindly on public displays of ambition.

When the Electoral College met in February 1789, Washington was chosen president unanimously with sixty-nine votes, and Adams was elected vice president with thirty-four votes. Although the tally placed Adams well ahead of ten other candidates, he was humiliated and hurt by what he considered to be a public rebuff of his long years of public service. The vote was in fact no measure of the public esteem with which he was regarded. Alexander Hamilton had been working quietly behind the scenes to convince leading politicians to withhold their votes from Adams. Hamilton's actions have never been explained satisfactorily. Exceedingly bright and ambitious, Hamilton perceived himself as Washington's political heir and some have viewed his intervention as an attempt to damage Adams and interpose himself in the line of presidential succession. Conversely, Hamilton may very well have acted so that Adams's popularity would not result in the outcome of the election being decided by the House of Representatives, thereby humiliating his mentor.

On April 21, 1789, Adams was formally received at Federal Hall in New York and escorted to the Senate chamber where he accepted the duties of vice president. There was no swearing-in ceremony for Adams, as the wording of an oath for the Senate was among the several matters yet to be resolved. On inauguration day, April 30, Adams stood by Washington's side as the latter took the oath of office as president. Washington's first cabinet was composed of revolutionary America's best and brightest: Hamilton as secretary of the treasury; Jefferson as secretary of state; Edmund Randolph of Virginia as attorney general; and Philander Knox of Massachusetts as secretary of war. Adams had not been consulted on the composition of the cabinet nor did he appear to have proffered any suggestions. He had little contact with Washington and the cabinet and virtually no influence. Adams was the first to experience the trials of "the most insignificant office that ever the Imagination of Man contrived or his Imagination conceived" that so many others following him were later to bemoan. The fiery and combative New Englander was temperamentally unsuited for an office that required no more of him than presiding quietly over Senate debates, making no formal speeches, and voting only in the event of deadlock among the members. Following an overhyped contretemps surrounding his advocacy of courtly pomp and royal-sounding titles for the president, however, an apparently chastened Adams settled down to presiding dutifully over the Senate.

The relative peace and quiet of masterly inactivity in the Senate would not last long. Adams was soon plunged again into controversy. In September 1789 news started to reach America of the storming of the Bastille and the French Revolution. More than by anything else, the Adams presidency was later to be defined by and preoccupied with the reverberations of this world-altering event in Franco-American relations. The majority of Americans greeted the French Revolution with enthusiasm. They saw in the events in France a kindred revolution. The United States would no longer be alone in the great experiment in freedom, and it was entirely apropos that America's friend and ally in its own revolutionary struggle should now embrace the cause. Adams, however, viewed the French Revolution with alarm and began work on a series of articles attacking it. These articles were eventually published as a book, *Discourses on Davila.* Warming to a theme first addressed in *Defenses,* in the *Discourses* Adams attacked the ideas of the radical philosophes as invidious and denied any similarities between the American and French Revolutions. He warned that the French Revolution, far from creating liberty, was headed for tragedy and terror. His critics accused him of hypocrisy and saw in *The Discourses* proof that he was a reactionary and a monarchist; Jefferson certainly thought so. That Adams supported one revolution while decrying the other placed him in the company of Edmund Burke, who had been one of the strongest supporters of America in the British Parliament but who now savaged the French Revolution. Both men foresaw the violent trajectory that the French Revolution would ultimately take, but whereas Burke sought a restoration of order and stability by turning to the nobility, Adams saw salvation in the idea of balanced government.

In December 1795, Adams learned that Washington planned to leave office after completing his second term. Washington could have sought and won a third term, but unlike the two previous occasions it would not have been by unanimous acclaim. The strains and stress of partisan attacks on his foreign and domestic policies had soured him on public life and reinforced his appetite for retirement. Although Adams was considered Washington's presumptive heir, his elevation to the presidency in 1796 was not a foregone conclusion. There were four possible successors to Washington: Adams, Hamilton, John Jay, and Jefferson. Adams had a distinguished record of public service as vice president and as a diplomat but was distrusted within High Federalist circles. Hamilton, the leader of the High Federalists, considered himself to be Washington's true political heir, but was as unpopular as he was brilliant. Jay's prospects of succeeding Washington were severely handicapped by the controversy surrounding the 1794 treaty he had negotiated with Britain. Jefferson, the former secretary of state, was now leader of the opposition Republicans and a strong contender.

The election of 1796 between Adams and Jefferson was the first between two opposing political parties and was characterized by scurrilous political invective and chicanery and foreign interference. Following custom, neither Adams nor Jefferson campaigned actively for the office. That, however, did not stop their supporters and surrogates from trading vicious slurs. The Republicans charged Adams with being a reactionary and a monarchist, and the Federalists retaliated by accusing Jefferson of being an atheist, a

Jacobin, and a coward. Hamilton was also once again up to his political intrigues. Without consulting Adams, he recruited Thomas Pinckney of South Carolina as the vice presidential candidate, ostensibly to bring regional balance to the Federalist ticket.

Prior to the Twelfth Amendment to the Constitution, the electoral system accommodated backroom maneuvers. Presidential electors cast ballots for candidates by voting twice, once for the president and once for the vice president, but without designating which candidate was being chosen for which office. The candidate with the highest number of votes overall became president; the runner-up became vice president. Hamilton urged strong support for Pinckney in order to deny his archenemy Jefferson the vice presidency, but also possibly to defeat Adams and make Pinckney president. Hamilton was not close to Adams and could not hope to play the role of advisor and confidante as he had with Washington. The New Englander was too independent and headstrong to be exploited by Hamilton; Pinckney appeared more pliable.

One of the key issues in the election was French interference. The French Directory (government of the French Revolution prior to the seizure of power by Napoleon) believed that the only way to restore the Franco-American alliance was to defeat the Federalists and to replace them with a pro-French Republican administration. The French minister Pierre Adet was therefore instructed by the Directory to intervene directly in electoral politics: to support the Republicans openly and attack the Federalists whenever possible. The French were acting on the belief that the Federalist administration's pro-British stance was opposed by public opinion, which was overwhelmingly pro-French. While that may not have been an inaccurate assessment of the situation, what Adet and his political masters in Paris failed to grasp was that his open politicking in support of Jefferson and the Republicans served only to confirm Washington's warnings against foreign interference contained in his Farewell Address. Adet's activities ended up harming the very cause he supported as Federalists seized the opportunity to patriotically denounce French interference in domestic politics and to accuse the Republicans of being pawns of a foreign government.

Washington's Legacy: The Quasi-War

The election was close. On February 8, 1797, Adams in his official capacity as president of the Senate tabulated the electoral returns and announced himself as the president-elect. He had won the presidency with seventy-one votes. Jefferson, however, was only three votes behind him and would be his vice president. Through intermediaries, Adams learned that Jefferson was happy and willing to serve under him, but privately Jefferson confided to James Madison that he was glad that Adams had won. There was no political advantage, he told Madison, in being Washington's immediate successor. It was a poisoned prize. The new president would have to deal with problems left over from Washington's administration and would have difficulty establishing a presidency on his own terms. Jefferson's prediction turned out to be immediately prophetic.

In his first decision as president-elect, Adams asked Washington's department heads to remain in his cabinet. This decision betrayed a stunning lack of political acumen. Not only was the cabinet comprised of mediocrities—Timothy Pickering of Massachusetts as secretary of state, Oliver Wolcott of Connecticut as secretary of treasury, James McHenry of Maryland as secretary of war, and Charles Lee of Virginia as attorney general—but all of them save Lee were High Federalists whose political allegiances laid with Hamilton rather than Adams. Jefferson wryly noted that the cabinet hated Adams only a little less than they did himself. Indeed, Adams would rue the retention of the Washington cabinet. Its members ultimately undermined his foreign policy initiatives and helped to destroy his presidency.

Adams took the oath of office on March 4, 1797. In his inaugural address he expressed his desire to maintain friendly relations with France. That was easier said than done, as almost immediately Adams faced a crisis with France. In 1793, when war had broken out between France and Britain, Washington insisted that the United States maintain a policy of strict neutrality. Neutrality, however, ran counter to American obligations to France contained in the Treaty of Alliance and Treaty of Commerce of 1778. The Republicans considered American neutrality as evidence that the Federalists were committed to taking the nation to war on the side of the British. Their suspicions appeared to be confirmed when Washington sought rapprochement with Britain on trade matters. Trade between the two countries had increased dramatically, but Britain was not respecting the right of neutral shipping on the high seas. American vessels were subject to harassment and seizure, and American sailors were pressed into service by the Royal Navy applying the Rule of 1756.

To prevent any further escalation in tensions, Washington dispatched John Jay to London to negotiate a treaty. This was undertaken in the face of public opinion, which clamored for a declaration of war against Britain. Jay, like Adams a decade prior, had little success in London. He was forced to concede virtually every point to the British in exchange for very little. He did, however, secure the immediate prospect of peace with Britain, which was sufficient to satisfy Washington. A treaty, however flawed, was preferable to a war with Britain. In June 1795, Washington called a special session of the Senate to consider the Jay Treaty.

Although Adams had served as first minister to Britain he had not been consulted on the Jay mission. Neither was he consulted when the treaty was submitted to the Senate for ratification, and he presided over one of the most rancorous sessions in Senate history. After thirteen days of angry debate, the Federalists mustered the requisite two-thirds majority to ratify the treaty.

The ratification of the Jay Treaty resulted in a rapid deterioration in relations with France. Aside from authorizing Adet to intervene directly in the elections on the side of the Republicans, the Directory had issued a decree on July 4, 1796, announcing its intention to treat neutral vessels, including American vessels, in the same manner that the Royal Navy treated them. This move by the Directory amounted to a repudiation of the Franco-American alliance and an unofficial declaration of war. Indeed, what resulted was a "quasi-war" as French warships began seizing American merchantmen carrying contraband.

Foreign Policy: Peace through Strength and Neutrality

The most important decision facing the incoming Adams administration was what to do about France. The situation deteriorated still further when the Directory refused to accept the credentials of Charles Cotesworth Pinckney as the new American minister to France and ordered him expelled. Many Federalists, including Hamilton, urged the president-elect to dispatch a special envoy or commission to seek a negotiated settlement with the French, along lines similar to the Jay mission. Adams required little persuasion; he had come to a similar conclusion independently. His foreign policy outlook was virtually identical to that of his predecessor's. War with either Britain or France was to be avoided if at all possible. War was not in the national interest; taking on the Great Powers of the time would be suicidal. Like Hamilton, Adams believed that commerce would ultimately provide the foundation for American strength beyond challenge by either Britain or France. Such a prospect, however, lay in the future. In the meantime, nothing should distract the country from the central tasks of cultivating trade, consolidating domestic political institutions, and exploiting the vast resources of an untapped continent. A war, whether for misplaced national pride or partisan advantage, would drain away American resources or, worse yet, destroy the republic itself. Adams was a realist and did not view either Britain or France as inherently more virtuous or venal than any other state. States, in his view, acted on the basis of a rational calculation of what was in their best interest. The United States could and should do nothing less than pursue its own interests. In these circumstances the national interest required maintaining a policy of strict neutrality and avoiding war.

Adams attempted to steer a middle course between the pro-British and pro-French factions at home to forge a bipartisan consensus on foreign policy. A few days before the inauguration, he approached Jefferson to sound him out about being an envoy extraordinary to France. Jefferson had been minister to France but, unlike Adams, was widely adored and respected by the French. Adams believed that if anyone were to have any hope of success in negotiating a settlement with the French, it would be Jefferson. In addition, a Jefferson peace mission held out other advantages. Any treaty negotiated by Jefferson, even if were to be as flawed as the one negotiated by Jay, would provide Adams with sufficient room to maneuver to avoid war. Even if Jefferson failed in his peace mission, Adams would still be in a better position if he ever required a congressional declaration of war against France.

When Jefferson notified Madison of Adams's offer, an alarmed Madison warned his mentor not to accept. There was no political advantage to be had in being implicated in Federalist diplomatic initiatives, and it would only complicate Jefferson's ability to organize effective Republican opposition to exploit Federalist missteps. Jefferson required little persuasion from Madison. He declined the mission, arguing that his constitutional duties as vice president precluded him from extended periods abroad. In any event, the point was moot. When Adams broached the possibility of including a Republican in the mission, possibly Madison or his friend Elbridge Gerry, Wolcott threatened to lead a mass resignation of the cabinet. Adams capitulated to the wishes of his treasury secretary. His hopes for a bipartisan foreign policy—always a long shot—were destroyed, and his middle course set him at odds not only with the Republicans but with his own party.

Even though his plan for a peace mission had to be set aside, at least temporarily, Adams still had to respond to French predations on American shipping which were starting to take a toll on the economy. There was a panic among American shippers as maritime insurance rates increased and underwriters refused to insure vessels sailing to French ports or areas where French warships or privateers were operating. There were several options: Adams could ask Congress for an embargo on French shipping; he could arm American merchantmen and license privateers to prey on French merchants vessels in retaliation; he could begin preparations for war; or he could ask Congress for a declaration of war. He decided to do nothing precipitant and instead played for time. He called for a cabinet meeting on March 14 and summoned a special session of Congress for May 15. Adams hoped that during that two month window he could find a way to avoid a war with France without sacrificing American honor.

At the cabinet meeting, Adams informed his department heads that he was still in favor of sending a peace mission to France and solicited their opinions and advice. The cabinet did not look favorably on this proposal. What Pickering, Wolcott, and McHenry did was to confide in Hamilton. Hamilton favored the dispatch of a peace mission. He doubted that it could be long avoided and could prove useful. If the French rejected American peace overtures, no one could then fault a decision to resort to arms. He also favored the inclusion of Republicans on the peace mission, for if it were to fail it would be preferable to implicate the opposition party as well. Hamilton's protégés took his advice to heart and submitted his recommendations as their own, in some cases virtually verbatim. Reversing course, the cabinet now favored a diplomatic peace initiative together with strong national defense measures. They advised Adams to arm American merchantmen and to strengthen the Navy so as to provide convoy escorts for shipping. The cabinet thus recommended a dual policy of continued negotiations and defense preparation, for in the event that diplomacy proved ineffective, the country would be prepared for hostilities. Adams was unaware that his cabinet had taken its marching orders from Hamilton; he instead inferred that they were committed to his policy of seeking a peaceful, negotiated outcome.

While Adams waited to address Congress, he sought to reassure the French of his intentions. In a lengthy meeting with Minister Adet, Adams tried to convince the French minister of his desire for peace. Other French diplomats meanwhile reported to the new French foreign minister, Charles Maurice de Talleyrand-Périgord, that Adams was an unreconstructed Francophobe. When Adams addressed Congress on May 16 he expressed outrage at French treatment of Pinckney and the predations on American maritime commerce. He insisted that the United States would defend its neutrality and asked Congress to expand the Navy, arm American merchantmen, and expand the militia. He also insisted, however, that a fresh attempt be made at a negotiated settlement to end the crisis. The speech was certainly more bellicose than his private communications with the French ambassador, but it was not the war-whoop that Republicans tried to make it out to be. Rather, it was a public enunciation of his dual policy of seeking a peaceful resolution to the crisis while taking all adequate measures for war should diplomacy fail.

The XYZ Affair

A few days after addressing Congress, Adams convened the cabinet to announce his choices for the peace mission: Charles Pinckney, who was still in Europe; John Marshall of Virginia, a staunch Federalist and future chief justice; and his friend, Elbridge Gerry. The cabinet objected fiercely to the choice of Gerry—he was a Republican. Adams did not back down; he knew Gerry and needed someone he could trust on the mission. Without further consultation with his cabinet, he forwarded the three names to Congress for ratification and proceeded to draft guidelines for his envoys. They would be empowered to negotiate a new treaty with France that accorded it the same commercial privileges that had been extended to Britain by the Jay Treaty. It was hoped that it was sufficient to mollify the French; failing that, the mission was to insist on America's right as a neutral to trade with whomever it chose. In addition, the envoys were instructed that there would be no loans or aid to France as long as it was at war.

Even as the peace mission was being dispatched, events in France altered the government and its attitude toward the United States. The coup of eighteen *Fructidor* removed two Directors who were sympathetic and replaced them with a pair of hardliners. As a result, the reconstituted Directory was even more hostile to the Adams administration than its predecessor. Furthermore, with the Habsburg monarchy having been forced out of the war against France, and with Napoleon's Armée d'Angleterre camped out on the Channel coast, it appeared that even Britain might be prepared to come to terms with the Directory. French hegemony over Europe did not bode well for the administration. Unencumbered by war on the Continent, France could turn all its attention and anger to the United States.

As Adams watched events in Europe unfold and waited for word from his envoys, he tried to persuade Congress to prepare for the worst by improving the nation's naval and military defenses. Congress considered the president's request but did nothing. Adams then turned to his cabinet for advice on what to do if peace negotiations failed. He had still not heard from Pinckney, Marshall, and Gerry, but he was aware of the rumors of their failure. McHenry immediately sought out Hamilton for counsel. Hamilton reiterated his previous advice and McHenry once again resubmitted it to Adams as his own, with a few modifications. The advice proffered by Pickering and Wolcott was similar, although Pickering was more aggressive; he argued in favor of an alliance with Britain and the seizure of Louisiana should the French reject the American peace mission.

Adams did not have time to digest fully his cabinet's—or more accurately, Hamilton's—recommendations. On March 4, the first anniversary of his presidency, he finally received word from his envoys. The mission had failed. The Directory had refused to meet with the American envoys. It had ordered that all French ports be closed to neutral shipping and that any ship carrying any British manufacture was subject to capture. Worse news was to follow as Adams read the secret dispatches. Talleyrand had kept the envoys waiting before receiving them for a scant fifteen minutes, after which he refused to have any further contact with them. They were then approached by three secret agents acting on behalf of Talleyrand—Jean Conrad Hottinguer,

Pierre Bellamy, and Lucien Hauteval—identified as X, Y, and Z in the secret dispatches. The agents informed the Americans that Talleyrand was prepared to initiate negotiation as long as a pot de vin, or bribe, of $250,000 was paid to him, and an apology was issued along with a loan of $100 million to France as compensation for their president's previous "insults." The Americans were aghast at this display of Gallic audacity and refused further negotiation; Pinckney's famous rejoinder to French insistence of a bribe was, "No; no, not a sixpence!"

Adams forwarded the decoded dispatches to Congress, but withheld information regarding X, Y and Z. Unsure of his next move, he consulted his cabinet. This time the cabinet was divided. Lee and Pickering advocated seeking a congressional declaration of war, whereas Wolcott and McHenry counseled restraint. They urged him instead to persist in his efforts to ready the nation for war and to permit the Navy to retaliate against French shipping in the Caribbean. Adams drafted a fiery and bellicose message, but before he submitted his address to Congress he calmed down, reconsidered his position, and drafted a new message with a very different tone. Adams did not want war. He continued to believe that a war would be disastrous for the United States and sought peace with honor. In his message of March 19, he attempted to guard against overreaction by telling Congress that he planned to recall Pinckney, Marshall, and Elbridge, but again withheld mention of the XYZ Affair. He also reiterated his call for improvements to be made to maritime and coastal defenses. Congress's reaction surprised him. On the one hand, the Federalist majority—supposedly spoiling for a war with France—did not move on his recommendations. On the other hand, the Republican minority, suspecting that Adams was concealing information to discredit the French and advance his own war plans, demanded the release of all relevant documents. A coalition of Republicans and High Federalists in the House succeeded in passing a resolution demanding the envoys' uncensored dispatches. Adams complied, concealing only the names of the French secret agents as X, Y, and Z.

Bayonets and Wooden Walls

The release of the secret dispatches unleashed the very passions that Adams had feared. The Republicans, realizing the enormity of their mistake in seeking full disclosure of the documents, attempted damage control—to little avail. Public opinion was now aroused against France, and the Federalists were only too glad to exploit the situation. Even Adams was swept by the general mood and appeared to lose his restraint. Basking in his newfound popularity with the public, his speeches were filled with bellicose rhetoric. The nation appeared poised on the brink of war with France. Hamilton urged the creation of an army of 50,000 under the

A painting depicts the battle between the USS Constellation *and the French frigate* L'insurgent *in the waters of the West Indies in February 1799 during the Quasi-War. (Naval Historical Foundation)*

command of Washington to counter the French menace. Adams was too much of a Whig to be enthused at the prospect of a large standing army or of Hamilton anywhere near its command. The political pressure on him from within his own party was nonetheless enormous, so he dropped his opposition. In July, Congress authorized the creation of an army under the command of Washington, with Hamilton as his deputy. This "Provisional Army" was not to be formed until the outbreak of full-scale war or when the president determined that national security required it.

Adams considered the army a distraction and a drain on scarce resources. The Quasi-War was being waged at sea and he believed that the nation's best line of defense was the navy, or what he called "floating batteries and wooden walls." On April 30, 1798, he signed a bill authorizing the creation of a Department of the Navy. Until that point, naval affairs had been under the auspices of the War Department, but McHenry's continued ineptness made that

arrangement unworkable. Adams appointed the able Benjamin Stoddert as the first secretary of the Navy. Congress also authorized increases in naval power and the use of the Navy against French warships and privateers, and Stoddert made the most of it. In February 1799, the USS *Constellation* encountered the fastest warship in the French navy, *L'insurgent*, off the coast of Nevis and gave battle. *L'insurgent* had previously outsailed and outfought all American and British warships, but more than met its match in the *Constellation*. Raked by broadsides, *L'insurgent* was rendered helpless and captured by the crew of the *Constellation*. By September 1799, Stoddert had deployed three battle squadrons to the Caribbean and the fighting abilities of the Navy grew from battle to battle.

The Alien and Sedition Acts

The XYZ Affair had meanwhile resulted in war fever and nationalist hysteria, and the Federalists seized the moment to attack and weaken their enemy. The Republicans had not ceased opposing what Jefferson called Federalist war measures designed to stampede the nation into hostilities with France. Many High Federalists considered the Republicans a threat to national security, a Jacobin fifth column ready to destroy the republic, overthrow the Constitution, and install a radical, egalitarian, democratic society modeled on revolutionary France. Although Adams did not subscribe to all the High Federalists' notions of Republican conspiracies, he shared with them a deep abhorrence of the French Revolution and the ideas underlying it. Beginning on June 18, 1798 and continuing for a period of two weeks, the Federalist majority in Congress passed the Alien and Sedition Acts over fierce Republican opposition. The Alien Friends Act was deliberately designed to deal with the problem of French agents in America. It gave the president power to arrest and deport aliens whom he considered a threat to national security. The Alien Enemies Act allowed the president to arrest and deport aliens from a country that was at war with the United States. The capstone of the Federalist measures was the Sedition Act, which attempted to define and prescribe punishment. It was clearly a violation of the First Amendment and the Republicans correctly called it a gag law, as it targeted only Republican journalists and presses.

The passage of the Alien and Sedition Acts marked the low point of the Adams presidency. Granted, he did not ask for or openly encourage the extreme measures, but neither did he oppose or veto the laws. John Marshall was the only Federalist to publicly denounce the measures. By publicly questioning the conduct of aliens and by repeated talk of Republican conspiracies and foreign intrigues, Adams helped contribute to the noxious political climate that made the Alien and Sedition Acts possible. In later years he spoke of the laws as necessary war measures, which is how he chose to remember them. The truth, however, was that they were partisan measures taken for the political advantage of maintaining Federalist dominance.

A New Peace Initiative

In a message to Congress on December 8, 1798, Adams declared that there would be no change in American policy toward France. He had no wish for war but urged continued defense preparations. The speech had been prepared by Wolcott, and Adams slipped in an important addition to the text. He told Congress that he had detected signs of moderation in France, which suggested that the Directory might be ready to receive an American ambassador. The burden of proof, however, lay with the French. He would not send another envoy to Paris until he received "determinate assurances" that France was serious about peace. If the French took the initiative, he would reciprocate.

Because the war fever following the XYZ Affair had dissipated, Adams believed that public opinion favored peace. On the one hand, the threat of a French invasion disappeared with news of Nelson's brilliant victory at the Battle of Aboukir Bay. On the other hand, the war measures put in place by his administration threatened domestic unrest and disunion as well as a crisis in American federalism. Domestic unrest stemmed in large part from the high costs of keeping the nation on a permanent war footing. By the third year of the Adams administration, the federal government was spending over twice what the Washington administration had spent in its final year. As the federal budget increased so too did taxation, and open protests soon flared up. The most dramatic of these occurred in eastern Pennsylvania where John Fries led a mob to free homeowners jailed for resisting payment of the so-called window tax, levied to pay for the upkeep of the Army and Navy. With the Whiskey Rebellion still fresh in his memory, Adams ordered part of the new army to assist the state militia in crushing Fries's Rebellion.

The Alien and Sedition Acts had also dampened any enthusiasm for war. The Kentucky and Virginia state legislatures passed two resolutions—the former drafted secretly by Jefferson, and the latter by Madison—declaring the Alien and Sedition Acts as unconstitutional and void. The resolutions depicted the measures as evidence of a Federalist conspiracy to destroy civil liberties and establish despotic rule and warned that, if the federal government persisted in exercising such illegal powers, it would drive the states into "revolution and bloodshed." The Federalists attacked the Kentucky and Virginia resolutions. Some High Federalists wished to combat what they considered sedition with force. They were prepared to start a civil war if necessary. Although the resolutions were aimed at issues of states' rights and federalism, and did not touch on the war crisis directly, they did warn that the republic would not long endure if repressive war measures remained in place and the rights of the citizenry were trampled.

The obvious solution to all these domestic disturbances was to end the Quasi-War. Adams had hoped to avoid war and now he believed that a conflict with France could be averted. This belief was shaped by private reports he received from Gerry, who had finally returned from France; his sons John Quincy and Thomas Boylston; William Vans Murray, the American minister at The Hague; and Joel Barlow in Europe. The reports indicated a change of attitude in Paris, which was now favorable to peace. Washington's note, which was appended to Barlow's report made a deep impression on Adams. The former president insisted that Barlow had correctly discerned that the Directory sought peace on terms that were honorable and acceptable to the United States. He added that he not only believed that the American people wished for peace but that it was also in the best long-term interest of the nation.

Washington's intervention provided much needed emotional release for Adams. It stiffened his resolve to take what his sense of right, his understanding of the national interest, and his horror of war and the role he would have to play in it, all told him was the correct course of action.

Embattled Mission to France

On February 18, without any prior consultation with any members of his cabinet or his party, Adams submitted the name of William Van Murray to Congress as minister plenipotentiary to France, empowered to negotiate a settlement putting an end to the Quasi-War. The message was received by Jefferson, who interrupted the business of the Senate to make the sensational announcement of Murray's appointment. The Federalists were mortified. Adams had expected a strong reaction to his decision, since he knew that a majority of his cabinet and the leaders of his party were hostile to the idea of a peace mission. But he was taken aback by the odium directed at him. He was excoriated in Federalist newspapers and there were even anonymous threats of assassination. The Federalist Party had no other issue of broad national appeal to replace the war crisis. Some High Federalists like Pickering had thought that they could exploit the Quasi-War to retain power indefinitely. They had constructed their entire political program on that single foundation, and Adam's peace initiative threatened to destroy everything. Not all Federalists opposed the Murray mission. Senior leaders like Washington, Jay, Henry Knox, and Patrick Henry supported the president, but their support was not sufficient to prevent a split in the party.

Unable to dissuade Adams from sending Murray to Paris, the High Federalists attempted to convince him to appoint additional envoys to assist Murray. Adams initially resisted this proposal but was forced to relent as High Federalists held up Murray's confirmation in the Senate. On February 25, Adams agreed to appoint Chief Justice Oliver Ellsworth and Patrick Henry as additional envoys. When Henry declined the post Adams replaced him with another southerner, William Davie, the Federalist governor of North Carolina. On March 9, the instructions for the Murray mission, prepared by Pickering under the president's direction, were completed. The American demands were tough: the French were to pay indemnities for all spoliation of American commerce, they had to recognize that American vessels were not bound to carry a *role d'equipage* (a list of the ship's company), they had also to concede that the United States would no longer be bound to guarantee France's territorial possessions in the West Indies as called for in the Alliance of 1778. After confirming the three envoys Congress adjourned, and Adams returned to Quincy to be with an ailing Abigail. He would not return to Philadelphia for another seven months.

This prolonged absence from the seat of government was controversial to say the least. Under normal circumstances it would almost certainly have provoked severe criticism; to his critics, absence in the midst of a national crisis was tantamount to a dereliction of presidential responsibilities. His friends advised Adams against the prolonged stay in Quincy, as he would lose effective day-to-day control of the government. Adams would not budge. He intended to stay with Abigail and insisted that he would remain in charge, as his department heads could and would carry out his policies as he directed from Quincy. His friends tried to warn him that some of his cabinet members would take advantage of the opportunity to try to scuttle his peace initiative. Adams would have done well to heed their counsel, since he remained ignorant as to the diminished extent of his control over his cabinet and over the execution of policy. Alexander Hamilton still called the shots for Pickering, Wolcott, and McHenry.

On August 6, Adams received word from Murray indicating that the French were receptive to peace along with a letter from Talleyrand assuring him that the American envoys would be received with all due respect. Adams ordered Ellsworth and Davie to prepare immediately to leave for France and then instructed Pickering to complete and send him a draft of their instructions. Pickering prevaricated; he took over a month to do what should have taken only a day or two. Before the instructions were complete, news arrived of the coup of thirty *Prairial*, which toppled all but one member of the Directory. It appeared that the Directory's days were numbered and that a Bourbon restoration was imminent. Pickering wrote Adams urging a suspension of the mission. He had already taken it upon himself to postpone carrying out the president's order to dispatch Ellsworth and Davie. Pickering argued that the envoys should remain at home until the situation in France stabilized. With an allied victory seemingly close at hand it would be better to wait and see how matters turned out. He also told Adams that the cabinet favored an indefinite suspension of the mission, which was a lie. Only the Hamiltonians were opposed to the mission; Lee and Stoddert urged the immediate dispatch of the envoys. Without the benefit of any advisors in Quincy, Adams had to make the decision alone. After weighing the various arguments for and against sending the new mission, he accepted Pickering's advice. Ellsworth and Davie were not to sail. He would make a final decision when he returned to Philadelphia in November.

Indeed, Adams would have remained in Quincy until November were it not for the urgent appeals of Secretary of the Navy Stoddert. He wrote Adams warning of "artful and designing men" who were intent on thwarting his peace initiative and damaging his chances for reelection, and pleaded for him to return to the capital. Adams, finally grasping that all was not well within his cabinet, decided to make the trip to the temporary capital at Trenton, Philadelphia having been evacuated due to an outbreak of yellow fever. When Adams arrived on October 10, he met with the cabinet. Lee and Stoddert argued that a suspension of the mission would disappointment the people and cast doubt on Adams's sincerity about the peace initiative. The Hamiltonians remained vigorously opposed to the initiative. Their leader, now inspector general of the Army, had made the trip to Trenton in an attempt to persuade Adams to call off the mission. After several hours of argument, Hamilton left having failed to change the president's mind. In a marathon cabinet session on October 15, the final details of the mission's instructions were hammered out. The next day Adams asked Pickering to deliver a copy of the instructions to the envoys and direct them to embark for France by the end of the month. The Hamiltonians were shocked. They believed that no decision had been taken regarding the timing of the mission's departure at the meeting and that Adams was once again making a unilateral decision on a matter of great importance without prior consultation.

Endgame

Ellsworth and Davie arrived in Lisbon on November 27, 1799. They hoped to rendezvous quickly with Murray and open negotiations with their French counterparts when they received news of the coup of eighteen *Brumaire*. Napoleon had overthrown the Directory and replaced it with a three-man consulate, with himself as the first consul; he was now effectively dictator of France. Ellsworth and Davie decided to proceed with caution, waiting for events to settle in Paris before approaching the French Foreign Ministry. It was not until March 1800 that they joined Murray in Paris. The American mission received a cordial welcome from Talleyrand, who remained minister, and Napoleon. Negotiations began at once and progressed smoothly until Joseph Bonaparte, Napoleon's brother and leader of the French delegation suffered a serious illness. Talks resumed in May but quickly stalled. Napoleon no longer appeared inclined to reach a settlement. He was preoccupied by the military campaign in Italy and seemed content to wait for a Republican administration under Jefferson to take office. In late summer, however, Napoleon changed his mind and negotiations resumed. Finally, on October 3, an accord was signed at Chateau Môrtefontaine.

The Convention of Peace, Commerce, and Navigation, also known as the Convention of 1800 and the Treaty of Môrtefontaine, ended the Quasi-War and restored peace between France and the United States. But peace arrived too late to salvage Adams's political fortunes. In a bitterly fought campaign, he lost his bid for reelection to Thomas Jefferson. He was, however, still president and on December 16, submitted the treaty for ratification by the Senate. Adams knew that the consent of the Senate would not be easily obtained. Although most senators favored ratification, the High Federalists had the votes to deny the two-thirds majority necessary for ratification. On January 23, the Senate voted sixteen to fourteen for ratification—four votes shy of the required majority. The High Federalists, on the other, were prepared to vote for the treaty with reservations. These called for the termination of the Franco-American alliance of 1778 and the indemnification of American property lost during the Quasi-War. On February 2, the Senate ratified the treaty with reservations by a vote of twenty-two to nine. Adams was not happy with the reservations, but to veto the amended treaty would destroy his legacy of peace. It was enough that the Quasi-War was over.

Legacy

In his dotage, Adams looked back at the securing of peace with France as the most "disinterested and meritorious" act of his long and distinguished life. His entire presidency had been absorbed by a crisis in American foreign relations. His domestic difficulties cannot be understood in isolation from his foreign policy, because the interaction of domestic and international politics propelled his presidency from one partisan and diplomatic predicament to another. This is attributable to the unique nature of the Quasi-War. It was more than a cold war yet fell short of a full outbreak of hostilities. It necessitated placing the nation on a permanent war footing, producing domestic disunity and exaggerated nationalism, but denying the nation either the emotional catharsis of war or the comfort of peace.

The foreign policy of the Adams administration did not cause the crisis with France. The Quasi-War was Washington's legacy, and Adams tried to resolve the crisis through negotiation. When that failed he aligned himself with hard-line elements within his party and supported their war program. It was an expedient and necessary, but unfortunate, alliance. It enabled him to pursue a dual-track policy of seeking peace while simultaneously building up the nation's defenses. Adams sincerely believed that the national interest of the United States lay in peace through neutrality. A policy of neutrality, however, could not be purchased through diplomatic niceties alone; it would require a powerful American fleet to defend it. Attachment to his party's war program also made John Adams complicit in the Alien and Sedition Acts. His final assertion of independence from his party's war program may have rescued the nation from certain disaster, but it failed to rescue him from political oblivion.

Adrian U-jin Ang

Chronology

1797

March 2: French warships directed to intercept all cargo bound for Britain.

May 31: President Adams seeks treaty of amity with France.

October 18: XYZ Affair in Paris results in an undeclared naval war with France.

1798

March 19: President Adams permits American merchant ships to arm.

March 27: Democratic-Republicans proclaim Sprigg Resolutions, opposing war with France.

April 7: Congress establishes Mississippi Territory.

April 27: Adams establishes Department of the Navy, Congress authorizes twelve warships.

May 28: Congress authorizes use of Navy to seize French ships.

June 13: United States embargos all commerce with France.

June 25: Alien Friends Act passed.

July 1: French army under Napoleon Bonaparte invades Egypt.

July 6: Alien Enemy Act passed.

July 11: United States Marine Corps established.

July 14: Sedition Act passed.

July 31: France seeks reconciliation.

August 1: British fleet wins Battle of the Nile.

December 2: Second Coalition—Austria, Britain, Naples, Portugal, Ottoman Empire, and Russia—formed against France.

December 14: Virginia legislature opposes Alien and Sedition Acts.

1799

February 9: USS Constellation captures French frigate Insurgente.

February 9: United States supports Saint Domingue revolt against France.

November 9: Napoleon made first consul, overthrowing the Directorate.

1800

June 14: Napoleon wins Battle Marengo.

September 30–October 1: Convention of Môrtefontaine restores friendly relations with France.

October 1: Second Treaty of Ildefonso gives Spanish Louisiana Territory to France.

December 3: Deadlocked presidential election decided by House of Representatives; Thomas Jefferson is president, Aaron Burr vice president.

References and Further Reading

DeConde, Alexander. *The Quasi-War: The Politics and Diplomacy of the Undeclared War with France, 1797–1801.* New York: Charles Scribner's Sons, 1966.

Diggins, John Patrick. *John Adams.* New York: Henry Holt, 2003.

Ellis, Joseph J. *Passionate Sage: The Character and Legacy of John Adams.* New York: W. W. Norton, 2001.

Ferling, John. *John Adams: A Life.* Knoxville, TN: University of Tennessee Press, 1992.

McCullough, David. *John Adams.* New York: Touchstone, 2001.

Skowronek, Stephen. *The Politics Presidents Make: Leadership from John Adams to Bill Clinton.* Cambridge, MA: Harvard University Press, 1993.

Smith, Page. *John Adams.* 2 vols. Garden City, NY: Doubleday, 1962.

Stinchcombe, William. *The XYZ Affair.* Westport, CT: Greenwood Press, 1980.

Thomas Jefferson (1801–1809)

Early Life and Political Career

Thomas Jefferson was born on his father's farm in what is today Albemarle County, Virginia, on April 13, 1743. He was the third of eight children, and the eldest of two sons born to Jane Randolph and Peter Jefferson. The father was a respected surveyor and mapmaker, but it was his marriage into the Randolph family that raised his prospects and status in Virginia. Soon after Thomas's birth, the family moved to Tuckahoe, a few miles north of the city of Richmond on the James River. Jefferson spent the first nine years of his life there, entering the "English school" at age seven. In 1752 the family relocated back to Albemarle. At this time, Jefferson began to study Greek, Latin, and French with Reverend William Douglas, but Douglas's abilities were limited and the young Jefferson was transferred to the care of James Maury, a more "correct classical scholar." In 1757, Peter Jefferson passed away, leaving young Thomas some 2,750 acres of land. At seventeen, he was admitted to William and Mary College where he came into contact with one of the leading enlightenment thinkers of the day, Dr. William Small.

Small was both mathematician and philosopher, and it was through his influence that Jefferson acquired his abiding interest in natural philosophy and science. He also came into the circle of colonial statesmen, and one of the leading legal scholars of the day, George Wythe. From Wythe, Jefferson imbibed the fundamentals of English common law, the history of English liberty and the ancient constitution, and an interest in political philosophy. These ideas served to round out the renaissance quality of Jefferson's intellectual endeavors, and set him on the path of later renown. While he excelled at horsemanship and the violin, it was his habit of rigorous study that propelled his academic and professional endeavors.

He read history voraciously as evidenced in his notes, or *Commonplace Book,* and this suited him well for his initially successful law practice. He was admitted to the Virginia bar in 1767, but was soon captivated by the early events leading up to the Revolution. The speeches of Patrick Henry, he recalled, were especially enthralling, and touched on all the themes of English liberty, constitutional history, and moral philosophy that formed the core of his study with Wythe. From early on he was an avid collector of books, and this remained with him all the rest of his days.

Founding father, diplomat, and Republican-Democratic president, Thomas Jefferson negotiated the Louisiana Purchase and proclaimed an American "Empire of Liberty." (Library of Congress)

Jefferson's family position and his evident intellectual talents made him a natural candidate for public leadership. In 1769, he was elected to be a representative to the House of Burgesses, the representative body of the colonial legislature of Virginia. In 1770, he was also made county lieutenant, and three years later was made a surveyor for William and Mary College. This was a momentous and formative time for the young representative. In 1772, he married Martha Skelton who would bear him six children over the next ten years, though only two, Martha and Mary, would survive to adulthood. Jefferson's skill as a writer quickly became evident to his peers and would soon propel him to the center of political events.

In 1774, he was elected to attend the convention in Williamsburg for appointing the delegates to represent the state of Virginia in the First Continental Congress. A brief illness prevented him from proceeding to the convention, but he sent ahead his notes for the instruction of the delegates. Most thought Jefferson's notes to be too radical, but his friends Patrick Henry, Peyton Randolph, and other members of the convention quickly recognized their merit and had them bound and printed as *A Summary View of the Rights of British America* (1774). The pamphlet was an instant success, and brought Jefferson's talents to the attention of the wider colonial resistance movement, and in the summer of 1775, he was selected by the Virginia legislature to provide additional representation for the state in the Congress in Philadelphia. His reputation as a writer firmly established, he was put to work on a number of committees, authoring or contributing to such documents as *Virginia's Resolutions on Lord North's Conciliatory Proposal* (June 10, 1775), and *The Declaration of the Causes and Necessity of Taking Up Arms* (July 6, 1775). These papers illustrated Jefferson's ability to weave together the major themes of English Whig opposition thought. The English Whig Party had traditionally sought to limit the power of the British monarchy. Through the works of John Locke, Algernon Sidney, John Trenchard, and Thomas Gordon, the Whigs had developed a variety of arguments for defending limited and constitutional government. Most of the leading members of the American cause were intimately familiar with these sources. Jefferson connected their widely different perspectives on historical legal rights and the ancient constitution with the more universal Enlightenment notions of natural rights, individual liberty, and political consent. He elegantly channeled all these perspectives into a seamless rationale for the American cause. That felicity of style was what convinced John Adams to assign Jefferson the task of drafting the Declaration of Independence, which was accepted by Congress on July 4, 1776. It is also what cemented Jefferson's public reputation, leading eventually to the presidency.

Jefferson served his state in other capacities, including being appointed to the committee charged with revising Virginia's statutes and laws in October 1776. One of Jefferson's most significant and successful recommendations was the abolition of primogeniture passed in 1785, and the bill establishing religious freedom adopted in 1786. His bill for establishing a system of public schools, though it wasn't passed, is a significant milestone in the history of public education. In 1779, he took over the governorship from Patrick Henry. His second term was made difficult by the British invasion of Virginia. After fleeing the capital of Richmond with the state legislature, Jefferson narrowly escaped capture by Colonel Banastre Tarleton, who seized Monticello briefly on June 4, 1781. Jefferson's conduct as governor was called into question by certain legislators who accused him of inadequately preparing the state for invasion. The allegations were soon dropped and on December 19, resolutions of thanks were issued, but the incident would be repeatedly referenced by later political opponents.

In 1783, Jefferson returned to Congress where he served on numerous committees, and authored papers on a range of important subjects such as money and the settling and governing of the western territories. Of particular interest was his paper on commercial treaties of December 20, 1783. This was a report recommending certain provisions for commercial treaties to America's ministers in France as they negotiated with European nations. The paper gives evidence of American confidence in reason as a basis for treaty negotiations. That faith traced back to the Plan of 1776, wherein Americans assumed that the world would willingly open its ports through an enlightened consideration of economic interests. The basic idea was that foreign nations at war with one another should simply allow the goods of noncombatant, or neutral nations, into their ports without hindrance, so long as no contraband items were aboard. Even though that expectation was quickly disappointed, Congress still hoped that the careful application of the principle of reciprocity by American ministers could open ports country by country, an enduring aspect of Jefferson's own thinking with regard to foreign relations in general.

Jefferson as Foreign Minister

In May 1784, Jefferson's abilities in and understanding of international law earned him an appointment to the foreign ministry, assisting Adams and Franklin in their work in Paris. Jefferson's time was well spent, successfully negotiating the Treaty of Amity and Commerce with Prussia in 1785 and otherwise helping to establish good relations with the French. Indeed, Jefferson was always more favorably disposed to France than John Adams, but this was largely because of a pragmatic realization that the United States would need to cultivate nations capable of checking the commercial and military power of Great Britain. England continued to harass American shipping, delayed the evacuation of its frontier forts, and closed her Caribbean colonies to American ships. If America was to be independent in more than just name, the young republic would need to enhance good relations with British rivals. Pragmatism thus formed a core part of Jefferson's thinking just as critical as the ideals of free trade and a peaceful, international order based on reason.

During his years in France, Jefferson remained in contact with developments back home, writing frequently to Madison and receiving regular communications about the Constitutional Convention in Philadelphia. It was in part due to Jefferson's urging that Madison came around to accepting the need for a Bill of Rights. Even before he returned, Jefferson was developing a reputation as a defender of limited national authority strictly bound to the functions of defense, securing individual rights from national interference, and federalism. On his return to the United

States in late 1789, he was appointed to serve in George Washington's administration as secretary of state.

Jefferson as Secretary of State

Friction arose between Jefferson and Secretary of the Treasury Alexander Hamilton almost from the beginning. Due in part to the French Revolution, Britain and France were again in conflict, and this raised fundamental questions about the nature of trade with neutral countries. Hamilton was adamant that revenues from imposts and duties on imports not be disturbed. Since most of America's commerce continued to be with Britain, he did not want to antagonize the former enemy, and that meant making concessions to British demands. What seemed necessary to Jefferson was to counter British restrictions on America with restrictions of the country's own. In February 1791, Jefferson was asked to prepare his *Report on the Privileges and Restrictions on the Commerce of the United States in Foreign Countries,* which was finally submitted in December 1793, after the British had swept away American ships from the Caribbean to prevent trade with the French West Indies. "Instead of embarrassing commerce," Jefferson argued, "under piles of regulating laws, duties, and prohibitions, could it be relieved from all its shackles in all parts of the world . . .the numbers of mankind would be increased, and their conditions bettered." But those nations that refused to free their ports of restrictions would have to be convinced by harsh measures: "Free commerce and navigation are not to be given in exchange for restrictions and vexations."

Both Jefferson and Hamilton counseled President Washington to maintain neutrality toward the British and the French, but the style of their recommendations varied dramatically. Hamilton recommended complete abrogation of the Franco-American Alliance of 1778. His reasoning was simple: that treaty was made with King Louis XVI. Since he was executed on January 21, 1793, the alliance was no longer operative. Jefferson's response revealed his understanding of international law and drew from a close reading of the texts of Grotius, Puffendorf, Wolf, and Vattel, concluding that nations have a right to change their governments and that treaties are made with nations, not specific men of state. However, the law of self preservation overrode any treaty since all actions by government are for the sake of preserving the society of which they are a part. Consequently, a treaty that threatened "great and inevitable danger" could be refused. Regardless, he noted, France had not invoked the treaty yet and probably would not.

Other differences arose with respect to their reactions to the controversial French minister, Edmund Genêt, and his activities to enlist Americans and American ships in the French cause. These were differences more of style and approach than of disagreement over outcome as recalled by

Jefferson in *The Anas.* Hamilton was more favorably disposed to the British while Jefferson inclined toward the French, but neither wanted to see America involved in a European war. Preservation of neutrality thus remained the dominant theme of the Washington administration.

On domestic issues, Hamilton's and Jefferson's differences were more implacable. Disagreement over the legality of a national bank, the financing of the national debt, and internal taxes rested on fundamental differences in the way each read the U.S. Constitution, whether strictly, as Jefferson preferred, or through what Hamilton deemed to be the necessary implication of essential powers. These differences only served to exacerbate tensions and spurred the formation of the Hamiltonian Federalist and Jeffersonian Republican parties. As Washington's own inclinations tended toward the Hamiltonian, Jefferson felt increasingly marginalized and decided to resign his post, delaying only until the end of 1793 at Washington's request.

Jefferson returned to the national stage in name only when he won the vice presidency under the election rules of 1796. With John Adams as the Federalist successor, Jefferson had little role to play but to remain at his beloved house in Monticello. He remained the leading opposition politician, but most of his activity was carried on through private correspondences. He was active behind the scenes by authoring the Kentucky Resolves in opposition to the Alien and Sedition Acts, which were designed to harass and silence Republican critics of the Adams administration and restrain French sympathy. Their actual result was just the opposite, serving to energize the Republican press and paving the way for Adams's eventual defeat. Little stood in Jefferson's way in 1800 when he was elected to the presidency.

Francophobia and the Quasi-War with France

The Adams administration was committed to preserving Washington's legacy of neutrality, but Adams was perhaps even more inclined against France than his predecessor. That fact, combined with growing French belligerence toward his administration and American commercial interests, brought America into undeclared hostilities with the revolutionary republic.

For a brief moment, Americans seemed to rally behind their chief executive when the French minister Talleyrand blundered by insulting America's commissioners through various dispatches demanding loans, in reality bribes, as a precondition for entering into discussions. The incident came to be known as the XYZ Affair, and it prompted Adams to break off further negotiations and ask Congress to be ready in the event of attack. In fact, Adams had considered a call to war but scrapped the idea at the last moment. Alternatively, a series of enactments were issued, some even authored by Hamilton, authorizing the outfitting of privateers and warships to defend American vessels preyed on by French ships. This Quasi-War, as it was called, and the impasse in negotiations amounted to a complete abrogation of the 1778 treaties and the consular convention of 1788.

Initially, Talleyrand had hoped merely to chasten America into recognizing its dependence on France, but his actions had the opposite effect. It now appeared that the Federalists in America were drawing the United States back toward England. Talleyrand had long-range designs on reestablishing the French Empire in North America, and these new developments simply would not do. Hoping to repair the damage caused by the XYZ Affair, he sent Louis Pichon to apologize to Adams and declare that France would henceforth receive American ministers with "the respect due to the representatives of a free, independent, and powerful nation." Adams now had a choice. Either he could appease the anti-French sentiments of his party and risk a full and open war with France, or maintain the peace and America's neutrality. He chose the latter path and sent commissioners to settle a new treaty that was finalized at Môrtefontaine on September 30, 1800. That act of statesmanship may have undermined support in his own party, contributing to his defeat in the election of 1800, but it proved to have positive longer-term results.

The new arrangements put an end once and for all to the troubling alliance of 1778 in exchange for America surrendering its legal claims against France for its attacks on American commerce. That was particularly fortuitous in light of the growing international conflict that brought Napoleon to power. America had once more escaped entangling itself directly in European conflict but it would find navigating the waters of neutrality ever more difficult. That was the continuing challenge bequeathed to the Jefferson administration.

Neutral Rights, the Law of Nations, and Western Expansion

As president, Jefferson would pursue the policies he had recommended to Washington as secretary of state. Needing a counterpoise to the British, he had often favored relations with France, but as he noted in his First Inaugural Address on March 4, 1801, America would seek "peace, commerce, and honest friendship with all nations, entangling alliances with none." Although he was certainly sympathetic to the early French Revolution as a vindication of republican principles, his primary aim was to keep America out of foreign wars, to strengthen its position within the North American continent, and to foster a basic respect for neutral rights on the high seas. France had proved useful to that objective in the past, but the course of events in Europe would pose increasingly more difficult challenges to this strategy in the future.

The execution of Louis XVI and the rise of the Directory and the Consulate in France ran counter to all Jefferson's thoughts on natural law and scientific progress. He used the results, as in the case of the Alien and Sedition Acts, to underscore the differences between Republicans and extreme Federalists, but his principles were completely at odds with later French developments and most especially with Napoleon. Nevertheless, because he held to the primacy of American independence, Jefferson would continue to deal with France, as Adams had done, when it served that larger purpose. That occasion arose again, dramatically and unexpectedly soon after taking office.

The Louisiana Purchase

Jefferson's thinking since the time of the Revolution extolled the benefits of personal independence and self-government. Those themes permeated his compositions from the Declaration forward and explain much about his attitude toward land, liberty, and government. Republican government in America, he wrote later in life, should always be divided and subdivided "from the great national one down through all its subordinations, until it ends in the administration of every man's farm by himself." It was this notion of the independence of the American on his own land that led him to extol the virtues of agriculture. He did not set himself against commerce, but valued the sort of life that could promote a degree of independence essential to republican citizenship—the sort of self-sufficiency that could not be easily intimidated by economic or political threats. To expand westward held the promise of fostering such independence down through the generations, establishing, in essence, an "Empire of Liberty."

Of paramount importance for this empire was the Mississippi outlet for the produce of the new settlers in the area of the Ohio Valley. Spain had been an occasional annoyance to trade, but it was thought too weak to be ultimately a permanent obstruction. Eventually, as Jefferson observed, it would yield up its holdings when it became expedient or profitable to do so.

In 1802, however, rumors spread that Spain might retrocede its holding of Louisiana territory back to France, which was an entirely different prospect. France was a powerful potential rival, and that prompted Jefferson to write to America's minister to France, Robert R. Livingston, on April 18, noting firmly that he should try to encourage the French to consider the long-term consequences of assuming control of the region. It would create friction between the two countries. It would pose little help to France in war, and provide no advantage she did not already enjoy in time of peace. "[A]ll these considerations," he wrote, "might in some proper form be brought into view of the government of France." The rumors were made official on October 16, when the Spanish, in violation of the 1795 treaty with the

United States, announced the closing of the Mississippi in preparation for transfer. The Federalists in Congress called for war, but Jefferson dispatched a new minister, James Monroe, to both France and Spain in an effort to avert crisis. Perhaps the Island of New Orleans and the Floridas might be obtained? Monroe was given a draft for $2 million, but the president, Madison noted, was prepared to go as high as $9 million or more. None anticipated that Napoléon, preparing to go to war with England, would offer sale of the entire region of Louisiana, but that he did. Monroe and Livingston communicated the news at once and agreed on a price that was only slightly higher than the president's upper limit, or $15,000,000. America would pay $11,250,000 and agree to assume the debts owed by France to Americans in the amount of $3,750,000.

Jefferson agonized over the constitutionality of the act. Many of the Federalists would pointedly ask from where he implied this power to make a purchase for the United States. Jefferson submitted the measure to the Senate for approval, but remained troubled by the question of the Constitution's silence respecting the purchase of new lands. His friends and cabinet tried to allay those fears. Secretary of the Treasury

Albert Gallatin advised on August 23, 1803, that such a power was to be found in "the general power given to the President and Senate of making treaties." Thomas Paine would observe in a letter one month later, that the purchase "only extends the principles of [the Constitution] over a larger territory, and this certainly is within the morality of the Constitution." Jefferson's later silence on the issue speaks to his own doubts on the validity of these arguments, but as he would reflect in his Third Annual Message to Congress on October 17, 1803, the purchase opened "a wide-spread field for the blessings of freedom and equal laws."

One sought after piece of real estate that persistently eluded the administration was the Floridas. Negotiations would persist with Spain, but the final acquisition of the area would not occur until 1819.

The Barbary Pirates

When a minister to France, Jefferson had tried to encourage an international coalition to subdue the piratical states of the Barbary Coast of North Africa. The project failed, as Jefferson said, because the American government was

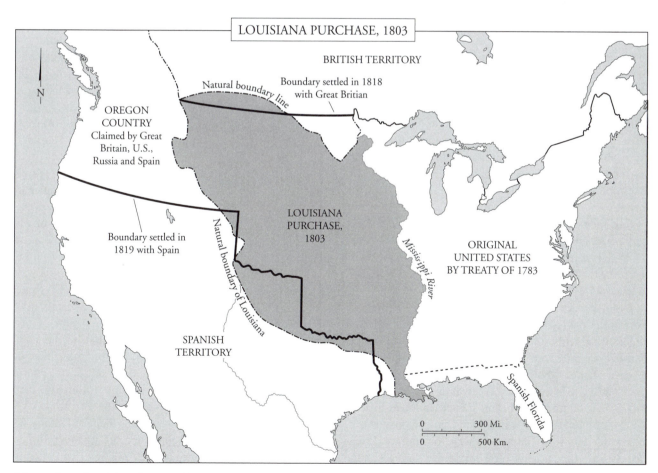

The purchase of Louisiana from Napoleon marked a major milestone in the continental expansion of the United States, building what Jefferson called "the Empire of Liberty."

unable to secure the requisite funds from the states under the Articles of Confederation to support a sufficient naval force. He remained, as a matter of principle, "unwilling that we should acquiesce in the European humiliation of paying a tribute to those lawless pirates."

As president, he had the opportunity to deal with the problem directly and attempt to apply the principles of the law of nations he had imbibed from his legal and philosophical readings. The worst incident occurred on October 31, 1803, when the pasha of Tripoli seized the America frigate *Philadelphia,* which had run aground off the African coast. The pasha took the crew prisoner and hoped to use them, along with increased harassment of American commerce, to secure a better deal respecting the amount of tribute paid to his kingdom under the 1796 treaty. Apparently his excellency, Pasha Yusuf Caramanli, discovered that Algiers had obtained a higher amount in its treaty. Wishing to make a case at least for the enforcement of international agreements, Jefferson chose to send a squadron of ships in May of 1801. The order was simply to destroy any vessels of the Barbary states found making war on American ships.

With only four vessels, the task proved logistically difficult if not impossible. American ships were better armed and faster, but the amount of coast to be covered made it particularly challenging to locate and intercept enemy vessels. A year later, there was little to show for the policy but the added expense of the mission. Albert Gallatin brought this to Jefferson's attention, and with the same reasoning of the European powers, asked if it would not be more prudent and inexpensive to negotiate a new tribute, rather than carry on the conflict. Jefferson was not ready to surrender what he considered a principle of law, and looked for a more aggressive commander, one who would inflict a more costly punishment on the Tripolitans. He obtained this person in Commodore Edward Preble. Preble took the ship *Constitution,* with its forty-four guns, and barraged the fortress and town. At the same time, Stephen Decatur entered the port, and finding the captured *Philadelphia,* set her ablaze, rather than leave her to the use of the pirates. Though a daring move, the administration was embarrassed by the loss of the ship, and the pasha simply refused to concede.

Little changed until 1804, when under further pressure from both Congress and within his administration, Jefferson appointed a new commodore, with a larger force. Samuel Barron was also given a free hand to employ the pasha's brother, Hamet, who had been deposed from the throne years earlier. Hamet and his loyalists along with the American commissioner to Tunis launched a successful mission to capture the Tripolitan town of Derne in the spring of 1805 while Barron stepped up attacks from the sea. Under that pressure, the pasha relented, obtained a hearing with the American commissioners, and agreed to a new treaty more advantageous to him than other powers. The prisoners were released on payment of $60,000. That fact and the retention of tribute, regardless of how well it compared to the arrangements of other nations, proved very unpopular at home and continued to be an embarrassment to later administrations. The fiscal reality, however, compelled even Jefferson to yield to the outcome no matter how much it grated against his understanding of the law of nations.

The Indian Nations

From colonial times, European settlers in the New World had either to treat with or to make war with the Native tribes of North America. The agents of negotiation were often military men, but also explorers and private agents for companies of trade and land. Treaties were negotiated first with crown and colonial officials, but later the formal responsibility for negotiation was assigned by the U.S. Constitution to the federal government. Jefferson attempted to use his position to stimulate an integration of the Indian nations with American culture. Thus his diplomacy addressed the headmen and councils of the tribes as separate powers, but his instructions to officers and governors of the United States revealed a policy of paternalism and dependence.

Much of his policy stemmed from the way Jefferson viewed Native Americans: equal in abilities to Europeans, but frustrated by their adherence to traditional ways. Of particular concern was their dependence on game. Jefferson felt strongly that the tribes should convert entirely "to agriculture, to spinning and weaving," as he wrote to Governor William Henry Harrison in Indiana territory on February 27, 1803.

For a time, the nations of the Illinois and Indiana regions were rumored to be under the influence of British intrigue to destabilize the western settlements. In particular, the administration worried about the Shawnee Chief Tecumseh and his brother the Prophet. Jefferson advised Harrison in February of 1803 to seize the land and drive off all those who would turn to the hatchet.

Friendlier relations characterized his dealings with those he thought were more cooperative. His communication to Handsome Lake in November 1802 assured him of the respect his administration had for their rights to the land: "We indeed, are always ready to buy land; but we will never ask but when you wish to sell." The other side of this policy was illustrated by Jefferson's instructions to Harrison that we should "push our trading uses, and be glad to see the good and influential individuals among them run into debt, because we observe that when these debts get beyond what the individuals can pay, they become willing to lop them off by a cession of lands."

The main thrust of Jefferson's relations with the Indian tribes was to secure western settlement for the independent agriculturalists who formed his ideal of republican citizenship. He wished either to integrate Native Americans into that vision or to remove them across the Mississippi. That hope would be more severely challenged than he expected from Tecumseh and his allies, but that would not become apparent until his successor's administration.

Embargo

The single most trying episode faced by Jefferson occurred in direct response to the ongoing challenges posed by the warring parties of France and England, and their harassment and interference with American shipping. The rights of neutral trading nations was an essential part of American foreign policy extending back to Washington, but as hostilities in Europe intensified with the consolidation of Napoleon's hold over Europe, American trading rights were repeatedly violated.

The Royal Navy persistently and frequently seized American crew members for service in the British fleet. This was the policy of *impressment*. The British held that many who served on American vessels were their own renegade crewmen. For Americans, it was an insulting violation of their right as an independent sovereignty. More fundamental, however, was the British application of the Rule of 1756, holding that neutral nations were not allowed to engage in trades that had been denied to them during peace. The Rule was relaxed for much of Jefferson's first term, but as the growth of American trade increased, pressure was placed on the British government to revive its enforcement with respect to France.

James Stephen's pamphlet, *War in Disguise; or The Frauds of the Neutral Flags* (1805) argued that American trade went directly to assist Napoleon's conquests. The basic point was to show that certain trades with French colonies would not have been allowed in peacetime, but were permitted to the Americans by the French because their own ships could not pass through the British lines. Even the American John Randolph referred to the enterprise as a "fungus of war." America, in essence, was enjoying an unnatural monopoly of the carrying trade because the rest of Europe was embroiled in conflict.

The revival of the Rule of 1756 was denounced by Jefferson's secretary of state, James Madison, in his 204 page pamphlet of the same year entitled, *An Examination of the British Doctrine, Which Subjects to Capture A Neutral Trade, Not Open in Time of Peace*. This was a weighty defense of the idea that a neutral vessel's cargo was free to travel from port to port so long as it was not carrying military contraband. It did not matter that these ports were closed in the time preceding conflict. What mattered was that nonbelligerents

be left unmolested. John Quincy Adams would later praise the work as a "standard Treatise on the Law of Nations," but it angered the pro-British elements in Congress. Near the same time as the publication of Madison's work, Madison presented to Congress the number of impressments of American sailors as 2,273 between 1803 to 1806.

The issue underscored a profound difference between the American and British concepts of citizenship. The United States accepted immigrants who professed loyalty to America, but England only recognized as American those British who had participated in the rebellion or war for independence. All others were presumed to remain under the authority of King and Parliament. The subject of impressment would bring to a standstill Monroe and Pinkney's efforts to ratify a new treaty to replace the expired Jay treaty of a decade earlier. Since they could gain no concession on impressment, Jefferson refused to accept the agreement, but this was overshadowed in late 1806 and early 1807 by Napoleon's Berlin Decree and Britain's Orders in Council. Both essentially prohibited the trade of neutrals with the other. Neutrality was essentially over as a viable policy.

Jefferson's course of action was in conformity with his past experience first in the American Revolution and later in Washington's administration. Embargos had embarrassed British merchants in the past and brought some limited pressure to bear on Parliament, but economic conditions had changed, and stores of essential supplies were ample enough in Britain that it could endure such restrictions over a longer period. American merchants could not. Yet there were few alternatives for the administration if it wanted to continue to pursue neutrality. Unable to challenge either French or English power, Jefferson could see no other option but that of prohibiting all trade with the belligerents and keeping American ships at home.

An incident involving the American ship *Chesapeake* cemented the president's resolve to act. On June 22, 1807, the British vessel *Leopard* demanded the return of four seamen known to have been British crewmen. The *Chesapeake* refused and was fired on for ten minutes by the *Leopard*, killing three and wounding eighteen. Six months later, on December 22, 1807, the embargo was enacted for fifteen months. It proved disastrous to the New England maritime economies and a hardship to the mid-Atlantic states. Though effectively enforced for the most part south of New York, it encouraged illegal trafficking. Over the fifteen months of the embargo, 150,000 barrels of flour were transported to Eastport, Maine, for carrying into Canada! Hostile letters from angry merchants abounded. It also revived the Federalist Party for a time. As Jefferson later recalled in a letter to Joseph C. Cabell dated February 2, 1816, while praising the power and importance of local governments, "How powerfully did we feel the energy of this organization in the case of embargo? I felt the foundations of the government shaken under my feet by the New England townships."

Many of the Federalists and the British themselves accused the embargo of playing into the hands of Napoleon because it denied the use of American ships as carriers of English manufactures to Europe. It thus effectively supplemented the emperor's Continental System. Some Federalists even mused about the possibilities of a New England secession from the Union. Still, petitions for repeal were repeatedly rebuffed by Congress, which remained firmly in the Republican camp. Only when the stories of secession and impending rebellion began to panic the leadership in the House was a resolution passed for the expiration of the policy on March 4, 1809. Jefferson felt that the only other honorable course was war, but the majority in both houses disagreed. Instead, the embargo was replaced by a Non-Intercourse Act, opening trade with everyone but Britain and France. This proved unworkable. Merchants had merely to transport their goods to noncombatant countries and from there they could be traded legally to either of the two belligerents. Jefferson's attempt to defend neutrality peacefully thus ended in failure. It was left to the next administration, that of his friend and political ally, James Madison, to attempt to find some way around the looming prospects of open warfare.

Legacy

Jefferson's own evaluation of his endeavors with respect to foreign policy are perhaps among the most critical. The Louisiana Purchase stands as his crowning achievement in diplomacy. Few dispute the fact that every aspect appeared to fall into place: the timing, the price, the extent of the territory acquired, and the security that it afforded to the fledgling republic on its western frontier. These were not small achievements, and any similar development would be welcomed by most presidents after Jefferson, but the third president remained troubled by the issue of its constitutionality and did not list Louisiana among the achievements for which he wanted most to be remembered.

His policy toward the Barbary States was ineptly executed. Even by the standards of his time, Jefferson detested the payment of tribute. It went against everything he thought appropriate for advanced nations, and a world that should be progressing toward the regular and peaceful administration of law. But he paid tribute to the Barbary States nonetheless, having handicapped his statecraft by undermining the navy throughout his administration.

Regarding the securing of the West and relations with Native tribes, his policy looked to the eventual elimination of the Indian nations as distinct sovereignties, and in to that end, he was willing to use both debt and force.

Finally, Jefferson remained convinced that if his policy of embargo had been endured for a short time longer, it would have forced Britain to respect neutral rights. Indeed, he thought it might even result in the promotion of local manufactures, and a further degree of national independence from the economy of the world. Clearly in this he forgot his own earlier acknowledgment to John Jay on August 23, 1785: "Our people are decided in the opinion that it is necessary for us to take a share in the occupation of the ocean, and their established habits induce them to require that the sea be kept open to them, and that that line of policy be pursued which will render the use of that element as great as possible to them. I think it a duty in those entrusted with the administration of their affairs to conform themselves to the decided choice of their constituents . . ." In a real sense, as Jeffersonian policies were acted out during the presidency of James Madison. Thomas Jefferson's most immediate foreign policy legacy was a grave and avoidable deterioration in Anglo-American relations, and even the ultimate disaster of the needless War of 1812.

Hans Eicholz

Chronology

1801

February 9: Franco-Austrian Treaty of Lunéville dissolves most of the Holy Roman Empire.

May 20: Jefferson orders naval force to be used against Barbary states.

August 1: American sloop *Enterprize* captures Barbary ship *Tripoli* off Malta.

1802

March 16: U.S. Military Academy established.

March 27: Anglo-French Treaty of Amiens.

November 2: France fails to suppress Saint Domingue revolt.

1803

April 30: Louisiana Purchase, for $15 million, the United States acquires the territory from France.

May 12: Anglo-American Boundary Convention.

May 16: Britain declares war on France.

August 31: Lewis and Clark expedition begins.

October 31: Tripoli captures U.S. frigate *Philadelphia*.

1804

February 24: Mobil Act, Congress claims West Florida for the United States.

May 18: Napoleon proclaimed Emperor of the French.

December 5: Jefferson reelected.

December 12: Spain declares war on Britain.

1805

April 11: Anglo-Russian Alliance.

May 22: British action against neutral U.S. shipping begins to increase.

June 9: Austria joins Third Coalition.

June 10: Peace with Tripoli after U.S. Marines capture Derna.

October 10: Napoleon victorious at Ulm.

October 21: Britain defeats Franco-Spanish fleet at Trafalgar.

December 2: Napoleon victorious at Austerlitz.

1806

April 10: Secretary of State James Madison protests British naval blockade and pressed service of Americans. Senate condemns "unprovoked aggression," passes First Non-Importation Act.

December 2: Congress bans all slave importation to the United States, effective January 1, 1808.

December 31: Monroe-Pinkney Treaty with Britain.

1807

June 22: Leopard-Chesapeake Affair brings Britain and the United States to the brink of war.

July 7–9: Victorious France concludes Treaties of Tilsit with Prussia and Russia.

December 22: First Embargo Act against all American overseas commerce.

1808

May 21: Canadian border incidents heighten tension with Britain

November 22: Congress reports Embargo Act a failure.

December 7: James Madison wins presidential election.

1809

January 9: Embargo enforcement tightened.

March 1: Jefferson signs Non-Intercourse Act in response to opposition to embargo.

References and Further Reading

Appleby, Joyce. *Thomas Jefferson.* New York: Times Books, 2003.

Appleby, Joyce, ed. *Jefferson: Political Writings.* New York: Cambridge University Press, 1999.

DeConde, Alexander. *This Affair of Louisiana.* New York: Charles Scribner's Sons, 1976.

Ellis, Joseph J. *American Sphinx: The Character of Thomas Jefferson.* New York: Alfred A. Knopf, 1998.

Ferrell, Robert H. *American Diplomacy, A History.* New York: W. W. Norton, 1975.

Kennedy, Roger G. *Mr. Jefferson's Lost Cause: Land, Farmers, Slavery, and the Louisiana Purchase.* New York: Oxford University Press, 2003.

Onuf, Peter S. Jefferson's Empire: *The Language of American Nationhood.* Charlottesville, VA: University Press of Virginia, 2000.

Peterson, Merrill D. *Thomas Jefferson and the New Nation.* New York: Oxford University Press, 1970.

Silverstone, Scott A. *Divided Union: The Politics of War in the Early Republic.* Ithaca, NY: Cornell University Press, 2004.

Tucker, Robert W., and David C. Hendrickson. *Empire of Liberty: The Statecraft of Thomas Jefferson.* New York: Oxford University Press, 1990.

James Madison (1809–1817)

Early Life and Political Career

James Madison was born in Port Conway, King George County, Virginia, on March 16, 1751, and died on June 28, 1836, at his Montpelier home in Orange County, Virginia. He was the first of ten children born to James Madison Sr. and Eleanor Rose "Nelly" Conway and grew up at the family home in Orange County. His father was a prominent man in Orange County who owned large landholdings there. The fourth president's early education began at age twelve and continued with his matriculation at the College of New Jersey (Princeton) in 1769. Madison was an active and serious student who studied government, history, law, ethics, and Hebrew. He also founded the American Whig Society—an important debate and literary club. He graduated with a BA in 1771, but remained at the college for an additional year of study in Hebrew and ethics. Returning home, Madison continued his studies and taught his younger siblings. However, this tranquil country life soon came to an end when he was caught up in the growing political turmoil between the colonies and Britain. Before long, Madison was on the road to a life of public service arguably unmatched in American history.

Madison's political career began in 1774 with his efforts on behalf of religious liberty in a local dispute over unlicensed preachers. His first election to office came in 1775 when he was chosen for the Committee of Public Safety in Orange County. A proud patriot of the Revolutionary cause, Madison was elected in 1776 as a delegate to the state convention and served on the committee that wrote one of the most important state constitutions in the Revolutionary era. He served in Virginia's House of Delegates for one year, but was defeated for reelection in 1777 (because of his failure to provide libations by tradition for the voters). His reputation already growing; the legislature elected him to the Council of State where over the next two years he assisted First Governor Patrick Henry and then his successor Thomas Jefferson. Madison was then selected as a delegate to the Continental Congress from March 1780 to December 1783. Madison was an important member of this body and acquired national prominence for his work there. One of his most important acts was to help settle Virginia's claims in the old Northwest (which helped secure passage of the Articles of Confederation). During his last year in Congress, he was instrumental in Congress's recommendation to the

James Madison's War of 1812 against Britain came dangerously close to a national calamity. (Library of Congress)

states that the national government be allowed to raise revenue via a 5 percent import tax. Madison was already showing a commitment to union and a stronger national government. He returned home following his retirement from Congress and again served with distinction in the state legislature from 1784 to 1787.

Worried about dangerous defects in the Articles of Confederation, Madison helped push the idea of interstate conferences that led to the Annapolis Convention of 1786 and the Philadelphia Convention of 1787 (both of which he attended). He returned to Congress in 1787, where his chief goal was "to bring about, if possible, the canceling of Mr. Jay's project for shutting the Mississippi." Fortunately, Jay's plan to trade to Spain navigation rights on the Mississippi for twenty-five years in exchange for commercial concessions was abandoned, though it cannot be said whether Madison was responsible for this. Madison was then called on by Virginia to represent the state at the Philadelphia convention. At what would come to be known as the Constitutional Convention, Madison supported replacing the Articles of Confederation with a stronger central government less dependent on the states. He was also one of the forces behind the Virginia Plan, which favored the large states in the new legislative scheme. Although Madison's ideas were not enacted in whole, he is often referred to as the "Father of the Constitution" for his efforts and influence on the framing of the new stronger and united American regime. After the convention and during the state-ratifying debates, Madison—along with John Jay and Alexander Hamilton—authored the *Federalist Papers,* which made the case for the Constitution. These papers represent a critical contribution to political thought and remain unmatched in the history of American political science. Madison also played a direct role in the state-ratifying convention in Virginia. Elected as a delegate from his home county, Madison defended the Constitution against prominent anti-Federalists such as Patrick Henry, Richard Henry Lee, and George Mason. His leadership in the Virginia convention certainly helped ensure its acceptance by this important large state.

Despite the efforts of his anti-Federalist opponents in Virginia to deny him a seat in either body of Congress, Madison was soon elected to the new House of Representatives. He was a leader in the House where, in the first session, he worked for passage of the promised Bill of Rights, fleshed out the executive branch of the new government, and tried to place the country on sounder financial footing with a revenue-producing tariff on imports. Madison generally believed in the ideal of free trade, thinking that "commercial shackles are generally unjust, oppressive, and impolitic." However, along with these revenue raising duties, he supported exceptions to the rule when justified by the national interest (which turned out to be fairly often in practice for Madison). He was particularly concerned with diversifying America's trade relations, given U.S. dependence on the British market, and unsuccessfully sought discriminatory measures that favored trade with France. He also argued for restrictions on the British, arguing in 1795 that U.S. trade and navigation should "not be free to her [Great Britain] without an equal and reciprocal freedom to us." He went on, providing an early indication of Jefferson's and Madison's later policy using trade as a tool of statecraft, by noting that such restrictions were "an intermediate experiment between negociation [sic] and war." Madison remained in the House until 1797. During his tenure in Congress, Madison moved away from his old Federalist allies and became a leader of the developing opposition movement.

Party Politics and Foreign Policy

Soon after that first session, Madison's remaining time in the House was consumed by the first party struggle in the United States that emerged between the Federalists and Jefferson's Democratic-Republicans. Secretary of the Treasury Hamilton's economic plans, including his proposed creation of a national bank, were particularly disturbing to Madison. On the bank, Madison thought the Federalists were interpreting the Constitution too loosely, threatening to undermine the principle of limited government and the barriers to excessive federal power enshrined in the Constitution's system of enumerated powers. Madison also grew disenchanted with his former political allies over foreign policy matters. In particular, Madison thought that the Washington administration, especially Hamilton, overly favored Britain. He saw France as a friendly ally and makeweight to British power. Hamilton, on the contrary, charged his new opponents with a "womanish attachment to France and a womanish resentment against Great Britain."

These foreign policy differences were heightened when Britain and revolutionary France went to war in 1793. The Washington administration's response was the Neutrality Proclamation, issued on April 22, 1793, that declared the United States would treat both belligerents in a "friendly and impartial" fashion. Madison disagreed with the Proclamation. He thought it "a most unfortunate error" that violated the United States's alliance with France and showed an excessive Anglophilia on the part of the administration. He also worried that this move represented executive encroachment on Congress' constitutional authority. He and Hamilton sparred in print over these matters in the famous Pacificus-Helvidius debate that followed Washington's Proclamation.

In early 1794, a war scare swept the country over British harassment and seizure of American commerce at sea. Madison moved to have Congress issue a nonintercourse act against Britain, but it was defeated in the Senate in a tie vote broken by Vice President John Adams. Despite the ominous clouds, perhaps even because of them, the Washington administration proceeded to negotiate a "Treaty of Amity, Commerce, and Navigation" with Britain on November 19, 1794. The Jay Treaty, as it came to be known, was not a smashing success, though it did pacify U.S.-British relations and led to increased Anglo-American trade. The treaty gave the United States little it was not already owed (such as British turnover of forts in the Northwest) and failed to secure agreement on neutral rights or impressment. The British, however, were able to win a halt to American efforts to restrict trade with Britain and even undermined America's long-standing view that "free ships make free goods." Madison viewed the treaty as a "ruinous bargain" and argued against it over the next year. However, he was unable to carry the House against the appropriations necessary to enact the treaty. The Federalists won the day and realigned American foreign policy in a pro-British fashion. Predictably, this policy angered the French and led to rough treatment of American shipping by them. The struggle with France led to the infamous XYZ Affair and the new Adams administration's engagement in a naval war (the Quasi-War with France). This served to further irritate Jeffersonian Republicans, including Madison. However, Madison was not to witness that war from Congress, as he retired from public life in 1797. The years of the late Washington-early Adams era were politically difficult for Madison, and the respite from politics was probably welcomed by the future president. However, there was at least one personal success during this trying time. On September 15, 1794, Madison married Dolly Payne Todd of Philadelphia, with whom he shared a long, happy marriage.

Madison's Return to Politics

Madison's retirement was short-lived. He returned to politics in 1798 by writing a vigorous response to the notorious Alien and Sedition Acts. It was soon adopted by the Virginia legislature. This Virginia Resolution declared the Alien and Sedition Acts to be unconstitutional, enunciated both a compact theory of the Constitution and a doctrine of interposition, and called on other states to follow Virginia in the defense of its peoples' and states' rights. Neither this resolution nor Jefferson's similar Kentucky Resolution inspired other states to follow suit. Madison then won election to the Virginia House of Delegates in 1799 and wrote his *Report of 1800,* which further spelled out and defended his views on the Constitution (in particular, the meaning of the First Amendment and his compact theory, according to which the national government was a creation of a compact among the individual states). Shortly before the election of 1800, the war with France ended with the Treaty of Môrtefontaine.

Madison returned to national office with the election of fellow Republican leader Thomas Jefferson to the presidency. Madison served as his friend's secretary of state from 1801 to 1809 and his chief advisor on foreign and domestic matters. Indeed, he played a key role in Jefferson's successful "Revolution of 1800" which transformed the country and the government more in keeping with the Revolutionary spirit of 1776 and the Constitution of 1789 than with the previous Federalist vision of an active, centralized state. It also meant a change in American policy vis-à-vis the British.

However, foreign policy would not come to the fore until 1803, as the first two years of the Jefferson administration coincided with a lull in the European war. After 1803, Jefferson and his secretary of state struggled with the problem of remaining neutral without forfeiting national rights and liberties in the face of both British and French harassment of American shipping. Indeed, the effects of the European war led to Jefferson's greatest foreign policy achievement, the Louisiana Purchase, and its chief legacy to his successor, continued maritime problems with the British and French.

The Jefferson Legacy: Unfinished Business

James Madison was easily elected president in 1808 over Federalist candidate Charles Cotesworth Pinckney. The Republican standard bearer trounced his opponent 122–47 in the Electoral College. Clearly, the "Revolution of 1800" was popular enough to carry one of its staunchest advocates into the White House as Jefferson's successor. Unfortunately for Madison, foreign policy was not one of the hallmarks of Jefferson's presidency despite the Louisiana Purchase, his call for "peace, commerce, and honest friendship with all nations, entangling alliance with none," and Madison's own efforts as secretary of state. Instead, the new president was left with a number of thorny issues that carried over into his term and almost ruined his presidency.

The chief legacy in foreign affairs was the continuing difficulty with Britain and France on the high seas and in the halls of power. In their own long struggle that had resumed in 1803, the British and French had sought to deny each other overseas trade, and the result was frequent harassment and depredations of American commerce. The British were particularly aggressive in trying to prevent American vessels from reaching French-controlled ports. In 1805, Britain changed its policy on "broken voyage" commerce that passed through a neutral to or from the Continent (essentially expanding Britain's Rule of 1756, which blocked direct trade). Such commerce had become particularly profitable for the Americans during the war. In response to the new British policy, Madison penned a long critical treatment of the Rule of 1756 titled, *An Examination of the British Doctrine, Which Subjects to Capture A Neutral Trade, Not Open in Time of Peace.* In this critique, Madison called into question the legality of the rule and forcefully defended neutral shipping rights. Regardless, in 1806, Britain issued an Order-in-Council that tightened its restrictions by declaring a blockade of the European coast. In the minds of Americans, this was an illegal act given that it was merely an unenforced "paper blockade" that led to further depredations at sea.

In 1807, another Order-in-Council was passed subjecting Continent-bound ships to seizure and confiscation. Finally, Anglo-American strife was intensified by another long-standing American grievance: Britain's continued practice of impressing American seamen for duty in the Royal Navy. Indeed, American and British obstinacy on the matter scuttled the Monroe-Pinckney Treaty of 1806, which would have won some relief from British restrictions on American trade. Jefferson and Madison opposed the treaty because it did not go far enough in safeguarding American rights, and kept it from reaching the Senate for ratification.

France was also guilty of belligerent actions against American shipping. Napoleon's Berlin and Milan decrees mirrored the British orders, though they did not have the same impact as British actions. Jefferson considered going to war with one or both of these powers in response to these edicts. However, he pulled back even when handed a casus belli on June 22, 1807, when the British warship *Leopard* attacked the USS *Chesapeake* resulting in twenty-one American casualties. Rather than go to war, the reaction of the Jefferson administration to all of this—born of both Republican philosophy and the weakness of the American state—was to use American trade as a weapon to force the two Great Powers to respect the United States's neutral rights. Specifically, the United States thought that it could use an embargo as a successful tool of statecraft while avoiding the costs and dangers of open war. Madison, as secretary of state, was an architect of this policy and was glad to see Congress enact the Embargo Act of 1807 and a nonimportation bill against the British. These laws cut off all of the country's export trade. Unfortunately for the administration, it was a complete failure, resulting in no change in French or British behavior and much harm to the nation, northern seaports and southern farms alike. This experiment in economic coercion was finally sent to pasture as Jefferson's presidency ended, yet the problems with Britain and France were a nagging hangover for Madison's administration. Moreover, Madison and the Republicans still hoped that well-crafted commercial weapons could work in place of gunpowder.

Another issue that carried over into Madison's administration concerned the Floridas. Since the Louisiana Purchase, the border between Spanish Florida and American territory remained unresolved. More important, the United States coveted both the disputed West Florida area and Spanish East Florida, hoping to eventually buy or wrest control of all of it from Spain.

Madison was also left to handle commercial difficulties in the Mediterranean. Since Washington's days in office, the United States—following European tradition—had paid tribute to the Barbary states to keep its commerce in the Mediterranean from being harassed by the four states. It

was also forced to ransom captured seamen on more than one occasion. Difficulties in the area finally led to U.S. military action under Jefferson in the war with Tripoli. Unfortunately, the practice of paying tribute did not end with the peace treaty ending the war in 1805. American troubles in the region did not cease either, leaving Madison with yet another difficulty that extended into his presidency. The last important foreign policy issue that extended from Jefferson into Madison's administration (and would remain on the American agenda for most of the century) was American-Indian relations. Indeed, problems with Native peoples were a contributing factor in the U.S. decision to go to war in 1812.

Foreign Policy: "The Assertion of National Rights and Independence"

Madison assumed the presidency with many thorny issues left unresolved by the Jefferson administration. In many ways, Madison's presidency was a continuation of the previous one, given his close working friendship with Jefferson and a shared mind-set with his fellow Virginian. Moreover, he kept many of Jefferson's cabinet officers on board, though only Albert Gallatin at the Treasury was a close and loyal advisor in the cabinet (James Monroe, later added in 1811 as secretary of state, was to a lesser extent an important advisor as well). As Jefferson's secretary of state, Madison had been long engaged with the same problems he faced as president, and thus was partly responsible for the legacy he inherited. Unlike his predecessor's tenure, though, Madison's presidency was dominated and defined almost exclusively by foreign affairs.

Madison spent nearly his entire presidency either trying to stay out of war or prosecuting war when peace could not be achieved short of national surrender. The chief problem he faced from the outset was how to deal with problems created by the twin battling powers of Europe: Britain and France. With American commerce deeply impacted by the hostile measures of both states, Secretary of State Madison tried to use an embargo to solve the problem. With the failure of the Embargo Act of 1807, President Madison and Congress went back to the drawing board to find a way to protect American interests short of war.

The Non-Intercourse Act of 1809 and the Erskine Agreement

The American embargo was quickly replaced by the relatively mild Non-Intercourse Act of 1809. This act reopened the world, minus Britain and France, to American commerce. More importantly, it offered to renew trading with either of those warring states if they would cease their harassment of and restrictions on American shipping. The administration was determined, as it related to its officers in London and Paris, "not to acquiesce in the edicts of either of the belligerents." Unfortunately, this weapon would not have any more success than the embargo in securing American trading rights. For a time, however, it looked like Madison's economic warfare would yield its desired fruit, and the United States would not have to fight for its rights at sea.

In response to the new American law and some weakening of the British position on the Continent, Britain's foreign minister George Canning authorized new talks to resolve the dispute with America. The new minister to the United States, David Erskine, was charged with negotiating the repeal of the Orders-in-Council and a settlement of the *Chesapeake* affair provided that the United States accept, among other things, British enforcement of U.S. laws at sea barring American ships from intercourse with France. Of course, British enforcement was a nonstarter with Madison given its attack on American sovereignty. As Madison later recalled, it was "too absurd and insulting ever to have been sincerely counted upon." Despite the apparent irreconcilability of British demands and American interests, Erskine and his American counterparts ploughed ahead with negotiations anyway. The British minister must have thought he had the flexibility to move forward without an American agreement on Canning's demands. Either that or he was so motivated by his desire to successfully conclude negotiations that he was blind to how it would be received in London. Without dealing with these irreconcilable issues, the negotiations quickly resulted in the Erskine Agreement that ended the Orders-in-Council, freed trade between Britain and the United States, and settled the *Chesapeake* affair. Consistent with the Non-Importation Act, this agreement allowed Madison on April 19, 1809, to declare an end to the dispute with Britain. It appeared that Madison's philosophy and policy had worked, and Americans rejoiced at the news. However, this joy was short-lived. The agreement was doomed in London since Erskine had not been able to meet Canning's requests of American acquiescence to British enforcement, restrictions on Franco-American trade, acceptance of the colonial trade law known as the Rule of 1756, and the end of the 1807 American ban on British warships operating in U.S. waters. Within two months, Washington learned that Canning rejected Erskine's agreement, recalled his minister, and kept the Orders-in-Council in place. By August 9th, the United States and Britain were right back where they started—or worse given the bad blood engendered by Canning's actions—as Madison reapplied the Non-Intercourse Act to the British. It also did not help that Erskine's replacement, Frances James Jackson, further antagonized the Madison administration with an exchange of nasty notes on the Erskine negotiations.

The Floridas

While the trade dispute between the United States and Britain deepened into a crisis that threatened to lead to war, the Madison administration was also engaged over the Floridas. West Florida's status had been in dispute since the Louisiana Purchase. The United States claimed that all of the Gulf Coast land between New Orleans and the Perdido River was American territory by terms of that treaty. Spain disagreed and maintained civilian and military authorities in Baton Rouge, Mobile, and elsewhere. In the meantime, little had been done to immediately resolve the issue, since American settlement and Spanish weakness meant it would likely fall into U.S. hands before long. Madison, as secretary of state, had said that "we are the less disposed to make sacrifices to obtain the Floridas, because their position and the manifest course of events guarantee an early and reasonable acquisition of them."

By 1810, Madison thought that the situation required more active attention. In January, his administration prompted Orleans Territory governor William Claiborne to move things along by instigating a call of West Floridians for U.S. occupation. Later in the year, American settlers went further and revolted against Spanish authorities at Baton Rouge (and set up a short-lived, independent republic modeled on the American regime). Fearful of British or French occupation, as well as the dangers of anarchy, Madison sent occupying forces into West Florida up to the Pearl River in 1810 in order to protect U.S. interests. He avoided a clash with Spain by not authorizing action against the Spanish forces at Mobile and Pensacola. Still worried about British interference in the Floridas in 1811, Madison asked for and was granted by Congress the power to occupy East Florida should it threaten to pass into foreign hands. This was one of the first articulations of the "no-transfer" policy that would guide American foreign policy in the Western Hemisphere. Then, in early 1813, the United States occupied the rest of West Florida up to the Perdido River. However, the East Florida situation remained unresolved since the Senate rejected a House bill that would have authorized Madison to send U.S. forces there. With the end of the War of 1812, the United States was again free to concentrate on fully absorbing the remainder of Spain's Florida territory. However, the Floridas issue would not be settled on Madison's watch. This would occur a few years later in 1819 when James Madison and Secretary of State John Quincy Adams concluded the Adams-Onis Treaty (what would later be called the Transcontinental Treaty with Spain).

The Path to War

The failure of the Erskine negotiations put the United States and Britain back on the road to war in 1810. Congress, though, failed to appreciate this and did not pass Madison's request for increased spending on the Army and Navy. However, in the same year, it did pass Macon's Bill Number 2 to replace the expired Non-Intercourse Act of 1809. This act allowed American shippers to trade with the British and French, but forbade ships of those states from U.S. ports. Most importantly, it also allowed the president to reimpose nonintercourse against one of the belligerents if the other renounced its restrictions. Napoleon took advantage of this part of Macon's Bill in the fall of 1810 by issuing the Cadore letter. This missive announced an end to French commercial restrictions and called on the Americans to punish British commerce if London did not reciprocate. Of course, Britain did not cave in to American demands to follow the French. Unfortunately for the United States, France was not acting in good faith, failing to live by its promises but meanwhile pushing the United States closer to war with Britain.

Despite evidence that France was not actually meeting the requirements of Macon's Bill, Madison issued a proclamation on November 10, 1810, imposing nonintercourse against Britain. Then in May 1811, the United States and Britain clashed at sea when the American ship *President* fired on Britain's *Little Belt*. This was not the first time that a naval incident had occurred since British ships were virtually blockading the American coast to enforce the Orders in Council. However, it was noteworthy because the *President* had been specifically ordered by Secretary of the Navy Paul Hamilton to be more proactive about protecting U.S. shipping. With no end in sight to the commercial struggle as 1811 closed, Madison and Congress readied for war.

Native American Relations

Fights over the treatment of commerce were not the only things fanning the fire in Anglo-American relations at this time. The United States faced trouble inland with some of the Indian tribes in the old Northwest and in the South. Most prominent among these was Tecumseh and the Prophet Tenskwatawa's attempt to unite Indians in the Ohio Valley. British agents were seen to be pushing these efforts, and British incitement of Indians in the West was mentioned later by Madison as one of the causes of the War of 1812. In 1811 these troubles in the West resulted in a significant armed clash. On December 18, Indiana territory governor William Henry Harrison attacked and defeated an Indian stronghold in the Battle of Tippecanoe. American-Indian clashes in the West continued during the War of 1812, including the Battle of the Thames in 1813, during which Tecumseh was killed (and with his death came the end of serious unified Indian opposition in the Ohio

Valley). Meanwhile, there were also Indian troubles in the South, specifically with the Creeks and the Seminoles. These problems were only exacerbated by the war with Britain. Especially significant fighting between Indian tribes and American forces under Andrew Jackson occurred from 1813 to 1814. One of the results of this nasty warfare was the harsh Treaty of Fort Jackson, which resulted in the Creeks giving up two-thirds of their land.

Despite these problems, Madison's general approach to Native peoples was to seek peaceful accommodations with and between Indian tribes and to try to convince them to live more like white men. In his First Inaugural, Madison called on Indians to "a participation of the improvements of which the human mind and manners are susceptible in a civilized state." He, like other presidents, received numerous tribal delegations at the White House. At one point, he even sought to quell Indian unrest in the South by sending in troops to protect Indian lands from encroachment. Moreover, toward the close of his presidency, he informed Commissioner Andrew Jackson that he was "determined to obtain no lands from either of those nations [Cherokee and Creek], upon principles inconsistent with their ideas of justice and right." However, the Madison administration was unwilling or unable to protect Creek lands that were supposed to be returned in accordance with Article IX of the Treaty of Ghent. Moreover, the government's view of Native tribes and frequent mistreatment of them during Madison's tenure as secretary of state and president is regrettable. Unfortunately, the most egregious offenses were still to come.

The War of 1812

Without any known British movement relaxing the Orders in Council or dealing with other important issues such as impressment, Madison and Congress approved the Embargo of 1812. This was seen a prelude to war. Madison finally called on Congress on June 1, 1812, to declare war, and the declaration was quickly delivered and signed on June 18, 1812. Unfortunately for the cause of peace, news that the British had rescinded the Orders in Council prior to the declaration did not reach Washington until July 27. It did not matter—Madison had already declared that "the rights, the interests, and the honor of our country" necessitated a martial response.

The primary causes of the declaration of war were the maritime grievances suffered by the United States at the hands of the British. This "series of acts hostile to the United States as an independent and neutral nation" included impressments, harassment and seizure of American commerce off the American coast and elsewhere at sea, and illegal blockades. Historians have also pointed to the goals of dealing with Indian troubles on the frontier and the desire for expansion. However, these were secondary motives, and expansion itself was probably motivated by defensive concerns. As one historian has sagely noted, "Had there been no war with France, there would have been no Orders-in-Council, no impressments, and, in all probability, no War of 1812."

Unfortunately, the course of the war did not go as smoothly as had been hoped by the Madison administration. Not only did Canada fail to fall into American hands as quickly as had been hoped, American forces actually lost ground on the border in the beginning stages of the war. In fact, American soldiers and militiamen fared poorly for most of the war. Two of the signal failures of American military history came during the war. On August 16, 1812, General William Hull surrendered his Detroit force and lost control over a wide swath of the Great Lakes region. Later on August 24, 1814, Washington, D.C., was easily taken by the British, and the White House and Capitol were torched. Despite much bad news on the ground, there were some important successes. Tecumseh was killed and his British allies were defeated at the Battle of the Thames on October 5, 1813. Baltimore held strong against a British attack following their successful march on Washington, D.C. And of course, following other important victories in the South, General Andrew Jackson utterly defeated a superior British force at the Battle of New Orleans (which had been made unnecessary by the end of the war two weeks prior). At sea, the American Navy fared quite well despite its smaller numbers. It won important victories on the Great Lakes (such as Oliver Hazard Perry's victory on Lake Erie) and on Lake Champlain as well as on the high seas (such as the *Constitution*'s sinking of the *Guerriere* and the *Java,* and Stephen Decatur's capture of the *Macedonia*).

The Treaty of Ghent

Soon after Madison's Second Inaugural in March 1813, Alexander I of Russia offered to mediate peace between Britain and the United States. Madison accepted the offer and quickly sent Senator James Bayard and trusted Treasury Secretary Albert Gallatin to join minister John Quincy Adams in St. Petersburg for a possible conference of peace. Unfortunately, Gallatin was rejected for appointment by the Senate, and the British declined the offer of mediation. At this point, Madison called for an embargo to prevent American goods from reaching the British one way or another. Congress rejected his call. Madison again asked for an embargo and other measures to thwart the British (and the New Englanders) in December 1813, stating that continuing the current trade regime would "favor the enemy, and thereby prolong the war." This time, Congress gave Madison what he wanted, much to the chagrin of the nearly treasonous New Englanders who had been profitably trading with the enemy. However, these economic weapons were surprisingly eliminated from the nation's arsenal the next spring.

As 1813 closed, a peaceful end to the war was again on the table. British foreign secretary Lord Castlereagh offered to discuss peace with the American commissioners already overseas for the scotched talks in Russia. Madison sent the letter and his acceptance of the talks to Congress. He then nominated Jonathan Russell, House Speaker Henry Clay, and Gallatin (who was still in Europe) to join Adams and Bayard for meetings scheduled for Gothenburg, Sweden. The talks produced little at first. The British asked for terms that Madison and the country could not accept: an Indian buffer state and nothing about impressment. The Americans, on the other hand, wanted at least part of Canada and an end to impressment. At that point, the talks moved to Ghent, Belgium, where they continued unsuccessfully for some time. Indeed, the British seemed unwilling to offer anything but harsh terms, and the talks almost broke down when the British insisted on fishing, border, and navigation concessions that no American could accept. Before any further progress on peace was made, events at home worsened considerably for the United States. The British had burned Washington, D.C. and assaulted Baltimore. Moreover, New England discontent continued to threaten the American war effort and even the union. Indeed, New England Federalists ultimately held a convention in Hartford, Connecticut, in December 1814, to discuss constitutional remedies to the problems Madison and the Republicans represented. However, soon there was good news on the military front as British forces were repulsed in key engagements in northern New York and at Baltimore. News of these critical events, not to mention European political developments and the Duke of Wellington's tepid view of the situation in America, helped rekindle British interest in the peace talks and led to signing a peace treaty on December 24, 1814. Unfortunately for those killed in the Battle of New Orleans, Madison and the rest of the country did not hear the official news until February 14, 1815.

The Treaty of Ghent was ratified by the Senate on February 16, 1815. It was a fairly modest treaty that did little but end the hostilities and return to the antebellum status quo. Although Madison did not get anything on neutral rights or impressments—the primary reasons for the war—he was able to truthfully claim that he had asserted "the rights and independence of the nation" against a major world power that threatened them. And whether it was true or not, the country believed what one pamphlet claimed: "Our character has been retrieved from ignominy and instead of an insulted and pusillanimous people, we rank exalted in the opinion of the surrounding world."

The Barbary States

On the heels of the close of the War of 1812, Madison decided to continue his defense of American rights and shipping by fighting back against the long-running bribery and piracy of the Barbary states. His move was precipitated by ongoing harassment of American ships in the region (despite U.S. tributary payments) and the dey of Algiers' declaration of war against the United States in 1812. The United States could do little about the dey until after the Treaty of Ghent. Soon thereafter, on April 12, 1815, Congress, prompted by Madison, finally declared "the existence of a state of war" between the two parties. Thereupon, Madison sent a naval force led by Commodore Stephen Decatur to the Barbary Coast.

Decatur's squadron of ten ships needed less than a summer to compel the dey to sign a treaty ending the war and granting American requests. In the course of the short war, the naval forces under Decatur successfully defeated the Algerians at sea, capturing two ships including the command ship of the Algerine admiral. American losses were minimal, with only one sailor killed in combat (and only four total U.S. deaths). Decatur then sailed into the port of Algiers, forcing the dey to submit. The treaty ending the Algerine War was signed on June 30, 1815, and called for the end of tributary payments and piracy, the return of all captives held for ransom, and other terms favorable to the United States. A larger American force moved into the region and was able to convince Tunis and Tripoli to cut similar deals with the United States.

When the dey tried in 1816 to regain tributary payments, Madison ended the discussion very quickly with a threat of war. In a strongly worded missive to the dey, Madison wrote in August: "the United States, whilst they wish for war with no nation, will buy peace with none. It is a principle incorporated into the settled policy of America, that as peace is better than war, war is better than tribute." A second treaty with Algiers followed in December, effectively ending Madison's and the United States's troubles with the Barbary states.

Postwar Foreign Policy Issues

As his presidency wound down, Madison attempted to deal with a number of other foreign policy issues. One of his chief successes after the war was the negotiation of the basis of an agreement with the British for disarmament on the Great Lakes (though the ultimate agreement, known as the Rush-Bagot Agreement, was not finalized and ratified until Monroe took office). As for trade, Madison was able to negotiate a commercial pact with the British, but was unable to win significant relaxation of British restrictions on American trade with the West Indies. This led to the passage

of a retaliatory law that placed the same restrictions and prohibitions on foreign vessels that were imposed on American shipping. Despite his previous concerns about trade barriers, Madison also saw through the passage of a protective tariff. Finally, given the wartime problems with the military, Madison attempted to reform the military and increase military spending.

Legacy

The single thread that runs through Madison's foreign policy was the assertion and defense of the rights and independence of the United States. This connects his war aims in both the War of 1812 and the Algerine War. It was also behind his attempts to eliminate the threat a foreign-held Florida might mean to the security of the expanding nation, particularly the recently purchased Louisiana Territory and the strategic city of New Orleans at the mouth of the Mississippi. In the process, Madison was able to prove to the world that the United States was a serious, if not yet great, power that deserved respect. Yet "Mr. Madison's War" in particular was hardly a great victory and included the humiliating burning of the White House and the Capitol. Moreover, it threatened to tear apart the union. Indeed, many scholars believe the War of 1812 was unnecessary and ineptly handled. Few actually defend Madison's handling of the crisis or the war. Many of these criticisms are valid, particularly those that center on his being diplomatically bested by Napoleon or those that focus on his role as commander-in-chief. However, it cannot be denied that the country that emerged from the struggle had more than survived what one scholar has called a "second war of independence" despite its military weakness, structural defects, and sectional rivalries (if not treasonous activities on the part of many New Englanders). Moreover, Madison should be credited with ending America's weak-kneed Barbary policy and building a new working relationship with the British following the war.

Madison inherited a number of serious problems from his predecessors. Though in hindsight we might wish that he had dealt with them in a different manner, one could not say that he failed the Ronald Reagan test: The United States was not worse off at home or relative to foreign powers at the end of his presidency. At the least, Madison should be credited with guiding the United States through a very difficult time. A more sympathetic conclusion would congratulate Madison for eliminating some thorny issues and facing down the British at little cost.

William Ruger

Chronology

1809

April 19: Madison reinstates trade with Britain.

August 9: Madison revives Non-Intercourse Act.

1810

January 20: United States seeks new talks with Britain.

October 27: United States annexes West Florida.

1811

February 28: United States and Britain recall ministers.

May 16: USS *President* attacks HMS *Little Belt*.

May 16: Reinstatement of nonintercourse policy against Great Britain.

July 31: Mexico defeats Hidalgo revolt.

November 4: Congressional "War Hawks" demand action against British and Indians in Northwest.

November 8: American forces defeat Indians at Tippecanoe.

1812

April 4: Congress approves full embargo against Britain.

May 28: Britain refuses to lift commercial restrictions.

June 18: Congress declares war on Britain, War of 1812 begins.

September 14: Napoleon's army in Moscow.

October 19: Napoleon's army begins retreat.

December 2: Madison reelected.

December 26: Britain blockades U.S. ports.

December 29: U.S. and British ships duel off Brazil.

1813

February 28: Treaty of Kadish, Russian and Prussia ally against France.

March 3: Britain and Sweden ally against France.

April 17: American forces burn York, Canada.

June 15: Treaty of Reichenbach, Britain, Prussia, and Russia ally against France.

September 10: U.S. Navy wins Battle of Lake Erie.

October 5: U.S. forces win Battle of the Thames in Canada.

October 16–19: Napoleon defeated by allies in Battle of Leipzig.

December 29–30: British burn Buffalo, capture Fort Niagara.

December 30: Britain offers peace talks.

1814

March 13: Allied armies enter Paris, Napoleon exiled to Elba.

May 30: Treaty of Paris, European war ends.

August 24–25: British capture and burn Washington, D.C.

September 12–14: British attack Baltimore, bombard Fort McHenry.

December 24: Treaty of Ghent signed by American and British negotiators.

January 8: Battle of New Orleans, unaware of peace Andrew Jackson leads American soldiers to spectacular victory.

1815

March 2: Congress declares war on Algeria.

June 8: Congress of Vienna.

June 18: Resurgent Napoleon defeated at Waterloo.

June 30: Algeria accepts American terms.

November 20: Second Treaty of Paris signed.

December 22: Spain defeats Morelos rebels in Mexico.

1816

April 27: Protective tariff imposed, Second Bank of the United States established.

December 4: James Monroe elected president.

References and Further Reading

Adams, Henry. *History of the United States of America during the Administrations of Thomas Jefferson and James Madison,* 9 vols. New York: Scribner's, 1889–1891.

Banning, Lance. *The Sacred Fire of Liberty: James Madison and the Founding of the Federal Republic.* Ithaca, NY: Cornell University Press, 1995.

Brant, Irving. *James Madison,* 6 vols. Indianapolis, IN: Bobbs-Merrill, 1941–1961.

Brown, Roger H. *The Republic in Peril: 1812.* New York: Columbia University Press, 1964.

Cox, Isaac J. *The West Florida Controversy, 1798–1813.* Baltimore, MD: Johns Hopkins University Press, 1918.

Horsman, Reginald. *The Causes of the War of 1812.* Philadelphia: University of Pennsylvania Press, 1962.

Ketcham, Ralph. *James Madison: A Biography.* Charlottesville, VA: University Press of Virginia, 1990.

Mahon, John K. *The War of 1812.* Gainesville, FL: University Presses of Florida, 1972.

Perkins, Bradford. *Prologue to War: England and the United States, 1805–1812.* Berkeley, CA: University of California Press, 1963.

Rutland, Robert Allen. *James Madison: The Founding Father.* New York: Macmillan, 1987.

Rutland, Robert Allen. *The Presidency of James Madison.* Lawrence, KS: University Press of Kansas, 1990.

Stagg, J. C. A. *Mr. Madison's War: Politics, Diplomacy, and Warfare in the Early American Republic, 1783–1830.* Princeton, NJ: Princeton University Press, 1983.

Stuart, Reginald C. *United States Expansionism and British North America, 1775–1871.* Chapel Hill, NC: University of North Carolina Press, 1988.

James Monroe (1817–1825)

Early Life and Political Career

James Monroe was born at Monroe Hall in Westmoreland County, Virginia, on April 28, 1758. He was the second and eldest male of five children of Spence Monroe and Elizabeth Jones. The ancestral home was located on the Potomac River tributary of Monroe Creek, and had been purchased in 1650 by Major Andrew Monroe. His parents were moderately wealthy planters, owning a 500-acre farm bordering forests and marshes, on which they raised cattle and produced tobacco and other cash crops. His father was also a cabinetmaker. Monroe was a patrilineal descendant of Edward III, his great-grandfather having been exiled to Virginia after fighting with Charles I during the Civil War. Monroe's early social environment was among Virginia's Northern Neck landed gentry. From the ages of eleven to sixteen he attended the academy of Scottish head teacher Archibald Campbell, where he and future Chief Justice John Marshall were fellow students. Both were influenced by a religiously inflected code of moral sternness. Monroe seems to have done particularly well in mathematics and in Latin. With the death of his father in early 1774, Monroe was encouraged to enter the College of William and Mary in Williamsburg by his uncle, Judge Joseph Jones. Matriculating that autumn, he read law there under George Wythe, a respected colonial lawyer, burgess, and Continental Congress delegate.

Leaving William and Mary in 1775, Monroe was commissioned lieutenant in the Third Virginia Regiment of the Continental Army. In August of the following year, the regiment was ordered north to Harlem Heights outside New York City, where it met the main body of the colonists' army on retreat from Manhattan, fighting with it at Harlem Heights and White Plains. On Boxing Day of 1776, during the Battle of Trenton, Monroe's captain was wounded and Monroe briefly assumed command. Monroe too was wounded soon after by a bullet that opened his auxiliary artery; he would carry the bullet in his shoulder the rest of his life. Later serving as aide-de-camp to Major General Lord Stirling, Monroe saw action again in the autumn 1777 battles of Brandywine and Germantown, accompanying General Washington to Valley Forge that winter and fighting the following June in the Battle of Monmouth. In early 1779, with the rank of major, Monroe left the Northern Army as it encamped outside New York with no immediate

James Monroe, an avid expansionist, issued the doctrine that appropriately bears his name. (Library of Congress)

prospects for action. Arriving in Virginia, he was commissioned a lieutenant colonel to lead a militia regiment there being recruited, but the unit never formed.

In Virginia, Monroe became an aide to Governor Thomas Jefferson, who, like Wythe, influenced the bent of his personality and profession toward the law. Settling in Prince Edward County, Monroe stood for the state legislature in 1782 and was elected. He was subsequently chosen for its executive council, and, at the age of twenty-four, was its youngest member. The following year, he was elected to serve in New York in the Congress of the Confederation, where he served for three years and chaired two committees concerned with American westward expansion: one with the formation of a government for the western territories and a second investigating free navigation on the Mississippi River. His interests in the territories lying between the Allegheny Mountains and the Mississippi thereby whetted, he journeyed through the Hudson River, Great Lakes, and Ohio River during a congressional recess in 1784, and helped draft a framework for western territorial governance enacted as the Northwest Ordinance in 1787. He contracted malaria in a swamp off of the Mississippi River, which would recur, though undiagnosed, in times of great physical strain in March 1815, early 1818, and August 1825. In February 1786, he married seventeen-year old Elizabeth Kortright, who was from an established Dutch family of New York.

Monroe resigned from Congress in October 1786, settling in Fredericksburg, Virginia. There he won successive elections to the town council and state legislature and, in 1786, attended the Annapolis Convention which convened to address issues of interstate commerce under the Confederation. Denied delegacy to the Constitutional Convention in 1787, a sourly disappointed Monroe blamed Madison and Governor Randolph of Virginia. Partially as a result, he initially adopted a neutral stand toward the Constitution as a delegate to the Virginia ratification convention, with Madison and Randolph as its principal advocates, and moved ultimately toward decided opposition with anti-Federalists George Mason and Patrick Henry, citing the absence of a Bill of Rights and the threat of centralized governance to free navigation of the Mississippi (the latter argument being crafted to appeal to western delegates). He was then defeated by Madison for the House of Representatives seat from Orange County by 366 votes on February 2, 1789. Curiously, the two men, beginning the campaign as political rivals, ended it as cordial friends. Madison was for his part impressed by their series of debates about the need for a strong Bill of Rights, which he then proceeded to shepherd through the newly convened Congress.

Selected in 1790 by the Virginia legislature to fill a vacant Senate seat, Monroe became a noted critic of the Washington administration's foreign policy, believing it too close to Britain. The near success of his opposition to the appointment of Gouverneur Morris as minister to France signaled to Washington that he should be consulted on future appointments. For reasons more procedural than substantive, Monroe decried the 1793 Neutrality Proclamation between Britain and France as a violation of congressional war powers. Monroe left the Senate in 1794 to replace Morris as minister to France; Washington appointed him in a time of French suspicion of his British leanings evidenced by his enthusiasm for the French Revolution, which Madison believed the successor of America's own. For a president remembered principally for his contribution to the American diplomatic discourse, his first tenure as a diplomat was not a success. An early speech to the French National Convention won from Washington the criticism, to Jay, that "considering the place in which they were delivered, and the neutral policy this country had to pursue, it was a measure that does not appear to have been

well devised by our Minister." He was on several occasions undercut by trade overtures toward Britain by Jay, of which he was not appraised, denting his credibility with the French government. When he was recalled in 1796 by Secretary of State Pickering to be replaced by Charles Pinckney, Anglo-American comity in the wake of Jay's Treaty had reversed the thaw in Franco-American relations which saw, after Monroe's convention speech, the American flag placed next to the French in the assembly hall. Monroe took the opportunity of his leaving ceremony to criticize Washington's Farewell Address.

Settling into a 3,500-acre Virginia plantation beside that of his mentor Jefferson, Monroe sought to fend off Federalist criticism of his tenure as minister to France by publishing an impassioned 407-page record and defense of his service entitled *A View of the Conduct of the Executive, in the Foreign Affairs of the United States.*

Elected as governor in a 1799 party-line vote after two years of superintending, alongside Jefferson and Madison, the coalescence of the anti-Federalist faction into the Republican Party, Monroe proved a reformist governor, expanding the powers of his office, reorganizing the militia, and checking Gabriel's Rebellion. His political fortunes rehabilitated at the end of his term in 1802, when Jefferson, now president, returned him to France as the United States' envoy extraordinaire. As envoy, his instructions were to negotiate the purchase of the port of New Orleans from France, solidifying American control of the Mississippi. (Pinckney's Treaty of 1795 had permitted American merchants "right of deposit" to use the Spanish-controlled port for their goods, but the retrocession of Louisiana to France under the Treaty of San Ildefonso increased American anxiety that its access would be annulled.) Deciding in March 1803 to abandon the rebuilding of France's New World empire in favor of attempting an invasion of Britain, Napoleon directed the Marquess de Barbé-Marbois to offer French Louisiana to United States for $15 million. With Livingston, Monroe negotiated the purchase treaty, then was translated to Britain where his unrealized instructions lay in obtaining relief from British harassment of U.S. shipping; his subsequent mission to Spain to secure Spanish assent for inclusion of West Florida in the Louisiana Purchase was equally frustrated. An 1806 Anglo-American trade treaty, which touched neither upon British blockading of French ports nor impressments, was not even submitted by Jefferson for Senate advice and consent. Soured against both Jefferson and Madison, Monroe returned from his mission in late 1807 and stood against Madison in the 1808 election, receiving no electoral votes and 2.5 percent of the popular vote.

Returning to Virginia politics—and spurning a conciliatory offer from Madison to accept the governorship of upper Louisiana—Monroe served again in the assembly in 1810, and in 1811 was again elected as governor. With time and through correspondence, the friendship between the three Virginians was reestablished and, resigning the governorship, in April Monroe accepted Madison's offer to become secretary of state. Though supportive within the cabinet of an equipoised relationship between Britain and France, Monroe was both overruled by Republican antipathy toward Britain and pressed on by territorial ambitions against British North America and Spanish Florida. Holding the war portfolio alongside that of state after the August 1814 invasion of Washington onward, Monroe oversaw the defense of Baltimore as well as the negotiation of the Treaty of Ghent. The Federalists were destroyed by their opposition to the War of 1812; on the expiry of Madison's second term, Monroe stood as natural successor and received the electoral votes of all but Massachusetts, Connecticut, and Delaware.

Tilting Toward France and Warring with Britain

Although elected in an era of good feelings and with his unequal campaign against Senator Rufus King showing none of the bitterness of previous drawn-out elections, Monroe entered the edifice that would, with his administration, first be known as the White House. He was dubious of his predecessor's policy of Anglo-American estrangement and a war which he had not favored.

Monroe was backed by John Quincy Adams, one of the most talented secretaries of state to have held the office. With firsthand experience in the Louisiana Purchase with diplomacy in service of territorial acquisition, Madison's presidency had marked a reversal in the French tilt of American policy since the Democratic-Republican rise to power in 1800. Skilled and often daring diplomatic maneuvers permitted the infant nation room amid the warring of the Great Powers to span the continent. Comity toward the British Empire permitted the declaration of the doctrine of western hemispheric noncolonization and nonintervention that would bear his name. Where warring with Britain permitted Madison nothing more at the conclusion of hostilities than the status quo ex ante, comfortable ties with Foreign Secretary George Canning allowed Monroe to bequeath the nation the western segment that had first interested him as a young legislator.

A Hemispheric Doctrine and a Transatlantic Nation

With less intellectual grandeur than his predecessors Jefferson and Madison, and by nature deferential and inclined to conciliation over boldness, Monroe's thinking nonetheless left a more enduring mark on subsequent American diplomatic tradition than the neutralism of Washington's Farewell Address. His behavior furthered the nation's territorial and economic interests more than Jefferson's ill-fated embargo or Madison's equally dolorous war.

The key lines of his diplomacy—reforming moderate but adequate land and naval forces, neutrality in great power conflicts, and furthering interests through comity toward the belligerents—were adumbrated in his First Inaugural Address. In a *sub rosa* repudiation of the foreign policy of his predecessor, he was unequivocal in ascribing present prosperity to neutralism:

> Under the benign influence of our republican institutions, and the maintenance of peace with all nations whilst so many of them were engaged in bloody and wasteful wars, the fruits of a just policy were enjoyed in an unrivaled growth of our faculties and resources.

Similarly he solicited amity with the European empires and a middle ground with regard to a standing military force:

> To cherish peace and friendly intercourse with all nations having correspondent dispositions; to maintain sincere neutrality toward belligerent nations; to prefer in all cases amicable discussion and reasonable accommodation of differences to a decision of them by an appeal to arms. . . . To keep within the requisite limits a standing military force, always remembering that an armed and trained militia is the firmest bulwark of republics—that without standing armies their liberty can never be in danger, nor with large ones safe.

He was remarkably well advised, abetted by one of the stronger sets of counsel assembled for any president. Jefferson and Madison, cordial friends and former presidents both, continued to offer prescriptions (though Monroe was not slavish about following them). His cabinet included Calhoun as secretary of war, William Crawford of Georgia with the treasury portfolio, and William Wirt of Maryland as attorney general.

The Rush-Bagot Treaty

The demilitarization of the Great Lakes and the groundwork for disarmed boundaries and peaceful coexistence between the United States and British North America was achieved as one of the Monroe administration's maiden acts. The Rush-Bagot Treaty imposed limits of four warships on each side, none to exceed 100 tons. The agreement, concluded in an exchange of notes between Acting Secretary of State Richard Rush and British minister Sir Charles Bagot, set a precedent for amicable resolution of Anglo-American contentions. It also inaugurated a policy of peace between the United States and Canada, which would be interrupted only by such minor boundary disputes as the Lumberjacks' War over the Maine-New Brunswick border. In broader significance, Monroe's

1817 treaty not only initiated an administration-long commerce in treaties with the United Kingdom, but also soundly put the two nations on a basis of amity that would grow into a special relationship, interrupted only by the American Civil War (in the Trent and *Alabama* affairs) and with Cleveland's threatened intervention in the Guianan-Venezuelan border dispute (as well as in the twentieth century by the Suez Crisis).

The Anglo-American Convention of 1818

The lasting demilitarization of the northern boundary accomplished, Monroe's diplomacy turned toward the western border in the London Convention of 1818. Richard Rush, America's minister at the Court of St. James, and envoy to Paris Albert Gallatin negotiated three major decisions along the western frontier with the Rt. Hon Frederick Robinson (later prime minister) and Conservative Under-Secretary Henry Goulburn. The question of ownership of the Oregon Territory, to which Britain and the United States were both claimants, was deferred for twenty years during which the two nations would follow a policy of joint occupation. (This territory corresponded to present-day Oregon, Washington, and British Columbia.) The Louisiana Purchase's northern frontier was established as 49° N latitude in the region from the crest of the Rocky Mountains eastward to the Lake of the Woods (the present day Minnesota-Canada boundary). The anomalous Northwest Angle, unspecified by the Treaty of Paris due to limitations of eighteenth-century knowledge of geography, was awarded to the United States, and U.S. fishermen were also given rights to fish the waters of Newfoundland and Labrador. The Convention also committed the nations to refer differences arising under the Treaty of Ghent to third-party mediation and extended the trade provisions of the Anglo-American Convention of 1815 for ten years. The Convention of 1818 furthered the pattern of pacific relations between the United States and the British Empire, though latent in its terms pertaining to the Oregon Territory would lie a vociferous struggle for control in that region realized in the 1830s and potent until the Oregon Treaty of 1846.

The Transcontinental Treaty of 1819

With his project of territorial consolidation thus concluded in the North and West, Monroe then followed it to the southern border. John Quincy Adams met in Washington with Don Luis de Onís for the Spanish Crown to settle control of East Florida and demarcation of the boundary between Mexico and the Louisiana Purchase. Spain reached the negotiating table in a position of weakness, its American territories in near or actual revolt. (Bolívar's *Campaña Admirable,* having begun in 1813 with the Second Venezuelan Republic proclaimed in that year, Bogotá being taken in 1814, and the remainder of Colombia falling into Bolivarian hands in 1819.) Where the United States claimed the Purchase extended its territories to the Rio Grande and the Rocky Mountains, the Spanish position remained that Spain's cession to France in the Treaty of San Ildefonso included only New Orleans and the west bank of the Mississippi. Complicating matters, the Treaty of San Ildefonso did not specify the boundaries of the territories being retroceded, referring only to "the colony or province of Louisiana." Monroe sought Oregon for the United States to allow the nation to develop as a Pacific power through its trade with Asia.

Onís, faced with the possibility of losing Florida without any compensation, agreed to the sale of East and West Florida, with surrender of its claims in the Oregon Country north of a line of demarcation (drawn at the Sabine River from the Gulf of Mexico to the 32nd parallel, then north to the Red River and Arkansas and thence along the 42nd parallel to the Pacific). His situation could hardly have been more desperate. Commanding Tennessee volunteers, Major General Andrew Jackson had pursued Seminole and Creek Indians as well as several non-Indian combatants from Georgia into Spanish Florida, writing to Monroe "Let it be signified to me through any channel (say Mr. John Rhea) that the possession of the Floridas would be desirable to the United States, and in sixty days it will be accomplished." Monroe sent orders that were left purposely ambiguous (" . . . the movement against the Seminoles will bring you on a theatre where you may possible have other services to perform . . . Great issues are at stake"), permitting himself plausible deniability if the letter were revealed but encouraging Jackson's ambition nonetheless. Entering Florida, Jackson easily seized Pensacola and deposed the Spanish governor on May 29, 1818. When Spanish Foreign Minister Pizarro demanded compensation and punishment for Jackson, Monroe permitted Adams publicly to respond on July 23 that the blame was Spain's for not controlling the Indians within its territory. Writing to Onís, Adams reproached the minister:

> Spain must immediately make her election either to place a force in Florida adequate at once to the protection of her territory and to the fulfilment of her engagements or cede to the United States a province of which she retains nothing but the nominal possession, but which is in fact a derelict, open to the occupancy of every enemy, civilized or savage, of the United States and serving no other earthly purpose, than as a post of annoyance to them.

Confronting this situation, and with Monroe threatening war and seizure of Texas when he hesitated, Onís felt fortunate to be permitted to keep Spain's colonies in Texas and a territorial buffer between Spanish California and New Mexico and the U.S. territories. With the signature of the

Adams–Onís treaty on February 29, 1819, West and East Florida were acquired for $5 million, this last paid to American citizens with claims against Spain. After the cession of Florida to the United States, Monroe installed Jackson as territorial governor.

In seizing Spanish Florida, Jackson had seized two British nationals, Lieutenant Robert Ambrister and the Scottish trader Alexander Arbuthnot, executing both on April 23 in Fort Marks. Arbuthnot had engaged in drilling and equipping Indian soldiers under the command of the Seminole chief Bowlegs, while Ambrister warned Seminoles of Jackson's advance. Either execution could have complicated Monroe's policies of Anglo-American comity and territorial expansion at the expense of Spain, but because Monroe had placed relations with Britain on sufficiently good footing, Viscount Castlereagh was happy to accept the convenient American explanation that the two British nationals were in Florida illegally, and indeed, exerted pressure subsequently on Madrid to ratify the Transcontinental Treaty. (This despite Arbuthnot and Ambrister having taken Castlereagh's own view, that the ninth article of the Treaty of Ghent entitled Creeks to restoration of lands they had relinquished at Fort Jackson.)

Liberia

Monroe's name is carried by not only a doctrine but also an African capital. Monroe, favoring a gradual end to slavery, served after returning to civilian life as first president of the American Colonization Society, a preponderantly southern organization favoring resettlement of free blacks in the West African coastal colony of Liberia. The Liberian project had its genesis in an 1800 correspondence between Monroe and Jefferson, following the Gabriel slave rebellion. Presbyterian clergymen Samuel Mills and Robert Finley succeeded in gaining some measure of support among New Jersey clerics for the idea. In 1819, Monroe succeeded in securing a congressional appropriation of $100,000 to resettle recaptured and illegally traded slaves to Africa. He appointed the Colonization Society's Rev. Samuel Bacon as agent, and on February 6, 1820, the *Elizabeth,* convoyed on Monroe's command by the U.S. sloop-of-war *Cyane,* set off from New York harbor with eighty-six settlers, who were required to seek refuge in Sierra Leone after encountering adversity. In March 1821, a second entourage of twenty-eight emigrants reached Freetown in the brig *Nautilus*. They identified Cape Montserado as a favorable location for settlement, but were unsuccessful in purchasing land there because its inhabitants were disinclined to break up the traffic in slaves. Monroe, immovably wedded to the idea and referring to Liberia as "a little America, destined to shine gem-like in the heart of darkest Africa," provided the Americo-Liberian settlers with military assistance in installing themselves in Cape Messurado in early 1822. Later that year, the brig

Strong, chartered by the Monroe administration, carried food, thirty-seven settlers, and ten liberated trafficked slaves from Hampton Roads. The capital city, formerly Christopolis, was renamed Monrovia in 1824. In the decade following the *Nautilus* settlement, 2,638 black Americans emigrated to the colony. Many abolitionists criticized the society as at best a palliative and at worst for strengthening the institution of slavery by removing free blacks. The American Colonization Society governed Liberia privately until 1847, when it became independent amid concerns of British annexation, with Joseph Jenkins Roberts as its first president. As president of the American Colonization Society, Monroe was succeeded by Henry Clay.

Second Term and the Russo-American Convention of 1824

Monroe was reelected in 1820 by a single-party polity in what would be the third and last uncontested American presidential election (former New Hampshire governor and senator William Plumer alone would cast a vote against him in the Electoral College, this purportedly to ensure only Washington would be elected unanimously). Monroe embarked on a second term that would, in retrospect, revolve around his doctrine: first the Russian territorial dispute and the American territorial ambitions of the Holy Alliance that predated and precipitated it and the continued closeness in Anglo-American relations that made it materially possible, and the debate in the cabinet that resulted in articulation of independent strategic principle in preference to an entangling alliance with Great Britain.

Russian North America began with Captain-Komandor Vitus Bering's stricken exploratory voyage of 1741. He accomplished a landing in the vicinity of Kayak Island and charted several of the Aleutian Islands. The first colony of Grigory Shelikhov was established in 1784, principally focused on the trade in sea otter fur. The Russian-American Fur Company received a charter from Czar Paul I in 1799. Orthodox missionaries followed, including Herman of Alaska and St. Innocent of Alaska. The Russian settlement's southernmost outpost was Fort Ross, on the California coast north of San Francisco in what is now Sonoma County.

In September 1821, Czar Alexander I released an ukase declaring a Russian zone of exclusivity on the western coast of North America extending from the Bering Sea to 51° N latitude, asserting ownership of coastal lands for Russia and the prohibition henceforth of foreign shipping within 100 miles of the claimed lands. As the Anglo-American territory of Oregon Country extended latitudinally between 54°40' and 42° N, the Russian claim overlapped with claims of the United States and United Kingdom. On the instructions of Monroe, Adams wrote and dispatched a diplomatic note to the Russian minister in Washington disputing the territorial claim: "We should contest the right of Russia to *any* territorial establishment on this continent." Adams also stated, in a prefiguring of the Monroe Doctrine's dominant motif, that "We should assume distinctly the principle that the American continents are no longer subjects for any new European colonial establishments." It was Adams's advice that led Monroe to contest the Russian claim: the president was initially willing to grant a boundary at the 55° line, but Adams had precognition of the trade potential of the northwest coast and his arguments convinced the president. In April 1824, Russia signed a treaty with the United States agreeing to no further settlement south of the 54°40' N latitude line, with the United States in turn promising no settlements north of that line, the line representing the southern tip of the Alaska panhandle and approximate boundary between Russian Alaska and the Oregon Country. Russia also gave recognition of joint British and American control of the Oregon Country.

The Latin American Republics

The second and more immediate provocation of his doctrine lay in the threat that the counter-revolutionary Holy Alliance—Russia, Austria, Prussia, and France—would dispatch troops to aid Spain in reasserting its control over its rebellious colonies. At their congress held in Troppau in 1820, the allied powers agreed their main common purpose was to maintain the principle of legitimacy of the existing dynasties, with the powers agreeing to preserve it by armed intervention when threatened. Austrian forces had thus suppressed popular uprising in Piedmont and Naples, with sanction from the alliance's 1820 congress at Laibach; French troops entered Spain to reinstate Ferdinand VII after a constitutionalist rebellion in 1822, on authority of the Congress of Verona.

The British role had been one of some complicity throughout the early Holy Alliance: though not aligned with the four allies formally, Castlereagh represented Britain in the Troppau and Laibach conferences during the final portion of his service as foreign secretary. Castlereagh was viewed domestically as an unpopular reactionary; upon his suicide, he was replaced with the more liberal George Canning. Canning led British policy to diverge from the allies over Verona and allowed Latin America to come within the French sphere of influence, for reasons both of principle and of commercial and strategic interest. Canning saw the reduction of Spain's colonies to be the natural subsequent application of the principle of intervention to follow the restoration of the Spanish king.

Canning made his overture to Madison in writing to the American minister, now Richard Rush, on October 9, 1823, proposing a joint Anglo-American declaration of five principles:

1. We conceive the recovery of the Colonies by Spain to be hopeless.

2. We conceive the question of the recognition of them, as Independent States, to be one of time and circumstances.

3. We are, however, by no means disposed to throw any impediment in the way of an arrangement between them, and the mother country by amicable negotiation.

4. We aim not at the possession of any portion of them ourselves.

5. We could not see any portion of them transferred to any other Power, with indifference.

Monroe retreated to his Virginia home at Ashlawn to consult Jefferson in Monticello and Madison in Montpelier; both advised accepting the Canning proposals.

Monroe was inclined to follow the advice of his predecessors, which agreed with the advice of much of his cabinet, particularly Calhoun; they feared the Holy Alliance would restore all South America to Spain, within a French sphere of influence. The cabinet met on November 7, with Adams noting Canning's proposal aimed also against the acquisition by the United States of any part of the Spanish American possessions. While Calhoun argued that Britain's greater ability to seize Spanish possessions by force made the agreement an advantageous bargain for the United States, Adams held out the possibility that Texas or Cuba might freely solicit union with the United States; thus by accepting, Monroe would give "a substantial and perhaps inconvenient pledge against ourselves, and really obtain nothing in return." Monroe's personal concern in these cabinet discussions was not to take any course placing the United States in a position subordinate to Britain. In this, his and Adams's thought were aligned: as the latter expressed it, "It would be more candid, as well as more dignified, to avow our principles explicitly to Russia and France, than to come in as a cock-boat in the wake of the British man-of-war." (A cockboat is a small boat towed behind a man-of-war and used for moving between ships or in small harbors.)

There was another level also possibly influencing these deliberations. The succession rivalries between Adams and Calhoun, which would debilitate the cabinet in its last year, were beginning to appear. Madison's principal foreign policy architect, Adams, found his candidacy opposed by Jefferson and Madison, who found the secretary of state objectionable because of his Federalist pedigree. With Madison and Calhoun also urging an alliance with Britain, and Madison furthermore supportive of extending recognition to Greece in its attempt to achieve autonomy from the Ottoman Empire, Adams was in the delicate situation of distancing himself from traditional Federalist attitudes in responding too favorably to British overtures, or adopting the position of many New England Federalists in extending Greek recognition. For Adams, a general principle provided a solution to this political conundrum. He successfully argued to Monroe that British interest would compel Britain to resist a European intervention in the Americas, even absent a "cockboat" alliance. The latter provided an easy appeal to national pride, and the principle of the distinctness of the European and American political systems allowed him to argue against Monroe's inclination to recognize Greece. For Monroe, this was a difficult step: he wrote Jefferson on October 17, 1823: "If a case can exist in which a sound maxim may & ought to be departed from, is not the present instance, precisely that case? . . . Has not the epoch arrived when Great Britain must take her stand, either on the side of the monarchs of Europe, or of the U.S. & in favor of Despotism or of liberty, & may it not be presumed that, aware of that necessity, her government has seized on the present occurrence to announce the commencement of that career."

Adams's influence was decisive. In the cabinet, Monroe offered a draft message praising the Greek rebels in their revolt against the Ottoman Empire, and lecturing France for the invasion of Spain. Both for considerations of statesmanlike dignity for the young United States and his own

political circumstances, Adams successfully opposed specific references to Greece and Spain, emphasizing instead the distinctiveness of the two hemispheres and their autonomy from one another. Monroe for his part agreed to rewrite the message for delivery to Congress as a statement of grand policy.

The doctrine as read to Congress in President Monroe's annual message of December 2, 1823, parsed into three terms:

1. "the American continents, by the free and independent condition which they have assumed and maintain, are henceforth not to be considered as subjects for future colonization by any European powers" *(noncolonization and hemispheric distinctiveness);*

2. "we should consider any attempt on their part to extend their system to any portion of this hemisphere as dangerous to our peace and safety" *(nonintervention and security linkage);* and

3. "in the wars of the European powers in matters relating to themselves we have never taken part, nor does it comport with our policy so to do." *(neutrality; entangling alliances)*

President James Monroe (standing) and members of his cabinet discuss the Monroe Doctrine issued in 1823. The policy was designed to deter European countries from future colonization in the Western Hemisphere. (Bettmann/Corbis)

This set of principles would first be known as the Monroe Doctrine in 1864, with the French installation of a client regime in Mexico. Canning responded to the rebuff affably, especially given it would fall to the Royal Navy to safeguard the doctrine's clauses. As it turned out, it helped that in the Canning-Polignac agreement of October 9, the foreign secretary had already secured an agreement with France (instigator of the proposal that the Holy Alliance intervene in Latin America) by which France renounced any intention of intervention, thus obviating the need for a joint U.S.-British protest. The language used in drafting the doctrine was softened, inasmuch as "Extension of the system of the allied powers" carried in its definite articles a possible connotation of the Holy Alliance rather than the quintuple Concert of Europe.

Ignored in its beginnings—apart from a repudiation by Britain in a protocol to the 1827 Anglo-American conference—the Monroe Doctrine would grow into its own. The Great Powers may have done well to ignore it, as both Monroe and Adams in large part did too. In spite of the security linkage component of the doctrine, Monroe declined to negotiate defensive alliances when his administration was approached by the newly independent republics of Colombia and Brazil. As president, the doctrine's principal drafter, Adams, dispatched delegates to a Bolivarian conference of American republics; he sternly cautioned them against the formation of alliances. It was not until 1845 that President Polk seized on the doctrine as precedent to resist British claims over the heretofore jointly settled Oregon territory, and then also to urge European and British abstention in the Mexican War of 1846–1848. Only with the withdrawal of French troops from Mexico in 1866 and restoration the previous year of Dominican independence after a short-lived Spanish reoccupation, did Europe begin to acquiesce in the political claims made in the doctrine. Thirty years subsequent, when President Cleveland invoked the doctrine in calling on Britain to submit to arbitration in a Guianan-Venezuelan boundary dispute, Britain yielded to the claim. Afterward, for a period from 1904 to 1929, American presidents held that under a Roosevelt corollary America had the right to intervene within the hemisphere to prevent European powers from exercising police powers over default on debts or mistreatment of nationals; the corollary was dispatched with by the Clark memorandum of 1928–1930. With the Great War, America was no longer a hemispheric power, and the doctrine became anachronistic, though it would continue to live on for rhetorical purposes.

A second legacy of the Monroe Doctrine is the tradition of doctrinalism it opened in American foreign affairs. What precisely is *doctrine*? It is neither law, nor strategy, nor policy. In common with legislation, doctrine imposes some straitjacketing on the creativity of statesmen, together with some discipline toward consistency, predictability, and adherence at times to high-minded principles. It does this while conferring a greater legitimacy on an action for deriving a diplomatic tradition. Alfred Thayer Mahan commented that "The virtue of the Monroe Doctrine, without which it would die deservedly, is that, through its correspondence with the national necessities of the United States, it possesses an inherent principle of life, which adapts itself with the flexibility of a growing plan to the successive conditions it encounters." As an indication of how firmly the doctrinalist seed was planted in the American diplomatic soil, in the latter half of the twentieth century, every president save Ford and the first Bush advanced a doctrine during his administration.

The Remainder of a Presidency

The recognition of the Latin American republics—the last of them postponed by the Monroe Doctrine speech until their viability and Spanish ratification of the Adams-Onís Treaty became apparent ("With the existing colonies or dependencies of any European power we have not interfered and shall not interfere")—took place in 1822 (Colombia, June; Mexico, December), 1823 (Chile and Argentina, January), 1824 (Brazil, May), and 1826 (Peru, May).

In May 1824, Congress narrowly passed a protective tariff that raised the cost of imported manufactured goods significantly, to the profit of the Northeast which was sheltered as it developed its manufacturing economy. Western states supported the tariff so its raw resources could also enjoy tariff protections and a sheltered internal market. The South, however, lacked a manufacturing industry and the resources of the West, and so suffered under the tariff. Henry Clay attracted marginal votes with promises of internal improvements, toward the formation of what Clay dubbed an American System. The most direct result for Monroe was the accentuation of sectional discord, to which the approach of elections added political division and intrigue within his cabinet.

Monroe complained to Madison: "The approaching election, 'tho distant, is a circumstance that excites greatest interest in both houses, and whose effect, already sensibly felt, is still much to be dreaded.... There being three avowed candidates in the administration is a circumstance which increases the embarrassment." These three avowed candidacies were those of Secretary of State Adams, Secretary of the Treasury Crawford, and Secretary of War Calhoun. Monroe, who could have preserved harmony in his administration by selecting a successor, remained scrupulously neutral, and his cabinet degenerated into rivalry and dissension. During his last winter in office, his Republican Party splintered into an Adams-Clay faction and another orbiting around Jackson (Calhoun and Crawford withdrew from the race). Adams, so influential under Monroe's administration, went on to have his own after an acrimonious tripartite election referred to the House of Representatives for want of a majority in the Electoral College.

Monroe was the last of the Virginia dynasts (of his predecessors only Adams was not a Virginian; his two immediate successors were from Massachusetts and the western frontier, and no Virginian would again occupy the White House until Wilson). His presidency expired on 4 March, 1825, and he moved to the farm he had occupied in 1788, which by then had become part of the grounds of the University of Virginia, Jefferson's foundation. In debt after a lifetime in the public's service, he sold the Highland plantation to pay off his debtors. With his wife Elizabeth's death on September 23, 1830, he moved to New York City to live with his daughter, dying there the next year on his nation's Independence Day.

Legacy

Monroe, a weak politician at the mercy of his cabinet and an unimaginative intellect reliant on his predecessors and secretary of state, gave the foreign policy of his nation its first, resplendent substantive foundation in the realm of ideas, with a doctrine both more pragmatic and visionary than Washingtonian nonentanglement, more confident than a simple alignment with Britain, and more principled and intellectually robust than a balancing of Great Powers along the lines of what Sir Edward Grey gave Britain. Monroe extended the writ of his country's laws to the Pacific, gave it negotiated boundaries on its northern, southern, and western frontiers, and established an alignment with an increasingly Whiggish and ideologically compatible Britain that in nearer decades would permit the United States the shelter to expand along lines in which his doctrine pointed and in the further years would develop into a special relationship. His accomplishments, considerable by any account, were all the more remarkable because he created them with neither the intellectual gifts of Jefferson and Madison nor the political endowments of his secretary of state. His contribution to his nation's external affairs was greater than any of theirs, and he drew on their talents while keeping a counsel of his own, with a genius that lay not in Jeffersonian exultations of mind, but in the soberer arts, more fitted to an established nation growing toward its maturity, of being *primus inter pares*.

Patrick Belton

Chronology

1817

March 13: Neutrality Act limits U.S. aid to rebel Spanish colonies in Latin America.

April 29: Rush-Bagot Agreement; Great Lakes demilitarized.

1818

February 12: Chilean independence proclaimed.

April 7: U.S. forces under Andrew Jackson capture Spanish posts in Florida.

October 20: Convention of 1818 resolves commercial issues with Britain.

November 28: Secretary of State John Quincy Adams blames Spain for Florida conflict.

1819

February 22: Transcontinental Treaty with Spain; Spain cedes East Florida and renounces claim to West Florida.

February 24: House defends Jackson's Florida campaign.

1820

March 3: Missouri Compromise approved.

May 15: Congress presses Britain to liberalize trade access to West Indian colonies.

May 15: Congress declares slave trade piracy.

December 6: Monroe reelected.

1821

February 25: Mexican independence proclaimed.

June 24: Simon Bolívar victorious at Carabobo; Venezuela independent.

November 21: Terranova Incident in China.

1822

June 24: British parliament opens West Indies ports to U.S. trade.

September 7: Brazilian independence proclaimed.

1823

February 28: House seeks international agreement against slave trade.

April 28: United States supports Spanish retention of Cuba and Puerto Rico.

July 1: Central American colonies declare independence from Spain.

June 17: Britain renews duties on U.S. shipping in West Indies.

July 17: United States opposes Russian claim to Pacific Coast territory.

August 16–20: Britain seeks Anglo-American agreement against European intervention in Spanish Americas.

October 9: Britain warns France against interventions in Spanish Americas.

December 2: State of the Union address includes Monroe Doctrine opposing any European intervention in the Western Hemisphere and pledging American noninterference in European affairs.

1824

April 17: Russia accepts 54° 40' as southern boundary of its North American territory.

December 1: Presidential election yields no majority winner.

References and Further Reading

Ammon, Harry. *James Monroe: The Quest for National Identity.* Charlottesville, VA: University Press of Virginia, 1990.

Bumgarner, John R. *The Health of the Presidents: The 41 United States Presidents Through 1993 from a Physician's Point of View.* Jefferson, NC: MacFarland, 1994, 32–35.

Cuningham, Noble E. *The Presidency of James Monroe.* Lawrence, KS: University Press of Kansas, 1996.

Lucier, James P., ed. *The Political Writings of James Monroe.* Washington, DC: Regnery, 2002.

May, Ernest R. *The Making of the Monroe Doctrine.* Cambridge, MA: Belknap Press, 1992.

McPherson, J. H. T., *History of Liberia.* [1891] Kila, Montana: Kessinger, reissued 2004.

Monroe, James. *Autobiography,* ed. Stuart. G. Brown. Syracuse, NY: Syracuse University Press, 1959.

Monroe, James. *Writings,* ed. Stanislaus. M. Hamilton, 7 vols. New York: Putnam's, 1898–1903.

Preston, Daniel, and Marlene C. DeLong, eds. *The Papers of James Monroe, Volume I: A Documentary History of the Presidential Tours of James Monroe, 1817, 1818, 1819.* Westport, CT: Greenwood Press, 2003.

Preston, Daniel, and Marlene C. DeLong. *Volume II: Selected Correspondence and Papers, 1776–1794.* Westport, CT: Greenwood Press, 2006.

John Quincy Adams (1825–1829)

Early Life and Political Career

John Quincy Adams may be seen, quite literally, as a "son of the American Revolution." Born in Braintree (now Quincy), Massachusetts, in 1767 to Abigail and John Adams, he was part of the generation that was born in the eighteenth century but was too young to have played any significant role in either the American Revolution or the drafting and adoption of the Constitution. This generation, which would emerge into national prominence in the years after the War of 1812, included most of Adams's future colleagues and rivals, notably Andrew Jackson and Henry Clay.

As a boy, Adams accompanied his father to Europe on two occasions, while the latter was involved in the negotiations that established in Europe, through diplomacy, the independence that had been won on the battlefield in America. Thus Adams as a teenager became acquainted with Benjamin Franklin, Thomas Jefferson, the Marquis de La Fayette, and others associated with the American cause. In 1781, he traveled to Russia along with Francis Dana, acting as the latter's interpreter in the French-speaking court of Catherine the Great. Upon his return from St. Petersburg two years later, he attended school in the Netherlands before joining his family in Paris. In 1785 he sailed from France alone, intending to enroll at Harvard College. Few, if any Americans of his age had seen as much of the world before their eighteenth birthday.

Adams spent most of the following year in the home of his uncle, the Rev. John Shaw of Haverhill, Massachusetts. Shaw's tutoring enabled him to enter Harvard in the spring of 1786 with advanced standing; he graduated a year later. Intending to follow in his father's footsteps as a lawyer, he studied in the Newburyport office of Theophilus Parsons, one of the outstanding practitioners of that trade and a future chief justice of the Massachusetts Supreme Court.

Unlike his father—who returned from Europe in 1788 to become the nation's first vice president—John Quincy Adams had little love for the practice of law. Settling in Boston in 1790, he found himself drawn increasingly to the political arena, attending the sometimes boisterous town meetings, and contributing newspaper essays on national topics, particularly foreign policy. In these essays, written under various pseudonyms like "Publicola," "Marcellus," and "Columbus," Adams developed many of the ideas and principles that would mark his foreign policies as secretary

John Quincy Adams drafted the Monroe Doctrine but counselled against going abroad "in search of monsters to destroy." (Library of Congress)

of state and president. In the emerging national debate over the proper relation of the new nation with revolutionary France and its war with Great Britain, Adams counseled strict separation from the current European struggle. The United States, he wrote in 1793, was "a nation whose happiness consists of real independence, disconnected from all European interests and European politics." He was particularly adamant in his insistence—in contrast to the position taken by his older friend Thomas Jefferson—that the current revolution in France and that in America of 1776 bore no relation to one another, and that Americans owed no more to France than to any other nation. This stance attracted the attention of President Washington, no doubt with some encouragement from his vice president, John Adams. In 1794, Washington rescued John Quincy Adams from the boredom and frustrations of his legal career by appointing him American minister to the Netherlands. Adams was twenty-seven years old.

Adams in Europe

For the next seven years, Adams resided in Europe, first at The Hague, and later in Berlin as American minister to Prussia. From these two cities he was able to observe European events from the tumultuous years of the French Revolution to the rise of Napoleon Bonaparte. What he saw only served to underscore his earlier convictions. While in the Netherlands, he witnessed the internal struggle between the two Dutch political parties, one of whom, Adams was convinced, was beholden to the British, while the other was allied to the French. The result, in 1795, was the loss of Dutch independence when the revolutionary armies of republican France, encouraged by their Dutch supporters, swept into the Netherlands. Pro-British elements, including the Dutch royal family, promptly fled to London. Such was the result, Adams wrote to his father, of the connection between domestic politics and foreign intrigue. At a time when many Americans seemed to be allying themselves either with the pro-British Federalists or the pro-French Republicans, Adams warned against a similar loss of independence in his own country, especially if it were drawn into the current Anglo-French war. "If we are once entangled in *this war*," he wrote his brother from The Hague, "we are irretrievably tacked to the destinies of Europe, and must be made the perpetual tools or victims of what avarice or ambition may stir up in this hemisphere."

The rising tide of partisanship in the United States had particular meaning for Adams. Events would maneuver his father into a contest for the presidency in 1796 with Thomas Jefferson, still a family friend, although differences over foreign policy had strained their relationship. Although deeply critical of Jefferson's Francophilia, Adams professed indifference to the outcome. He was confident that Jefferson, for all his faults, would not be manipulated by the French. It would not be until early 1797 that he learned that his father had narrowly defeated Jefferson to become the nation's second president, with Jefferson, under the rules of that day, becoming vice president.

One of George Washington's last acts as president was to nominate John Quincy Adams as minister to Portugal, a position that the new President John Adams switched, much to his son's consternation, to Prussia. John Quincy Adams thus arrived, not in Lisbon, but in Berlin later that same year, along with his newly acquired wife, Louisa Catherine Adams, daughter of the Maryland-born American consul in London, Thomas Johnson. The Adamses were met at the gate to Berlin by a "dapper lieutenant" who had never heard of the United States.

For the next three years, John Quincy Adams directed his observations on European affairs as much to his father, the president, as to his ministerial superior, the secretary of state. Franco-American relations deteriorated, especially in the wake of the controversial Jay Treaty, which the French interpreted as being a virtual Anglo-American alliance. When French officials demanded a bribe to continue diplomacy with the revolutionary Directory, President Adams angrily withdrew his delegation, and an undeclared naval war broke out between the two nations. His son's contempt for those Americans who continued to side with the French at home only increased.

But President John Adams had not closed the door on diplomacy. "We will have neither John Bull nor Louis Baboon," he had told his wife Abigail. And from his Berlin listening-post, the younger Adams was receiving intelligence that suggested the French were indeed willing to back off from their earlier confrontational style and seek to resolve the differences between the two republics. As President Adams moved toward diplomacy instead of war, he became the object of criticism from the Anglophile elements within his own party, including his secretary of state. Encouraged by his son, the president sent a second delegation to Paris, which, with the ascendancy of Napoleon, resolved most issues.

President Adams paid a price for his accommodation with the French. His diplomacy was very nearly sabotaged by his own cabinet, two members of which he eventually fired. In his son's view, writing from Berlin, the new threat to American independence came less from the republican French than from the arrogant British and their American allies. During his last months in Berlin, John Quincy Adams directed most of his fire against the Anglophiles who had attempted to undermine his father's diplomacy, and, as it turned out, contributed to his defeat at the hands of the Jeffersonians in 1800. In this there was a consistency established from his earliest writings: that American owed nothing to any power, and that allying politically or even psychologically with any other nation was a threat to American independence. In this, Adams was well in line with the ideas expressed in Washington's Farewell Address, and, ironically perhaps, with Thomas Jefferson's future warning against "entangling alliances."

U.S. Senator

Returning to Boston in 1801, Adams resumed his law practice and went through the motions of swearing off politics. There was no political party, he told his brother, that he could take seriously. But his disinterest in the law remained unabated. Within a year he ran unsuccessfully for Congress. The following year, 1803, saw him elected by the Massachusetts legislature to a full term in the U. S. Senate. In each case, he reluctantly aligned himself with the dominant Federalist Party, but it soon became clear that in matters of foreign policy, he would pursue an independent course. Indeed, even before his arrival in Washington, he announced his support for the recent treaty with Napoleon that resulted in the Louisiana Purchase. He was the only Federalist to do so.

So long as Britain and France remained at peace, the possibility of any "foreign entanglement" was remote. But when they resumed their warfare, the crisis of the 1790s threatened to reassert itself. Once again, the United States found itself challenged by both nations in its attempt to establish the right of neutral powers to trade with belligerents in non-contraband goods. And once again, Americans were dividing along partisan lines in their sympathies.

It was clear to John Quincy Adams that this time the British, rather than the French, posed the greater threat to American independence. Following the battle of Trafalgar in 1805, the French had no navy to speak of. The British, on the other hand, resumed their role as the world's leading naval power and proceeded to take advantage of it by reasserting its alleged right to "impress" fugitives from the Royal Navy on American vessels, and by restricting American trade with Napoleon and his continental allies. Events reached the boiling point in 1807 when the British frigate *Leopard* fired point-blank on the American *Chesapeake,* resulting in the loss of several American lives.

The tensions between the United States and Great Britain were exacerbated by the growing tension between Adams and the Federalist Party. When the Jeffersonian Republicans in Boston called a protest meeting in reaction to the *Leopard-Chesapeake* affair, and the local Federalists refused to join, Adams not only participated, but chaired the meeting. A year later, when President Jefferson called for an embargo on all American trade with Europe, Adams reluctantly supported him, again, the only Federalist to do so. The Federalist-dominated Massachusetts legislature responded by electing a successor to Adams well in advance of the expiration of his term. Adams promptly resigned his seat, leaving the Federalist Party for good. In both his actions and writings, Adams believed himself to be consistent. Neither the French nor the British should be allowed to manipulate American domestic politics, and while in the 1790s he believed the greater threat to have come from the former, in the most recent decade the challenge had come from the latter.

Minister Abroad

Having reluctantly returned yet again to his legal practice, the forty-one-year-old Adams was in Washington in 1809 when he learned that the new president, James Madison, had nominated him to the post of American minister to Russia. Over the objections of most of his family, Adams accepted the position and would spend the next eight years abroad, representing the Republican administration in St.

Petersburg and London, and vigorously defending the American position, even when it resulted in a second war with Great Britain. Indeed, he chaired the American delegation that would conclude the Treaty of Ghent, ending the War of 1812.

In his years at the court of the Russian Czar Alexander I, Adams found himself face-to-face with the representatives of the Great Powers (a critic later described him as a "bulldog among spaniels"); as a representative of a neutral power he was able to hold his own, with the covert support of the Czar. Nominally an ally of Napoleon, Alexander found himself slipping into the growing opposition to French hegemony, finally resulting in Bonaparte's fatal gamble in 1812 when he invaded Russia. At the same time, the United States was slipping into war with Britain over its alleged abuse of neutral rights and its encouragement of Indian warfare on the American frontier. That he represented a nation at war with Alexander's new ally did not affect his relations with the Czar, whom Adams came to admire among all the leaders of the Great Powers of the day.

His letters from St. Petersburg were uncompromising in their defense of the war with Britain and their denunciations of the war's critics, most of whom came from his native New England, some of whom were contemplating secession from the Union. "No nation," Adams told a fellow New Englander, "can be independent which suffers its citizens to be stolen from her at the discretion of the naval and military officers of another nation." As for the secessionists, they had to be crushed. Otherwise, the great republican experiment created by the Founders would wither on the vine. "Instead of a nation coextensive with the North American continent, destined by God and nature to be the most populous and most powerful people combined under one social contract," he told his aging father in 1813, "we shall have an endless multitude of little insignificant clans and tribes at eternal war with one another for a rock or a fish pond, the sport and fable of European masters and oppressors." Here Adams revealed the second component of his American foreign policy. In suggesting that "God and nature" had destined the Americans to occupy the entire North American continent, he became one of the first public figures to express what a later generation would call the ideology of *Manifest Destiny.*

Adams would have the opportunity to defend these ideas when President Madison appointed him and four others to negotiate an end to the War of 1812. Meeting at Ghent in what is now Belgium, Adams, chairman of the delegation, led the resistance to the British proposal that Indians be given a quasi-independent buffer zone in the American West. Adams recognized the proposal for what it was: an attempt to curtail U.S. expansion. If the British expected to stop the Americans from expanding, he pointedly told a member of the opposing delegation, "she must not think of doing it by a treaty. She must formally undertake, and accomplish, their utter extermination." The proposal was quietly dropped.

The issues that had allegedly provoked the war—impressments and the trading rights of neutral powers in wartime—were likewise dropped, since with the end of the Anglo-French wars they were no longer relevant. Adams and his colleagues concluded an agreement on Christmas Eve, 1814, embracing the principle of status quo ante bellum for each of the two nations. Adams expressed the hope that the Treaty of Ghent would be the last peace treaty between America and Great Britain. President Madison then rewarded him with an appointment as minister to Great Britain, the same position his father had held in the 1780s.

Adams's final two years abroad were relatively uneventful. As American minister in London it was his responsibility to see to it that the Treaty of Ghent was carried out in ways as advantageous to the United States as possible. This included the establishment of an agreed-on border between the United States and British North America, and the restitution of slave "property" allegedly kidnapped by the British during the recent war. If Adams had any moral reservations about slavery at this point, he did not express them, either publicly or privately. At this stage in his career, both his nationalism and expansionism outweighed any other considerations.

Secretary of State

Nationalism and expansionism were the key elements of his policies as secretary of state, a position to which he was appointed in 1817 by the new president, James Monroe. This was demonstrated when, a year later, General Andrew Jackson, hero of the spectacular American victory over the British at New Orleans, launched an incursion into Florida, then a part of the crumbling Spanish empire. On Spanish soil, the Tennessean tried and executed two British subjects and a number of Indians, accusing them of plotting warfare against the United States. Most of Monroe's cabinet and a large contingent of congressmen led by Henry Clay, Speaker of the House of Representatives, were ready to condemn Jackson. But Secretary Adams defended him, citing both the unwillingness of the British to control their own subjects and the inability of the Spanish to control their own territory. In a brilliant series of diplomatic dispatches, ignoring the difficulties created by an American general trying and executing British subjects on Spanish soil, Adams managed to remove the onus from Jackson and place it on the British and the Spanish. He more than hinted that the time had come for Spain to cede Florida to the United States. A third war with Britain, the Prime Minister

later told Adams's successor in London, could have been had "by merely holding up a finger." But there was no war. In 1819, John Quincy Adams negotiated the sale of Florida to the United States.

Friction soon emerged again between Britain and the Americans over disputed territory in the American Northwest. Again, Adams was bellicose in asserting of American claims. In a series of stormy confrontations with Stratford Canning, the British minister to the United States, Adams conceded that the British may have had some right to their claims in Canada, but, he told Canning, "leave the rest of the continent to us." To Monroe's cabinet, Adams declared that the world should be "familiarized with the idea of considering our proper dominion to be the continent of North America. From the time we became an independent people, it was as much a law of nature that this should be our pretension as that the Mississippi should flow to the sea." In the treaty he negotiated with Spain over Florida, Adams managed for the first time to establish American claims to the Pacific Ocean.

In the early 1820s, Adams and others turned their attention to events in both Latin America and Europe. The liberationist ideologies spawned by the American and French Revolutions sparked upheavals in the Portuguese and Spanish empires and briefly in Spain itself. Further to the East, the Greeks sought to free themselves from Turkish rule. These movements for self-determination inspired a sympathetic response among most Americans. Some, led by Speaker Clay, wanted to extend more than mere sympathy, offering diplomatic recognition to those elements seeking freedom from oppression.

Adams rejected these notions. Although sympathetic to the liberationist goals, Adams took the position that the nation's future lay in the New World in general and North America in particular. Moreover, although he was no friend of colonial empires, he was skeptical of the chances for true freedom among the remnants of the Spanish and Portuguese empires. He explained his position in an interview with Henry Clay, who was emerging as his major critic in Congress. The history of the Latin American colonies was different from North America: "Arbitrary power, military and ecclesiastical, was stamped upon their education, upon their habits, and upon their institutions. War and mutual destruction was in every member of their organization, moral, political, and physical . . . . The United States would have little to gain from any future connection with them, political or commercial."

On July 4, 1821, Adams delivered by invitation the annual Independence Day address to the citizens of Washington. In it he gave a classic expression of the thinking that governed his diplomacy. Intervention in foreign wars, even on the right side, he argued, would undermine the nation's unique position in the world. She had become a symbol of liberty to all, both friend and foe. To intervene in a cause not her own would alter this symbol "from *liberty* to *force*. . . . She might become the dictatress of the world. She would no longer be the ruler of her own spirit." War could be justified, as in the case of the recent war with Britain, only when American security and independence was directly threatened. "Wherever the standard of freedom and Independence has been or shall be unfurled," he told his listeners, "there will her heart, her benedictions and her prayers be. But she goes not abroad, in search of monsters to destroy. She is the well-wisher to the freedom and independence of all. She is the champion and vindicator only of her own."

Two years later, in 1823, the opportunity arose for a further expression of Adams's views on the relationship of the United States to the rest of the world, but particularly to Latin America. With the approval of the so-called Holy Alliance (Russia, Austria, and Prussia), a French army had invaded Spain and restored the Bourbon monarchy recently overthrown by Spanish liberals. Further discussion ensued as to whether the next step should be a European intervention in the revolt of the Spanish colonies in the New World as well. The prospect of a massive armada bent upon restoring Spanish rule so alarmed the British—who not only could not countenance such a threat to the naval supremacy, but who saw trading advantages with the newly-independent nations of Latin America—that they proposed a joint Anglo-American declaration, warning against European intervention in the New World's affairs.

To many, it seemed a good idea. Overcoming lifetimes of Anglophobia, the aging ex-presidents Jefferson and Madison urged President Monroe to take up the offer. So did most of his cabinet. But the British proposal placed Monroe in a dilemma, for to accept it would violate the principle of "no entangling alliances." This was the position taken by Secretary Adams, who never believed that the member states of the Holy Alliance were capable of invading Latin America, especially over the opposition of Britain's Royal Navy. There was no need, he told the cabinet, for a joint declaration. It would be much better to stand alone, "to avow our principle explicitly . . . than to come in as a cockboat in the wake of the British man-of-war."

Thus it was that in his Annual Message for 1823, President Monroe unilaterally warned against European intervention in the colonial revolts to the south. The ideas, and in some cases the words, of what later became known as the *Monroe Doctrine* were those of John Quincy Adams. "In the wars of the European powers in matters relating to themselves," Monroe asserted,

> we have never taken any part, nor does it comport with our policy to do so. It is only when our rights are invaded or seriously menaced that we resent injuries

or make preparation for our defense. With the movements in this hemisphere we are of necessity more immediately connected, and by causes which must be obvious to all enlightened and impartial observers. . . . We owe it, therefore, to candor and to the amicable relations existing between the United States and those powers to declare that we should consider any attempt on their part to extend their system to any portion of this hemisphere as dangerous to our peace and safety.

The Monroe Doctrine was both a promise and a threat: a promise not to take sides in European quarrels, and a threat—backed up silently by the Royal Navy—to resist any further colonization in the New World.

Annexing Florida, extending American claims to the Pacific, and crafting the Monroe Doctrine stand as Adams's three major achievements as secretary of state. In the opinion of one of his biographers, Adams established the "foundations of American foreign policy" at least for the next century. They also are the basis for the claim that Adams was among the nation's greatest secretaries of state.

Yet Adams has had his critics, both in his lifetime and ever since. His fierce resistance to the establishment of a Native American Indian buffer state during the negotiations at Ghent in 1814 was mixed with the casual contempt for Indian culture typical of most white Americans of his day. His defense of Andrew Jackson's incursion into Florida was an example of the best defense being a good offense rather than an argument consistent with international law. And more than one critic of the Monroe Doctrine has seen it, not as a ringing assertion of the right of self-determination in the New World, but as the first assertion of American hegemony there.

At least two phrases used by Adams in the 1820s have been taken up in the twentieth century and beyond by those who wished to be seen as standing in his shadow. His plea that the American declaration against European interference in the New World be made unilaterally and not in conjunction with Britain—that the United States not come in "as a cockboat in the wake of the British man-of-war"—was cited in 2001 by secretary of state designate Colin Powell in his confirmation hearings of that year. And Adams's July 4, 1821, oration, asserting that America "goes forth not in search of monsters to destroy" has provided rhetorical ammunition for isolationists, pacifists, and various noninterventionists, from the United States entry into World War I in 1917 to the invasion of Iraq in 2003.

The Presidency

John Quincy Adams was one of five candidates for president in the election of 1824. Not surprisingly, none of them received the necessary majority of electoral votes. The leading candidate was Andrew Jackson, whom Adams had supported in 1818 when few others would, and for whom he had expressed continued admiration and support. The general had reciprocated similar respect for Adams. But Henry Clay, who had established a reputation as the leading critic of both Adams and Jackson, threw his support to Adams, thus assuring him of election. Adams subsequently appointed Clay as his secretary of state, thus permanently alienating Jackson, leading to charges of a "corrupt bargain," and ultimately laying the basis for a pro-Jackson coalition that would limit Adams's presidency to one term. It also contributed to frustrating any further advancement of his goals in foreign affairs.

In his First Annual Message in December 1825, Adams called for the United States to participate in the proposed inter-American conference to be held in Panama the following year. On its agenda was, among other things, a discussion of neutral rights in time of war (a long-held goal of American foreign policy), and the suppression of the African slave trade (to which Congress, with Adams's prodding, was on record as favoring). The Jacksonians succeeded in sabotaging American participation through delaying tactics mixed with racial slurs that resulted in the American delegation arriving in Panama after the conference was over. Disputes with Britain over American trade with the British West Indies left Adams vulnerable to criticism from northern merchants injured by restrictions on that trade. He pursued his goal of American expansion by attempting to purchase the Mexican province of Texas (increasingly populated by American citizens), but this came to naught. Yet, with the leadership provided by Secretary Clay, no less than nine commercial treaties were negotiated with foreign powers (more than any comparable period prior to the American Civil War) and a large number of individual American claims against foreign powers were settled amicably. If his presidential record in foreign affairs did not match that of his career as secretary of state, this was due to the changed situation in both American and Europe. With some notable exceptions, both continents would turn toward internal matters for the next century.

Legacy

Two years after his defeat in 1828, the sixty-three-year-old Adams, much to the concern of both friends and family, returned to Washington as a congressman from Massachusetts. He served in that capacity until his death in 1848. He became the most notorious congressional advocate of the antislavery cause and the fiercest opponent of the annexation of Texas and the war with Mexico that followed. His numerous critics accused him of hypocrisy—pointing

to his presidential attempts to purchase Texas from Mexico. Adams explained that at the earlier time Texas was nominally free from slavery, but by 1844 the proposed annexation of slaveholding Republic of Texas only meant extension of the empire of slavery, not the "empire of freedom" proclaimed by the annexationists. As American minister to Great Britain, his nationalism had trumped whatever antislavery feelings he may have had. By 1844 the reverse was true. But he had no difficulty in supporting American claims to the Oregon Country in 1846, even if it meant a third war with Great Britain.

His critics maintained that Adams's opposition to Texas annexation was sparked more by his need for revenge against those who had defeated him in 1828, but Adams always denied this. He could point to his support of President Jackson in 1833 in the latter's dispute with France over that nation's failure to meet its obligation arising from a treaty pledging compensation for American financial claims arising from the Napoleonic period. Adams's support for Jackson's hard line against the French probably cost him a promotion to the United State Senate.

His last public speeches were in opposition to the Mexican wars. When he died in the Capitol building in 1848, there were few Americans left who remembered when there had not been a John Quincy Adams. In American foreign policy he left a legacy of fierce patriotism mixed with republican virtue, and of vigorous expansionism mixed with moral principle. It would provide both inspiration and challenge for generations of American diplomats yet to come.

Lynn Parsons

Chronology

1825

February 9: House elects John Quincy Adams president.

February 16: Russia and Britain sign treaty on 54° 40' boundary.

March 4: Erie Canal completed.

June 27: Britain bans all U.S. trade with West Indies.

August 6: Bolivia declares independence from Spain.

October 25: United States warns France not to occupy Cuba.

December 26: Adams nominates two delegates for the Panama Congress.

1826

March 14: Senate approves delegates to the Panama Congress against strong opposition.

July 15: Panama Congress adjourns with no U.S. attendance.

1827

March 27: United States closes ports to British vessels from ports in the Western hemisphere.

August 6: Anglo-American convention on Oregon Territory.

1828

January 12: Mexican-American treaty recognizes Sabine River boundary.

May 19: Congress approves "Tariff of Abominations."

December 3: Andrew Jackson elected president.

References and Further Reading

Bemis, Samuel Flagg. *John Quincy Adams and the Foundations of American Foreign Policy.* New York: Knopf, 1949.

Bemis, Samuel Flagg. *John Quincy Adams and the Union.* New York: Knopf, 1956.

Bolkhovitinov, Nikolai. *The Beginnings of Russian-American Relations.* Cambridge, MA: Harvard University Press, 1975.

Dangerfield, George. *The Era of Good Feelings.* New York: Harcourt, Brace and World, 1952.

May, Ernest. *The Making of the Monroe Doctrine.* Cambridge, MA: Harvard University Press, 1975.

Parsons, Lynn Hudson. *John Quincy Adams.* Madison, WI: Madison House, 1998.

Perkins, Bradford. *Castlereagh and Adams.* Berkeley, CA: University of California Press, 1964.

Russell, Greg. *John Quincy Adams and the Public Virtue of Diplomacy.* Columbia, MO: University of Missouri Press, 1995.

Weeks, William Earl. *John Quincy Adams and American Global Empire.* Lexington, KY: University Press of Kentucky, 1992.

Andrew Jackson (1829–1837)

Early Life and Political Career

Andrew Jackson was born on March 15, 1767, in the Lancaster District of South Carolina. He was the third son of Andrew and Elizabeth Jackson. The elder Andrew Jackson died shortly before the birth of his son, and following his death, Elizabeth Jackson abandoned the family farm in the Waxhaws and moved into the home of her sister Jane Crawford. Elizabeth entertained hopes that her youngest son would someday enter the Presbyterian ministry, but such hopes were abandoned when Jackson's hot-tempered nature became evident, even at a young age. Jackson attended a local school run by the Presbyterian minister, but he was not studious and received little formal education, even by the standards of the late eighteenth century. What formal education he received was interrupted by the American Revolution. Jackson's eldest brother Hugh had enlisted in the colonial cause and was killed at the Battle of Stono Ferry. Jackson, age thirteen, along with his older brother Robert, signed up for the patriot cause as well. Following an especially bloody engagement, Jackson was wounded; the brothers were captured by the British and contracted smallpox while in captivity. Elizabeth managed to secure her sons' release in a prisoner exchange, but Robert succumbed to smallpox. She then decided to go to Charleston to help nurse prisoners of war held aboard ships in the harbor. Just as the war ended with the surrender of Lord Cornwallis at Yorktown, however, Elizabeth contracted cholera while tending to the sick and died, leaving Jackson an orphan.

Jackson was sent to live with his cousin Thomas Crawford in Charleston, where he led a dissolute life, gambling away a small inheritance from his grandfather at the tender age of fifteen. Jackson then returned to the Waxhaws where he finished his education and taught school for a couple of years. In 1784, he decided to become a lawyer and moved to Salisbury where he apprenticed under Spruce McKay. Completing his legal training in the office of Colonel John Stokes, Jackson was admitted to the North Carolina bar in September 1787. In 1788, Jackson accepted an offer from his friend John McNairy, the recently elected superior court judge of the Western District of North Carolina, to serve as public prosecutor for the district. In Nashville, Jackson settled down to his duties as prosecutor, but found time for a vigorous social life. He courted Rachel Donelson Robards, the youngest daughter of one of the most prominent families in

Andrew Jackson, pugnacious and instinctively expansionist, nevertheless resisted the annexation of Texas for fear of war with Mexico. (Library of Congress)

Tennessee and the estranged wife of Lewis Robards. Jackson's subsequent marriage to Rachel was mired in controversy and came to haunt him in his later political career amid charges that she had failed to secure a timely divorce from Robards and the lack of any records of the marriage.

In 1795, Jackson was elected as a delegate to the Constitutional Convention to prepare Tennessee for entry into the Union. The following year, facing little serious opposition, Jackson was elected as Tennessee's first and sole representative to the U.S. House of Representatives. Jackson's term in Congress was solid if unspectacular; by all accounts he was a conscientious representative who was devoted to the interests of his constituents and home state. In 1795, having failed to secure election as major general of the Tennessee militia, Jackson was elected by the state legislature to a six-year term in the U.S. Senate. Jackson found his

Senate experience to be absolutely miserable and resigned his seat in 1798. Shortly after returning to Tennessee, Jackson was elected without opposition to a seat on the superior court and served with distinction for six years. In 1803, Jackson secured his election as major general of the Tennessee militia and concentrated on developing his commercial interests.

The War of 1812 finally provided Jackson with the active military command he so desperately craved. Old Hickory, as Jackson was affectionately called by his troops, first led a campaign to destroy the power of the Cree Nation, removing a potential source of danger to the southern United States as it faced the threat of a British invasion from the Gulf of Mexico. On December 1, 1814, Jackson arrived in New Orleans with his army to supervise the defense of the city against the British invasion. On January 8, 1815, the British forces attacked and were decimated by the Americans. The British suffered 2,037 casualties including their commanding general, Sir Edward Pakenham; Jackson, on the other hand, reported a total of 13 Americans killed, 39 wounded, and 19 missing in action. The Battle of New Orleans was a stunning victory for American arms in a war that had hitherto produced a series of unmitigated military defeats; it made Jackson a national military hero. The Hero of New Orleans was voted the thanks of Congress and awarded a gold medal. When the United States Army was reorganized in the spring of 1815, Jackson was given command of the southern division; one of his principal duties was supervising the removal of Indian tribes to facilitate the settling of the fertile delta lands of the west-central Mississippi.

Jackson's command of the southern military district brought him into conflict with the Spanish in Florida. The Spanish position in Florida had become increasingly untenable following the War of 1812; abandoned by their British allies, they did not possess adequate resources to defend or administer the province. One cause of friction between Spain and the United States was the presence of a fort alongside the Apalachicola River in Florida, near the border occupied by fugitive slaves who incited other slaves to escape and join them. A more pressing cause of friction was the safe haven Florida afforded to marauding Seminole Indians after their periodic raids of Georgia settlements. The massacre of over forty men, women, and children near Fort Scott in November 1817, marked the beginning of the First Seminole War and provided the pretext for American intervention in Florida. Jackson took command of the expedition to invade Florida and received tacit authorization from President James Monroe to seize the Spanish province. In May 1818, Jackson captured Pensacola, the center of Spanish rule, and established a provisional government for Florida on his own initiative. Jackson's exploits prompted strong protests from the Spanish government and Monroe sought to deny any responsibility for the general's actions. Secretary of State John Quincy Adams,

however, defended Jackson's actions on the grounds of self-defense and military necessity, and deflected Spanish demands for his punishment.

As Adams entered into negotiations with Spain for the acquisition of Florida, Congress launched an investigation into Jackson's actions, and there were calls for his censure. Some members were genuinely incensed that congressional authority had been circumvented by waging an undeclared war with Spain, but others had baser political motives for attacking Jackson. Jackson's enormous popularity, especially in the West, posed a threat to the political ambitions of men like Secretary of the Treasury William H. Crawford and Speaker Henry Clay of Kentucky. Members of Congress, however, keenly aware of the popular mood, decided not to risk incurring the public's wrath by censuring its beloved war hero, and in February 1818, four resolutions condemning Jackson's actions in Florida were voted down by comfortable margins. Jackson's seizure of Florida was vindicated and Adams completed its acquisition with the conclusion of the Transcontinental Treaty of 1819. Spanish intransigence in the course of negotiations was overcome by Adams's threat to unleash "the Napoleon of the Woods"(as the Spanish dubbed Jackson) and the United States acquired all Spanish territories east of the Mississippi, excluding Texas.

Jackson accepted Monroe's offer to be the territorial governor of Florida; he received his commission in March 1821 and resigned from the army. Jackson's most important task was to establish a territorial government on a firm basis. One of his first decrees organized the territory into two counties: Escambia and Saint Johns. He also established three revenue districts: Pensacola, St. Marks, and St. Augustine. He set about creating a civil administration for each county by appointing mayors, aldermen, clerks, sheriffs, prosecuting attorneys, and commissioning justices of the peace. In judicial matters, Jackson served as the court of final appeal. He also established a board of health, ordered repairs to hospital buildings, and issued ordinances for the "preservation of health." In a foretaste of Jacksonian democracy, Jackson extended the franchise to all freemen to guarantee a democratic process and to ensure that the government would be run for the benefit of all citizens. He served as territorial governor of Florida for approximately three months—a relatively short period but still longer than he had intended. Despite some signal accomplishments, his term as territorial governor was not devoid of unpleasantness; he had several run-ins with Spanish officials that embarrassed the Monroe administration. Jackson's resignation was officially accepted by the president on December 1, 1821.

Jackson returned to Nashville, exhausted and sick. While recuperating, he received a constant flow of disturbing reports detailing the misconduct and corruption that pervaded the Washington establishment. Jackson was particularly upset by reports that certain members of Congress were determined to use the King Caucus to nominate his old nemesis William H. Crawford as the next Republican presidential candidate. The use of the congressional caucus to select presidential candidates was neither new nor unusual; it had been in use for decades. However, in the Era of Good Feelings, when the Republican Party ruled the country with no opposition, the nomination of a presidential candidate by means of the King Caucus was tantamount to electing the next president of the United States by extra-constitutional means and would make a mockery of the idea of free elections. Jackson's fears appeared to be confirmed when the Republican caucus persisted in nominating Crawford despite his having suffered a stroke that left him paralyzed, dumb, and blind. Jackson was also greatly troubled by the scandal surrounding fraud in the Second Bank of the United States and its role in triggering the Panic of 1819. Jackson's political correspondence during this period outlined the salient features that would come to characterize his philosophy of government. He affirmed and embraced the conservative doctrine of limited government, opposing a broad definition of constitutional power for the federal government. While Jackson advocated states' rights—viewing it as the most efficient means of checking the growing power of the federal government—he did not consider states to be superior to the central government and opposed their right to secession. Debt reduction was another major element of Jackson's political thought. Unlike Alexander Hamilton, Jackson considered the national debt to be a national bane and a threat to republicanism; the total elimination of the national debt would be one of the major accomplishments of his administration.

Jackson's political allies in Tennessee started a campaign to elevate him to the presidency. In 1822, Jackson secured the presidency of the Tennessee legislature; the following year, his allies prevailed on him to once again run for a seat in the U.S. Senate, which he won by a vote of thirty-five to twenty-five. This time around, Jackson took his senatorial duties seriously, hoping to convince his colleagues that he was a legitimate contender for the presidency. At the popular level, Jackson's candidacy generated an unprecedented outpouring of support throughout the nation and made him a viable candidate alongside Adams, Crawford, Clay, and John C. Calhoun. His campaign document, known as the *Letters of Wyoming*, struck a responsive chord with the public. The general theme of the *Letters* echoed his earlier private correspondence; it lamented the displacement of the virtue and morality of the Revolutionary generation and its replacement with misrule and corruption. The pamphlet also served as something of a blueprint of the ideology of the burgeoning Jacksonian movement, providing a powerful assertion that only a return to the first principles of republicanism could serve as a legitimate basis for the

maintenance and perpetuation of liberty. Jackson's reform message started to have an impact. On February 14, 1824, a congressional caucus was convened to nominate the Republican Party's presidential candidate, but only 68 out of a possible 261 members acknowledged the summons. Even though Crawford received 64 votes, Adams received 2 votes, and Jackson and Nathaniel Macon of North Carolina each received 1 vote, the King Caucus was ultimately an exercise in futility. The unity of the Republican Party was shattered, and with Calhoun dropping out of the race to seek the vice presidency instead, it became a four-man competition for the presidency between Crawford, Adams, Jackson, and Clay.

The election of 1824 demonstrated that Jackson was a political force to be reckoned with. It marked the first presidential election in which popular voting was maintained, and the results demonstrated the American public's preference for Jackson; he polled 152,901 votes against 114,023 votes for Adams, 47,217 for Clay, and 46,979 for Crawford. However, Jackson's popular vote was less than the combined tally of his opponents, and more importantly the president was (and still is) selected by the Electoral College. Jackson won a plurality of the electoral votes (99) but fell short of the requisite majority of 131. As a result, according to the provisions of the Twelfth Amendment, the House of Representatives, with each state having one vote determined by its congressional delegation, would decide the outcome of the presidential election. Jackson expected to win the election in the House, but Henry Clay, having been dropped from the run-off by virtue of garnering the least electoral votes, used his considerable influence in the chamber to swing the election in favor of John Quincy Adams. Clay rejected Jackson as being substantively and temperamentally unsuited for the presidency. He calculated instead that Adams, with whom he shared a commitment to an expansive program of national public works, was the best candidate to put his American Systems proposal into action. Thus, the final electoral count in the House showed Adams with thirteen states, Jackson with seven, and Crawford with four. Publicly, Jackson took his defeat with grace and dignity; in private, however, he railed against the corruption of the political process. Jackson's fears of corruption appeared to be borne out when Adams, in an apparent quid pro quo, named Clay as Secretary of State, traditionally the quickest route to presidential succession. Jackson's supporters decried this "Corrupt Bargain" and labeled Clay "the Judas of the West."

The outcome of the House election of 1825 reinforced in Jackson's mind the urgent need for reform and a return to the principles of republicanism as characterized by the Revolutionary era. In the immediate aftermath of the election, Jackson made common cause with Calhoun, who was now vice president. An alliance with Calhoun would enhance Jackson's standing in the South and made sense if he was to regroup his forces for another run at the presidency in 1828. On Calhoun's part, his political fortunes were now tied to Jackson, as Clay was now positioned to succeed Adams. Having reached an accord with Calhoun, Jackson returned to Tennessee to lay the groundwork for the next election. He resigned his Senate seat and the Tennessee legislature promptly renominated him for president in October, 1825. Jackson did not personally campaign for the presidency, but he did supervise the activities of the so-called Nashville Central Committee. This committee served as the principal coordinating body of the Jackson campaign; its members functioned as they would in any modern political campaign: preparing statements for the press, liaising with a network of sympathetic politicians across the nation, and coordinating the activities of state and local committees supporting Jackson. The Jacksonian movement, as it developed, was more than a practical campaign to purge American politics of corruption and malfeasance and restore popular government to the people. It was also an ideological crusade that reframed the old divisions between the goals of Jefferson and Hamilton as a moral struggle between a corrupt elite bent on further aggrandizement and a virtuous citizenry determined to preserve its right to life, liberty, and property. As such, the attacks on the Clay-Adams coalition and the Corrupt Bargain served to unite seamlessly both elements of the Jacksonian movement. The movement eventually coalesced into a new political party—the Democratic Party—organized for the purpose of turning out Adams and Clay and placing Jackson and republicanism at the head of the government.

The 1828 presidential elections were hard fought. The National Republican press attacked Jackson, dredging up past controversies including his marriage to Rachel, alleging that he was guilty of adultery if not complicit in bigamy. Even Jackson's vaunted military record was not spared partisan abuse. The Jacksonian press retaliated by accusing Adams of having procured female companionship for the Czar while he was the United States minister to Russia. When the election returns were tallied in the late fall, Jackson polled 647,276 votes against 508,064 votes for Adams; in the Electoral College, Jackson crushed Adams with 178 electoral votes to 83. Jackson's electoral victory, however, was tinged with tragedy when Rachel Jackson died on December 22 of a heart attack; her death devastated him and he would mourn his wife for the rest of his life. On March 4, 1829, on the east portico of the Capitol, Andrew Jackson took the oath of office from Chief Justice John Marshall and was sworn-in as the seventh president of the United States.

The Adams Legacy

Foreign policy had not been a public issue in the presidential elections of 1824. Jacksonians, however, exerted great influence on the direction of American foreign policy during the Adams administration. One of the major immediate issues facing the Adams administration was the question of recognizing Greek independence from the Ottoman Empire. An influential segment of public opinion, which included former presidents Jefferson and Monroe, favored support for the Greek revolution, and Daniel Webster brought the issue to the House floor, urging American support for the Greeks. The Jacksonians, however, favored a conservative interpretation of Washington's Farewell Address and believed that the national interests were best served by advancing America's commercial relations while eschewing involvement in foreign alliances, wars, or revolutions. Webster's measure was therefore opposed by both Jacksonians as well as radical Republicans, and died in a House vote. Jacksonians also clashed with the Adams administration over the president's attempt to align the United States with Latin American republics in the Pan-American Conference. In his first annual message to Congress, Adams announced that he had accepted an invitation from Simon Bolivar to participate in a conference in Panama with the intention of creating an association of states in the hemisphere. This prompted cries of outrage from Jacksonians and resulted in a battle that lasted for fifteen months in both houses of Congress. The Jacksonians were led by Martin Van Buren of New York and Thomas Hart Benton of Missouri in the Senate, and in the House by James Polk of Tennessee and James Buchanan of Pennsylvania. In May 1826, despite the stalling tactics of the Jacksonians, Congress finally authorized the Panama mission; one of the American representatives died en route to the conference, while the other arrived in Panama after it had adjourned.

Although the Jacksonians disagreed with the Adams administration on the extent of American involvement in the Greek revolution and inter-American affairs, they were united on the subject of advancing American commercial interests. The Adams administration achieved a modicum of success by negotiating commercial treaties with Denmark, Norway, Sweden, the republics of the Hanseatic League, Prussia, the Central American Republic, and the Empire of Brazil. The administration, however, failed to advance American commercial and political interests in Mexico in the face of stiff British competition. By the end of the Adams administration, Britain had secured a most-favored nation commercial treaty, and became the principal foreign investor in Mexico, providing a substantial loan to the Mexican government, as well as investing millions in Mexican industry. Furthermore, Adams had failed to acquire Texas, and the Mexican government, in a calculated rebuke to its northern neighbor, planned to abolish slavery in the province and strengthened military and economic ties to the area. The administration also failed to resolve the pressing West Indian trade issue with Britain. The British had excluded foreign shipping from their Caribbean ports since the American Revolution; when they reopened their West Indian and Canadian colonies to foreign trade, they attached discriminatory provisions aimed at American commerce. When the Adams administration refused Parliament's offer to reciprocate domestic port trade with British commercial port trade, commerce collapsed. Adams's failure to resolve the West Indian trade dispute became an issue of contention in the 1828 elections.

Foreign Policy

At the start of his administration, Jackson made it clear that his program for reforming government would extend to foreign as well as domestic affairs. In his first message to Congress in December 1829, Jackson outlined his approach to foreign policy: "To ask nothing that is not clearly right, and to submit to nothing that is wrong." In practical terms, Jackson's policy deviated little from that of his predecessor's; it was centered on the advancement of American commercial interests and the recovery of spoliation debts, but never at the cost of American national honor. Shortly after his inauguration, Jackson summoned the various ministers representing foreign countries to a meeting at the White House. He assured them that the United States harbored no designs on the safety of other nations but warned that America would not back down from insisting that its rights be respected fully by others.

Rapprochement with Britain

Jackson made the resolution of the Anglo-American dispute his highest diplomatic priority. Reaching an understanding with Britain was considered key to achieving his goals of settling claims against various countries for violations against American vessels during the Napoleonic Wars, as well as advancing American commercial interests. Britain was the preeminent maritime power, with a powerful navy and the world's largest merchant marine. In addition, British political and commercial influence was an important factor in many smaller countries like Portugal, Spain, the Netherlands, and Belgium; a British veto made the negotiation of treaties with those countries impossible. Jackson understood that Britain could not be bullied or cajoled into a settlement, and defying stereotypes regarding his supposed Anglophobia and his famous temper, the frontier Democrat remained calm and dispassionate throughout the negotiations. Jackson moved quickly to resolve the West Indian trade dispute, appointing Louis McLane of Delaware, a former Radical Republican, to serve as minister to Britain. In June 1829, McLane informed Secretary of State Martin Van Buren that if the administration abandoned the failed policies of its predecessor, the British might consider negotiating a treaty to resolve the West

Indian issue. Jackson was prepared to risk the partisan wrath of the National Republicans and repudiate the failed diplomacy of Adams to adopt a new course of action. In a memorandum to Van Buren dated April 10, 1830, Jackson explained that American diplomacy ought to be conducted along conciliatory lines with a willingness to accept compromises and practical solutions to foreign disputes whenever possible, but to be always ready to act to vindicate the proper respect and rights due to the United States.

When negotiations with the British stalled, McLane suggested that American legislative initiative might undo the deadlock. He argued that if Congress moved to end American restrictions against British vessels sailing from the West Indies on a reciprocal basis as a gesture of American good faith, the British might quit their stalling. To expedite the diplomatic process, Jackson sent a message to Congress on May 26, 1830, stating that he expected to resolve the West Indian trade issue successfully on the basis of reciprocity and requested permission to act independently on the issue after Congress adjourned. Jackson lacked the requisite authority to lift American sanctions on his own, and to avoid having to call a special session of Congress, he requested authority to remove restriction by executive order once Britain agreed to allow American vessels into Caribbean ports. Congress passed a bill on May 29 setting forth reciprocity as the basis for an agreement with Britain. The British responded to the congressional action with a pledge that all trade restrictions between the United States and its West Indian colonies would be removed once Jackson implemented the law by proclamation. On October 5, 1830, Jackson issued an executive order opening American ports to British trade; on November 5, Britain lifted its restrictions on American vessels. The resolution of the West Indian trade issue was a stunning success for the administration. In substance, Jackson offered little more than Adams had, but he had resolved the issue successfully on a fair and reciprocal basis while vindicating both national honor and interests. Jackson understood that more than mere trade was at stake. He removed a source of long-term irritation in Anglo-American relations and laid the foundation for increased cordiality and prosperity between the two countries.

Resolving Indemnity Claims

Jackson also moved swiftly to settle American spoliation claims against various European powers. During the Napoleonic Wars, the United States suffered heavy commercial losses at the hands of France as well as a host of smaller nations who were required to carry out Napoleon's Continental System as laid out in the Berlin and Milan Decrees of 1806 and 1807. American spoliation claims existed against France, Russia, Denmark, Portugal, the

Netherlands, and the Kingdom of the Two Sicilies. Previous administrations had sought a settlement of American claims but had been rudely rebuffed by the European powers. It was now Jackson's turn to try to recover the debts, and he was not prepared to take no for an answer. He believed in the simple frontier credo that an honest man always paid his just debts; he also believed that this principle extended to the conduct of nations. For Jackson, the debts constituted a legitimate obligation on the part of the European countries and he wanted them paid. The claims against Russia and Portugal were resolved easily enough through executive agreements; both countries accepted and paid the amounts negotiated. Resolving claims against the other countries proved more difficult.

American claims against Denmark dated to when Danish cruisers set upon neutral American commerce as part of the Continental System. Denmark did not dispute the legitimacy of American spoliation claims, but it challenged the right of the United States to dispute the decision of its prize courts. The chargé d'affaires in Copenhagen, Henry Wheaton, was a distinguished international lawyer and a holdover appointment from the Adams administration. Wheaton argued that while prize courts had the authority to affix responsibility, their decisions extended only to private litigation, whereas the United States was now pressing its claim on a state-to-state basis. News of the Russian Czar's settlement of reparations claims helped induce a mood of compromise; the Danish minister of foreign affairs and president of the chancery eventually came round to Wheaton's position. They accepted American spoliation claims against Denmark from 1808 to 1811 and agreed to a lump sum payment of $650,000 as indemnity. This was a victory for Jackson; given the impoverishment of the Danish government, the settlement was $150,000 more than American merchants had hoped to receive as indemnity. The convention was signed in Copenhagen on March 27, 1830, and submitted to the Senate for ratification on May 27; the Senate gave its consent. Jackson's hopes that the Danish settlement would serve as a precedent of a nation paying its honest debts were dashed; it had minimal impact on negotiations with the Kingdom of the Two Sicilies and France.

American claims against the Kingdom of the Two Sicilies stemmed from the seizure of forty-nine American vessels and their cargoes by Joachim Murat, the Bonapartist ruler of Naples in 1809. In October 1831, Jackson selected former representative John Nelson of Maryland as minister to the Kingdom of the Two Sicilies. Nelson was instructed by Jackson to offer the Neapolitans a "carrot"—upon resolution of spoliation claims the United States would enter into negotiations for a commercial treaty that would benefit Neapolitan wines, silks, and artworks; further, recognizing the financial straits of the government, payment of the indemnity could be spread over a four-to-six year period. Jackson's instructions also included a "stick"—should the Neapolitans continue to deny responsibility for the debt, Jackson would ask Congress to take "such measures as to insure full compensation." Nelson arrived in Naples in January 1832, accompanied by four warships. Still, the Neapolitans continued to dissemble, alternately pleading impoverishment, denying responsibility for Murat's actions, and urging negotiation of the commercial treaty. In March, a frustrated Nelson suggested in a letter to Secretary of State Edward Livingston that only a demonstration of American naval power would convince the Neapolitans of American resolve on the claims issue. In early September, the American Mediterranean squadron sailed into Naples harbor bearing Jackson's reply to Nelson. Jackson's new instructions surprised Nelson. The president did not ask Congress for harsh measures of reprisal. Instead, he counseled restraint and understanding; Jackson favored giving the Neapolitans one more chance. To demonstrate, however, the seriousness of the American position and that the president's patience was not infinite, more American warships were dispatched to Naples. The Neapolitan position had become untenable, and on October 14, the government concluded a treaty that settled the debt at approximately $1.7 million to be paid over nine installments and at an annual interest rate of 4 percent. Because 1832 was an election year, Jackson had hoped to add the Neapolitan settlement to an already impressive diplomatic record in his first term in office for his bid for reelection. It was not needed; Jackson cruised to reelection over Henry Clay, polling 687,502 votes against 530,189 votes for Clay and winning 219 of the 289 electoral votes cast.

Reckoning with France

The most difficult negotiations to resolve American spoliation claims involved France. Under the Continental System, Napoleon had seized over 300 American vessels and their cargo valued at over $7 million. Franco-American relations deteriorated to such an extent that in 1812, the Madison administration seriously contemplated whether to declare war on France as well as Britain. Even though Franco-American diplomatic and political ties had frayed, neither country could afford to jeopardize the very lucrative economic ties that continued to bind the countries together. The United States was the largest importer of French goods while France was America's second largest export market. Jackson, on the advice of Van Buren, selected William Rives of Virginia, a dedicated party man, as minister to France in 1829. In July 1831, after nearly two years of negotiations,

Rives finally secured a treaty from the French to settle American indemnity claims. The French agreed to the sum of $4.6 million as indemnity payable in six equal installments. When the first installment came due in February 1832, however, the French exchequer refused to honor the draft issued by the secretary of the treasury, claiming that the Chamber of Deputies had neglected to authorize the payments. Jackson was furious. He appointed former Secretary of State Edward Livingston as minister to France with instructions to remind the French that the United States had acted to fulfill its obligations under the treaty, and Jackson now expected them to in act in good faith and fulfill theirs. To underscore the seriousness of the mission, Livingston arrived in France onboard the seventy-four-gun warship *Delaware*.

In his fifth annual message to Congress of December 3, 1833, Jackson expressed disappointment that the terms of the treaty remained unfulfilled, but did not seek reprisal measures, hoping that the appropriation of funds would be forthcoming in the next session of the French chamber. The appropriations bill did not come to the attention of the deputies until January 13, 1834, when it was immediately sent to committee and ignored for two months. In early April, the deputies finally voted on the bill, defeating it by a vote of 176 to 168. Jackson fumed; he considered the French action a national and personal insult. He considered requesting from Congress "Letters of Marque and Reprisal" that might have resulted in war. Fortunately cooler heads prevailed on Jackson to give diplomacy more time. His patience was finally exhausted when the Chamber of Deputies failed to address the indemnity issue during its summer or fall sessions despite the assurances of the French minister in Washington. In his sixth annual message to Congress dated December 1, Jackson condemned the French government for failure to abide by its treaty obligations and sought congressional approval for the confiscation of French ships and property should the French chamber fail to appropriate the funds during its next session. The French government took immediate exception to Jackson's message and recalled its minister, but it nonetheless proceeded to request the Chamber of Deputies for an appropriations bill to indemnify the Americans. The bill was introduced in the chamber on January 15, 1835, and passed on April 15 by a vote of 289 to 137.

Passage of the appropriations bill did not put an end to the dispute. The deputies had attached an amendment requiring Jackson to provide an explanation of his December message before any indemnification would be paid. Many saw this as a face-saving gesture on the part of the French and of little consequence, but not Andrew Jackson. Jackson's response was direct: "no apology." In his seventh message to Congress on December 7, 1835, Jackson sounded a more conciliatory tone. He stated that he had never intended to threaten or insult France, but insisted that American independence and sovereignty would be defended. He argued that no nation could question how and in what language the president communicated with Congress, and there would be no apology for his assertion and defense of American rights. That was the extent of Jackson's contrition. The dispute ended when Britain offered to mediate between the two parties, and prevailed on France to accept Jackson's latest message as the "explanation" that it demanded in exchange for payment of the indemnification. On February 15, the British informed the administration that the first installment of the indemnity would be paid whenever the American government demanded it, and on February 22, Jackson informed Congress that the dispute with France was over.

Expanding American Commerce

Although Jackson devoted considerable attention to resolving American indemnity claims against the various European powers, he did not neglect the advancement of American commercial interests worldwide. Jackson saw the potential of Asia as a vast untapped area for American commerce, and in December 1831, commissioned Edmund Roberts, a grizzled naval veteran, as a special envoy to negotiate formal commercial treaties with Cochin China (present-day Vietnam), Siam (present-day Thailand), Muscat (present-day Oman), and Japan. Roberts's refusal to adopt a tone of supplication in his salutation to the emperor of Cochin China resulted in the failure of that mission. He had better luck in Siam, where on March 30, 1833, he concluded a Treaty of Amity and Commerce with the government. Roberts then proceeded to the spice-rich sultanate of Muscat and signed a treaty on October 3, 1833. Both of the treaties negotiated by Roberts granted most-favored nation status to American commerce and were ratified by the Senate in June 1834. Jackson was delighted at Roberts's progress and in April 1835, authorized him to enter into negotiations with Japan. Unfortunately, Roberts died in Macao on June 12, 1836. Asia was not the only region targeted for expanding American trade. Commercial treaties existed with several Latin American countries; between 1831 and 1833, Chile and Colombia concluded a series of treaties extending reciprocal trade benefits to the United States. In Europe, James Buchanan signed a treaty with Russia on December 18, 1832, which granted most-favored nation status to American commerce; it was the first such treaty ever signed by the Russians. By the time Jackson left office he could rightly boast that his administration had made significant progress in furthering American commercial interests; trade agreements were in place with Siam, Muscat, Britain, Chile, Colombia, Venezuela, the Peru-Bolivia Federation, Mexico, Turkey, and Morocco.

Texas

The most notable failing in Jackson's diplomacy was his inability to acquire Texas from Mexico. Jackson believed that Texas was a legitimate part of the United States under the Louisiana Purchase and earnestly sought to "re-annex" the province, as he put it. He denounced Adams for relinquishing American claims to Texas in the Transcontinental Treaty and for failing to acquire it from Mexico during his term in office. Despite Jackson's criticism of Adams's failures, once in office, his approach to the Texas question was very similar to that of his predecessor except that he quintupled the price the United States was willing to pay for the acquisition of the province to $5 million. Jackson's minister to Mexico, Anthony Butler, tried various nefarious means, including bribery, to bully or cajole the Mexicans to part with Texas. He failed, and in the process, alienated the Mexican government. Jackson, too, balked at Butler's illicit methods. As much as he craved the acquisition of Texas, Jackson's sense of personal and national honor forbade the use of less-than-honest means. Besides, if Congress got wind of the affair it would result in scandal. Jackson, already facing congressional difficulties over his handling of the rechartering of the Second Bank of the United States, was in no mood for further scandal. His vacillations, however, pleased no one. Mexican suspicions were raised and the government moved to crush Texas home rule by centralizing control over all parts of the province. That in turn sparked a movement for Texas independence, which was proclaimed on March 2, 1836. The Texans defeated the Mexican army dispatched to crush their independence at the Battle of San Jacinto on April 21, 1836. The president of the Mexican Republic, General Antonio de Santa Anna was captured and forced under duress to sign a treaty recognizing Texan independence, which was subsequently repudiated.

The Texans were doing everything in their power to gain American recognition of their independence, and Mexican-American relations reached a nadir; war was a real possibility. Jackson, however, was having second thoughts about the annexation of Texas. He was not prepared to resort to war to acquire Texas. Again, his sense of national and personal honor required that the United States acquire Texas freely and fairly with the consent of the Mexican government and not by means of aggression. A war to seize Texas from Mexico would stain the nation's honor and cause immeasurable harm to its standing in the community of nations. Despite strong affection for his old friend Sam Houston, Jackson rejected all overtures to recognize the independence of Texas, instead deferring the decision to Congress. On February 28, 1837, the House of Representatives passed several bills authorizing funds for the formal recognition of Texas as well as directing the president to dispatch an agent to the republic. The next day the Senate, voting twenty-three to nineteen, recommended to the president the formal recognition of Texas. On March 3, the eve of his departure from the presidency, Jackson received word that the Senate had confirmed his nomination of Alcée La Branche of Louisiana as chargé d'affaires to the Republic of Texas. Jackson had failed to acquire Texas for the United States, but he had at least secured its recognition, and that was an important step; he would live just long enough to see Texas enter the Union in 1845.

Legacy

Andrew Jackson ranks high among presidents for his impressive domestic accomplishments, but his foreign policy achievements have been underappreciated. Unlike John Quincy Adams, Jackson possessed virtually no diplomatic experience when he became president, but he did not let that deter him; he had other life experiences to draw upon. As a boy and as a man, Jackson had been a soldier defending America's honor and interests; as president he continued to do the same. Jackson had also been a capitalist and businessman, and as president he understood the importance of expanding American commerce abroad. The success of Jackson's foreign policy is not in his settling of outstanding foreign debts and expanding American trading ties—although they were signal accomplishments that had eluded his predecessors—but is in his raising of the nation's international reputation. There can be little doubt that after Jackson, the United States was a power to be respected, and even feared.

Adrian U-jin Ang

Chronology

1829
August 25: Renewed effort to purchase Texas from Mexico.

August 27: Treaty of Commerce and Navigation with Austria-Hungary.

1830
May 7: Commercial Treaty with Ottoman Empire.

May 28: Congress approves Indian removal policy.

July 5: French army captures Algiers, deposes the dey.

July 28: Revolution in Paris topples Charles X.

October 5: Jackson secures partial resolution of West Indies trade dispute.

1831
April 5: Boundary and commercial treaties with Mexico.

December 7: Jackson and Senate reject arbitrator's decision on Northeast boundary.

1832

January 26: Falkland Islands crisis with Argentina.

May 16: Treaty of Peace, Amity, Commerce and Navigation with Chile.

July 14: Tariff of 1832 passes Congress, rejected by South Carolina.

December 5: Jackson reelected.

December 15: Britain sends sloop of war to reclaim Falkland Islands.

1833

February 12: Henry Clay's Compromise Tariff resolves disputes of 1832.

1834

February 17: Van Ness Convention with Spain.

1835

November 6: United States severs relations with France over spoliation dispute.

1836

February 5: France agrees to pay spoliation claims.

March 2: Texas declares independence from Mexico.

March 6: Alamo falls to Mexican army.

April 21: Texans win Battle of San Jacinto.

May 31: Treaty of Peace, Friendship, Navigation and Commerce with Venezuela.

September 16: Treaty of Peace with Morocco.

December 7: Martin Van Buren elected president.

References and Further Reading

Belohavek, John M. *Let the Eagle Soar: The Foreign Policy of Andrew Jackson.* Lincoln, NE: University of Nebraska Press, 1985.

Ellis, Richard E. *Andrew Jackson.* Washington, DC: CQ Press, 2003.

Remini, Robert V. *Andrew Jackson and the Bank War: A Study in the Rise of Presidential Power.* New York: Norton, 1967.

Remini, Robert V. *Andrew Jackson and the Course of American Empire.* New York: Harper and Row, 1977.

Remini, Robert V. *Andrew Jackson and the Course of American Democracy.* New York: Harper and Row, 1984.

Martin Van Buren (1837–1841)

Early Life and Political Career

Martin Van Buren, the eighth president of the United States, was born on December 5, 1782, in the village of Kinderhook, New York, which straddled the Hudson River along the route between New York and Albany. Raised in the Dutch Reformed religion, Van Buren was the first president not born a British subject or of British ethnicity. Abraham and Maria Van Buren, his parents, managed a small family farm, as well as a local tavern where passing politicians often gathered. His father was a rare Jeffersonian in a region devoted to the early Federalists. Van Buren thus grew up without wealth or family connections, isolated from urban life, but not unaware of politics and its possibilities and controversies. He was educated in the village school, the fancifully named Kinderhook Academy, from which he graduated in 1796. From his hometown, where he was later buried, and from his red hair and lifelong habit of concealing a shrewd mind behind impeccable manners, he garnered the nickname "The Red Fox of Kinderhook." From his short stature (his full height at adulthood was five feet-six inches) and deft political touch, he was also known as "The Little Magician." He began studying law at age fourteen, in 1796. He completed preparatory studies in 1802 and passed the bar in 1803 (age twenty-one), with the assistance of William Peter Van Ness, a New York lawyer best known for serving as Aaron Burr's second during the vice president's infamous duel with Alexander Hamilton. Van Buren married Hannah Hoes in 1807. After bearing five children by 1817, she died in 1819 at age thirty-six. Van Buren never remarried, instead raising his children alone. Two of his sons, Abraham and Martin Jr., later played important roles as his personal secretaries during his presidency.

After establishing a successful law practice, Van Buren entered local politics. He first served as a surrogate of Columbia County from 1808 to 1813. As a rising star and party organizer within Democratic-Republic circles, he led the Bucktails in opposition to the policies and corruption of Governor De Witt Clinton. Running in opposition to the Clinton faction within the party, Van Buren was elected to the New York State Senate in 1812. He served two terms in the state senate before advancing to the office of state attorney general from 1815 to 1819. By 1820, he was a successful and prosperous member of the Albany Regency, a select group of upstate New York politicians and a budding political machine

Martin Van Buren's moderation enabled him to avoid conflict with Britain over Canada, but it accomplished little else. (Library of Congress)

that increasingly dominated state politics and exerted a growing influence on the Democratic-Republicans even on the national level.

In 1821, Van Buren parlayed his state party connections into election to the U.S. Senate. He was a vocal opponent of the policies of President John Quincy Adams, whom he opposed in the presidential election of 1824. Van Buren solidified his role as a party leader in the Senate by transferring his state party-building skills to the national level. In 1828, he again threw his support behind the western populist reformer, Andrew Jackson, though not without misgivings that Old Hickory might prove more a general in office than a Jeffersonian. Not an overly capable public speaker, but always a superb party organizer, Van Buren prospered in traditional political settings. His legal training led him to prepare his opinions and positions carefully. His Jeffersonian instincts compelled him to support state projects such as building the Erie Canal, but also to seek limits on the federal government. In 1827, he was reelected to the Senate by a large majority. Newly elected President Andrew Jackson then selected him to serve as secretary of state in March 1829. His term in the first Jackson cabinet was uneventful, as was the nation's foreign policy at that time. In cabinet meetings, Van Buren urged Jackson to veto federal improvement schemes, cleaving as always to fading Jeffersonian principles of limited government.

The early historiography portrayed Van Buren as a fervent admirer of Jackson, but more recent research belies that view. The two men were political allies, but never personally close. In fact, Van Buren played at best a marginal role in most of the major issues of the Jackson presidency: Indian clearances, the national bank, and the nullification crisis. In the cabinet shake-up that took place toward the end of Jackson's first term, Van Buren was sent to London to serve as minister to the Court of St. James. He returned to Washington during Jackson's second term to serve as vice president, largely because Jackson saw him as both loyal and lacking true independence of mind or position. This prepared the way for Van Buren's later difficulties with John C. Calhoun and Daniel Webster. During his tenure as secretary of state and later as vice president, Van Buren reached agreements with Great Britain concerning free-trading rights with British colonies in the Caribbean. He also calmed Jackson's bellicose rhetoric toward France, helping thereby to arrange an amicable settlement of the longstanding dispute over spoliation claims dating to the Napoleonic Wars.

The Presidency and Foreign Policy

Van Buren was unanimously selected as the 1836 Democratic nominee for president, which did not mean that he enjoyed anywhere near Jackson's level of personal and political popularity. He did, however, have broad support among party activists, stemming from many years of cultivating the Regency. Hand-picked by Jackson as his successor, Van Buren accepted the nomination at a national convention held in Baltimore in May 1835. He continued to advocate traditional Jeffersonian policies of states' rights and limited federal government. He was generally liked by the public, and was elected to the presidency with a higher popular vote than all of his opponents combined, largely because he promised to continue Jackson's core policies. He was immediately faced with a national monetary, and by extension, also an economic crisis—the fiscal disaster and attendant economic depression of the late 1830s known as the Panic of 1837. The Whigs again called for a national bank to help manage the money supply and national economic affairs. Van Buren opposed the measure, as Jackson

had done, proposing instead an independent Treasury and making federal deposits in state banks. He thus presided over several more years of economic upheaval before his sub-treasury scheme was passed in 1840.

Van Buren worked to maintain his political base in the South in part by actively opposing radical abolitionists, while trying to appease northern politicians and voters alienated from the party during the nullification crisis. On the other hand, he declined to support the anti-Mexican revolution in Texas that had strong southern support, and opposed annexation of the new Texas republic, fearing that sectionalism over the slave question would be the most likely result. Van Buren faced a nation divided to shrill levels of disagreement over the Texas question. Jackson was a strong supporter of Texas independence and had reveled in the revolt against Mexican authority. As the fledgling Texas republic began to fight the Mexican military, expectations grew on both sides of the border that Texas would be soon annexed by the United States. Mexico refused to recognize an independent Texas, and Van Buren saw annexation as a probable catalyst to an unnecessary war. On March 3, 1837, Congress recognized the independence of the Republic of Texas, but Van Buren rejected a request to annex Texas made on August 25, 1837. Although many southern Democrats in particular were unhappy with his decision, Van Buren successfully avoided war with Mexico by deferring the annexation issue until 1842.

Van Buren also worked to downplay tensions with Great Britain over a comical border dispute with Canada, sometimes called the Aroostook War (February–May 1839). This dispute began as a war over private economic interests along the then-uncertain U.S.-Canadian border between Maine and New Brunswick in the Aroostook River valley. The "war" was not much more than a sustained brawl between American settlers aroused to irresponsibility by Maine's Governor John Fairfield, and Canadian lumberjacks similarly overstimulated by New Brunswick's Lieutenant Governor John Harvey. As the argument over land use dragged on, it threatened to escalate into a more serious conflict involving American troops dispatched north by Van Buren under the command of General Winfield Scott (as much or more to restrain the men of Maine than to confront the Canadians and British), and British regulars whom local Canadian opinion had demanded show the flag along the disputed border. Although Van Buren supported Maine's position on removal of the interloping lumberjacks, he was not amused or moved to aggressive action by that fact, or by the jingoistic authorization by Congress of 50,000 volunteers and $10 million in war funds, far more men and money than Van Buren requested. General Scott and the British worked out an agreement on-site, and both sides enforced this against local filibusters and would-be troublemakers. Each agreed to hold the territory it currently occupied and to seek no change on the ground before negotiation of final resolution of the dispute. The boundary was eventually set permanently in the Webster-Ashburton Treaty (1842). At no point was war seriously contemplated in London or Washington, and thus it cannot fairly be said that Van Buren prevented war with Great Britain; he did facilitate a more tidy end to a longstanding disagreement over trees and a few acres of snow.

On December 29, 1837, the American steamship *Caroline* was cut loose from its moorings on the Niagara River by Canadian agents who set the ship ablaze and adrift. It sunk just above Niagara Falls, killing one U.S. citizen. The Canadians had targeted the ship because it was actively supporting an ongoing insurrection in Upper Canada (Ontario) led by William Lyon Mackensie. In retaliation, the British ship *Sir Robert Peel* was burned on May 29, 1838, by angry American nationalists. Small raiding parties also crossed the border into Canada. In response, Van Buren again dispatched Winfield Scott to the northern border. He again calmed the situation by enforcing border security against would-be American filibusters and inept Canadian insurgents. The quarrel festered as a legal matter for two more years, but was ultimately settled to the satisfaction of both sides when the insurrection expired, local law enforcement on either side of the Falls arrested the worst agitators, and British representatives issued a formal apology for the sinking of the *Caroline*.

On September 6, 1839, the U.S. Navy stopped the *Amistad,* a Spanish-flagged ship whose cargo of slaves had rebelled and taken control of the vessel while sailing off the coast of Cuba. The U.S. Navy took the ship into custody off Long Island, New York. The slaves insisted on their freedom and demanded to be taken back to their homes in Africa. Although abolitionists in the United States insisted on granting legal freedom for the *Amistad's* slaves, Van Buren sought to avoid alienating his southern base, and to deter an international dispute over the affair, he permitted the judicial process to run its course, with former president John Quincy Adams taking a prominent part in the legal defense of the captives. In 1841 a federal trial court ruled that the transport of Africans across the Atlantic was illegal; thus the former slaves had always been free. Following an appeal to the Supreme Court, the ship was finally allowed to sail away from New York in 1842.

Legacy

The Whig Party learned much from the Jacksonian Democrats, and by 1840 were close to matching the party organization and mass politics pioneered by Democrats. In the 1840 campaign against Van Buren, the Whigs ran William Henry Harrison as a "log cabin and hard cider" candidate. Van Buren was an easy target for Whig political caricature and ridicule: portly, excessively fussy in dress and manners, and overly sympathetic to foreigners. That Van Buren's origins were more humble than Harrison's did not matter a jot. Dissatisfaction with Van Buren's handling of the banking and economic crisis, grumbling about his supposed appeasement of foreigners along both land borders, and a sense that he stood too small and weakly in President Jackson's inherited boots, did him in. "Van, Van's a used up man!" was the Whig taunt of 1840. Van Buren thus lost not just the national election; he failed even to carry his home state of New York, the locale of his Regency party machine. Although Van Buren remained politically active and hoped for some future electoral vindication, he was never renominated by his party. In 1844, he again opposed annexation of Texas, a position that helped bar him from the Democratic nomination for president. In 1848, he ran for office on a Free Soil ticket, but only as a ploy to aide his old allies in the New York Democratic Party. He thereafter retired to his home town of Kinderhook, where he died on July 24, 1862, and was buried.

Arthur Holst

Chronology

1837
March 3: Congress recognizes independence of Texas.

August 25: Van Buren rejects request to annex Texas.

December 29: Caroline incident with Canada.

1838
March 10: Revision of Neutrality Laws

April 25: Texas-American Boundary Convention.

May 29: Sir Robert Peel incident with Canada.

August 18: Wilkes expedition leaves for South Seas.

1839
January 14: Secretary of State John Forsyth declares United States neutral over Falklands.

February 27: "Aroostook War" along Canadian border

September 6: Amistad incident with Spain.

November 3: Anglo-Chinese Opium War begins.

1840
December 2: William Henry Harrison elected president, John Tyler as vice president.

References and Further Reading

Holt, Michael F. *The Rise and Fall of the American Whig Party.* New York: Oxford University Press, 1999.

Hoyt, Edwin Palmer. *Martin Van Buren.* Chicago: Reilly and Lee, 1964.

White, Leonard D. *The Jacksonians: A Study in Administrative History, 1829–1861.* New York: Macmillan, 1954.

Widmer, Ted, and Arthur M. Schlesinger. *American Presidents: Martin Van Buren.* New York: Times Books, 2005.

Silbey, Joel H. *Martin Van Buren and the Emergence of American Popular Politics.* Lanham, MD: Rowan and Littlefield, 2002.

William Henry Harrison (1841)

Early Life and Military Career

William Henry Harrison was a military leader, politician, and the ninth president of the United States. He was born to a family of wealth and political renown on February 9, 1773, in Berkeley, Charles City County, Virginia, the third son of Benjamin Harrison and Elizabeth Bassett. As the son of a Virginia planter who had been a delegate to the Continental Congress from 1774 to 1777, the governor of Virginia, and one of the signers of the Declaration of Independence, Harrison was exposed at an early age to the many facets of political life. His brother, Carter Bassett Harrison, was a member of the Virginia state House of Delegates from 1784–1786 and 1805–1808. In addition, Carter was elected to the United States House of Representatives as a representative of Virginia for the Third Congress and also to the two succeeding Congresses, serving from March 4, 1793, to March 3, 1799. In this sense, it is clear that Harrison was born into a recognized political family. On November 25, 1795, he married Anna Tuthill Symmes, the daughter of Judge John Cleves Symmes of Ohio.

In 1787, Harrison entered Hampden-Sydney College where he studied classics and history. This college required that its students pursue a rigorous, traditional liberal arts curriculum and become proficient in the written and oral expression of the English language. Harrison then began to study medicine in Richmond, but his father's death in 1791 left him without any money to continue his studies. During that same year, at the age of eighteen, he was commissioned as an ensign in the United States Army and moved to the Northwest where he spent much of his life. Harrison served as aide-de-camp to General "Mad Anthony" Wayne and participated in Wayne's decisive victory at the Battle of Fallen Timbers in 1794. Shortly afterward he became lieutenant, and on August 3, 1795, was one of the signers of the Treaty of Greenville, which put an end to the Northwest Indian War of 1785–1795. It is important to recognize that this war was fought between the United States and a large confederation of Native Americans for the control of the Old Northwest. One of the major goals of the treaty was to open much of present-day Ohio for white Americans to inhabit. The treaty ended almost twenty years of hostilities in the region until the Battle of Tippecanoe in 1811.

Harrison, after resigning from the Army in 1798, became the secretary of the Northwest Territory. Also, he acted as

William Henry Harrison, a hero of the War of 1812, came to the presidency an old man and died a month after inauguration. (Library of Congress)

the governor when Arthur St. Clair, ninth president of the Continental Congress under the Articles of Confederation, was absent. In 1799, Harrison was elected as the first delegate representing the Northwest Territory in the Sixth United States Congress, where he served from March 4, 1799, to May 14, 1800. As a delegate, he successfully promoted the passage of the Harrison Land Act of 1800, which made it less difficult for whites to acquire land that belonged to Native Americans by permitting them to buy property on credit. Between 1795 and 1809, in fact, the tribes of the Northeast surrendered some 48 million acres.

In addition, Harrison helped pass legislation to break up the Territory into the Northwest and Indiana Territories and in 1801 became governor of the Indiana Territory (a massive territory covering the present-day states of Indiana, Illinois, Wisconsin, and Michigan), a post he filled for twelve years. As the governor, he continued to facilitate the acquisition of land by white settlers, the main purpose of which was to increase the white population for the attainment of statehood. Harrison was nevertheless often unpopular among the settlers because he tolerated slavery in the territory and, although he permitted the establishment of a territorial assembly in 1805, he usually ignored its authority. It was not until 1809 that Washington separated present-day Indiana from the rest of the territory and the legislature was able to assert itself, among other things outlawing both slavery and the property qualification for electoral suffrage in 1810.

The Battle of Tippecanoe

In the meantime, land-hungry settlers and speculators kept moving ahead of government survey and sales in search of fertile soil. Because Harrison functioned as superintendent for Indian Affairs as well as governor, he was in a position to use his political skills to convince Native Americans to abandon ever more land in the Northwest, much of which had actually been guaranteed to them by the Treaty of Greenville. They signed treaties they did not always fully understand. As a result, quarrelling broke out among them over the surrender of territory. It was not surprising, then, that they ultimately decided to retaliate. Retaliation took the form of the emergence of two Shawnee leaders, Tecumseh, a persuasive and vigorous chieftain, and his twin brother Tenskwatawa, "the Prophet." Harrison spoke reverently of Tecumseh as "one of these uncommon geniuses, which sprang up occasionally to produce revolutions and overthrow the order of things."

Tecumseh sought to form a confederation of the various tribes west of the Appalachians in an effort to rightfully defend traditional hunting grounds. Additionally, he insisted that no land cession was valid without the consent of all the members of the confederation—not an unusual stipulation, as all Native American peoples held the land in common. On the other hand, Tenskwatawa provided the inspiration for a religious revival. He called on his followers to sincerely worship the Master of Life in the belief that, in so doing, they would be able to resist the white man's firewater and his territorial predations. He attracted followers from the Shawnee, Canadian Iroquois, Fox, Miami, Mingo, Ojibway, Ottawa, Kickapoo, Lenape, Mascoutin, Potawatomi, Sauk, and Wyandot Nations. Harrison continued nonetheless to shamelessly defend new settlements. With the singing of the Treaty of Fort Wayne, he secured the purchase of more than 2,500,000 acres of Native American land.

By 1809, resistance to white settlement had became serious. In November 1811, Tecumseh and Tenskwatawa sought to strengthen the confederation in an effort to prevent further infringement on their land. Tecumseh journeyed south to try to persuade other tribes to join the confederation and won the support of the Creeks, Cherokees, Choctaws, and Chickasaws. In his absence, Harrison led about 1,000 men against Tecumseh's capital on the Tippecanoe River. Before dawn on November 7, 1811, Tenskwatawa and a band of Shawnee braves attacked Harrison's camp, although Tecumseh had warned against any fighting in his absence. After serious fighting that left about 190 of Harrison's men dead or wounded, the Shawnees were finally repulsed. The Battle of Tippecanoe, on which Harrison's fame thereafter rested, reinforced many unwarranted suspicions that the British in Canada were inciting the Native Americans against the United States. The provocations were in fact almost entirely Harrison's. British authorities in Canada had, in fact, steered a careful course to dampen the conflict because they wanted to avoid any damage to the lucrative fur trade.

Eventually, Harrison disrupted Tecumseh's confederacy but failed to diminish the number of raids. Nonetheless, in the War of 1812—fought between the United States and Great Britain with more than half of the British forces made up of Canadian militia—he won more military glory. He was given the command of the Army in the Northwest with the rank of brigadier general. At the Battle of the Thames, north of Lake Erie, on October 5, 1813, Harrison defeated the combined British and militia forces, killed Tecumseh, and invaded Canada. In Harrison's mind, the conquest of Canada served a twofold purpose. It would eliminate the British authority and influence among the Indian nations and put more territory at the disposal of land-hungry Americans. Also, Canada was the only place where Britain was vulnerable to direct attack from the United States. The defeat he inflicted on British and Canadian forces in the Battle of the Thames released the American Northwest from any further British threat. Thus, Harrison had won an apparent victory at Tippecanoe and an indisputable victory at the Thames. In combination, these engagements led to the collapse of Tecumseh's confederacy, so the security of the American military frontier in the Northwest was reestablished. Even so, ongoing disagreements with Secretary of War, John Armstrong, caused him to resign from the army and return to private life on his farm in North Bend, Ohio.

Politics and Diplomacy

Harrison then had a comparatively obscure career in politics and diplomacy that lasted for twenty years. From October 8, 1816, to March 3, 1819, he served in the U. S. House of Representatives from Ohio. In 1820, he ran for governor of Ohio and was defeated, but served in the Ohio State Senate from 1819 to 1821. In 1824, Harrison was elected to the U.S. Senate, where he served until May 20, 1828, when he resigned to take up the post of minister to Colombia.

Harrison's stay in Colombia was cut short when President John Quincy Adams lost the 1828 presidential election to Andrew Jackson, who promptly recalled Harrison. Remaining in Colombia pending the arrival of the new American minister, Harrison was indiscreet in his sympathy for Colombians plotting against President Simón Bolívar and came close to being arrested. He also breached diplomatic etiquette by writing a letter to Bolívar critical of his authoritarian rule and urging him to follow the example of American republicanism—an example to which Harrison himself had not been notably true.

The period between his recall from Colombia and the rise of the Whig Party in the late 1830s represents the lean years of Harrison's life. In 1834, in fact, he accepted the job of clerk of courts for Hamilton County in southwestern Ohio for financial reasons. The emergence of the Whig Party in the late 1830s, however, permitted him to parlay previous political experience and his military exploits into presidential potential. To a certain extent, Jackson himself—a nationally recognized figure uncommitted on most controversial issues—provided the model for Harrison. Indeed, his most forthright defense of any principle had been the undiplomatic lecture to Bolívar, which, offensive as it was to Colombians, burnished the image of a plain-speaking appeal to American voters. Although Harrison did not have the stature of Whig leaders such as Henry Clay or Daniel Webster, the divided Whig Party had little chance of defeating Jackson's successor in the White House, Martin Van Buren, in the 1836 presidential election. A good showing, however, could make the difference for the 1840 contest. Harrison made by far the best showing of the Whig candidates, capturing 25 percent of the vote.

In 1837, an economic depression gave the Whigs their best chance to defeat Van Buren and capture the White House. As they prepared for the election of 1840, both Democrats and Whigs were organized for campaigning on a national scale. In a ballot that turned out an astounding 80 percent of a greatly expanded electorate, the campaigners sought to appeal to a wide range of voters. The contest between Van Buren and Harrison marked the first truly modern presidential campaign, with methods that are still used in today's campaigning for presidential elections.

The Whigs made an early start on their campaign when they met at Harrisburg, Pennsylvania, on December 4, 1839, to choose a candidate. The Whigs needed a national hero, and Harrison's showing in 1836 convinced them that they at last had one. It was clear that although the Whig Party had no platform, it did have a slogan. The campaign essentially rewrote Harrison's biography from that of the planter's son from Virginia to that of an Indian fighter, hero of the War of 1812, and a frontier farmer—a Whig Jacksonian to take on the "aristocratic" Van Buren, "Old Tippecanoe as the

rightful heir to Old Hickory." Aided by the prevailing public sentiment that a Democratic administration had brought on a depression it was unable to master, the Whigs nominated Harrison with John Tyler as the vice-presidential running mate and launched the presidential campaign under the slogan "Tippecanoe and Tyler too." The popular vote was close, but the Electoral College gave Harrison a 234–60 vote victory. Whig leaders such as Clay and Webster expected Harrison to be a unifying figurehead they could manipulate. Ultimately, he turned out to be even less.

When Harrison arrived in Washington in February 1841, and took office at the age of sixty-eight, he was the oldest president to be elected to date (until the election of President Reagan in 1980). It was an extremely cold and windy day on March 4, when he delivered his Inaugural Address. He faced the weather without his overcoat and spoke for nearly two hours, the longest inaugural in American history. Webster, who edited the speech, had good reasons to be satisfied, for while Harrison was nationalistic in his outlook, he emphasized he would uphold the Constitution and be obedient to the will of the people as expressed through Congress. He also promised to "restore the government to its pristine health and vigor, as far as this can be affected by any legitimate exercise of the power placed in [his] hands." The task of the republic, he maintained, is "to limit the service of that officer at least to whom she has entrusted the management of her foreign relations . . . to a period so short as to prevent his forgetting that he is the accountable agent, not the principal; the servant, not the master." Before he had been in office three weeks he caught a cold that developed into pneumonia and pleurisy. In spite of the many efforts by his doctors to cure him, he died on April 4, 1841.

Legacy

Harrison was the first president to die in office after serving the shortest term of any chief executive, a total of thirty-two days. With his death, the Whig program came to a complete halt, despite his last words: "Sir, I wish you to understand the true principles of the government. I wish them carried out. I ask nothing more." Harrison's death in office set into motion a debate about who was next in line to become the president, about which the Constitution was vague. John Tyler's succession to the office nonetheless had the support of the majority of the cabinet and Congress, although the constitutional issue of succession was not officially put to rest until the ratification of the Twenty-Fifth Amendment in 1964.

If there was ambiguity surrounding where Harrison stood on political issues, there was none about Tyler. He had a long political career as legislator, governor, congressman, and senator where he had stated his opinions on many important issues without any compromise. Harrison had no chance to develop a foreign policy, and his principal legacy to American diplomacy was, for better and for worse, the ascendancy of Tyler. An additional contribution was Harrison's appointment of Daniel Webster as secretary of state, the only Whig to remain in Tyler's cabinet after his arrival in office. Webster served with dedication and ability until June 1843, when he resigned in protest over Tyler's Mexico policy. In 1842, he negotiated the Webster-Ashburton Treaty, which settled a dispute with Britain dating to 1782 over the border between Maine and New Brunswick.

Sherrow Pinder

Chronology

1841

March 9: U.S. Supreme Court frees *Amistad* slaves.

April 4: President Harrison dies of pneumonia, Tyler succeeds.

References and Further Reading

Cleaves, Freeman. *Old Tippecanoe: William Henry Harrison and His Time.* New York: Scribner, 1939.

Davis, John, and Peter Edwards. *The True History of Presidential Campaigns.* New York: Watts, 1982.

Doak, Robin Santos. *William Henry Harrison.* Minneapolis: Compass Point, 2004.

Edmunds, R. David. *Tecumseh and the Quest for Indian Leadership.* Boston: Little, Brown, 1984.

Gilbert, Robert, E. *The Mortal Presidency: Illness and Anguish in the White House.* New York: Fordham University Press, 1998.

Peterson, Norma Lois. *The Presidencies of William Henry Harrison and John Tyler.* Lawrence, KS: University Press of Kansas, 1989.

Walker, Daniel. *The Political Culture of the American Whigs.* Chicago: University of Chicago Press, 1979.

John Tyler (1841–1845)

Early Life and Political Career

John Tyler was born into a prominent family of colonial Virginia on March 29, 1790. He received his formal education at the College of William and Mary, from which he graduated at seventeen years of age. He received his informal education at the shoulder of his father, a plantation owner, friend of Thomas Jefferson, judge and, in John's youth, governor of Virginia. The younger Mr. Tyler read law with his father for two years after college, before being admitted to the bar at nineteen, setting up his practice near the capitol in Richmond.

From the age of twenty-one, to his retirement from the presidency at the age of fifty-five, Tyler held elective office continuously, except for three years: 1822, 1837, and 1838. Even after his term in the White House, he was not through with elections. In the last year of his life, he was elected to the Confederate Congress, though he died before it convened.

Politics was John Tyler's pride as well as his passion. In politics, he found excellent opportunities for expressing his personality and demonstrating his character to all who might bear witness. His first act as an elected official set Tyler on the path he would follow in his adult years. As a young member of the House of Delegates in Virginia, Tyler proposed a resolution condemning the state's two U.S. Senators, the one for having recently voted "wrong," the other for having voted "right," but refusing in the process to acknowledge the right of his state legislature to instruct him how to vote.

John Tyler was proud of his self-professed "old fashioned views" about government and exhibited a fierce sense of independence and rectitude in their defense. Tyler believed, as did all good followers of the "republican" philosophy in government (not to be confused with the Republican Party, which came later), that the goal of government was preservation, not innovation. Time brought change, and change brought corruption; the "old ways" must be preserved. In Tyler's case, the old ways meant the government of the Founders, which he took to be a government of states' rights, in which, significantly, the rights of slave owners were sacrosanct.

As a member of the House of Representatives, Tyler rejected the American System of Henry Clay, and stood solidly against such apparently wild schemes as a new national bank and even the Missouri Compromise on the

John Tyler played down the festering issue of slavery in urging the advantages of annexing Texas. (Library of Congress)

ground that it violated the immutable rights of slave owners as guaranteed in the Constitution. As a member of the United States Senate, Tyler lost confidence in the administration of Andrew Jackson over the Force Bill, which granted the president authority to use the military, if necessary, to enforce federal law in South Carolina, which had threatened secession in response to the Tariff of 1832. Tyler's pride of defiance was evident when he, alone among all senators in opposition, stayed in the Senate chamber for the vote, rather than walk out in protest. Tyler wanted his opposition to be recorded for posterity. When Senator Tyler was instructed by the Virginia legislature, two years later, to vote in the affirmative for a resolution to expunge from the congressional record the vote of censure against President Jackson that had resulted from the struggle over the threatened use of force, he resigned.

John Tyler's opposition to "King Andrew" made him of interest to the Whig Party that grew up in opposition to President Jackson. First promoted for the vice presidency by a convention of Maryland Whigs in 1836, Tyler was the unanimous choice of the Whig's national convention four years later. In that famous election, the Indian fighter and former governor of the Indiana Territory, William Henry Harrison, was promoted as the proper antidote to the incumbent Martin Van Buren, who, the Whigs said, had brought the nation to ruin—and drunk French champagne in the White House. Harrison, famous for his exploits in the Battle of Tippecanoe, needed a man of the South on the ticket for geographical balance. Tyler was that man, and "Tippecanoe and Tyler Too" were swept to office in an emotional campaign that was long on slogans and short on substance. When Democrats challenged the Whigs to justify Tyler's place on the ticket, since he had never expressed favor for the party's policy agenda of a national bank, a protective tariff, and internal improvements, the Whigs replied with a song with the catchy refrain, "We'll Vote for Tyler Therefore, Without a Why or Wherefore." They would come to regret that sentiment when, only a month into his presidency, William Henry Harrison died.

Acting President

As the first vice president to assume the duties of the presidency, John Tyler inherited a unique constitutional problem: Was he truly the president, or merely the "acting president," or perhaps not even that? Tyler answered this question himself by asserting his right to the full range of responsibilities and duties of the chief executive, even giving his own self-styled inaugural address. But what was his policy to be? The Whig Party's leaders in Congress, led by Henry Clay of Kentucky, thought the answer was clear: he should sign bills that the Whig-controlled Congress might present to him, repudiating the policies of the previous twelve years of Democratic rule. If Clay truly thought this was possible, he did not understand the president. Tyler would do what *he* thought was right, nothing more and nothing less. And he would have to begin right away, because there was a sort of cold war going on, which threatened to become hot.

In the late 1830s, British-American competition for disputed timberland in the Northeast had erupted into armed conflict. The Aroostook War was a bloodless affair, but in 1839, the governors of New Brunswick on the Canadian side of the border and of Maine on the American, called out their militias and threatened battle. The United States Congress, at the urging of Maine, authorized a force of national volunteers. Britain and the United States had then agreed, near the close of the Van Buren presidency, to settle their respective claims diplomatically. It was now up to President Tyler to make this happen.

To the south and west, there was the issue of an enormous expanse of land, much of it held only weakly by the newly independent republic of Mexico. Should the United States gain possession of these territories, its power might grow to a point at which the British would have reason to regret that it had ever sent settlers to the continent in the first place. Demographic pressure in the United States, and the rival interests of the slave-owning South and the fast-industrializing North, made it unlikely that the Americans would simply stop at their present borders. In Texas, settlers, mostly from the United States, had rebelled against the Mexican government and won their independence. Mexico had not yet accepted the outcome of the war, and forces from Texas and Mexico continued to battle one another, threatening to drag the United States into war. If the prospect of war with Mexico was not alarming enough to many, added to that was the fear that the British might interfere.

Even before he could address these pressing issues, President Tyler was compelled to do something about the finances of the government and the international trade on which they depended.

International Trade: The Tariff

Tariffs, an often decisive issue defining political parties and their membership in the nineteenth century, divided the new president from his new party. Under the tariff bill of 1833, tariffs were to be reduced gradually until, in 1842, they were on average at or below 20 percent. The 1832 tariff law had been enforced, and tariffs were on the whole low, but it was time for a new tariff bill. Whigs wished to increase protection for native industry by raising rates. They had the votes in Congress to pass a new tariff bill, but the president had recently proved his willingness to veto legislation with which he disagreed, if he thought principle was at stake. Was principle at stake in a new tariff?

It was. The Tariff of 1833 was heralded as a "sacred" compromise in the South. As a consequence, to move back to rates above 20 percent would be a grave matter for this president from Virginia. Tyler, surprisingly, indicated that he was willing to make this sacrifice. The nation's government was quite simply going broke, and he was bound by oath to execute the laws of the land. He could not do so if he could not pay the government's meager bills, in an age before entitlements, mass standing armies, and other major categories of modern government expense.

There was, however, a catch. In the first year of his presidency, Tyler had signed a bill making certain changes in the program through which the federal government sold land. It specified that distribution to the states of the proceeds, which was generally favored by Whigs and distrusted by Democrats, would be suspended if the government ever raised tariff rates above 20 percent. The idea was to keep tariffs and Whigs in line by threatening to take away distribution in the event of a rise in tariff rates. President Tyler demanded that if the Whigs were to have their tariff increase, they would have to surrender, as per the law he had signed just the year before, their cherished policy of "distribution." Secretary of State Daniel Webster had reported to Tyler that European financiers would not issue the United States the loans it desperately needed unless distribution were in fact suspended, and the revenues from land sales dedicated to the repayment of any new loans. The pro-administration presses warned, moreover, that without enactment of higher tariffs and the suspension of distribution, the United States would invite stronger nations with ill intent (most prominently, Great Britain) to interfere in its affairs, perhaps even to initiate war.

President Tyler, having secured an opinion from his attorney general that he could continue to collect revenue even without the renewal or the replacement of the expiring tariff law, vetoed the bill Congress delivered to him, which dared to nullify the suspension provision in the recent distribution law. Whig leaders in Congress, already furious at the president for having twice vetoed bills to reestablish a national bank, were now apoplectic. After daring Tyler to veto this bill also a second time, which he did, the congressional majority surrendered, for the time being. The result was a new tariff law, the "Black Tariff" to its detractors, the Tariff of 1842 to all others. The law raised duties to an average of almost 40 percent and covered a much wider range of goods than the previous law. The consequences for international trade included a reduction by half in American imports, and a decline of 20 percent in exports the following year.

"All Hail, King John," cried the Whigs. If there had been any doubt before this episode that the new president was stubbornly independent and willing to go to extremes in the exercise of presidential power, there was no longer reason for doubt. The Whigs railed against the executive's alleged abuse of the veto; they initiated unsuccessful impeachment proceedings the following year.

The Webster-Ashburton Negotiations

When Tyler assumed office, he asked all the members of Harrison's cabinet to remain. They did, but shortly thereafter, following Tyler's second veto of a banking bill, all but one resigned. The one who stayed was Secretary of State Daniel Webster. The Massachusetts "arch Federalist" was involved in delicate negotiations with Great Britain over the northeastern boundary and other points in dispute. Webster had established an exceptionally cordial relationship with his counterpart, special envoy Alexander Baring, a tremendously wealthy man who sported the title Baron Ashburton. The baron was fond of the United States, so much so that he had married an American. Webster, a scion

of Boston, was an Anglophile. They worked together so closely, in fact, that their bargaining sometimes had more the character of a conspiracy. Coming to agreement among themselves, they then expended their energies devising ways to persuade their own governments, especially the testy Anglophobe Tyler, to accept their compromises. Ashburton's superior, Foreign Secretary Lord Aberdeen, who played a direct role in the negotiations at various times, and Prime Minister Sir Robert Peel, were on the whole more agreeable to what Ashburton and Webster devised, but then they had the advantage of superior force to set their minds at ease. There were four issues that were thus settled. The first two were settled outside their treaty, the second two within its text, as agreed to August 9, 1842.

The Caroline

After the Canadian rebellion of 1837, a band of defeated rebels, joined by a small number of American adventurers, settled on Black Rock and Navy Island near Niagara Falls. There they contracted with a small American steamer, *The Caroline*, to provision them. The ship, in port on the American side of the Niagara River, was seized on December 20, 1837, by seventy to eighty armed agents of the British-Canadian government and set loose to descend over the famous falls. In the process, an American crew member, Amos Durfee, was killed.

American complaints, and British defiance, threatened to escalate when in March 1841, a citizen of Great Britain, the deputy sheriff of the Niagara District (Canadian), Alexander MacLeod, was arrested in New York, having been overheard boasting of taking part in the affair. The British government claimed MacLeod as their agent, said that he was acting on orders of the British government, that the raid on the ship was a matter of national self-defense, and that grave consequences would follow if MacLeod was not released. New York authorities replied that, not only would he not be released, but he would be tried for the murder of Durfee and, if found guilty, be executed.

The Tyler administration was in a bind. The president and his secretary of state agreed, in principle, with the British, but lacked the means to usurp the criminal courts of New York. To the immense relief of President Tyler, MacLeod was acquitted by a jury in Utica. Webster and Ashburton reached agreement on the principles of law involved in this celebrated affair, and exchanged notes on the matter. As a result, the president recommended legislation to Congress that would remedy the defects of American law. Henceforth, federal courts would possess jurisdiction in all such cases.

Webster's position in favor of the American side in *The Caroline* affair was so well researched and argued that it became the basis for a doctrine in customary international law. Under the "Caroline Doctrine," a nation might claim self-defense for otherwise illegal acts only in the event of "a necessity . . . instant, overwhelming, leaving no choice of means, and no moment for deliberation."

The Creole

The American slaver, *The Creole*, was not mentioned in the treaty that Webster and Ashburton negotiated either, but they were forced to resolve a controversy over the ship for the treaty to have a chance of being accepted by President Tyler. Nineteen of the 135 slaves held as cargo onboard *The Creole* mutinied, killed one of the ship's crew, and gained control of the vessel. Taking refuge in the British Bahamas, the slaves, including those who had taken part in the mutiny, were freed by British officials. Southerners in the United States were furious at this British affront. Tyler, on grounds of sympathy as well as national interest, agreed with their point of view and demanded an apology, compensation, and a pledge never to act in this way again.

Webster and Ashburton agreed to refer the matter of compensation to a commission (compensation was paid in 1855) and on language sufficiently vague as to satisfy both English and American honor. The English pledged no "officious interference" with American ships taking refuge in their harbors. What exactly this meant was left to the readers, on both sides of the Atlantic, to surmise. The two sides also settled on an extradition agreement that became the tenth article in the treaty. It provided for extradition for seven crimes, including murder, though it did not mention mutiny or slave rebellion.

The Maine/New Brunswick Border

Unfortunately, the Treaty of Paris (1783) had not clearly settled the boundary in parts of the Great Lakes region and the Northeast, including that between Maine (then a district of Massachusetts) and New Brunswick. It did not much matter until loggers from both these states moved to occupy and use the disputed land, some 12,000 square miles of timber. When Canadian authorities arrested American loggers, the Aroostook War had been the result. What was the solution?

Webster and Ashburton consulted what they believed to be definitive maps and documents. The map that the American side used was thought to be from the period of the Treaty of Paris. On it was a red line marked, it was thought, by Benjamin Franklin, indicating the border that the Americans were prepared to accept. The red-lined map would have granted the entire disputed territory to the British. On the British side, ironically, its map is thought to have shown the opposite. Both sides were thus eager to compromise, lest the "truth" come out and the other side claim the whole.

On the American side, it was not, this time, the president, but the chief negotiator from Maine, Judge William P. Preble, who was the obstacle to an orderly settlement. No soldier had died on either side from combat in the late border war, but as many as two score militiamen of Maine had given their lives to disease and unknown causes while on expedition. Their sacrifices demanded a favorable return. The final settlement, as detailed in the treaty, granted roughly 7,000 square miles to the Americans, and 5,000 to the Canadians, and specified the rights of both parties to water navigation routes in the region.

The American federal negotiators sweetened the deal for the state of Maine by agreeing to compensate it for its sacrifice. In addition to money that it would receive, as would New Brunswick, to compensate the state for expenses incurred in surveying and attempting to hold the disputed land, the residents of Maine and Massachusetts would receive $150,000 apiece "on account of their assent to the line of boundary described in this Treaty."

The Illegal Slave Trade

British "visitation" of American ships had been a cause of complaint, and indeed war, ever since the Americans had won their independence. Going into these negotiations, the British hoped to gain a sanction to that right, in the case of American ships suspected of engaging in the illegal international slave trade, while the Americans wished that the British might once and for all renounce the practice. The result was a compromise that avoided the issue of "visitation" altogether in the text of the treaty.

Under Article VIII, both nations agreed to maintain naval forces off the coast of Africa to enforce "the laws rights and obligations of each of the two countries, for the Suppression of the Slave Trade." For that purpose, each navy would deploy a force possessing no fewer than eighty guns. The British were surprised to learn that President Tyler believed that the British had, in fact, agreed to more than this, if not in the treaty, then in notes exchanged during its negotiation. In his Annual Message to Congress of December 6, 1842, Tyler boasted that Article VIII had removed "all pretense . . . for interference with our commerce for any purpose whatever by a foreign government."

Tyler's reasoning was lawyerly. Though the British Foreign Secretary, Lord Aberdeen, had asserted during negotiations a right "to visit and inquire" of American ships suspected of bearing slaves, such a right was tantamount, the president stated, to a right to "detain," which Aberdeen had expressly *disclaimed*. After all, if one visits a ship, one must of necessity detain it for at least a little while. Therefore, the president intimated, the British had, whether that was their intent or not, at long last surrendered the much-hated right of visit. The British Parliament and press were not in the slightest moved or amused by the president's logic. The bad feeling that resulted would hamper future negotiations.

The Webster-Ashburton negotiations were somewhat short of momentous. A number of issues that had threatened the peace had been resolved, and in the process the two nations had displayed considerable mutual regard. This might have been a confidence-building exercise, but it was not for two principal reasons. First, John Tyler had a Jeffersonian skepticism about British intentions. Like Jefferson, he suspected that the British meant his nation harm. Tyler's boastful misrepresentation of the British position regarding the slave trade component of the treaty diminished British confidence in the Americans and the value to be had from negotiating with them, which was problematic, as the treaty had left unresolved the perplexing question of Oregon.

The ambivalence that both governments continued to feel toward one another was evidenced in the disposition of their envoys. In Britain, Baron Ashburton was rewarded for his efforts in the treaty with a mere viscounty. He had expected an earldom, at the least. In the United States, shortly after the treaty was signed and submitted to the Senate, a statement appeared in the administration's press, that the president had granted his approval for the secretary of state to resign.

The continuance of a competitive and suspicious relationship between the two powers was also demonstrated in a peculiar incident in California. Thomas Jones, USN, commander of the Pacific Squadron, received a communication from the U.S. consul in Mazatlan, Mexico, that war between the United States and Mexico was "imminent." This alone was insufficient to prompt the commander to action, but at the same time, he heard a truly disturbing rumor: that Mexico had secretly ceded California to England. Jones knew that Californios had resigned themselves for some time to a future alliance with some foreign nation—if not the United States, then France or England—feeling that Mexico could neither hold nor protect the province. Jones also knew that at that moment, the English, as well as the French, had naval forces in the Pacific Ocean. Believing that his ultimate mission was to promote the security of the nation, he seized Monterey, California, negotiated a private declaration of surrender with a group of Monterey citizens, and proclaimed American possession of the Monterey District of California. Jones held the port for one day, October 20, 1842, before realizing his mistake and reversing his actions. Though Jones was relieved of his position as a result of his peremptory move, he was not driven from the Navy. Many of his superiors approved of what he had done. The English menace, they felt, was real, and Mexico's control of the region so weak as to invite trouble.

Oregon

The American secretary of state and the English baron (soon to be earl) attempted, but failed, to resolve their countries' dispute over Oregon. Both nations occupied the disputed land, in accordance with a Convention of Joint Occupation, but as with the contested land in the Northeast, increased settlement, mostly from the American side, made the issue ripe for solution. Unfortunately, Ashburton was handicapped by the instructions he worked from, which had been written by an English ministerial official who had an apparent disdain for the conciliatory policies of the Peel government. The veteran permanent undersecretary in the foreign ministry had recently resigned due to illness, and his replacement purposely kept Ashburton and even Peel in the dark about the history of Oregon negotiations. As a result, Ashburton arrived in the United States bearing, as a secret fall back "final offer," a settlement line that had previously been submitted to, and rejected by, the Americans.

As another drawback to the settlement of Oregon in these negotiations, Webster was ambivalent about American expansion, and proposed a settlement that made Oregon an afterthought. His proposal was that Great Britain would use its influence to help secure San Francisco for the United States from Mexico, and the United States would divide Oregon at the Columbia River (well below the eventual line of settlement). Webster's proposal would have dismayed most American expansionists, who wanted far more than a port for trade in the West. They wanted land for settlement. If Oregon's future was to be settled under President Tyler, it would have to be resolved independent of the Webster-Ashburton negotiations.

Negotiations continued under Webster and his successor, Abel Upshur, but were ineffectual. Failure did not signify a lack of interest in Oregon on the part of either party, certainly not the United States. The American interest in Oregon land was spurred shortly after Webster's resignation by the completion, in 1842, of a four-year expedition led by an officer of the United States Navy, Lieutenant Charles Wilkes. Wilkes was greatly impressed by the bay of Puget Sound. Of that and other harbors in Oregon Territory, he wrote that "no country in the world . . . possesses waters equal to these." In his official report on his lengthy journey to explore the Pacific, the lieutenant suggested that the United States claim all the disputed territory in Oregon, up to the line of 54° 40' latitude, and hold it by force if necessary. Secretary of State Upshur suppressed publication of the document, but unofficial versions soon appeared in the press, and added to the public's interest. (Though Wilkes himself was not so popular; he became a model for Herman Melville's character, Captain Ahab.)

President Tyler further diminished prospects for an agreement on Oregon when, in his December 1842 Annual Message to Congress, he seemed to chastise Great Britain for the failure to come to terms. As he had at that moment a fresh proposal from the British on the very subject, the president's remark greatly embarrassed the English government. A leader of the opposition gave a three hour speech in Parliament decrying Aberdeen's diplomacy, and mocking attempts to be cordial with the Americans, for whom he said it was true that, "Undue concessions, instead of securing peace, only increase the appetite for aggression." Tyler repeated the exercise the next year, once again laying blame for the failure to conclude a settlement on the British, while failing to acknowledge British initiatives to negotiate.

The British, for good reason, suspected a trick, for although the two parties continued to talk about whether or not they were in fact talking, American settlers continued to break ground, build houses, and establish communities throughout Oregon. Abel Upshur died in an accident aboard an American naval vessel, February 28, 1844. His replacement, John C. Calhoun, professed ignorance of negotiations and declined to state plainly his country's terms for settlement, thus rebuffing the final efforts made while Tyler was president to settle the affair through diplomacy.

Texas

Against this backdrop of domestic political chaos and mutual suspicions that persisted despite partially successful negotiations, President Tyler plunged his nation into the single biggest issue of his presidency, and of American politics during his and the succeeding presidency: Texas. John Tyler wanted Texas for the nation for a host of reasons. There were three motivations deriving principally from a consideration of domestic politics. First, the physical expansion of the nation was in keeping with his cherished republican principles, as expounded and acted on by the revered Thomas Jefferson. Like Jefferson, Tyler associated cities with disease and corruption, both physical and spiritual. By bringing new land into the nation, the United States might retain its virtue indefinitely by remaining primarily an agricultural society. Like a great many Democrats, moreover, Tyler believed in what would soon be termed the Manifest Destiny of his nation to spread across the continent.

Second, Tyler also believed that the addition of Texas would promote the nation's economic power, by expanding the domain of "King Cotton." Cotton, he and most other Southern gentlemen were certain, was the nation's greatest economic resource. With cotton as its lever, the United States could influence events around the world, most particularly in Great Britain. The British, it was assumed, would do nothing to harm their chief supplier of this vital commodity. Texas's admission to the Union would make the English even more dependent on the Americans. That it would have the added benefit of making the North even more dependent on the South surely did not escape Tyler's mind either, though in his public pronouncements and even his private correspondence, he spoke preeminently of the *national* interest to be served by bringing Texas into the Union.

Finally, Tyler subscribed to what was known as the diffusion theory. According to this ingenious, if ludicrous, argument put forth by Robert J. Walker, a confidant of the president and Democratic senator from Mississippi, the annexation of Texas would promote the eventual abolition of slavery in the United States. Tyler, like most Southern planters in the 1840s, acknowledged slavery as an evil institution and wished to see it expunged, but not, of course, at the expense of the slave owner. What they longed for was a natural, progressive end to slavery. This is how it would work: As the soil in the southern slave states was exhausted, slaves would be sold or taken to Texas. Eventually, slavery would reach its limit there as well. As that happened, the slaves would find their way across the border and *off American soil*. Because the people of Mexico and other nations south of the border are themselves of mixed race, they would welcome the former slaves without prejudice. The alternative, Walker announced, was that slavery would remain enclosed in the American South. Once it had run its course there, slaves would be emancipated and flood the North.

The problem, however, was the same as it had been ever since Texan independence in 1836. Texas's addition was widely opposed in the North. A fight for its admission might well break apart the party that supported it, before ultimately failing in the Senate, where a two-thirds majority would be required to ratify any treaty with the independent republic. These obstacles proved less onerous for Tyler than for other presidents. First, Tyler no longer had a party. Having left the Democrats and having been written out of the Whig Party, he dreamed of mobilizing a new party behind his own person. Second, as he demonstrated in his use of the veto power, Tyler was willing to dare greatly in his interpretation of the Constitution. But, without the addition of a motivation arising from the perception of a foreign threat, even Tyler might not have been moved to action.

The British Menace Looks to the South

Tyler had first brought up Texas's annexation with Secretary of State Webster, just months into his presidency, as he prepared to deliver his First Annual Message to Congress. Tyler made favorable mention of Texas in that speech, but did nothing about Texas beyond talking until shortly after he met, in early 1843, with a representative of the Texas government. On behalf of President Sam Houston of Texas, the envoy began to play "the British card."

Houston's envoy warned Tyler, as did Houston in subsequent correspondence, that, without formal affiliation with the United States, Texas would have no choice but to accept British offers of assistance. At the same time, Houston cultivated the British so as to make the "threat" of British diplomatic predation seem more convincing. When Houston needed an emissary from a third country to negotiate for the release of Texan prisoners from Mexico, he went to the British, not the Americans, for help. To negotiate a truce in their constant war of harassment, Houston again rebuffed American offers of assistance, and accepted those of the British. Most cleverly, Sam Houston played on Tyler's fear that, in any affiliation that Texas forged with Britain, it would demand as the price of its protection the abolition of slavery in the republic.

Texas abolitionists were pursuing such a plan at the very moment. In the summer of 1843, a delegation of abolitionists from Texas attended a worldwide conference on the subject in London. They were received by Aberdeen himself. In the House of Lords, a member prophesied that should slavery fall in Texas, it would fall in all the United States, and asked Lord Aberdeen what he was doing to help this process along. The foreign secretary, in reply, expressed support for abolition in Texas. Informed of these events by a friend of John C. Calhoun, who was in London at the time, President Tyler and Secretary of State Upshur were alarmed. Upshur instructed the American ambassador in England to press Aberdeen regarding his intent, and at the same time opened informal talks with representatives from Texas.

In his Annual Message to Congress of December 10, 1843, President Tyler chided Mexico and encouraged the growing number of advocates for Texas's annexation. (In a recent public letter, Andrew Jackson had called for incorporating Texas to check Britain.) Referencing Mexico's threat of war should annexation occur, Tyler said "It must be regarded as not a little extraordinary." After all, Texas and the United States were just talking at this point, the president asserted. Moreover, Mexico's belligerence could only enhance American interest in Texas, for constant warfare along the border must eventually render both Mexico and Texas, "and especially the weaker of the two—the subject of interference on the part of stronger and more powerful nations—intent only on advancing their own peculiar views . . . ."

Mexico posed a peculiar problem for the United States, both in California and in Texas. Its weakness, combined with its ambition, made for an unstable political environment, which invited stronger nations to attempt to intercede. Mexico was a new republic, and it had followed a chaotic path, to American eyes, since independence. During Tyler's presidency alone, the famous Santa Anna resumed and resigned the presidency three times, before being captured and exiled—not for the last time—in November 1844. Rebuking Mexico as a newcomer to independence, Tyler continued his Annual Message in a lecturing tone. "I can not but think that it becomes the United States, as the oldest of the American Republics, to hold a language to Mexico upon this subject of an unambiguous character. It is time that this war had ceased." Tyler then went on to complain of a recent edict from President Santa Anna banning foreign retail business in the nation.

Tyler's ambition, Houston's diplomacy, and Mexico's condition all created momentum for Texas's annexation. Lord Aberdeen had unwittingly played his part as well. He was perhaps never entirely serious in his apparent abolitionist designs on Texas. Aberdeen certainly wished for abolition in Texas and for a formal alliance with Texas. Texan independence would check the growth of American power, and would also provide an alternative market for England in the Americas. As a diplomat of the Texas Republic later recalled Aberdeen stating to him, Great Britain desired to find in Texas a market for her merchandise "without having to climb over the United States tariff." But was he, or the Peel government, really willing to forge a treaty with Texas that would guarantee abolition, in addition to trade? It seems doubtful. In 1844, Britain proposed that France and England guarantee Texas's independence (against the United States) on condition that Mexico recognize Texas's sovereignty. As Mexico clearly had no intention of making this concession, it seemed an empty gesture. Indeed, Aberdeen's purpose seems to have been to lay the foundations for better relations with France. France and England had come close to war, again, during Aberdeen's tenure, and he and Peel were eager to establish what the minister termed an *entente cordiale* with the French. Toward that end, he sought to work with France diplomatically where their interests coincided. Keeping a lid on American power by preventing its acquisition of Texas was one such area. In thus subordinating British-American relations to British-French concord, Aberdeen underestimated American hostility regarding European encroachment on its borders. Through the second half of Tyler's term, pro-annexationist editors and politicians kept up a steady drumbeat of allegations against British machinations.

Following the lead of the revered Jackson, Democratic politicians in particular, though they derided Tyler as "His Accidency," echoed his sentiments about Texas. "Great Britain must not control Texas," roared Democratic Representative Charles Ingersoll of Pennsylvania, chair of the House Foreign Affairs Committee. "If such is the alternative, the United States must insist on immediate annexation." This was, he proclaimed, "the last struggle for American independence."

The Treaty for Texas

When John C. Calhoun took his place as secretary of state, negotiations for Texas were well advanced. Calhoun urgently completed the task. Unfortunately for the president, his secretary of state submitted on his behalf to the Senate on April 22, 1844, not just the treaty, but a letter he had written to the British minister in Washington, Richard Packenham, defending slavery as an institution and criticizing British advocacy of abolition in Texas. In this letter, Calhoun justified American interest in Texas "in order to preserve a domestic institution."

Were the high-minded, nationalist arguments for Texas's annexation merely a smoke screen? Was Texas annexation just a project of the slave power? Calhoun's missive certainly gave this impression, and added fuel to what surely would have been a fire of controversy in any event. Incredibly, Calhoun had sought precisely the effect his maneuver precipitated, for he had come to believe that the survival of slavery, the South, and the nation, depended on the mobilization of Southern opinion.

Calhoun's attempt to break apart the parties and forge a new power along sectional lines may have been visionary, in its own way, but it was not good politics in 1844. One wonders if the secretary of state was already looking beyond the Senate's consideration of the treaty at this point, or whether he had just forgotten his political arithmetic. Even a solid South could not produce a two-thirds majority in the Senate. When the vote was at last taken, June 8, the treaty failed thirty-five to sixteen. Most Southern Whigs ignored Calhoun's provocation and voted with their party, not their region, while seven Northern Democrats voted "no" as well. If Texas were to become the twenty-eighth state, it appeared that it would not happen during the 28th Congress.

If some of the elders of the two major parties had had their way, the Senate rejection of annexation would have been the final word on Texas for the time being. Well before the vote, in fact, both Henry Clay and Martin Van Buren came out in opposition to the treaty. Clay was the national leader of the Whig Party and that party's presumptive nominee for president. Van Buren, by his action, promoted himself as Clay's counterpart. Rather than risk the unknown—a national contest over Texas's admission to the Union—they preferred simply not to speak of Texas.

Van Buren misjudged the mood of his party. Texas was a more popular issue than it ever had been, and the apparent threat that Texas might invite Britain, and abolitionism, into the American South was an urgent inducement to action. When Andrew Jackson himself repudiated Van Buren's position, Van Buren's chances for the party's renomination were dealt a severe blow. Tyler hoped that Jackson might throw Democratic support behind *him,* but no party wanted the difficult Mr. Tyler at its head. James K. Polk, a protégé of Jackson and an advocate of Texas annexation took the nomination of the Democrats, and Tyler—after failing to excite interest as an independent candidate—settled for Jackson's written assurance that his followers would be welcomed back into the Democracy without taint of association. As a result, Tyler dropped out of the race for election, but not out of the race for Texas. But what could be done by a lame-duck president and a lame-duck Congress after the Senate had already rejected the treaty so decisively?

Texas Becomes the Twenty-Eighth State

The electoral victory for the pro-annexationist Polk and the Democratic Party in 1844 gave Tyler the opportunity that perhaps only he among presidents of the first half of the nineteenth century would have dared to take. (Even Tyler had to be urged on by his secretary of state, Calhoun.) In his last Annual Message to Congress, delivered December 3, 1844, Tyler made his bid for the immediate acquisition of Texas.

In that document, Tyler first warned, again, of British designs. "The United States," he pointed out, "are becoming too important . . . not to attract the observation of other nations. It therefore may in the progress of time occur that opinions entirely abstract in the States which they may prevail [opinions of no practical consequence in other nations, who nonetheless voice them] and in no degree affecting their domestic institutions may be artfully but secretly encouraged with a view to undermine the Union." Such, presumably, was the case with British advocacy of abolition in Texas. As for Mexico, Tyler reiterated his earlier remarks about the ill effects to be anticipated should that nation "renew the war." An invasion of Texas, Tyler cautioned, even without a treaty of annexation, "would arouse the attention of all Christendom." "A war of desolation, such as is now threatened by Mexico, can not be waged without involving our peace and tranquility." With these cautions to foreign nations behind him, Tyler moved on to propose a remarkable innovation: the admission of a new state, formed from a formerly independent nation, by joint resolution of Congress.

His argument in favor of this proposal revealed its weakness. The Constitution, Tyler observed, grants the president full authority to negotiate treaties. Thus it is "untenable" to argue that a treaty should be "submitted to the ordeal of public opinion." Nevertheless, this had been "one of the chief objections" against the recently defeated treaty for Texas's admission to the Union. Seeing how "the decision of the people and the States on this great and interesting subject has been decisively manifested" in the recent elections, Tyler concluded that "It is the will of the both the people and the States that Texas shall be annexed to the Union promptly and immediately." This could be accomplished, the president helpfully concluded, "in the form of a joint resolution . . . ." The Joint Resolution for Annexing Texas to the United States was signed Sunday, March 1, 1845, two days prior to the inauguration of the new president.

Legacy

John Tyler was a stubborn man, proud of his independence and sure of his rectitude. He was also keenly ambitious. Though he had come to the presidency by accident, he was determined to be president in his own right. Through his repeated vetoes of first banking, and then tariff legislation, he alienated himself from his new party, the Whigs. His first secretary of state, Daniel Webster, was able and diligent, and it was largely through his efforts and those of his British counterpart, Baron Ashburton, that a number of quarrels in British/American affairs were resolved, including the location of the border of Maine.

Despite this diplomatic success, President Tyler remained suspicious of America's principal potential antagonist, Great Britain. Anglophobia joined national interest and a republican belief in national destiny to promote the annexation of Texas and the deferral of agreement on the division of Oregon. In Oregon, postponement seemed calculated to benefit the American claim, as American settlers were greatly interested in the land and voted with their feet to claim more of it with each passing month. With regard to Texas, Tyler and many other Americans feared that, if the United States did not admit Texas to the Union, Texas would seek an alliance with Great Britain. Constant warfare with Mexico had weakened the republic, and its president, Sam Houston, seemed interested in a compact with the British. Southerners were particularly anxious at the prospect that Britain might demand, in a bargain with Texas, the abolition of slavery.

At first, President Tyler had one more reason for pursuing the admission of Texas under his presidency. He hoped that it would prove so popular a move that either the Democrats would welcome him back into their party and nominate him for another term as president, or that a new party might mobilize in his support. Even when Tyler dropped out of the race for election in 1844, though, he continued to push for Texas annexation, finally securing his legacy, if not his continuance in office, through the unconventional means of a joint congressional resolution.

John Tyler never seemed to take war with Mexico seriously. He continuously ridiculed Mexico's claims on Texas, and did not ask Congress to prepare for a possible war. Tyler seemed sincerely to believe his public rhetoric: that the disposition of Texas was of no rightful concern to Mexico. Texas had won and maintained its independence, and was a sovereign nation. That Mexican political leaders might feel about the United States much the same as many Americans felt about Great Britain, especially in regard to the association of one of these large powers with Texas, seems not to have occurred to Tyler or his inner circle. The results would be observed in the next administration.

Thomas Langston

Chronology
1841
March 9: U.S. Supreme Court frees *Amistad* slaves.

April 4: President Harrison dies of pneumonia, Tyler succeeds.

1842
March 30: Congress raises tariffs to 1832 levels.

August 9: Webster-Ashburton Treaty settles Northeast boundary issues.

August 29: Britain wins Opium War; China cedes Hong Kong in Treaty of Nanking.

October 20: Commodore Thomas Jones temporarily seizes Monterey, mistakenly claims California for the United States.

December 30: Tyler asserts U.S. interest in Hawaii.

1843
August 23: Mexico protests U.S. interest in annexing Texas.

September 23: Mexican President Santa Anna bans foreign retail business in Mexico.

December 16: U.S. Navy conducts punitive operations against African coastal villages.

1844
February 15: Texas wants annexation treaty.

April 12: Texas Treaty of Annexation.

June 8: Texas annexation treaty rejected by Senate.

July 3: Treaty of Wanghia with China.

July 18: Britain aborts efforts to keep Texas independent.

September 29: *Sancola* incident with Argentina.

October 31: Santa Anna overthrown in Mexico.

December 3: Tyler advocates Texas annexation to Congress.

December 4: James Polk elected president on annexation platform.

References and Further Reading
Crapol, Edward. "John Tyler and the Pursuit of National Destiny," *Journal of the Early Republic* 17 (Fall 1997): 467–491.

Haynes, Sam W. "Anglophobia and the Annexation of Texas," in Sam W. Haynes and Christopher Morris, eds., *Manifest Destiny and Empire: Antebellum American Expansionism*. College Station, TX: Texas A&M University Press, 1997, 115–145.

Holt, Michael F. *The Rise and Fall of the American Whig Party: Jacksonian Politics and the Onset of the Civil War*. New York: Oxford University Press, 1999.

Jones, Howard. *To The Webster-Ashburton Treaty: A Study in Anglo-American Relations, 1783–1843*. Chapel Hill, NC: University of North Carolina Press, 1977.

Jones, Wilbur Devereux. *The American Problem in British Diplomacy, 1841–1861*. Athens, GA: University of Georgia Press, 1974.

Monroe, Dan. *The Republican Vision of John Tyler*. College Station, TX: Texas A&M University Press, 2003.

Peterson, Norma Lois. *The Presidencies of William Henry Harrison and John Tyler*. Lawrence, KS: The University Press of Kansas, 1989.

Seager, II, Robert. *And Tyler Too: A Biography of John and Julia Gardner Tyler*. New York: Easton Press, 1963.

Silbey, Joel H. *Storm Over Texas: The Annexation Controversy and the Road to Civil War*. New York: Oxford University Press, 2005.

James K. Polk (1845–1849)

Early Life and Political Career

Born on November 2, 1795, in Mecklenburg County, North Carolina, James K. Polk was the first of nine children of Samuel and Jane Polk. Ten years later, in 1805, the family relocated to Maury County, Tennessee, about sixty miles south of present day Nashville. Initially schooled at home by his mother, Polk absorbed her strict adherence to the Presbyterian faith and also learned to control his emotions, characteristics that became life-long. Young Polk rebuffed his father's nudge into the business world in favor of scholarly pursuits. He advanced rapidly through the local schools and entered the University of North Carolina at Chapel Hill at the age of sixteen in January 1816. Two and one half years later, Polk delivered the salutary address at his graduation where he received honors in mathematics and the classics.

Polk returned to Columbia, Tennessee, to pursue a career in law and then politics. Following his admission to the state bar in 1820, Polk opened a law office in Columbia where he continued to practice law throughout his career, primarily as a means to subsidize his political aspirations. In 1824, Polk married Sarah Childress, the daughter of a prominent Murfreesboro merchant and planter. Like James, she maintained an unbending commitment to the Presbyterian faith. Unlike James, she had been schooled in feminine cultural affairs that provided her with social skills that balanced her husband's aloofness throughout his political career.

Polk's political career began in 1819 as a clerk in the Tennessee State Senate, where he earned the reputation as an excellent and detailed record keeper, another characteristic that he kept throughout his life. In 1822, he easily won a seat in the lower house of the state legislature. Despite his family name, Polk took to the campaign trail, visiting many farms throughout Maury County. His oratorical skills earned him the title "Napoleon of the Stump," another skill that would later serve him well. As a legislator, Polk favored the interests of small farmers and workers at the expense of those of bankers and land speculators. He supported a statewide public school system, internal improvements, implementation of a progressive tax code, and writing a new state constitution.

Regarding the Constitution, Polk was a "strict constructionist." Simply put, the federal government had no legal authority to perform functions not clearly spelled out in its Constitution. In fact, Polk contended, the less government, the better. From the start, Polk also was a fiscal conservative,

James K. Polk brought vast new territories under American control. (Library of Congress)

demanding that government spending stay within restricted limits. Another Tennessean and popular war hero, Andrew Jackson, also held these views, prompting Polk to support Jackson's appointment to the U.S. Senate in 1823. From then until Jackson's death in 1845, Polk remained an unwavering Jackson supporter.

In August 1825, Polk was elected to the U.S. House of Representatives. He took his constructionist view of the Constitution with him to Congress, where he used it to justify his opposition to President John Quincy Adams (1825–1829) and his expansive government programs. As a leader of the Democratic Party's "factious opposition" to Adams, Polk enhanced his reputation as a great orator and master of details. His political career advanced further with

Jackson's presidential victory in 1828, a presidency marked by the growing controversy over constructionist interpretations of the Constitution, and the growing sectionalism that subsequently impacted the Polk presidency. Congressman Polk stood with Jackson in rejecting federally funded intrastate roads, opposing protective tariffs, and against rechartering the National Bank. Polk also supported programs that signaled his support for U.S. expansion: lower land prices, extension of the federal court system to western states, and the removal of Indians to areas far beyond the Mississippi River. Recognizing the rancorous debate about the westward extension of slavery, in 1835 Polk instituted the "gag rule" that permitted the introduction of antislavery resolutions in the House but provided that they be tabled immediately, a move that favored Southern interests. This and his link to Jackson, however, cost Polk consideration for higher office in the 1836 presidential campaign. In the congressional elections that same year, Polk survived the purge of the Democrats by the Tennessee electorate only because he ran unopposed in his district. Polk returned to Congress for two more years, where, as Speaker of the House of Representatives, he was at his political zenith.

Polk left Congress to accept his party's nomination to run for the Tennessee governorship in 1839, an election he won by a mere 2,462 votes. Despite the narrow victory, many state politicos viewed the triumph as a stepping-stone to the Democratic Party's vice presidential nomination in 1840, but Polk withdrew from the competition amid a plethora of feuding candidates. When Polk lost his bid for reelection to the Tennessee governorship in 1841 and again in 1843, his political career appeared to be over.

As the Democratic National Convention convened in Baltimore in May 1844, Polk was at best a distant, dark horse candidate for the vice presidential nomination. But when the convention split over a presidential nominee, it turned to Polk and Pennsylvanian George M. Dallas to provide the image of sectional balance to the divided party. The Polk-Dallas ticket bested the Whigs nominees Henry Clay and Theodore Frelinghuysen by a 170–105 electoral vote count. The count belied the narrowness of Polk's victory—only 38,180 votes. Polk came to Washington without a mandate to preside over a divided nation.

Polk was nonetheless convinced that he represented all the people of the United States, and that he possessed a more important role in shaping the legislative program than Congress, whose membership he viewed as representing only various portions of the entire nation. He also felt obliged to introduce legislation that benefited the whole nation and to veto congressional actions that favored only singular or sectional interests. As could be expected, congressmen on both sides of the aisle did not share Polk's view of presidential leadership over the legislative process. This conflict played out in the struggle over a lower tariff, an independent treasury system, and federal support for infrastructure projects that dealt only with international commerce or national defense. The 1846 Walker Tariff contained more protectionist features than the president wanted, but he recognized that Congress would not produce anything different. With only the Whigs in opposition, Congress established an Independent Treasury in late 1846. Throughout his presidential term, Polk vetoed several domestic reform proposals on the grounds of strict constructivism—proposed roads, for example, that served only Western, Southern, or Eastern interests rather than national commercial or security needs.

Emerging National Self-Confidence: Economics, Politics, and Reform

While Polk clung to principles that guided the nation's early development, in the two generations since its birth, the United States experienced bewildering domestic changes that contributed to national self-confidence on the eve of his presidency. The country's economic patterns changed significantly between 1800 and 1840; the economies of the northeastern and Middle Atlantic states became more diversified as agriculture mixed with fledgling industries. During the same generation, the South became increasingly dependent on cotton production for export to mills in the U.S. Northeast and in Great Britain. In the Midwest, small farms abounded, and riverfront towns like Louisville, Cincinnati, and St. Louis developed into commercial centers. Railroads, turnpikes, and canals connected these sections, particularly between the Northeast, the Middle Atlantic, and Midwest.

As the nation's economy developed and changed, so too did the patterns of political behavior. Politics became more democratic, with a rapidly growing number of people participating in local, state, and national elections. In the older states, increased participation resulted from lifting property holding and taxpaying qualifications for the franchise, while the constitutions of newer states provided for universal white male suffrage. Although women, blacks, and Native Americans continued to be excluded from voting, men flocked to the polls in unprecedented numbers. Other factors that stimulated voter participation included the growing strength in democratic beliefs, the active role of state governments in building roads and canals, selling public land, chartering corporations, and interactions with Native Americans. Beginning in the 1820s, politicians of every persuasion vied with each other for voter support. The result was an outpouring of interest in elections, as voter turnout increased markedly. Only 27 percent of the eligible voters cast their ballots in the 1824 presidential election; 58 percent did so in 1828; 55 percent in 1832; 58 percent in 1836; and 80 percent in 1840.

Manifest Destiny and the Principles of Foreign Policy

In addition to the changing economic and political dynamics, the 1830s ushered in a reformist spirit that contributed to a more egalitarian society. The introduction of public education, the quest for women's rights, the development of labor unions, the drive for temperance, and prison reform all characterized the pursuit of a better America. Americans demonstrated great confidence that its progressive society was far more advanced than that of Europe and Latin America. Only in the slaveholding South did the planter class cling to the past to preserve its political power and place in the established social order. For most Americans, the United States had, by 1840, become a true republic in which the supreme power of government resided with the citizens and whose society was more egalitarian than any other in the world. This self-confidence in the superiority of its own system was not new. Pamphleteer Thomas Paine expressed the same thought on the eve of the American Revolution and, as president, John Quincy Adams described the United States as the "beacon on the hill" for the world to imitate. Journalist John O'Sullivan symbolized the spirit of the 1840s when he wrote that it was the Manifest Destiny of the United States to spread the advantages of its society across the continent to the Pacific Ocean. For some, that destiny included Mexico and Central America; democracy would follow the flag. The Native Americans residing in the Great Plains, the Mexicans, and the Central Americans—until now considered "inferior peoples"—would come to enjoy the benefits of the American way of life.

The moral crusade paled by comparison with the hunger for land, markets, and accompanying international overtones. This was most evident with Texas, which was coveted by Southern slave owners for the expansion of cotton plantations and as a state to send like-minded political representatives to the national Congress where they would defend low tariffs and the "peculiar institution" of slavery, the backbone of the Southern economy and social order. At the same time, Midwestern farmers and their children crossed into the territories beyond Missouri toward the Pacific. The search for new lands brought wagon trains to the Oregon and California territories. Beyond the Pacific coastline lay the vast potential markets of the Far East. New England merchants, anticipating the Orient's treasures, sought ports along the California coast. This desire to expand the national horizon brought America into the international arena, where it again met its old European nemeses. Since the birth of the nation, the Americans distrusted the European powers and remained determined to keep them from American shores and periphery. In the eyes of most Americans, including Polk, Great Britain was the most sinister of the European powers. Every British move was interpreted as part of a grand plan to thwart American national interests. National security became a hallmark of U.S. foreign policy.

On March 4, 1845, before a rain-soaked crowd in front of the Capitol Building in Washington, D.C., Polk took the oath of office as the eleventh president of the United States. At forty-nine, he was at the time the youngest man ever to do so. And in his inaugural address he made reference to all three principles for the conduct of his foreign policy: spreading democracy, the opportunity for economic expansion, and the need to secure the nation from European interlopers. Polk appeared poised to answer the call of Manifest Destiny. The challenge to do so greeted him as he entered the White House later that same day.

Texas

Americans began to venture into Texas within a year of the 1803 Louisiana Purchase in search of commerce and land. Some even intrigued with Mexicans for independence when the battle against Spain began in 1810. After achieving its independence in 1821, the Mexican government encouraged American settlers to enter the territory, although its policies were restrictive. The most notable of the grants went to entrepreneur Moses F. Austin who, along with his son Stephen, brought 300 families to settle between the Brazos and Colorado Rivers by 1824. The number of Anglo-Americans (as the Mexicans referred to them) in Texas swelled to 15,000 by 1830 and 30,000 by 1836, along with an estimated 5,000 slaves. According to the Moses Grant, the Anglos were to swear allegiance and pay taxes to the Mexican government, convert to Roman Catholicism, and pay ten cents an acre for their land on easy credit terms. But the Anglos rejected everything Mexican and detested the presence of Mexican government officials and military personnel in their midst. By the mid-1820s the cultural conflict became violent, with lives and property threatened and in some cases destroyed. The Anglos blamed the Mexican government for not controlling those responsible.

In the east, New England merchants coveted trading links with Chihuahua and Zacatacas through Santa Fe in present-day New Mexico. By 1821, a permanent trading route connected St. Louis, Missouri, with Santa Fe and Taos, and by 1828, an estimated $150,000 worth of consumer goods from the United States arrived in these Mexican cities annually. Several hundred Anglos settled in the New Mexico territory and some migrated to California. While the local Mexicans welcomed the new arrivals, the government in Mexico City viewed these developments as bad omens.

At the time James K. Polk began his congressional career, the U.S. government commenced its quest to acquire Mexico. President John Quincy Adams authorized Minister Joel Poinsett to offer $1 million for the territory. In 1829

President Andrew Jackson dispatched Anthony Butler on the similar mission and, in 1835, Jackson expanded the American territorial horizons to include San Francisco Bay. The Mexican government rejected the U.S. offer and in fact demanded both that the United States stem the influx of Anglos into the Texas territory and that those already resident there abide by Mexican law. As a result, a nationalist rivalry emerged.

In December 1834, General Antonio Lopez Santa Anna seized the Mexican presidency with the determination to centralize the government and bring Texas back into the Mexican fold. The Texans were equally determined to resist Mexico's authority. Skirmishes soon followed that escalated into Santa Anna's brutal victories at the Alamo in San Antonio and at Goliad in March 1836. These victories were short lived, for on April 21, Texan forces, led by Sam Houston, forced the Mexican's capitulation at San Jacinto and wrung from Santa Ana treaties that, among other things, placed the Texas boundary at the Rio Grande River. In the midst of the military struggle, Texas declared its independence on March 19 and, following the defeat of the Mexican army in April, Houston led a delegation to Washington, D.C., to seek annexation to the United States.

The mission was to no avail. Neither Jackson nor his successor, Martin Van Buren wanted to deal with annexation primarily because of the slavery issue. The Texas legislature legalized slavery, which pleased Southerners and contributed to a political balance regarding any future states carved out of the Northwest Territory. But abolitionists and congressional representatives from the Northeast and Midwest did not share that view; they feared that several slave states might be carved out of a territory as large as Texas. The annexation also raised the possibility of war with Mexico. Matters rested there until late in the presidency of John Tyler in 1844.

With an eye on his own 1844 presidential reelection bid, Tyler submitted a Texas annexation treaty to the Senate in April 1844, at a time when the national parties convened their nominating conventions in Baltimore, Maryland. While the Senate soundly defeated the treaty and the Whigs avoided the issue in their party platform, the Democrats did not. As their candidate, Polk favored westward expansion, and the party platform called for the "re-annexation" of Texas. During the ensuing presidential campaign, abolitionists and anti-abolitionists drew the most public attention, and only a few gave notice to the supporters of Manifest Destiny, who advocated spreading democracy across the continent. In the emotion of the moment, the campaign was blind to other issues: a central bank and domestic and protective tariffs. Although Polk's razor thin victory in November 1844 could not be attributed to any single issue, he interpreted the result as a referendum victory for annexation. Polk went to Washington

determined to carry out a continental policy, and his inaugural address reflected that determination.

Outgoing President John J. Tyler also interpreted Polk's victory as one for expansion, including the annexation of Texas. So too did the Texans who played the British card; the Lone Star Republic cautioned the United States that, if it did not act favorably on annexation, Great Britain would guarantee its independence from Mexico. Such a British presence at the American back door would not only constitute a menace to security but could also serve to thwart continental expansion. Tyler recognized that he could not muster the necessary two-thirds vote to approve an annexation treaty but could secure a congressional resolution toward the same end. On January 25, 1845, the House of Representatives passed such a resolution and one month later the Senate did the same. On March 1, with only three days left in his presidency, Tyler signed the resolution.

Before his presidential nomination, Polk made it known that he favored the incorporation of Texas into the Union and that he thought John Quincy Adams had erred in 1819 when he negotiated away the Rio Grande River as the territory's boundary. Once he arrived in Washington in January 1845, to prepare for his inauguration, Polk met privately with some of the leading congressional advocates of westward expansion, including Senator Thomas Hart Benton. Once in the White House, he quickly implemented the joint congressional resolution by dispatching Andrew Jackson Donelson to Texas to complete the annexation details and Charles Wickliffe and Archibald Yell to whip up popular enthusiasm for that objective. Anxious to derail American westward expansion, in May 1845, Britain persuaded the Mexican government to recognize Texas independence with the proviso that it not be attached to a third country. It was too little, too late. On June 16, the Texas Senate approved the Lone Star Republic's annexation to the United States. For a moment, Mexico considered going to war over its lost territory, but with an undermanned army and no foreign support, it quickly dropped the option. Shortly thereafter, the Anglos and the Mexicans clashed. In the meantime, the United States focused its attention on the Pacific Coast.

Oregon and California

American claims to the Oregon Territory dated to 1792, when Captain Robert Gray discovered the mouth of the Colombia River. The Lewis and Clark expedition further cemented the claim when it reached the river's mouth in 1806. Hunters and trappers soon followed, the most notable being John Jacob Astor, who in 1811 established a trading fort bearing his name on the south side of the Columbia River. Legal claims were laid out in the Treaty of Ghent of

1815 that brought the War of 1812 to an end; the treaty recognized rights of the United States to the territory south of the Columbia River.

The Americans were not without competitors. Spain's claims dated to its colonial explorations but gave little attention to the Pacific Northwest. Spain finally abandoned all interest in the Pacific Northwest in the 1819 Adams-Onis Treaty. The Russian American Company had a string of trading outposts along the Pacific Northwest Coast that caused a war of words with the United States until 1824, when the Russian company collapsed financially and withdrew from the territory altogether. That left the British, whose interest can be traced to the explorations of Sir Francis Drake in 1579, but thereafter gave little attention to the distant territory. In 1827, the United States and Great Britain signed a ten-year agreement for the joint occupation of the territory, with options for ten-year renewal and a proviso requiring a one-year's notice to abrogate the agreement. Thus, at the time Polk was completing his second year in Congress, the Pacific Northwest between the 42nd parallel and 54° 40' settled into an Anglo-American dispute.

Since the 1820s, the British-owned Hudson Bay Company had been the dominant commercial firm in the Oregon Territory, but it faced growing competition from American entrepreneurs who made their way into the territory, first for sea otter pelts, then fur trading, and finally, in the 1830s, for whale oil. In the 1830s a few missionaries and settlers followed the businessmen into what was now called the Oregon Territory. The need for seaports in the region led to an 1826 report by a Boston merchant that called for the United States to insist upon the 49th parallel as its northern boundary in any forthcoming settlement. Subsequent studies reaffirmed the 1826 report. Before Polk entered the White House, the United States had, on three different occasions, offered to settle the territorial boundary at the 49th parallel.

Despite the interest, by 1841 only an estimated 500 Americans resided in the territory. A year later "Oregon Fever" gripped the nation, so that by the time Polk took his oath of office, nearly 5,000 Americans had settled in the Oregon Territory, almost all of them south of the Colombia River, but without a locally organized government or a link to the U.S. Army for military protection. The Hudson Bay Company served as their chief source of supplies, but company officials feared that the continued influx of American residents would lead to a confrontation between the governments in London and Washington, D.C.

The stakes moved higher with the 1844 Democratic Party national platform that declared the right of the United States to Oregon to be "clear and unquestionable" and held further that "no portion of the same ought to be ceded to England or any other country." This became the basis for Polk's demand for settlement of the issue at 54° 40', not the 49th parallel.

Concerned with the rising American jingoism, on the eve of Polk's presidency the British proposed that the issue be submitted to arbitration. Outgoing Secretary of State John C. Calhoun refused the offer. The British also interpreted the Democratic Party platform and Polk's inaugural address as policy statements, not a reflection of the republicanism gripping the nation. As a result, the British viewed the American stance as a defiant challenge. The British minister to Washington, Robert Packenham, also contributed to the problem. In July 1845, he rejected, without referring to London, Secretary of State James Buchanan's proposal to set the Oregon boundary at the 49th parallel. Over the next several months American jingoism became more strident. Polk and congressional representatives, newspapers, and flysheets all demanded that America possess the entire Oregon Territory. After four months of acrimonious debate, on April 17, 1846, only weeks before the outbreak of the Mexican War, Congress instructed Polk to give the required one-year notice to abrogate the 1827 joint occupation treaty.

During the same period, the British government reassessed its own position. When it learned that the Hudson Bay Company foresaw a rapidly deteriorating future in the Pacific Northwest, the need to defend economic interests with military might lessened. The British also confronted a serious logistical problem if they engaged in a war so distant and in a territory so inaccessible. Closer to home, the Irish potato famine that began in 1846 only promised to worsen. More importantly, the United States was the chief market for British manufactures and also the major source of raw cotton for the British textile industry. London had reason for compromise. British Foreign Secretary Lord Aberdeen used the U.S. abrogation of the 1827 agreement to restart negotiations. Polk was equally eager and, in fact, had a treaty prepared for British consideration. The proposed new treaty set the 49th parallel as the northern boundary of Oregon for the United States. Aberdeen accepted. The settlement came at a propitious time. Mexico and the United States were at war, and the thought of the British abandoning the Oregon settlement to aid the Mexicans remained on the American mind. Against this backdrop, Polk asked the Senate to advise him whether the treaty was acceptable before he submitted it to the full Senate for approval or rejection. After two days of closed-door discussions, on June 12, 1846, the Senate reported that the treaty was acceptable. Three days later, June 15, it was ratified. The British Parliament assented to the treaty a few weeks later. Oregon, as originally defined, now belonged to the United States.

American interests on the Pacific Coast also included California, where experience paralleled that of Oregon. The Spanish presence dated to the sixteenth century conquest of the New World, but, owing to an absence of natural wealth or highly organized Indian societies, Spain neither gave significant attention to the vast western territories nor exercised tight political control over them. The same was true for Mexico when it acquired these territories with its own independence in 1821. Similar to Texas in the first part of the nineteenth century, local governments on the periphery often acted independent of the government in Mexico City. French interest in California dated to 1786 and the British to 1792, but the Russians were the first to establish settlements as far south as Fort Ross in 1812. All recognized the importance of San Francisco Bay for trading in the region, and Britain's Hudson Bay Company also saw its importance as a stepping-stone to trade in the Pacific. Yet none went far beyond exploration.

At the time Polk entered Congress in 1825, American fishermen and merchants were establishing trade contacts with California's coastal cities from Yorba Linda in the north to San Diego in the south. By 1837, Boston merchants dominated this trade. During the same period, American explorers, fur trappers, and opportunity seekers made their way across the Sierras into California where they lived quietly and on good terms with local government officials and Spanish-Mexican rancheros. The American residents in California did much to increase the Eastern awareness of the opportunities on the West Coast. By the time Polk was assessing his political future in 1843, thousands of American migrants had trekked the California trail and, clearly, the future promised to bring many more. The growing American presence prompted Lord Aberdeen in 1844 to momentarily consider guaranteeing California for Mexico if it recognized Texan independence. Thus, as Polk's political star began to rise again in1844, the United States faced no real opposition to its designs on California, although policymakers continued to fret about possible British intrigue.

While Polk may have coveted California when he came to the White House in March 1845, he did not have a plan to acquire it. Only after the finalization of Texan annexation in October 1845 did his policy take shape. It was, however, based on erroneous information received from the U.S. consul in California, Thomas O. Larkin and sources in Mexico City that indicated there was a Mexican-British partnership to keep California in the Mexican system. As a result, Secretary of State James Buchanan directed Larkin to work for the prevention of foreign control over the territory, because the result would deny the American residents "the blessings of liberty." Polk also made it known that if California became independent and expressed a desire to join the Union, the U.S. government would move quickly. Although he did not expect war, Polk prepared for it by dispatching naval ships to the California waters with instructions to seize the ports in case of an outbreak of hostilities. Polk also sent Army Colonel J. Gillespie to visit General John C. Frémont with instructions that remain unknown to this day. When in February 1846 Frémont moved close to Monterey, California, the move raised suspicions regarding those instructions.

On the diplomatic front, Polk dispatched John Slidell to Mexico in November 1845 with an offer to pay $5 million above the American claims for damages suffered in Texas at the hands of Mexicans; if the settlement included San Francisco, $20 million; and $25 million if it also included Monterey. Polk's aspirations to purchase any part of California momentarily ended with Slidell's humiliating reception in Mexico City in December. The acquisition of California had to await the peace treaty that officially ended the war with Mexico.

War and Peace with Mexico

President Polk interpreted the failed Slidell mission as the termination of peaceful efforts to settle all disputes with Mexico. Henceforth, his policies became more assertive. Committed to defending the Texas boundary claims, on January 13, 1846, Polk ordered General Zachary Taylor to move his 4,000 troops from Corpus Christi to a position near present day Brownsville on the northern side of the Rio Grande River, the state's southernmost boundary claimed by the Texans and within striking distance of Matamoras, Mexico. Polk also ordered a naval blockade of the mouth of the Rio Grande River. On the diplomatic front, he directed Slidell to make one more effort at negotiations and, failing that, to return home.

Polk reasoned that the American show of force would prompt the Mexicans to back down. The Mexicans did not. In fact, the jingoism whipped up by the Slidell mission markedly increased in response to Polk's threatening gestures and prompted President Mariano Paredes y Arrillaga to order General Pedro Ampudia to the region. Upon his arrival on April 12, 1946, Ampudia ordered Taylor to evacuate his position within twenty-four hours. Taylor did not, and on April 25 the Mexicans entrapped sixty-three of Taylor's men while on reconnaissance; sixteen were killed, a few escaped, and the remainder were imprisoned in Matamoros. Taylor's report on the incident arrived at the White House Saturday evening May 9, 1946, just as the Oregon question was reaching its climax, one day after Slidell reported to Polk on his failed mission and only four hours after Polk and his cabinet had concluded that, should the Mexicans attack Taylor, Polk had no recourse but to ask Congress for a declaration of war. At midday Monday May 11, 1846, Polk sent his war message to Congress, a message that included the assertion that "American blood had been spilt upon the American soil." After a brief debate, the House approved a war measure by a 174–14 vote; the Senate approved the war resolution by a 40–2. The congressional approval gave the impression of widespread support for the war, but there was not, particularly in the Northeast where the conflict was interpreted as the expansion of Southern interests.

The United States entered the conflict without adequate preparation or a clear military plan but the capacity to develop both. Mexico, by contrast, lacked the ability to create political cohesion and an industrial base to support a war. In time, the weight of the U.S. economy and the efforts by Secretary of War William Marcy in preparing and supplying an army numbering some 200,000 men proved too much for Mexico. Polk played a dominant role in making military plans that initially called for a strike at Santa Fe in the Southwest, incursions into Mexico's northern states, and a blockade of Veracruz and other ports. He expected the war to last up to 120 days and that Mexico would sue for peace. The plan was carried out, but Mexico did not sue for peace. In a cabinet meeting on May 13, 1846, two days after asking Congress for a war declaration, Polk spelled out his war objectives: the Texas border would be at the Rio Grande River, and California and New Mexico would become part of the United States. At this time, Polk made no reference to money transfer, stating that land concessions were the only way the enfeebled Mexico could reimburse the United States for its war costs.

While attention was focused on the slow pace of the conflict in northern and central Mexico, the United States achieved victories elsewhere. By July 1846, Frémont and Commodore John D. Sloat secured San Francisco and Monterey in California, and General Stephen F. Kearny faced little opposition in reaching Santa Fe. These victories, along with Taylor's success in northern Mexico, prompted Polk to make an unsuccessful effort to start peace negotiations. He then approved a new strategy that directed General Winfield Scott to take Veracruz and march on Mexico City. After seizing the seaport in March 1847, Scott then trekked to Mexico City with his 10,000 troops accompanied by the State Department's Chief Clerk Nicolas Trist, who was selected by Polk to negotiate a peace treaty with the Mexican government. Scott took control of Mexico City on September 13, 1847, but the inexperienced Trist failed to conclude a treaty. A frustrated Polk ordered his recall in October. Trist ignored the order. He remained in Mexico City while Polk fumed in Washington.

Finally, on February 2, 1848, in the city of Guadeloupe Hidalgo near Mexico City, Trist reached a peace agreement with the Mexicans. By then, the Mexican northern periphery had succumbed to the United States. According to the terms of the Cahuenga Capitulation on January 20, 1847, local authorities in California agreed to lay down their arms and

U.S. Army troops under General Winfield Scott land at Vera Cruz, Mexico in March 1847. (Library of Congress)

to submit to American authority. And a year later, in January 1848, the citizens of New Mexico voted to join the United States. The treaty itself granted these two territories to the United States and established the Rio Grande River as the southern boundary of Texas. Mexico surrendered nearly half of its territory. In return, the United States agreed to pay Mexico $15 million and assumed the claims of its citizens against Mexico up to $3.25 million. Although unauthorized to do so, Trist completed American continental expansion, and an embarrassed president submitted the treaty to the Senate for ratification. It approved the treaty on March 10, 1848. Manifest Destiny had triumphed. For the moment, Americans lost interest in gaining additional territory.

Rejecting the Periphery

When John O'Sullivan, editor of the *Democratic Review*, coined the term Manifest Destiny in 1845, some Americans believed that the United States should extend its benefice beyond the Rio Grande River as far south as Central America, because the people there suffered the legacy of Spanish colonial policies. That sentiment reemerged in February 1848, as Polk prepared to submit the Treaty of Guadeloupe Hidalgo to the Senate. Rather than going to the isthmus, the "All Mexico Movement" set its sites solely on the Republic of Mexico. Newspapers across the country picked up the battle cry, and Polk feared that it might cause the rejection of the treaty and an extension of the war. But the movement was poorly organized and it quickly fizzled.

Polk confronted another problem on Mexico's Yucatán Peninsula, when the local province seceded from Mexico in 1846—an act that led to the so-called Caste War. In April 1848, the local criollo-led Yucatecan government appealed to the United States for annexation; a similar appeal was made to Britain and Spain. Initially, Polk intimated he favored annexation but accepted his cabinet's advice to provide only military assistance. He asked for congressional action based on the principle of the Monroe Doctrine that denied the transfer of any territory in the western hemisphere to a European power. The issue provoked a sharp debate in and outside Congress. Proponents of Manifest Destiny called for bestowing the benefits of American society on the Yucatecans. Edward Hannegan, a Democrat from Indiana, led the call for temporary American occupation of Yucatán in face of the alleged British threat, while South Carolinian Whig John Calhoun led those opposed to any role for the United States on the peninsula. The issue was resolved locally, when in May 1848, the Yucatecan adversaries concluded their own peace terms and the British government stated that it had no designs on the peninsula.

The problem in Yucatán, however, rekindled the longstanding American interest in Cuba. The renewed interest came at a time when some of Cuba's elite criollo families supported Narciso López in his plot to sever the island from Spain and annex it to the United States. Slave owners in several Southern states saw this as an opportunity to create new slave states that would counter those free states to be carved from the territories acquired from the Treaty of Guadeloupe Hidalgo. John O'Sullivan asserted to President Polk in May 1848 that, in order to thwart British designs on the island, the United States should purchase Cuba for $150 million. Polk took O'Sullivan's advice and offered Spain $100 million for Cuba, an offer the Spanish quickly rejected with the comment that they would rather see the island sink into the Caribbean Sea than fall into the hands of another country.

Just as Polk prepared to depart the White House for his Tennessee home, the United States awoke to the British presence in Central America. Ever since its independence in 1823, Central America remained outside the sphere of American foreign concerns. Not so the British, whose minister to the five republics, Frederick Chatfield, built a solid relationship that gave Britain a near monopoly on trade with the region. American agents William Murphy and Henry Savage pleaded with their superiors in Washington to take countermeasures, but to no avail. Only after the Senate's ratification of the Treaty of Guadeloupe Hidalgo in 1848 did Secretary of State Buchanan become alarmed by messages sent from Murphy and Savage. A course of action awaited the arrival of President-elect Zachary Taylor, but when he took office in March 1849, the American enthusiasm for foreign affairs had dissipated. Manifest Destiny had, for now, run its course.

Legacy

James K. Polk came to the presidency in 1845 just as Manifest Destiny reached the zenith of its appeal and the divisiveness of sectionalism asserted itself. Americans residing in Texas sought admission to the United States, but until late in the Tyler administration, previous presidents had avoided the issue owing to the sectional controversy over slavery. For the same reason, Tyler could muster only a congressional resolution in favor of annexation and left it for Polk to implement. Polk did just that. Americans also stormed into the Oregon Territory on the eve of the Polk presidency, sparking a demand that the United States make the 54° 40' parallel, not 49th, its boundary as had been the long-stated government policy. Thus, when Polk completed the Oregon treaty, with the latter as its boundary, he sanctified the long-standing American objective. The sparsely populated California and New Mexico territories rounded out the completion of the national destiny—a fact Polk emphasized in his final State of the Union address on December 5, 1848.

In Texas and Oregon, Manifest Destiny meant protecting the Americans and the culture they took with them against potential foreign intruders who threatened to destroy the American way of life. In California and New Mexico, where only a few Americans then resided with the promise of more to come, it meant extending the American benefice to the Mexicans and Native Americans who lived there. But the moral crusade of Manifest Destiny reached its limits when some suggested that the United States uplift the residents in parts or all of Mexico, Central America, and Cuba with much larger and mostly nonwhite populations. While the legacies of Spanish colonialism may have been difficult to overcome, American racist attitudes of the time made these residents inferior peoples. Thus, Polk was not anxious to expand beyond the borders he defined as the American war objectives in May 1848.

Manifest Destiny also teased out the sectionalism that divided the nation and that promised to worsen over time. If the annexation of Texas satisfied Southern interests and the acquisition of Oregon the midwestern appetite for land, California and New Mexico momentarily satisfied the New England merchants. It was they who alerted the nation to the importance of the California ports, the northern entry-way into Mexico, and the potential economic benefits they offered. Polk understood this too, as demonstrated by his willingness to seek congressional advice and consent before making political or diplomatic decisions.

When Polk left office in March 1848, the American appetite for additional land did not go with him. In the following decade, the United States cast a covetous eye in the direction of the Caribbean and Central America, but no additional territory was acquired until after the Civil War.

Thomas M. Leonard

Chronology

1845
March 1: Texas annexed by joint House and Senate resolution.

March 3: President John Tyler signs congressional joint resolution providing for admission of Texas to the Union.

March 4: Polk is inaugurated

July 2: Britain rejects 49° Oregon boundary.

December 2: Polk asserts U.S. right to 54° 40' Oregon border.

1846
January 2: Mexican president Herrera overthrown in a coup.

January 13: Polk orders General Taylor to station his troops on the north bank of the Rio Grande River.

April 25: First clash between U.S. and Mexican troops.

May 13: Congress declares war on Mexico.

June 15: Oregon Treaty settles Anglo-American boundary dispute.

August 15: United States occupies New Mexico.

1847
January 13: Treaty of Cahuenga ends fighting in California.

February 23: United States wins battle of Buena Vista.

March 27: Vera Cruz surrenders to General Winfield Scott.

August 24–27: Armistice of Tacubaya.

September 14: U.S. troops capture Mexico City.

December 6: Trist refuses Polk's order to return home.

1848
February 2: Trist completes the Treaty of Guadalupe Hidalgo, which satisfies all of Polk's war objectives in return for $15 million in compensation to Mexico.

February 22: Revolution in France, Louis Philippe abdicates.

March 10: Senate ratifies the Treaty of Guadalupe Hidalgo.

March 13: Republican uprising in Vienna.

May 18: Frankfurt National Assembly.

August 14: The Territory of Oregon is organized by an act of the U.S. Congress.

November 7: Zachary Taylor elected president, Millard Fillmore is vice president.

References and Further Reading

Bergeron, Paul H. *The Presidency of James K. Polk.* Lawrence, KS: University Press of Kansas, 1987.

Bergeron, Paul H., et al. *The Correspondence of James K. Polk,* 8 vols. Nashville, TN: Vanderbilt University Press, 1981–1993.

Hays, Sam W. *James K. Polk and the Expansionist Impulse.* New York: Longman's, 1997.

Jones, Howard, and Donald A. Rakestraw. *Manifest Destiny: Anglo-American Relations in the 1840s.* Wilmington, DE: Scholarly Resources, 1997.

Leonard, Thomas M. *James K. Polk: A Clear and Unquestionable Destiny.* Wilmington, DE: Scholarly Resources, 2001.

Pletcher, David M. *The Diplomacy of Annexation: Texas, Oregon and the Mexican War.* Columbia, MO: University of Missouri Press, 1973.

Quaife, Milo M., ed. *The Diary of James K. Polk During His Presidency, 1845–1849,* 4 vols. Chicago: A. C. McClurg, 1910.

Weinberg, Albert K. *Manifest Destiny A Study of Nationalist Expansionism in American History.* Baltimore, MD: Johns Hopkins University Press, 1935.

Zachary Taylor (1849–1850)

Early Life and Military Career

Zachary Taylor was among the most popular presidents of the decades between the Founding and the Civil War. Serving only sixteen months in office, his presidency nevertheless drifted quickly into obscurity after his sudden death of gastroenteritis on July 9, 1850. He was elected largely due to his reputation as a war hero and his homespun personality, but neither of these assets made Taylor a natural fit for politics. Arriving in office with no practical experience in public office and deprived by his early death of the time to acquire it, he is remembered as a tough but naïve chief executive who too often preferred to act as if he were above politics.

Taylor was born on November 24, 1784, to Sarah and Richard Taylor, a wealthy Virginia planter who had served with the First Virginia Regiment during the Revolution. Despite the aristocratic pedigree, Taylor's formative years were spent in Kentucky, where his family moved to take up farming on Beargrass Creek, near Louisville. His perceptions and personality were molded by a frontier life in which skills with horses and muskets were more important than formal education. Taylor therefore took naturally to a military career and was commissioned as first lieutenant in the United States Army at the age of twenty-three. He married Margaret Mackall Smith in 1810, and subsequently had six children with her, four of whom survived infancy. He was given command of Fort Harrison in the Indiana Territory, and in the War of 1812 earned a reputation for both courage and tactical leadership skills in engagements against British and Indian forces. Although his army career kept him away from home for extended periods, Taylor secured ownership of a plantation and eventually built a considerable fortune in land and slaves in Louisiana and Mississippi.

Taylor held commands in the Black Hawk War of 1832 and the Second Seminole War of 1835–1842, but it was in the Mexican War that his military skills earned him national renown. Now at the rank of general, Taylor was ordered by President James Polk in January 1846 to establish a camp on the Rio Grande River, a provocative action in that it signaled Polk's rejection of Mexico's claim to land all the way up to the Nueces River north of the Rio Grande. On April 25, 1846, a Mexican force of 1,600 crossed the river and fell upon a scouting party of sixty-three Americans, killing sixteen and capturing nine. This was the skirmish that enabled

Zachary Taylor, a hero of the Mexican War, served just one year in presidential office. (Library of Congress)

Polk to secure a war declaration from Congress on May 13, five days after Taylor had scattered a Mexican force of 6,000 with only 2,300 American troops at Palo Alto. On May 17, he caught up with the retreating Mexican army at Resaca de la Palma and chased it south across the Rio Grande. On May 18, Taylor then occupied the Mexican fort at Matamoros. The following September he captured Monterey.

Taylor's victories made him a national hero of Manifest Destiny with the press, but his popularity, outspoken personality, and Whig views simultaneously began to transform him into a political threat to Democratic control of the presidency. Polk therefore kept Taylor in northern Mexico and gave overall command of the war effort in Mexico to General Winfield Scott—also a Whig but not as attractive politically as Taylor—with orders to march on Mexico City from Vera Cruz, a plan that had been rejected to this point in favor of Taylor's campaign. Now the situation was reversed. Scott was to carry the war to the Mexicans while Taylor was confined to defensive operations in the north. Starved of supplies and stripped of some of his troops, Taylor was, in fact, hard pressed to take the offensive. But he was not helpless. When Mexican forces under Santa Anna sought to exploit Taylor's weakened condition with a march of 20,000 men northward against him, he disobeyed orders and took 5,000 troops southwest of Monterey to confront Santa Anna on more favorable ground. Near a ranch called Buena Vista, Taylor stopped the Mexican army in two days of hard fighting; more than 700 Americans died, but Mexican losses were more than double this figure. Polk's plan therefore backfired politically, as Taylor's victory enhanced his national reputation and presidential potential.

A Whig for Any Season

Taylor's Mexican exploits were followed closely by Thurlow Weed, the manager of the Eastern Whig party, who saw in Taylor a natural presidential candidate as much as two years before the election of 1848. While Taylor denied presidential ambitions and avoided taking clear positions on contentious issues, enthusiasm for his nomination grew not only among Whigs but also among Democrats and followers of the Native American Party, a precursor of the anti-immigration Know-Nothing movement of the 1850s. Taylor politely accepted endorsements for a presidential candidacy from public figures across the political spectrum, yet continued to deny any partisan loyalties. Only six weeks prior to the Whig national convention did he publicly acknowledge his affiliation and even then adroitly avoided taking positions on policy issues such as slavery or territorial expansion, insisting that in presidential office he would not be dictated to by a party platform. Another associate of Thurlow Weed, Millard Fillmore, balanced the ticket as a vice-presidential candidate with much less color but infinitely greater political experience and the backing of the northern business community.

The Democratic Party nominated Senator Lewis Cass of Michigan, a strong Manifest Destiny candidate. Because neither the Whigs nor the Democrats had a proper electoral platform—and avoided above all any formal declaration on the evermore-volatile matter of slavery—the electoral contest boiled down more than usual to a choice between personalities. Taylor's ownership of slaves offended three Whig factions: New York Whigs led by Martin Van Buren, "Conscience Whig" abolitionists from Massachusetts, and a rival abolitionist faction under the flag of the Liberty Party, that banded together to form the Free Soil Party and nominated Van Buren. Under normal circumstances, the Van Buren nomination would have split the Whig vote and handed the presidency to Cass. But in 1848, Taylor was so popular in the South that he managed to carry eight slave states against Cass's seven; in New York, meanwhile, the Free

Soil factor split both the Democratic and Whig vote and permitted Taylor to capture the state with only a plurality of the ballots. The three-corned contest and Electoral College math gave the presidency to Taylor by 163 to 127 electoral votes.

Expansion and Slavery

The central issues facing Taylor's administration were the interrelated pressures for territorial expansion of the United States on the one hand and the gathering national crisis over slavery on the other. In his inaugural address of March 5, 1849, he fielded no agenda for foreign policy beyond the balanced observation that American freemen could not but sympathize in efforts "to extend the blessings of civil and political liberty," but that "at the same time we are warned by the admonitions of history and the voice of our own beloved Washington to abstain from entangling alliances with foreign nations." He then added that "It is to be hoped that no international question can now arise which a government confident in its own strength and resolved to protect its own just rights may not settle by wise negotiation.... It eminently becomes a government like our own, founded on the morality and intelligence of its citizens and upheld by their affections, to exhaust every resort of honorable diplomacy before appealing to arms"—a hope as applicable to the resolution of the slavery issue as to any quarrel beyond American shores.

Slave insurrections were intermittently as much of a nightmare to the Southern states as abolition. The latter, however, seemed more and more to loom as a certainty. The Missouri Compromise banning slavery from the Northern states and the creation of a slave-free Oregon Territory in 1848, together with the swelling population of the North, promised to tip the balance in the country and the Congress in favor of abolition. In the face of the Free Soil movement's determination to thwart any extension of American territory to the west and the south that could enlarge the ambit of slavery, Taylor instinctively sought compromise. But despite the fact that he was himself a slaveholding president, his obvious sensitivity to the North's apprehension over the spread of slavery quickly began to erode Taylor's political support in the South, while his lack of political experience left him ill-equipped to master the conflict with the prestige of the presidential office alone. Thus, it was not Taylor but the congressional leadership of Henry Clay that ultimately put forth the Compromise of 1850. As a result of Clay's proposals, Congress established a western boundary for Texas and abolished slave trading in the District of Columbia. It also passed a fugitive-slave law and relinquished the authority to legislate slave trading across state lines.

The tension between territorial expansion and the Southern attachment to slavery was at its most volatile over the terms of California's statehood. Taylor rejected the notion that Congress ought to legislate for the territories of the United States on the status of slavery and dispatched agents to both California and New Mexico with the message that they should organize their own governments and apply for statehood on their own terms. By November 13, 1849, California had ratified a constitution as a free state, and on December 4, Taylor recommended its admission, changing the balance of states represented in the Senate in favor of free states. California did not actually apply for admission until March 1850, but Taylor nonetheless increased the pressure by encouraging New Mexico to apply for statehood as a free state as well. In response to Southern threats of secession, Taylor raged that "if there are any such treasonable demonstrations on the part of the Southern leaders, I will hang them . . . I will hang them as high as hung spies in Mexico, and I will put down any treasonable moves with the whole power of the government, if I have to put myself at the head of the army to do it." According to the congressional compromise brokered by Clay—in legislative substance five separate bills in an omnibus package—the territory of New Mexico was organized without any explicit prohibition of slavery. This was a violation of the Wilmot Proviso of 1846, adopted by the Republican Party, according to which slavery was to be outlawed in any territory gained as a result of the Mexican War. Taylor was poised to veto the congressional package.

Caribbean and Pacific Horizons

At the same time, the appetite of the Whig Party for American commercial expansion beyond the North American continent directed the administration's diplomatic attention toward the Caribbean and across the Pacific. In January 1849, U.S. Naval Commodore James Glynn was ordered to Nagasaki to secure the release of eighteen American seamen being held as spies from Japanese authorities. After Glynn's triumphant return to the United States, Taylor asked the commodore to prepare a report on his experiences. The final draft included a recommendation that the United States seek as soon as practicable a commercial treaty with Japan, a recommendation that led to Commodore Perry's expedition of 1853. Similar overtures were made in Cochin China and in Southeast Asia in pursuit of expanded trade.

In June 1849, the New York–chartered Panama Railway Company received a commission from the government of Colombia to build a railroad across the Isthmus of Panama. Elisa Hise, a special envoy dispatched by President Polk to Nicaragua, negotiated a treaty with its government giving the United States exclusive rights to build a canal across its territory. John Clayton, Taylor's secretary of state, wanted no part of the treaty's reciprocal commitment to an American guarantee of Nicaragua's territory. Clayton judged that Hise had exceeded his authority and promptly

replaced him with another envoy, E. George Squier. Squier secured another treaty protecting the Nicaraguan rights of Cornelius Vanderbilt's Atlantic and Pacific Trading Company but avoiding an American guarantee of Nicaragua. Both episodes were influenced by American concern over British designs on Central America, concerns that were heightened in October 1849, when a Royal Navy ship seized Tigre Island off the Pacific Coast of Honduras. To avoid open Anglo-American conflict over rights to an isthmian canal, Clayton worked out an agreement with Sir Henry Lytton Bulwer, Britain's minister to the United States. According to the agreement, neither country was to build a canal in Central America without the consent of the other; neither was to fortify or found new colonies there; and both powers were to guarantee the neutrality of any interoceanic canal. The Clayton-Bulwer Treaty was signed on April 19, 1850, and approved by the Senate on May 22.

Taylor applied a forthright nationalistic policy to relations with two other European powers, Portugal and Spain. In July 1850, Secretary Clayton attempted to redeem American claims against Portugal dating to the War of 1812, specifically for damages on behalf of the owners of the *General Armstrong*, an American privateer attacked by a British naval squadron while in a neutral Portuguese harbor. Claims against Britain had been settled by the Treaty of Ghent in 1815. Clayton instructed the American minister to Lisbon to arrive at a round sum settlement with the Portuguese government. When Lisbon offered to submit the dispute to arbitration, Clayton withdrew his minister and in effect threatened to sever diplomatic relations. The affair was not settled until the Fillmore administration agreed to arbitration in 1851, a process that concluded in favor of Portugal.

The quarrel with Spain was more serious and spoke of the American future rather than the past. Taylor opposed filibuster expeditions by American expansionists in the Caribbean, but the appetite of expansionists for new territory in the Caribbean and Central America made freelance expeditions by American entrepreneurs and adventurers a recurring problem for successive administrations. In May 1850, three ships under the command of Narciso López—a Venezuelan-born Spanish general who sought to liberate Cuba from Spain and preserve slavery there—managed to elude U.S. naval patrols sent to intercept them and launched raids against Cardena in Cuba and Contoy, a key off the coast of Yucatán. In the latter episode, Spanish forces captured fifty Americans and took them to Cuba to be tried despite the fact that Yucatán was a Mexican possession. Clayton protested to Spain that the arrest was illegal and persuaded Taylor to threaten Spain with war. Although the administration carried on with its diplomatic protest through the U.S. minister to Madrid and the Spanish representation in Washington, Taylor ordered an American warship to Cuba to underscore the warning that the American prisoners should not be harmed. The trial proceeded nonetheless. On July 8, Spain released all the prisoners except a captain and two mates who received prison terms. The affair was concluded peacefully the following October when the Spain's queen pardoned all three as a gesture of friendship to the United States; but Taylor did not live either to accept the gesture or to witness California's admission to statehood in September. On July 9, 1850, he died suddenly of acute gastroenteritis.

Legacy

Zachary Taylor's contribution to the foreign relations of the United States was minimal, that of a transitional figure between the Polk and Fillmore presidencies during the uncertain maturation of the Whig tradition and the Free Soil movement into the Republican Party. The task of his time was to keep the project of territorial expansion on a politically prudential timetable while avoiding open conflict over the status of slavery. Initiatives to extend American commerce across the continent and the Pacific Ocean were commendable, but they were premature for a nation now subject to repeated crises over its domestic political economy. Neither Taylor's temperament nor his military experience prepared him for the challenges of presidential office in the 1850s. He was both baffled and enraged by the strength of feeling over the slavery issue. It is symptomatic of Taylor's times that in the crisis with Spain over Cuba the Lopez expedition had the support of Southerners who sought to preserve and extend the "peculiar institution."

Carl Cavanagh Hodge

Chronology

1849

June 12: Panama Railroad Company secures authority to build across Panamanian Isthmus.

December 4: Taylor recommends annexation of California.

1850

April 19: Clayton-Bulwer Treaty on Central American Canal.

July 9: Taylor dies, Fillmore is president.

September 9: Compromise of 1850: California a free state; New Mexico and Utah territories.

References and Further Reading

Bauer, K. Jack. *Zachary Taylor: Soldier, Planter, Statesman of the Old Southwest.* Baton Rouge, LA: Louisiana State University Press, 1985.

Dyer, Brainerd. *Zachary Taylor.* New York: Barnes and Noble, 1949.

Holman, Hamilton. *Zachary Taylor: Soldier of the Republic.* Indianapolis, IN: Bobbs-Merrill, 1941.

Edwin Hoyt. *Zachary Taylor.* Chicago: Reilly and Lee, 1966.

John C. Waugh. *On the Brink of Civil War.* Wilmington, DE: Scholarly Resources, 2003.

Millard Fillmore (1850–1853)

Early Life and Political Career

The "forgotten president" was born January 7, 1800, in Cayuga County in the Finger Lakes district of New York State, the second of eight children of an industrious but poor tenant farming family. He attended one-room schools and worked on his father's farm. His formal education was modest and he was briefly apprenticed as a clothier. At age eighteen he made the acquaintance of a local lawyer who convinced him of the potential for social and professional advancement offered by a career in law. After working as a law clerk, he moved to Buffalo, completed his formal legal training, and was called to the bar in 1823. In 1826, he married a minister's daughter, Abigail Powers, started a family, and pondered a life in public office.

Fillmore joined the Anti-Masonic party and in 1828 was elected to the New York legislature, where he served three terms. He developed close relations with the Whig leader, Thurlow Weed, who in 1831, supported Fillmore's successful candidacy for a seat in the U.S. House of Representatives. Fillmore served in the House from 1833 to 1835. In 1834, he became a member of the Whig Party and subsequently secured three more terms in the House. His star continued to rise when the Whigs captured the presidency under William Henry Harrison in 1840. As chair of the House Ways and Means Committee, he promoted high trade tariff legislation in 1842 and was considered for the vice presidential nomination of 1844. Weed advised him instead to run in the gubernatorial race of New York State, a close election in which Fillmore suffered his first defeat. Although Whig fortunes in 1844 were in part damaged by the reputation of their presidential candidate, Henry Clay, it was also Clay who backed Fillmore for the vice presidential nomination during the contest of 1848, with Zachary Taylor at the head of the Whig ticket. With the Whig victory of that year, Fillmore became a living vindication of the hallowed notion that in America, humble origins were not a barrier to achieving a position of high office by citizens who combined both intelligence and hard work with political ambition.

Sectionalism and Expansion

In the truncated Taylor administration, Fillmore generally supported the president's policies, but had very little personal influence. With Taylor's sudden death, Fillmore came

Millard Fillmore was a selfless civil servant, but lacked the vision for the presidential leadership of a nation drifting toward dissolution over the issue of slavery. (Library of Congress)

into his own. Though his single term as president lasted fewer than three years, Millard Fillmore made a handful of crucial foreign policy decisions. In relations with Latin America, he consistently opposed endeavors to acquire new territories for the United States by filibuster or revolution, often in the face of enormous public support for such schemes. In relations with Europe, Fillmore resisted attempts by British and French diplomats to bind the United States to a treaty concerning the status of Cuba, and he threw cold water on an enthusiastic movement to implicate the United States government somehow in the drive for Hungarian independence from Austria. Undoubtedly, the most significant and enduring consequence of Fillmore's foreign policy was to expand American influence and trade in the Pacific, where he effectively thwarted the designs of the French Emperor Napoleon III to acquire control of Hawaii, and commissioned Commodore Matthew C. Perry's historic mission to open the Empire of Japan to diplomatic and trade relations with the United States. As the last Whig president, Fillmore embodied his party's consistent faith in the expansion of commerce as the most effective means of assuaging sectional disputes and ensuring more amicable international relations. When Millard Fillmore declared in 1851 that, "I am entirely in favor of all means by which States and countries can be bound together by ties of mutual business interests and relations," he defined the single overriding goal of his administration's foreign policy.

Upon the death of Zachary Taylor in the contentious summer of 1850, the administration of Millard Fillmore began with a prayer of sorts: "God save us from Whig vice presidents!" Antislavery Whigs, who opposed the Compromise of 1850, were immediately concerned that as president, the pragmatic lawyer from upstate New York, would cater to the Southern branch of the party, the so-called Cotton Whigs. They were right. The administration of Millard Fillmore bowed with such regularity to Southern demands on domestic matters that it split the Whig party irrevocably between its proslavery and antislavery factions. In international relations, on the other hand, Millard Fillmore's policies were dramatically different. With a consistency that enraged Southern proponents of a more adventurous foreign policy, the Fillmore administration thwarted the designs of proslavery factions to acquire Cuba or any other territories by filibuster, intrigue, or revolution, and sought to maintain the rule of law in U.S. relations with Spain and Latin America.

For his first secretary of state, Millard Fillmore was not afraid to select a man with a considerably larger reputation than his own, the nationally renowned lawyer and statesman Daniel Webster. By 1850, however, Webster was approaching seventy and was soon frequently confined by health problems to his estate in Massachusetts. This situation demanded that Fillmore handle foreign policy concerns directly much of the time. When the noted scholar Edward Everett became his secretary of state on Webster's death in 1852, Fillmore continued to manage a series of urgent diplomatic situations and crises in Europe, Latin America, and the Pacific with close attention and a steady hand.

Resisting Entanglements

During the early 1850s, the aftermath of the Mexican War engendered a growing fever for the acquisition of Cuba, especially among proslavery interests who saw the largest island of the Antilles as both a source of new slave labor and as another potential slave state to augment Southern power in the Congress. Expansionist sentiment was also fueled by the argument that if Cuba was somehow acquired by a

European nation more powerful than Spain, or if it underwent a slave revolution similar to what had happened in Haiti, it would become a significant threat to the security of the United States. President Polk had attempted to buy the island from Spain for 100 million dollars, and, after the failure of that initiative, a number of designs emerged to acquire the Pearl of the Antilles by force.

A particular concern for the Fillmore administration was Narisco Lopez, a Venezuelan adventurer who had attracted support from Southern planters in the United States for his scheme to invade Cuba and foment a revolution there. When the president learned of plans to launch a filibuster led by Lopez from the port of New Orleans, he alerted customs officials there and ordered them to stop Lopez and his army of about 400 armed men before they could depart. These orders proved ineffective, however, and when Lopez and his men landed at Playtas, within striking distance of Havana, they quickly found themselves overwhelmed. Lopez and his lieutenants were soon captured and summarily executed in Havana, and among rank and file who were not killed in the field, more than 160 were made prisoners and shipped to Spain.

Because so many of the killed and captured were not only U.S. citizens but the sons of influential Southern families, the Fillmore administration faced intense public and political pressure to act in support of the expedition and to retaliate against Spain for its actions. Had Fillmore entertained expansionist designs, the public outcry over this incident, as evidenced by riots in New Orleans and destruction of the Spanish consulate there, would have afforded him the perfect opportunity to commence a military adventure modeled on the template of Polk's war with Mexico. Instead, Fillmore refused to offer any support to the survivors of the filibuster, declared that Spain had acted completely within its rights, and had the State Department issue a formal apology for the destruction of the Spanish consulate.

On the other hand, when Fillmore declined to sign a treaty proposed by the British guaranteeing that neither the United States nor Britain nor France would ever take possession of Cuba, he indicated very clearly that he was not opposed in principle to the idea that the United States might one day acquire direct or indirect control of the island. What he did object to was any armed action or provocative intrigue by private citizens or corporations that might draw the United States into an international confrontation or war. Consistent with this policy, the Fillmore administration rebuffed pleas for support from the maritime businessman George Law when he was denied the right to trade in Havana because of his ties to a Cuban revolutionary organization. Likewise, when U.S. railroad developers, seeking to build a line across Mexico, sought to employ a few hundred armed men to bolster their negotiating power with President Santa Anna, Fillmore refused to countenance the scheme. And when a group of well-connected Northern businessmen sought the protection of the U.S. Navy for a plan to harvest tons of bird guano from a small chain of Peruvian islands without permission from the government of Peru, they failed to obtain the blessing of the White House for this imaginative enterprise. Whether the object in question was the Pearl of the Antilles, a railroad route from the Gulf of Mexico to the Pacific, or tons of guano from Peru, President Fillmore's guiding principles remained the same. He rejoiced in the orderly expansion of American trade and commerce, but he would not countenance the acquisition of wealth that was "only to be obtained by . . . bloodshed, war, and revolution."

Even revolutionary movements that were infused with republican idealism and supported by a broad cross-section of the American public received little more than tepid support from President Fillmore, who remained careful to abide by Washington's injunction to remain aloof from foreign entanglements, however eloquent and influential the advocates of American engagement might be. During the early 1850s, as European capitals were still reeling from the revolutionary movements of 1848, many Americans were caught in a wave of fervent support for republican causes in Europe. When the Hungarian nationalist and revolutionary Lajos Kossuth visited the United States in the autumn of 1851 for example, he was met by cheering crowds when he crossed the gangplanks in New York. He was greeted with the same enthusiasm in many other American cities. Kossuth's earlier release from a Turkish prison as a result of American negotiations and his enormous popularity in the American press did not go unnoticed in Vienna. When the Austrian government expressed its displeasure at American support for Kossuth, Daniel Webster relished the opportunity to belittle the Hapsburg monarchy by declaring that the United States comprised "one of the richest and most fertile" portions of the globe, while the entire Austrian Empire was merely "a patch on the earth's surface." This sort of bluster notwithstanding, the real policy of the Fillmore administration was to provide no real aid, materially or politically, to the cause of Hungarian independence. When Kossuth, dubbed "the Noble Magyar" by the American press, sought an audience at the White House, President Fillmore set the terms very clearly in advance. He would treat him "with respect," but would "give him no encouragement that the established policy of this country will be in any degree departed from." Fillmore also told Webster to caution Kossuth that, "If he desires simply an introduction, I will see him, but if he wants to make a speech to me, I most respectfully decline to see him." Fillmore did receive Kossuth, who, in spite of his promise not to harangue the president, gave a long speech replete with specific requests for aid from the United States. President Fillmore listened politely and even expressed a personal sympathy for the Hungarian patriot, but he stuck to his policy as stated at the outset. In spite of

all the fanfare and international controversy that had attended his sojourn in America, Lajos Kossuth left his appointment at the White House empty handed.

Commerce Goes West

If Fillmore was destined to disappoint proslavery enthusiasts for expansionist adventures in Latin America or idealistic advocates of republican revolutions in Central Europe, there was at least one constituency who would not be disappointed by the foreign policy of the Fillmore administration. These were the maritime merchants seeking the dramatic expansion of U.S. trade in the Pacific. Since the British had waged the Opium War in the early 1840s and opened several Chinese ports to Western trade, the seemingly limitless promise of East Asian trade had loomed large in the American imagination. Access to the Pacific port of San Francisco had been a major motive in the Mexican War, and the goal of expanded trade was the one aspect of Manifest Destiny to which Fillmore's Whig administration could give its unqualified support.

Fillmore's foreign policy would attempt to enhance American trade in the Pacific in the three ways. First, it would attempt to shorten the distance from the U.S. eastern seaboard to the Pacific by developing rail or canal projects across routes in Mexico and Central America. Second, it would use U.S. influence to create greater stability in the Pacific wherever possible. Third, it would seek to open new markets in East Asia to gain traction on the rapid expansion of British trade in that region.

In attempting to meet the first of these goals, the Fillmore administration had mixed results at best. The idea of a canal across Colombia's Panamanian isthmus had been contemplated but remained too daring a project for mid-nineteenth century engineering. Fillmore backed a rail link across the Panamanian route. Attempts to build a canal across the geographically more attractive passage through Nicaragua were impeded by instability inside Nicaragua and by Britain's self-declared protectorate of the Mosquito Indians of eastern Nicaragua, which dovetailed conveniently with British imperial goals of restraining U.S. expansion in the region. Meanwhile, the construction of rail route across Mexico's Tehuantepec Isthmus ran into obstructions from the government of Santa Anna. Though Fillmore refused to back the use of a private army as proposed by the American railroad contractors working in Mexico, he did employ the U.S. Navy to make a show of force when the British attempted to levy an illegal port charge on the American merchant ship *Prometheus* in the British-occupied city of San Juan on the Mosquito Coast of Nicaragua. Fillmore succeeded in having the demand for a port charge retracted, and the new British foreign minister, Lord Granville, promised that the British Navy would not interfere with American shipping in the area again. While neither the Nicaraguan nor the Mexican project bore any fruit during Fillmore's administration, the president reported with great satisfaction in December 1851 that the rail line across the Panamanian isthmus was moving steadily toward completion. The project, dubbed "the wedding of the rough Atlantic to the fair Pacific Ocean" by the *New York Mirror,* was not completed until 1855, two years after Fillmore had left office.

Fillmore's second goal of promoting stability in the Pacific met with greater success. Due to rapid evolution of new maritime technologies such as more efficient steam engines and the use of the screw propeller on seagoing vessels as pioneered by the U.S. Navy in the 1840s, the speed and range of both American merchant and military ships in the Pacific was greatly enhanced. The British were undoubtedly the preeminent naval power in the Pacific, but the U.S. Navy had a growing share of influence. In 1851, Napoleon III, whose attempted occupation of Honolulu had been thwarted by the United States in 1849, now sought to force the Hawaiian kingdom into accepting the status of a protectorate of the French Empire. When the French Emperor received Daniel Webster's unambiguous warning that Hawaii must remain independent in the spirit as well as the letter of the law, the French quietly backed away from their claims. Meanwhile, the agitation for U.S. annexation of Hawaii reached a fever pitch in the American press, but the Fillmore administration ignored the din. Although U.S. economic influence would continue to grow, Hawaii would remain independent for the better part of the next half-century.

Instead of seeking to conquer new territories in the Pacific, the president, consistent with his stated faith in the steady expansion of commerce, sought to complete his third goal for enhancing American trade in the Pacific: the opening of new markets for American trade in East Asia. The China trade had long loomed large in the American imagination, but as the British had gotten there first, they possessed what seemed at the time to be a perennial advantage in terms of political influence and market share. If American traders could open the as yet untapped market of Japan, a closed nation that had only strictly limited trade with the Dutch since the seventeenth century, then U.S. merchants would have a new market in which they could operate with much less competition than they faced in China.

In December 1850, just a few months after assuming office, Fillmore began laying the groundwork for a U.S. mission to open Japan to trade. Commodore John H. Aulick, who had been an early and persuasive advocate for opening trade with Japan, was the first choice to lead the mission; Commodore Matthew C. Perry, an august and very commanding New Englander who had earned wide acclaim as "the father of the steam navy," was ultimately assigned the task. The return of some shipwrecked Japanese sailors who

had been rescued by an American ship and brought to San Francisco provided the perfect pretext for a mission to the Shogun capital of Edo, at the site of modern-day Tokyo. With a letter to the Japanese Emperor from his "great and good friend" President Fillmore seeking "friendship, commerce, a supply of coal, and friendship for our shipwrecked people," Commodore Perry set sail in 1853 with four "black ships," as the Japanese would call them. These modern vessels, combining steam and sail power, were fitted with impressive artillery, but they were also loaded with gifts designed to entice the Japanese empire into commerce with the United States: two telegraph transmitters and hundreds of feet of wire; a quarter scale railroad with 370 feet of track; four beautifully illustrated editions of Audubon's *Birds of America;* a wide array of American foods and wines; and 100 gallons of Kentucky bourbon whiskey.

The mission launched by Fillmore's administration was entirely successful, but it came to fruition after the Whig party had been irrevocably split over the issue of slavery and the Democrat Franklin Pierce had succeeded Fillmore as president. In the 1854 Treaty of Kanagawa, Perry obtained four important and precedent-setting guarantees from the Japanese Shogun: First, a declaration of peace and friendship between the United States and Japan. Second, the opening of two ports to American ships at Shimoda and Hakodate. Third, help for any American ships wrecked on the Japanese coast and protection for shipwrecked persons. Fourth, the permission for American ships to buy supplies, coal, water, and other necessary provisions in Japanese ports. The actual impact of the new trade with Japan was not as great in its near-term economic benefits as first expected, but Perry's mission and subsequent treaty had the catalytic effect of helping to inspire the Meiji Restoration, and thus its long-term cultural, political, and economic impact on the Pacific region and the world is beyond calculation.

Legacy

In the years following the Mexican War, the expansionist foreign policy of the United States could have tended toward one of two broad directions: south, toward further military adventures and the acquisition of new slave states in the Caribbean or Central America; or west, toward expanded trade and diplomatic involvement with East Asia. The foreign policy of the Fillmore administration set the path for U.S. foreign policy on a westward course into the Pacific. However, Millard Fillmore's term was so short and overshadowed by domestic crises that he has received little credit from historians for the steadiness and vision of his foreign policy. While Fillmore's pliancy to Southern demands on domestic issues cost him vital support among

Northern Whigs, his refusal to acquiesce to proslavery interests in the field of foreign policy also alienated Southern Whigs and helped hand the presidency to the Democrats in the election of 1852. Nonetheless, Fillmore's unswerving allegiance to the rule of law and his tireless efforts to expand American trade into new markets produced tangible achievements in foreign policy and earned his administration perhaps its only claim to enduring fame. In its obituary for Millard Fillmore published more than two decades after his brief term as president, the *New York Times* cited Perry's mission to Japan as Fillmore's single greatest achievement, concluding that "The general policy of his administration was wise and liberal, and he left the country at peace with all the world and enjoying a high degree of prosperity."

R. S. Deese

Chronology

1849

June 12: Panama Railroad Company secures authority to build across Panamanian Isthmus.

December 4: Taylor recommends annexation of California.

1850

April 19: Clayton-Bulwer Treaty on Central American Canal.

July 9: Taylor dies of acute gastroenteritis, Fillmore is president.

September 9: Compromise of 1850: California a free state, New Mexico and Utah territories.

1851

December 2: Louis Napoleon seizes power in France, Second Republic falls.

1852

April 30: Webster-Crampton Convention refines Clayton-Bulwer Treaty.

November 2: Franklin Pierce elected president.

References and Further Reading

Howe, Daniel Walker. *The Political Culture of the American Whigs.* Chicago: University of Chicago Press, 1979.

Rayback, Robert J. *Millard Fillmore: Biography of a President.* East Aurora, NY: Published for the Buffalo Historical Society by Henry Stewart, Inc. 1972.

Scarry, Robert J. *Millard Fillmore.* Jefferson, MO: McFarland, 2001.

Smith, Elbert B. *The Presidencies of Zachary Taylor and Millard Fillmore.* Lawrence, KS: University Press of Kansas, 1988.

Wiley, Peter Booth. *Commodore Perry and the Opening of Japan.* New York: Viking, 1990.

Franklin Pierce (1853–1857)

Early Life and Political Career

Franklin Pierce was born on November 23, 1804, in Hillsborough, New Hampshire. He was one of nine children born to Anna Kendrick Pierce and General Benjamin Pierce. His father was a Revolutionary War veteran, New Hampshire pioneer, and prominent local Jeffersonian. At the time of Franklin's birth, he was also the sheriff of Hillsborough County, and an implacable opponent of the Federalist Party. Pierce was raised in this highly charged political atmosphere. Later, as a member of the Federalist-controlled New Hampshire Governor's Council, General Pierce was intimately embroiled in the partisan strife that characterized the politics of the new nation, a struggle that intensified when Republican president James Madison called for a declaration of war on Great Britain in 1812. In 1814, as the war drew to a close, ten-year-old Franklin enrolled at Hancock Academy, and later concluded his studies at Francestown Academy in order to prepare for college admission.

In 1820, as Maine achieved statehood in the great political compromise of that year, Pierce matriculated at Bowdoin College in Brunswick, Maine. Initially, he proved himself to be a unremarkable student, spending more time at the local tavern than attending to the rigors of Latin and the classics. Indeed, on the publication of the class standings in his junior year, Pierce discovered himself ranked in last place. Nonetheless, with the help of his more diligent classmates—including Nathaniel Hawthorne, who would remain one of his closest friends—he ultimately graduated fifth in his class in the fall of 1824. After graduation, Pierce returned to Hillsborough and immediately benefited from the political patronage of his father, who relinquished his position as postmaster to his son. At the same time, Pierce undertook legal studies with a distinguished local jurist, John Burnham. Shortly thereafter, he moved to Portsmouth to continue his studies in the law practice of Levi Woodbury, a future Supreme Court justice. After concluding his legal studies in Northampton, Massachusetts, and Amherst, New Hampshire, Pierce was admitted to the bar in September of 1827.

Following in the path of his father, who was elected governor of the state in March 1827, Pierce spent the next five years forging a political career in New Hampshire. In January of 1829, he attained his first state political office

Franklin Pierce sought new commercial relations with Britain and secured a treaty with Japan. (Library of Congress)

when he was elected as the Hillsborough representative to the New Hampshire legislature. In May of that year, Pierce accepted his first committee appointment, that of chairman of the Committee on Education, a legislative responsibility he would assume frequently during his nearly thirty-year political career. That same month he was also appointed as a justice of the peace.

Pierce quickly consolidated his reputation as an unyielding Jacksonian Democrat, rising swiftly through the local political ranks to become speaker of the legislature in June 1831 at the age of twenty-six. Given his abiding loyalty to the Democratic Party and his father's party connections, it is not surprising that in 1832, just three years after his election to the New Hampshire General Court, Pierce was elected to the United States House of Representatives. He entered Congress in the aftermath of Jackson's resounding victory in the election of 1832, amid fierce partisan and sectional antagonism engendered in part by South Carolina's nullification threats and Jackson's unreserved enmity toward the Bank of the United States. During his time in Congress, Pierce maintained a staunch partisan voting record and was especially vigorous in his opposition to the expansion of congressional power, consistently voting against internal improvements and forcefully denouncing any federal interference in slavery.

His tenure in the House was unexceptional, however, with much of his time devoted to his responsibilities on the House Judiciary Committee.

In November 1836, despite a relative dearth of legislative achievements and for reasons that reflected the vagaries of the New Hampshire Democratic Party, rather than any evidence of his extraordinary aptitude in the House, Pierce was elected to the United States Senate by the New Hampshire legislature. In March of 1837, at the age of thirty-four, he entered the Senate as its youngest member. His senatorial career was short-lived, however, as a combination of primarily personal pressures coalesced to compel Pierce to resign his office in February 1842. Foremost among these pressures was his wife's opposition to his political career. In November 1834, he had married Jane Appleton Means, the daughter of a former president of his alma mater, Bowdoin College. Her physical and emotional frailty, and distinct aversion to Washington, D.C.—especially where the social activities of her husband were concerned—coupled with the expected birth of their third child, eventually persuaded Pierce that it was necessary to return to the more lucrative and stable foundation of his law practice in New Hampshire.

Pierce could not escape the lure of political life, however, and for the next five years he combined the responsibilities of his successful legal practice with ever-increasing responsibilities in the New Hampshire state Democratic Party. Indeed, Pierce was appointed chairman of the Party's central committee, and consistently loaned his energetic support to local and national Democratic political campaigns. He also became involved in the furor of temperance reform that swept antebellum American society, perhaps reflecting an anxiety about his own alcoholism. In June 1844, Pierce became chairman of the state Democratic Party, and campaigned strenuously for James K. Polk's presidential bid in the election of 1844. Polk rewarded Pierce in 1845 by appointing him New Hampshire district attorney. The following year, he offered Pierce the position of United States attorney general, an appointment Pierce declined.

He could not, however, decline the opportunity to fight for his country after war broke out with Mexico in 1846. When he was offered a colonel's commission in February 1847 and was asked to raise a New Hampshire regiment for deployment in Mexico, he enthusiastically accepted. A swift promotion to brigadier general came just days later, and by May 1847, Pierce and his new brigade were on their way to Veracruz, Mexico. Pierce was an earnest and dedicated soldier, although a battlefield accident limited his involvement in the campaign; his agitated horse threw him during an artillery barrage. Though determined to make a glorious contribution, Pierce was consistently hindered by bad luck and illness. When he finally returned to the United States in December of 1847, he nonetheless felt assured that he had proved himself a competent and worthy leader of men.

Following the Mexican campaign, Pierce resumed his responsibilities at his legal practice and continued to augment his reputation as a capable trial lawyer. He remained active in New Hampshire politics, shepherding the careers of aspiring young Democrats and serving in 1849 as chairman of the New Hampshire Constitutional Convention, which was convened in November with the aim of modernizing the state's antiquated constitution. He continued, however, to resist those in the Democratic Party who sought his return to national politics, and when the National Democratic Party Convention convened in Baltimore in June of 1852, Pierce informed a friend that he would find any use of his name at that convention "utterly repugnant." It was therefore a considerable surprise to many, including Pierce, when he was selected as the Democratic nominee for the upcoming presidential election after forty-nine ballots. Following a dull and insipid campaign, in which he faced his old commanding general in Mexico, Winfield Scott, Pierce achieved an unqualified Electoral College victory, becoming president with 254 electoral votes. Despite this clear victory, the popular vote margin had been slight, and opinion remained divided on whether Pierce was the appropriate man for the job. As his friend Nathaniel Hawthorne opined, "There are scores of men in the country that seem brighter than he is, but [he] has the directing mind, and will move them about like pawns on a chessboard, and turn all their abilities to better purpose than they themselves could do." Others, however, expressed less confidence. Renowned Boston lawyer and Free-Soil Party cofounder, Richard Henry Dana, expressed incredulity at the election of "a New Hampshire Democratic, doughface, militia colonel, a kind of third-rate county, or at most, state politician, President of the United States!"

Sectionalism and Restraint

The foreign policy implications of the 1852 election were negligible, and domestic issues dominated the politics of the period. A Northerner with solid pro-Southern credentials, Pierce in many ways seemed to be the ideal solution for a nation eager to heal the sectional wounds exacerbated by the acquisition of Mexican territory in 1848 and further intensified by the famous Compromise of 1850.

The foreign policy record of his predecessor, Millard Fillmore, was negligible. Wrenched from the vice-presidency upon the death of Zachary Taylor in July of 1850, Fillmore was preoccupied with the increasingly costly domestic repercussions of slavery and the continuing repercussions of the Polk administration's territorial expansion at the expense of Mexico.

Nevertheless, Fillmore's Whig administration instigated several foreign policy initiatives that commanded the attention of the new Democratic president. Continued tension with Great Britain, for example, required Pierce's constant consideration, especially concerning the control of crucial transcontinental transit routes in Latin America and the status of North American fishing rights. Fillmore had also dispatched Commodore Matthew C. Perry to Japan in 1852, initiating a sequence of events that culminated in that nation's historic opening to Western ideas and influence during the Pierce administration. Moreover, Whig opposition to American expansion in the Caribbean and Latin America contributed to the increasing proclivity of individual filibusters—a term derived from the Dutch and Spanish expressions for "free booty"—to take matters into their own hands.

Restrained Expansionism

With the exception of his military service during the war with Mexico, Pierce had little international experience prior to his presidency. He nevertheless espoused a vigorous, expansionist, and nationalistic conception of American foreign policy in his Inaugural Address, delivered on March 4, 1853. The address was replete with the tenets of the Young America movement, whose Democratic Party adherents saw commercial and territorial expansion abroad as a potential panacea for sectional antagonism at home. The Young Americans also echoed the rhetoric of European nationalism as it emerged in the Revolutions of 1848–1849. In particular, Pierce alluded to the sporadic American attempts to annex Cuba, and boldly stated the policy of his administration. "It is not to be disguised that our attitude as a nation and our position on the globe," he announced, "render the acquisition of certain possessions not within our jurisdiction eminently important for our protection, if not in the future essential for the preservation of the rights of commerce and the peace of the world."

Pierce appointed William L. Marcy as secretary of state, and in June 1853, Marcy issued a seemingly benign instruction to American representatives abroad that in many ways encapsulated the strident nationalism of the Pierce administration. His so-called Dress Circular asked U.S. diplomats to eschew the formal, ceremonial dress that was commonplace in European diplomatic circles, and instead appear "in the simple dress of an American citizen" using only "the American language" in consultations with their counterparts. This relatively modest request made it clear both at home and abroad that Americans were, quite literally, cut from a different cloth.

Mexico and the Gadsden Purchase

American relations with Mexico continued to be strained by the persistent avarice of American railroad speculators, the pressure of Southern advocates for the expansion of slavery, and audacious filibusters, who were often driven by a combination of economic and ideological motivations. Still, in 1853 the conditions seemed propitious for a resolution of outstanding claims between the United States and Mexico, and Pierce seized the opportunity offered by the financial desperation of Mexico's military dictator, Santa Anna, to initiate negotiations for the further acquisition of Mexican territory. In May of 1853, Pierce appointed James Gadsden, a Southern railroad promoter, to be his minister to Mexico. Gadsden had a mandate to settle Mexican claims resulting from Indian attacks originating in American territory, to obtain territory in northern Mexico that would facilitate construction of a southern transcontinental railroad, and to acquire American transit rights across the Isthmus of Tehuantepec—an important transportation route that linked American trade in the Pacific.

The resulting Gadsden Purchase Treaty, concluded with Santa Anna on December 30, 1853, provided for the sale of a portion of Mexican territory that would eventually become part of southern Arizona and southern New Mexico. In exchange, Mexico would receive $15 million, and the U.S. government would apportion $5 million to compensate American citizens with outstanding claims against Mexico. The United States would receive transit rights across the Isthmus of Tehuantepec under certain conditions, and the American government would no longer be responsible for the behavior of Indians in Mexican territory.

The treaty was a great disappointment to many in the Pierce administration, including the president himself. The land obtained under its terms did not assuage the extensive territorial aspirations of those in the thrall of Manifest Destiny. Nevertheless, after a period of debate within the cabinet, the treaty was presented to the Senate on February 10, 1854. Much to the chagrin of the president, the Senate rejected the treaty that April amid charges of fraud on the part of a member of the delegation, Christopher L. Ward. Ward, it transpired, was closely linked to an American consortium—led by Albert G. Sloo—that owned a claim on the Isthmus of Tehuantepec for the purposes of constructing a railroad there. Despite this setback, the treaty was passed on April 25 with the support of three Southern senators who had been absent during the previous deliberations. The final version of the Gadsden Purchase Treaty, implemented on June 30, 1854, stipulated that Mexico receive

$10 million for its territory. Washington undertook henceforth to support the claims of the Sloo group in constructing its railroad.

The Koszta Affair

In the summer of 1853, the Pierce administration seized on another opportunity to demonstrate the patriotic credentials of the Young Americans. Martin Koszta, a Hungarian refugee wanted by Austrian authorities for his involvement in the 1848–1849 Revolution, was arrested by agents of the Empire while on a business trip in Turkey and deposited on an Austrian ship anchored in Smyrna Harbor, bound for Trieste. Prior to his capture, Koszta had filed papers announcing his desire to obtain American citizenship. At the behest of the American chargé d'affaires, Captain Duncan N. Ingraham of the USS *St. Louis* demanded that the Austrians release Koszta—a demand reinforced by a threat of fire from the American ship. When Austrian representatives in Washington registered their grievance, Secretary of State Marcy issued a seventy-three-page rebuttal on September 26 that purported to draw on international law to support the American claim that "Koszta when seized and imprisoned was invested with the nationality of the United States, and they had therefore the right, if they chose to exercise it, to extend their protection to him." Marcy's robust declaration of American suzerainty in this matter delighted the American people and even won the begrudging assent of former British Foreign Secretary Lord Palmerston, a renowned skeptic of American policies. Three days after the publication of Marcy's rebuttal, the Austrian government announced its intention to eschew its claim to Koszta, a decision they had apparently reached prior to the publication of Marcy's note. Nevertheless, the affair underscored the nationalistic tenor of the Pierce administration and asserted American rights vis-à-vis a major European power.

The Opening of Japan

Commodore Matthew C. Perry and his four imposing "black ships" had been dispatched to Japan by President Fillmore to survey Japanese waters and to obtain treaties pertaining to the treatment of shipwrecked sailors, coaling stations, and trading rights. On his arrival at the entrance to Edo Bay on July 8, 1853, however, representatives of the increasingly decrepit Tokugawa regime rebuffed Perry's entreaties. In response, and with the implicit threat of force should he be denied a second time, Perry declared his intention to sail directly into Edo Bay. This was an inconceivable proposition to the previously isolated Japanese Shogunate. In the meantime, Perry sailed south with the intention of spending the winter in China. On his way, he independently

seized control of the Bonin Islands, and established a coaling station on the island of Okinawa in the Ryukyus. Despite its expansionist tendencies, the Pierce administration rejected Perry's efforts to establish American dominion over the Bonin Islands, the Ryukyus, and the island of Formosa.

On February 12, 1854, Perry returned to Edo Bay as promised, this time with nine ships, and on March 31 obtained a treaty of friendship from Japan. The Treaty of Kanagawa facilitated restricted American trade at two ports, Simoda (now Shimoda) and Hakodade (now Hakodate). The treaty also provided for an American consul at Shimoda, and Japan agreed to treat shipwrecked American sailors with decency. Townsend Harris became the first American consul general and arrived in Japan in August 1856. Somewhat tentatively, the treaty also provided for most-favored-nation status for the United States, in the event that Japan granted concessions to other powers in the future—something it soon did. Although the final terms of the Treaty of Kanagawa severely circumscribed American activities in Japan, Perry's mission established the foundation of American influence in the previously cloistered country. It culminated in the first commercial treaty with Japan in June of 1857, the genesis of the "unequal treaties" that would continue to antagonize Japanese relations with Europe and the United States.

Cuba: The Failure of Annexation

The island of Cuba represented a significant prize to the proponents of expansion. Even before the partisans of Manifest Destiny fully articulated their vision, the promulgation of the Monroe Doctrine in 1823 was seen by many to herald the beginning of the end of Spanish dominion in the western hemisphere. Pro-slavery advocates imagined the further extension of that institution into the Caribbean, while strategically oriented Young Americans envisaged an important naval base for American operations in Latin America. The Polk administration, however, had failed in its attempts to purchase Cuba and the repeated filibuster expeditions of Narciso López simply incurred the indignation of the British and the French.

Notwithstanding these obstacles, Pierce and his cabinet were almost unanimous in their commitment to the acquisition of the island by force or negotiation. With this objective in mind, Pierce appointed Pierre Soulé to be his minister to Spain. Soulé was an avowed supporter of the Young America project and a vociferous proponent of the expansion of slavery.

Almost immediately on the change of administration yet another filibuster operation was organized with the support of the president, this time by John A. Quitman, a pro-slavery former governor of Mississippi. The recurrent fear that Britain and France sought to abjure American expansionism in Latin America also intensified the determination of the administration to oust Spain from Cuba. Most troubling to pro-slavery expansionists was the common assertion that the three European powers were intent on the wholesale emancipation of Cuban slaves in order to render the island unpalatable to American expansionists through a process of Africanization.

On February 28, 1854, as Britain and France were preoccupied with preparations for war in the Crimean Peninsula, an opportunity arose for the culmination of these various intrigues. Claiming that the American ship *Black Warrior* had violated harbor regulations, Spanish authorities in Cuba confiscated the ship's cargo and arrested the captain. The incident was seen by some in the Congress as the very *causus belli* that would justify an American military engagement with Spain. On March 15, Pierce delivered a speech to the House of Representatives and asked Congress for authority to "obtain redress for injuries received, and to vindicate the honor of our flag." Two days later, Soulé received his instructions from Marcy. On April 8, Soulé issued the American demand for a $300,000 indemnity to the Spanish authorities in Madrid. Not content to await a Spanish response, however, Soulé relayed the American note in the form of a forty-eight hour ultimatum and further insisted on the discharge of those responsible for the seizure of the *Black Warrior*. This exceeded his admittedly ambiguous instructions from Marcy, but the Spanish authorities did not buckle to the American emissary's pressure and ignored the ultimatum. When it became clear, as the Spanish foreign secretary suspected, that Soulé had exceeded his authority from Washington, the Spanish settled directly with the owners of the *Black Warrior* and the crisis abated. In the meantime Marcy authorized Soulé to broach the possibility of an American purchase of Cuba, approving up to $130 million for the island.

Though the *Black Warrior* crisis subsided in the summer of 1854, Pierce was unwilling to forgo the acquisition of Cuba. The furor surrounding the Kansas-Nebraska Act, signed by Pierce on May 30, 1854, cooled his enthusiasm somewhat, continuing pressure from the Young America faction of the Democratic Party and supporters of Quitman's threatened filibuster operation compelled his administration to convene a diplomatic commission mandated to explore the possibility of, and justifications for, American control of the island. Aware of the broader international implications of American expansion into the Caribbean, Marcy assembled the American minister to Great Britain, James Buchanan; the minister to France, John Y. Mason; and Soulé in Ostend, Belgium, in October of 1854, to formulate a coherent approach to the question of Cuba. Beset by reporters in Ostend, they reconvened in

Aix-la-Chapelle, and on November 4, 1854, the product of their deliberations arrived in Washington. The so-called Ostend Manifesto reasserted the now familiar claim that Cuba was essential to the commerce and security of the United States, and further affirmed that Cuba "belongs naturally to that great family of States of which the Union is the providential nursery." The three diplomats proposed that the United States should continue in its attempts to purchase the island. In the event that Spain refused and the Africanization of Cuba proceeded, however, they forcefully concluded that, "we shall be justified in wresting it from Spain if we possess the power, and this upon the very same principle that would justify an individual in tearing down the burning house of his neighbor if there were no other means of preventing the flames from destroying his own home." Unfortunately for its advocates, the statement arrived in the midst of crucial congressional midterm elections, in which the Democrats suffered heavy losses in the North to the newly formed Republican Party. In the midst of this sectional drama, Marcy repudiated the manifesto, forcing Soulé to resign; pressure was applied on Quitman to disband his expedition to Cuba. Not until April 1855, following a meeting with Pierce and Marcy, did Quitman finally announce the end of his unofficial efforts to seize Cuba by force.

The Pierce administration met with similar disappointment in its efforts to acquire the Hawaiian Islands, or the Sandwich Islands as they were then known. Anglo-French resistance and ambiguous overtures from the Hawaiian monarchy ultimately precluded annexation of the Pacific territories. American ambitions for overseas dominions were partly compensated by the Guano Islands Act of August, 1856. The act proclaimed that any American citizen could take possession of any uninhabited island, loosely defined, containing deposits of guano, a natural fertilizer derived from bird droppings. Any such possession would, "at the discretion of the president, be considered as appertaining to the United States." Such possessions, however, were to be considered insular or unincorporated territories of the United States, that would not be incorporated into the federal union. This legislation provided the legal justification for the American claim to the Midway Islands, Baker Island, Jarvis Island, the Christmas Islands, and over seventy other claims in the latter half of the nineteenth century.

A Strained Rapprochement with Britain

As evident in the continued suspicion over American expansion in Latin America, British statesmen refused to accept unconditionally the American de facto declaration of suzerainty over Latin America articulated in the Monroe Doctrine of 1823. American relations with Great Britain remained strained during the Pierce administration, but the two governments managed to finesse one of the most con-tentious problems that had embittered Anglo-American relations throughout the early nineteenth century. Anglo-American relations over Canada were complicated by the continuing covetousness of the exponents of the doctrine of Manifest Destiny.

Again, sectional tensions inhibited the worst excesses of those who sought to annex Great Britain's dominion on the North American mainland. Just as important was the severe economic crisis that shook Canada during the 1850s. Buffeted by American tariffs and undermined by British trade liberalization following the repeal of the Corn Laws in 1846, some Canadians even began to consider the wisdom of joining the United States. Ultimately, diplomacy settled the most urgent questions of American fishing rights and reciprocal trade and thus ameliorated Canada's economic woes. On June 5, 1854, Great Britain and the United States concluded the Marcy-Elgin Treaty, which permitted American access to the fishing grounds of the North Atlantic previously had been denied. Moreover, the treaty enumerated a considerable list of previously restricted nat-ural products that would henceforth be reciprocally free of duty, including grain, livestock, timber, and coal. The Senate ratified the Marcy-Elgin Treaty on August 4, 1854.

The exigencies of the Crimean War troubled Anglo-American relations. Although the United States remained neutral during the Anglo-French conflict with Russia, it retained the right to ship American goods on belligerent ships, and vice versa. The British and the French adhered to this principle for the duration of the conflict, and the bel-ligerents even incorporated it into the Declaration of Paris that was promulgated on April 16, 1856, after the conclu-sion of hostilities. The Pierce administration, however, refused to sign the declaration, objecting to the inclusion of a stipulation that abolished privateering and the refusal of the other signatories to accept that all belligerent private property, except contraband, be exempt from capture.

A diplomatic crisis emerged in May of 1856, when Pierce expelled the British minister in the United States, John F. Crampton, along with British consuls in New York, Philadelphia, and Cincinnati, in response to perceived infractions against American neutrality during the war. The expulsions were actually the culmination of three years of tension and diplomatic wrangling over the legality of British recruitment efforts in North America. Due to the difficulty of recruiting men into the armed forces in Great Britain, the British government authorized the recruitment of foreign soldiers in 1853 for deployment in the Crimean conflict. Crampton, under strict orders to legally circum-vent American neutrality laws, arranged for American recruits to enlist and depart from Canada. Although the activities of British recruiters in the United States were offi-cially aborted in June 1855, the crisis continued to intensify

following diplomatic squabbling and even talk of war in the more belligerent American newspapers. Though the tension subsided following the removal of the British diplomats, the British government declined to dispatch any further repre-sentation to the United States until after the change of administration in March 1857.

American Power in Nicaragua

In July 1854, an American warship bombarded the free city of Greytown at the mouth of the San Juan River in Nicaragua. The city was populated largely by European and American entrepreneurs, fortune hunters, and speculators. The captain of the USS *Cyane* fired on the town, nominally under the protection of Great Britain, in response to an insult against the American minister to Nicaragua, Solon Borland, by an angry crowd. Following a two-hour naval bombardment, a contingent of U.S. Marines was deployed and proceeded to demolish the remains of the town. Despite international and domestic criticism, Pierce defended the barrage in his annual address of December 1854, disparaging the town's anarchic and restive inhabi-tants and minimizing the attack in comparison to the actions of other governments against "communities far less offending and more defenseless than Greytown."

Nicaragua also briefly fell victim to an American fili-buster expedition in 1855. William Walker, perhaps the most famous and successful of these unofficial agents of American foreign policy, had already established a short-lived filibuster government in Baja California, and in 1855, he was invited to intervene in Nicaragua by a revolutionary group fighting in the civil war then underway. In May of 1856, Walker succeeded in taking control of Nicaragua, and promptly installed a puppet regime that almost immediate-ly received the recognition of the Pierce administration. The following July, Walker became president of Nicaragua, whereupon he promptly repealed its emancipation laws and instituted slavery, hoping to gain the support of sympathet-ic Southern slaveholders in the United States. His dream of a Central American slave empire was fleeting, however, for on May 1, 1857, Walker surrendered to the U.S. Navy after a cholera epidemic and the undermining of his power base by a fellow American adventurer in Central America, Cornelius Vanderbilt, who had extensive railroad interests in Nicaragua. He was eventually executed in Honduras in 1860 following another attempted filibuster expedition.

Legacy

After a presidential term that was troubled by sectional ten-sions and foreign policy miscalculations, Pierce suffered an ignominious defeat at the 1856 Democratic Convention, losing the party's nomination to his minister to Great

Britain, James Buchanan. Following his term in office, Pierce dedicated himself to caring for his increasingly sick wife, who died in 1863. It is perhaps not surprising that the president, when asked what came after the presidency, supposedly remarked "there's nothing left to do but get drunk," died of cirrhosis of the liver in October 1869 in New Hampshire.

In many ways, the Pierce administration pursued foreign policy goals that exceeded the capacity of the nation's power and influence. Despite consistently defending American honor against the perceived encroachment and offenses of the European powers, the Pierce administration could do little to restrain their activities, especially in Latin America and the Pacific. Despite the intransigence of Great Britain, France, and Spain, the long-standing American desire to annex Cuba did not subside in the aftermath of the Ostend Manifesto. When war with Spain finally came in 1898, American influence over Cuba reached its peak, and the legacy of the Ostend Manifesto came closest to fulfillment.

Nonetheless, in the years that followed the brief but ultimately unfulfilled dynamism of the Young America movement that had informed so much of Pierce's term in office, American foreign policy was increasingly subordinated to domestic policy. The escalating sectional conflict, which Pierce could do little to resist, subsumed the once potent rhetoric of nationalism and expansionism, and eventually propelled the nation into civil war. Ultimately, the Pierce administration's attempts to realize what many perceived to be America's Manifest Destiny beyond the United States ended largely in failure. The potential domestic repercussions of extra-continental expansion were simply too divisive amid the seething sectional tension of the 1850s, and the great power realities of international politics overshadowed the rhetoric of the Young Americans, humiliating the more ostentatious claims of the Pierce administration.

David Atkinson

Chronology

1853

January 20: British forces capture Rangoo and Pegu, Anglo-Burmese war ends.

July 8–13: Admiral Perry's fleet anchors in the Bay of Edo, Tokyo.

September 7: Taiping rebels capture Shanghai.

December 30: Gadsden Treaty with Mexico.

1854

February 28: *Black Warrior* incident in Havana, crisis in U.S.-Spanish relations.

March 28: Crimean War begins.

March 31: Perry signs Treaty of Kanagawa with Japanese officials.

April 3: Secretary of State William Marcy offers U.S. purchase of Cuba.

May 30: Kansas-Nebraska Bill passes Congress.

October 18: Ostend Manifesto favors U.S. purchase of Cuba.

December 18: Spanish Cortes rejects sale of Cuba.

1855

January 28: Panama Railroad Company of New York begins service across Isthmus of Panama.

October 15: Accessory Transit Company uses mercenaries to topple Nicaraguan government.

1856

April 16: Declaration of Paris ends Crimean War.

November 4: James Buchanan elected president.

November 16: U.S. gunboats attack Chinese Barrier forts.

References and Further Reading

Bemis, Samuel Flagg, ed. *The American Secretaries of State and Their Diplomacy. Volume VI.* New York: Pageant, 1958.

Dowty, Alan. *The Limits of American Isolation: The United States and the Crimean War.* New York: New York University Press, 1971.

Gara, Larry. *The Presidency of Franklin Pierce.* Lawrence, KS: University Press of Kansas, 1991.

Nichols, Roy Franklin. *Franklin Pierce: Young Hickory of the Granite Hills.* Philadelphia: University of Pennsylvania Press, 1931.

Perkins, Bradford. *The Cambridge History of American Foreign Relations: Volume 1: The Creation of a Republican Empire, 1776–1865.* New York: Cambridge University Press, 1993.

Sloan, Irving J., ed. *Franklin Pierce, 1804–1869: Chronology-Documents-Bibliographical Aids.* Dobbs Ferry, NY: Oceana, 1968.

Stephanson, Anders. *Manifest Destiny: American Expansionism and the Empire of Right.* New York: Hill and Wang, 1995.

Wallner, Peter A. *Franklin Pierce: New Hampshire's Favorite Son.* Concord, NH: Plaidswede, 2004.

Weeks, William E. *Building the Continental Empire: American Expansion from the Revolution to the Civil War.* Chicago: Ivan R. Dee, 1997.

James Buchanan (1857–1861)

Early Life and Political Career

James Buchanan, Sr. emigrated to the United States in 1783, settling in an as yet untamed part of Pennsylvania. He married Elizabeth Sears, daughter of a wealthy local farmer. James Buchanan, Jr. was born into this affluent Irish immigrant family on April 23, 1791, at Cove Gap, near Mercersburg, Pennsylvania. Young James attended local schools until age sixteen, when the affluent Buchanans sent him to complete his education at Dickinson College in Carlisle, Pennsylvania. He was an undisciplined student who was twice nearly expelled from Dickinson, but who held on until his graduation (with academic honors) in 1809. The future president subsequently studied law. He was a solid debater and an able law student, and he passed the bar examination in 1813. He volunteered to serve in the War of 1812, but it was too late to see any action. Instead, his law practice in Lancaster, Pennsylvania prospered. His investments also paid off handsomely, so he was independently wealthy at a young age. Despite the attractions and respectability of his education, profession, and wealth, Buchanan never married: he was the only American bachelor president. He vowed to remain a lifelong bachelor (though not a celibate) after Ann Caroline Coleman, a young woman to whom he was engaged, but from whom he was also estranged, died under unexplained circumstances. (It is possible she committed suicide after she broke off their engagement, which her family opposed.) Later, Buchanan spent much of the wealth and time he might otherwise have devoted to private family life supporting a surrogate extended family of poor cousins and other blood relations. He reveled in his role as patriarch, a position of benevolent mastery that colored his views on slavery in both his personal and public life, and later on secession.

James Buchanan's legal and political careers progressed in tandem. He took populist positions whenever possible, while avoiding comment on the key problems and most controversial debates of the day. It is likely that from an early age, his eye was on the prize of the presidency. His first successful election was to the Pennsylvania State Legislature in 1814, as a Federalist, when he was just twenty-three. He was reelected several times, serving in the state House until 1819. As political winds shifted, he crossed over and ran as a Democrat. In 1821, he was elected to the House of Representatives in Washington, where he served five consecutive terms, until

As secretary of state, James Buchanan helped to settle the Oregon Question. As president he watched in befuddlement as the nation slid toward the Civil War, the most tragic war in its history. (Library of Congress)

1831. In 1824, he supported Henry Clay for president, earning real animus from Andrew Jackson even while supporting him and shifting from the moribund Federalists to the Democratic-Republicans. Buchanan backed Old Hickory again in 1828, bringing Pennsylvania into Jackson's column and thus positioning himself to benefit from Jackson's victory. In 1831, Jackson appointed Buchanan minister (ambassador) to Russia. While serving in St. Petersburg and Moscow, Buchanan's singular success was to negotiate a commercial treaty that had eluded U.S. diplomats in Russia for over thirty years. But he was also a rank apologist for czarism. He downplayed the illiberal implications of Russia's bloody repression of a national rebellion in Poland in 1831, even though he never deigned to travel to or observe the events in Poland firsthand. In his aloof dispatches, he assumed the tone of apologist for the czarist system, mainly passing along court gossip and opinion picked up at diplomatic parties in the twin capitals. He defended the worst excesses of czarism and of serfdom in terms that echoed his support for slavery in the American South, writing approvingly about the "calm of despotism" that blanketed Russia. He painted Russian serfs and American slaves as similarly childlike and utterly incapable of self-government, and thus as far happier and better off under the "benevolent" masters who ordered their lives than they would be if forced to endure emancipation.

Buchanan returned to the United States in 1833. Bland both personally and politically, but a shrewd and ambitious operator working within the Democratic Party machine, he reentered public politics and won election to the Senate. There, he continued his strong support of the Jackson administration. He remained in the Senate through the administration of President Martin Van Buren. Thereafter, his own presidential ambitions were both obvious and frustrated: he sought the presidency unsuccessfully in 1844, 1848, and 1852. Under President James K. Polk, Buchanan served without distinction as secretary of state. Although he showed initial independence in opposing Polk's "fifty-four forty or fight" demands on the Oregon question, he also drafted an argument in favor of that demand and eventually assisted in working out the final compromise with Great Britain. Prior to the Mexican War, he cooperated with Polk's advocacy of secret talks with California that aimed at secession of the west coast territory from Mexico to be followed by application for admission to the United States on the Texas model. Buchanan expressed fears that Great Britain had annexationist designs on California that needed to be forestalled by a U.S. annexation. His major contribution was to encourage Polk not to begin his war with Mexico until it was certain that resolution of the Oregon question had eliminated the possibility of war with Great Britain. At the end of the Mexican war, Buchanan called for more limited annexations than his president supported; he then expressed fear that Polk would not demand enough territory, and ended up opposing the peace treaty that was actually agreed on, insisting that it did not obtain enough Mexican territory for the United States. The sole common thread tying this tapestry of indecision together was his pandering to popular opinion in the hope of subsequently converting this into support for his presidential ambitions.

Buchanan fought Douglas for the Democratic nomination in 1852, with the ugly affair lasting through thirty-four ballots at the National Convention in Baltimore before a third and compromise candidate, Franklin Pierce, won the nomination on the forty-eighth ballot. Pierce appointed Buchanan minister to the Court of St. James in London. There, he sought unsuccessfully to negotiate settlement of various minor Anglo-American disputes over Central American issues. In October 1854, he met in secret with French and British diplomats in Ostend, Belgium, where he drafted the pro-slavery Ostend Manifesto, reviving arguments for the purchase of Cuba by the United States from Spain. That affair linked broad annexationist designs with the interest of the Southern Democratic Party and Young America movement in annexation of Cuba and expansion into territory that was suitable for an extension of slavery. Northern public opinion was outraged when news of the secret memorandum leaked, and that, along with electoral defeats for the Democrats in the November 1854 Congressional elections, killed the proposal. Nevertheless, two years later Buchanan ran on a national platform that included a call for annexation of Cuba.

Presidency and Foreign Policy

In June 1956, Buchanan was chosen as nominee for the presidency by a badly divided Democratic Party, winning on the seventeenth ballot. In the general campaign, the Republican candidate, California senator and famed explorer John C. Frémont, won a Northern popular majority, but lost a narrow national plurality to Buchanan (45.3 percent), whose strength was in the slave states: he lost ten of fourteen Northern states but won all the slave and border states except Maryland, which voted Know-Nothing. The final tally in the Electoral College was 174 votes for Buchanan to 114 for Frémont, and 8 votes for the Know-Nothing candidate Millard Fillmore. Buchanan was sixty-five years old, and had finally achieved his life's ambition. The pity was that he did not know what to do next or do with the powers of his office. Perhaps that is why he promised to serve only one term, a promise no one would later ask him to break. Buchanan's clear task as president was to avoid disintegration of the Union; in that, he would fail abysmally. A second key task was to reunite the Democratic Party, to prevent more defections to the rising Republicans in the next presidential election, which would make secession and civil war far more likely. Instead, he quarreled with Stephen A. Douglas, whom he resented and envied as a major rival for leadership of the Democratic Party. Buchanan made no effort to woo Davis. To the contrary, he appointed anti-Douglas men and radical slavery supporters to key posts in his administration. This powerful inner group, or "Directory," is usually portrayed as having Buchanan kowtow to its narrow interests and dictates. But this was not always true: as president, Buchanan wielded considerable power on the sheer basis of his high office, if not ever due to his wits or personality. In any case, his cabinet choices left out most Northern Democrats, denied representation to large cities, and excluded the business community in favor of the Southern planter class.

On a narrow, Southern, and pro-slavery basis then, Buchanan launched a disastrous national and foreign policy of even more territorial expansion, trying several times to persuade Congress to buy Cuba. The best that might be said of this effort was that it aimed to distract the nation from a worsening civil and constitutional crisis by ringing the bells of jingoistic nationalism. But a policy of mere distraction could only delay the inevitable and did nothing to avoid the coming crisis. That Buchanan failed to appreciate that the slave vs. free soil status of the territories acquired in the Mexican War, along with the new doctrine of popular sovereignty of the states, was what started the country down the road to civil war in the first place. Making matters worse, he personally intervened in the process leading to the *Dred Scott* decision, urging the Supreme Court to adopt a wholly Southern view of the case, which denied citizenship anywhere in the United States to free blacks and wholly discarded legal precedent, including the Missouri Compromise. Buchanan further compounded his error by asking Congress to admit Kansas as a slave state, aggravating the civil unrest already underway in "Bleeding Kansas."

While this political and constitutional crisis built in the West, Buchanan had to deal with a widening economic depression. He proposed authorization of the sale of Treasury revenue bonds to Congress. His reconstructed Tariff of 1857 was his most aggressive action to solve the revenue problem. It reduced rates to an unprecedented low of 20 percent and enlarged the list of duty-free items. This move was applauded by Southern states that did not rely on export of manufactures, but it damaged the North, where Abraham Lincoln and other Republicans and former Whigs called instead for a protectionist national tariff. Although lowering the tariff encouraged trade, its negative effects were far more widespread in the North than the South, lending false hope to the belief of many Southerners that their agrarian economic system was superior to that of the industrialized North. The net effect of Buchanan's tariff reform was thus to heighten tensions within the Union. Buchanan was similarly inept in dealing with pro-slavery filibusters such as William Walker, who was abetted in his serial invasions of weak Central American republics by nullifying Southern courts. As an expansionist Democrat, Buchanan several times proposed sending in U.S. troops to support Walker's wildcat actions, but he was deflected from actually doing so by antislavery and anti-annexationist opposition in Congress. After a British officer handed Walker over to face a Honduran firing squad in 1860, the United States and Great Britain settled most of their Central American disputes. Britain abandoned its claim to the Mosquito Coast and returned several disputed Bay Islands to Honduras. Buchanan boasted in his 1860 State of the Union message to Congress that he had thereby improved

Anglo-American relations, when in truth his earlier support for Walker had badly damaged them. Indeed, several times Buchanan flirted with war with Great Britain, which could only have been disastrous given the domestic situation in the United States. He sent naval forces into the Caribbean to warn off British adventurers. Wisely, the British recognized that the stakes in Central America did not warrant war, and made the necessary concessions.

The Treaty of Kanagawa between the United States and Japan was signed on March 31, 1854, and ratified on July 11, 1854. This commercial treaty was forced on Japan by Commodore Matthew C. Perry. It forced Japan to establish diplomatic relations with the United States (that is, to accept a U.S. consul based at Shimoda) and granted trade access at two designated Japanese treaty ports. Since the most-favored-nation principle applied internationally, this treaty opened Japan to other Western trading powers after more than two centuries of Tokugawa enforced economic autarky and political and cultural isolation. It was quickly mimicked in agreements with European trading nations and naval powers that scrambled to follow the American lead, with the British and Russians alike securing similar agreements in 1855. The Buchanan administration followed-up with additional agreements that opened more Japanese ports to direct trade, granted residential rights to U.S. citizens in Shimoda and Hakodate, and confirmed extraterritorial legal rights of foreign nationals within the treaty port zones. Although the agreement was significant, Buchanan received little credit because the main initiative had been President Pierce's, with Buchanan only completing the negotiations.

Concerning growing European aggression toward China, Buchanan mostly remained indifferent and detached. He declined British and French efforts to involve the United States in a bitter Chinese dispute with Russia over the Amur River basin. Instead, he ordered the U.S. representative, William B. Reed, to maintain strict neutrality. In 1858 the United States attached its interests to the Treaty of Tientsin forced on Qing China by other foreign powers. The treaty was forced on China following a display of British gunboat diplomacy during the Second Opium War. Tientsin led to comparable "unequal treaties," negotiated on the most-favored-nation principle, with France, Russia, and the United States (the latter signed on June 18, 1858). These treaties permitted foreign ambassadors to take up residence in Beijing, opened ten more coastal cities to foreign trade as official treaty ports, allowed foreigners to import opium for sale to Chinese addicts, gave additional Qing guarantees and access to the interior of the country for traders and to Christian missionaries, and set tariff terms that were highly disadvantageous to China. The U.S-China treaty did not greatly affect Sino-American relations in Buchanan's day, partly because the United States did not use force to gain its privileged terms and did not lay claim to Chinese ports. However, the United States had clearly hitchhiked into Chinese concessions on the warhorse of European aggression and military intervention. Buchanan's acceptance of forced Chinese concessions thus set in motion longer-term animosities and a clash of interests over China's sovereignty and independence from penetration by foreign powers that would have enormous, and largely deleterious, effects on Sino-American relations in later years and decades.

While American diplomacy was chalking up cheap diplomatic and trade victories across the Pacific, closer to home it saw Spain and France take advantage of American divisions and preoccupations to assay expansion of the Spanish Empire and a return to French Empire in the Americas. Buchanan did not even symbolically invoke the Monroe Doctrine (that was left to Abraham Lincoln's secretary of state, William H. Seward, on April 2, 1861). Thus, on March 18, 1861, barely two weeks after Buchanan left office and in the midst of the secession crisis, the Dominican Republic was annexed to Spain without effective U.S. opposition. Similarly, Buchanan had done nothing effective about the "War of the Reform" in Mexico, which began on his watch in 1858 and lasted into 1861. The effect of this, and the American Civil War, was to encourage and permit later French military intervention in an effort to establish a Catholic monarchy south of the Rio Grande. In the far north, a Russian offer to sell Alaska to the United States in 1860 was welcomed by Buchanan, who offered $5 million, but the Civil War interrupted negotiations before a deal could be consummated.

Legacy

Buchanan's fundamental ineffectiveness as president played out at home as he presided over the dissolution of both the Democratic Party and the American Union. His hatred for Stephen A. Douglas split the Democratic Party and denied its candidates any chance to win the 1860 election, which was thereby lost by a plurality of votes to Abraham Lincoln and the Republicans. Additionally blinded by pro-slavery and pro-Southern sentiments, and baffled by the constitutional issues presented by the wave of state secessions that began in South Carolina in December, 1860, Buchanan merely looked on as the nation split asunder and both sides prepared for civil war. He did nothing as a new slave republic was declared on part of American soil, or when all Southerners in his cabinet resigned to join the rebellion. On the other hand, he clung to Fort Sumter and other Federal garrisons, displeasing the fire-eaters in the South. For his core ineptitude on the cental issue facing his presidency and the nation, for his months long delay that permitted the

Confederacy to organize politically and for war, James Buchanan is correctly ranked by most historians as the worst president ever to occupy the White House. On March 4, 1861, Buchanan was replaced as president by Abraham Lincoln, arguably the *most* decisive and perhaps the best man and the greatest president to ever sit in the Oval Office. Neither the immediacy nor the historical importance of the contrast between these two men can be exaggerated. In great political disfavor (his portrait in the Capitol was vandalized, and he was widely regarded as a Northern traitor), Buchanan retired to his estate in Wheatland, Pennsylvania. From there, he watched the Civil War play out. In 1866 he published a long defense of his presidency, blaming the war wholly on Lincoln, the Republicans, and Northern abolitionists. He died on June 1, 1868.

Cathal J. Nolan

Chronology

1857

February 5: Liberal government of Benito Jurez established in Veracruz, Mexico.

March 3: Tariff of 1857 reduces tariffs and enlarges tariff-free list.

May 1: ATC regime in Nicaragua overthrown.

June 17: United States and Japan sign commercial agreement.

1858

May 28: Russian and China sign Treaty of Aigun.

June 18: Treaty of Tientsin with China.

July 29: Second commercial treaty with Japan.

August 2: India Act brings India under British political control.

August 8: Transatlantic cable completed.

November 8: United States signs commercial treaty with China.

1859

April 7: United States recognizes Juarez government in Mexico.

May 19: Vicksburg Convention demands an end to all measures against the slave trade.

June 25: Taku incident in China, followed by Anglo-French military intervention.

July 30: United States fails in its attempt to purchase more Mexican territory.

October 19: John Brown's raid on the federal arsenal at Harper's Ferry.

December 19: Congress denies Buchanan authority to intervene in Mexican civil war.

1860

August 31: United States warns France not to intervene in Mexico.

October *12:* Peking occupied by Anglo-French troops.

November *6:* Abraham Lincoln elected president

December 20: South Carolina adopts Ordinance of Secession.

References and Further Reading

Baker, Jean H. *James Buchanan.* New York: Times Books, 2004.

Birkner, Michael J., ed. *James Buchanan and the Political Crisis of the 1850s.* Selinsgrove, PA: :Susquehanna University Press, 1996.

Smith, Elbert B. *The Presidency of James Buchanan.* Lawrence, KS: The University Press of Kansas, 1975.

Abraham Lincoln (1861–1865)

Early Life and Political Career

Samuel Lincoln emigrated from England to Massachusetts in 1637. His descendants moved to Virginia, where they were successful farmers for seven generations. In the early 1780s Abraham Lincoln, Sr., the later president's grandfather and namesake, moved to break and settle new farmland in Kentucky (which was then still part of Virginia). On the other side of Lincoln's paternal family tree were Pennsylvania Quakers who also migrated to Kentucky in the 1780s. Abraham, Sr. was killed during an Indian raid in 1786. Under Virginia's law of primogenitor, his death disinherited all his younger sons, including Lincoln's father, Thomas, wholly in favor of the oldest boy. As a disinherited illiterate, Thomas struggled to scratch out a living as a manual laborer and sometime cabinetmaker, until he could afford to buy a homestead. In 1806 he married Nancy Hanks, the illegitimate daughter of a Virginia planter from a long line of modest farmers. Three years later Thomas started a new farm, where he built a 16- by 18-foot, dirt floor, log cabin in the rough style common to most frontier homes at that time. Abraham Lincoln was born there on February 12, 1809.

A few years after his birth, he briefly attended a rural "ABC school" with his older sister, Sarah, but was still unable to read or write. In 1816 Thomas Lincoln moved the family across the Ohio River to the newly formed "free soil" state of Indiana, where slavery was excluded by the Northwest Ordinance. Thomas did this mainly because he was too poor to secure legal title to the family's Kentucky farm, but also because of antislavery views rooted in his Baptist faith reinforced by the natural economic antipathy of a free farmer to competition from slave labor.

Thomas built another log cabin on the new farm. The next year, Abraham was nearly killed when a mare kicked him in the head, leaving him unconscious, then speechless, for many hours. He grew up distant from, and ultimately disdainful and unappreciative of, his hardworking father. He was drawn more to his mother, a highly intelligent woman who could read but not write. But two years after the move to Indiana, when Abraham was nine, his mother died during an outbreak of cow's milk poisoning ("milk fever") that also carried off several close relatives. Death was thus all around the young Lincoln, and touched him deeply: as a youth he was highly and unusually sensitive to any spilling of blood, including in hunting and animal husbandry, and to

Abraham Lincoln, with his rare combination of idealism and pragmatism, guided the nation through its gravest crisis and facilitated its emergence as a Great Power. (Library of Congress)

casual cruelty, including to all beasts. The next year, his father returned to Kentucky to secure a new mother for his waif children. He returned with a recent widow, Sarah Bush Johnson, who had three needful children of her own. Abe (a boyhood nickname Lincoln did not like, but which stuck) quickly grew devoted to her, even beyond the deep but less mature love he felt for his natural mother. These were happy years during which Abe absorbed western patterns of speech and his justly famous storytelling ear and style, along with physical toughness born of numerous fistfights and much hard manual work, and of the personal tragedy and poverty endemic to frontier life. Abe was a normal boy in most ways, but unusual in several key respects. Unlike most frontiersmen and westerners, he did not hunt (he gave up hunting at age eight, in moral self-disgust upon shooting a wild turkey in 1817). Nor did he smoke, and all his adult life he abstained from liquor and from gambling. His father hired his tall, strong son out as a laborer to other farmers to supplement the family's income. At home, Lincoln grew evermore distant from his father but was adored by, and adoring of, Sarah. Though illiterate, she appreciated the value of education and understood Abe's thirst for books and learning. During nine months of schooling in the "blab" or rote recital style, scattered across two years of unceasing work on the farm, but mainly through private persistence and Sarah's encouragement, Abe learned to write and to enjoy logic and mathematics. Still, at age fifteen his crude education was over; in all, it amounted to less than a full year's formal instruction.

So where did Lincoln acquire his great learning and rare agility with language? He taught himself, starting from elementary grammar and arithmetic books, proceeding through deep (rather than wide) reading in American history and biography, the *Bible, Aesop's Fables,* John Bunyan's *Pilgrim's Progress,* and the works of William Shakespeare. Decades later, Lincoln would recall extended passages of these works from memory. An extraordinary autodidact, he never ceased to read throughout his life. He would learn, if not master, new subjects as he saw the need. He thus later taught himself law well enough to practice successfully. During his term as a Whig member of the House of Representatives, he drew notice for spending his spare time reading in the Library of Congress. Even as president, when he felt it necessary to better evaluate and argue strategy with his generals, Lincoln read deeply until he gained a respectable command of military theory, tactics, and strategy. In his mature writing and speeches he displayed an exceptional and discriminating intellect that penetrated far more deeply than most, to the root of important things, and with accompanying disdain for trivia and fashion.

Like many gifted people, Lincoln was most comfortable with his own internal life. Unlike some, he did not exhibit a need to display his intellectual superiority over others. To the contrary, he made considerable political use of a general underestimation of his abilities. On the other hand, during his teen years his precocious intellectuality led to permanent deterioration of his relationship with his father. Unfairly, as a boy and young man, he resented and seemed ashamed of his father's lack of erudition. They also argued over religion, after Abe was caught mocking and parodying for other children sermons he had been compelled to attend. Though raised in a region of the country and in an era that frequently succumbed to ecstatic Christian revivalism and equated mere evangelical fervor with holiness, Lincoln never joined and seldom ventured into a church as an adult, other than for funerals. He cleaved to agnosticism or perhaps a faint deism from his early years, keeping these views well into, and possibly all through, his presidency. Lincoln thereby demonstrated early in life what emerged as

a core characteristic of his adulthood and presidency: highly unusual independence of thought and judgment accompanied by a hard conviction about the rightness of his own opinions and a quiet scorn for the unlettered, ignorant, and fools.

From age sixteen Lincoln began to hire out on his own, splitting rails for fences, killing hogs, and plowing fields for daily or weekly pay. His first encounter with slaves came when he and a friend took a small cargo barge down the Ohio River. Along the way they fought off a night attack by, in Lincoln's recollection, "seven negroes with intent to kill and rob" them. When the young travelers reached New Orleans they observed the enormous slave markets of that city, though it is not known what impression this made on Lincoln. Part of the return journey was spent in the presence of seven chained slaves; again, little is known of Lincoln's reaction. He left his father's farm for good in 1831, moving to the village of New Salem, Illinois. There he spent the next six years in varied occupations: store clerk, sometime carpenter, riverboat hand, local postmaster, volunteer militiaman in the Blackhawk War (though he saw no action), and county surveyor. Later, in Vandalia and then in Springfield, he studied and practiced law and served for the first time in political office as a state representative.

As in his personal life, Lincoln's political career was marked by independence and pragmatic, rather than visceral, equal pursuit of principle on the great, lesser, and merely local issues of the day. His region was dominated and controlled by Jacksonian Democrats, yet Lincoln was an avid admirer of Henry Clay's anti-Jacksonian American System that promoted a national bank, private investment on railways, canals, and other western infrastructure, and a national protective tariff, all intended to promote national economic integration and to erode divisive sectional antagonisms. In 1832, at age twenty-three, Lincoln ran for the Illinois state legislature on a platform that called for dredging the Sangamon River and against a railway project that would bypass and kill the river trade of New Salem. Out of work during the campaign, Lincoln enlisted in the Illinois militia that formed to wage the Blackhawk War, and was quickly elected an officer—his first ever victory by ballot. He joined mainly for the pay, and for the same reason reenlisted twice. The state election was held after his final discharge. He finished eighth out of thirteen candidates. Again penniless, he returned to rail-splitting and odd jobs until he secured a position as county surveyor, which gave him a more secure income while also making him known around the state circuit. He again ran for the state legislature in 1834. Lincoln received 1,376 votes, which was enough to place him second on the electoral list. In the months before he was due to take up his new position as a state legislator, he began to teach himself law (a path to the practice of law not as unusual then as it sounds today). In order to attend the legislature, he took a room in isolated, unexciting

Vandalia, the state capital. In his first term he was unnoticed and ineffective, but learned much. But even as his career and income improved, death stalked him. Ann Rutledge, a young love interest to whom he felt vaguely pledged, died of typhus on August 25, 1835. Her passing thrust Lincoln into a deep melancholia, which lasted through his campaign for reelection. This time, he finished first on the list, an apparent rising star in state politics. In 1837 he was licensed to practice law and moved to Springfield, which he had helped make the new state capital in the previous session. Having emerged from his earlier romantic grief, he courted Mary Owens. Too soon, and ineptly, he proposed marriage, and was firmly rejected.

Lincoln gained prominence within Whig Party circles in Springfield, and was twice put forward (though in failing efforts) as the Whig candidate for speaker of the state house. By 1838, he was confident and experienced both as a legislator and public speaker, a fierce partisan who now favored spending public funds on big infrastructure projects across the state. However, as leader of the Whigs in the Illinois legislature, he failed to block a Jacksonian-Democratic bid to kill the Whig-supported state bank. Lincoln acquiesced in Whig abandonment of Henry Clay, a man for whom he had professed admiration all his life, as presidential candidate in favor of nomination of William Henry Harrison (of the Battle of Tippecanoe fame), to run against the Democratic candidate Martin Van Buren in the 1840 presidential election. On November 19, 1839, Lincoln began a series of debates on national campaign issues with state Democratic leader Stephen A. Douglas. During these debates, Lincoln criticized Martin Van Buren for supporting the right of free blacks in New York to vote. But he also spoke against growing social disorder, lynchings, and sectionalism of any kind, against which he opposed an American nationalism based upon the rule of reason and reverence for law as the "political religion of the nation." He softly criticized the abolitionist movement as threatening to lead to the overthrow of popular government and dissolution of the Union, although he opposed slavery. He did this in the same spirit of admired rationality by which he opposed prohibition as excessively romantic and overly emotional, although he did not drink at all. Like Thomas Mallory's knight errant, Sir Lancelot, Lincoln remained something of an ill-made knight. He strove to impose the rule of cool reason as much on himself as on the boiling and tumultuous public realm, even as he also struggled with enormous personal ambition and to flee his past and his image as a crude and vulgar frontiersman.

In 1837, Lincoln began a long courtship of Mary Todd, the well-educated daughter of a prosperous Kentucky merchant and banker, who had been raised in a household filled with slave servants. She shared his Whig convictions and many of his interests, and was a lively intellectual in her own right. Lincoln's shyness and clumsiness around women complicated the development of their relationship. His prospects were not aided by the fact that in 1840, his political fortunes began to fail: he fell from first place on the Whig list, and this determined him not to stand again. Without an income or a home suitable to a new bride, and from feelings of inadequacy as a man and potential husband, he wavered in his devotion to marrying Mary Todd. He awkwardly broke off their engagement, an act he instantly regretted when it clearly wounded Mary. Lincoln then sank into another of his periodic deep depressions and withdrawals from his social circle. So severe was his melancholy on this occasion that several friends feared he might kill himself. He recovered slowly, and regained his old interest in politics. That led him to publicly mock a Democratic opponent and to absurd acceptance of a duel with the offended man (even more ridiculously, with broadswords, the weapon chosen by Lincoln upon acceptance of the challenge). The fight, which was moved out-of-state for legal reasons, was only stopped by last minute intervention by a more mature man, who mediated an end to the argument. The main effect of the affair was to impress Mary Todd with Lincoln's chivalric nature and thus to restore the couple's engagement. They married hurriedly, as if afraid to delay, on November 4, 1842. Lincoln grew less moody with marriage and later, with fatherhood, but was never openly demonstrative about his affections. The birth of Robert Todd Lincoln, then several more children, followed in due course. Lincoln spent several years as a happy town bourgeois, patriarch of a modest but respectable family and partner in a solid though not lucrative practice of circuit lawyering. He had, utilizing great natural talents but also with determined effort, escaped his father's poverty and occupation and surpassed his lowly social station.

In 1846, Lincoln was persuaded to stand as a Whig candidate for Congress. His Democratic opponent made Lincoln's lack of religious conviction an issue, as it would be in all his campaigns, but Lincoln still won the Seventh District by a record majority, the only Whig member elected from Illinois. He served a single term in the House of Representatives, from late 1847 until 1849, where he met John Quincy Adams just before that great man died. Lincoln joined in the Whig attack on President James K. Polk's problematic role in instigating the Mexican War, but this failed to carry over into an advance in Lincoln's political career as the assault failed in face of popular enthusiasm for Polk's expansionism and territorial annexations. To close the political gap in the 1848 presidential election, the Whigs nominated General Zachary Taylor, hero of the Mexican War they had opposed. Lincoln urged Taylor, whose views were both shallow and unknown, to adopt a nationalist Whig ideology that he and others were promoting, but in this he failed. The Whig Party thus broke apart in following years, along sectional lines and over the issue of "free soil," paralleling the deep sectional fissures that began to yawn ever more widely.

Lincoln and Slavery

Lincoln first attracted some national attention as a result of a speech he delivered on September 12, 1848, in Worcester, Massachusetts, in which he proclaimed opposition to the expansion of slavery to any new state carved from annexed, former Mexican territory. This was one of those rare, and electorally inspired, occasions prior to 1854 on which Lincoln gave voice to antislavery views. Otherwise, he did not show signs that this issue was dominant in his political thinking nor did he seek or attain a leadership role in the antislavery movement. He accepted the legal and constitutional basis for the institution of slavery, and that Congress therefore could not legislate it out of existence in the slave states, even though he found slavery morally repugnant and opposed to the natural freedom he believed America historically and morally represented. Though he hated slavery his whole life, he was never a fire-eating abolitionist, and prior to the outbreak of the Civil War he sought only to contain slavery to its constitutionally and politically (Missouri Compromise) defined area, where he believed it was destined to wither on the cotton bush within a few decades—an obnoxious anachronism barricaded into the agrarian, southeast corner of an otherwise free labor, and emerging industrial and commercial, nation.

It was the new question that arose in 1848, that of the *expansion* of slavery to territories accruing from the Mexican War, that moved Lincoln more openly into the overt antislavery camp. But as always, he first sought compromise based upon a strict application of reason and law. He proposed legislation that provided for emancipation of all slaves within the District of Columbia, but with full compensation to slave owners by the U.S. Treasury for their lost property. His hopes for passage and reform rested on the assumption that "nearly every man . . .would sell his slaves if he saw that slavery was to be abolished." However, fire-eaters on both sides opposed the plan, with abolitionists objecting to payment to slave owners and slave owners rejecting what they saw as a first step toward legal abolition of slavery in the whole country. Defeated and thus unheralded, and also despairing of the failing fortunes of the Whigs, Lincoln kept his word to serve only one term in Congress. He returned to private life in Springfield where, from 1849 to 1854, he further developed his law practice. He argued cases often before the state Supreme Court, and earned a reputation for both fairness and honesty, and hence the moniker "Honest Old Abe." During this period he again dealt with multiple deaths in his family: his father passed in 1849; Mary's father and grandmother also died that year, aggravating Mary's emotional instability; then Abe and Mary's second son, Edward, died of tuberculosis in February, 1850. Mary gave birth to a third son, clearly planned as a replacement child, William, late in 1850. The Lincoln's had a fourth son, Thomas (nicknamed by Lincoln

"Tadpole," which shortened to "Tad") in 1853. Given such domestic turmoil and the ill-fortune of the Whig Party in Illinois, Lincoln played a small role in the presidential campaign of 1854.

It was the Kansas-Nebraska Act that drew Lincoln back into public life and elevated him to a genuinely national leadership role in the great debate over the future of slavery in America. Passed by Congress in May, 1854, and backed by Stephen A. Douglas, the Kansas-Nebraska Act proposed to open most of the trans-Mississippi region (the northern half of the Louisiana Purchase, constituting much of the western United States) to legal slavery. That vast region was as yet undecided as to statehood or slavery; this proposed expansion of the "slave power" threatened to unravel all prior constitutional compromises and to upset the internal balance of power within the federal union. It was to oppose this great legal change abetting a huge expansion of slavery that Lincoln reengaged in national politics, and on which he delivered the first truly important and also great speech of his life. Before a crowded Whig convention in Winchester, Illinois, Lincoln denounced slavery in general and its territorial expansion in particular, as contrary to the spirit and historical mission of America as a beacon of liberty to a dark, unrepentant and mostly unfree world. As a lawyer, Lincoln understood that the Constitution guaranteed the rights of slave owners rather than slaves. He did not, therefore, argue for radical, immediate abolition of slavery. Instead, he spoke eloquently of opposing its further expansion, through legal and constitutional means such as sustaining the Missouri Compromise and repeal of the Kansas-Nebraska Act. Why? Because slavery was the great corruptor of all American ideals—of self-government, of fair play, and of liberty from exploitation, and freedom from expropriation of the results of one's own labor. On the other hand, Lincoln was still not entirely clear on the question of racial equality. Early in his political career he had opposed extending the franchise to Illinois' small community of free blacks, and had rejected interracial marriage. In these matters he either failed to escape local thinking—a rare thing, given his more usual intellectual independence—or, more likely, he bowed expediently to prejudice as the lesser of political evils, if the only other outcome was his own political defeat. Even so, he now emerged as a clarion voice on the dangerous crisis of sectarian division over slavery the nation had finally engaged.

Most of Lincoln's local and time-bound prejudices were eventually—though perhaps never wholly—overcome by his ongoing self-education, his unusually agile and open mind, and his evolution as a moral and political pragmatist. Whatever he thought in private, Lincoln was always a moral realist when acting in the public realm. He was a politician in the best sense, who sought realistically achievable moral outcomes in a specific historical time and place. Lincoln was no mere abstract moralist, no thundering but ineffective, self-absorbed and also self-important caricature of responsible ethical action that is so common to democratic polities and great moral issues. As William Lee Miller had aptly phrased it: "There would never come a time when Abraham Lincoln abandoned the role of politician, or rose above it to some allegedly higher moral realm. What he did instead as a lifelong politician was to realize that role's fullest moral possibilities." This became even more clear during his 1858 debates with Stephen A. Douglas, exchanges during the Illinois Senate race which elevated Lincoln to top national prominence. Where Douglas made overtly racist appeals to the gathered crowds by proclaiming the ineluctable inequality of blacks, Lincoln reminded listeners of the core American creed that natural rights inhered in all men, rights which were enumerated in the Constitution. To complete his argument he explicitly embraced the credo of the abolitionist movement, that the negro slave was both "a man and a brother." On the other hand, he was not yet prepared to suggest that he or other whites would accept that freed slaves were "politically and socially our equals." Nor did he yet have a solution to the problem, as he saw it, of what to do with African Americans once they were freed.

That was because, while Lincoln did not believe (as Max Weber later argued) that tragedy is the inescapable precursor to moral progress, he took pains to incorporate into his core positions those baser inclinations of his fellow Americans, which promised to set sharp limits to achievable reform. In Lincoln's day, and much later, there remained rank and open racism even among the majority of Northerners who favored abolition. That is why Lincoln supported—for far too long, in the eyes of most modern observers—what he argued was the best pragmatic and humanitarian solution to the real world situation of slavery: resettlement of freed slaves to offshore colonies. He rested this proposal on the view that most white Americans would not accept social, political, or economic equality for freed slaves. Yet, the proposal probably also reflected his lack of social contact with African Americans, free or slave, prior to coming to Washington. In either case, he advanced colonization schemes in several prewar speeches, discussed the idea in cabinet meetings while president, mentioned it in two State of the Union addresses, and argued about it with leading black politicians—who were unanimously and vehemently opposed—in the White House in 1862. Colonization, including deportation, was an idea Lincoln abandoned only once it became obvious that it was impracticable, and perhaps because he was convinced by William Douglas that it was also un-American and immoral. That he changed, even changed utterly, on this issue is best revealed in the following facts: by the time of his assassination, Lincoln publicly abandoned schemes for black colonization; facilitated the enlistment of several hundred thousand free blacks in the Union Army; emancipated Southern

slaves by presidential decree, and followed this up with successful constitutional amendments emancipating all slaves everywhere in the United States, and securing for them freedom and equality in law (though it would take many decades more for these legal rights to be accepted by most whites and realized in daily practice). Lincoln ultimately came to accept that black Americans should remain, and have the same rights and liberties of white Americans in a society that had undergone a "new birth of freedom" and must henceforth evolve as a multiracial country.

But much of that lay in the presidential future. More immediately, Lincoln sought a return to public office, this time as Whig candidate for an Illinois seat in the Senate, which was voted out of the state legislature. He ran as a Whig moderate, not as one of the new radical antislavery Republicans. He tried to straddle all factions in the legislature, accepting the Fugitive Slave Act and failing to publicly renounce rumors of secret support for him by the nativist, anti-immigration and anti-Catholic Know Nothings. Lincoln also courted Democrats who broke with Douglas over the Kansas-Nebraska Act. Lincoln led on the first ballot, forty-five votes to forty-one for the Democrat James Shields, and five for Lyman Trumbull. By the ninth ballot, however, Lincoln's support had fallen to just fifteen votes, with Trumbull gaining thirty-five and a new candidate, the corrupt Governor Joel Madison, taking forty-seven. Lincoln withdrew and tossed his support to Trumbull on the next ballot, in order to stop Madison.

During the late 1850s, Lincoln finally found his moral voice on the slave question, as well as a new vehicle for his personal political ambitions: the Republican Party. He took the lead in founding the Illinois branch of the new Republican Party, at first in opposition to more radical Republicans who represented the full-throated abolitionist wing of the fractured and failed Whig Party. In a key speech in Springfield, Lincoln identified slavery as the singular source of the national crisis. For the first time, he also publicly linked his opposition to the slave power to an implied willingness to use federal force to preserve the integrity of American principles as enshrined in an indissoluble constitutional Union. He thus closed a fiery speech by quoting the old Whig leader and firebrand, Daniel Webster: "Liberty and Union, now and forever, one and inseparable." Like most other Republicans, Lincoln did not easily or quickly formulate a position on the *Dred Scott* case, partly due to its sheer complexity, but in Lincoln's case also from an exceptional reluctance to challenge judicial proceedings. However, it eventually became clear that in overriding state laws and denying citizenship to free blacks anywhere in the country, a legal condition enjoyed in some states since the founding, the *Dred Scott* decision had discarded decades of legal precedent and directly contradicted the Declaration of Independence and the Constitution. Lincoln was stunned, and against all his higher ambitions and instincts for the rule of law, abandoned his long-standing deference to a Supreme Court that had shown itself to be a base political instrument of the slave power.

Lincoln was acclaimed by the Illinois Republican convention, held in Springfield, as the sole choice to run for the U.S. Senate in 1858. In his acceptance speech and later, he painted his opponent, Stephen A. Douglas, as part of a grand conspiracy to nationalize slavery. This was the real significance of the deviant *Dred Scott* decision, he argued, adding ominously that "a house divided against itself cannot stand . . . I believe this government cannot endure, permanently half slave and half free. I do not expect the Union to be dissolved. I do not expect the house to fall. But I do expect it will cease to be divided. It will become all one thing or all the other." Such dramatic rhetoric propelled Lincoln to the front ranks of the national Republican Party, because it anticipated a coming grand and even violent sectional conflict with slave-owner interests. Seven debates followed between Lincoln and Douglas, a reprise of their 1840 argument, but played out on a national stage and at an advanced moment of national crisis. Lincoln used the opportunity to flesh out his developing constitutional and moral arguments, and his principled opposition to the expansion of slavery that nevertheless stopped short of calling for its abolition in the South. He stumbled once more over acceptance of racial equality, in the face of popular and possibly also personal prejudice against that position, and what to do socially and politically with free blacks. Lincoln lost the Illinois Senate race when the Democrats won the State House and its fifty-four Democratic members voted for Douglas, with forty-six Republicans voting for Lincoln. Still, the campaign laid the basis for his bid for the top position on the Republican ticket in the 1860 presidential election, although Lincoln did not yet take himself at all seriously as a candidate for that office, his capacious but well-concealed ego and deep personal ambition notwithstanding.

President Buchanan's Legacy

President James Buchanan (1791–1868), who held the presidential office from 1857 to 1861, was singularly ill-equipped to resolve the escalating national crisis of the late 1850s. In 1855, the argument over slavery had turned violent, starting in "Bleeding Kansas" and continuing through the fanatic John Brown's attack on Harper's Ferry in October 1859. Buchanan had served as minister (ambassador) to Czarist Russia in the 1830s, where he negotiated a commercial treaty which had eluded U.S. diplomats for over thirty years. But he also acted as a rank apologist for the worst features of czarism, including bloody repression of a liberal rebellion in Poland in 1831. In pompous, morally abstract dispatches written without benefit of visiting the areas on which he reported, he defended serfdom in terms akin to his strong support for slavery in America—as ultimately conducive the well-being of serfs and slaves alike, and of society as a whole, and not just the economic interests of landowners. As secretary of state to President Polk, Buchanan helped settle the "Oregon Question" but was also tied to the Mexican War, which split open what became a chasm in American politics by raising the issue of whether to admit new territories as slave-rights or free soil states. He had avoided the divisions of the Kansas-Nebraska Act by the good fortune of his appointment as minister to Great Britain. But as president he had no such luxury. Instead, he watched with utter ineptitude and tragic—for the nation—befuddlement as the great crisis of the later 1850s unfolded, leading to dissolution of the United States in his final months in office, the creation of the Confederate States of America, and thereafter to the awful suffering and carnage of the American Civil War.

On paper, Abraham Lincoln was the most ill qualified major candidate to ever seek the presidency, which he did at the urging of most western Republicans and those eastern Republicans who wished to stop the frontrunner, the former Senator and Governor of New York, William H. Seward. At the age of fifty-one, Lincoln had less than a year's formal schooling and little experience in Washington, and was one of the youngest men to seek the White House to that point. He had never held a major government post or administrative office, not even as mayor of a small town. He was poor and came from an inconsequential family. For the prior decade, he had been out of public office and he had lost the last two senatorial elections in Illinois. Having spent thirty years running hard from his impoverished, rail-splitting youth, Lincoln embraced the legend of his tough physicality and log cabin origins as politically useful, which it proved to be both among delegates to the Republican Convention in Chicago and with the voting public. Seward (whom Lincoln would later name to his cabinet as secretary of state) won the first ballot by 173 ½ votes to Lincoln's 102 (with 233 needed to win). The second ballot gave Seward 184 ½ to Lincoln's 181. Lincoln passed Seward on the third ballot, surging to 231 ½ votes. He went over the top when four Ohio delegates switched from a third candidate (Salmon P. Chase, longtime bitter rival of Seward) to Lincoln, precipitating a rush that gave him a final total of 364 out of 466 delegates. As was then tradition, Lincoln did not actively campaign during the general election, but Republicans held huge rallies in the major Northern cities for their ticket of Lincoln and Hannibal Hamlin, shouting out "For Lincoln and Liberty Too." That most Republicans also opposed anti-immigration laws helped secure a crucial share of the foreign-born vote. When it was over, Lincoln secured a plurality of less than 40 percent of the popular vote, as the Democratic Party (and the country) split along sectional lines. The vote count was 1,866,452 for Lincoln to 1,376,957 for Douglas, 849,781 for John C. Breckinridge, and 588,879 for John Bell. In the Electoral College, Lincoln won 180 votes to 72 for Breckinridge, 39 for Bell, and just 12 for Douglas.

News of Lincoln's election enraged the South. Within two weeks, South Carolina and Georgia authorized state conventions to consider secession. Within a month, the movement spread to eight Southern states. Buchanan remained inert and inept as the country split apart, neither envisioning nor offering any solution to secession. As President-elect, Lincoln remained quiet, suspecting that the secessionists were merely bluffing. He grew a beard, assembled his cabinet, and watched events unfold as he waited for formal elevation by the Electoral College on February 13, 1861. He was convinced that there was a quiet majority of Unionists, many former Whigs and political comrades, in the South. Events proved him woefully wrong on that score: South Carolina seceded from the Union on December 20, 1860. It was followed by Mississippi (January 9, 1861), Florida (January 10), Alabama (January 11), Georgia (January 19), Louisiana (January 26), and Texas (February 1). Representatives of six of these seven states gathered in Montgomery, Alabama. They enacted a constitution and declared an independent Southern republic, the Confederate States of America, on February 8th, immediately setting up a provisional government to rival and oppose Washington. As early as January 9th, Confederate hot-heads fired on reinforcements heading for the Federal garrison at Ft. Sumter. Lincoln opposed all suggested appeasement schemes, instead considering the rebellion to lie outside the law and in forfeit of a natural right to revolution because of the core immorality of its cause. For Lincoln, the moral and legal promise and superiority of the Union trumped and predated even the Constitution. The Union had been forged in the War of Independence upon the promise of the Declaration of Independence that all men had a natural right to liberty. Reinforcing this bedrock conviction was his uncompromising opposition to expansion of slavery into new regions of the West, the platform on which he and the Republicans had stood and were elected. Lincoln did not keep company with those who proposed to end slavery in the South, rents in the national fabric and likely civil war be damned. Nevertheless, he was perceived as such by many in the South, who failed to appreciate his refined and careful legal language and his instinctive search for a pragmatic compromise that might avert civil war.

Lincoln traveled to his inauguration in Washington by slow train, stopping frequently to stoke support for the Union and the policies he intended to implement. He was warned by Alan Pinkerton of an assassination plot, and agreed to pass through Baltimore at night and in disguise in a sleeping car as an invalid passenger. He thus arrived unheralded in Washington, in the still of night. Ten days later, on March 4, Lincoln was sworn in and delivered his First Inaugural Address. In it, he called upon both sides to reach for "the better angels of our nature." The call fell on Southern ears deafened by cries for secession and the thunderous expectation of war. The next day, Lincoln was presented with an urgent request to resupply or relieve a small federal garrison at Fort Sumter, an island outpost in the harbor of Charleston, South Carolina. It was his moral desire as well as a deep political need not to have federal forces fire the first shots, to avoid playing the part of aggressor should war come despite his best efforts to prevent it and his hope that it would not. Supported by a majority of his cabinet, Lincoln ordered a naval expedition to sail on April 6th in relief of Fort Sumter, knowing that this would likely provoke open fighting. It did: secessionist fire-eaters bombarded Fort Sumter on April 12th. The assault gave Lincoln clear maneuvering room to call, on April 15th, for a volunteer army of 75,000 to suppress the rebellion. In the short-term, his call to arms by the North provoked a deeper crisis, as a second wave of four more slave states seceded: Virginia (April 17), Arkansas (May 6), North Carolina (May 20), and Tennessee (June 8). That brought eleven states into open rebellion and completed membership of the CSA, which moved its capital to Richmond. Four slave states, Delaware, Maryland, Kentucky, and Missouri, remained or were forcibly held in the Union. Later, free soil West Virginia seceded from pro-slavery Virginia and was accepted into the Union. But already, within five weeks of Lincoln's inauguration, the American Civil War was underway.

Foreign Policy: The Union Forever

The national crisis surrounding Lincoln's inauguration was a rare moment, a time of potentially fatal division in the affairs of a great but still unstable nation, and of the radical idea that free men could govern themselves without producing anarchy. Fortunately, the ethics of political responsibility and of moral intention combined in the inspired leadership of an American president singularly capable of continuing personal growth, both in office and as a politician and statesman of acute moral sensibility. For Lincoln, the crucial moment came when he took the oath of office to "preserve, protect and defend" the Constitution and the Union, even as the Union was being rent asunder by the rabid response of Southerners to his lifelong commitment to territorial containment of slavery. That is why Lincoln made the decision to embrace war in 1861, once the South insisted upon and started the armed conflict. This was the single most important decision ever made by an American president. What was its motivation? Lincoln wrote in 1862: "My paramount object in this struggle is to save the Union, and is not either to save or to destroy slavery. If I could save the Union without freeing any slave, I would do it; and if I could save it by freeing all the slaves, I would do it; and if I could do it by freeing some and leaving others alone, I would also do that." Yet, the Union was threatened solely by division over slavery, meaning that the two questions—of slavery and union—were conjoined at all their vital points. After Fort Sumter, Lincoln could not save one without killing the other. The country might not survive the deep cutting that had to be done, but Lincoln understood that neither could it live any longer as it had been born, half-slave and half-free. Yet, for all that, Lincoln did not believe in an overly powerful executive. He cleaved to the old Whig tradition, unlike that of tyrants like Andrew Jackson, which favored a weak executive and a strong Congress: Lincoln seldom interfered in congressional matters, and he used the veto power carefully and infrequently.

As Lincoln groped to assemble a cabinet and install effective government in the midst of national crisis and expanding civil war, he made a major mistake: he declared a Union blockade against Southern ports. In terms of international law and practice this contradicted his official theory of the war as a wholly domestic conflict and affair. It unintentionally elevated the CSA to the status of belligerent, which gave the South rights of international commerce and to wage war at sea that were immediately recognized by Great Britain, France, and other maritime and naval powers. Foreign powers extended this limited recognition on the basis of new maritime law codified in the Declaration of Paris of 1856, which the United States had declined to sign. The alternative to a formal, *de jure* blockade was to impose a *de facto* blockade without actually declaring one *de jure*, by proclamation the legal fiction that all Southern ports were henceforth placed under a total embargo. Lincoln was rescued from serious confrontation with Great Britain, as he was again during the Trent Affair, by his own sense of prudence, but also by Secretary of State William Seward, a shrewd and able, if overly ambitious and sometimes insubordinate, statesman and cabinet minister. In addition, the British saw future value in a principal historical neutral shifting toward the more expansive British view of naval power in wartime. This change in American maritime foreign policy would pay Great Britain huge dividends during the two world wars of the twentieth century. Lincoln's error carried potential for a naval confrontation with Great Britain. It also led to reversal of the traditional doctrine upheld by both countries on maritime rights. The British now enunciated and defended the rights of neutrals, which as the dominant naval power, it had hitherto and always sought to sharply limit. Meanwhile, the United States suffered the travails of Confederate privateering, abetted by the British and French, a method of war at sea Americans had previously relied upon to supplement a weak peacetime Navy. The damages done to Union commerce by the depredations carried out by the *C.S.S. Alabama*, a Confederate commerce raider built in Great Britain, and other CSA ships fighting as privateers, was considerable. The fact that these ships found sanctuary and supplies in European ports was a point of diplomatic aggravation throughout the war, and not fully resolved until the "Alabama claims" settlement clauses of the Treaty of Washington signed with Great Britain in 1870.

The core diplomatic question of the Civil War was international recognition of the CSA. This depended, in the final analysis, on whether or not Confederate armies could sustain *de facto* independence in arms long enough for *de jure* status to be accepted internationally. Lesser status as a formal belligerent gave the CSA certain rights to wage war, including purchasing warships and guns from European nations, but this did not imply recognition as an independent nation. The clash between Lincoln's view of the rebellion and its international status in law, stemming from the error of the blockade decision, led to the gravest international crisis of the war. Generally known as the Trent Affair, this diplomatic dispute came close to provoking war with Great Britain, which might have in turn allowed the CSA to break away, just as French and Dutch intervention had aided the independence of the United States during the Revolutionary War. A Union warship intercepted a British mail steamer, the *Trent*, on the high seas off the Bahamas in August, 1861, and illegally seized two Confederate "diplomats" who were onboard. Britain reacted with profound anger to this "insult to the flag." The Royal Navy prepared its squadrons for war and some 8,000 troops were sent on transports to Halifax. All of Europe backed the British interpretation of the affair, including Russia, which otherwise was the most pro-Union (if also distant and detached) of the Great Powers. Given Seward's pronounced tendency to bluster in the face of British threats to recognize the CSA, Lincoln had already begun to consult on foreign policy with the more even-tempered Charles Sumner. Lincoln did not want to appear to be bullied by Great Britain, and looked for a face-saving solution. But once the full extent of British anger became clear, Lincoln shifted his position. In private, he told Seward: "One war at a time." The war cabinet also came around, reluctantly but unanimously, to the view that the United States must bend and release the prisoners. At a cabinet meeting held on Christmas Day, 1861, when it was clear that Britain intended war if its ultimatum for return of the diplomats was not met, Lincoln and his government agreed to hand over the two Confederates to British custody.

A second crisis with Great Britain, and to a lesser extent with France, developed toward the end of 1862. Following the Union loss at Second Bull Run (August 29–30, 1862), the British cabinet concluded that the North could not win the war and offered to mediate a peace settlement. Together with France, where Napoleon III was eager for intervention to divide the United States and thereby sustain his military misadventure in Mexico, the British prepared a mediation offer. However, in the interim, Robert E. Lee had invaded the North only to be turned back after a bloody fight at

Antietam (September 17, 1862). This gave the British pause, and they backed away from further antagonizing the North by seeming to come to the diplomatic aid of the South with an untimely offer of mediation. Napoleon III, however, pressed the issue of recognition hard even after Antietam. However, he was not strong enough to recognize the CSA without support from Great Britain. Napoleon tried to obtain cooperation from Russia and Britain for simultaneous recognition of the CSA, but neither government accepted his proposal. The British were already more cautious about the military prospects of the CSA, while the Russians had little desire to see a growing American counterweight to the British Empire broken apart and weakened. In February, 1863, Napoleon openly offered a more friendly mediation proposal to Washington. Lincoln and Seward emphatically rejected the offer, as they did all other international efforts to mediate what they insisted was solely an internal American affair. By the middle of 1863, British and French domestic opinion about recognition grew more divided, as the American Civil War took on more clearly the character of a campaign to end slavery in addition to preserving the Union. Also, from 1863 the French were too heavily occupied with a failing military effort in Mexico to seriously contemplate intervention in the great war being fought north of the Rio Grande. On the other hand, there was nothing Lincoln could do about French (and Spanish) attempts to take advantage of America's bloody division to return to empire in North America. The task of scaring the French out of Mexico fell instead to Lincoln's Vice President and successor, Andrew Johnson, who later sent 50,000 Union veterans to "demonstrate" along the border after the Civil War ended.

Beyond the major crises with Great Britain and France, the two Great Powers who most favored the Southern cause and whose elites looked to break-up the United States, foreign policy did not occupy much of Lincoln's time or attention. The majority of nations remained friendly to the Union and none recognized the Confederacy. Russia sent two fleets to winter in American ports, one in New York and the other in San Francisco. This was misinterpreted by many Unionists as an indication of Russian support for the Northern cause, when in fact it was an effort by Russia to keep its fleets out of the reach of the Royal Navy during a crisis over Poland. Otherwise, Russia remained a detached Great Power concentrating on its own internal problems, most notably emancipation of the serfs. Absorbed with daily conduct of the war, Lincoln left daily tedium of diplomatic exchanges and meetings to Secretary of State Seward, intervening only in matters of true international crisis. There were minor exceptions to this pattern. Lincoln struck up an odd correspondence with the King of Siam, who first wrote to express support for the Union (and in the hope of gaining American support for the continued independence of his country in face of European imperialism in southeast

Asia). On one other matter Lincoln struck out on his own, in his first State of the Union message delivered to Congress on December 3, 1861. Openly repudiating the foreign policy of several past Democratic administrations, he called for diplomatic recognition of the only two black republics, Haiti and Liberia.

Despite occasional missteps, overall Lincoln proved a quick study and ultimately also a sound wartime president and strategist. He understood well before most that critical advantages enjoyed by the Union in industry and manpower dictated an offensive war, just as he understood that political and diplomatic superiority would not be sustainable unless the rebel armies were beaten in the field. He was also an excellent judge of character, though he was not always in a position to act on his perceptions. At the start of the war, Lincoln was afflicted with excessively cautious generals, especially in the eastern theater of operations. Such men headed his armies by virtue of formal training at West Point, or simple seniority, or because they were influential at the state level where most regiments were raised and maintained. Lincoln thus once bitterly remarked: "If [General George B.] McClellan is not using the Army [of the Potomac], I should like to borrow it for a while." From 1862 to the middle of 1863, Lincoln and the Union suffered dark days of successive Confederate victories, conjoined with serious threats of foreign intervention and Northern moral division or exhaustion. Lincoln therefore rejoiced not just over victories won by more determined commanders in the western theater, but also over the toughness and even the clear-eyed ruthlessness shown by a former Democrat, Ulysses S. Grant and other western generals. A few months after Grant's victory at Vicksburg (July 4, 1863), Lincoln brought him east to assume overall command of all Union armies, and to prosecute the war to a ruthless but victorious finish. When straightlaced Christian gentlemen in the cabinet objected to Grant's reputation for drunkenness, Lincoln is said to have shot back: "Find out what he drinks, and send a case to each of my generals."

The important error of the blockade aside, Lincoln's insistent view of the war as an internal rebellion guided his foreign policy throughout the conflict. He consistently refused any direct negotiations with the CSA because in his view it did not exist as a legal or moral entity. For the same reason, he deflected all foreign attempts to mediate a truce or arrange a peace treaty with the rebel states. At a legal extreme, Lincoln regarded the eleven states of the CSA as still full members of the Union, whose citizens enjoyed full rights under the Constitution. That meant, prior to his Emancipation Proclamation and later, the formal amendment of the Constitution to ban slavery, even Southern slave-holders retained a right to their slaves as "property." However, starting in 1862 lists of dead or gravely wounded sons, brothers, husbands, and fathers grew to astonishing length in Northern newspapers. Anger toward the slave power that started this awful war also grew around the hearths of Northern households, and in pews and town halls from Maine to Pennsylvania. The strategic logic and moral demand to redefine the war as a moral crusade for emancipation, to make it a war for liberty as well as union, grew inexorable. Lincoln timed his Emancipation Proclamation (preliminary draft on September 23, 1862, and formal proclamation on January 1, 1863) to speak to this rising mood that saw the war as a redemptive national act, but also to advance the diplomatic effect in Europe of the Union victory at Antietam (September 17, 1862), which in fact was closer to a bloody draw. By freeing slaves initially solely in secessionist territory Lincoln aimed to hurt the CSA economy without inspiring additional secession by the slave states which remained in the Union. In also appealing to popular antislavery opinion in Europe (huge crowds celebrating the Proclamation took to the streets in British and French cities), by converting the Civil War into a crusade for universal freedom as well as against internal rebellion, Lincoln undercut those in high office in London and Paris who wished to intervene diplomatically, or even militarily, to divide and weaken the United States and prevent its emergence as a rival to their own empires.

Lincoln's domestic life was troubled during his White House years by Mary's increasingly moody and erratic behavior. A crisis was reached in early 1863, when two of the Lincoln boys, Willie and Tad, came down with "bilious fever." Lincoln sat up with his ill children every night for two weeks, but Willie finally slipped away on February 20th. Lincoln broke down and cried openly, even as he sat still vigil with Tad. The funeral was held in the White House, after which Lincoln shut himself away in a small room for hours every day, privately sobbing over his lost son and lingering sorrows. It may have been at this time that Lincoln sought solace in contemplation of the divine. It was a new mode of religious thinking for him that clearly affected his speech and writing to the end of his presidency, though he never converted to conventional Christian beliefs or became a churchgoer. Lincoln slowly came to terms with the death of a second son, as he dealt also with the hundreds of thousands of deaths all around for which he bore a measure of moral responsibility. Mary Lincoln could not do the same. She collapsed, overwhelmed by grief. Unable to attend the funeral or even to look after Tad, she took to bed for three weeks. Afterward, she never entered the room where Willie died. Lincoln hired a personal nurse to care for Mary, who temporarily abandoned her secret, spendthrift ways. For over a year the White House, too, ceased to host any social functions. In 1864, Mary's hysterical worrying shifted to the eldest boy, Robert, who wanted to enlist upon graduating from Harvard. Grant solved the problem by taking the young man onto his staff.

In deceptively plain speech, throughout his presidency Lincoln gave voice to the highest ideals of American statehood and civilization. Nowhere was this more clearly done than when consecrating the Union cemetery and battlefield at Gettysburg, in November 1863, or in his justly famed Second Inaugural Address. The short address at Gettysburg captured the essence of his presidency and the deeper meaning of the Civil War:

> It is for us the living . . . to be dedicated here to the unfinished work which they who fought here have thus far so nobly advanced . . . to be here dedicated to the great task remaining before us, that from these honored dead we take increased devotion to that cause for which they gave the last full measure of devotion, that we here highly resolve that these dead shall not have died in vain, that this nation, under God, shall have a new birth of freedom and that government of the people, by the people, for the people, shall not perish from the earth.

Legacy

Even before Grant's several Union armies encircled Richmond and final victory drew near in the spring of 1865, Lincoln took the last step into greatness: he persuaded Congress and the states to pass the Thirteenth Amendment abolishing slavery everywhere in the United States as of January 31, 1865. Through four years of war that killed over 620,000 Americans (still more than in all other U.S. wars combined), Lincoln's deeply principled yet pragmatic idealism both saved the nation and freed a race. In saving the country, Lincoln also remade it.

Lincoln hoped and planned for a tolerant, forgiving Reconstruction "with malice toward none and charity for all." It was not to be: six days after the surrender of Lee's Army of Northern Virginia on April 9, 1865, Abraham Lincoln, too, gave "the last full measure of devotion" to his great cause and country. He was shot in the head at Ford's Theater in Washington by John Wilkes Booth. A tragic victim of a conspiracy of misfit, unreconstructed Confederates, Lincoln lingered through the night, then died. His funeral train retraced much of his clandestine journey to Washington four years earlier, but this time the 1,600-mile route was lined by hundreds of thousands of admirers and mourners. Lincoln's deeply principled yet pragmatic idealism while president preserved both liberty and union, and finally slew the serpent of slavery that had despoiled the moral idealism of the New World since before the founding of the United States. After Lincoln, and in great measure because of him, the brittle iron of a young country hammered into a misshapen vessel in Philadelphia in 1789, which therefore broke apart in 1861, reemerged from the forge of civil war as tempered steel: "a new nation, conceived in Liberty, and dedicated to the proposition that all men are created equal." Lincoln, the man and the president, should be recalled not only as a great statesman but as the master moral thinker of the American political tradition. That lesser men and women did not achieve as much in the years and decades that followed does not diminish the magnitude, or the magnanimity, of Lincoln's accomplishment.

Cathal J. Nolan

Chronology

1861

January 9–26: Mississippi, Florida, Alabama, Georgia, and Louisiana, secede from the Union.

February 1: Texas secedes from the Union.

February 4: Six Southern states form the Confederate States of America (CSA).

February 19: Alexander II, of Russia, emancipates the serfs.

March 2: Morrill Tariff raises duties on manufactured imports.

March 4: Lincoln takes oath of office.

April 13: Fort Sumter taken by Confederate forces.

July 21: CSA wins First Battle of Bull Run (First Manassas).

October 31: Convention of London between Britain, France, Spain, and Mexico.

November–December: Trent Affair

December 17: Veracruz occupied by British, French, and Spanish troops.

1862

April 6–7: Grant wins Battle of Shiloh.

July 31: Confederate commerce raider Alabama permitted to leave Britain.

September 17: Battle of Antietam: tactical draw but political victory for Lincoln.

September 22: Otto von Bismarck appointed prime minister of Prussia.

September 23: Lincoln issues preliminary Emancipation Proclamation.

November 1: Napoleon III proposes Britain, France, and Russia mediate U.S. Civil War.

December 13–15: CSA wins Battle of Fredericksburg.

1863

January 1: Lincoln issues full Emancipation Proclamation.

January 22: Russian troops put down Polish uprising.

February 6: Secretary of State Seward rejects French mediation offers.

May 1–3: CSA wins Battle of Chancellorsville.

June 7: French troops occupy Mexico City.

July 1–3: Meade wins three-day Battle of Gettysburg.

July 4: Vicksburg surrenders to Grant after sustained siege.

September 5: Britain agrees cease ship sales to the CSA.

September 18–20: CSA wins Battle of Chickamauga.

August 11: Cambodia becomes French protectorate.

November. 23–25: Union wins Battle of Chattanooga.

1864

April 4: House protests French actions in Mexico.

May 5: Sherman begins march to Atlanta and on to Savannah

September 5–8: U.S., British, Dutch, and French warships fire upon Japanese fortress of Shimonoseki.

September 23: *Bakufu* opens Yokohama and Inland Sea to foreign trade.

October 19: United States protests Confederate raids launched from Canadian (British) territory.

November 8: Lincoln is reelected president.

September–December: Union armies besiege Richmond and Petersburg, Virginia.

1865

January–March: Union armies press siege of Richmond and Petersburg.

April 9: Lee surrenders to Grant at Appomattox Court House.

April 14: President Lincoln dies; Andrew Johnson sworn in as president.

May: Final Confederate surrender in the Trans-Mississippi Region; Civil War ends.

References and Further Reading

Donald, David. *Lincoln.* New York: Simon and Schuster, 1995.

McPherson, James. *Battle Cry of Freedom.* New York: Oxford University Press, 1988.

Miller, William Lee. *Lincoln's Virtues: An Ethical Biography.* New York: Alfred A. Knopf, 2002.

Oates, Stephen B. *With Malice Toward None.* New York: Harper Perennial, 1977.

Andrew Johnson (1865–1869)

Early Life and Political Career

Andrew Johnson was born in a log cabin in Raleigh, capital city of North Carolina, on December 29, 1808. He was the second surviving child of Jacob and Mary Johnson, a landless and illiterate couple who earned their livings working odd jobs around the tiny capital. Tragically, just a few days after saving three of his townsmen from drowning, Jacob died suddenly when Andrew was only three. His mother was too poor to afford him a private education, and there were no public schools available, so Andrew never received a day of proper schooling in his life. From childhood, then, Andrew occupied a relatively low rung on the social ladder in an area dominated by the aristocratic planter class. His resentment of them became a lifelong fixation. Still, such "poor white trash," as he and his family were scornfully called, were not the lowest of the low in the antebellum South. That distinction was of course reserved for blacks, whether slave or free, and the young Andrew acquired the (all too common) belief in white supremacy that he carried with him all the way to the White House.

In 1818, Andrew followed in his older brother William's footsteps and became apprenticed to a local tailor in Raleigh. He was taught to read and write while apprenticed, during which time he also learned to love politics and oratory through his exposure to the many debates on local politics held at the shop. Having gotten into trouble for some juvenile vandalism in 1823, however, the fifteen-year-old Johnson and his brother ran away from Raleigh and their apprenticeships. After living and working as a tailor in South Carolina for two years, Johnson finally settled down in Greeneville, Tennessee, in 1826. A year later, he married Eliza McCardle, a shoemaker's daughter, and opened his own tailor shop. Interestingly, the justice of the peace who performed the marriage ceremony was Mordecai Lincoln, first cousin of Abraham's father. Andrew and Eliza had their first child in 1828, going on to have three sons and two daughters in all.

As his tailoring business began to thrive, Johnson increasingly participated in local public debates and soon became sufficiently well known that he was elected an alderman of Greeneville in 1829. In 1834, he was the Board of Aldermen's choice for mayor, and the following year, at age twenty-seven, he was elected without party affiliation to the Tennessee state legislature in Nashville. By 1839, Johnson

Andrew Johnson forced France out of Mexico but was nearly forced from office for his attempts at reconciliation with the defeated South. (Library of Congress)

had officially come out as a Democrat, and he earned a statewide reputation during the following year's presidential contest by campaigning throughout Tennessee for Martin Van Buren, who was ultimately defeated by William Henry Harrison. Nevertheless, capitalizing on his new fame, Johnson ran successfully for state senate in 1841, and United States House of Representatives in 1843. His steady climb up the political ladder from penniless tailor had finally taken him to Washington.

Once in the halls of Congress, Johnson, always defensively proud of his humble origins, became known as a tireless advocate for the rights of the poor against what he considered to be an overbearing aristocracy. In introducing his Homestead Bill in 1846, which gave every willing poor man 160 acres of free land, he revealed his Jeffersonian view of the nobility of the small (white) farmer, which shaped much of his congressional career. At the same time, Johnson never faltered in his defense of slavery. Indeed Johnson himself, by then a wealthy proprietor and landowner, eventually came to own some eight or nine slaves. He also revealed at this time the expansionism that was a major pillar of his foreign policy as president. Debate was raging over the annexation of Texas and soon thereafter over war with Mexico—two policies that Johnson ardently supported.

In 1853, Johnson turned his attention back to Tennessee, where he was elected governor. The governorship was largely ceremonial, but it did hold one distinct advantage for an ambitious politician: exposure. After two terms as governor, then, Johnson ran successfully for United States Senate in 1857. He returned to a Washington that was very different from the one he had left in 1853. Sectional tensions had risen to a fever pitch after the Kansas-Nebraska Act of 1854, and Johnson was placed in the increasingly awkward position of being a Southerner who was both proslavery and pro-Union. During the secession crisis of 1860, Johnson argued passionately that secession was unconstitutional, especially in light of Lincoln's fair election, and that the South ought to fight for its principles from *within* the Union. Moreover, his Jeffersonian-Jacksonian philosophy further informed his pro-Union stance: "I have an unshaken confidence," he told his fellow senators in December 1860 in words that both recalled Jackson and anticipated Lincoln, "in man's capability to govern himself. I will not give up this Government that is now called an experiment . . . . In the language of the departed Jackson, let us exclaim that the Union, 'the Federal Union, it must be preserved.'" Johnson was hailed as a genuine patriot throughout the North, while he was excoriated in most of the South.

Once his home state of Tennessee seceded in June 1861, Johnson returned to Washington to take his seat in the Senate—the only senator from a seceding state to do so. President Lincoln rewarded his loyalty by appointing him military governor of Tennessee, a state that in 1862 was largely (though far from wholly) under Union occupation. The governor succeeded, albeit after several delays, in creating a new civil government for the state, and in 1864 Lincoln asked Johnson to be his running mate in his upcoming bid for reelection. Despite his former defense of slavery, by this time Johnson was endorsing emancipation by constitutional amendment; he blamed aristocratic secessionists for their own misfortune and even went so far as to call slavery "a cancer on our society." He continued to believe fully, however, in government by white men alone—one of many positions he held that, during his presidency, led to bitter clashes with the Republican Congress and ultimately to his impeachment in 1868.

The Lincoln-Johnson ticket was triumphant in 1864. Johnson, feeling under the weather on inauguration day in March 1865; took some whiskey—three full glasses of the stuff—to make himself feel better before the ceremony. Needless to say, the intoxicated vice president-elect embarrassed himself by making a rambling and half-coherent speech that left little doubt as to his state of inebriation. But life would soon become much more serious. Only weeks later, on April 14, 1865, Abraham Lincoln was shot in the back of the head by John Wilkes Booth while attending a play with his wife at Ford's Theatre. Johnson, who had gone to bed early that night, was awakened by a friend at 10:15 with news of the shooting. Lincoln died the following morning at 7:22 a.m., and Andrew Johnson became the seventeenth president of the United States several hours later.

The Lincoln Legacy

Every aspect of Abraham Lincoln's tenure in office was dominated by the Civil War, and foreign policy was no exception. The primary foreign policy objective of Lincoln and his secretary of state, William Seward, was to prevent recognition of and intervention on behalf of the Confederacy by the two most powerful countries in Europe, Britain and France. Jefferson Davis, president of the Confederacy, was confident that he could win such recognition, especially after Britain and France took the initial steps of recognizing a state of war between the Northern and Southern states and declaring their neutrality. The Lincoln-Seward team, however, was able to use a combination of diplomacy and military victories to prevent this eventuality. On the diplomatic end, for example, Lincoln wisely decided to release two imprisoned Confederate agents that a Union captain had plucked illegally off the Europe-bound British mail ship *Trent*. The insulted British protested by sending 8,000 troops steaming toward North America. Lincoln concluded that "one war at a time" was enough, and complied with the British demand that the two be released. Militarily, the Union victory at Antietam in 1862 proved a turning point in the war, not just because it allowed Lincoln to issue his preliminary Emancipation Proclamation, but also because it forestalled a mediation proposal from the European powers based on Southern independence that Seward almost certainly would have rejected, a rejection that might have led to the intervention of Britain and France.

Tensions with Britain and France did not entirely disappear after Antietam. Over U.S. protests, the British had repeatedly violated their neutrality laws by permitting the building of raider ships for the Confederacy by British shipyards. The most notable of these were the *Alabama, Florida,* and *Shenandoah,* which together burned and sank over 250 Union merchant ships. The British finally ceased such construction under threat of war from the United States, but tensions over what came to be known as the Alabama Claims long outlived the Lincoln administration. The French, meanwhile, had occupied Mexico City in 1863 as part of an expedition ostensibly aimed at reclaiming unpaid debts.

When Napoleon III named Austrian Archduke Maximilian as emperor of Mexico in 1864, a flagrant violation of the Monroe Doctrine, Lincoln's government registered no formal protest. Though Lincoln continued to recognize the deposed Benito Juárez as the legitimate ruler of Mexico, neither he nor Seward wished to provoke France into recognition of the Confederacy by demanding a French withdrawal. The problem of the French puppet regime in Mexico was to be resolved not by Lincoln, but by his vice president and successor, Andrew Johnson.

Foreign Policy

One of Johnson's first decisions as president was to retain Lincoln's cabinet, which prominently included Secretary of State William Seward. In late May 1865, Johnson and Seward came to an agreement whereby Seward was essentially given a free hand to continue to conduct U.S. foreign policy. As president, Johnson reserved the right to make final decisions, but the details were left mainly to Seward. The two men agreed on some fundamental principles: Both thirsted for U.S. territorial expansion at a time when most of the country was more interested in repairing the wounds wrought by the Civil War. Add to the lack of support for expansionism in the country as a whole the venomous relations between the executive and legislative branches during Johnson's administration, and it is easy to see why Johnson and Seward failed in almost all their major attempts to acquire new territory. There is one notable exception to this rule: the purchase of Alaska from Russia in 1867. Perhaps Johnson's only other noteworthy foreign policy success was getting the French out of Mexico without U.S. troops having to fire a shot.

Mexico: The Monroe Doctrine Preserved

When he accepted the nomination for vice president in 1864, Johnson, though of course he had no idea that he would be commander in chief so shortly after the Civil War, promised to "attend to this Mexican affair" once the war was over—even if it meant using force. General Ulysses S. Grant was of the same mind. Indeed, the day after taking Lee's surrender at Appomattox, he declared to his staff, "Now for Mexico!" Grant himself soon ordered over 50,000 U.S. troops to the border with Johnson's tacit approval. Seward, however, did not want war with France and was convinced that diplomatic pressure alone would be sufficient. The more experienced statesman prevailed on Johnson to stay Grant's hand, pending further diplomatic efforts. The French asked for U.S. recognition of Maximilian in exchange for a French military withdrawal, but Seward responded in November 1865 that to recognize the overthrow of a republican government in the Western Hemisphere by a European-backed monarchy would be in direct opposition to the basic principles of U.S. foreign policy. At the same time, Johnson was growing increasingly impatient with Seward's lack of progress, and the president came close to taking over the whole matter and ordering a more aggressive policy. Thereafter, Seward took a markedly firmer tone with the French. The ratcheted-up pressure from the United States finally combined with armed resistance from supporters of Juárez and the threat of war with Prussia at home to convince Napoleon to withdraw his forces. Maximilian foolishly decided to stay and defend his throne against a resistance that had previously been held at bay only by French power, and the erstwhile emperor was captured and executed by firing squad in June 1867.

It should be noted that throughout this episode, Johnson and Seward were under considerable pressure from hawkish Republicans to take immediate military action to overthrow Maximilian and expel the French, but Johnson persisted in allowing Seward to work his diplomatic channels, though all the while prodding him to be tougher. By so doing, he was able to achieve the desired result without resorting to a war with France. That result was an impressive victory for the Monroe Doctrine. For the first time in its history, the United States actually had both the will and the power to enforce Monroe's famous declaration that no European power was to be allowed to colonize or interfere in the affairs of any nation in the Western Hemisphere. Not only had the principles associated with the Monroe Doctrine been preserved, they had also been irrevocably strengthened.

Alaska: "Johnson's Polar Bear Garden"

Johnson and Seward wished not only to preserve republicanism where it existed in the Western Hemisphere, they also wished to expand it. A golden opportunity to do so appeared in early 1867 when the Russian minister to the United States, Edouard de Stoeckl, fully aware of Johnson and Seward's expansionism, began to signal to Seward that he was interested in discussing the future of Alaska (then called Russian-America). In reality, the Russians, seeing Alaska as an unprofitable and indefensible mass of land, had decided in December 1866 to seek out a buyer. The logical customer was the United States; Russia sought to strengthen the Americans as a geopolitical counterweight to the British. Moreover, the Russians knew there was gold in Alaska (though they did not have the means or the patience to find it), and they were convinced that once Americans learned of the possibility of finding gold, they would flock to Alaska and take it over as they had Texas. Johnson gave Seward the approval to go ahead with talks, and he and Stoeckl met to discuss the matter on March 8, 1867. Seward first inquired whether it might be possible for the United States to gain trade and fishing concessions in Alaska; Stoeckl replied in the negative. The secretary of state then asked whether the Russians were willing to sell the territory

A painting depicts the signing of the treaty for the purchase of Alaska in 1867. (Bettmann/Corbis)

outright, and this time Stoeckl replied more favorably. The two agreed on a price of $7 million—$2 million more than Seward had initially offered and than Stoeckl had been instructed to accept at minimum.

On the evening of March 29, Stoeckl called upon Seward to inform him that the Tsar had cabled his approval of the deal, and that he would be delighted to write up the formal treaty the following day. Seward exclaimed, "Why wait till tomorrow, Mr. Stoeckl? Let us make the treaty tonight!" Off they went to the State Department, and at 4:00 a.m. on March 30, 1867, the two signed the treaty. Initially, the U.S. press viewed Alaska as worthless frozen tundra and ridiculed the unratified purchase as "Seward's Folly," or "Johnson's Polar Bear Garden." Undaunted, Seward praised the rich fish, fur, and lumber resources there, as well as pointing out that it would be an insult to Russia, a friendly power, not to follow through on the treaty. Johnson made a less mundane argument, proclaiming, "The acquisition of Alaska was made with a view of extending national jurisdiction and republican principles in the American hemisphere." Indeed, Johnson and Seward believed that a U.S. Alaska would not only rid North America of one more Old World monarchy, it would also be a significant step toward hemming Canada in, prying it away from Britain, and

bringing it into the arms of the United States. Still, it was the support of Charles Sumner, fierce enemy of the administration and chairman of the Senate Committee on Foreign Relations, that was ultimately required for the treaty's approval by the Senate. Although the House dragged its feet on appropriating the money for the purchase until July 1868, the U.S. annexation of Alaska was effectively complete when the United States took formal control of the territory on October 18, 1867. Within a few short decades, profits from gold, fish, and timber had far surpassed the purchase price. Johnson's Polar Bear Garden, twice the size of Texas and bought at approximately two cents an acre, had become a bargain second in value only to the Louisiana Purchase.

Expansionism Thwarted

Given the acrimony over all manner of issues surrounding Reconstruction, it is hardly surprising that Congressional cooperation with Johnson and Seward on matters of foreign policy proved to be the exception rather than the rule. In addition to the Alaska treaty, Seward negotiated the purchase of two of the three islands of the Danish West Indies (today the Virgin Islands), with the hope of using the location for a U.S. naval base in the Caribbean. The Senate refused to ratify the treaty. Johnson and Seward's plans to annex the Dominican Republic and Haiti were also killed in Congress, as were their plans to purchase Hawaii. The administration did succeed in taking the tiny and uninhabited Midway Atoll in the Pacific, but the failure to establish a naval base in the Caribbean was a far greater failure than this was a success. Finally, Seward succeeded in obtaining treaties to secure a location for a future isthmian canal in Central America with both Colombia (which included what is today Panama) and Nicaragua, but the Colombian Senate rejected the former, and the latter remained in force for decades with no effect. In advocating such expansionist schemes, Johnson and Seward were, for better or worse, men ahead of their time. Nowhere is this clearer than in Seward's moves toward the construction of a U.S.-controlled canal connecting the Atlantic and Pacific Oceans across the Central American isthmus.

Canada: Unrequited Annexationism

As already noted, Johnson and Seward hoped that the purchase of Alaska would hasten the fulfillment of what they and many other Americans assumed to be Canada's destiny—to join the United States. This fulfillment was made more difficult, however, by raids launched into Canada beginning in 1866 by an Irish-American organization known as the Fenian Brotherhood. The Fenians had as their ultimate end Irish independence from Britain, so they attacked Canada in the hope that doing so would provoke a war between the United States and Britain, resulting in their cherished goal. Despite the Fenians' violation of U.S. neutrality laws, many Americans, possibly even including the president, viewed these raids as just reprisals for the attacks launched by Confederates into New York and Vermont from Canadian soil during the Civil War. In Canada, however, these raids, combined with open talk in the United States of annexing its neighbor to the north, hardened anti-annexationist sentiment, ultimately led to the British North American provinces passing the British North America Act of 1867, which officially created the Dominion of Canada. Ironically, in their thirst to expand their own nation, Johnson, Seward, and others like them (not to mention the Fenians), had unwittingly helped create a new one.

Alabama Claims Unresolved

The major point of tension between the United States and Britain in the immediate postwar years was the issue of U.S. demands for compensation for the losses suffered due to Britain's lax enforcement of its neutrality laws during the Civil War (e.g., by permitting British shipyards to provide the Confederacy with such raiders as the *Alabama*). At first,

Britain refused even to discuss the matter, but the government in Britain changed twice, and the U.S. Congress passed a law that implied that the United States reserved the right to sell warships to Britain's enemy, Russia. Finally, the two English-speaking countries made some progress toward settling the claims. Under President Johnson's direct instructions, American diplomat Reverdy Johnson negotiated and signed the Johnson-Clarendon Convention on January 14, 1869. The agreement did not cover indirect American losses resulting from Confederate raiders built in Britain, nor did it include an apology for the construction of the *Alabama*. President Johnson's senatorial enemies were outraged, and the treaty was rejected by a vote of 54–1 in April. By then, of course, the United States had a new president—Ulysses S. Grant—and it fell to his administration to settle the matter of the *Alabama* claims.

Legacy

Andrew Johnson left the White House a failure, though for reasons far more related to his Reconstruction policy than to his foreign policy. Indeed, though foreign policy failures were certainly part of the equation, he did achieve some successes. Much of the credit for the purchase of Alaska and the peaceful withdrawal of the French from Mexico must of course go to William Seward, but Johnson played an important role as well. He was as expansionist in sentiment as Seward (to the extent this was possible), and thus eagerly gave his blessing to the negotiations over Alaska. And it was his measured approach to the Mexico situation that helped both avoid war with France and preserve the integrity of the Monroe Doctrine. There can be little doubt, however, that Johnson and Seward's attempt to secure a naval base in the Caribbean was an utter failure. Moreover, their open rhetoric about wanting to annex Canada, combined with Johnson's unwillingness to fully suppress the Fenians, led to an outcome the exact opposite of their policy goal. Finally, Johnson's poisoned relations with Congress helped delay resolution of the *Alabama* claims, allowing Grant's success in resolving them to go down as perhaps his finest foreign policy achievement. Sadly for Johnson and the country, his larger legacy is one of failure, impeachment, and white supremacy.

Dane Cash

Chronology

1865
April 14: Johnson sworn in as president.

May 1: Uprising in Santo Domingo defeats Spanish forces.

November 6: United States refuses to recognize Maximilian as Emperor of Mexico.

December 5: United States pressures France to remove troops from Mexico.

1866

March 17: United States terminates *Marcy-Elgin Treaty* of 1854.

April 15: France announces withdrawal from Mexico.

May 31: The French begin their phased withdrawal from Mexico.

May 31: Irish Fenian Brotherhood conducts unsuccessful raids in Canada.

June 25: U.S. signs joint tariff convention with Japan.

June 27: Seven Weeks' War between Austria and Prussia begins.

July 3: Prussia wins *Battle of Königgrätz.*

1867

March 30: Russia sells Alaska to US.

June 13: U.S. warships conduct punitive actions in Formosa.

June 19: Maximilian executed by firing squad.

June 21: Dickenson-Ayon Treaty with Nicaragua provides for free transit between oceans.

July 1: British North America Act creates The Dominion of Canada under British rule.

August 28: U.S. takes possession of Midway Island.

October 24: Denmark agrees to sell Virgin Islands to United States.

1868

January 3: Emperor takes direct control of Japan, Tokugawa Shogunate ends, Meiji Restoration begins.

March 5: Impeachment hearings against Andrew Johnson begin.

July 28: Burlingame Treaty with China is signed.

October 10: Civil war breaks out in Cuba.

November 3: Ulysses S. Grant elected president.

1869

January 14: Johnson-Clarendon Convention signed with Britain.

References and Further Reading

Campbell, Charles S. *The Transformation of American Foreign Relations 1865–1900.* New York: Harper and Row, 1976.

Castel, Albert. *The Presidency of Andrew Johnson.* Lawrence, KS: Regents, 1979.

DeConde, Alexander. *A History of American Foreign Policy.* New York: Scribner, 1963.

Trefousse, Hans L. *Andrew Johnson: A Biography.* New York: W. W. Norton, 1989.

Ulysses S. Grant (1869–1877)

Early Life and Military Career

Ulysses S. Grant, whose presidency was almost an anticlimax in comparison to a heroic military career, was borne by Hannah Simpson to Jesse Grant, a tanner, in Point Pleasant, Ohio, on April 27, 1822. He was christened Hiram Ulysses Grant, a name he found embarrassing, and he later changed to reverse the first and middle name. At West Point, a clerical order then substituted his mother's maiden name for Hiram, and he became Ulysses Simpson Grant for life.

A year after Ulysses's birth, Jesse moved his business to Georgetown, Ohio. A quiet, retiring personality, Ulysses spent his boyhood in Georgetown, attending school regularly until the age of seventeen, working in his father's tannery, and acquiring a reputation for an innate ability to handle difficult horses. When his father sought a professional education for him at government expense by sending him to West Point, Grant initially refused a military education and then attended the academy without enthusiasm. Grant was an indifferent student who received numerous demerits for slovenly dress and unmilitary bearing and spent more time reading fiction than applying himself to the academic curriculum. He excelled only at horsemanship; in 1843 he rode a particularly powerful but truculent mount, York, to an academy high-jumping record that stood for twenty-five years. Grant placed twenty-first of thirty-nine in his graduating class. Although he was promoted to sergeant in his third year, he confessed that the responsibility was too much for him and managed to accumulate sufficient demerits to be demoted to private for his senior year.

After graduation, Grant was made a brevet second lieutenant in the 4th U.S. Infantry and posted to Jefferson Barracks near St. Louis. It was here that he met Julia Boggs Dent, the daughter of Frederick Dent who owned a nearby plantation. They married in August 1848, a union that lasted almost thirty-seven years and produced four children. Grant served in the Mexican War under the command of Zachary Taylor and Winfield Scott, and was distinguished for bravery in hand-to-hand combat. He was personally opposed to the war, judging it an unprovoked adventure of conquest, and served as a matter of duty, maintaining that any man who obstructed his nation in war would come to occupy "no enviable place in life or history." Grant came to view the great Civil War that made him a national hero as a

Ulysses S. Grant was the architect of Union victory in the Civil War. His foreign policy was more quietly successful. (Library of Congress)

punishment for the national transgression of adding Texas to the Union at the expense of Mexico and thereby expanding the American empire of slavery.

After the Mexican War, Grant was posted to Sackett's Harbor, New York, and thereafter to a series of frontier postings on the West Coast. Grant's management of the transport of an infantry regiment from the Atlantic to the Pacific coast, including a crossing of the Isthmus of Panama in the company of incessant rain and cholera, cultivated his talent for cool and implacable determination under pressure. Posted thereafter to Fort Vancouver in present-day Oregon, Grant grew melancholy at the long separation from his family and fell into a habit of excessive drinking. In 1854, Captain Grant was discovered drunk by his commanding officer at Fort Humboldt, California, and was offered the choice between resignation and court-martial. Opting for resignation over the humiliation of a trial, Grant began six years of failure. He initially tried farming 60 acres near St. Louis, then took a series of short-term, dead-end jobs. Desperate to save his family from destitution, he turned to his father for a job as a clerk in the family leather goods shop in Galena, Illinois.

In April 1861, when President Lincoln called for 75,000 volunteers, Grant offered to drill a company of Galena volunteers. After serving as a clerk in the Illinois adjutant general's office, he offered his services to the War Department and to General George B. McClellan, soon to command the Union Army of the Potomac. McClellan refused to see him. In June 1861, Grant was finally made a colonel at the head of the 21st Illinois Volunteers, and in August, a brigadier general over Union forces in southern Illinois and southeastern Missouri. Thereafter, Grant's military career proceeded from minor victories at Fort Henry and Fort Donelson, through a pivotal near-defeat at Shiloh, to a major victory at Vicksburg on July 4, 1863, that did more substantively to secure the doom of the Confederacy than did the more storied Union victory at Gettysburg on the same day. In November 1863, Grant's victory at Chattanooga, Tennessee, opened Georgia to invasion by the Union Army. On March 9, 1864, President Lincoln made Grant a lieutenant general. Only three days later he was put in command of the entire Union Army.

Although Grant's reputation for drinking followed him throughout the war, his increasing renown for fighting eclipsed it altogether. Beyond his ability to maintain emotional equilibrium and mental clarity under pressure, he possessed the comparatively rare capacity to learn from past mistakes. Additionally, Grant's appreciation of the nature of the armed struggle between the Union and the Confederacy was more comprehensive than that of his principal foe, General Robert E. Lee. "The art of war is simple enough," he noted. "Find out where your enemy is. Get at him as soon as you can. Strike him as hard as you can and as often as you can and keep moving on." This will-to-combat, combined with an understanding of grand strategy, enabled Grant to bring to bear the Union's greater firepower for the complete destruction of the Confederate Army. While Lee sought set-piece battles in Virginia and Pennsylvania, and often secured brilliant tactical victories, Grant moved relentlessly in a series of engagements to move Union forces south along the Mississippi and then east into the heart of the Confederacy. It is no exaggeration to say that his systematic application of overwhelming force established the strategic doctrine used by the United States in the great wars of the twentieth century. By June 1864, it had brought him to the siege of Petersburg, Virginia, and by April 1865, to the Confederate capital of Richmond. When, on April 9, 1865, he accepted Lee's surrender at Appomattox Courthouse, Grant's status in the victorious Union was second only to Lincoln's. Grant might well have perished with his president at Ford's Theater on the fateful Good Friday of April 14, 1865, but he and Julia declined an invitation to attend at the last moment in order to be reunited with their children.

The Politics of Reconstruction

There followed immediately a difficult period in which President Andrew Johnson, a tactless and ill-tempered individual on his best day, assumed his constitutional powers in an atmosphere of national bitterness and vengefulness over Lincoln's assassination. Grant stood much higher in public esteem than the president and was widely considered a possible Republican nominee for the White House in 1868. Johnson came under pressure from Radical Reconstructionists in Congress to impose sweeping changes on the defeated South; it was the beginning of a struggle between the executive and legislative branches in which Johnson was nearly removed from office in an impeachment trial. Grant came into conflict with the president almost immediately over a presidential amnesty proclamation that violated the terms promised by Grant at Appomattox. Johnson wanted to exclude Confederate generals from amnesty and, more to the point, sought to arrest General Lee for treason. In a personal confrontation at the White House, Grant compelled Johnson to back down, placing all his prestige on the line by threatening to resign command of the army rather than execute an order to arrest Lee.

Johnson also fought against the Fourteenth Amendment, which made all persons born or naturalized in the United States American citizens. He had no intention of permitting the political reconstitution of the South to overturn the social fact of white supremacy there. Grant attempted to stay clear of the conflict between Johnson and Congress over Reconstruction, but national circumstance and his personal anger at the outbreak of racial violence in the South would not permit it. As general-in-chief, he could not tolerate the lawlessness and became increasingly impatient with Johnson's reluctance to intervene. As the victor at Appomattox, he was outraged by white mobs attacking black suffrage meetings in apparent defiance of the military verdict of the war. In fact, Grant had initially been uncertain about enfranchising freed slaves and was moved to endorse it in large part because of the violent resistance to it by white Southerners.

For his part, Johnson saw Grant's disapproval of his policy in the South as a challenge to its legitimacy and Grant's national popularity as a potential threat to his own authority. He could not afford to dismiss Grant, so he sought instead to diminish his influence. First he ordered Grant on a diplomatic mission to Mexico. Grant refused the assignment on the grounds he was obliged to follow military orders from the president but that the president had no authority to send him on a purely diplomatic mission. He feared that Johnson was planning a presidential coup d'état to prevent a Republican victory in the congressional elections of 1866 and thought it prudent to remain in Washington. After the Republicans won decisively in an election that had become a referendum on the Reconstruction Act, Grant urged Johnson to seek a compromise. Despite the obvious repudiation of the vote, Johnson refused. At this point Grant's support for the Reconstruction Act made him a political figure in his own right with the Radical Reconstructionists in Congress as his natural allies. When they overrode Johnson's veto of the Reconstruction Act, Grant gravitated further in their direction and became the symbol of Reconstruction's enforcement. Johnson's next move was to fire Edwin M. Stanton as secretary of war and call on Grant to replace him. This was designed to shield the administration from criticism by identifying Grant with Johnson's policy while simultaneously compromising Grant's base of support among Republicans for the same reason. Grant accepted the position only on an interim basis and was promptly labeled a "cat's paw" for the president by the Republican press. When Congress refused to permit Stanton's dismissal, Grant resigned his post immediately and was in a position both to oppose Johnson openly and to run for the Republican presidential nomination of 1868.

War Hero as President

With House Speaker Schuyler Colfax as his running mate, Grant won the Republican nomination by acclamation on the first ballot of the party's Chicago convention. Republican posters celebrated the nominee as the hero of Vicksburg and the savior of the Union. His Democratic opponent, Horatio Seymour, had, as the wartime governor of New York, referred to antiwar rioters as his friends. The result was predictably lopsided. Grant captured 214 Electoral College votes to Seymour's 80.

Grant thus took up presidential duties during the national turmoil of Reconstruction, but also at the beginning of a period of extraordinary economic prosperity. The pace of westward expansion was accelerating as industrial innovation intensified. American society was flush with optimism, awash in accumulating wealth, and proportionally vulnerable to corruption. The Grant administration became infamous for the latter. Too many of his cabinet appointments were based on personal friendship and Grant's apparent assumption that trusted friends would, in public office, approximate the honesty of their president. Instead, adventurers flocked to the administration while Grant committed some titanic errors of judgment and trust. It is no exaggeration to say that his presidency was mired in scandal from beginning to end, but also that Grant's popularity remained high and placed him, if not beyond suspicion, at least beyond vengeful public outrage.

His cabinet was unremarkable, with Elihu B. Washburn initially as secretary of state, George S. Boutwell in the Treasury, and Grant's wartime adjutant John A. Rawlins as secretary of war. A notable exception to the rule of mediocrity or impermanence was Hamilton Fish who replaced Washburn as secretary of state after only two weeks. Fish subsequently figured prominently in Grant's modest record of foreign policy achievement.

The Dominican Venture

When Grant took up his presidential duties, he inherited the problem of determining a position on the possible annexation of the Dominican Republic as well as toward a gathering Cuban insurrection against Spanish rule. Interest in the former dated to the Civil War and President Lincoln's conviction that the United States would be prudent to establish naval bases in the Caribbean, both to prevent hostile intrusion and to nurture growing East Coast trade with the Pacific by protecting transit across the Isthmus of Panama. In 1865, Secretary of State Seward had proposed to the Danish government the purchase of the Virgin Islands and had expressed an equal interest in the harbor at Samaná Bay in the Dominican Republic. In the latter case, the Dominican government sought American protection against invasion by Haiti, its French-speaking neighbor. Seward discussed the purchase or annexation of the city of Santo Domingo with the Dominican authorities while serving in the Johnson administration. Johnson's many enemies in Congress, however, had opposed the annexation. In early 1869, the House twice defeated resolutions to authorize the protection or annexation of Santo Domingo. Grant was content to let the venture lapse.

Others were not. As acting secretary of the navy, Admiral Horace Porter expressed a continuing interest in a coaling facility at Samaná Bay. Grant was skeptical. His opposition to the Mexican War and calculation of its consequences made him reluctant to hazard any territorial expansion that did not enjoy the support of the local population. He nonetheless dispatched a warship to the Dominican Republic with instructions to report on finances, economy, political circumstances, and the attitude of the people toward annexation by the United States. In addition, Grant sent his White House secretary and a former aide-de-camp, Brevet Brigadier General Orville Babock, as a special agent with a letter of personal instruction to the Dominican president, Buenaventura Báez. When Babcock returned with a draft protocol for either the annexation of Santo Domingo or the sale of Samaná Bay, Grant instructed Secretary Fish to prepare a treaty of annexation. Fish personally opposed the annexation, but agreed to let the venture proceed in order to retain a free hand in his diplomacy with Great Britain, specifically the *Alabama* claims against the British government for damages to Union shipping during the Civil War done by Confederate warships that had been built by British shipyards.

The treaty with which Babcock returned to Washington in December 1869, after securing Dominican approval, gave the Senate the option to approve either the outright annexation of Santo Domingo or the lease of Samaná Bay as a naval base. With Dominican approval, indeed enthusiasm, for annexation in place, Grant now seized the opportunity and lobbied personally for the treaty's passage to no avail. It was defeated largely through the efforts of Senator Charles Sumner, chair of the Foreign Relations Committee, who argued that the Dominican acquisition would be only the first step in a larger and costly Caribbean expansion that would make the United States "an Anglo-Saxon Republic," sovereign over a new possession where the nonwhite population was predominant. Grant fought back, urging Congress to establish a special commission to investigate both the conditions in the Dominican Republic and the advantages afforded by an American presence there. He was successful, and after three months on the island, the commission vindicated Grant's claims. By this time, public opinion in the United States had hardened against the annexation, so Grant submitted the commission report to Congress without a recommendation and the Dominican venture died. Determined to have the last word, he announced in 1870 that "hereafter no territory on this continent shall be regarded as subject to transfer to a European power." The principle of nontransferability had been applied in 1811 by President James Madison to the case of Florida, but Grant's declaration made this principle an integral corollary to the Monroe Doctrine.

The Cuban Insurrection

The travails of Spain in its Caribbean possession Cuba offered another opportunity for new territory. When a Cuban revolt against Spanish rule broke out in 1868, over half a million Africans were working as slaves on the island's plantations; slave trading continued there in the face of British and American efforts to eradicate it. Thus, abolitionist sentiment dating from the Civil War, combined with revolutionary resentment against Old World oppressors dating from 1776, gave a special wholesomeness to the idea of American intervention. Prodded by public sentiment, many congressmen urged that the United States recognize a Cuban rebel government, or at the very least acknowledge a state of belligerency. Secretary Fish was loath to do so because of his diplomatic efforts to secure damages from Britain for its aid to the South during the Civil War. In April 1869, the Senate rejected the Clarendon-Johnson Treaty, signed by President Johnson during his last days in office, as insufficient payment for American Civil War damage claims against Great Britain. How was the United States now to support an insurrection in Cuba while demanding compensation from Britain for supporting the Confederate insurrection only a few years earlier?

By contrast, Secretary of War John A. Rawlins pushed the Cuban cause very hard. As Grant's wartime adjutant, Rawlins always had the president's ear. Prior to the insurrection, Rawlins had spoken in favor of the elimination of all European power in the Americas, but his advocacy of the Cuban cause now was tainted by his acceptance of $28,000 in Cuban bonds from the Cuban exile community in the United States. As Congress passed a resolution of sympathy with the rebels and public meetings in support of intervention caught on across the country, Grant's cabinet remained divided. There was also a danger that the situation could slip beyond Grant's capacity to contain national sentiment, much less determine American policy, as private intervention operations were launched from American shores. In response, he issued an executive order prohibiting all filibuster expeditions while the Treasury and Justice departments tightened up their enforcement. Even when the *New York Sun*—now published by Charles Dana, one of Grant's most dedicated supporters during the Civil War—called for immediate intervention in Cuba and bemoaned an administration "barren of great ideas" and "so deficient in character," Grant refused to be hectored into war.

In June 1869, Fish authorized the American minister in Madrid to negotiate a settlement based on Cuban independence and the abolition of slavery. Madrid rejected the offer. In August of the same year, Grant wobbled somewhat in his resolution when he drew up a proclamation recognizing Cuban belligerence, but Fish convinced him that such a proclamation would be imprudent as long as the major European powers had refused to recognize the Cuban rebels. The year of uncertainty finally ended on December 6, when Grant informed Congress that United States could not presently intervene in Cuba regardless of American sympathy for the rebel cause; he added that Washington could not acknowledge a belligerent situation in Cuba until the insurgents had established a political organization worthy of recognition. The matter did not rest there. Under pressure from Cuban lobby groups, Congress debated a resolution recognizing a state of war with Cuba and Spain. Because such a resolution implied recognition of Cuba as a sovereign state, Grant and Fish fought to thwart its passage. When this looked futile, Republican legislative leaders managed to gut the resolution with a series of amendments that protested Spanish policy and indicated sympathy for Cuba, yet removed formal recognition of the rebels. The resolution passed 101–88 on June 16, 1870.

The administration's circumspection on Cuba paid diplomatic dividends in 1871. In late 1870, the Tory government of Benjamin Disraeli in Britain was defeated and replaced by a Liberal cabinet headed by William Gladstone. Gladstone was eager to mend fences with United States, a change in attitude that coincided happily with the defeat of the Dominican treaty and the successful efforts of Fish to depose the Anglophobe Charles Sumner from the chair of the Senate Foreign Relations Committee in retaliation for his opposition to it. Gladstone wanted to put to rest a number of Anglo-American aggravations in one comprehensive package and took the initiative through the Foreign Office to have Sir John Rose, unofficial Canadian representative in London and a well-known figure in Washington, put it forward. After a preliminary exchange of views, Fish and Rose decided to appoint a joint high commission to develop a resolution of outstanding grievances among the United States, Britain, and Canada, the latter having become a self-governing Dominion in 1867. They then signed the Treaty of Washington prepared by the commission on May 8, 1871. The essentials of the treaty included an expression of regret by Her Majesty's Government for the predations of the *Alabama* and other British-made warships during the Civil War; the creation of a tribunal to arbitrate the *Alabama* claims; the readmission of American citizens to inshore fishing in Canada and the opening of American waters north of 39° latitude to Canadian fishing; and the submission of the dispute over San Juan Island to arbitration by the Emperor of Germany. The Senate ratified the treaty by 50–12 on May 24, 1871. In October 1872, Kaiser Wilhelm I ruled that San Juan Island in the straits between Vancouver Island and the North American mainland rightfully belonged to the United States.

Expansion Deferred

The Anglo-American dispute over San Juan Island was only a footnote in the intensified competition among established and emerging powers in the nineteenth century. The United States belonged to the latter group, and the ambition of the U.S. Navy for offshore bases did not confine itself to the Caribbean. In May 1872, Grant asked Congress to approve a treaty with Samoa, negotiated by Commander Richard W. Meade, that would give the United States exclusive rights to a coaling station in the harbor of Pago Pago and place the native population under American protection. Halfway between Hawaii and Sydney, Australia, the base would be ideally situated between the North American West Coast and British colonial possessions in the southwestern Pacific. However, Congress failed to act on the treaty. Grant continued contact with Samoa by sending Colonel A. B. Steinberger as a special agent, but it was not until 1878 that the Hayes administration was able to get a treaty of amity and commerce with Samoa that included nonexclusive rights to a naval station at Pago Pago. In the meantime, the Grant administration secured a treaty with Hawaii in January 1875 that provided for freer trade between and the United States and the Pacific islands. Hawaii also agreed not to lease any of its territory to a third party. This treaty was thus a diplomatic down-payment on a U.S. protectorate in Hawaii. Grant's initiatives reflected a consciousness that the United States could not long delay the establishment of a presence in strategically important waters. Both Britain and Germany were also interested in Samoa. In 1869, the Suez Canal, built by the French engineer and entrepreneur Ferdinand Lesseps, connected the Mediterranean with the Rea Sea for the first time. Lesseps wanted to build a similar waterway across the Isthmus of Panama between the Atlantic and Pacific oceans. In January 1869, the Senate rejected a treaty with Colombia granting the United States rights to a Panamanian canal in large part because legislators at the time wanted no part of a treaty connected with Andrew Johnson. But a year later it also rejected an amended version of the treaty sent to it by Grant, this time because the treaty did not permit the United States to close the canal in time of war.

Grant's efforts to defeat American intervention in Cuba did nothing to undermine his chances of reelection in 1872. A central issue in the campaign was the violent activity of the Ku Klux Klan in the former Confederacy intended to intimidate the newly freed and enfranchised black population from voting and to consolidate the social reality, if not the constitutional legitimacy, of white supremacy. Grant seized the initiative in dealing with the Klan by declaring the situation in the South beyond the control of state authorities, thus providing Congress with political cover for anti-Klan legislation as Grant ordered troops to the South. In the 1872 presidential campaign, the Liberal-Democratic nominee, Horace Greeley, made Grant's treatment of the South key to his bid to oust the incumbent and reaped a colossal defeat for his efforts. With federal officials standing watch as African Americans voted in record numbers, Grant was reelected in a landslide of 286 electoral votes against Greeley's 66.

Cuba Redux

Early in Grant's second term, Cuba once again loomed large on the diplomatic agenda due in large part to instability in both Spain itself and in its colony. Late in 1872, Secretary Fish had instructed the American representatives in Madrid to warn the Spanish government that it must implement reforms to end the anarchy in Cuba. But before King Amadeo was able to act on the reassurances given, he was forced to abdicate by a republican revolution whose leaders announced that domestic reforms would take priority over conditions in Spain's colonies. To this, Fish responded in August 1873 that groups inside the United States were eager to invade Cuba and that President Grant was in a difficult position to oppose them so long as the situation there continued to outrage American public opinion. In November 1873, Spain and the United States came close to war when an American-registered ship, the *Virginius,* was captured by a Spanish cruiser near Cuba. Spain maintained that the ship had been transporting arms to the Cuban rebels, but, counter to orders from Madrid, Spanish officials in Cuba executed fifty-three men caught aboard the *Virginius,* including its captain and thirty-six crew members. Only the arrival of a British warship, whose captain threatened to bombard Santiago, prevented more executions. In the United States, rallies of public indignation took place all along the eastern seaboard while newspapers such as the *New York Sun* bayed for war. Cooler heads prevailed in the administration as Fish initially posted an ultimatum demanding an apology from Madrid. Between November 27 and 29, he reached a negotiated settlement with the Spanish ambassador to the United States, Admiral José Polo de Bernabe, wherein Spain was to surrender the *Virginius* along with all surviving prisoners and was additionally to pay an indemnity of $80,000 to the families of the executed Americans. It subsequently emerged that the ship had no right to fly an American flag, because its owners, Cuban exiles, had obtained U.S. registration by falsely claiming American citizenship. By 1878, the Spanish military had ended the insurgency in Cuba, and the matter of American involvement awaited the McKinley administration.

World Weary

For an administration continually troubled by scandal, the crowning humiliation came in March 1876 when the news broke that Grant's secretary of war, William Belknap, had been profiting personally from leasing trading posts through his department. Belknap resigned, but an angry House voted for impeachment proceedings against him nonetheless. Belknap was acquitted by the Senate, notwithstanding the volume of evidence of his guilt, and Grant's national popularity was only slightly diminished by the affair. Still, the burden of defending administration officials—who in many cases deserved no defense from their president—eroded Grant's enthusiasm for executive office. Although a Republican Party convention in 1875 endorsed him for another term, Grant announced that he would not seek a third term any more than he had sought the first. Years later, recalling the day he turned over the reigns of the presidential office to his successor, Rutherford Hayes, he said that "I felt like a boy getting out of school."

Legacy

The foreign policy of the Grant administration is as noteworthy for its limits as its achievements. The opportunity for the territorial expansion of the United States was present throughout Grant's term in office, but the national mood as reflected in Congress was ambivalent about exploiting it. Grant was a conservative president in the sense that he defined the constitutional authority given to the president to set the foreign affairs agenda narrowly. His role as supreme commander in war had taught him the importance of delegating authority, and he sought in the presidency to apply the same principle by providing general guidance while surrendering

detail and day-to-day diplomatic duties to his secretary of state. Because many of Grant's other cabinet appointments were unremarkable, he was therefore fortunate that Secretary of State Fish combined professional competence and thoroughness with an instinctive caution similar to Grant's own. Resisting the war cries of a bellicose press, the administration applied patience to the Cuban crisis and avoided war with Spain while pursuing a policy of reconciliation with Great Britain. The Treaty of Washington was a significant diplomatic triumph, both for the breadth of the Anglo-American differences addressed and for the arbitration procedure it established.

In the 1870s, the United States was unprepared to assert American power in the Pacific or the Caribbean with the vigor it would be able to exercise in the 1890s. Reconstruction consumed much of the Grant administration's attention and energies. Territorial consolidation in the continental United States was as yet incomplete. It was not until late 1876, after all, that U.S. forces finally ended the Sioux Wars with the capture of Sitting Bull and Crazy Horse. The Apache Wars were not yet nearly over. The country was, in other words, neither mature nor united enough to assume a high profile on the international stage.

But that day would not wait much longer. In 1871, a united Germany emerged triumphant from the Franco-Prussian War. In 1875, Great Britain purchased majority control of the Suez Canal, and the next year, an American interoceanic canal commission recommended a canal through the territory of Nicaragua. In 1875, insurrections broke out in the Ottoman territories of Bosnia and Herzegovina. As Turkish power in the Balkans waned, Russia moved to exploit the opportunity, and Britain became progressively nervous about a threat to the Mediterranean. Finally in 1878, Ferdinand Lesseps, the architect of the Suez waterway, gained from Colombia the right to build a similar canal across Panama. Competition among the Great Powers was intensifying as technology made the world smaller. It was fast becoming a matter of when and how, but not of if, the United States was to join the first rank of nations.

Carl Cavanagh Hodge

Chronology

1869

January 14: Senate rejects Panamanian canal rights treaty with Colombia.

April 13: Senate rejects Clarendon-Johnson Treaty.

November 17: Suez Canal opens.

1870

January 20: Senate rejects amended Panamanian canal rights treaty with Colombia.

July 19: France declares war on Prussia.

September 2: Prussian and German armies win Battle of Sedan.

September 4: French Third Republic proclaimed.

1871

January 18: Under Prussian leadership German states unite to form German Empire.

January 18: Wilhelm II proclaimed German Emperor, Bismarck is chancellor.

April 30: U.S. Army begins campaign against Apache in Arizona.

May 8: Anglo-American Treaty of Washington over *Alabama* claims.

May 10: Treaty of Frankfurt ends Franco-Prussian War.

1872

May 22: Senate rejects treaty with Samoa.

October 21: Germany arbitrates Northwest border dispute in favor of United States.

November 5: Japan obtains control of Ryukyu Islands.

November 5: Grant is reelected president.

1873

February 12: First Spanish republic proclaimed.

August 27: United States urges Spain to reform colonial regime in Cuba.

November 29: Virginius incident in Cuba.

December 31: Military coup topples Spanish republic, Alfonso XII is King.

1875

January 30: Hawaii becomes U.S. protectorate.

July 5: Insurrection against Ottoman rule in Bosnia-Herzogovina.

November 25: Britain buys controlling interest in Suez Canal.

1876

February 26: Sino-Japanese treaty on Korean independence.

March 1: U.S. attempt to mediate Cuban insurrection fails.

June 25: U.S. Army defeated by Sioux at Battle of Little Big Horn.

June 30: Serbia declares war on Turkey.

October 31: U.S. forces capture Crazy Horse and Sitting Bull, Sioux Wars end.

November 7: Presidential election produces Hayes-Tilden deadlock.

November 20: Porfirio Diaz overthrows President Tejada in Mexico.

References and Further Reading

Fuller, J. F. C. *Grant and Lee: A Study in Personality and Generalship.* Bloomington, IN: Indiana University Press, 1957.

Grant, U. S. *Personal Memoires.* Lincoln, NE: University of Nebraska Press, 1996.

Nevins, Allan. *Hamilton Fish: The Inner History of the Grant Administration.* New York: F. Ungar, 1957.

Perret, Geoffrey. *Ulysses S. Grant, Soldier & President.* New York: Modern Library, 1997.

Simpson, Brooks D. *Let Us Have Peace: Ulysses S. Grant and the Politics of War and Reconstruction.* Chapel Hill, NC: University of North Carolina Press, 1991.

Smith, Jean Edward. *Grant.* New York: Simon and Schuster, 2001.

Rutherford Birchard Hayes (1877–1881)

Early Life and Political Career

Rutherford Birchard Hayes was born in Delaware, Ohio, on October 4, 1822, after his parents had moved from Dummerston, Vermont, in 1817. Hayes was one of five children, though only sister Fanny Arabella and he lived to adulthood. He was educated in Connecticut at Webb's Preparatory School in Middletown—sent by the most influential person in his life, his uncle Sardis Birchard (1801–1874)—and later at Kenyon College in Gambier, Ohio, where he graduated as valedictorian in 1842. Hayes developed many lifelong friends from his school days and travels in New England, the Midwest, and the South, including Guy Bryan from Texas and Stanley Matthews, who Hayes eventually nominated to the Supreme Court. As he traveled in the 1840s, he became increasingly interested in Whig politics. After studying law in the law offices of Thomas Sparrow in Columbus, Ohio, he was encouraged by his uncle Sardis and enrolled in the law school of Harvard University in the fall of 1843. His teachers included Simon Greenleaf and Supreme Court Justice Joseph Story, and he read Blackstone, Aristotle, John Locke, and the Scottish common school philosophers. Hayes finished his studies in January 1844 and was admitted to the bar after passing his examinations in Ohio, March 10, 1845. He undertook his legal practice in Lower Sandusky (later Fremont), eventually forming a partnership with another young lawyer, Ralph P. Buckland, in April 1846.

Between 1846 and the outbreak of the American Civil War in 1861, Hayes practiced law and became increasingly involved in politics, married Lucy Ware Webb on December 30, 1852, and started a family. Rutherford and Lucy had a remarkably close and affectionate marriage and raised a large family of eight children, though three died at young ages. Hayes practiced law continuously in the 1850s, primarily in Cincinnati, developing a civil practice, but also arguing cases before the Supreme Court of Ohio, and worked with clients developing railroad lines in Ohio and Indiana. He was elected to his first office as city solicitor of Cincinnati in 1858 and served until 1860. Throughout the 1850s, Hayes

Rutherford Birchard Hayes used moderation as his guiding principle and was moderately successful with it. (Library of Congress)

became an increasingly influential figure in the Republican Party in Ohio, and helped found the party in Cincinnati and then Ohio as a whole. He became an acquaintance and supporter of Abraham Lincoln in the presidential election of 1861, opposing slavery and its extension in the territories.

In the spring of 1861, Hayes enlisted in the 23rd Regiment of the Ohio Volunteers, and started training at Camp Chase, near Columbus. In a famous remark he said "I would prefer to go into it [the Civil War] if I knew I was to die or be killed in the course of it, than to live through and

The author is grateful for the expertise and help with this article of Thomas Culbertson, executive director of the Rutherford B. Hayes Presidential Center.

after it without taking any part in it." He served as a Union officer until the end of the war in 1865, saw frequent action in campaigns in Western Virginia, Virginia, and the Maryland theaters, and was wounded four times, once seriously. He rose through the ranks from major ultimately to the rank of brevet major general, and valued his service as one of the most important episodes of his life.

For Hayes, the "war is forced on us," and the Confederacy of seceded slave states "has not by its acts sought a peaceful separation" but attacked the federal government. Hayes believed that "rebellious citizens" in the upper South were "bent on forcing out of the Union States whose people are not in favor of secession." The war was "to defend the rights of Union, and to strengthen the Union men in the doubtful States." Such a war was "necessary, wise, and just."

Hayes resigned from the Army in April 1865, as he had been elected as a Union Republican congressman from Cincinnati, and went to Washington, D.C., where he served from March 4, 1865, until October 31, 1867. When Governor Jacob Cox decided not to run for reelection as governor of Ohio in 1867, Hayes ran and won the governorship, which he held from January 1868 through January 1872. Hayes supported voting rights for blacks in all states and the ratification of the Fourteenth Amendment. He also became very involved in the state's educational, benevolent, and welfare policies such as prison reform and industrial schooling. Hayes described the governor's office "as the pleasantest office I have ever had." He supported legislation to create the Ohio State University in 1870, serving as a very influential trustee and moving figure in the 1880s until his death in 1893. After a period of retirement from 1872 to 1875 at Spiegel Grove, his estate and community in Fremont, Ohio, Hayes yielded to the call of the Republican Party and was elected to a third term as governor from 1875–1876. Free schools for all and a sound money system were his two campaign issues.

Rutherford B. Hayes was one of several leading candidates for the Republican nomination for the president at the Republican National Convention in Cincinnati, which met on June 14, 1877, and included James Blaine of Maine, Roscoe Conkling of New York, Secretary of the Treasury Benjamin Bristow, Oliver Perry Morton of Indiana, and Governor John Hartranft of Pennsylvania. Hayes won on the seventh ballot and subsequently ran against the Democratic reform governor of New York, Samuel Jones Tilden. In the presidential election of 1876, which has drawn much controversial debate, Hayes won the electoral vote 185 to 184 but lost the popular vote to Tilden. Louisiana's eight votes, Florida's four votes, and South Carolina's seven votes were contested, and there were election irregularities, Democratic intimidation of black Republican voters, and other issues. Not until Congress had appointed an Electoral Commission on January 29, 1877, did the Commission meet and eventually award all contested

electoral votes by an eight to seven Republican-Democratic party line to Republican Hayes. Amid calls of corruption and foul play, Hayes' advisors affirmed his pledge to appoint a Southern Democrat to his cabinet, to withdraw federal troops in the South to their barracks after receiving assurances that all civil rights would be honored, and to consider internal improvements in the South. On March 5, 1877, Rutherford B. Hayes became President of the United States and pledged to bring peace, honor, and respect to government, and to serve his country—not his party—with his most famous remark "he serves his party best who serves his country best."

Domestic Concerns

During his one term of office from 1877 to 1881—he declared in the 1876 campaign that he would serve only one term—President Hayes was mainly concerned with civil service reform, monetary and sound money policies, reconciliation with the South, and matters of business and industry in the midst of the Gilded Age and the making of modern America. He also fought strenuously to make strong and fair cabinet and presidential appointments and to make the Republican Party a truly national party, frequently battling perennial Republican leaders like Conkling and Blaine. Secretary of the Treasury John Sherman, Secretary of the Interior Carl Schurz, and Secretary of State William M. Evarts were the three most influential members of his cabinet, and provided President Hayes an excellent core of advisors. With regard to the South, Hayes recognized that Northern public opinion no longer supported Radical Republicans and also that Congress no longer supported the enforcement of equal rights. Under these circumstances, Hayes created a new Southern policy based on conciliation rather than confrontation. Consequently, he issued orders transferring the few remaining federal officers and soldiers still stationed in South Carolina and Louisiana to the nearest army barracks. By so doing, he hoped "to get from those States by their governors, legislatures, press, and people pledges that the Thirteenth, Fourteenth, and Fifteenth Amendments shall be faithfully observed, that the colored people shall have equal rights to labor, education, and the privileges of citizenship. I am confident that this is a good work. Time will tell." Because Hayes believed "universal suffrage should rest upon universal education," he called for "liberal and permanent provision . . . for the support of free schools by the State governments, and, if need be, supplemented by legitimate aid from national authority."

There were issues of civil reform in 1877 and 1878, and Hayes believed in using patronage fairly. In 1877, he faced a labor relations crisis in the Great Strike and relied on the pressure of federal and state guard troops to restore order. From 1878–1881, Hayes also turned to reevaluate federal policy toward Native American rights in response to the Nez

Perce War that broke out in 1877. In his first annual message, Hayes admitted that "many, if not most, of our Indian wars have had their origins in broken promises and acts of injustice upon our part." He worked with Congress to aid Native Americans with prompt and liberal aid on reservations, while often battling with the U.S. Army, which wanted a much firmer policy of removal and suppression. In the summer of 1880, at the end of his term, Hayes took the first presidential tour of the West Coast, which lasted two months and took him through Utah, Nevada, Oregon, Washington, California, New Mexico, and Arizona.

General Diplomatic Affairs

During the administration of President Hayes from 1877 to 1881, no grave or serious diplomatic issues threatened the peace and stability of American foreign relations with traditional European powers such as Great Britain, France, Spain, or Germany. After the Treaty of Washington with Great Britain in 1871, only fishery issues and lingering claims with regard to Canadian territories disturbed Anglo-American affairs, although some initial Irish-American terrorist and international monetary conference concerns started to appear and became more serious issues during the Arthur, Cleveland, and Harrison administrations. By contrast, Latin American affairs—including border disputes and annexationist sentiments with regard to the Texas-Mexican border, a Panamanian canal proposition, Argentinian-Paraguayan arbitration, and lingering debates in California over Chinese exclusion—foretold the emergence of the new international and American imperial foreign policy agenda that burst forth in the 1890s.

Hayes never traveled to Europe as had many of his contemporaries such as James Blaine, Samuel Tilden, General Grant, William Evarts, and Roscoe Conkling. Even so, he was intimately concerned and knowledgeable about foreign affairs through his prolific readings and close relations with the talented former attorney general who served as his secretary of state, William M. Evarts. Mexican affairs had long been an interest since the days Hayes traveled in Texas and the South in the 1840s and 1850s; he was very familiar with the annexationist sentiments of Manifest Destiny and the Whig Party in the 1840s and 1850s.

Diplomatic and consular affairs were handled in the 1870s and 1880s by a small department of the secretary of state and a modest number of foreign secretaries, consular officers, and aides. In March 1877, there were twenty-eight legation heads, which included a range of Republican and Democratic leaders, including Southerners such as Henry Hilliard of Georgia who was sent to Brazil; Cassius Goodloe of Kentucky to Belgium; and two black diplomats, John M. Langston to Haiti and John H. Smyth to Liberia. President Hayes's able appointments included James Russell Lowell (the literary figure), John Hay, William Hunter, Frederick

W. Seward, Bayard Taylor, and Bret Harte. They also included such educational leaders as the former president of Cornell University, Andrew D. White, and the former president of the University of Michigan, James B. Angell, to Germany and China, respectively. Secretary of State Evarts was aided by senior department secretaries and foreign expert aids such as Alvery Adee, James Conley, John Kasson, and Edward Stoughton.

Although diplomatic appointments were awarded with regard to patronage and party loyalty, Hayes was notorious in choosing good, responsible leaders of any party. Under Evarts, there were many departmental improvements. Evarts was a New Englander, a former attorney general and lawyer who had been to Europe four times before assuming his office and knew many British, French, and European leaders personally. His relations with the Republican Party had been fractured when he defended Andrew Johnson at his impeachment trial, but President Hayes valued Evarts's expert and conscientious advice on both foreign policy and domestic affairs. Diplomatic departmental business in the secretary of state's office had been reorganized in the mid-1870s under Hamilton Fish, with business distributed among three assistant secretaries, six bureaus, two agencies, a private secretary, and various clerks. In January 1878, there was a total executive and clerical foreign diplomatic force of only slightly over fifty individuals.

Foreign Business and Commerce in the Gilded Age

In the midst of the Gilded Age and the rise of big business, urbanization, and commerce, it is not surprising that foreign policy under President Hayes sought to promote foreign business, commerce, and trade abroad—not only in traditional Europe, but in Central and Latin America, Asia, and the Pacific. Under Secretary of State Evarts, there were more requests for consular reports and studies of the history, language, and traditions of foreign countries around the world. As business and industry prospered in the United States, the quest for foreign markets for domestic surpluses was greater than any effort by the administration to acquire foreign territories. Between 1870 and 1880, American export trade increased by more than 200 percent as new markets were opened, particularly in Latin America, Asia, and the Pacific. Secretary Evarts requested that all South American consuls, for instance, send regular reports "outlining some practical resources to increase United States trade in Latin America." The State Department published monthly reports in pamphlet form that were then circulated to American businessmen and merchants to encourage American business abroad. Instructions were also sent to all American consuls in Europe to investigate five areas: the rate of wages, cost of living, comparison of wages for the preceding five years, amount of money in circulation and condition of trade, and the system of business.

With regard to American-Canadian border concerns, Evarts sought somewhat unsuccessfully to negotiate with Great Britain over fishing rights in Newfoundland and Fortune Bay. The Treaty of Washington of 1871, between Britain and the United States, contained provisions concerning fishing rights for New England fisherman, seeking to treat them in a similar fashion to British-Canadian citizens. In 1877, President Hayes discharged the outstanding debt of $5.5 million to Great Britain under the Halifax fishery assessment agreed on in the Treaty of Washington after a three-member commission determined the validity of the award. But this did not resolve the issue, as incidents arose about a section of Newfoundland, and American fishermen complained that their rights to fish were violated. Lord Salisbury, the prime minister of Britain, insisted that American fishermen should be subject to the same restraints as British fisherman. While Evarts refused to accept Salisbury's conditions, his successor James G. Blaine was more willing to acquiesce to Lord Salisbury's demands as well as those of the new Liberal Gladstone ministry. Subsequently, in 1881, the British government awarded the United States £15,000 pounds for American fishermen's losses in the Fortune Bay incident.

With respect to trade in the Pacific and Asia, President Hayes and Secretary of State Evarts forged closer friendships and relations with Samoa, China, and Japan. Washington refused Samoa's request for annexation but signed a treaty of friendship and peace that also allowed the United States to establish a naval station in Samoa. Amicable trading and commercial relations were maintained with Great Britain and Germany, despite their different territorial settlements in Samoa.

Latin America and the Panama Canal Issue

Latin American relations were also important. Following the tenets of the Monroe Doctrine, Hayes made increasingly bold references throughout 1877 and 1878 to the importance of American hemispheric affairs for the protection of American business and commercial interests. His policies, taken together, constituted a preliminary declaration of American western hemispheric hegemony, which were later underscored in President Theodore Roosevelt's 1904 Corollary, the annual message to Congress on December 6 in which he justified American intervention in the affairs of the Dominican Islands to exercise its "international police power."

In 1879, the Frenchman Ferdinand Lesseps, the builder of the Suez Canal, proposed a canal across the Isthmus of Panama connecting the Pacific Ocean with the Caribbean Sea. This brought to a head a whole range of existing American agreements with Central American governments regarding the meaning of the Monroe Doctrine in the area—treaties with Colombia (1846) and Nicaragua (1847)—and especially with regard to Anglo-American interests in the Clayton-Bulwer Treaty of 1850. In a special message to Congress on March 8, 1880, Hayes responded that an isthmian canal would be "virtually a part of the coastline of the United States" and that "the policy of this country is a canal under American control." Throughout his administration he "steadily evolved the concept of the paramount interest" of the United States in western hemispheric affairs.

Lesseps sought to promote his canal project in 1879–1880 by traveling to the United States, appearing before the House of Representatives, and appealing to American businessmen and investors to subscribe in stock or assume important leadership positions in his company. While President Grant refused the presidency of the company, Lesseps successfully persuaded Hayes's Secretary of Navy, Richard W. Thompson, to accept the job of chairman of the American Committee of the Panama Canal Company. Thompson had sought a conference with Hayes while the president was on his western trip in the summer of 1880. Upon hearing Thompson had accepted, Hayes asked for Thompson's resignation, believing that cabinet members should not accept such foreign or diplomatic offices with possible financial gain at stake. Subsequently, Hayes appointed Nathan Goff, a West Virginian, for the final two months of the term as secretary of the Navy.

To further enforce his decision that the United States would not consent to any European power to construct a canal or railroad in Central America, and to secure American commercial and trade interests, Hayes sent two naval vessels to establish naval and coaling stations at the Chiriqui Grant. In his diary on January 13, 1880, Hayes observed that this "will give us a foothold which will be of vast service in controlling the passage from Ocean to Ocean either at Panama or at Nicaragua Lake." Subsequently, after consulting and attaining full support of his cabinet, Hayes sent a message on March 8 to the Senate. He asserted:

> The policy of this country is a canal under American control. The United States cannot consent to the surrender of this control to any European power, or to any combination of European powers. If existing treaties between the United States and other nations, or if the rights of sovereignty or property of other nations stand in the way of this policy—a contingency which is not apprehended—suitable steps should be taken by just and liberal negotiations to promote and establish the American policy on this subject, consistently with the rights of the nations to be affected by it.

In the end, the Lesseps project went bankrupt by 1888, but in the course of events, Hayes had helped assert American hemispheric interests in the region.

In a different issue, the nineteenth president entered a Latin American international border dispute between

Argentina and Paraguay in 1878. For years there had been border disputes between Paraguay and the Triple Alliance of Argentina, Brazil, and Uruguay. The Paraguayan War lasted from 1865 to 1870, and Argentina claimed the entire Chaco region bounded by the Pilcomayo and Verde rivers. Rather than sliding toward an international incident of serious nature like the Venezuelan boundary dispute of 1896 between Great Britain and the United States, Argentinian and Paraguayan plenipotentiaries journeyed to Washington, D.C., in the autumn of 1878 to present their respective positions to President Hayes for arbitration. International arbitration had become increasingly popular as a means to resolve disputes peacefully among American nations over territorial and commercial rights and led to increasing dialogue about settling disputes peaceably by the end of the nineteenth century. On November 12, 1878, Hayes announced his decision that the Argentinian troops must leave the Chaco territory and cede the area to Paraguay. In gratitude, the Paraguayan Congress later named the principal city of Villa Occidental as Villa Hayes. In 1944, when provinces were established and then expanded in 1973, the largest was named Presidente Hayes. In Paraguay today, generations remember Hayes out of great respect, even naming leading soccer teams after him.

Mexican Relations and the Diaz Government

Since the end of the Civil War, tensions had increased along the U.S.-Mexican border, and during the Hayes administration, no foreign issue more consistently created diplomatic problems than Mexican affairs. But unlike what would happen under President Woodrow Wilson, Mexican-American disputes were settled by a combination of diplomatic negotiations and growing internal stability in Mexican domestic affairs. Problems arose when Mexican marauders crossed into Texas to steal the cattle of American ranchers, and there were persistent border troubles. On November 20, 1876—two weeks after the Hayes-Tilden presidential election—Porfirio Díaz overthrew Lerdo de Tejeda and assumed the office of president of Mexico by May 1877. Increasingly, Díaz moved to assume absolute power over Mexican affairs and held that power unswervingly for more than thirty years until the emergence of new tensions with the United States shortly before World War I.

On June 1, 1877, Hayes ordered General Edward Ord to keep "lawless bands" from invading the United States and refused to recognize the new Díaz government in Mexico—although Díaz was recognized fairly quickly by most major European powers. The Díaz government, on the other hand, demanded recognition, and frequent diplomatic missions ensued between Secretary of State Evarts and the Mexican government between 1877 and 1881.

Former colleagues of President Hayes such as William S. Rosecrans—also former U.S. minister to Mexico under President Johnson (1868–1869)—pressured Hayes to promote mining and railroad interests in Mexico. He even tried as an annexationist to urge American purchase of parts of northern Mexico: Sonora, Chihuahua, Coahuila, Nuevo Leon, Tamaulipas, and the Territory of Lower California. While Hayes had made remarks to the effect that the annexation of adjacent territory both north and south "seems to be, according to the phrase of 1844, our 'manifest destiny,'" he was "not in favor of artificial stimulants to this tendency." Neither Hayes nor Diaz was willing to go to war over these vexing border problems, even though Hayes's antagonist James Blaine claimed that Hayes was an aggressive annexationist. On July 6, 1877, President Hayes made clear that "nothing hostile to Mexico or detrimental to her interests is intended. As to annexing any part of the Mexican territory, there is no thought of it, and the United States does not want any more territory in that direction even if offered as a gift."

Negotiations between the United States and Mexico were deadlocked through much of 1877, as the Díaz government insisted on official diplomatic recognition as a precursor to the settlement of the border raids and incidents. John W. Foster, the American minister to Mexico, also believed strongly that the United States should grant recognition, and in early January 1878, testified to that effect before the House in Washington, D.C. It wasn't until April 1878 that Hayes and Evarts formally recognized the Díaz government, prolonging estranged negotiations.

The Texas-Mexican frontier remained calmer in 1878 and 1879, as Díaz removed Indians into the interior of Mexico and suppressed Mexican raids into Texas. General Ord noted in his 1879 report that there were no longer urgent needs to cross the border to suppress bandits and marauders. On March 1, 1880, Evarts notified the Mexican minister to the United States, Manuel de Zamacona, of Hayes's decision to revoke the controversial order of June 1, 1877. It is quite clear that the improvement in U.S.-Mexican border relations came about primarily because of the ability of the absolutist power of the Díaz government to handle border issues. For its part, the Hayes administration can be credited with contributing to improved relations supporting such projects as two American-financed railroad companies in Mexico.

Chinese Immigration and Exclusion

The last major foreign relations issue to face the administration—equally as important as the Panama canal, business and trade, and Mexican affairs—was the lingering debate over Chinese immigration to California in the mid-nineteenth century. Anti-Chinese sentiment grew in San

Francisco in the 1860s and 1870s. In October and November 1876, a joint congressional committee chaired by Oliver P. Morton, a human rights champion, held public hearings in San Francisco on Chinese immigration, character, and labor. The majority called for renegotiation of the Burlingame Treaty of 1868 and the elimination of unrestricted Chinese immigration to the United States. In 1876 and 1877, a special California Senate report argued that the Chinese failed to assimilate into American society and contributed to the decay of American character and values. In 1877, the Great Railroad Strike inspired anti-Chinese riots in San Francisco. In 1878, the California State constitutional convention supported restricting the Chinese from voting and working on state or local public works. Both the U.S. House and Senate approved a bill allowing each vessel to land no more than fifteen Chinese passengers, amended further by the Senate to further restrict general rights of Chinese citizens by repealing articles five and six of the Burlingame Treaty.

Hayes vetoed the Chinese Exclusion Bill on March 1. In many parts of the country, especially the West, Hayes was denounced as un-American and burned in effigy. He argued that the Burlingame Treaty was advantageous to the United States, especially with respect to business and trade, and that rights of Americans in China would be injured if it were violated. He also thought that Chinese immigration to the West Coast was not threatening to American society and that diplomatic solutions, negotiations, and even arbitrations should be pursued jointly between the United States and China.

Moreover, Hayes indicated strong sympathies to both white Californians and the Chinese as it was his life's habit to be sensitive to the issues of race and equality. He had argued consistently in his positions on black equality and voting rights in the South, and with his support of Native American rights, he commented on the Chinese-American race relations in California: "If we would put ourselves in the place of white Californians, it is absolutely certain that we should think and feel as they do." But as a firm supporter of equal rights and the principles of the Declaration of Independence, he also proclaimed that "our experiences in dealing with weaker races—the negroes and Indians for example—is not encouraging. We shall oppress the Chinamen, and their presence will make hoodlums or vagabonds of their oppressors." Nonetheless, Hayes recognized that foreign immigration presented likely long-term and substantial problems with regard to assimilation into American society. His trip to the West in the fall of 1880 presented Hayes with a chance to meet California labor, Chinese immigrant workers, and state legislative leaders.

Life after Presidency

In retirement at Spiegel Grove, Ohio, from 1881 until his death on January 17, 1893, Hayes remained very much devoted to educational reform and causes benefiting black Americans. More so than his nineteenth century predecessors, he was the model of the modern ex-president.

In national, state, and local affairs he sought to give his service in order to bring "presence, prominence, and dignity to each organization." Whether presiding over the Board of Trustees of the Ohio State University, the Birchard Public Library, the Slater Fund for Negro Education, the meetings of the Military Order of the Loyal Legion, the Sandusky County Bible Society, or the National Prison Congress, Hayes roamed the nation. In particular, he helped Civil War veterans associations, the National Prison Association, spoke at dedications and events, and was a moving force behind the Lake Mohonk Conference starting in 1890 in New York to frame platforms for Native American and black schooling, opportunity, and rights. Lucy Hayes passed away at Spiegel Grove on June 25, 1889, but the former president continued to serve his community, state, and nation by welcoming visitors, and handling a voluminous personal correspondence more typical of eighteenth and nineteenth presidential leaders than their twentieth and twenty-first century counterparts. Often taking strong and controversial positions, Rutherford Hayes sought to give stability, character, and the care of a moderate reformer to the most important issues of the Gilded Age in America.

Legacy

Throughout his administration, Rutherford Hayes displayed a genuine attentiveness to foreign and diplomatic affairs. American trade, commerce, and exports increased substantially with Europe, Asia, and Latin America. While the 1870s and 1880s didn't draw Hayes's attention to foreign affairs as much as they did Cleveland and McKinley, these presidents addressed the modern age of the 1890s—an age of American imperialism and global concerns. Nonetheless, Hayes's foreign relations policies indicated that the American hemisphere was both a valued and vital concern and that the United States should involve herself as a great business and commercial force in the world, heralding the emergence of new foreign relations tensions with Great Britain, France, Spain, and Germany in the 1890s.

Murney Gerlach

Chronology

1877

March 2: Rutherford Hayes declared president by Congress; William Wheeler is vice president.

April 24: Russia declares war on Turkey.

June 1: U.S. troops ordered to patrol Mexican border.

1878

January 17: United States signs treaty with Samoa, establishing naval base at Pago Pago.

February 8: British fleet protects Istanbul from Russian capture.

February 10: Convention of El Zanjon, Cuban insurrection ends.

March 23: United States recognizes Diaz regime in Mexico.

May 18: Colombia grants French company exclusive Panama Canal rights.

1879

October 7: Germany and Austria sign Dual Alliance.

1880

February 24: Mexican border tension ends.

March 8: House protests French Panama Canal project.

October 27: United States fails to mediate war between Chile and Bolivia/Peru.

November 2: James Garfield elected president; Chester Arthur vice president.

November 17: Treaty with China permits immigration restrictions.

References and Further Reading

Barnard, Harry. *Rutherford B. Hayes and His America.* Newtown: CT: American Political Biography, 1992.

Barrows, Chester L. *William M. Evarts: Lawyer, Diplomat, Statesman.* Chapel Hill, NC: University of North Carolina Press, 1941.

Davison, Kenneth E. *The Presidency of Rutherford B. Hayes.* Westport, CT: Greenwood, 1972.

Dyer, Brainerd. "Secretary of State," in *The Public Career of William M. Evarts.* Berkeley, CA: University of California Press, 1933.

Hoogenboom, Ari. *Rutherford B. Hayes, Warrior and President.* Lawrence, KS: University Press of Kansas, 1955.

Lewis, William Ray. "The Hayes Administration and Mexico." *The Southwestern Historical Quarterly* 24/2 (1920): 140–153.

McCullough, David. *The Path between the Seas: The Creation of the Panama Canal.* New York: Simon and Schuster, 1977.

Saxon, Alexander. *The Indispensable Enemy: Labor and the Anti-Chinese Movement in California.* Berkeley, CA: University of California Press, 1971.

Williams, Charles Richard. *The Diary and Letters of Rutherford B. Hayes: Nineteenth President of the United States,* 5 vols. Columbus, OH: State Archaeological and Historical Society, 1922–1926.

Williams, Charles Richard. *Life of Rutherford Birchard Hayes: Nineteenth President of the United States.* 2 vols. Columbus, OH: Ohio State Archaelogical and Historical Society, 1914.

Williams, T. Harry. *Hayes: The Diary of a President, 1875–81.* New York: David McKay, 1964.

James Abram Garfield (1881)

Early Life and Political Career

In office for just six months and fifteen days from his inauguration to his assassination, James Abram Garfield made only the first tentative steps in an administration that was completed after his death by his vice president, Chester Arthur. Had he lived to serve a full term, there was nothing in his political career prior to the presidential office to suggest that Garfield would have been a more forceful leader than Arthur. His natural temperament was that of a conciliator and his primary political skills were more legislative than executive. His contribution to American foreign relations was therefore modest and came chiefly in the form of initiatives begun by his secretary of state, James Blaine, some of which were revised or abandoned by Arthur.

He was born in Orange Township in Cuyahoga County, Ohio, to Abram Garfield and Eliza Ballou on November 19, 1831. Abram Garfield died suddenly when James was only two years of age, leaving a widow and son to a hard life on the farm. Eliza Garfield nonetheless noticed that her son was intellectually gifted and encouraged him to acquire strong secular and religious educations. Garfield became a member of the evangelical Disciples of Christ at the age of eighteen and attended the church's Western Reserve Eclectic Institute, later Hiram College, in Hiram, Ohio. After attending and graduating from Williams College in Massachusetts, Garfield began a teaching career in West Troy, New York. He later returned to Hiram College as a professor of ancient languages—he was reputed to be able to write simultaneously Greek with one hand and Latin with the other—and became the college president before his thirtieth birthday. He married Lucretia Rudolf in 1858. They had five sons, one of whom later engaged in a political career and served as secretary of the interior under Theodore Roosevelt.

Garfield's own career in public office began in 1859 with his election to the Ohio senate, but was promptly interrupted by the outbreak of the Civil War. He enlisted in the Union Army and was given the command at the rank of colonel of the 42nd Ohio Volunteer Infantry. He served with distinction at Middle Creek, Kentucky, and then at Shiloh and Chickamauga, finishing the war as a major general. Garfield reentered the political arena in 1863 with a successful run for a seat in the U.S. House of Representatives, and became Republican floor leader of the House in 1876. In the same year, Garfield was a member of

James Abram Garfield was a conciliator committed to sound policies yet was robbed of the chance to test them. (Library of Congress)

the electoral commission that awarded the twenty-two contested Electoral College votes to Rutherford Hayes in his campaign against Samuel Tilden for the presidency.

The Dark Horse Presidency

In 1880, Ohio Republicans sent Garfield to a seat in the U.S. Senate, a seat that he was never able to take. Instead, he was drawn into the internal struggle over the nomination of the Republican Party for the presidential election of that year and ultimately was nominated himself by the same convention that he had attended initially as manager and spokesman for the candidacy of the Ohio Senator John Sherman. The favorite of the conservative "Stalwart" faction of the party was two-term president Ulysses S. Grant, while the moderate "Half Breed" faction backed Senator James

Blaine of Maine. Defending Sherman as the candidate of con-ciliation, Garfield's eloquent call for party unity to the assembled delegates was so well received that New York Senator Roscoe Conkling, who backed Grant, called Garfield "Ohio's real candidate and dark horse." When successive ballots yielded no clear winner from the three front-runners, Garfield was urged to offer himself as a compromise candidate but declined. The Wisconsin delegation finally cast a score of votes for Garfield, and a slow stampede toward his non-candidacy began. He was finally nominated on the thirty-sixth ballot.

The presidential election of 1880 yielded the closest outcome to that date, but Garfield took 214 Electoral College votes to the 155 of the Democratic nominee, Winfield Scott Hancock, due to the support of Conkling's party machine in New York and the Republican victory in that state. In the high summer of the "spoils" era on American politics, Garfield's real problems began after the election with the task of building a cabinet. In part because he had been the compromise nominee, the president-elect was besieged from all sides of the Republican Party for key executive appointments. The expectations of the Conkling Stalwarts in particular were disappointed, possibly because they were so high to begin with; they considered Vice President Chester Arthur their only reliable contact in the cabinet. The most noteworthy appointment was that of James Blaine, one of the Half Breed Republicans, as Garfield's secretary of state, both because of Blaine's minimal qualifications to preside over American foreign relations and because Blaine ultimately made significant contributions to foreign policy under President Benjamin Harrison.

Commerce and the Hemisphere

Garfield's primary concern in foreign affairs was with commercial expansion. He inherited from the Hayes administration a concern over European ambitions in the Western Hemisphere generally, and the designs of France and Britain in particular. In a period of intensified imperial competition among the European powers for influence overseas, the credibility of the Monroe Doctrine of 1823 was being tested anew. In 1879, Ferdinand Lesseps, the visionary engineer of the Suez Canal, had announced the plan for a French-financed canal linking the Atlantic with the Pacific Ocean across the isthmus of Panama and attempted to elicit support for the project in the United States. In response, Hayes had cautioned that it would consider any such canal to be part of the coastline of the United States and acceptable only under American control. To underscore his point he deployed naval vessels to cruise off the coast of Panama. An American company had meanwhile secured the rights from the government of Nicaragua to construct a rival interoceanic waterway. The

Nicaraguan project, however, was troubled by a disinterested Congress influenced above all by the powerful transcontinental railway lobby as well as the inconvenient fact that the Clayton-Bulwer Treaty of 1850 required the United States to share control of an isthmian canal with Great Britain.

In June 1881, Secretary of State Blaine therefore sought to amend the treaty, first by circulating a memo to U.S. embassies in Europe maintaining that in light of the changed international circumstance the United States alone should administer any interoceanic waterway in Central America, provided that it guarantee freedom of transit to all nations, and additionally by inviting the British government to renegotiate the 1850 treaty. The British government had no interest in renegotiation. Garfield appreciated that over the long term, the matter of American control could not be left unresolved. He believed in the principle of reciprocity in trade, arguing to Congress that "we want all fair chances that the markets of the world can give us for selling our surplus supplies" and cautioning Britain against any attempt to penetrate the "great tropical world" of Central America. Furthermore, Garfield anticipated that with the completion of the transcontinental railway and the acquisition of Alaska, the United States would emerge as the dominant power not only of the Western Hemisphere but also as the arbiter of the Pacific Ocean, "the controller of its commerce and chief nation that inhabits its shores." With the exception of Canada, he generally repudiated territorial expansion. He preferred the hope that commercial power would bring under American influence territories and markets that the European powers competed to conquer militarily and govern as overseas colonies. This outlook was partly Republican Party cant and partly an attempt to make a virtue out of weakness, because in 1880, the United States did not possess a navy of any significance and was in no position to be arbiter of power in the Pacific.

The administration's diplomacy nonetheless anticipated the future of American influence in the Pacific with its initiatives just as the president himself did with strong words. Blaine genuinely believed in hemispheric solidarity and acted accordingly. Most prominent among his attempts at meditative diplomacy was in the War of the Pacific involving an expansionist Chile against Bolivia and Peru in a territorial dispute over the Atacama Desert. Chile was supported by Britain, while Blaine favored Peru and insisted that no territorial change should take place without the consent "of all the powers whose people and whose national interest are involved." Meanwhile, the government of Guatemala requested that United States intervene on its behalf in its dispute with Mexico over the province Chiapas and the district of Soconusco. Blaine strongly favored the Guatemalan position, but Mexico rejected American mediation.

Legacy

Blaine's ambitions for mediation diplomacy suited President Garfield's conciliatory approach to contentious issues, so the idea of a Pan-American conference to be hosted by the United States (ostensibly for the purpose of preventing future wars and insurrections) might have found favor with him had he lived out his term. Garfield was with Blaine at the Baltimore and Potomac railway station in Washington on July 2, 1881, when he was gunned down by Charles J. Guiteau, a mentally unstable and disappointed office seeker from the Stalwart faction of the Republicans. Although Garfield clung to life for several months, his presidency was effectively over. Neither Blaine's career nor his diplomatic initiatives, however, died with Garfield—both awaited a future president. In 1881, the nation had neither the will nor the power to support a diplomacy seeking the kind of prestige Blaine sought for the nation and himself. The best evidence of that was the fact that its president had been felled not by the rigors of office at the head of an emerging great power but rather by a family feud within the Republican Party.

Carl Cavanagh Hodge

Chronology

1881

May 12: France establishes protectorate in Tunisia.

June 2: Britain pays an indemnity to U.S. fishermen for 1878 Newfoundland fisheries quarrel.

June 18: Austria, Germany, and Russia form Three Emperors League.

June 24: Secretary of State Blaine seeks revision of the Clayton-Bulwer Treaty.

July 2: President Garfield shot.

September 19: President Garfield dies; Chester Arthur sworn in as president.

References and Further Reading

Doenecke, Justus D. *The Presidencies of James A. Garfield & Chester A. Arthur.* Lawrence, KS: The Regents Press of Kansas, 1981.

LeFeber, Walter. *The American Search for Opportunity, 1865–1913.* New York: Cambridge University Press, 1993.

Peskin, Allan. *Garfield: A Biography.* Kent, OH: Kent State University Press, 1999.

Taylor, John M. *Garfield of Ohio: The Available Man.* Newtown, CT: American Political Biography, 2005.

Thayer, William Makepeace. *From Log Cabin to White House: The Life James A. Garfield.* New York: Hurst, 1908.

Chester Alan Arthur (1881–1885)

Early Life and Political Career

The twenty-first president was born on October 5, 1829, in Fairfield, Vermont, to Malvina Stone and William Arthur, a Baptist minister. The Reverend Arthur's search for a permanent parish kept his family on the road for ten years before he landed a ministry at Union Village, New York, and later at Schenectady when Chester Alan Arthur was fifteen. Chester then studied Greek and Latin at Union Village, graduated in 1848, and worked in teaching posts in Vermont and New York while studying law at home. He finished his training at the law office of Culver & Parker in New York City, was called to the bar in 1854, and made a partner at Culver, Parker, & Arthur in 1856.

Having inherited a dedicated opposition to slavery from his abolitionist father, Arthur found many like-minded and politically active colleagues in New York, not the least of whom was his firm's founder, Erastus Culver, a fervent opponent of the Fugitive Slave Act of 1850 that required Northern states to deny shelter to slaves fleeing from the South. Arthur attended the meetings of the Free Soilers Party, which opposed the admission of additional slave states to the Union, and signed on as a party member to serve as an inspector of elections in 1856. Through Thurlow Weed, the leader of the New York State Whig Party, Arthur learned the subtle arts of the "spoils system" of urban politics and came into the political orbit of Edwin D. Morgan, whom Weed helped to elect governor in 1858. Morgan made Arthur state engineer-in-chief and then his personal adjutant at the head of the New York State Republican Party.

In 1859, Arthur married Ellen Lewis Herndon, an Episcopalian from Virginia whose family sympathized with the Confederate cause as the prospect of civil war loomed closer. After the attack on Fort Sumter, Arthur was commissioned at the rank of brigadier general and made quartermaster general for the state. Suddenly responsible for the feeding and supply of tens of thousands of Union troops, Arthur saved the cash-strapped state money by contracting out the requisitioning of supplies to the lowest bidder. By all accounts Arthur lived well during his tenure as quartermaster but did not abuse the advantages of the business contacts he cultivated for personal gain. Because his position depended on his place in the patronage machine of the New York Republican Party, Arthur nonetheless found himself suddenly out of work when the Democrats won the 1862 election and Morgan left office. Arthur returned to his law

Chester Alan Arthur, chiefly a domestic reformer, also began the modernization of the U.S. Navy. (Library of Congress)

practice and established a reputation for settling war claims as well as for drafting legislative bills for compensating claimants more justly, the proceeds from which helped to sustain the prominent profile he and his wife maintained in the upper reaches of Manhattan society. The Arthurs' astute socializing facilitated a rapid ascent in the state Republican Party, even as Arthur finessed the tension between his own ambitions and "Nell" Arthur's Confederate sympathies by opposing the increasingly popular sentiment that the war was a crusade to abolish slavery. Among Arthur's greatest political skills, in fact, was stealth in matters of policy; he avoided taking principled stands over contentious issues and concentrated on making himself indispensable as an efficient subaltern to more charismatic personalities.

Far and away the most important of these personalities was Roscoe Conkling, a rising star of the conservative wing of New York Republicanism that included Lincoln's secretary of state, William Seward, and Thurlow Weed, whose patronage power was now becoming the stuff of legend. In the years immediately following the Union victory in the Civil War, when a triumphant Republican Party could offer new horizons of opportunity to well-positioned loyalists like Arthur, this pragmatic faction of party "stalwarts" vied with the more ideologically fervent Radical Republicans for control of the national post-bellum agenda. In the late 1860s, the influence of the Radical Republicans began to fade after the death of Thaddeus Stevens, their most effective congressional leader. With the election of Ulysses S. Grant to the presidency in 1868, the national dominance of pragmatic Republicanism was secured for a generation. With Conkling's support, Arthur was made the collector of the New York State Customs House, which was the largest federal office in the United States at that time. From his office in the Merchants' Exchange Building on Wall Street, Arthur broadened his contacts with wealthy businessmen while diligently serving the Conkling party machine. When in 1876 Conkling sought the Republican presidential nomination, Arthur worked in his campaign but quickly transferred his talents to that of the eventual nominee, Rutherford Hayes, by raising political assessments from Customs House workers for the Hayes campaign.

In the aftermath of the most controversial presidential election to that date—the Democratic nominee Samuel Tilden won the popular vote, but the Republican Rutherford Hayes won the Electoral College—the newly inaugurated Hayes launched a campaign of civil service reform of which an investigation of corrupt practices in custom houses of the United States was a centerpiece. Strictly speaking, Arthur had done nothing that was illegal, but the report released in 1878 called for his suspension as collector. Far from ruining his career, the affair actually made Arthur a figure of national attention for the first time and drew sympathy not only from Republican stalwarts but also from Democrats seeking to exploit divisions within the Republican Party. Arthur resigned his post and returned to his law practice, yet suffered a much greater blow with the sudden death of his wife in January 1880.

In the same year, however, Arthur's political fortunes reversed dramatically. At the Republican national convention he led the campaign to nominate President Grant for a third term. When the nomination instead went to James Garfield, Arthur was himself approached for the vice presidential nomination and accepted. His role in the campaign was modest, concentrated on his home ground of New York, and any sense of celebration over a Republican victory that propelled him to national office was darkened by continuing depression over Nell's absence. Arthur had little influence in the business of the Garfield administration and was instead immediately drawn into a conflict over presidential appointments that enraged his traditional Stalwart

allies from New York, Conkling in particular. When one of the Stalwarts, the mentally unstable Charles Guiteau, went so far went so far as to assassinate Garfield on July 2, 1881, the problem of the Garfield appointments evaporated. Arthur had now to contemplate assuming the duties of the nation's highest office.

A Diplomacy of Caution

The stricken president lingered until September 19, 1881, at which point President Arthur appointed an entirely new cabinet. But it was not the cabinet that Conkling would have appointed, and Arthur retained an old Conkling enemy, James Blaine, as secretary of state until December, when he finally chose Frederick Frelinghuysen to replace him. Furthermore, Arthur announced in his first annual message as president his intention to make civil service reform a major feature of his domestic agenda. The resulting Pendleton Act of 1883, named for its congressional sponsor, Senator George H. Pendleton of Ohio, began the process of dismantling the spoils system by establishing competitive examination to determine the fitness of appointees to federal offices on a merit basis. Arthur also advocated a cautious revision of tariff laws and supported the War Department's advice that the army be increased to full strength of 30,000 to protect settlers and property against Indian attack in the West. He balanced the latter by calling for legislation to prevent encroachment on lands set aside for the Indians as well as for measures to make them citizens of the United States—a call that was largely ignored by Congress. In addition, Arthur vetoed legislation promoted by John F. Miller, a fellow Republican from California, that excluded Chinese labor from migrating to the United States and denied citizenship to those already in residence on the grounds that it violated the Burlingame Treaty of 1868 which gave the Chinese the right of unlimited immigration.

The replacement of James Blaine with Frelinghuysen as secretary of state signaled a significant change. Although Frelinghuysen had little experience in foreign affairs, his native caution steered him away from ventures that the flamboyant Blaine sought for American prestige that required the United States to punch above its weight diplomatically. He abandoned Blaine's mediation diplomacy in the War of the Pacific involving Bolivia, Chile, and Peru, but did this while William H. Trescot, dispatched to South America by Blaine during the transitional phase from the Garfield to the Arthur administration, was in Santiago. Additionally, Frelinghuysen published diplomatic correspondence covering discussions of the Pacific War from 1879 to 1882 along with a message recalling the Trescot mission—yet never cabled Trescot about this development. Apart from Trescot's personal embarrassment and professional humiliation in learning of this news from the Chilean foreign minister, the mediation mission was undercut, and any Chilean fear of American pressure was removed in one stroke. Chilean forces promptly picked up the effort to seize as much Bolivian and Peruvian territory as possible. Frelinghuysen then revoked the invitations to the peace conference scheduled by Blaine for November 22, 1882, to which nine Latin American countries had already issued their acceptance.

Awkwardly articulated though it was, this belated policy of neutrality did reflect the White House position. In his annual message to Congress of December 12, 1882, Arthur attacked Chile's stubbornness. He cautioned that a dictated peace would have to be "supplemented by the armies and navies of the United States" and would "almost inevitably lead to the establishment of a protectorate—a result utterly at odds with our past policy, injurious to our own present interests, and full of embarrassments for the future." Any Peruvian hope for American intervention was thus dashed. In 1883, the new American minister to Chile persuaded its government to moderate its demands and to meet Peru at the negotiating table. In the Treaty of Ancon, Chile obtained Tarapaca and occupied Tacna and Arica for ten years; in 1884 Bolivia then signed the Truce of Valparaiso with Chile in which it lost Tarapaca and Atacama.

The Arthur administration also reversed the direction of American diplomacy in the Mexican-Guatemalan dispute by turning down a treaty jointly proposed by Guatemala, Honduras, and El Salvador. According to its text, the United States was to offer the three countries protection from attack in return for the right to occupy ports and to garrison troops on their territories. When, in May 1882, the Guatemalan foreign minister offered low tariffs and rights to build a canal in return for U.S. protection, Frelinghuysen again declined. Thwarted in its attempt to draw on American strength, Guatemala sought a settlement with Mexico and in September 1882 signed a treaty calling for direct negotiations.

The Highways of Commerce

In contrast to his policy on other hemispheric issues, Arthur remained on the course set by Blaine concerning American interest in a canal across Central America linking the Atlantic and Pacific coasts. Frelinghuysen, in fact, sought not a revision of the Clayton-Bulwer Treaty concluded with Great Britain in 1850, but its abrogation. He argued that joint rights could only give rise to quarreling, and that the 1850 treaty had in any case never applied to Panama. The British government, however, maintained that the treaty had applied to all isthmian canal routes and refused to surrender significant treaty rights on demand. In light of this failure, mounting concern over European and possibly Chilean interest in a Central American canal brought the administration's attention to focus on a Nicaraguan canal as

the best way to keep Europe out of the isthmus. After lengthy bargaining with the Nicaraguan government, a treaty was signed on December 1, 1884, that would give the United States co-ownership over a 2.5-mile strip for the canal and a defensive alliance with Nicaragua, whose authorities were to have civil jurisdiction—in substance, an American protectorate over Nicaragua. For a variety of reasons, ranging from the charge that bribery had been used in the negotiations to the more important factor—too many congressmen rejected the idea of assuming responsibility for the construction and defense of such a waterway—the Nicaraguan scheme was unpopular in Congress. The treaty failed ratification by nine votes and was subsequently withdrawn by the Cleveland administration.

American desire to have control over a Central American canal was heightened by the emergence of the United States as a major commercial power, while national caution about shouldering hemispheric burdens reflected a consciousness of its weakness as a naval power. In the years since the Civil War, the condition of the U.S. Navy had declined to that of a flotilla of wooden antiques. By 1880, every European power and several Latin American states possessed superior fleets. As Britain and France were rapidly constructing steel navies, Captain Alfred Thayer Mahan, later to become the founder of modern naval strategic theory, observed that "we have not six ships that would be kept at sea in war by any maritime power." Morale in the Navy was so poor and the Navy Department so incompetently run that the fleet had become a national joke. And yet national prestige, the credibility of the Monroe Doctrine, and any prospect of American control of an isthmian canal depended on robust sea power. Without reform and modernization of its Navy, the critics argued, the United States could be defeated at sea by Britain, France, German, Chile, or even China. Ultimately, export trade would be lost unless it was protected.

A holdover from the Garfield administration, William H. Hunt initially served as Arthur's secretary of the Navy. Hunt began the process of naval modernization by appointing a planning board to assess the Navy's needs. When the board's report called for the construction of sixty-eight warships, a large number of them steel, Arthur made naval modernization a presidential cause. Citing "the highways of commerce, the varied interests of our foreign trade," Arthur made the plea for a strong Navy and brought in William E. Chandler, a ruthless party organizer from New Hampshire, to replace Hunt at the head of the Navy Department.

The appointment was an extraordinary success. Chandler's executive talents included an ability to get quickly to the heart of a challenge. He observed that the United States had a "natural, justifiable and necessary ascendancy in the affairs of the American hemisphere," from which it followed that its Navy ought to be "capable on brief notice of being expanded into invincible columns." Chandler stripped the officer corps of over 400 men; closed redundant Navy yards around the country while supervising plans for erecting new gun foundries; established the Naval War College at Newport, Rhode Island; and created the Office of Naval Intelligence. The naval advisory board, headed by Chandler-appointee Commodore Robert Shufeldt, acknowledged that Congress would not fund the immediate construction of sixty-eight ships and astutely scaled back the number while recommending commissioning three armored cruisers with the speed, endurance, and firepower capable of protecting far-flung commercial interests. On March 3, 1883, Congress authorized the construction of the ships so that development of a modern navy could begin. Though significant in light of the state affairs when Arthur came to office, it was a modest start. It was not until the 1890s that the United States constructed its first battleships.

On the same day that it authorized the new warships, Congress voted to continue protecting American commerce by way of its more traditional method of trade tariffs. In response to agitation in favor of lowered tariffs to help reduce consumer cost of both European imports and American manufactures, Arthur had appointed a nine-man commission to provide recommendations on the nation's import duties. To universal surprise, the commission's report called for substantial reductions, averaging between 20 and 25 percent, and in some instances as much as 50 percent. Arthur made no specific recommendations and sought instead a general enlargement of the list of goods to be declared duty-free along with substantial reductions of the duties on several commodities. The lack of more specific presidential goals for tariff reduction may have weakened the cause from the outset. In any event, protectionist lobbies converged on Congress to undermine, clause by clause, the substance of the recommendations. The resulting legislation, the Tariff Act of 1883, dropped the average duty by 5 percent, and the tariffs remained between 35 and 40 percent on most items. The act was a dog's breakfast of special provisions, and in fact earned it the nickname "Mongrel Tariff" because nobody wanted to acknowledge responsibility for it. Arthur's reputation was also damaged by the widespread perception that he had been a passive bystander.

In the closing weeks of his presidency, he sought the renewal of the 1875 treaty with Hawaii, calling on Congress in his second and third annual messages to act decisively. Frelinghuysen rightly believed that Hawaii was vital to the American highways of commerce and that it was eminently qualified by virtue of geography to become an American protectorate. On December 6, 1884, the 1875 treaty was renewed, but a new article was included to give the United States the exclusive right to the harbor of the Pearl River and to establish a naval coaling and repair station there.

Legacy

This revised treaty was agreed on after the election of the Democrat Grover Cleveland to the presidency in November 1884. In this affair, too, Arthur was often reduced to the role of bystander. Without an election mandate, he had instead completed the Garfield presidency without ever establishing a presidential coalition of his own within the Republican Party. In 1884, the party was badly divided, and Arthur was only one of several contenders. For all the controversy he drew, James Blaine had more support than either Arthur or the other rivals could hope to marshal. After a respectable showing on the first ballot, Arthur's support faded quickly.

The contribution of his presidency to American foreign policy was therefore that of a caretaker who had at least managed to avoid major setbacks or national humiliations and had ventured modest improvements on which future presidents could build. In the 1880s, foreign policy was still determined by a combination of party politics and parochial economic interests. There is no evidence that Arthur would have overcome the prevailing national comfort with commercial protectionism and disinterest in an assertive international diplomacy had he attempted more robust presidential leadership. In the event, he did not, and Chester Arthur surrendered the executive office as quietly as he had taken it over.

Carl Cavanagh Hodge

Chronology

1882

January 26: Release of confidential documents thwart U.S. mediation efforts in Chile-Bolivian dispute.

May 6: Congress suspends Chinese immigration for ten years.

May 20: Austria, Germany, and Italy form Triple Alliance.

May 22: U.S. commercial treaty with Korea.

September 15: British troops occupy Cairo.

1883

February 22: Congress votes to repay Japan 1864 Shimonoseki indemnity.

March 3: Tariff of 1883 retains high duties.

March 3: Congress authorizes construction of a modern U.S. Navy.

October 20: Treaty of Ancon ends war between Chile and Peru.

1884

April 4: Truce of Valparaiso ends war between Chile and Bolovia.

June 6: Treaty of Hue gives France control of northern Vietnam.

July 5: Congress further tightens Chinese immigration.

November 4: Grover Cleveland elected president; Thomas Hendricks vice-president.

December 6: United States secures naval base at Pearl Harbor, Hawaii.

References and Further Reading

Karabel, Zachary. *Chester Alan Arthur.* New York: Henry Holt and Company, 2004.

Doenecke, Justus D. *The Presidencies of James A. Garfield & Chester A. Arthur.* Lawrence, KS: The Regents Press of Kansas, 1981.

LeFeber, Walter. *The American Search for Opportunity, 1865–1913.* New York: Cambridge University Press, 1993.

— Stephen Grover Cleveland (1885–1889, 1893–1897) —

Early Life and Political Career

Stephen Grover Cleveland was born on March 18, 1837, in Caldwell, New Jersey, the fifth of nine children of Richard Falley and Ann Neal Cleveland. Named after Stephen Grover, a minister whom Richard had succeeded in the local church, young Cleveland grew up in a strictly maintained household. The family gathered for nightly worship in the house, and attended Sunday school, prayer meetings, and two lengthy worship services every Sunday. Richard Cleveland, though educated at Yale, and apparently a knowledgeable and pious man, was not considered a highly motivating preacher. Because he could not rise above his station as a lay-preacher at small country churches, he could not afford to put down roots in any one place and expect to make a living for his large family. As a result, the Cleveland family moved around several times during Grover's youth.

By all accounts, Grover was a good child, considered large for his age, and was known to love sports and playing pranks. He favored fishing excursions as a pastime, but also worked at odd jobs to aid his family financially. Cleveland was not a brilliant student, but he loved the pursuit of knowledge. To that end, he studied hard and learned his lessons as well as he could to find his way into college. His work ethic, dependability, and honesty made him a perfect candidate to follow in his father's footsteps as a respected preacher, but when Richard died in 1853, Grover saw his visions of a college education disappear. The family was left nearly destitute; so Grover, now only sixteen, and his older brother, William, became teachers at the New York Institute for the Blind. They made little money, but managed to send their mother whatever they could spare.

Life in New York City was not all that Cleveland had expected. Hours spent working at the Institute were long, and left little time for Grover to do anything but widen his own education through reading books he found at the school. By the time he was released from service in 1854, he had begun to take an interest in studying law. Cleveland was undereducated and unemployed when, in spring 1855, he accepted a loan for $25 from a church elder to help cover the costs of a westward expedition. Cleveland made it as far as Buffalo, New York, where he visited an uncle, Lewis F. Allen, a prolific stockman. It did not take much coaxing from Allen to persuade Cleveland to stay on at the farm as a sort of bookkeeper for $50 for five months of labor. At the

Stephen Grover Cleveland opposed the rising tide of imperialist sentiment in the United States. (Library of Congress)

end of the agreed-upon term, Allen introduced Cleveland to the partners of the Buffalo firm of Rogers, Bowen, and Rogers, who gave the young man a job as office clerk, and gave him free reign of the firm's library in his spare time. Cleveland began immediately to immerse himself in the law, a step that would begin his journey to the White House.

Following nearly four years of study, Cleveland was admitted to the New York bar in May 1858. Rather than strike out on his own path, he remained with Rogers, Bowen, and Rogers while still maintaining his uncle's books. When the national issue of slavery began coming to a head in the same year, Cleveland began working for the local Democratic organization in his free time. He chose this party affiliation most likely because of his father's aversion to abolitionism, the Democratic views of his employers (staunch Jacksonians), and the fact the he believed that the

Democrats were, at the time, more steadfastly conservative than the followers of Republican presidential candidate John C. Fremont.

In October 1862, Cleveland's reputation as an honest, dependable worker, and his frequent appearances at Democratic functions helped him gain the position of delegate from Buffalo's second ward at the age of twenty-five. After a year in that post, he was nominated and elected ward supervisor in November 1863. The same month saw him appointed assistant district attorney, a job he performed for the next three years. Cleveland was nominated for district attorney in 1865, but was defeated in the election. In 1870, while practicing law in a large firm in Buffalo, Cleveland was elected sheriff of Erie County. When his term was up in 1873, he again busied himself with practicing law.

Cleveland's meteoric rise to the White House began with his 1881 nomination and election to the office of mayor of Buffalo, New York. Following a landslide victory, Cleveland took the oath of office in Buffalo at the age of forty-four. He carried on his penchant for stopping government waste and fraud by passing bills to get a full day's work out of government employees, ceasing bribes and contract swindles, and having the city auditor actually look into the merits of city accounts and claims rather than just crunching numbers blindly. The same summer, Cleveland was nominated to run for New York's next governor. That November, splits within the state's Republican caucus allowed Cleveland to cruise to Albany in another landslide election. His previous manner in governing Buffalo translated well to the governor's office, and Cleveland wasted no time exposing scandal and corruption as well as appointing forthright individuals to various government posts. Having broken with the deceitful traditions of Tammany Hall, Cleveland was seen as the saving grace of the Democratic Party. Less then two years after gaining the highest office in New York, Cleveland was nominated for and elected president of the United States in 1884.

America's Steel Navy

Perhaps the most significant foreign policy measure enacted by the Cleveland administration was the modernization of the United States Navy from wooden sailing ships to wholly steel-hulled vessels. In 1883, during Chester A. Arthur's tenure in office, a naval advisory board determined that the Navy was dangerously archaic. Congress authorized and appropriated funds for three steel cruisers to be christened the *Atlanta, Boston,* and *Chicago,* as well as a dispatch boat named *Dolphin.* Arthur's Secretary of the Navy, William E. Chandler, awarded the building contracts to John Roach, an elderly shipbuilder who had done some work on the first ironclad boats constructed during Ulysses S. Grant's administration in the White House. By the time Arthur's term had ended, Congress had authorized the construction of four

more ships, which Cleveland's Secretary of the Navy, William C. Whitney, was to oversee.

The *Dolphin* was the first vessel to be completed, but examiners concluded that the overall construction of the ship was subpar. Attorney General Augustus H. Garland ruled that the government was not bound to accept delivery of the boat as the contract had not been complied with, and that the same contract had been illegally awarded by Chandler, who awarded the contract to his friend, Roach, without looking at other bids. As a result, the Department of the Navy took over Roach's business and workforce to complete the building of the authorized vessels.

On Cleveland's orders, Whitney began a massive overhaul of the department, making it more efficient, knowledgeable, and experienced in the construction of modern warships. Bureaus were consolidated and coordinated to cut down on wasteful spending, needless duplication of tasks, and minimize confusion within the department. Cleveland's push for a fresh agenda for the Navy resulted in appropriations for a new cruiser, two armored warships, and a torpedo boat. Soon after, contracts for five more cruisers—the *Baltimore, Charleston, Philadelphia, Newark,* and *San Francisco*—were awarded through a proper bidding process.

The new Navy, or White Squadron, as it was called, helped the United States become less reliant on foreign steel manufacturers and created jobs domestically, but Cleveland's interest in retooling the Navy was not financial. Cleveland, not a man interested in the offensive capabilities of naval vessels, was simply concerned with ensuring that his country's extensive coastlines and shipping lanes could be adequately defended. America's rebuilt Navy was a drastic change from its former dilapidated self, but it was certainly no match for a fleet such as Britain's. In time this would change, as Cleveland's policy started the country on a path toward building a naval force capable of maintaining a forward presence for the good of not only the interests of the United States, but also those of her allies across the globe.

The North American Fishing Dispute

The second major foreign policy issue encountered during Cleveland's first term in the White House involved a clash between the United States and Canada over their respective territorial waters and fishing rights. The Treaty of Washington, established in 1818, contained clauses allowing American fishermen the right to fish, ship cargo, and purchase supplies within Canadian waters in return for monetary duties. In July 1885, the clauses dealing with U.S.-Canadian fishing entitlements were abruptly rescinded due to concerns over the extremely high cost of duties and the influx of Canadian fish into the American market. In response, Canadian authorities began seizing American fishing ships and their crews for working in what were considered to be Canadian territorial waters.

Cleveland knew that the Canadian government was amenable to negotiating a new treaty, and further knew that the British government was also willing to find a diplomatic end to the problem. The biggest roadblock to accomplishing the task was the United States Senate, whose majority party, the Republicans, was not about to let Cleveland win the day. The Republicans believed that Canadian fishing privileges diminished the profits of American fishermen and unfairly depleted populations of the various fish found in the disputed territorial waters. They were pushing for retaliation against Canada for the warlike seizure of American vessels and sailors. This retaliation, they believed, should be in the form of permanent exclusion of Canadian goods and ships from American ports. In 1887, the Senate passed legislation to that effect—barring Canadian boats and Canadian-caught fish from entering U.S. ports.

The benefactors of such legislation would undoubtedly be the fishing concerns in and around New England, who were championed in the Senate by their Republican delegates. Cleveland believed that any retaliation was not to be made solely in the interest of a single facet of American society, but was to "maintain the national honor" of all Americans. Eventually, Cleveland sent the tough-talking Senate his own demand for immediate retaliation against Canada. He proposed an expansion of executive powers to control all laws and regulations dealing with all goods passing to or from the United States and Canada. While this would give the president augmented powers, which the Republicans would not condone, it also took potential profits away from all American fishing concerns, even those in New England. The bill proposed by Cleveland quickly passed through committee and floor passage in the House of Representatives, but was immediately quashed when it got to the Senate.

In February 1888, a treaty was finally drafted between the U.S. and Canada delineating Canada's territorial waters at a line three miles distant from its shoreline. The Bayard-Chamberlain Treaty granted American fishermen free navigation of the waters separating Cape Breton Island and Nova Scotia, as well as the right to buy supplies on trips back to the United States. Additionally, American vessels in distress were now allowed to seek Canadian aid. The removal of duties guaranteed Americans the right to buy bait and supplies and to hire additional crewmembers from Canadian ports. In the end, Cleveland had not only handled the Canadian dispute, but had also successfully handled his Republican detractors in the Senate.

A related dispute involved the seizure of British Columbian sealing schooners by authorities of the U.S. Treasury Department. Because the United States restricted not only domestic sealing on the Pribilof Islands off the coast of Alaska but also granted a monopoly to the Alaska Commercial Company in return for restrictions on the seal slaughter, the interest of foreign sealers in pelagic sealing—killing seals in the ocean rather than onshore—intensified. Both to preserve the seal population against wasteful slaughter and to protect the Alaskan company's monopoly, U.S. Customs ships began seizing foreign sealing ships in the vicinity of the Pribilofs, in effect declaring that the waters of the Bering Sea were American. Canada and Britain rejected any American authority to seize vessels outside the three-mile limit of the Alaskan waters, and in January 9, 1887, the British minister to Washington cautioned Secretary of State Thomas Bayard that Britain would not tolerate the seizure of Canadian pelagic sealing vessels. Bayard called for an international conference over the issue, but Canada refused participation. In March 1889, Cleveland signed legislation claiming U.S. sovereignty over the Bering Sea, and the crisis flared again during the Harrison administration.

The Samoan Crisis

The competition for sealing rights in the Bering Sea was only part of a larger picture of intensified international competition around the frontiers of American expansion. In 1878, the United States had acquired a naval station at Pago Pago in Samoa. Great Britain and Germany had also established a presence in Samoa, and in 1879 the three countries had agreed to regulate activity in the town of Apia jointly. But in 1885, the German consul reacted to what he perceived as an anti-German sentiment among the local native chiefs by deploying forces to seize control of Apia and the Mulinuu Peninsula. Assurances that these actions posed no challenge to American interests in Samoa proved to be false when the Samoans petitioned the U.S. consul in Samoa, Berthold Greenbaum, for assistance against Germany's claims. Without authorization, Greenbaum promptly declared Samoa under American protection, an action Bayard disowned in preference for a three-nation conference to resolve the crisis.

In June and July of 1887, the Washington Conference failed to bridge the gap between American support for King Malietoa and his Samoan assembly as the legitimate authority on the island and Germany's insistence that Chief Tamasese serve as king with an advisor appointed by Germany. In August, Germany pressed the issue by landing a force to topple Malietoa and place Tamasese on the throne. The United States dispatched a warship, the USS *Adams*, to Apia in October, but Cleveland and Secretary Bayard retained an otherwise neutral position on Germany's actions until a native rebellion against Germany's regime in Samoa erupted in September 1888. This position was no longer tenable after German warships shelling Samoan coastal villages seized an American vessel, forcing a response from the United States. Cleveland deployed additional ships, denounced the German action before Congress as "inconsistent with every prior agreement or understanding" between the two countries, and received funding to develop the Pago Pago station into a genuine naval base. In January 1889, German Chancellor Otto von Bismarck proposed another three-nation conference over Samoa. The conference convened in Berlin in late April. A hurricane struck Samoa in March, sinking three American, three German, and one British warship, helping establish the climate of cooperation among the participants that by June 14, 1889, produced the General Act of Berlin. This in effect created a three-nation protectorate over Samoa; restored Malietoa to the throne; reestablished an Apia council to include the king, a Samoan chairman and a representative from each one of the powers; and established a chief justice to mediate disputes over the status of the king and his relationship to the three powers.

At the time of his acceptance of Bismarck's proposal for the Berlin conference, Cleveland had already suffered defeat in his reelection bid of November 1888 at the hands of the Republican nominee Benjamin Harrison—a defeat in which his foreign policy played a role. During the campaign, several newspapers published the "Murchison Letter"—a letter written by Lord Sackville-West, the British minister to Washington, advising a naturalized Englishman living in the United States to vote for Cleveland; this aggravated anti-British sentiment aroused by the Canadian and Bering Sea disputes. The initial letter soliciting Sackville-West's advice had in fact been drafted by George Osgoodby, a California Republican posing as one Charles Murchison, so that the minister's answer could be used to vindicate the Republican charge that Cleveland had been weak with Britain. Cleveland promptly declared Sackville-West *persona non grata*, but the damage was done. It is impossible to measure the impact of the Murchison letter on the election, but Cleveland's loss in the state of New York, with its large Irish-American vote, could well have been a factor.

Grover Cleveland reentered the White House for the second time as a result of the Democratic Party's landslide victory in the presidential election of 1892. As in his first administration, he sought to keep his foreign policy low-key and to focus on domestic problems such as fair business practices and lower taxes. Instead, Cleveland again ended up correcting mistakes and cleaning up messes made by his predecessor in the Oval Office. His foreign policy quickly became estranged from the isolationist policy he desperately wished to pursue.

Hawaiian Annexation

Queen Liliuokalani, hereditary monarch of the Hawaiian Islands, was influenced by advisors to attempt a return to autocratic native rule in her country. This would have done away with what little constitutional rule existed, and would have also eliminated any foreign sway over the government. At the time this decision was made, only 2,000 of Hawaii's nearly 81,000 inhabitants were Americans; however, American money was the overriding economic power in the islands. In 1893, just prior to Cleveland's reappearance in the White House, revolutionaries ousted Liliuokalani in favor of a modern constitutional government, and pressed the United States for annexation and protection.

John Stevens, minister to Hawaii under President Harrison, perpetrated a few ambassadorial improprieties following the revolt. He hastily recognized the revolutionary government while Liliuokalani still sat on the throne. He also had the American flag flown over the house of government while declaring Hawaii the newest American protectorate and asked the captain of the USS *Boston* to land troops to protect it. On January 16, a battalion of U.S. Marines landed and was deployed to the U.S. legation and consulate while another force proceeded to the offices of the Hawaiian government and the royal palace, thus facilitating the occupation of the government offices by the revolutionaries and the surrender of Queen Liliuokalani the following day. On February 1, 1893, Stevens announced that the United States would make Hawaii an American protectorate and drafted a treaty for the advice and consent of the Senate.

Cleveland returned for his second term one month later, and immediately withdrew the treaty from the Senate, because annexation of Hawaii was not in keeping with his interpretation of American foreign policy interests. He was against the appearance of American imperialism in assigning Hawaii the status of a protectorate and doubted that the U.S. Constitution could be made to work for a non-Caucasian society so far away. Rather, he saw Hawaii as an ideal location for a naval base to help defend America's Pacific Coast. In keeping with his isolationist beliefs, Cleveland tried to reverse the actions taken during Harrison's term by restoring Liliuokalani to her throne. As it turned out, she was not willing to regain her station without taking revenge on those who had displaced her, and the revolutionary government, led by sugar growers dependant on American money, was not going to give up power on its own. Cleveland recognized that troops would be needed to bring about a regime change. This would be seen as an act of war; in the event of failure, Liliuokalani could deny the United States a strategically advantageous position in the Pacific Ocean after a good deal of blood had been shed for it. Cleveland therefore maintained his disallowance of the annexation while continuing to recognize the revolutionary government in Hawaii.

Additionally, he dispatched James H. Blount to Honolulu as a special commissioner to replace Stevens and reverse his policy. After withdrawing the Marines and lowering the U.S. flag over Honolulu, Blount began a personal study of the political situation in Hawaii, and after four months concluded that the rebellion lacked popular support and that the prevailing native Hawaiian sentiment was with Liliuokalani. Cleveland then sent Albert S. Willis to

U.S. Marines from the cruiser USS Boston *after landing in Honolulu to aid in the overthrow of the monarchy of Queen Liliuokalani and establish a provisional government in January 1893. (U.S. Navy)*

Hawaii with the mission to placate the queen, but her brusque rejection of Willis' plea for amnesty for the rebels actually strengthened the hand of the annexationists back in the United States. Cleveland's final report to Congress advised that the administration would support neither Liliuokalani nor the rebels but would accept any morally respectable plan for Hawaii that Congress could devise. Ultimately, the House and Senate voted against annexation but split over the matter of exonerating Stevens. For their part, the rebels refused to accept Liliuokalani's authority and voted to establish a Hawaiian republic under Sanford B. Dole. The United States recognized the republic in August, 1894.

The Anglo-Venezuelan Boundary Dispute

In 1814, Britain gained control over the Dutch-held portion of Guiana, an unsettled area bordered on the west by Venezuela. Each year following Britain's acquisition, the Venezuelan government pushed for a final determination of just exactly where the boundary was to be drawn. Britain

refused to discuss any border, choosing instead to await civil disorder or the ascension of a corrupt government so that Venezuela as a whole might become British property. The United States offered assistance in arbitrating the boundary dispute, but Britain kept stalling on the matter.

Cleveland felt that the time had come to stop skirting the issue, so the business of arbitration was put into motion in late 1894. Letters and visits to various British ministers and secretaries yielded no results. Therefore, in mid 1895, the administration informed Britain that the United States was in a position to force arbitration under rights granted through the Monroe Doctrine's assertion that European nations could be dealt with forcibly if found to be depriving American states of self-government. Richard Olney, who replaced Walter Gresham as Cleveland's secretary of state when Gresham died suddenly of pneumonia in May, instructed Thomas Bayard, U.S. ambassador to Britain, to demand that London submit the Venezuelan dispute to arbitration. In so doing he alluded to "the doctrine of an American public law" that required the United States "to treat as an injury to itself the forcible assumption by any European power of political control over an American state."

December arrived with no reply from Britain regarding U.S. demands to allow arbitration, so on December 17 Cleveland delivered a message to Congress requesting the funds to form a commission to research Venezuela's actual boundary. He further stated emphatically that it was the duty and intention of the United States to aid in the defense of this boundary. Despite the expected uproar of a few high-ranking legislators and a few members of Cleveland's cabinet, Congress appropriated $100,000 for the requested commission. Much of the press offered harsh criticism of Cleveland's policy, which it saw as a direct threat of war against Britain. Cleveland, in fact, merely wished to state that the United States was going to aid Venezuela in its assertion of its right—peacefully if possible, forcibly if necessary. In substance, the administration acted above all in the interest of the United States. Olney acknowledged in that in principle the entire disputed border area should be discussed, but he did want the United States to act as an ally for Venezuela and believed that its government would have to accept any decision that London and Washington finally settled on. Strategically, the administration sought to prevent Britain from acquiring control of the mouth of Orinoco River in Venezuela; diplomatically it wanted British acknowledgment of American dominance in the Americas. It was not until Parliament met in the following February that Britain took Cleveland's forcefulness seriously and began to resolve the issue. In October 1896, the two countries agreed to establish an arbitration commission. In 1899, the commission finally settled the Venezuelan boundary peacefully, deciding substantially in favor of Britain's position yet leaving the mouth of the Orinoco in Venezuelan territory. Venezuela was outraged at the settlement, but London and Washington welcomed the outcome in a new spirit of Anglo-American rapprochement.

Cuban Independence

Spain's control of the island nation of Cuba was seriously threatened in 1895 when Cubans, determined to gain independence, instigated a revolt. As the revolt became more intense, Cubans reasoned that if they were to start destroying the island's crops and infrastructure there would be no other recourse than for Spain to abandon the country altogether. As this seemingly mindless destruction would be felt deeply by American importing and investment houses, the White House would be pressured to step in to offer aid to Cuba. Cleveland sought to maintain his policy of neutrality in the affairs of foreign governments while recognizing the democratic rights of Cubans living in both Cuba and the United States.

While neutrality was kept at the fore of Cleveland's mind, he decided to offer Spain a plan for arbitration of the revolt. He knew that Spain's demands for outright Cuban surrender were irrational and that peace would only arrive through the institution of Cuban home rule. Cleveland reasoned that continued violence against Cuba would eventually cause America's obligation to Spain to be overcome by a moral responsibility to Cubans everywhere. Meanwhile, the Senate Foreign Relations Committee was working to adopt a joint resolution forcing Cleveland to recognize Cuba, thereby creating a possible state of war with Spain. Cleveland was rescued from having to veto such a resolution when the story was given to the press. Attacks by media sources on the resolution obliged the Senate to shelve the proposal. If the Senate were to have voted for a declaration of war, Cleveland was determined to decline to mobilize America's armed forces against Spain.

The Cuban Revolution raged on after Cleveland left office, effectively leaving the decision to intervene in the hands of his successor, William McKinley. Continued fighting between Spain and Cuba forced McKinley's hand, and within a year of being sworn into office, he was dealing with what would be known as the Spanish-American War—a commitment Cleveland fought strenuously to avoid.

Legacy

A case can be made the Grover Cleveland was the most significant president between Abraham Lincoln and William McKinley, a leader of character and conviction whose policies nonetheless cut against the spirit of his time. This was certainly true in the case of Cuba, a popular cause McKinley would find politically impossible to resist. As the only president ever to serve two nonconsecutive terms, Cleveland is uniquely difficult to assess. Over the period of two presidencies interrupted by the Harrison administration he attempted to strike a balance between competing principles and forces, opposing imperialist sentiments over Samoa, Hawaii, and Cuba but invoking the Monroe Doctrine against Britain in the case of Venezuela. His position on trade was more enlightened than most of his contemporaries. In August 1894, for example, he signed the Wilson-Gorman Tariff, passed by Congress over his objections because it generally reduced the average duty on imports by 10 percent from the high reached under Harrison. The bill was protectionist in spirit, but at the time it was the best Cleveland could have achieved. A national rethinking on the relationship between trade, prosperity, and security was still decades in the future.

John G. Martin

Chronology

1885

February 26: U.S. delegation sent to Berlin conference on Congo.

March 27: Anglo-German entente on East Africa, Samoa, and Egypt.

March 30: Russian attack on Afghan forces in Penjdeh, Britain threatens war.

April 18: Sino-Japanese agreement to withdraw forces from Korea.

May 2: Leopold II of Belgium becomes ruler of Congo Free State.

November 13: Serbia declares war on Bulgaria.

1886

January 1: Britain annexes Upper Burma.

August 3: Congress provides for construction of twenty-two steel ships for U.S. Navy.

1887

January 9: Anglo-American/Canadian seal dispute.

February 12: Britain seeks Mediterranean agreements with Austria, Italy, and Spain.

February 20: Austria, Germany, and Italy renew Triple Alliance.

March 3: United States bars Canadian fishing/shipping vessels from American ports.

June 18: Germany and Russia sign Reinsurance Treaty.

June 25: Washington conference over Samoan dispute convenes.

August 19: German marines seize control of Samoa.

October 11: United States declares neutrality on Samoan issue.

1888

February 15: Bayard-Chamberlain Treaty ends U.S.-Canadian fishing/shipping dispute.

March 12: Treaty with China excludes Chinese laborer immigration for twenty years.

October 21: Murchison letter damages Cleveland's reelection hopes.

October 29: European powers sign Suez Canal Convention.

November 6: Benjamin Harrison elected president.

Second Presidency
1893

January 17: Queen Liliuokalani of Hawaii overthrown, provisional government requests U.S. annexation.

April 23: Onset of 1893 stock market crash.

1894

January 4: France and Russia.

January 29: U.S. Navy assists republicans in Brazil.

May 31: United States recognizes new Hawaiian government but refuses annexation.

July 4: Republic of Hawaii proclaimed.

August 1: War breaks out between China and Japan over Korea.

August 28: Cleveland lowers U.S. trade tariffs.

1895

February 20: Congress recommends arbitration of Anglo-Venezuelan boundary dispute.

February 23: Renewed rebellion against Spanish rule in Cuba.

April 17: Treaty of Shimonoseki ends Sino-Japanese War, Japan triumphant.

April 27: British marines seize Corinto, Nicaragua.

June 28: United States officially neutral in Cuban rebellion.

June 25: Joseph Chamberlain becomes British colonial secretary.

July 20: United States demands arbitration in Anglo-Venezuelan dispute.

December 17: Britain refuses Venezuelan arbitration, Cleveland threatens action under Monroe Doctrine.

1896

January 3: Anglo-German Kruger Telegram incident.

January 15: Britain and France agree on Siamese independence.

March 1: Battle of Adowa, Ethiopians defeat Italian army.

April 4: United States offers Cuban mediation.

April 6: Congress calls for Cuban independence.

June 3: China and Russia sign Manchurian Treaty.

November 3: William McKinley elected president.

November 12: Anglo-American agreement on Venezuelan arbitration.

December 30: Spain executes Philippine rebel leader José Rizal y Mercado.

References and Further Reading

Brodsky, Alyn. *Grover Cleveland: A Study in Character.* New York: St. Martin's, 2000.

Ford, Henry Jones. *The Cleveland Era: A Chronicle of the New Order in Politics.* New Haven: Yale University Press, 1919.

Hollingsworth, J. Rogers. *The Whirligig of Politics: The Democracy of Cleveland and Bryan.* Chicago: University of Chicago Press, 1963.

Merrill, Horace Samuel. *Bourbon Leader: Grover Cleveland and the Democratic Party.* Boston: Little, Brown, 1957.

Nevins, Allan. *Grover Cleveland: A Study in Courage.* New York: Dodd, Mead, 1933.

Welch, Richard E. *The Presidencies of Grover Cleveland.* Lawrence, KS: University Press of Kansas, 1988.

Benjamin Harrison (1889–1893)

Early Life and Political Career

Benjamin Harrison, the grandson of President William Henry Harrison, the twenty-third president of the United States was born in North Bend, Ohio, on August 20, 1833, the second of the nine children of John Scott Harrison and Elizabeth Ramsey Irwin. Although he served in the House of Representatives, John Harrison's primary vocation was farming, and Benjamin was initially enrolled in the Farmers' College in Cincinnati before transferring to Miami University in Oxford, Ohio. In 1852, he graduated with distinction, married Caroline Lavinia Scott, and moved back to Cincinnati to study law. He was admitted to the bar in 1854 and opened a law practice in Indianapolis later the same year.

Harrison was immediately attracted to public life. In 1856, he joined the newly founded Republican Party and was elected to the office of the Indianapolis city attorney, before running, again successfully, for the post of the state supreme court reporter just as the Civil War was about to erupt. In 1862, the state charged Harrison with the recruitment of men for the 70th Indiana Volunteers and made him colonel of the regiment. Harrison was an aloof disciplinarian not at all popular with his troops, but by 1865 he had nonetheless been promoted to a brigadier general, and at the war's end was able to pick up his political career where it had left off. In fact, he was reelected state supreme court reporter in 1864 while still serving in uniform. The Indiana Republican Party was impressed by Harrison's political talents and selected him in 1876 to run for governor when the original Republican nominee was forced to withdraw under a cloud of corruption allegations. Harrison lost by some 5,000 votes, but a strong electoral showing under difficult circumstances enhanced his prestige within the party.

President Rutherford Hayes initially considered Harrison for a seat in his cabinet before appointing him to head the Mississippi Power Commission in 1879. The position gave Harrison national exposure and doubtless helped him in his successful bid for a seat in the United States Senate. Serving from 1881 to 1887, Harrison chaired the Senate Committee on Transportation Routes and the Senate Committee on Territories. He also led the Indiana delegation to the Republican National Convention in 1880 and used his influence to promote James Garfield's bid for the presidential nomination. Once elected, Garfield offered Harrison a place in his administration, but Harrison declined.

Benjamin Harrison laid much of the groundwork for more active American involvement in international affairs. (Library of Congress)

Patriotism and Protection

During the 1880s, the groundwork for a Harrison presidential campaign was laid, both by the prospective candidate himself and by Louis Michener, chairman of the Indiana Republican State Committee. In 1888, Harrison was at last in a position to launch a campaign for the Republican nomination, but the challenge was daunting. Although Harrison's most formidable rival, James G. Blaine, was forced from the race by poor health, there remained no fewer than nineteen aspirants for the nomination. Harrison was aided by two factors: Michener's negotiations with other delegations to make Harrison their second choice when their own candidates were forced out of the race and a message from Blaine, convalescing in Scotland, that Harrison was his personal choice for the nomination. On the third ballot Harrison won, and the vice-presidential nomination went to Levi P. Morton.

The election against the incumbent, Democrat President Grover Cleveland, was close, but Harrison was helped by the trade tariff issue. During his first term Cleveland had continued the Republican policy of high tariffs in order to foster American industry, but by 1888 he was under pressure from Democrats in the "Solid South" in particular to advocate lower tariff protection. Harrison's campaign therefore openly courted the business vote by extolling trade protection as a national interest. Protection was probably critical to the outcome in so far as Harrison won large northeastern and midwestern states such as New York, Pennsylvania, Ohio, Illinois, Michigan, and Indiana by narrow margins, whereas Cleveland rode large Democratic majorities to victory in southern states. This meant that Cleveland actually captured a majority of the popular vote, but also that Harrison beat him handily in the Electoral College, 233–168.

Not surprisingly, tariff protection had a place of privilege in Harrison's inaugural address, delivered on March 4, 1889, as Cleveland held an umbrella to shield his successor from a driving rainstorm. Harrison intoned the traditional Republican message of the "patriotic interest in the preservation and development of domestic industries and of the defense of our working people against injurious foreign competition." But he also cited "the evil example of permitting individuals, corporations, or communities to nullify the laws because they cross some selfish or local interest or prejudices" as a danger to the nation "but much more to those who use this pernicious expedient to escape their just obligations or to obtain an unjust advantage over others." As candidate and as president, Harrison is reputed to be among the least charming figures to grace national public life, but he was a serious and honest chief executive who lived up to the promise of the speech with two acts of historic importance: the McKinley Tariff and the Sherman Anti-Trust Act. Just as he shielded American industry from foreign competition, so too did he seek to liberate it from limits on domestic competition.

In the first of these, the leading congressional proponent, Senator William McKinley of Ohio, initially claimed that tariff reform would lead to lowered barriers. However, amendments attached to the bill during its passage—amendments in which Harrison took an abiding interest—responded to the pleadings of business lobbyists to the ultimate effect that the bill passed and signed into law by Harrison raised the ad valorem tariff duty from that of 47 percent in 1869 to 49.5 percent in 1890. The act authorized the president to negotiate reciprocity trade agreements and thus mitigate its effects selectively from retaliation against America exporters by other countries, but its overall effect was to raise prices inside to United States to an extent that may have damaged Harrison's popularity among wage earners. The tariff also identified the Republican Party with protection at a time when the advocacy of lower tariffs was gathering popularity as a possible palliative to the world depression of 1873–1896.

By contrast, the administration's antitrust legislation was ahead of its time. Authored by Senator John Sherman, also of Ohio, the act of 1890 was, in its own words, "to protect trade and commerce against unlawful restraints and monopolies," and it declared illegal "every contract, combination in the form of trust or otherwise, or conspiracy, in restraint of trade or commerce among the several States, or with foreign nations." Harrison was not so much providing national leadership with its signature as endorsing, with a federal law initiatives already taken by the states, twenty-seven of which had by 1890 passed some form of antimonopoly provision. The Sherman Anti-Trust Act therefore provided for fines and imprisonment for those deemed guilty of monopoly practices and permitted plaintiffs to recover as much as three times the figure of damages sustained as a result of such practices. Harrison hoped that it would balance the effect of the McKinley Tariff by lowering prices through intensified competition. Initially, the act was not very effective other than in its use against trade unions in the Pullman Strike of 1894, but Theodore Roosevelt subsequently allied the Sherman Act with his own antitrust efforts while President Taft applied it to the American Tobacco Company and Standard Oil.

Sea Power

In the first half of his term, Harrison devoted more attention to domestic than to international affairs. This order of priorities was reversed by the congressional elections of 1890 in which a strong shift of legislative power in favor of the Democrats limited the president's capacity to set the national agenda. But Harrison was not inactive in foreign policy even with the shift of focus. Having commissioned James Blaine as his secretary of state in March 1889 in recognition of Blaine's support in his presidential campaign, Harrison was able to exert considerable direct influence on foreign affairs, mostly because of Blaine's failing health.

To begin with, there was the matter of tying up the diplomatic strings of the Samoan crisis, partly but not completely resolved by the Cleveland administration. In late April 1889, Britain, Germany, and the United States convened a conference in Berlin and on June 14 agreed to treaty terms. In effect, the General Act of Berlin established a three-nation protectorate over Samoa. It was the first time that the United States consented jointly to govern a foreign people, and the precedent was influenced by developments beyond American control but with implications for American interests. In May 1889, the British Parliament formally approved the two-power naval standard, according to which the British fleet was to be as strong as the combined strength of the two next-strongest naval powers. Moreover, Cleveland's agreement to settle the Samoan crisis was reached with German Chancellor Bismarck, and the Berlin General Act was one of Bismarck's last diplomatic achievements before Kaiser Wilhelm II dismissed him in March 1890. The dismissal of the cautious Bismarck presaged a more aggressive German pursuit of overseas colonies that ultimately led to a plan to build a world-class navy. Last, on March 2, 1889, President Cleveland had signed legislation asserting American sovereignty over the Bering Sea, partly as a result of sealing disputes with Canada dating to 1877. Harrison followed through on Cleveland's initiative on March 22 by declaring that sealers entering American jurisdiction "in the waters of the Bering Sea" would be liable to arrest.

Together, these developments enhanced the importance of Alfred Thayer Mahan's three-volume work, *The Influence of Seapower Upon History, 1660–1783,* which was published between 1890 and 1892. The book maintained that a timeless lesson of history was that dominant powers required commercial and martial command of the high seas to protect trade routes and to interdict predations to maintain their position. Mahan noted:

> The eyes of the country have for a quarter of a century been turned away from the sea: the results of such a policy and of its opposite will be shown in the instance of France and of England. Without asserting a narrow parallelism between the case of the United States and either of these, it may safely be said that it is essential to the welfare of the whole country that the conditions of trade and commerce should remain, as far as possible, unaffected by an external war. In order to do this, the enemy must be kept not only out of our ports, but far away from our coasts.

Harrison agreed with Secretary Blaine that the nation's growing industry compelled it to develop new overseas markets, but it was obvious from the Samoan crisis that American overseas interests could depend on neither the protection nor the benign neutrality of European powers plying the oceans for new colonies and bases. Harrison recognized the importance of rescuing the United States Navy from the neglect it had suffered since the Civil War but also the prudence of establishing coaling stations on the Caribbean, the annexation of Hawaii, and the construction of a canal linking the Atlantic and Pacific Oceans across the isthmus of Central America.

Hemispheric Affairs

These objectives, however, would require commitments over the long term. In the short term, Blaine suggested, it would be prudent to establish more calculable diplomatic relations with the countries of the Western Hemisphere. The administration therefore hosted eighteen nations at the first Pan-American Conference in Washington in October and November of 1889. Blaine welcomed the delegates with his hope that the conference would enhance mutual respect and collective confidence among the participating states "in the spirit of just law and not the violence of mob." The lofty rhetoric notwithstanding, the conference's substantive achievements were modest. Blaine sought a customs union but got only a commitment to promote reciprocity. His proposal for an arbitration mechanism to settle disputes aroused the suspicion among many that the United States saw itself as that mechanism. The delegates ultimately did vote in favor of creating a Pan-American Union to nurture cooperation among themselves, but Harrison and Blaine agreed that they had attempted too much and that future meetings should focus more narrowly on trade reciprocity.

Still, the conference was timely in that it recognized that relations with the Latin American states, quite apart from those with the European powers, could take unanticipated turns with dire consequences that were frequently not the result of malign intent from a foreign government. In January 1891, this point was underscored dramatically by the outbreak of civil war in Chile. The *Itata*—a ship captured by the rebel forces opposing the Chilean government—docked at San Diego, California, to load arms and supplies for the rebel war effort. When a U.S. federal marshal boarded the ship to inspect it for violations of American neutrality, the *Itata* left port with the official on board. The episode was now a crisis. Harrison ordered the U.S. Navy to apprehend the *Itata*, which it did by pursuing the Chilean ship, capturing it in the Chilean port of Irquique, and returning it to San Diego. When the rebel cause in Chile prevailed, the administration released the *Itata* to the new regime. A U.S. court subsequently ruled that the detention of the ship had been unlawful, and Chilean public sentiment was still aroused. It did not help that the U.S. legation in Chile sheltered several leaders of the deposed regime. The USS *Baltimore* arrived at Valparaiso in October 1891, and local mobs attacked American sailors on shore leave, killing two. The incident was embarrassingly similar to an incident in New Orleans in which a local mob had lynched three Italian nationals recently acquitted of the murder of the New Orleans police chief. The incident was not resolved until April 1892 when the United States offered the Italian government a $25,000 indemnity.

A State Department note demanding from Chile an apology and an indemnity provoked only an investigation of the incident from the government in Santiago. For some weeks, Blaine's counsel of patience prevailed, but on December 9, Harrison charged that the Chilean police had been involved in the incident and drew the countercharge from Manual Matta, Chile's foreign minister, that Harrison's accusation was deliberately false. The crisis then escalated to the brink of war, in official terms at least, when on January 25, 1892, Harrison laid the nation's case before Congress with the observation that Chile had attacked the uniform and therefore the very nationality of the United States and recommended that Congress take such action "as may be deemed appropriate." The speech was in part theater, because Chile had, on January 1, already replaced Matta with a new foreign minister, Luis Pereira, who was prepared to withdraw Matta's accusations as well as to offer reparations. Three Chileans were sentenced to prison and Santiago paid $75,000 in reparations. The sealing dispute with Canada, meanwhile, had ended peacefully with an agreement between Blaine and the Salisbury government in London on an interim *modus vivendi* on seal kills pending an arbitration convention.

The bellicose spirit of Harrison's approach to the Chilean crisis prompted the Democratic press to accuse him of attempting to exploit a foreign policy issue to political advantage in a presidential election year. The evidence was strong, certainly, that Harrison's presidency was in trouble in the autumn of 1892. The Republican Party was divided and generally disappointed in Harrison's very limited use of his patronage powers to stroke the ambitions of its bosses and factional leaders, while the president himself was despondent over the death of his wife from tuberculosis just weeks before the ballot. But the central issue of the campaign was the same as in 1888, as was Harrison's Democratic opponent: the Republican tariff versus Grover Cleveland's more moderate position on duties. Public reaction to the McKinley Tariff and labor unrest—most notably a bitter strike against Carnegie Steel—carried the day for Cleveland. While the third party Populist candidacy of James Baird Weaver captured several states in the West, the South remained solidly Democratic while industrial states in the Northeast, including New York, flipped for Cleveland and gave him the revenge of a 277–145 Electoral College margin.

Legacy

Having inherited a crisis from Cleveland's first administration, Harrison passed on a crisis of its own making to Cleveland's second. In Hawaii, Queen Liliuokalani had been attempting to recover her dynasty's authority since 1887 when King Kalakua had surrendered much of it to sugar planters, mostly American. The McKinley Tariff had meanwhile wiped out the reciprocity advantages hitherto enjoyed by Hawaiian planters and intensified their interest in the outright American annexation of Hawaii, a goal favored by Blaine and the U.S. minister to Hawaii, John L. Stevens. Stevens had kept the State Department abreast of the struggle with Liliuokalani throughout 1892, but neither Blaine nor Harrison had responded with instructions as to what position Stevens should adopt. Nor did this change when

John Watson Foster became secretary of state on Blaine's sudden retirement in July 1892. In November of that year, the Hawaiian legislature temporarily gained the whip hand over Liliuokalani by forcing on her a cabinet generally favorable to the planters. In January 1893, after Harrison had lost the election to Cleveland but before Cleveland had assumed office, Liliuokalani struck back by dissolving the legislature and dismissing the cabinet. It was at this point that Stevens took the matter into his own hands. When the legislature proclaimed a constitution and asked Stevens for protection, he asked the U.S. Navy to deploy troops on shore to protect American property. Only two weeks after Stevens announced a U.S. protectorate did Foster explicitly disavow such a commitment.

The resolution of the crisis, therefore, was on Cleveland's desk when he returned to the White House. The Harrison administration ended as it had begun, rather untidily. While some of the uncertainty about the direction of U.S. diplomacy was attributable to a measure of neglect of some issues in preference for others—especially in the lack of guidance on Hawaiian policy during 1892—it was also a product of the fact that between the Civil War and 1900, the long-term developments in the American role in the world required more vision and vigor than successive administrations were prepared to devote to them. This was to be as true of Cleveland's second administration as it was of his first. In Harrison's case it was evident that, fascination with Mahan's prescriptions on sea power notwithstanding, the commercial appetite for American expansion exceeded that of political leadership.

Carl Cavanagh Hodge

Chronology

1889

March 2: United States claims jurisdiction over Bering Sea.

May 31: British Parliament passes Naval Defense Act, applying two-power naval standard.

June 14: General Act of Berlin ends Samoan crisis.

October 2: First Pan-American Conference convenes in Washington.

1890

March 18: Bismarck resigns as chancellor of Germany.

July 2: Sherman Anti-Trust Law enacted.

October 1: McKinley Tariff hikes import duties as high as 49.5 percent.

1891

March 3: Civil war breaks out in Chile.

June 15: United States and Britain settle Bering Strait fishing dispute.

July 4: U.S. Navy captures Chilean rebel ship *Itata.*

October 16: Chilean mob attacks U.S. seamen in Valparaiso.

1892

January 25: Chile agrees to reparations for Valparaiso incident.

November 8: Grover Cleveland elected president.

References and Further Reading

LaFeber, Walter. *The New Empire: An Interpretation of American Expansion, 1860–1898.* Ithaca, NY: Cornell University Press, 1963.

Socolofsky, Homer Edward, and Allen B. Spetter. *The Presidency of Benjamin Harrison.* Lawrence, KS: University Press of Kansas, 1987.

Tyler, Alice. *The Foreign Policy of James G. Blaine.* Hamden, CT: Archon Books, 1927.

William McKinley (1897–1901)

Early Life and Political Career

William McKinley was born in the small town of Niles, Ohio, on January 29, 1843, the seventh of nine children. McKinley's father managed a local metal-works factory; his mother was a deeply religious person actively involved in the Methodist Episcopal Church. Due to her influence, religion played an important role throughout McKinley's life. The family's strong belief in the importance of education led them to move near the town of Poland, Ohio, in 1852, where their children could receive a better education at the Poland Academy. In 1860, McKinley entered Allegheny College in Meadville, Pennsylvania, but returned home after only one term. According to many accounts, William studied so hard that he fell ill. Others maintain that McKinley left college because he was depressed. McKinley quickly recovered his lost health, yet due to family financial troubles was unable to return to college immediately and took a job as a teacher in the fall of 1861. He supplemented his teacher's income by working afternoons as a postal clerk.

Like many others of his generation, McKinley's early adulthood was strongly influenced by the quarrels between the South and the North which finally led to the Civil War. In June 1861, Poland's town meeting was characterized by a patriotic atmosphere and excitement about the conflict. Caught up in the fervor, McKinley decided to volunteer his services to the cause of the Union and served as a private in the 23rd Ohio Volunteer Infantry Regiment. From the beginning, McKinley showed an aptitude for the soldier's life. According to his commander and future close friend, Lieutenant Colonel Rutherford B. Hayes, McKinley was a man of rare capacity. He was promoted several times and ended the war as a twenty-two-year old brevet major.

After the war, McKinley seriously considered the career of a professional soldier but instead chose to become a lawyer. He started work as a law clerk in Youngstown, Ohio, and in the fall of 1866 moved to Albany, New York to study law at Albany Law School. In March 1867, McKinley passed the Ohio bar examination and set up a law office in Canton where he soon became a respected lawyer. Soon local Judge George W. Belden recognized McKinley's qualities and offered him a partnership in his already established law firm. In Canton, McKinley also met his future wife Ida Saxton, the daughter of a banker. They married in January 1871 and their first daughter, Katherine, was born the following

William McKinley wanted to avoid foreign entanglements, but gave the country the "splendid little war" it wanted. He thereby made the United States a Pacific and imperial power. (Library of Congress)

December. In 1873, Ida's mother suddenly died. Soon Ida, who was still deeply depressed by her mother's death, gave birth to their second daughter, whom they named Ida. Daughter Ida died just a couple months later and in 1876, four-year old Katherine died as well. This was the final stroke for Ida. Throughout the rest of her life, she suffered mental depression and epilepsy. These tragedies also changed McKinley himself. Always hard working, he threw himself to an even greater extent into his work.

In 1867, McKinley launched his political career as a campaigner for his former commander and friend Rutherford Hayes in his run for governor of Ohio. McKinley, a rising Republican star in Ohio, was helped immensely by a strong network of influential people who had served with him in the same regiment during the Civil War. Hayes was elected governor and McKinley became the Republican Party's Stark County chairman. In this position, he helped form many Ulysses Grant-for-President clubs.

McKinley became an elected official for the first time as a prosecutor in his county in 1869, holding the office until 1871. From 1874 to 1875, he focused on expanding his law practice, but still found time to support Hayes in another campaign for the governorship and later in his ambition to become president. In 1876, McKinley won a Congressional seat as a result of his hard work and broad popularity and a year later moved to Washington to start work in the Forty-Fifth Congress. The new congressman and his work quickly gained respect, although he was still seen primarily as a protégé of the newly-elected President Hayes, at whose suggestion McKinley became involved in supporting the policy of protective trade tariffs. His work was rewarded by appointment to the House Ways and Means Committee. In 1889, McKinley lost a bid to become Speaker of the House of Representatives to Thomas Brackett Reed by one vote. Reed, however, named McKinley the Chairman of the Ways and Means Committee and the Republican floor leader. In both positions, McKinley pushed a bill to raise tariffs and saw his efforts rewarded in October, 1889, when President Harrison signed the bill into law. It became known as the McKinley Tariff Bill.

In 1890, McKinley lost his congressional seat by a mere 300 votes. The Republican Party promptly nominated him for the gubernatorial elections in 1891, which he won with a clear majority of votes. From 1892 to 1896, McKinley was widely considered a successful and popular governor. His agenda was broad, but he paid special attention to tax reform and new labor laws. In 1896, McKinley withdrew from the office so that he could focus fully on the Republican presidential nomination. A few months later, at the age of fifty-three, he was nominated and quickly established his legendary front porch campaign, carefully led by the brilliant strategist and wealthy McKinley supporter Marcus Hanna.

McKinley's opponent was Democrat William Jennings Bryan. The major issues were the controversial currency question and the trade issue. McKinley supported the gold standard policy and trade protectionism, whereas Bryan advocated free silver policy and free trade. McKinley defeated Bryan, partly because of divisions within the Democratic Party over its radical candidate, partly due to a depression under the last presiding Democratic president Grover Cleveland, and partly too on the strength of a well prepared and financed Republican campaign. McKinley, for example, was the first presidential candidate filmed for campaign reasons. Another clear reason for McKinley's victory was the character of the candidate. The fact that nearly three quarters of a million people came to listen to McKinley's speeches made on his porch clearly demonstrated his ability to draw attention, command respect, and communicate with Americans as a national leader.

The Unfinished Cleveland Agenda

To better appreciate McKinley's achievements as president, it is necessary to acknowledge the most important achievements of his predecessor, the famously incorruptible Grover Cleveland. Cleveland was the first Democratic President elected in twenty-eight years and to this day is still the only president elected for two nonconsecutive terms, serving from 1885 to 1889 and again from 1893 to 1897.

According to Cleveland, the major function of the White House office was to maintain watch over the nation's morality. Cleveland also believed that "the people should support the government [and that] the government should not support the people." Many also perceived Cleveland to be an obstructive president, as he exercised the right to veto quite often. During his first term, Cleveland devoted his energy to lowering tariffs, whereas the Republican presidential nominee of 1888, Benjamin Harrison, based his campaign on the preservation of protective tariffs and won the election. Four years later, the voters generally supported the ex-president's economic program, and Cleveland defeated Harrison in 1893 to become president for the second time. Unfortunately for Cleveland, his term brought a financial panic, followed by a serious depression and significant labor strife.

Cleveland's activities in foreign affairs strengthened the presidential position and helped the White House regain some of its lost prestige in the eyes of Americans. Prior to Cleveland, Congress set much of the tone and substance of American foreign affairs. But Cleveland's interest and personal involvement in diplomacy meant that he took a more active role than most presidents had before him. His well-intentioned stress on fairness in foreign affairs earned him widespread respect. Cleveland's noteworthy achievement was his supervision of the negotiations between Venezuela and the British colony of Guiana concerning their border dispute. Still, Cleveland was under enormous pressure to apply the Monroe Doctrine—not only from Venezuelan officials, but, more importantly, from the American public, press, and influential politicians, who criticized him for his indecisiveness and apparent pro-British attitude. In spite of this pressure, President Cleveland maintained his arbitration plan.

In March, 1893, only five days into his second term as president, Cleveland again confirmed that he was a man of high principles. He withdrew a treaty from the Senate that would have formally annexed the Hawaiian Islands to the United States as a dependent territory. Cleveland considered the January 1893 revolution orchestrated by the pro-American sugar planters with the help of the U.S. marines to be immoral. In another case, Cleveland suggested that the

United States leave Samoa to Britain and Germany and thereby avoid American involvement in their international rivalry. During his presidency, other events such as the 1895 Cuban revolt and the Sino-Japanese War in 1894–1895 had significant aftershocks on American foreign affairs and McKinley's term as president. Although Cleveland was more actively involved in foreign affairs than most of his predecessors, he still acted as if "foreign relations were composed of incidents, not policies."

The New Manifest Destiny

At the time of McKinley's inauguration, new theories on the future of American foreign relations and dealing with Manifest Destiny from various perspectives were being developed. These were influenced by Alfred T. Mahan's *The Influence of Sea Power on History,* Josiah Strong's *Our Country,* Frederick J. Turner's *Frontier Thesis,* and Brooks Adams' *The Law of Civilization and Decay.* Although their reasons for supporting further American expansion varied, these authors agreed that, in contrast to the original concept of Manifest Destiny, the United States should take a significant and active Great Power role in the world. Since its territory now stretched across the continent to the Pacific Ocean, some Americans felt that the United States must extend certain aspects of the concept of Manifest Destiny overseas. Furthermore, other Americans viewed themselves as being part of the culturally superior Anglo-Saxon "race" (a term contemporary theorists and rhetoricians often used synonymously with "civilization" and "people"). They believed that the United States had a right and an active duty to spread its culture of democracy and civilization beyond its shores. The national mood of "expansionist fervor" could not be ignored either in the White House or in Congress. It was mainly President McKinley's responsibility to maintain the right balance between the expansionists and moderates.

The Spanish-American War

It is a historical paradox that President McKinley presided over a war against Spain in which strategically significant territorial gains were won. In his Inaugural Address in March 1897, McKinley proclaimed that "we want no wars of conquest; we must avoid the temptation of territorial aggression. War should never be entered upon until every agency of peace has failed; peace is preferable to war in almost every contingency." The conflict between Spain and the United States was the first war with a European country since the War of 1812 with Great Britain.

The origin of the Spanish-American War lay in a nationalist uprising on behalf of an independent Cuba that began in 1895. The underlying cause of the rebellion, in American eyes, was the brutal treatment of the Cubans by the Spanish colonial regime, aggravated by economic depression and high levels of poverty. The Spanish government charged General Valeriano Weyler with the responsibility of dealing with the revolt. Weyler not only fought the Cuban revolutionaries, he also used atrocious methods to undermine the morale of the rest of the Cuban population. His tactics included the incarceration of thousands of Cubans in concentration camps designed to separate the population from the guerillas. These camps had poor sanitary conditions, little food, and high death rates among civilians. The American public read often exaggerated news stories, many fed by effective Cuban nationalist propaganda agents, about the clashes between the "freedom fighters" and Spanish soldiers with interest and increasing romantic sympathy for the rebels. They especially sympathized with Cuban civilians, even more so because of their shocking treatment at the hands of a power alien to the Western Hemisphere, the last European power with significant territories in the Americas. Each year, an increasing number of Americans supported taking action against Spain, while many felt that McKinley was overly cautious and indecisive about American involvement in Cuban affairs. McKinley had never ignored the Spanish-Cuban conflict; he believed that if the right diplomatic efforts were made there was a strong possibility that Spain would allow Cuban independence without engaging in war with the United States. This view was justified in part by the results of his firm diplomatic pressure on Madrid, which resulted in the recall of General Weyler and the elimination of the detention camps. This policy also provided extra time to prepare for the possible war. In the meantime, McKinley organized a humanitarian relief effort for Cuba.

On February 15, 1898, the U.S. battleship *Maine* blew up in Havana harbor, killing approximately 260 sailors. The slogan, "Remember the Maine!" became a rallying cry of the yellow press calling for intervention in Cuba against Spain. Theories about the cause of the explosion vary from a faulty boiler (in which case the United States *casus belli* was spurious), to a mine or torpedo planted by the Cubans to draw the United States into their rebellion, or by the Spanish, for unclear motives. At the time, most Americans reacted in anger, believing the explosion to be the work of Spanish saboteurs; goaded on by a jingoist press and by imperialists within the Republican Party, they demanded a military confrontation with Spain. The outbreak of public anger and calls for revenge still did not provoke McKinley to declare war, however. He regarded war as a last option to be explored only after other options no longer proved viable and understood that, with the exception of Britain, the United States had no sympathizers in Europe. As a veteran of the Civil War who had personally witnessed massive killing, he was also disinclined to lead Americans into another bloody conflict. In addition, he had doubts about the Spanish involvement in the destruction of the *Maine*. An investigation later concluded that the blast was caused by an internal combustion of coal gases.

The turning point for McKinley's support of the war was the influential speech given by the Republican Senator from Vermont, Redfield Proctor, in which he vividly described the difficult situation for civilians in Cuba. Before Proctor's speech, only yellow press publications—represented above all by Joseph Pulitzer's *World* and William Randolph Hearst's *Evening Journal*—called for war. After the speech mainstream news publications, religious publications, and Wall Street called for war as well. Realizing that the issue could play a significant role in the future elections, President McKinley felt he had to act. However, he did not immediately declare war. He delayed for important reasons, such as the need to give enough time for the Americans in Cuba to leave and the need to prepare the American forces, mainly the U.S. Navy, for war. During this interval, the government bought two modern cruisers and assembled the U.S. Asiatic Squadron in preparation for the likely combat against the Spanish Navy.

On April 22, 1898, the U.S. Navy blockaded Cuba, claiming that it was acting "in aid of independence forces." Two days later, the United States declared war on Spain. A key moment in the war occurred when the American fleet, under the command of Commodore George Dewey, destroyed the Spanish fleet in the Philippines on May 1. A victorious ecstasy filled the press and public. The battle also demonstrated to the European countries supporting Spain—France, Germany, Russia, and Austria-Hungary—that the United States was not a second-rate power and that arbitration was probably out of the question. The destruction of the second Spanish flotilla off Santiago again confirmed the capacity of the U.S. Navy. In addition to the battles at sea, there were a few land battles, most notably at El Caney and San Juan Hill, that were well-covered in the press. The battle of San Juan Hill also gained notoriety because of the participation of Theodore Roosevelt and his Rough Riders. The two battles at sea, however, had the most impact on the outcome of the war. On August 12, Spain and the United States signed a protocol with a clause that included the signing of a peace treaty in Paris the following fall. The document also provided specific conditions under which hostilities would end. These included the condition that Spain leave Cuba and cede Puerto Rico and Guam to the United States along with the right to occupy Manila in the Philippines.

The U.S. Ambassador to Paris, Horace Porter, correctly pointed out that "no war in history has accomplished so much in so short a time with so little loss." At the end of the conflict, it was apparent that McKinley had shown himself to be an efficient and competent commander-in-chief. The first

"war room" in the White House, equipped with telegraphs and telephones, provided the headquarters for the president and his staff, from which he led the transformation of the United States from a regional to a world power.

Empire in the Pacific

In the beginning of October 1898, peace negotiations began between the United States and Spain in Paris, France. They lasted for several weeks, the main dispute being about the future of the Philippines. The American delegation included several U.S. senators appointed by the president; McKinley hoped that it would be easier to get his agenda through Congress if the senators felt involved in the process. It is noteworthy that this created a precedent of involving senators in diplomatic negotiations. The Treaty of Paris was signed in December 1898, transferring the control of the Philippine Islands to the United States. This disappointed Japan as its government too had imperial designs on the islands. The Filipinos felt the greatest amount of displeasure, however, as the agreement did not grant independence.

After a passionate debate between the expansionists and their opponents, the Paris Treaty was ratified by a narrow margin on February 6, 1899. With this, McKinley and Congress officially confirmed the ambitions of the new Manifest Destiny and the willingness to "take up the white man's burden" (as Rudyard Kipling had phrased the notion of responsible imperialism). In McKinley's words, this meant that the United States would "educate the Filipinos, and uplift and Christianize them," a pronouncement not welcomed in the Philippines where nationalist guerrillas had been well on their way to liberation from Spain before the American intervention, and where most of the population was already Catholic. In February, Filipino Emilio Aguinaldo launched a revolt against the new American overlords that lasted nearly four years and cost the lives of more than 500,000 Filipinos and approximately 5,000 Americans. At the end of the bloody conflict, in which the American army resorted to Spanish methods of repression, the United States retained control over the islands.

Since the 1840s, the United States had been interested in the Hawaiian Islands as a key stop along the trade route to China. Honolulu had earned the nickname "The Crossroads of the Pacific." It is therefore not surprising that Washington announced that the Monroe Doctrine would also shield this remote territory from foreign influence. In 1885, the United States obtained an exclusive right to Pearl Harbor. The local Hawaiian government understood that to keep its independence it would need guarantees from the United States, Britain, and France.

While moderates were satisfied with the policy of no foreign control of the Hawaiian Islands, expansionists continued their long-standing demand for annexation to the United States. There had already been several unsuccessful attempts at annexation. In January 1893, a group of Americans on Hawaii seized power and established a provisional government. On July 4th of the following year, they proclaimed the "Republic of Hawaii" with the goal of making it part of the United States as soon as possible, based on the historical model of the brief independence and annexations of Texas and California. A plan to annex these islands was also a vital part of the Republican Party's agenda.

The rapidly growing Japanese population in Hawaii caused the White House and Congress to take the annexation plan more seriously. By March 1897, the relationship between the Hawaiian government and Japan had grown quite tense over the immigration issue. The Hawaiian government asked Washington to annex the islands as a way to protect them from Japan. On June 16, President McKinley therefore asked the Senate to consider a treaty of annexation. He did not favor expansionism but neither did he want to see Hawaii under Japanese control. Although some Americans were strongly opposed to annexation, the "splendid little war" with Spain had fired the spirit of expansionism in others and fueled the desire to add the Hawaiian Islands to the territory of the United States. Eventually, the Senate approved the annexation of the Hawaiian Islands and they became American territory on August 12, 1898.

According to some scholars, Samoa was the first example of the American hunger for a new territory beyond the North American continent. In 1889, American, British, and German representatives signed an agreement in which they agreed to share control over Samoa. In 1899, a civil war started among various Samoan tribal chiefs, the United States and Britain supporting those tribes that had sympathized with them and Germany doing the same. The conflict led to strong anti-German feelings in the United States and simultaneously nurtured a sense of friendship and intimacy between the Americans and the British. At the end of the war, the islands of the Samoan archipelago were divided between the United States and Germany. The British agreed to abandon their claim to the Samoan Islands under the condition that Germany would compensate them elsewhere. Eventually, the Germans ceded to the British the Tonga Islands, some islands in the Solomon chain, and additional territorial concessions in West Africa. Since the U.S. Navy Department had long stressed the importance of Pago Pago as the key harbor in the Pacific Ocean, President McKinley turned these islands over to direct administration by the Navy in February 1900.

The Hague Peace Conference

On March 18, 1899, the American delegation joined the international conference in the Netherlands city of The Hague. Organized by the Russian Czar Nicholas II, the conference included twenty-five other countries. When the United States received an invitation to the event, it showed little interest in participating and discussing the conference's major topic: disarmament and prevention of war. But McKinley was pleased by the czar's request for American participation. It illustrated the growing international prestige of the United States. Although McKinley was skeptical about the ability to achieve peace in a time of expansionary fever, he remained an ardent supporter of any diplomatic activities that supported peace. Although opinion varied concerning whether Americans should attend the conference, Washington finally decided to send representatives, mostly due to the growing pressure of the reformers and the peace movement at home. Although the delegates did not sign any disarmament agreements, they still achieved some valuable results, such as the declaration to humanize war. Another great achievement was the creation of a Permanent Court of Arbitration. Even though the court did not have any legal means to enforce its future decisions, it did provide a place in which countries in disagreement could come to resolve their disputes through negotiation rather than by war. Of all the participating countries, the United States was perhaps the most careful not to become involved in any international commitments and to maintain a policy of nonentanglement.

Anglo-American Rapprochement

During McKinley's presidency, the United States remained firmly committed to its growing friendship with Britain. However, a cordial relationship was not always easy to maintain. Some situations, such as the Boer War and the dispute concerning Alaska's frontier, challenged the relationship.

In the case of the Boer War between Great Britain and the whites of the erstwhile independent Boer Republics in South Africa, the McKinley administration remained on the side of Britain from the beginning. It was a difficult stance, as domestic public opinion—most notably among Americans of Dutch, German, and Irish descent—supported the Boers. Most of the public throughout the world also sympathized with the Boers, and in the presidential election of 1900, anti-British sentiment was so strong that the Democratic Party tried to use the government's pro-British position against the Republicans by attacking "the ill-concealed Republican alliance with England." For London, American favor was essential, as the majority of European governments criticized the British military action against the Boers. There were two major factors that explain McKinley's pro-British attitude. First, the president did not forget that Britain was the only country among the great powers that had shown friendliness and diplomatic backing toward the United States during its war with Spain. Second, both the United States and the British Empire were in similar positions at the time—coping with overseas uprisings organized by the locals against their authority. For Britain it was the uprising in South Africa, for the United States, the revolt in the Philippines.

Another source of friction was the dispute about Alaska's border. The Russian-Canadian frontier, established prior to 1867, had never been clearly defined. The original agreement stated that "the boundary ran inland thirty miles from the Pacific Ocean." This clarification worked well until gold was discovered in Canada's Klondike River near Alaska. After the discovery, Canada challenged the poorly delineated border between the two countries with a new interpretation that could disturb American control of trade. In August 1898, a commission met in Quebec to solve this problem and others that had arisen between Canada and the United States, including a dispute over fisheries. However, all attempts at negotiations between the two countries failed.

In October 1899, U.S. State Secretary Hay took charge of the affair and negotiated a temporary agreement with Britain that brought needed stability for those countries involved in the dispute. Only later, during Theodore Roosevelt's administration, was the dispute permanently solved.

The Open Door Policy in Asia

The United States had been interested in trade with China for decades. The outbreak of the first Sino-Japanese war in 1894 and the easy victory of Japan over China in 1895 sent two important messages to Washington regarding its relationship with both the victor and the vanquished. First, the war revealed Japan's growing ambitions to join the great powers. Second, the conflict revealed that, although China was large, it was tremendously weak and vulnerable. The administration understood that the political, military, and economic weaknesses of China could mean that it could easily lose its independence and become a colony of a country with greater strength and power than its own. If this were to occur, then the United States might not have access to the Chinese market. When the McKinley administration debated the status of the Philippines, it therefore took into account the fact that the new territory could become a key base from which the United States could protect its interests in China and other parts of Asia. These analyses led to the formulation of the Open Door policy toward China.

In September 1899, the administration announced the Open Door policy in a circular diplomatic note by the Secretary of State John Hay directed at Britain, France, Germany, Italy, Japan, and Russia. The note stated three basic guiding principles: to make China an open international market while avoiding interference with trade in the respective spheres of influence of the seven powers; to retain tariff duties at all treaty ports with duties collected for the Chinese government; and to treat all nations equally in harbor dues and railway charges. The fact that the United States worked on this issue closely with Britain is additional evidence of the growing friendship between these two countries

as well as a mutual concern about the potential of the Japanese challenge. In March 1900, John Hay announced that Britain, France, Italy, Germany, Russia, and Japan agreed with the Open Door policy for China.

In the following month, the policy was unexpectedly tested. In May 1900, the Boxers, one of the many secret societies in China that disliked any foreign presence in the country, moved from their base in Northern China to Peking to fight the numerous foreigners in Peking. In reaction, the European powers and Japan sent forces to Peking to squash the rebellion and protect their citizens and property. McKinley felt that he had to react promptly as well. Although his decision brought some criticism at home, McKinley ordered 2,500 soldiers to join the international armed forces. In August, the uprising was suppressed and the survival of the weak Chinese government was preserved.

Legacy

On September 4, 1901, William McKinley visited the Pan-American Exposition in Buffalo, New York. The following day, McKinley gave a speech to 50,000 people about America's role in the world. The speech marked significant change in McKinley's policy toward free trade. Previously an ardent protectionist, McKinley now called for reciprocity in trade treaties. On September 6, the president enjoyed a less formal day. He visited Niagara Falls and the fair itself. In the afternoon, he viewed the Exposition's Music Temple, where he wanted to greet some of the visitors. As McKinley was shaking hands with visitors, anarchist Leo Czolgsz assassinated him with two gunshots. The president lingered and then died on September 14, 1901.

The last resting place of President William McKinley and his wife Ida McKinley is located on Monument Hill in Canton, Ohio. Beneath a bronze statue of McKinley, a visitor can read the inscription "Good Citizen–Brave Soldier–Wise Executive–Helper and Leader of Men–Exemplar to His People of the Virtues That Build and Conserve the State, Society, and the Home." Many people born in the twentieth century might see this as an unfitting appraisal of the deceased president. Overshadowed by popular presidents such as Theodore Roosevelt and Franklin D. Roosevelt, or even Ronald Reagan, McKinley's achievements are often neglected or forgotten.

President McKinley, however, initiated many of the policies that would become well known under the leadership of subsequent presidents. It was McKinley who started to build the office of the modern presidency. In addition, McKinley brought the United States into the elite club of world powers that included Britain, France, Germany, Russia, and Japan. McKinley's presidency was also characterized by a time of domestic economic prosperity and social peace. He reconnected the North and South into one nation again. From the Republican point of view, McKinley was second only to Abraham Lincoln in terms of important presidents in the nineteenth century. McKinley helped build a powerful and successful Republican Party that continued to play a major role in domestic and foreign affairs from 1896 until 1932.

McKinley's political work was characterized by the use of indirect pressure and careful, almost hidden diplomatic suggestions. To many observers, this discretion and subtlety often appeared as indecisiveness. McKinley was known to be unusually kind, a virtue often mistaken for weakness. Finally, McKinley's well-guarded privacy and his distaste for documenting his plans and ideas on paper did not contribute to a scholarly interest in McKinley by future generations. But William McKinley was certainly a successful president. It was McKinley who realized that as president he needed more secretaries and clerks—not just an army of servants and cooks—to be an effective leader. Within a few months of becoming president, McKinley fashioned an efficient, modern executive apparatus. He was aided by his outstanding selections for his cabinet.

The political, economic, and military expansion that permanently transformed the United States from a regional power to the status of a great power occurred during the McKinley administration. His presidential decisions influenced not only his contemporaries, but future generations as well. Rapprochement with Britain built a strong base for the Anglo-American alliance that proved decisive in world affairs throughout the remainder of the twentieth century. Likewise, the Open Door policy definitively secured American involvement in Asia, as his war with Spain secured a long-lasting commitment to the affairs of Cuba. Finally, McKinley's diplomatic work on the Isthmian Canal project paved the way for the eventual construction of the Panama Canal and its control by the United States through the Hay-Pauncefote Treaty of November 1901.

Zbysek Brezina

Chronology

1897

April 17: War breaks out between Turkey and Greece.

April 30: Austro-Russian Agreement about maintaining the status quo in the Balkans.

May 5: Japan demands end to immigration discrimination in Hawaii, sends warship.

June 16: United States signs annexation treaty with Hawaii.

July 7: Dingley Tariff raises duty rates to 57 percent.

September 18: United States demands Spain bring peace to Cuba.

November 14: German troops occupy Kiaochow and Tsingtao, China.

December 14: Russian fleet ordered to proceed to Port Arthur.

December: Diplomatic conflict between Russia and Britain over China.

1898

January 12: Rioting in Havana, United States sends USS *Maine.*

January 25: Salisbury's note to Russia offering a compromise over Asia.

February 15: Maine destroyed by explosion in Havana harbor.

February 25: U.S. Navy Asia Squadron on alert.

March 27: China leased Port Arthur and Talienwan to Russia.

March 27: China leased Weihaiwei to Britain.

March 28: First Naval Bill funds expansion of Kriegsmarine.

April 10: China leases Kuangchowwan to France.

April 11: McKinley asks congressional authority for military action in Cuba.

April 19–20: Congress approves military action to support Cuban independence.

April 25: United States declares war on Spain

April 25: Nishi-Rosen Agreement between Russia and Japan over Manchuria and Korea.

May 1: U.S. Navy defeats Spanish fleet in Manila Bay.

May 25: U.S Army expeditionary force departs for the Philippines.

May 29: U.S. Navy blockades Spanish fleet in Cuba.

June 29: U.S. Navy captures Guam.

July 3: U.S. Navy destroys Spanish fleet in Cuba.

July 4: U.S. occupies Wake Island.

July 6: U.S. annexes Hawaii.

August 12: Spain requests armistice, Spanish-American War ends.

August 30: Britain-German Agreement about the Portuguese colonies.

September 9: Filipinos declare independent republic.

September 18: Fashoda incident between Britain and France.

November 21: Commercial treaty signed between France and Italy.

December 10: Treaty of Paris signed by United States and Spain.

1899

February 4: Fighting breaks out between U.S. and Filipino troops in Manila.

February 6: United States annexes Guam, Puerto Rico, and the Philippines.

March 11: United States, Britain, and Germany in dispute over Samoa.

May 18: First Hague Conference on Disarmament convenes.

August 9: The Franco-Russian Alliance is extended.

September 6: United States asks European power and Japan to reaffirm Open Door policy in China.

October 9: Boer Republics of Transvaal and Orange Free State issue ultimatum to Britain.

October 11: Boer ultimatum expires; Second Anglo-Boer War begins.

October 14: Windsor Treaty between Britain and Portugal renews previously established treaties between the two countries.

November 25: Baghdad Railway concession granted to Germany.

December 2: Anglo-American-German treaty partitions Samoa.

1900

February 5: First Hay-Pauncefote Treaty is established between the United States and Britain about an interoceanic canal project.

May 17: Boxer Rebellion in China increases attacks of foreigners.

May 31: U.S. Marines arrive in China to help suppress the Boxer Rebellion.

June 12: German Reichstag authorizes second major naval expansion.

August 14: Boxer siege of Peking lifted.

September 4: Russian deploys 100,000 troops to Manchuria.

October 16: British-German Yangtze Agreement supports the Open Door policy in China.

November 6: McKinley reelected president.

December 14: Franco-Italian Agreement about Morocco and Tripoli is signed.

1901

March 2: Congress passes Platt Amendment to Army appropriations bill.

September 6–14: President McKinley is shot and dies eight days later; Vice-president Theodore Roosevelt is sworn in as president.

December 16: Senate approves Hay-Pauncefote Treaty.

References and Further Reading

Armstrong, William. *Major McKinley: William McKinley and the Civil War.* Kent, OH: Kent State University Press, 2000.

Gould, Lewis, L. *The Spanish-American War and President McKinley.* Lawrence, KS: University Press of Kansas, 1982.

Hay, John. *William McKinley: Memorial.* New York: Crowell, 1902.

Leech, Margaret. *In the Days of McKinley.* New York: Harper and Brothers, 1959.

Morgan, H. Wayne. *William McKinley and His America.* Syracuse, NY: Syracuse University Press, 1963.

Musicant, Ivan. *Empire by Default: The Spanish-American War and the Dawn of the American Century.* New York: Henry Holt,1998.

Olcott, Charles, Summer. *The Life of William McKinley,* 2 vols. Boston: Houghton Mifflin, 1916.

Phillips, Kevin. *William McKinley.* New York: Times Books, 2003.

Sievers, Harry, J. *William McKinley 1843–1901: Chronology-Documents-Bibliographical Aids.* New York: Oceana, 1970.

Spielman, Willliam, Carl. *William McKinley: Stalwart Republican.* New York: Exposition Press, 1954.

Theodore Roosevelt (1901–1909)

Early Life and Political Career

Theodore Roosevelt, Jr., the second of four children and the older of two sons, was born into wealth and comfort in New York City on October 27, 1858. His father was a businessman and a philanthropist whose family's Dutch roots in the area were over two centuries deep; his mother, the former Martha Bulloch, had grown up on a moderately prosperous plantation in antebellum Georgia. The Roosevelts were an extremely close-knit family.

Theodore was educated at home by private tutors. Extended sojourns abroad in 1869–1870 and 1872–1873 which took him to Great Britain, continental Europe, and the Near East—and frequent visits to the countryside helped develop a cosmopolitan spirit and a passionate, lifelong interest in nature. (Though an amateur, Roosevelt would become one of the nation's foremost natural scientists.) In 1880, Roosevelt graduated Phi Beta Kappa from Harvard.

In his early adult years, Roosevelt's family life was marked by tragedy. He lost his beloved father—his role model and best friend—in 1878. He married Alice Lee in 1880, but on February 14, 1884—two days after the birth of a baby girl, Alice—both his wife and his mother suddenly died. In 1886, Roosevelt married Edith Carow, a close childhood friend, and took up permanent residence in Oyster Bay, New York, in the spacious, comfortable new house that they called Sagamore Hill. By 1897, five children—four sons and a daughter—had joined daughter Alice in the Roosevelt family.

Roosevelt's career over the two decades after Harvard was varied and interesting. Beginning in politics as a Republican reformer in the New York State Assembly, Roosevelt then spent time as a rancher and hunter in the Dakota Badlands. Following a defeat in the New York mayoralty race in 1886, Roosevelt returned to politics in 1889 by accepting an appointment to the U.S. Civil Service Commission. Six years later he became president of New York City's Board of Police Commissioners. From 1897 to 1901 he served as assistant secretary of the navy, the heroic (and fortunate) colonel of the Rough Riders fighting Spanish forces in Cuba, governor of New York, and, for six months, vice president of the United States.

Throughout these twenty years, Roosevelt wrote prolifically on a wide range of subjects, including United States history and life in the American West. *The Naval War of 1812,* published in 1882, revealed Roosevelt as a budding

Theodore Roosevelt advocated diplomacy backed by military strength—"speak softly and carry a big stick"—and was mostly successful in applying it to his foreign policy. (Library of Congress)

strategic thinker, while *The Winning of the West* (1889–1896), a four-volume history of the frontier from 1769 to 1807, was his most significant scholarly endeavor.

Well before assuming the presidency, Roosevelt became a prominent figure among leading American expansionists. These influential men were big-navy advocates who believed strongly in American political and cultural superiority and American beneficence. Very attentive to the foreign relations of the United States, they met and corresponded frequently.

As assistant secretary of the navy during 1897–1898, Roosevelt took full advantage of opportunities to express his views and to affect naval and diplomatic decisions. He regularly outmaneuvered his lethargic superior, John D. Long, most memorably in February 1898 when he sent off a famous telegram to Admiral George Dewey concerning operations in the Philippines in the event of a war with Spain.

The assassination of William McKinley brought Theodore Roosevelt to the presidency on September 14, 1901. A charismatic and politically adept progressive Republican, an avid conservationist, and a "practical idealist," Roosevelt retained the presidency for seven and a half years, decisively winning the election of 1904. He almost certainly would have been reelected had he decided to seek another term in 1908.

Legacy of the 1890s

Historians tend to identify the Spanish-American War of April–August 1898—or, less commonly, the Venezuelan boundary crisis of 1895–1896, which featured sharp rhetoric toward Great Britain by U.S. leaders—as marking the emergence of the United States as a Great Power. The United States had begun building a modern navy in the 1880s and had accelerated this work in the 1890s, providing the country with a fleet substantially superior to Spain's by the time President McKinley opted for war.

The Spanish-American War would prove to be a transformative event in the history of U.S. foreign relations. The wartime annexation of Hawaii, the postwar establishment of a protectorate over Cuba, and the outright acquisition of Puerto Rico and the Philippines (sparking a bloody guerrilla war in the case of the latter) rendered the victorious United States a recognized imperial power. And Great Britain's distinctly pro-American stance during the U.S.-Spanish contest opened up the possibility of a new and valuable U.S. partnership with a long-standing adversary.

President McKinley was not a particularly active agent of this transformation, but ultimately, he did much more to advance it than to impede it. Reluctant to go to war with Spain, he nonetheless eventually succumbed to a rising popular demand. And despite having thought little about imperialism, strategy, or the imperatives of being a Great Power, in the end he sided with the articulate and insistent expansionist group that included Theodore Roosevelt, Captain Alfred Thayer Mahan, and a number of prominent congressional Republicans. As for Anglo-American relations, by placing the conduct of U.S. foreign policy primarily in the hands of Secretary of State John Hay (the Anglophile U.S. ambassador to Britain in 1897–1898 who was appointed to head the State Department shortly after the Spanish-American War), McKinley inadvertently created conditions very favorable to building friendly Anglo-American ties. Most notably, the unpopular but politically sustainable pro-British neutrality policy charted by Hay during the Boer War that began in 1899 was enormously appreciated by the embattled British government, engendering in London a very cooperative spirit. Roosevelt would also inherit from Hay and McKinley the British-supported Open Door policy in China, which called for equal commercial opportunity and the preservation of beleaguered China's territorial integrity and political independence.

Engagement, Power, and Anglo-American Preeminence

A set of broad objectives underlay the foreign policy of President Theodore Roosevelt. Most prominent among these were sharply expanding the international role played by the United States; greatly increasing U.S. naval power; and building and solidifying a partnership between Great Britain and the United States. The achievement of these broad objectives would enable the president, in his view, to promote peace, stability, U.S. interests, and the progress of civilization.

Roosevelt believed in the necessity of active U.S. engagement with the world. As one of the Great Powers, the United States was affected by important events occurring around the globe; hence, Roosevelt considered it not merely fruitless but also harmful to U.S. interests to try to shield the country from major overseas developments. And the United States needed not only to engage but to take initiative; it needed to seek to influence and to shape important overseas events to its advantage rather than simply observing them passively and reacting to them later. Considering the deeply entrenched and potent legacy of George Washington's farewell address of 1796 urging Americans to "steer clear" of foreign entanglements, Roosevelt's belief in active U.S. internationalism stands among the most radical departures of his presidency.

Although Roosevelt defined U.S. interests in a global context, he did so discriminatingly. In his scheme, the Western Hemisphere—particularly the Caribbean region, where he saw U.S. hegemony as a self-evident strategic imperative—and the western Pacific were the two areas of the world most vital to the United States. In other areas, Roosevelt was especially attentive to situations where there was conflict or the potential for conflict among two or more of the Great Powers. While a steadfast proponent of the "just war" doctrine, Roosevelt harbored no illusions about the horrors and the unpredictable consequences of war and considered it his moral obligation to do all that he realistically could to prevent or to stop unnecessary Great Power wars.

Roosevelt looked upon arbitration as a useful device for resolving international disagreements, but only if they did not involve questions of vital interests, territorial integrity, or national honor. When a dispute did fall into one or more of these three excluded categories, he was adamant that the United States must be free to act as it saw fit. And not only free, but sufficiently strong militarily—for ultimately, Roosevelt clearly recognized, it was power more than any other factor that determined the course of international affairs.

Consistent with this perspective, Roosevelt believed that the most civilized and most righteous nations (as he defined these terms) should always be well armed and should take particular care to build up and preserve a preponderance of naval power to be able to deter aggression and defend their interests. He considered the United States and Great Britain—which shared, in his view, a duty to extend civilization and an attachment to the principles of freedom and self-government—to be the two most civilized and most righteous nations. Moreover, he realized, the two countries' interests tended to coincide. Britain, therefore, was an essential friend for America.

Indeed, the cornerstone of Rooseveltian statecraft was the cultivation and fortification of a special relationship between the United States and the British Empire. Roosevelt was both a proud American nationalist and, in important respects, an internationalist. But as his presidency moved along, and as his devotion to U.S.-British unity was continually reinforced by events, he became in a sense an *Anglo*-American nationalist as well. Without reservation, therefore, Roosevelt considered the unrivaled power of the Royal Navy to be an asset to the United States, and in his private correspondence he frequently proclaimed his support for Britain's maintenance of its overwhelming naval superiority.

In contrast, Roosevelt perceived Germany, Russia, and Japan to be potential enemies of the United States. Not only did their interests often clash with those of Britain and the United States, but they had not yet attained America's or Britain's (or France's) level of civilization. Imperial Germany was militaristic and aggressive, while czarist Russia was reactionary and utterly untrustworthy. Roosevelt's outlook on Japan was more positive, but his respect and admiration for that country were tempered by uncertainty and suspicion regarding its intentions and future course.

It should be added that economic concerns were never very prominent in Roosevelt's foreign policy. Thus, amicable U.S.-Japanese relations always took precedence over the Open Door for commerce in Manchuria. As for imperialism, it could be justified by strategic considerations and especially by the idealistic imperative of advancing civilization and improving the human condition, but never as a vehicle for economic exploitation. Paternalistic though it may have been, President Roosevelt's policy toward the Philippines demonstrated the sincerity of his concept of benevolent imperialism.

On the subject of process, two points are central. First, Roosevelt himself dominated his administration's diplomacy. Although very ably assisted by Secretaries of State John Hay and Elihu Root, Roosevelt was an energetic chief executive who held strong, well-defined foreign policy views. When dealing with the foreign policy matters he saw as most important, Roosevelt charted the broad course of American diplomacy *and* attended personally to the significant details of its execution. Second, the president generally preferred an informal, personal approach to diplomacy. He utilized a sizable and varying network of American and foreign (especially British) friends and associates as he carried out foreign policy. Even with the small number of overseas U.S. diplomats in whom Roosevelt had great confidence, major communications tended to be in the form of private letters dispatched outside the established channels.

1901–1903: Focus on the Western Hemisphere

During the early years of his presidency, Theodore Roosevelt's diplomacy focused primarily on the Western Hemisphere, where he was determined to establish U.S. hegemony. The three biggest foreign policy issues of 1901–1903 were the acquisition of a canal route across the isthmus of Panama and the resolution of crises with Germany over its Venezuelan intervention and with Great Britain over the disputed boundary between Alaska and Canada.

Upon assuming the presidency, Roosevelt—an outspoken opponent of the first Anglo-American Hay-Pauncefote Treaty of February 1900—continued to support the effort to revise it. He then played an active role in the successful drive for Senate ratification of the second Hay-Pauncefote Treaty of November 1901, under which the United States could build, control, and fortify an isthmian canal.

Roosevelt's dealings with Colombia were more complicated and dramatic. By September 1903—after many fruitless months of endeavoring in good faith to reach an agreement with the government of José Marroquín, which had recently rejected the Hay-Herrán Treaty (according to which the United States was to pay Colombia $10 million in gold plus $250,000 per year for a 100-year lease on a 6-mile-wide canal zone)—Roosevelt lost patience with what he confidentially termed "the foolish and homicidal corruptionists in Bogota." Well aware of the strong and rising secessionist ferment in Colombian-ruled Panama, Roosevelt and Secretary of State Hay now encouraged this revolutionary movement—but only in private and even then only by indirection. Beginning on October 17, the president ordered U.S. naval vessels to sail toward Panama—not to take an active part in the revolution, but, as stipulated in a U.S.-Colombian treaty of 1846, to "maintain free and uninterrupted transit" across the isthmus. The essential purpose of this U.S. action was to prevent Colombia from deploying troops to suppress the uprising. As a result, the practically bloodless Panamanian rebellion was carried out in less than three days, concluding on November 6.

The United States promptly granted recognition to the new Panamanian government and bolstered its naval presence in the area to prevent Colombia from overturning Panama's separation; there would be no further pretense of

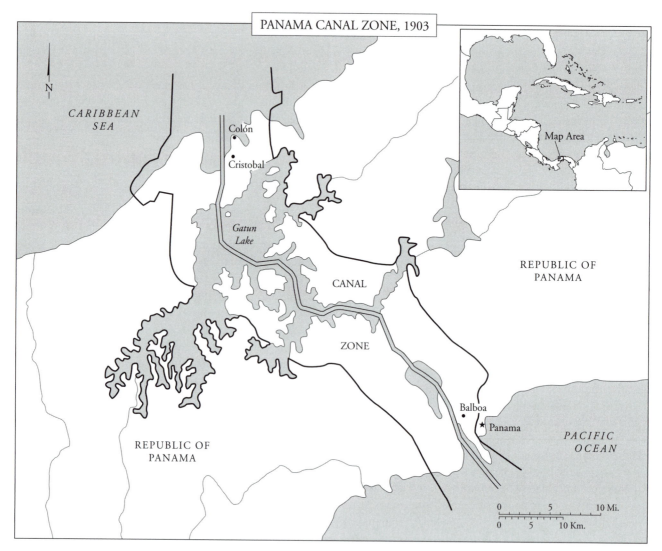

PANAMA CANAL ZONE, 1903

The inter-oceanic waterway was built between 1903 and 1914 by U.S. Army engineers in response to strategic interests first made clear during the two-ocean Spanish-American War.

American neutrality. The Hay-Bunau-Varilla Treaty, granting the United States sovereignty "in perpetuity" over a ten-mile-wide canal zone (in exchange for payments identical to those earlier rejected by Colombia) and making Panama a virtual U.S. protectorate, was signed on November 18, 1903, and ratified by the Senate on February 23, 1904. The construction of the Panama Canal, a mammoth undertaking in which President Roosevelt was deeply interested and became heavily involved, soon commenced.

Roosevelt was extremely proud of his diplomacy relating to the controversial acquisition of the Panama Canal Zone, believing that he had absolutely nothing to hide, and that he not only had advanced the interests of the United States but also had thwarted Colombia's attempt to impede the progress of humanity. He would never cease to defend his actions vigorously, most notably in the autobiography he published in 1913.

In December 1908, toward the end of his presidency, Roosevelt wrote these words in a letter to Whitelaw Reid, his trusted and valued ambassador to Great Britain: "The foreign policy in which I believe is in very fact the policy of speaking softly and carrying a big stick." As practiced by its architect, Rooseveltian big-stick diplomacy had at its foundation five central principles. The first was the possession of a formidable military capability, which during the opening decade of the twentieth century meant, especially, a large, well-equipped, well-trained U.S. Navy. The second principle was to act justly toward other nations. The third was never to bluff, and the fourth was to strike only if prepared to strike hard. Fifth and finally, big-stick diplomacy required its practitioner to allow an honorable adversary to save face in defeat.

One of Roosevelt's classic displays of big-stick diplomacy was directed against Germany during the Venezuelan crisis of 1902–1903. Roosevelt blamed Germany for the joint

Anglo-German military expedition against Venezuela that began in December 1902, and he saw the expedition as a German challenge to the Monroe Doctrine. (Roosevelt judged Britain merely foolish, and he rapidly prevailed on the British government to recognize its error and alter its policy.) Roosevelt dispatched a battleship squadron to the waters near Venezuela, insisted on arbitration (for which the Venezuelan government was calling), and privately issued in mid-December and in early February two timely and stern ultimatums to Germany. The first gained German acceptance of the principle of arbitration, while the second, communicated following a German bombardment of a Venezuelan fort (with a U.S. battleship squadron still poised for action), helped bring about agreement on the terms of arbitration, ending the crisis. Adhering to all the tenets of big-stick diplomacy, Roosevelt had found Germany's conduct unjust and unacceptable, had readied the necessary military forces, had personally delivered unambiguous warnings, and by keeping those warnings private had made it possible for the German government to back down without losing face.

Right from the beginning of (and even before) his presidency, Roosevelt looked upon the Canadian interpretation of the Alaskan-British Columbian border as "an outrage pure and simple." Thus, he saw the boundary question as an issue of national honor and was adamantly opposed to abandoning any essential elements of the American claim. Yet the Anglo-American friendship he had been cultivating was also immensely important to Roosevelt. The reconciliation of these conflicting imperatives would require statecraft of the highest order.

The story of the resolution of the Alaskan boundary quarrel reveals a determined American statesman adroitly employing personal and big-stick diplomacy to attain the result at which he was aiming. Having "quietly and unostentatiously" dispatched troops to the disputed region in 1902, Roosevelt acceded early in 1903 to the establishment of an "impartial" six-person tribunal, including three Americans appointed by himself, to settle the boundary question. However, his selections—Secretary of War Elihu Root, Senator Henry Cabot Lodge, and former Senator George Turner, upon all of whom Roosevelt could depend to sustain the U.S. claim—made it apparent that he perceived the tribunal merely as a means of making it as easy as possible for Britain to manage Canada's defeat. The president then launched a multipronged diplomatic offensive, utilizing a number of personal agents, to drive home two crucial messages to the British government and to Lord Chief Justice Alverstone, the lone Briton on the tribunal. In the absence of a settlement affirming all the essential aspects of the American stance, Roosevelt would deploy sufficient numbers of U.S. troops to "take possession of the disputed territory" and would ask Congress for "an appropriation which will enable me to run the boundary on my own hook."

However, there were "two or three lesser points on which there is doubt," and on these he was prepared to countenance U.S. concessions to provide England with a dignified way out. The key American and British participants picked up Roosevelt's signals, and an agreement—supported by the one British and three American tribunal members but not by the two Canadians—was reached in October 1903.

Roosevelt would never cease to view his assertive Alaskan diplomacy as decisively advancing the cause of Anglo-American unity. As he claimed retrospectively in 1911, the settlement of the Alaskan boundary resolved "the last serious trouble between the British Empire and ourselves as everything else could be arbitrated."

1904–1906: Global Activism for Peace, Stability, and American Advantage

By the onset of 1904, Theodore Roosevelt's commitment to U.S. dominance in the Caribbean had been strengthened by his concerns about the security of the future Panama Canal and by his determination to prevent another episode similar to the Venezuelan intervention crisis. Motivated by these considerations and spurred by both the British government's urging and the chaotic conditions in the Dominican Republic, he introduced the Roosevelt Corollary to the Monroe Doctrine, proclaiming in June the obligation of the United States to counteract "gross wrongdoing" in the hemisphere. "If we intend to say 'Hands off' to the powers of Europe, . . . we must keep order ourselves."

Actually Roosevelt was very reluctant to exercise this new international policing authority, and he initially resisted the Dominican government's overtures for U.S. intervention. By the beginning of 1905, however, he believed it was imperative to act, and he arranged to establish a U.S. customs receivership in the Dominican Republic. When partisan politics impeded Senate ratification of the Dillingham-Sanchez Protocol, the president fell back on his broad constructionist principles and through an executive agreement with the Dominican government instituted a *modus vivendi* embodying the terms of the protocol. In the Dominican Republic the U.S. customs receivership was kept limited by Roosevelt and functioned very well, enabling the Caribbean nation to repay debts owed to foreigners and to finance government operations. Finally, early in 1907, the Senate ratified a slightly modified U.S.-Dominican treaty. The only other intervention by Roosevelt under his Corollary, likewise limited and successful, took place in Cuba from September 1906 to January 1909 in response to a civil war in which both the Cuban government and its armed opponents requested U.S. military involvement.

As is suggested by both the infrequency and the restraint with which he intervened under his Corollary, Roosevelt considered it a priority to minimize Latin American resentment and suspicion of the United States. His most proactive initiative in this regard was Secretary of State Root's goodwill tour of seven Latin American countries during the summer and early fall of 1906. Roosevelt was delighted with his trusted secretary's "wonderful trip," following which Root continued to work hard and effectively on behalf of better U.S.-Latin American relations. (The common image of a rampant, heavy-handed U.S. interventionism in Latin America under Roosevelt—perhaps an outgrowth of the far more widespread and intrusive interventionism practiced by Roosevelt's successors—is wildly inaccurate.)

Increasingly suspicious of Russia's designs in East Asia and Germany's ambitions in Europe and elsewhere, Roosevelt was very favorably disposed toward both the Anglo-Japanese Alliance of January 1902 (revised and strengthened in August 1905) and the Anglo-French Entente Cordiale of April 1904. Roosevelt viewed the former as a check on Russia and the latter as a counterweight to the growth of German power. Both he saw as advantageous to Britain and also, therefore, to the United States.

As he assessed the Russo-Japanese War, launched by Japan in February 1904 in response to perceived Russian encroachments on Japanese interests in Manchuria and Korea, Roosevelt readily grasped the complex international context of the hostilities. While much more sympathetic to Japan than to Russia, he believed it would be destabilizing for either combatant to be pushed entirely out of the East Asian competition. Since France was allied with Russia and Britain was allied with Japan, Roosevelt also perceived a danger to the new Anglo-French understanding. From the outset, Roosevelt was determined to do all he could to bring the war to a conclusion that would restore an East Asian balance of power and preserve the existing balance in Europe. By December 1904 he had begun thinking seriously about trying his hand as a mediator, and when an opportunity arose in the spring of 1905 he stepped forward. After plenty of discreet preliminary work by Roosevelt, the door opened in May when Japan—financially strapped and militarily overextended despite a string of decisive victories—requested that Roosevelt offer mediation to Russia "on his own initiative." Through the intensive and extremely adept application of personal diplomacy involving British, French, and German as well as Russian and Japanese officials—using the summer White House in Oyster Bay, New York, as his base of operations—Roosevelt arranged for a Russo-Japanese peace conference to convene in early August in Portsmouth, New Hampshire. There he proceeded to overcome formidable obstacles as he shepherded it to the triumphant conclusion of the Treaty of Portsmouth of September 2. This treaty, which ended a bloody Great Power war and reinstituted an East Asian balance of power, earned Roosevelt the Nobel Peace Prize for 1906 and may have been his foremost single achievement as a statesman.

Roosevelt's equally remarkable mediation of the Franco-German dispute over Morocco in 1905–1906 would have to rank a close second, as this highly flammable crisis very conceivably could have brought on World War I nine years before it actually began.

The Moroccan crisis began in the spring of 1905 when Germany, seeking to wreck the Anglo-French Entente, aggressively defied the Anglo-French agreement on French control in Morocco by calling for an independent Morocco with an open door and requesting an international conference on the Moroccan question. This crisis unfolded in two phases. During the first and more dangerous phase, lasting until July 1905, Roosevelt, operating completely out of the public eye, was instrumental in preventing war by arranging for a conference to be held in Algeciras, Spain. France was assured privately that Roosevelt would sustain its most fundamental Moroccan interests at the coming conference, while a trusting Germany pledged to defer to Roosevelt's judgment should a deadlock arise. Inevitably Kaiser Wilhelm II and his government learned of the president's pro-French outlook during the second phase of the crisis, the Algeciras Conference of January–April 1906. But even as Roosevelt deftly engineered Germany's defeat, he characteristically did his utmost to disguise the reality of the outcome and thereby soften the blow. In the wake of the German capitulation, Roosevelt was generous with encomiums for German diplomacy.

The years 1904–1906 mark the most intense and important period for Rooseveltian foreign policy. Roosevelt boldly declared and skillfully effectuated U.S. predominance in the Caribbean. On a larger stage, the president established himself as a mediator par excellence by ending one major war and preventing another. Roosevelt's well-conceived, well-executed, activist statesmanship thrust the United States into the center of global diplomacy and (notwithstanding Britain's relative unhelpfulness during Roosevelt's Russo-Japanese and Moroccan mediations) fortified the Anglo-American bond. Roosevelt was justifiably very pleased with these accomplishments.

1907–1909: Partnership with Britain, Understanding with Japan

In the area of highest priority, Anglo-American relations, the final years of Theodore Roosevelt's presidency were a time of consolidation. This process was facilitated by a Liberal victory in the British election of December 1905, which removed Lord Lansdowne as foreign secretary and brought in Sir Edward Grey, a leader substantially more attuned to the value to Britain of an Anglo-American friendship and more compatible with Roosevelt. Grey, in turn, acted on Roosevelt's private but persistent request that Sir Mortimer Durand, the incompetent British ambassador to the United States, be replaced; in January 1907 Roosevelt's friend James Bryce assumed control of the embassy.

By 1907 the most challenging remaining problem for U.S.-British relations was the long-standing Newfoundland fisheries question. This on-and-off dispute had been renewed by Newfoundland in 1905 in retaliation for the U.S. Senate's unfriendly treatment of a U.S.-Newfoundland reciprocity (bilateral tariff reduction) treaty. Roosevelt had not reacted hastily. Indeed, he considered his own country to be primarily to blame. America's course, he explained to Senator Lodge, "has given deep offense to Newfoundland, and most naturally. If the circumstances had been reversed, this country in its turn would have been deeply angered." The United States, he continued, should "try to show such patience and forbearance as possible until the exasperation caused by our very unfortunate action has worn off." When Newfoundland had placed additional restrictions on American fishermen in 1906, Ambassador Whitelaw Reid, representing the president, had worked out a temporary *modus vivendi* with the British government. When negotiations reached an impasse in the summer of 1907, Roosevelt proposed to resolve the fisheries issue through binding arbitration by the Hague Tribunal. Britain agreed; formal arrangements were set early in 1909; the following year (after Roosevelt had left the presidency) the tribunal rendered a compromise verdict. Roosevelt's sense of proportion and fairness, along with his creativity and his thoughtful evaluation of U.S. interests, had brought to a satisfactory conclusion this previously intractable dispute with the best and most important friend of the United States.

The special Anglo-American relationship that Roosevelt had been forging was tested by two small-scale episodes during the closing years of his presidency. Both the Jamaica incident of 1907 and the Olympic Games controversy of 1908 drew the president into intensive and delicate back-stage diplomacy designed to avert damage to Anglo-American ties.

In a concrete display of British support for U.S. hegemony in the Caribbean, in 1904 Great Britain's government had initiated a nearly total withdrawal of its naval forces from that region, leaving the protection of British colonial and other interests there in American hands. Thus there were no British warships in the vicinity when a devastating earthquake and fire struck Kingston, Jamaica, on January 14, 1907. The U.S. government responded to urgent British requests for assistance by dispatching a squadron from the American naval base at Guantanamo, Cuba. Despite performing in Kingston with great energy, selflessness, and efficiency, the U.S. relief mission was forced to depart only two days after landing on account of a startlingly offensive letter written by the British governor of Jamaica, Sir Alexander Swettenham, to the commander of the American squadron, Admiral Charles H. Davis. This letter, dated January 18, was

published in British and American newspapers on January 21. Notwithstanding his great pride in the U.S. Navy and his sensitivity about insults to the national honor of the United States, Roosevelt unhesitatingly accepted the British government's prompt disavowal of Swettenham's rude act and took the leading American role in the execution of a joint U.S.-British policy of damage-control diplomacy aimed at isolating Swettenham and downplaying the episode as an aberration. Bizarre behavior by the aggrieved Swettenham complicated this endeavor, but within several months Anglo-American diplomacy achieved its objectives. In the process, the extent of the devotion to the Anglo-American partnership of both Roosevelt and leading figures in the British Foreign and Colonial Offices had been vividly demonstrated.

The following year, at the Summer Olympic Games in London, vehement American charges of grossly biased British officiating produced great bitterness between Britain's and the United States' athletes and managers. Initially determined to avoid engagement, Roosevelt nonetheless was drawn into a rather extensive behind-the-scenes involvement. In a letter of November 17 to a Briton with whom he was privately exchanging correspondence about the dispute, Roosevelt included this revealing lament: "Throughout the time I have been President I have steadily striven for a better sympathy and understanding between the United States and Great Britain, and to have me take any part whatever in this exceedingly unfortunate controversy would simply tend to undo just what I have been striving to accomplish." By the end of that same month, due largely to the president's skillful work, the relatively small threat to Anglo-American harmony posed by the quarrel had entirely faded. As a relieved Roosevelt wrote to Ambassador Reid in January 1909, "the Olympic game squabble is dying a natural death."

Prior to and throughout his presidency, Roosevelt viewed and wrote about the mammoth British Empire as a decidedly positive force for the advancement of civilization. But it was only toward the end of his presidency that he actively employed his admiration and affection for the British Empire in his unceasing quest to bolster the special Anglo-American relationship. By far the most important of Roosevelt's pronouncements in support of the empire—prompted by a series of private British requests to the president to speak publicly in praise of British rule in India during a difficult period—was delivered in Washington on January 18, 1909, at the African Diamond Jubilee of the Methodist Episcopal Church. Within a long address extolling the benefits of enlightened imperial government, Roosevelt's remarks about the British Empire's "crown jewel" were unambiguously laudatory, even celebratory. "Every true friend of humanity," he summed up after offering many glowing words, "should realize that the part England has played in India has been to the immeasurable advantage of India, and for the honor and profit of civiliza-tion, and should feel profound satisfaction in the stability and permanence of English rule."

Roosevelt's address had the intended effect of cementing still more firmly what by that time was already a well-estab-lished, durable friendship between the British Empire and the United States. The British reaction was captured partic-ularly well by a *London Times* editorial. "We have long been conscious," declared the *Times,* that British rule in India was "a monument . . . to our highest qualities as a nation. . . . But it is new to us to have its greatness . . . proclaimed in unhesitating accents by the Chief Magistrate of the people whose esteem and good opinion we prize beyond those of any other foreigners." Moreover, Roosevelt's "testimony . . . is an impressive proof of the happy change which has taken place of late years in the relations of the American people to us"—a change so far-reaching as to render it "possible for the President of the United States to express in a public speech his unstinted admiration of the British administra-tion of alien races." Roosevelt, naturally, was delighted by Britons' overwhelmingly enthusiastic response to his address. For he would shortly be vacating the White House, and he wished to leave Anglo-American relations in the healthiest possible condition in every single respect.

The U.S. relationship with Japan also was accorded care-ful and sustained presidential attention during the closing years of the Roosevelt administration. A crisis in U.S.-Japanese relations sparked by the San Francisco school board's passage in October 1906 of a resolution segregating Asian schoolchildren was being stoked by the continuing immigration to the United States of substantial numbers of Japanese laborers. Roosevelt took a well-conceived, multi-faceted approach (which included an only partially success-ful effort to draw in Britain, Japan's ally) to this very serious problem.

Roosevelt cultivated Japanese goodwill by pressuring the Californians to end the blatant discrimination (and accom-panying violence) while emphasizing to Japan his thorough disapproval of Californian behavior. Meanwhile, he worked with Japanese officials to find an amicable way to halt the flow of Japanese workers to the American mainland, finally bringing the immigration problem under control in 1908 via a "Gentlemen's Agreement" stipulating the "mutual" exclusion of Japanese and American laborers from each other's country.

In addition, Roosevelt's dealings with Japan featured his single most illustrious act of big-stick diplomacy: He sent the American battleship fleet (the "Great White Fleet") on a fourteen-month world cruise beginning in December 1907. Not a threatening word was spoken—indeed, Japan invited the fleet to its shores and extended it a grand welcome in October 1908—but the message that America was strong and ready was unmistakable.

The world cruise of the Great White Fleet advanced another Rooseveltian foreign policy objective. From the start, Roosevelt's ambitious diplomatic agenda had been undergirded by his buildup of the United States Navy. Between 1901 and 1905 Roosevelt had pushed Congress into authorizing the construction of ten battleships among more than thirty total warships. Then, after slowing down temporarily, he responded to the dreadnought revolution (marked by larger battleships carrying uniform batteries of big guns, of which the Royal Navy's HMS *Dreadnought,* completed in December 1906, was the prototype) and to increasing tension in U.S.-Japanese relations by calling for a stepped-up pace of naval building, with an emphasis on adding dreadnoughts to the battleship fleet. By 1907, the U.S. Navy, the world's sixth in size in 1901, had grown into the second largest (and was also far better trained). In this regard, the Great White Fleet not only waved a big stick at Japan but also functioned as a magnificent public relations spectacle that extracted from an antagonistic Congress in 1908 an authorization for two dreadnoughts (Roosevelt astutely had demanded four) and a commitment to fund two per year in the future.

The signing of the Root-Takahira Agreement in November 1908 was a major event in U.S.-Japanese rela-tions. In this accord, while giving lip service to "the inde-pendence and integrity of China," the governments of Japan and the United States "firmly" resolved "reciprocally to respect the territorial possessions belonging to each other" and to uphold "the existing status quo" in East Asia and the Pacific: Japan would continue to stay away from the Philippines; the United States would continue to support Japanese control of Korea; and it was transparently implied that where Japan's predominant position in southern Manchuria clashed with America's Open Door policy in China, the former would take precedence. More broadly, the Root-Takahira Agreement demonstrated to the world the achievement of respectful and amicable relations between the United States and Japan and marked a climactic tri-umph for Roosevelt's Japanese policy. (Roosevelt's succes-sors as president—beginning with William Howard Taft, despite Roosevelt's protests—would undo his fine handi-work in building a friendly U.S.-Japan relationship.) In December 1908, Roosevelt immodestly but very accurately summed up his accomplishment in a letter to a close English friend: "My policy of constant friendliness and courtesy toward Japan, coupled with sending the fleet around the world, has borne good results!"

Legacy

Ex-President Roosevelt never really retired. Continually, he wrote about his experiences and his perspectives on con-temporary issues. In 1909, he embarked on a long African safari and a tour of England and continental Europe. In 1912, he dramatically broke with the Republicans to lead his new Progressive ("Bull Moose") Party to a second-place finish in the presidential election. A year later he headed an expedition into previously unexplored areas of Brazil, irretrievably impairing his health. As an outspoken proponent of preparedness and a pro-Allied policy during World War I and a detractor of President Woodrow Wilson, Roosevelt eventually drifted back into the Republican Party. He was considered a prime contender for its 1920 presidential nomination at the time of his death on January 6, 1919.

Roosevelt was a consummate diplomatist. He was almost uniformly successful both in addressing specific foreign policy challenges and in advancing his broader objectives. He kept his country at peace while consistently upholding what he defined as its vital interests, and he was directly responsible for restoring or preserving peace between other powers. Moreover, his statecraft significantly enhanced the United States' image in the world. Indeed, it is difficult to escape the conclusion that in the foreign policy arena, Roosevelt may have been the greatest of all U.S. presidents.

From a longer-range perspective, Roosevelt displayed a degree of perspicacity that transcended his era. It would take the disastrous failure of isolationism and appeasement and the terrible experience of World War II to revive Roosevelt's way of thinking about U.S. foreign relations and to bring his guiding precepts—formidable and credible deterrent power, broadly conceived U.S. interests, and Anglo-American solidarity and preeminence—into the mainstream, where they have been ever since.

William N. Tilchin

Chronology

1901
March 2: Congress passes Platt Amendment to Army appropriations bill.

September 6–14: President McKinley is shot and dies eight days later; Theodore Roosevelt is president.

December 16: Senate approves Hay-Pauncefote Treaty.

1902
January 18: Walker Commission recommends Panama Canal scheme to Congress.

January 30: Britain and Japan form an alliance.

June 26: Congress approves Panama Canal project.

June 28: Austria, Germany, and Italy renew Triple Alliance for six years.

July 4: Roosevelt proclaims Philippine Government Act.

December 8: Roosevelt issues ultimatum to Germany over Venezuelan intervention.

1903
January 22: United States and Colombia sign Hay-Herran Treaty to facilitate Panama Canal construction.

February 13: Venezuelan crisis ends

July 16: Roosevelt criticizes Russian persecution of Jews.

August 12: Colombian Senate rejects Hay-Herran Treaty.

August 12: Japan denounces Russian presence in Manchuria.

October 20: U.S.-Canada Alaskan boundary dispute settled.

November 3: Panamanian revolt against Colombian rule breaks out.

November 6: United States recognizes Panamanian government.

1904
February 8: Russo-Japanese War breaks out.

February 23: Senate approves Hay-Bunau-Varilla Treaty for construction of the Panama Canal.

April 8: Anglo-French entente established.

September 7: Britain establishes protectorate in Tibet.

November 8: Roosevelt reelected.

December 6: Roosevelt announces Corollary to Monroe Doctrine.

1905
February 7: United States intervenes in Dominican Republic's debt crisis.

March 31: First Franco-German Morocco crisis.

May 25: Japanese Navy defeats Russian fleet in Battle of Tsushima Strait.

June 10: Roosevelt convinces Russia and Japan to negotiate.

July 8: Roosevelt secures Franco-German Algeciras Conference on Morocco.

July 24: Germany and Russia agree to Björkö Treaty.

July 29: United States and Japan sign secret Taft-Katsura Agreement.

August 9: Roosevelt chairs Russo-Japanese peace conference.

August 12: Britain and Japan renew alliance.

September 2: Russia and Japan sign Treaty of Portsmouth

October 20–30: General strike in Russia.

1906
February 10: Britain launches HMS *Dreadnought*.

April 7: France and Germany conclude Algeciras Treaty.

December 4: Roosevelt advocates naturalization rights for Japanese immigrants.

1907

January 15: United States advocates reforms in Belgian Congo.

January 21: Anglo-American Jamaica incident

August 31: Britain and Russia agree to an entente.

October 18: Second Hague Conference adjourns.

December 12: U.S. Navy begins round the world cruise.

1908

April 11: Root-Bryce Treaty signed for U.S.-Canada boundary settlement.

July 5: Young Turk revolt in Turkey.

October 6: Austria annexes Bosnia-Herzegovina.

November 3: William Howard Taft elected president; James Sherman is vice president.

November 30: Root-Takahira Executive Agreement with Japan.

December 4: London Naval Conference.

References and Further Reading

Beale, Howard K. *Theodore Roosevelt and the Rise of America to World Power* 1956. Reprint. Baltimore: Johns Hopkins University Press, 1984.

Brands, H. W. *TR: The Last Romantic.* New York: Basic Books, 1997.

Burton, David H. *Theodore Roosevelt: Confident Imperialist.* Philadelphia: University of Pennsylvania Press, 1968.

Collin, Richard H. *Theodore Roosevelt's Caribbean: The Panama Canal, the Monroe Doctrine, and the Latin American Context.* Baton Rouge, LA: Louisiana State University Press, 1990.

Cooper, John Milton, Jr. *The Warrior and the Priest: Woodrow Wilson and Theodore Roosevelt.* Cambridge, MA: Belknap Press of Harvard University, 1983.

Esthus, Raymond A. *Theodore Roosevelt and the International Rivalries.* 1970. Reprint, Claremont, CA: Regina Books, 1982.

Marks, Frederick W., III. *Velvet on Iron: The Diplomacy of Theodore Roosevelt.* Lincoln, NE: University of Nebraska Press, 1979.

Morris, Edmund. *Theodore Rex.* New York: Random House, 2001.

Neu, Charles E. *An Uncertain Friendship: Theodore Roosevelt and Japan, 1906–1909.* Cambridge, MA: Harvard University Press, 1967.

Ricard, Serge. *Théodore Roosevelt: principes et pratique d'une politique étrangère.* Aix-en-Provence: Université de Provence, 1991.

Roosevelt, Theodore. *Theodore Roosevelt: An Autobiography.* 1913. Reprint, New York: Da Capo, 1985).

Tilchin, William N. *Theodore Roosevelt and the British Empire: A Study in Presidential Statecraft.* New York: St. Martin's, 1997.

Trani, Eugene P. *The Treaty of Portsmouth: An Adventure in American Diplomacy.* Lexington, KY: University Press of Kentucky, 1969.

Zimmermann, Warren. *First Great Triumph: How Five Americans Made Their Country a World Power.* New York: Farrar, Straus, and Giroux, 2002.

William Howard Taft (1909–1913)

Early Life and Political Career

William Howard Taft was born in Cincinnati, Ohio, on September 15, 1857. He was the first of the four surviving children of Alphonso and Louisa Taft, who had lost their first son to whooping cough shortly after his first birthday. William also had two older half-brothers from his father's first marriage. Louisa, a highly educated and strong-minded woman, took tremendous interest in William's education and development as a child, making little secret of her expectation that he would achieve great success. Alphonso was a prominent lawyer and member of the Republican Party who would later serve as secretary of war and attorney general under President Grant, as well as minister to both Austria-Hungary and Russia under President Arthur. From a young age, then, the insecure Taft had much to achieve to satisfy his ambitious parents.

Taft graduated high school in 1874, second in his class. He then matriculated at Yale, where he again graduated as salutatorian in 1878. After Yale, Taft returned to Ohio, where he enrolled at Cincinnati Law School. In large part due to the connections his father had built up in the area, Taft was appointed assistant prosecutor of Hamilton County shortly after he passed the bar in 1880. This was followed up by his appointment as collector of internal revenue in 1883. Taft was heading in the right direction toward fulfilling his judicial ambitions, but political ambitions were far from his mind. That began to change in 1886, when he married Helen "Nellie" Herron, a woman from a prominent Cincinnati family who had dreamed of becoming First Lady since age seventeen, when she and her parents, friends of President Hayes, had spent time in the White House. Nellie saw in Taft a promising vehicle to satisfy her aspirations of leaving Ohio for a life of importance in Washington. Taft received in Nellie a woman who constantly pushed him to succeed (as his mother still did), but who was usually cold and unaffectionate. Throughout the remainder of his career, Taft would often be faced with having to decide between pursuing his own desires and fulfilling his wife's dreams.

In 1887, at age thirty, Taft was appointed to serve as a judge on the Ohio Superior Court, a position his father had once held. Taft loved the life of a judge, and set his heart on securing a seat on the United States Supreme Court. To that end, in 1889, Taft pressed Ohio Governor Joseph Foraker to request of President Harrison that he be appointed to the

William Howard Taft's attempt to use commercial and economic incentives in foreign affairs was dubbed "dollar diplomacy." (Library of Congress)

Supreme Court. Harrison countered by offering Taft the position of United States Solicitor General. Taft was disappointed and wished to remain in Ohio, but Nellie saw a potential move to Washington as an opportunity too golden to pass up, and she prevailed on her husband to accept the president's offer. Once in the nation's capital, Taft met Civil Service Commissioner Theodore Roosevelt and the two became fast friends. Arguing before the Supreme Court as solicitor general, however, required a competitiveness that was alien to the amicable Taft, and so he was quick to accept President Harrison's offer of a seat on the Sixth Federal Circuit Court of Appeals back in Cincinnati in 1892. Until 1900, Taft spent eight productive and enjoyable years on the bench, while his reputation among the elite of the Republican Party continued to grow.

Meanwhile, the American acquisition of the Philippines as a result of the Spanish-American War was about to alter William and Nellie Taft's lives profoundly. In January 1900, President McKinley asked Taft to serve as civil commissioner of the new American possession. Taft felt uncomfortable with the idea of serving in an executive rather than a judicial capacity, and told McKinley that he did not even approve of the United States keeping the islands. To this the president replied, "You don't want them any less than I do, but we have got them and . . . I think I can trust the man who didn't want them better than I can the man who did." Still, it was Taft's wife Nellie and not President McKinley who ultimately convinced him to accept the job.

Taft arrived in a Philippines controlled by General Arthur MacArthur, military governor of the islands. During the next year the two clashed over whether a civil or military administration should exercise ultimate authority over the islands, which were in the midst of an insurrection led by Emilio Aguinaldo. The disagreement was solved when Aguinaldo was captured in April 1901. Three months later, on July 4, 1901, Taft was sworn in as governor of the Philippines. The transfer of authority from military to civil government was complete. By all accounts, Taft's tenure in the Philippines was a successful one. He enjoyed the Filipino people, his "little brown brothers," as he fondly called them, and they were eager to return his affection. By May 1903, Taft's administration had implemented a criminal code, an internal revenue program, incorporation laws, and a districting scheme for electing the legislative assembly that would later convene in 1907. Taft did not believe that the Filipinos were likely to be capable of self-government within his lifetime, but he nonetheless governed them with an eye toward their eventual independence, and worked hard to develop the islands' economy and infrastructure. For her part, Nellie immensely enjoyed the prestige of being the lady of the "First Family" of the Philippines.

Taft's service in the Philippines did not come without a price. His old friend Theodore Roosevelt assumed the presidency upon McKinley's assassination in September 1901, and had twice since offered Taft a seat on the United States Supreme Court. Though tempted with the realization of his life's dream, Taft refused both offers, intent on fulfilling his duty to the Filipinos. When Elihu Root resigned as Roosevelt's secretary of war in 1903, however, the cabinet position was offered to Taft. Nellie supported the move, seeing it as a potential stepping-stone to the presidency. What convinced Taft, however, was Roosevelt's promise that, as secretary of war, he would retain ultimate control of the Philippines, and would therefore not be abandoning his duties there. In 1904, then, William Howard Taft moved back to Washington to become Theodore Roosevelt's secretary of war.

As secretary of war, Taft served Roosevelt as principle troubleshooter. Indeed, he had already begun to assume such a role while still governor of the Philippines. Then, in 1902, Roosevelt sent Taft to Rome to negotiate the sale of church-owned lands in the Philippines with Pope Leo XIII. Roosevelt now sent his secretary of war on similar missions, such as that to Japan in 1905. This trip resulted in the Taft-Katsura "Agreed Memorandum," informally approving the status quo in Asia (i.e., Japanese dominance in Korea, American in the Philippines). Taft was again sent around the world in 1907, including a second trip to Japan to investigate rumors that Japan wanted war with the United States. Taft concluded it did not. He then continued on to the Philippines to be present, as he promised he would be, at the opening of the Filipino Legislative Assembly.

Upon his return to Washington in December 1907, Taft learned that Roosevelt had publicly endorsed him to be his successor as president. Roosevelt had by then begun to regret his 1904 announcement that he would not seek a second full term, but he stuck to his word and turned to the next best thing: a Taft presidency. Taft, after all, had consistently supported Roosevelt's major positions, and would be sure to continue the policies of his friend and mentor. Although Taft had little desire for the presidency, he refused to publicly disavow his candidacy. Despite his lack of obvious ambition for the office and the popular quip that "Taft" stood for "Take Advice From Theodore," he easily won both the Republican nomination and the general election of 1908, defeating Democrat William Jennings Bryan by a count of 321 electoral votes to 162.

The Roosevelt Legacy

Taft entered office expecting to carry on most of Roosevelt's major policies; foreign affairs were no exception. In Latin America, Roosevelt had caused widespread resentment of American power by military interventions in Panama and the Dominican Republic. Roosevelt used American force to deter Colombia's reacquisition of Panama, its erstwhile province. This was prompted by his designs on securing rights to construct a canal across that newly created country. The Panama Canal Treaty was signed in 1904, and construction promptly began. Taft was thus left with the obligation to ensure the peace and stability of Central America in preparation for the opening of the canal, while much of the region was already beginning to chafe against "Yankee imperialism." Such sentiments were only exacerbated by the Roosevelt Corollary to the Monroe Doctrine, articulated in May 1904, which declared that the United States, in the interest of preventing European intervention, had the right to intervene in the internal affairs of any Latin American country if that country failed to repay its debts or otherwise misbehaved. This new policy was put into action in 1905, when the United States took control of Dominican customs to prevent a repeat of the recent British,

German, and Italian intervention in Venezuela. Despite the period of relative political and economic stability that resulted in the Dominican Republic, anti-Americanism continued to grow throughout the Western Hemisphere.

In China, Roosevelt's policy was nominally guided by the principle of the Open Door, which was supposed to guarantee equal trading rights to all countries in all parts of China. Roosevelt, however, had little problem acquiescing to the strengthening of Japanese special interests in Manchuria (as tacitly recognized in the Treaty of Portsmouth in 1905). Indeed, Roosevelt's commitment to the Open Door was strong only insofar as it did not mean trouble with one of the other interested powers or disrupt the balance of power in China. In his advice to the incoming Taft, Roosevelt warned that preservation of the Open Door was not worth war, as the United States essentially had no vital interests in China. While Taft never went so far as the brink of war over the Open Door, he was certainly more proactive in China than Roosevelt had been. The result would be the alienation of Russia and Japan and revolution in China.

While the beginning of the construction of the Panama Canal and the brokering of the Treaty of Portsmouth between Russia and Japan were two of Roosevelt's more obvious lasting foreign policy achievements, he and Secretary of State Elihu Root also largely eliminated the few remaining thorns in the side of Anglo-American relations. Under Roosevelt's administration, nagging border disputes between the United States and Canada (along the Alaskan border with British Columbia, and between Maine and New Brunswick at Passamaquoddy Bay) were submitted for arbitration. In addition, the decades-long disagreement over fishing rights in the waters off Newfoundland was also submitted to the Hague Tribunal for arbitration. Although all these issues were brought to a successful conclusion while Taft was in office, Roosevelt deserves much of the credit for initiating these settlements.

Finally, it is noteworthy that Roosevelt himself played an extremely active role in foreign affairs while president. Taft, on the other hand, preferred to set broad policy and leave the details to his secretary of state, Philander C. Knox. Due to his experiences in the Philippines and as secretary of war, Taft seemed perfectly suited to being a strong foreign policy president, but he nevertheless left office in 1912 with few lasting achievements. Dedicated above all to "Dollar Diplomacy," Taft accomplished none of his goals in China, left many open questions in Latin America for his successor, and largely ignored Europe.

Foreign Policy: "Substituting Dollars for Bullets"

In his Inaugural Address, Taft said relatively little about foreign policy, but summed up the heart of his views by stating, "I sincerely hope that the incoming Congress will be alive, as it should be, to the importance of our foreign trade and of encouraging it in every way feasible." Indeed, the promotion of American trade interests was Taft's top foreign policy priority. He viewed the Spanish-American War as an epochal event that placed the United States in a position of global influence that it had never previously enjoyed. As such, Taft sought to take advantage of that influence by using his government to promote private loans from American bankers for developments like railroad construction and currency reform in countries where American interests were greatest, namely China and the republics of Central America. Taft's tenure as executive of the Philippines clearly informed the direction of his policy toward China and its teeming billions. While visiting Asia as Roosevelt's secretary of war in 1907, Taft had occasion to address the American Association of China in Shanghai. There he proclaimed that "the attitude of the United States toward China must be regarded not alone as a country interested in the trade of China, but also as a Power owning territory in China's immediate neighborhood." In other words, the United States had become a Pacific as well as an Atlantic power. Moreover, the opening of the Panama Canal would only augment this new international role for America.

Central America, as the immediate neighborhood of the canal-to-be, was Taft's other main region of concern. His inaugural address included mention of the need to maintain the Monroe Doctrine, and the following four years would provide him with several opportunities to demonstrate this necessity, most notably in Nicaragua. On the whole, Taft's vision of foreign policy was one of expanding American economic influence in Asia, keeping Europe out of the Western Hemisphere, and using arbitration when appropriate to preserve world peace. Guided by the faith that American economic aid would serve the interests of both the United States *and* the people of the countries receiving such aid (a la the Filipinos), Taft summed up his administration's policy thusly in his final annual message: "The diplomacy of the present administration has sought to respond to modern ideas of commercial intercourse. This policy has been characterized as substituting dollars for bullets. It is one that appeals alike to idealistic humanitarian sentiments, to the dictates of sound policy and strategy, and to legitimate commercial aims." Upon taking office in March 1909, then, the reluctant president set out to serve both America's and the world's interests by increasing American global influence through dollars rather than guns.

The Hukuang Loan

In 1904, China signed an agreement with the United States and Great Britain, giving those two countries priority in securing loans for the construction of a possible railway from Hankow to Chungking. In addition, the two were promised an equal share of any loan they might be able to negotiate. Shortly thereafter, in 1905, the British inquired of the United States whether American capital might be interested in bringing such a loan to fruition, but the Roosevelt administration was apparently unenthusiastic about encouraging American bankers to participate. London, then, entered into negotiations with other interested powers, and by the summer of 1909, British bankers had come to a preliminary agreement with their counterparts from France and Germany to provide China with a loan for the construction of just such a railway. Upon learning of the impending closure of the European loan, the Taft administration immediately protested to the British government that previous American demurrals in no way constituted "a relinquishment of the right of American capital to participate." The United States had reversed course on the issue, and now wanted at the eleventh hour to elbow its way into an equal share of a loan agreement in which it had previously shown no interest.

The British, French, and German governments were initially noncommittal as to whether the United States should be allowed to participate at such a late stage of the negotiations, but the Taft administration had another avenue it could pursue. To this end, on June 5, 1909, American Chargé d'Affaires in Peking, Henry Fletcher, requested a hearing on the matter with the Chinese government. Fletcher notified the Prince of Ch'ing that the United States "insists that the assurances of 1904 be observed, and that American capitalists be consulted and allowed to participate in the loan about to be floated." Chang Chih-tung, the Chinese official most directly responsible for negotiating the loan, was soon convinced to delay an Imperial Edict on the loan until a satisfactory solution could be reached through negotiations involving the Americans. Little did Chang know that this promised delay would wind up costing him eleven months—precious time for a dynasty with only thirty months left until its demise.

The negotiations soon became deadlocked when the Taft administration insisted that American bankers accept nothing less than full equality in financing the loan—a demand to which the Europeans would not agree. Into this imbroglio stepped President William Howard Taft himself. In a personal letter to Prince Regent Chun, Taft cited the agreement of 1904 as the reason he was "disturbed" at "certain prejudiced opposition to your Government's arranging for equal participation by American capital in the present railway loan." The President acknowledged that he had resorted to a "somewhat unusually direct communication" because of the "high importance" that he attached to the successful result of the loan negotiations. "I have an intense personal interest," Taft continued, "in making the use of American capital in the development of China." Such an

arrangement, Taft assured the Prince, was motivated by the United States's concern for China's welfare, prosperity, independent political power, and the preservation of her territorial integrity.

To accompany Taft's letter, Knox instructed Fletcher to tell China on the same day that the American government deplored that certain individuals (i.e., European bankers) were acting in opposition to the spirit of the open door and equal opportunity. The time had arrived, suggested Knox, when China should "determine the matter by confining her dealings to those who are willing to respect her highest interests." Moreover, the United States would be willing to take up the entire loan, if necessary, "by reason of further persistency of the individuals who refuse to meet the situation broadly." The force of this diplomatic onslaught convinced the Prince Regent to acquiesce to the United States, and the Wai-wu Pu (the Chinese Foreign Office) was instructed to negotiate directly with Fletcher to resolve the issue. Taft had won the upper hand in the negotiations. The first test of his Dollar Diplomacy was going well.

In October 1909, however, Chang Chih-tung died—an ominous sign for foreign interests in China. As Fletcher observed, Chang was strong enough to keep the growing opposition to the borrowing of foreign capital in the Yangtze Valley to little more than talk. But now that he had died, the "woefully weak" central government might hesitate "to adopt the strong line with these Provinces." By December, a British-German dispute had been resolved, but France was displeased with the kilometers of track allotted to it. Knox grew increasingly uneasy, as further delays were sure to play into the hands of the anti-foreign Chinese. Indeed, as negotiations dragged on into the spring, riots erupted in the Yangtze Valley and throughout Hunan Province. During a one-week period in mid-April in Changsha, all foreign property was burned or otherwise destroyed, including several foreign missions. No foreigners were themselves harmed, but the unrest lent a tremendous sense of urgency to the loan negotiations. For this reason, in fact, the United States hastened to sign the final agreement, despite dissenting from a British proposal that would in effect lessen the Americans' overall mileage on the railway.

The Hukuang Loan agreement was signed on May 24, 1910, but not before it had fanned the flames of revolutionary antiforeign and antidynastic sentiments in China that would culminate the following year in the advent of a Chinese republic. Ironically, the revolution ultimately prevented the implementation of the very loan agreement for which Taft and Knox had pushed so hard.

Proposed Neutralization of Manchuria

The Hukuang Loan was but one half of the Taft administration's two-pronged strategy for increasing American influence in China. Just prior to Chang Chih-tung's death in October 1909, the United States, Great Britain, and China agreed on a construction plan for a railway running from Chinchow to Aigun in Manchuria, the traditional area of Japanese and Russian special interests. This agreement, while significant in itself, was used by Knox as leverage with the other powers to attempt to neutralize all railways in Manchuria. The idea was that Japan and Russia, being presented with the fait accompli of the Chinchow-Aigun line, could be led to give up control of their own railways in the region in the interest of working toward a common good rather than being forced to compete with the would-be Anglo-American line. To this end, in November and December 1909, Knox instructed his ambassadors in London, St. Petersburg, Paris, Berlin, and Tokyo to propose the following to the governments to which they were accredited:

> [P]erhaps the most effective way to preserve the undisturbed enjoyment by China of all political rights in Manchuria and to promote the development of those provinces under a practical application of the policy of the open door and equal commercial opportunity would be to bring the Manchurian highways, the railroads, under an economic, scientific, and impartial administration by some plan vesting in China the ownership of the railroads. . . .

Although China would have titular ownership of the railroads, that ownership would be under the guarantee and supervision of the interested powers. Moreover, Knox argued that the scheme would benefit all the powers, including Japan and Russia, as those countries would be freed from the sole burdens of funding the existing Manchurian railways. Neutralization would guarantee the open door, would preserve Chinese territorial integrity, and would allow powers other than Japan and Russia to share in the profits of trade in Manchuria.

Whereas Roosevelt had little desire to risk upsetting Japan and Russia by insisting on American influence in Manchuria, Taft saw tremendous potential in the region for American business and was not willing to stand idly by while Japan and Russia continued to dominate the region. Roosevelt's laissez-faire policy, however, had perhaps been wiser. By mid-January 1910, both Russia and Japan had rejected Knox's proposal. Soon, France too rejected the idea on the grounds that its adoption would have first required Russian and Japanese approval. The neutralization scheme had come apart at the seams. Moreover, Russia also registered a protest against the pending Chinchow-Aigun project. Not only would the railway line, slated to run right up to the Chinese-Russian border, be injurious to Russian interests, but its construction would fly in the face of an 1899 agreement whereby the Chinese gave Russia first priority in the construction of any railways north of Peking. Finally, by the summer of 1910, in the face of Russian and

Japanese objections to the Chinchow-Aigun project, the British had cooled to the idea of pressing ahead. Not only had neutralization failed, but the United States now seemed to have been frozen out of Manchuria altogether. In the end, the abortive proposals had the effect of driving erstwhile enemies Russia and Japan into greater cooperation with one another in order to prevent future incursions of other powers into Manchuria. The two signed a convention in St. Petersburg on July 4, 1910, in which they agreed to the preservation of the status quo in Manchuria.

The Failure of Dollar Diplomacy

By early 1912, the United States was aware that it had antagonized the other powers by its policies in China. Its forced participation in the Hukuang Loan and the neutralization proposal left Britain, France, Germany, Japan, and Russia suspicious of American motives and thinking Taft's policies to be "active and aggressive," and "competitive if not hostile to all other foreign interests in China." But the real trouble was not with those countries. It was with China herself. Throughout 1910 and 1911, popular discontent with China's imperial government grew. Not only was the government moving too slowly on promised political reforms, but it was seen as excessively weak in dealing with foreign powers. By the summer of 1911, rumors ran rampant in China that the ancient country was about to be partitioned. Antiforeign sentiment had certainly been simmering in China at least as far back as the Boxer Rebellion of 1900, but the recent conclusion of several foreign loans was one of the main factors exasperating "the radical element of the people to an extreme degree." As an increasingly potent and well-organized rebellion began to spread throughout China in the fall of 1911, the United States remained neutral. It also made moves to ensure the neutrality of the other powers, for example, extracting a promise from Japan that it would not take any action against either side without first consulting the State Department. As the revolutionaries gained more and more control over the apparatus of local government, Knox gave Minister Calhoun permission to enter into informal relations with the provisional government, and on February 12, 1912, the Manchu Emperor abdicated his throne. China had become a republic.

The revolution left Taft's China policy in shambles. All that remained was the possibility of participating in a "reorganization loan" to the new government. Belgium moved more quickly than the traditionally interested foreign powers by negotiating its own loan to the Republic of China. But under threat that the United States, Great Britain, France, and Germany would refuse to negotiate a larger loan to China so long as it was working with Belgium, the Chinese cancelled the Belgian loan. The four powers were later joined by Russia and Japan, though Belgium continued to be excluded from the group. The open door, it seems, was not open to all. In any event, the group of six agreed on terms for a reorganization loan in June 1912, which included plans for their supervision and control of expenditures. Refusing to bow to foreign influence in the same way that the previous regime repeatedly had, the Chinese "emphatically" rejected the arrangement. Taft left office before a solution could be reached, and under President Wilson, American participation in the reorganization loan was withdrawn. Taft's Dollar Diplomacy had been repudiated.

Nicaragua: Dollars and Gunboats

In Latin America, Taft's overarching goal was to preserve the political and economic stability necessary to pave the way for the opening of the Panama Canal, as well as to keep European influence out of the region. Nicaraguan dictator José Santos Zelaya was an obstacle to such stability. He had invaded Honduras in 1907, and continued to pose a threat to Nicaragua's neighboring republics. In addition, he increasingly looked across the Atlantic rather than to North America for assistance when in economic trouble. Shortly after Taft was sworn in, a revolution broke out against Zelaya that was partially instigated by American firm owners in Nicaragua. In November 1909, two Americans fighting with the rebels were captured and executed by Zelaya's forces. No law existed in Nicaragua that permitted the execution of POWs, yet Zelaya personally insisted on the executions—"not so much because they were revolutionists, but because they were Americans." The Taft administration responded by promptly breaking off relations with Nicaragua.

By mid-December, the besieged Zelaya was forced to step down as president of Nicaragua. In his message of resignation, he blamed "the hostile attitude of a powerful nation which, against all right, has intervened in our political affairs and publicly furnished the rebels the aid which they have asked for . . .." Exactly how much official support the revolution received from the United States is unclear, but in his final annual message, Taft explained that he was opposed to revolutionary movements except when occasionally justified by "a real popular movement to throw off the shackles of a vicious and tyrannical government" such as the Zelaya regime. The replacement of Zelaya with his Minister of Foreign Affairs José Madriz, however, did little to end hostilities. In October 1909, rebel leader General Juan Estrada proclaimed an independent republic in the eastern half of the country. Despite protests by the Madriz government, the United States continued to ship goods, including arms, to territory controlled by Estrada, thus providing him with fresh supplies for his revolt. In August 1910, Madriz fled the country and was replaced by Estrada as president. The popular and American-backed revolution was finally complete, and the stability that Taft so desired

could begin to return to Central America. In Managua, Estrada's arrival was celebrated with fireworks and bells, and Consul Moffat reported "intense enthusiasm" throughout Nicaragua.

Despite the fact that American envoy T. C. Dawson subsequently extracted an agreement with Estrada that promised elections, a liberal constitution, the negotiation of a loan guaranteed by Nicaraguan customs, and the prohibition of any Zelayista elements in the new government, peace and stability did not come easily. Estrada soon resigned over a battle with Minister of War Luis Mena, and Adolfo Díaz became a caretaker president until he was confirmed by election in 1913. In May 1911, he requested that a U.S. warship be sent to Nicaragua's Pacific coast to deter a rumored plot by the exiled Zelaya. The USS *Yorktown* promptly arrived in Nicaraguan waters. The Taft administration was apparently willing to use more than just dollars to ensure the stability of a vital region. As Mena, who commanded the loyalty of a majority of the national assembly, grew more ambitious, American diplomats were put in the position of trying to keep a lid on the rising tensions between Díaz and Mena. Fearing the loss of power, President Díaz requested an agreement with the United States along the lines of the Platt Amendment for Cuba. He asked for American intervention in Nicaragua whenever necessary "in order to maintain peace and the existence of a lawful government."

The opportunity for intervention presented itself in August 1912. Díaz asked the increasingly frustrated Mena to resign as minister of war. Mena responded by launching a rebellion and seizing a portion of an American-owned railway in the process. Díaz requested American assistance, ostensibly to guarantee the security of American property in Nicaragua so that Nicaraguan forces could be freed to put down the revolt. Whatever Díaz's motives, Knox urgently recommended action to President Taft. Taft approved, and marines began to arrive in Nicaragua. One Central American diplomat suggested that it was only the arrival of American forces that prevented the situation from widening into a region-wide conflagration. This assertion is perhaps borne out by President Araujo of Salvador's ploy to effect the withdrawal of the Americans by suggesting to Taft that the contingent of marines was not only unnecessary, but actively harmful to Central American stability. Taft replied that the United States was intent on protecting the lives of its citizens in Nicaragua as well as preventing the advent of a new Zelayaism. Finally, Taft hinted that, due to suspicions that Salvador served as a base for the anti-Díaz revolt, the level of friendship of Salvador to the United States was to be judged on its further actions regarding the rebellion. Little more trouble was made by Salvador.

Mena surrendered in early September, and by October the 2,700 marines in Nicaragua had effectively occupied all towns formerly held by his forces. Although four marines laid down their lives for it, Taft had successfully managed to return Nicaragua to some measure of political stability. But the Senate had still not ratified the loan contracts signed in the summer of 1911. Taft had repeatedly urged the Senate to ratify the loan to Nicaragua (as well as one to Honduras), but to no avail. In his final annual message, he argued that the Nicaraguan insurrection of 1912 could have been avoided had the State Department been given approval by the Senate to go ahead with the loan. Financial stability, for Taft, could prevent useless loss of life, destruction of property, and the suffering of thousands. In the absence of Senate action, the State Department turned to two American businesses to lend money to Nicaragua and take control of its customs. Once the gunboats withdrew, if dollars could not be substituted for bullets through government channels, there were always private channels.

Mexico: Qualified Neutrality

In October 1909, Taft became the first American president in history to set foot in a foreign country while in office. His visit to Ciudad Juarez, Mexico, lasted but a few hours and took him only just across the border from El Paso, but it afforded Taft and Mexican dictator Porfirio Díaz the opportunity to exchange diplomatic pleasantries and proclaim the strong friendship between the two men and their two countries. As events would bear out, however, that friendship was perhaps not as strong as Taft led Díaz to believe. Slightly more than a year after his meeting with Taft in Juarez, Díaz requested American assistance in keeping Mexican revolutionaries from purchasing arms in the United States. Despite American knowledge that revolutionary leader Francisco Madero was in San Antonio buying and shipping arms to his forces in Mexico, the State Department maintained that Madero had not technically violated American neutrality laws, as he was not using American territory as a base for rebel operations but merely carrying on legitimate acts of commerce. Thus, repeated Mexican requests that U.S. authorities arrest Madero went unfulfilled, even as the strength of the revolutionaries grew.

In March 1911, American Ambassador to Mexico Henry Lane Wilson personally met with Taft and Knox to explain the gravity of the situation in Mexico. To Wilson, the growing revolutionary fervor and potential resulting disorder imperiled the sizable American colony and its property in Mexico. Taft responded to this alarming news by ordering a three-month deployment of American troops to Texas in case it became necessary to protect American lives and property in Mexico. And if not, Taft hoped and reasoned, at least the military would have the opportunity to engage in educational maneuvers while deployed. Taft attempted to make it clear to both Díaz and the Mexican people that this deployment was in no way suggestive of an impending American intervention, but his assurances did little to convince most Mexicans of his benign intentions. In fact, Taft

only intended to intervene if the Díaz government, if and when it fell, was replaced with an irresponsible one—that is, a government that refused to guarantee the safety of American lives and American-owned property in Mexico.

Events took a dangerous turn in April 1911. Two Americans were killed and eleven wounded by stray bullets from a battle that took place in Mexico, but within feet of Douglas, Arizona. Taft responded with direct warnings to both the Mexican government and rebel forces that he would be compelled to act in defense of American lives on American soil if such an incident were repeated. Three days later, five more Americans were wounded in a similar incident, but Taft held firm to his policy of nonintervention. Although American forces might be compelled to cross the border or fire on forces on either side of the conflict, such actions might lead to a much larger intervention—one, Taft urged, that "we must use the greatest self-restraint to avoid."

Fortunately for Taft, no further incidents involving the loss of American life occurred. Unfortunately for Díaz, Madero gained strength, set up a provisional government in Juarez, and in May 1911, began his march on Mexico City. At this point, Taft informed Knox that this crisis for Díaz in no way altered American policy of allowing the legitimate shipment of arms through the customs house at El Paso. Taft recognized that such a policy may in fact give the rebels a great advantage, "but it grows out of the weakness or the misfortune of the Mexican Government, for which we are not responsible, and it does not change . . . the right of persons in our jurisdiction to carry on legitimate business." The United States was officially neutral, but remained so with the full knowledge that its policies were in effect favorable to Madero and the revolutionaries. Madero, after all, seemed "anxious to favor Americans and work in harmony with them in the establishment of law and order." By the time Díaz resigned in late May, then, Taft had skillfully avoided a potentially messy intervention in a conflict between two parties, both of which were relatively friendly to American interests.

It was not long before counterrevolutionary forces began to gather against Madero. Ironically, General Bernardo Reyes took the same path that Madero had the year before by making his way to San Antonio to plot against the Mexican regime. This time, however, the Taft administration intervened, arresting Reyes for violating American neutrality laws. Whereas the United States had stood idly by while Madero schemed against the dictator Díaz, it had no intention of allowing Reyes or anyone else to prepare a second revolution from Texas soil and further disrupt Mexican stability. With congressional approval, Taft did for Madero what Díaz had begged him to do a year earlier: he prohibited the export of all arms to Mexico except those destined for members of the American colony.

Madero, however, soon fell out of Taft's favor by making such arms deliveries to Americans in Mexico difficult, by increasingly gravitating toward European rather than American commercial markets, and by taking little action to suppress the anti-American press in Mexico. Taft personally expressed disappointment with the Mexican leader, who he thought should have "a more hearty consideration" for American interests given that he owed his very survival as president to Taft's nonexport law. In fact, the law turned out to be insufficient to ensure Madero's survival, both politically and literally. In February 1913, Taft's final month in office, General Victoriano Huerta overthrew Madero and had him killed. In the fighting leading up to the counterrevolution, despite some pressure to intervene, Taft's policy remained one of strict neutrality. A second revolution in Mexico had occurred on Taft's watch, but Huerta was soon to become Woodrow Wilson's problem.

Arbitration Treaties and Other Disappointments

Taft was a firm believer in arbitration as a tool for the preservation of world peace. Among his more notable achievements in this regard was the successful conclusion of the aforementioned fishery arbitration with Great Britain. In addition, American arbitration in 1910 peacefully settled a border dispute between Peru and Ecuador, as well as between Haiti and the Dominican Republic in 1911. But one of the greatest disappointments of Taft's presidency was his failure to shepherd through the Senate the arbitration treaties he signed with France and Great Britain in 1911. To Taft, the treaties "set the highest mark of the aspiration of nations toward the substitution of arbitration and reason for war in the settlement of international disputes." This failure, however, opened the door for him to turn down Britain's request to submit to arbitration the dispute over the Panama Canal tolls. In brief, in August 1912, Congress exempted American ships from having to pay tolls in the soon-to-be-opened canal, despite treaty language suggesting the canal should be open to ships from all nations "on terms of entire equality." The British protested, fearing that such an exemption would result in increased tolls for other countries, and asked for arbitration. In response, Taft said, "owning the canal and paying for it as we do, we have the right and power, if we so choose, to discriminate in favor of our own ships." When the canal opened in 1914, President Wilson repealed the exemption and the dispute was settled without resort to arbitration.

Another agreement that Taft failed to bring to fruition was that concerning tariff reciprocity with Canada, signed in 1911. Taft argued that the agreement would turn Canada's gaze and trade increasingly southward toward the United States instead of eastward towards its mother country. More mundanely, it would allow the United States cheap access to Canada's plentiful timber. But congressional concern that the deal would adversely affect the American fishing industry caused substantial modifications to be made, to the point where Taft no longer favored the agreement. The point turned out to be moot, however, as the Canadian parliament roundly rejected the treaty.

Legacy

Taft entered office reluctantly, but with a vision of expanding American commercial influence in Asia and preserving it in Latin America, especially in the immediate vicinity of the Panama Canal. His policy in Asia can only be seen as a failure. The neutralization scheme not only failed, but antagonized Russia and Japan, driving them into closer cooperation in Manchuria. His demand that American bankers be included in the Hukuang Loan both forestalled and ultimately doomed its implementation, as well as fanned the flames of revolution in China. Taft achieved his greatest foreign policy success in Nicaragua. Zelaya was removed from power and a new American-friendly regime took his place. Moreover, a potential regional conflict had been avoided. Still, a civil war might not have happened had he been able to convince the Senate of the importance of the loan contract to the new government. Taft's non-policy in Mexico surely saved the lives of many an American soldier, but it did little to effect lasting stability in that country, as Woodrow Wilson was soon to discover. As for Europe, Taft remained disinterested in the Turkish-Italian war, the Balkan Wars, and the second Moroccan crisis, as the United States had few interests in any of those disputes. He did negotiate arbitration treaties with Britain and France, but neither of those countries that would force the United States to war in the coming years. Still, war was coming, and for better or worse, it was not William Howard Taft who would lead America into it.

Taft's former friend and mentor Theodore Roosevelt decided to run against him in the election of 1912, splitting the Republican Party and allowing Democrat Woodrow Wilson to be elected. The loss came as a relief to Taft, who went on to have his lifelong dream fulfilled when President Harding appointed him chief justice of the Supreme Court in 1921. Taft remains the only American to have served as both chief executive and chief justice.

Dane J. Cash

Chronology
1909
February 8: Franco-German agreement on Morocco.

April 9: Payne-Aldrich Tariff lowers some duties.

November 6: United States proposes international neutrality for Manchuria.

December 16: United States assists Nicaraguan rebellion against Zelaya regime.

1910

August 22: Japan annexes Korea.

October 5: Portuguese republic proclaimed.

1911

May 21: French troops occupy Fez; Second Moroccan Crisis.

May 25: Revolutionary government of Francisco Madero takes power in Mexico.

July 26: United States offers trade reciprocity to Canada, Canada rejects offer.

September 28: Tripolitan War breaks out between Italy and Turkey.

November 29: Russia invades northern Persia.

December 30: Sun Yat-Sen elected president of the United Provinces of China.

1912

January 9: Insurrection in Honduras, U.S. Marines protect American property.

August 2: Lodge Corollary extends Monroe Doctrine to Japan and commercial ventures.

August 14: Unrest in Nicaragua, Taft sends U.S. Marines.

August 24: U.S. coastal shipping exempt from Panama Canal tolls.

October 8: Montenegro attacks Turkey, First Balkan War begins.

November 5: Woodrow Wilson elected president, Thomas Marshall is vice president.

References and Further Reading

Anderson, Judithe Icke. *William Howard Taft: An Intimate History.* New York: W. W. Norton, 1981.

Coletta, Paola E. *The Presidency of Wlliam Howard Taft.* Lawrence, KS: University Press of Kansas, 1973.

DeConde, Alexander. *A History of American Foreign Policy.* New York: Scribner, 1963.

Haley, P. Edward. *Revolution and Intervention: The Diplomacy of Taft and Wilson with Mexico, 1910–1917.* Cambridge, MA: Massachusets Institue of Technology Press, 1970.

Minger, Ralph Eldin. *William Howard Taft and United States Foreign Policy: The Apprenticeship Years, 1900–1908.* Urbana, IL: University of Illinois Press, 1975.

Scholes, Walter V., and Marie V. *The Foreign Policies of the Taft Administration.* Columbia, MO: University of Missouri Press, 1970.

Thomas Woodrow Wilson (1913–1921)

Early Life and Career

Woodrow Wilson was born in a manse in Staunton, Virginia, on December 28, 1856, the third child, and eldest son, of the Reverend Dr. Joseph Ruggles Wilson and Jessie Woodrow Wilson (who was the daughter and sister as well as the wife of a Presbyterian minister). This background certainly left a lasting mark on the style of Wilson's oratory and has been thought by some historians to explain the inspiration of his later policies—although it is at least equally plausible to see these as shaped by pragmatic political considerations. The family left Staunton two years after Wilson was born, but his upbringing remained entirely in the South, as his father moved successively to positions in Augusta, Georgia; Columbia, South Carolina; and Wilmington, North Carolina. As an adolescent, Wilson dreamed of being a political leader. From his father, whose parents had been Scots-Irish immigrants from Ulster, he derived a fascination with oratory as well as a love of English literature and poetry. At each of the three colleges he attended (Davidson College, Princeton, and the University of Virginia law school), he founded debating societies.

Wilson became a lawyer because he saw it as a route into politics, but after a brief unhappy time practicing in Atlanta, he enrolled at Johns Hopkins University as a graduate student in history and political science. Here he developed ideas from his undergraduate days into a book-length critical analysis of the way the American political system had come to work in practice; in 1885 this was published as *Congressional Government*. The central argument was that both efficiency and democratic accountability suffered from the lack of clearly identifiable and adequately empowered leadership, such as was provided by the cabinet in Britain. The book attracted national attention and laid the basis for Wilson's career as an academic political scientist. In the year of its publication, he married Ellen Axson, the daughter of another Presbyterian minister, and accepted a post at the new women's college of Bryn Mawr. After five years teaching there and at Wesleyan University, during which time his three daughters were born, he returned to Princeton as a professor in 1890. Here he acquired an outstanding reputation as a lecturer and published prolifically in the fields of politics and American history. In these voluminous writings, he expressed opinions about many issues, but the

Thomas Woodrow Wilson's initiatives for international peace went down in ruins in the 1920s and 1930s, but his long-term legacy, both to U.S. foreign policy and to the conduct of international relations generally, is enormous. (Library of Congress)

nature of successful leadership in a democracy remained a particular preoccupation.

In 1902, Wilson was elected president of Princeton, which he saw as an opportunity to put his ideas about leadership into practice. The trajectory of Wilson's presidency at Princeton has been seen as foreshadowing his later years in the White House—a period of remarkable accomplishment and acclaim followed by failure to achieve overambitious goals and final defeat in an atmosphere of bitter personal conflicts and animosity. In reforming the undergraduate curriculum, introducing the "preceptorial" system and strengthening the faculty, Wilson did much to raise Princeton's standing, but a rather high-handed attempt to replace the established eating clubs with residential quadrangles evoked a strongly negative reaction from alumni. In public speeches, Wilson presented the issue as one of democracy against privilege and the power of money, thus aligning himself with the progressive movement that seemed to be the prevailing force in the country at the time.

The bosses of the New Jersey Democratic Party, facing a difficult election, offered him the gubernatorial nomination in 1910, and Wilson, aged fifty-three, at last entered the political arena directly. After winning the election, he furthered his progressive credentials by publicly breaking with the bosses and securing the passage of several pieces of reform legislation. He became a leading contender for the Democrats' presidential nomination, which he secured on the forty-fourth ballot at a tumultuous convention at Baltimore in 1912. Aided by the split in the Republican Party that led to Theodore Roosevelt's candidacy on a Progressive Party (or "Bull Moose") ticket, Wilson carried forty of the forty-eight states in the subsequent election with only 42 percent of the popular vote.

A Democratic Foreign Policy

"It would be an irony of fate if my administration had to deal chiefly with foreign affairs." Wilson's reported remark to a friend before going to Washington has been much quoted because of the heaviness of the "irony" fate had in store for the man who was to lead the United States through World War I. It was certainly true that domestic affairs had dominated the election campaign and that they were to be Wilson's principal concern during his first eighteen months in office when he secured the passage through Congress of four major reform measures, a legislative achievement matched only by Franklin Roosevelt and Lyndon Johnson among his twentieth-century successors. From the beginning, however, he devoted considerable attention to foreign affairs, in which sphere he saw the president's authority as virtually absolute. Unlike Theodore Roosevelt, Wilson had not given much thought to international relations before reaching the White House, and had visited Europe (apart from Britain) only briefly, and no other continents at all. But he approached the conduct of foreign policy with some assumptions and beliefs that were perhaps more deeply rooted than his views on domestic economic and social issues, as well with some more general predispositions and values that were to prove equally relevant. He held a fundamental belief in the virtue and power of his own country. Like most Americans he had no doubt that the political and social system of the United States was superior to that of other countries and, more than most, he believed in the nation's historic mission to lead the world on to a higher plane. It was to do this chiefly by example, and an aspect of this example should be a foreign policy designed to serve broad human interests rather than narrow selfish ones. Wilson also was very impressed by the scale of American power, and thought that this in itself impelled a more active

involvement with world affairs than had been traditional. Although he had been uncertain at the time whether the United States should take the Philippines after the War of 1898, he had come to see its doing so as marking the country's "full maturity" and the end of its "isolation." He recognized that America's new power was the product of the nation's tremendous economic advance since the days of Washington and Jefferson, and believed that this advance had in itself widened the scope of the nation's interests.

Yet Wilson's foreign policy was by no means simply the product of his own attitudes and views. It also reflected his understanding of the role of a leader in a democracy and his party affiliation. In charting his course, Wilson believed it to be his duty—and recognized that it was in his political interest—to represent the preponderant sentiment of the American people. However, at a time when few Americans gave much attention to foreign affairs, there was a consensus only on certain basic principles such as upholding the Monroe Doctrine, not becoming involved in Europe's wars, and defending the rights of Americans abroad. It had been in the Republican Party that support had developed since the 1880s for strengthening the U.S. Navy, constructing an isthmian canal, and a generally more energetic and expansionist foreign policy. The fact that proponents of this more active diplomacy often favored some degree of cooperation with Great Britain only increased the antagonism to it within Democratic ranks, where Anglophobia was strong among Irish-Americans and some agrarian radicals. The Democratic Party had opposed the acquisition of the Philippines and other overseas territories in 1898 as a violation of the principles of the Declaration of Independence. That campaign had been led by William Jennings Bryan who was the party's presidential candidate in three elections. Bryan had thrown his weight behind Wilson at the Baltimore convention and, in recognition of this and Bryan's standing in the party, Wilson granted him the premier cabinet position of secretary of state, notwithstanding his lack of experience in foreign affairs. Bryan, who was deeply committed to the cause of world peace, set about negotiating bilateral "cooling-off" treaties with other states in which the parties agreed to submit any disputes to a commission of inquiry and not to resort to war for six months or a year.

Like several later American presidents, Wilson began by seeking to show how different his foreign policy was going to be from that of his predecessors. Within days of taking office, he had withdrawn support for the participation by American bankers in an international consortium to make a large loan to China. The Taft administration's attempt in this way to use private American capital to buttress its policy objectives—the preservation of China from the formal or informal imperialism of other powers—was a prime example of what the Democrats had condemned as "dollar diplomacy," and Wilson's move was hailed in progressive circles as a blow against profiteering exploitation. But the lack of

American financial assistance rendered the government of the new Chinese republic (which Wilson was quick to recognize) vulnerable to Japanese expansionism, and by 1917 the administration was attempting to organize a new consortium. Repudiation of Republican actions was also involved in the treaty that Bryan negotiated with Colombia, by which the United States undertook to pay $25 million and expressed regret for its part in the process by which the province of Panama had broken away in 1903, but ex-President Roosevelt's friends in the Senate prevented this treaty ever being ratified. However, in securing the repeal of a measure that exempted American shipping from the payment of tolls in the newly-opened Panama Canal in 1914, Wilson took on Democratic leaders in the House of Representatives and enjoyed the support of prominent internationalist-minded Republicans.

Notwithstanding this readiness to subordinate material American interests to the principle of fair dealing between nations, Wilson was to authorize military interventions in Haiti, Santo Domingo, Nicaragua, and twice in Mexico. The interventions resulted from events in the countries concerned, particularly the Mexican revolution, but they also reflect the attitudes with which Wilson and Bryan approached policy-making in the Caribbean and Central America. Their anti-imperialism by no means implied isolationism, and certainly not in a part of the world where they were determined to maintain American hegemony, but felt that it brought responsibilities—in this respect manifesting continuity with their Republican predecessors, including Theodore Roosevelt's Corollary to the Monroe Doctrine. In Haiti and Santo Domingo, the interventions started with efforts to oversee the management of the customs revenue and proceeded by way of somewhat naïve attempts to secure freely-elected and uncorrupt governments.

Mexico

Throughout Wilson's first term, Mexico was as subject to internal instability and disorder as the smaller states in the region. The Mexican revolution had begun in 1911 with the overthrow of the long rule of Porfirio Díaz, whose policies had attracted much foreign investment, particularly from the United States. A few weeks before Wilson entered the White House, the revolutionary president, Francisco Madero, had been deposed and murdered in a coup led by General Victoriano Huerta. Shocked by the methods by which Huerta had come to power and suspicious of the interests behind him, Wilson refused to recognize his government, a stand that gained additional justification when Huerta's effective control of the country could be questioned after revolutionary leaders under Venustiano Carranza launched a military movement against him, calling themselves the Constitutionalists. Defying Wilson's demand that he schedule elections, Huerta assumed dictatorial powers in

October 1913. Determined to prevail in a public contest of wills in which he evidently felt his own prestige, as well as that of his country, was at stake, Wilson recognized the belligerent status of the Constitutionalists, allowing them openly to buy arms. In April 1914, after some American sailors had been arrested by a junior Mexican officer in Tampico, Wilson firmly backed the commanding U.S. admiral's demand for a twenty-one gun salute from the Mexicans as well as an apology. Veracruz was quickly seized, but only after fighting in which 19 Americans and over 100 Mexicans lost their lives. Regardless of their internal divisions, Mexicans reacted angrily to what they perceived as American aggression, and Carranza talked of war. Wilson had no wish to be drawn into a full-scale conflict, especially as most public opinion in the United States as well as Europe regarded the issues at stake as trivial, but the United States retained control of Veracruz until Huerta resigned in July 1914.

However, instability continued as Carranza's lieutenant, Francisco Villa, made a bid for power. During the ensuing conflict, foreigners in Mexico City suffered much hardship. This, and attacks on church institutions and personnel by the anticlerical revolutionaries, led to demands, particularly from Catholic spokesmen, Roosevelt, and some Republicans, that Wilson do more to restore order in Mexico. The administration sought to bring unity to the various revolutionary factions, initially unilaterally and later in collaboration with other Latin American governments. However, Wilson frequently expressed sympathy with the basic aims of the revolution and now insisted that social reforms needed to be enacted before elections could be held. By October 1915, Carranza's forces had clearly prevailed and his government was granted recognition by the United States and the major Latin American countries. When protests continued about affairs in Mexico, Wilson gave emphatic expression to the principle of self-determination: "If the Mexicans want to raise hell, let them raise hell. We have got nothing to do with it."

In 1916, however, the issue was not Mexico's right to determine its own government in its own way but the conflict between its sovereign prerogatives and the duty of the American government to safeguard the lives of its citizens. Blaming the United States for his defeats, and perhaps hoping that provoking military intervention would embarrass Carranza, Villa began attacking Americans, killing eighteen in Mexico in January, and in March leading a raid on Columbus, New Mexico, in which seventeen more Americans lost their lives. Although Wilson had responded calmly to the first event, placing the responsibility on Carranza to punish the perpetrators, the second outrage obviously demanded a direct response, and a punitive expedition led by General J. J. Pershing penetrated 350 miles into Mexico in pursuit of the elusive Villa. Weeks of mounting tension, with increasingly insistent demands by Carranza that the Americans withdraw, climaxed in a battle between an American unit and Carranza's troops at Carrizal, Chihuahua, in June, in which fourteen Americans were killed and another twenty-five taken prisoner. In response to an ultimatum, Carranza released the American prisoners, and a joint commission was established to resolve the issues. When the commission abandoned its work in early 1917 without having reached an agreement, Wilson accepted its members' advice to withdraw Pershing's force.

Wilson's experiences with the Mexican revolution left him convinced that outside intervention in such situations was not only wrong in principle but likely in practice to be both counterproductive and the source of intractable difficulties and serious embarrassments. These attitudes were to shape his response to pressure for military intervention to affect the outcome of the revolution and civil war into which Russia was plunged in 1917.

Neutrality and Its Problems

As World War I broke out in Europe, the president of the United States was sitting by the bedside of his dying wife. Ellen's death from Bright's disease on August 6, 1914, devastated Wilson, who had held out hope of her recovery almost to the end. Yet it was not because of the President's distraction that the United States played no part in the European crisis sparked by the assassination of Archduke Franz Ferdinand in Sarejevo on June 28, 1914. Like most Americans, Wilson certainly saw war between the Great Powers as a disaster for civilization. Earlier that summer, his friend and confidant, Colonel Edward M. House, had been in Europe seeking to ease tensions between England and Germany. But House had been able to offer no more to the cause of European peace than the good offices of the United States and his own services as a mediator. More extensive participation in the power politics of Europe would violate a hallowed tradition and was not generally perceived to be in the national interest.

Wilson initially adhered to this position. Indeed, he erected neutrality into more than a technical status by calling on the American people to be "impartial in thought as well as in action." Wilson argued that this would enable the United States to play the role of a trusted mediator when the time came. But more immediately he feared the effects on domestic harmony of the naturally divided sympathies of a people "drawn from many nations, and chiefly from the nations now at war." In seeking to override these divisive sentiments by appealing to a higher loyalty to America, Wilson based official policy strictly on the nation's interests and rights as a neutral.

In the first months of the war, it was the British who impinged upon these as they tightened their naval blockade until it amounted to a more or less complete embargo on both direct and indirect trade with Germany. In December 1914 and March 1915, the United States sent lengthy official notes protesting the infringements on the legal right of neutrals to trade in noncontraband goods. Although these notes warned of the bad effect on American opinion of British practices, they were couched in a friendly manner and contained no hint of retaliatory action. Wilson recognized that the material interests involved were small in scale, particularly as the British kept cotton off the contraband list until August 1915, and that the economic loss was more than compensated for by the increased Allied purchases of American goods. Any retaliatory sanctions would certainly have damaged the American economy (currently suffering from recession) and were unlikely to have persuaded the British to moderate the blockade, which was the principal means by which they hoped to bring Germany to its knees. Moreover, at a time when most Americans (and, privately, Wilson himself) saw the Allies as fighting against aggression, any action that hampered their war effort would have faced fierce domestic opposition.

This would no doubt have been led by some of Wilson's most prominent political opponents, such as Theodore Roosevelt and Senator Henry Cabot Lodge (Republican of Massachusetts), who were much more emotionally committed to the Allied cause than he was. Although they did not advocate intervention, such men did stridently support the agitation for greater military "preparedness" that developed in late 1914. In his annual message in December, Wilson deplored this response to "a war with which we have nothing to do, whose causes cannot touch us, whose very existence affords us opportunities of friendship and disinterested service which should make us ashamed of any thought of hostility or fearful preparation for trouble."

In February 1915, Germany proclaimed a war zone around the British Isles, within which commercial vessels as well as warships would be liable to be attacked by submarines. This clear disregard of the rules of war was justified as a reprisal for the British "food blockade." (It is this that provides the somewhat shaky link in the later argument that the failure to resist Allied violations of international law more effectively paved the way to America's eventual involvement in the war.) The United States declared that it would hold the German government to "a strict accountability" for its navy's acts, though the wording of its note did not make it entirely clear whether this applied to the safety only of American ships or also of Americans taking passage on ships of the belligerent nations. This issue arose sharply in late March when a small British liner, the *Falaba*, was sunk and an American, Leon Thrasher, was among those who lost their lives. This case set off a fierce debate within the administration. The counselor of the State Department, Robert Lansing, drafted a note demanding that Germany disavow the act and make reparation. On the other side,

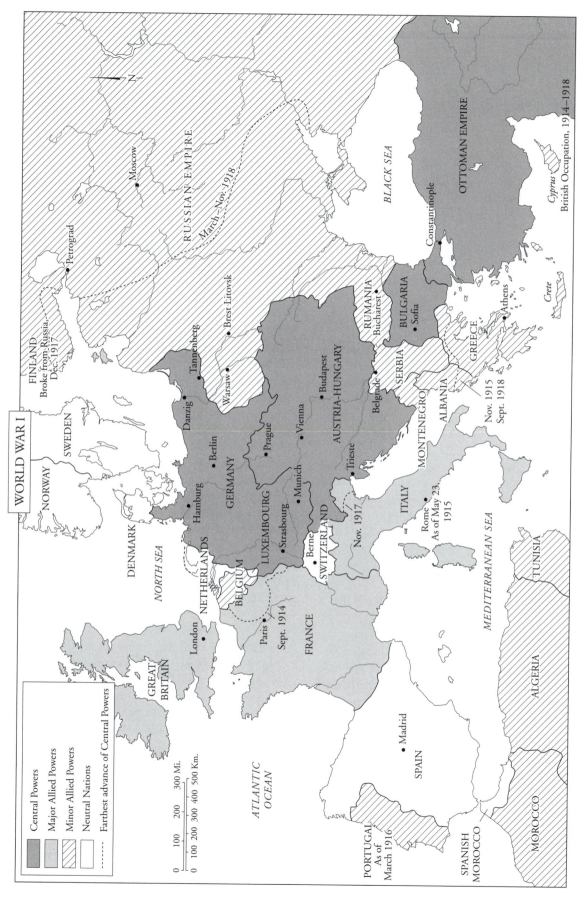

From August 1914 to November 1918, every major power in Europe, and ultimately the United States as well, found itself in a death struggle that radically changed the face of global affairs and the conduct of diplomacy.

Bryan argued that an American citizen pursuing his business interests in a risky situation should not expect his country to protect him. Wilson at first inclined toward Lansing's position but was apparently impressed by Bryan's insistence that an ultimatum that might lead to war would lack public support. No action had been taken when on May 7, 1915, the premier British liner, the *Lusitania*, was torpedoed with the loss of 1,200 lives, including 128 Americans.

The outrage created by this event produced demands for firm action from newspapers and politicians, and Wilson's apparently coincidental remark in an impromptu speech three days later that "there is such a thing as a man being too proud to fight" was not well received. In this atmosphere (and at a time when he had just proposed to the woman who would become his second wife), Wilson drafted on his own typewriter (as was his wont) a note demanding that Germany not only disavow the act and make reparation but also abandon submarine warfare against merchant ships entirely. Bryan, who was extremely anxious that war be avoided, recommended that Americans be officially warned against traveling on belligerent ships. When Wilson rejected his suggestions, Bryan resigned rather than sign a second note reiterating the demands of the first. Lansing was appointed to the post despite some doubts on Wilson's part as to whether he was up to the job.

Wilson's strong stand was almost unanimously applauded, but he was well aware that Americans generally did not wish to become involved in the war. In a private letter in late July, he observed that "the opinion of the country seems to demand two inconsistent things, firmness and the avoidance of war, but I am hoping that perhaps they are not in necessary contradiction and that firmness may bring peace." This hope was shaken when another British liner, the *Arabic,* was sunk on August 19, with the loss of two further American lives, and Wilson feared for a time that a break with Germany was unavoidable. However, the Germans were at this juncture anxious not to bring the United States into the ranks of their enemies, and they disavowed the sinking, publicly pledged that liners were safe from attack, and secretly suspended submarine operations.

This conclusion left Wilson apparently triumphant. With Germany's public abandonment and repudiation of the use of submarines against passenger ships, his handling of the crisis that began with the *Lusitania* sinking was widely praised. But he was well aware that the danger of a conflict that the great majority of Americans did not want had been averted only by the actions of the German government. By securing "peace with honor" he had placed himself in a strong position for his reelection campaign in 1916, but he never lost sight of the fact that Berlin could at any time force him to choose between these values—and he recognized that either choice would divide the American people and lose him support. Consciousness of this danger was the

dominating background of Wilson's policy for the rest of the period of neutrality. It impelled him to take steps that moved the United States significantly nearer to a full and active participation in international politics.

In the first place, he reversed his position over "preparedness." Although the president did not publicly make the case for increases in the size of America's armed forces until November 1915, he had indicated an abrupt change of mind on this issue within two weeks of the *Lusitania* sinking. Faced with determined opposition to his program in Congress, Wilson took his case to the country in a series of speeches in early 1916. In these, he explained that an increase in America's armed forces was essential because of "the double obligation you have laid upon me"—"to keep us out of this war" and "to keep the honor of the nation unstained." The actions of other countries might make it necessary "to use the force of the United States to vindicate the right of American citizens everywhere to enjoy the protection of international law." On his return to Washington, Wilson supplemented his strengthened position with a readiness to compromise with congressional critics. After he had dropped the controversial proposal for a reserve "Continental Army" of 400,000 men, a bill passed both houses that substantially increased the regular Army and also provided for a greatly enlarged National Guard under more effective federal control. Even more impressive was the Navy Act of 1916 which authorized a building program (sixteen capital ships over three years) larger than any ever previously undertaken by any nation.

Wilson also modified the administration's position on loans by private American citizens and institutions to the belligerent governments. In 1914, Bryan, declaring money to be "the worst of all contrabands because it commands everything else," had announced that such loans were inconsistent with neutrality. This policy was soon interpreted as allowing private commercial credits, but the enormous growth of Allied purchases created a trade deficit that could only be met by borrowing and the sale of gold and American securities. In September 1915, Wilson tacitly permitted floating a large public loan by the Allies in the American market. In doing so, he was acceding to the pleas of Lansing and Secretary of the Treasury William G. McAdoo that this was necessary to maintain America's own prosperity, but it may not have been coincidental that the change of stance occurred during the *Arabic* crisis.

Seeking Peace and Challenging Tradition

The greatest effect of the crisis of 1915 on Wilson's policy was that it added urgency and force to his efforts to bring the war to an end. This was the only secure and lasting way in which he could avoid having to choose between humiliation and an unpopular war. In the attempt to achieve this goal, he departed from the tradition of nonentanglement in a very dramatic way—by committing the United States to participation in a postwar league of nations.

Initially, Wilson sought to end the war through collaboration with the Allies. But when House approached British foreign secretary Sir Edward Grey, in September 1915, with the suggestion that Wilson call for a peace "upon the broad basis of the elimination of militarism and navalism and a return, as nearly as possible to the status quo," Grey replied by asking directly whether the United States would be prepared to take part in "a League of Nations binding themselves to side against any Power which . . . refused, in case of dispute, to adopt some other method of settlement than that of war?" Although a similar suggestion the previous winter had been dismissed by House as contrary to America's "fixed policy not to become involved in European affairs," he and Wilson now responded positively to this request, and sought to use this potential commitment to persuade the Allies to agree to an early peace. In February 1916, House persuaded Grey to sign a secret memorandum embodying an agreement that Wilson would call for peace when the Allies thought the moment was opportune and then force Germany, if necessary by war, to accept reasonable terms.

Since the appeal of this plan to the Allies would obviously depend in part on the credibility of the American commitment, House had to counter any impression that it was motivated by America's desire to avoid being dragged into war by the submarine dispute. This may well have contributed to Wilson's rejection in early 1916 of two moves to minimize that danger. In the face of Allied opposition, he withdrew his support of a *modus vivendi* suggested by Lansing under which German submarines would undertake to abide by the law of visit and search in return for the Allies' removing guns from their merchant vessels. The president also deployed all his authority to defeat congressional resolutions sponsored by Bryanite Democrats warning American citizens not to travel on armed belligerent ships. Germany had now resumed its submarine campaign, announcing that armed merchantmen would be treated as warships. Another crisis was precipitated by the torpedoing of a cross-Channel passenger ship, the *Sussex*, on March 24. In response to a virtual ultimatum from Wilson, Germany undertook to suspend submarine warfare but declared that it now expected Washington to compel the British also to observe international law.

This crisis added urgency to Wilson's drive for peace. In an attempt to persuade the Allies to activate the House-Grey agreement, he made his readiness to join a postwar league of nations public in a speech on May 27, 1916, to the League to Enforce Peace (an organization promoting such a plan). In this first attempt to persuade his own countrymen to make this commitment, he argued that the war had shown that isolation was no longer an option: "we are participants, whether we would or not, in the life of the world." It followed that the United States had a real interest in seeing peace restored and given "an aspect of permanence." This would require a "universal association of nations" to prevent aggressive war as well as the adoption of such traditional American principles as "that every people has a right to choose the sovereignty under which they shall live."

Despite this speech and House's repeated urgings, the Allies made it increasingly clear that they had no wish either for an early peace or for American mediation. Wilson now saw their war aims, too, as selfish and imperialistic and this, together with Britain's cavalier disregard of American protests about new blockade practices, led to a marked deterioration in relations with the Allies from the summer of 1916. In September, the administration secured from Congress authority to restrict trade with countries illegally interfering with the movement of American goods or ships. In his election campaign that fall, Wilson portrayed the war as the product of the European system in general rather than of German aggression and as a simple contest for dominance with no wider significance. Contemporary observers agreed that the election, which Wilson did well to win with the Republican Party reunited after its split in 1912, demonstrated the depth and breadth of anti-interventionist sentiment. With the German government clearly signaling that it would launch a new and more ruthless submarine campaign if peace was not made soon, this evidence of the balance of American opinion only strengthened Wilson's desire to bring the war to an early end.

He now sought to do this through an independent and public peace initiative. Both House and Lansing opposed such a move, fearing it would be welcomed by the Germans and resisted by the Allies, thereby placing the United States on what they regarded as the wrong side. Their objections delayed but did not prevent Wilson's addressing a note to all belligerent powers in mid-December that combined an eloquent denunciation of the war's human and material costs with a plea for a statement of "the precise objects" for which each side was fighting. When he received replies that left no opening for a peace conference, the president responded with an address to the Senate on January 22, 1917, in which he openly sought to force the belligerent governments to make peace by appealing over their heads to their presumably war-weary populations. At the same time, he attempted to maximize the leverage he could gain from his readiness to bring the United States into a postwar league of nations by making it conditional on there being "a peace without victory" based on liberal principles. Following the speech, Wilson assured House that he could bring about an end to the war if the Germans (who had themselves proposed negotiations to their enemies in December) came up with reasonable terms. He seems to have been confident that he could put pressure on the Allies by exploiting their increasingly desperate need for dollars, as he already had in November by strengthening a warning by the Federal Reserve Board against the purchase of British and French government bonds.

War Leader

Given these hopes, it is not surprising that Wilson confessed to House that "he felt as if the world had suddenly reversed itself" when Germany announced an unrestricted submarine campaign, against neutral as well as belligerent shipping, beginning February 1, 1917. The president at once made clear his reluctance to respond with war. In breaking diplomatic relations with Germany, which he recognized as inevitable after his earlier notes, he stated that "only actual overt acts" would lead him to go further. When U.S. ships hesitated to enter the war zone, he adopted an "armed neutrality" that would give them guns and naval protection. But the Zimmermann telegram, offering Mexico territorial compensation if she would join a war against the United States, not only aroused fury in the most isolationist part of the country but also indicated that Berlin would not back down this time. When, in mid-March, three American ships were sunk, Wilson accepted his cabinet's unanimous view that there was "no alternative" to belligerency. The Germans had removed the option of "peace with honor." And, as Wilson declared to Congress when he called for a declaration of war, "there is one choice we cannot make, we are incapable of making: we will not choose the path of submission."

At no time did Wilson suggest that intervention was necessary to prevent a German victory that would threaten America's own security. American commentators did not see the submarine campaign as a winning weapon, and the administration had no idea of the seriousness of the Allies' military and financial position until after U.S. entry into the war. Nor was belligerency required to sustain the nation's export trade, as the Allies transported most of the goods they purchased in their own ships. What was at stake was the nation's prestige and diplomatic credibility, and with it the president's. In making the case for war, Wilson blended appeals to several different elements in American opinion. Detailing the hostile actions of the German government aroused patriotic indignation, and, in linking these to that government's autocratic character, Wilson adopted the pro-Allied ideological interpretation of the European conflict that he had previously eschewed (something made easier by the recent overthrow of the Tsar in Russia). At the same time, the president reassured the progressive internationalists who had become his particular supporters that he was still committed to a liberal and lasting peace—one that would make the world "safe for democracy."

Notwithstanding this claim to continuity, entry into the war involved a significant change in Wilson's policy in that he no longer desired "a peace without victory." In rejecting calls for such a peace from the Petrograd Soviet in May and from the Pope in August, Wilson argued that "it was the *status quo ante* out of which this iniquitous war issued" and that no agreement with "the present rulers of Germany" could be relied on. This did not mean that he endorsed the war aims of the Allies, but nor did he try to force them to abandon their territorial ambitions by exploiting their critical need for American support. Quarrelling with the Allies at this point would not serve either to build domestic support for the war or to bring it to a swift and successful conclusion. For Wilson, as for all war leaders, the priority now was victory.

It soon became apparent that this would require a full-scale mobilization of American resources. Conscription was introduced from the beginning, though it may not have been until after pleas from the Allies that Wilson decided to send an expeditionary force to France under Pershing's command. Even more urgent was the need for American money, and eventually loans totaling $11.2 billion were made to the various governments fighting Germany. In late 1917, the Italian disaster at Caporetto and the antiwar Bolshevik Revolution in Russia in November led to Allied requests for many more American divisions to be sent to France as soon as possible. By July 1918, Pershing had more than a million men under his command, a number that doubled by the time the war ended in November 1918.

It was not only by collapsing the eastern front that the Bolsheviks threatened the anti-German war effort. In furtherance of their agitation for a general "peace without annexations or indemnities on the basis of the self-determination of peoples," they published secret treaties in which the Allies had promised each other territorial gains. The need to counter this propaganda and justify the war to liberal and labor circles in the Allied countries as well the United States provided Wilson with an opportunity to promote his own conception of the peace. In a speech to Congress on January 8, 1918, he set out a program consisting of fourteen points. Some of these were general, such as freedom of the seas, the lowering and equalization of trade barriers, and disarmament, but the majority concerned the territorial settlement in Europe. In his 1917 address to the Senate he had largely confined himself to broad principles such as "the consent of the governed" and that "every great people" should have access to the sea. In now applying these to specific situations, Wilson accommodated some of the Allies' objectives (such as the return of Alsace-Lorraine to France) while implying opposition to others, notably with respect to what Italy had been promised as reward for entering the war in 1915. Finally, Wilson called for "a general association of nations" to afford "mutual guarantees of political independence and territorial integrity to great and small states alike."

In this speech Wilson condemned Germany's "military leaders" but spoke sympathetically both of the Bolshevik representatives who had just broken off truce negotiations with the Germans and of "the more liberal statesmen" of the Central Powers. If he was hoping either for a revival of the eastern front or a change of regime in Germany that would make possible an early peace, both hopes were comprehensively dashed by the draconian Treaty of Brest-Litovsk in

March 1918, which enabled the Germans to move troops to the west and launch a formidable offensive. Responding to these developments, Wilson called for "Force, Force to the utmost, Force without stint or limit." The Allies pressed strongly for military intervention in Russia, and Wilson eventually agreed to the participation of U.S. units in limited missions to North Russia and Siberia. The Siberian expedition, undertaken together with a Japanese force, was to aid the Czech Legion, former prisoners of war who wanted to fight for their nation's freedom from the Austro-Hungarian empire on the western front. Shortly afterward, the United States recognized the Czech National Council, a move that deepened Wilson's association with the cause of national self-determination.

The arrival and engagement of American troops helped to turn the tide of battle on the western front in the summer of 1918 but also lengthened casualty lists. As war fever rose in the United States, Theodore Roosevelt and other Republican leaders called for a punitive peace to be dictated in Berlin. In a major speech in late September, Wilson insisted that there must be "no discrimination between those to whom we wish to be just and those to whom we do not wish to be just." Soon afterward the German government asked for peace on the basis of Wilson's program. An exchange of notes followed, in which Wilson implicitly pressed for a change of regime in Berlin. Thereafter, House in Europe secured the Allies' agreement to Wilson's program as the basis of the peace, subject to reservations on the freedom of the seas and reparations. But success abroad had been preceded by failure at home when, despite Wilson's plea for a Democratic Congress to support his leadership in the peacemaking, the Republicans won control of both houses in the midterm elections.

Peacemaking in Paris

By participating personally in the Paris peace conference, Wilson became the first president to leave North America while in office. Indeed, notwithstanding later "summit diplomacy," it remains a unique episode in the history of the presidency as he was out of the country for all but two weeks between December 3, 1918, and July 8, 1919. Both

Allied leaders meet at the Paris Peace Conference on May 27, 1919. Pictured (from left) are British prime minister David Lloyd George, Italian prime minister Vittorio Emanuele Orlando, French premier Georges Clemenceau, and U.S. president Woodrow Wilson. The Paris Peace Conference resulted in the Treaty of Versailles and the formation of the League of Nations. (National Archives)

House and Lansing advised against Wilson's decision to lead the U.S. delegation, and it has been subsequently criticized by historians, as has the failure to include any prominent Republican politician. These mistakes, it is argued, contributed to Wilson's failure to achieve either the kind of peace settlement he had called for or Senate approval of American membership in the League of Nations. Yet these criticisms, like those made of Wilson's performance in the negotiations, may underestimate the difficulties he faced, and also his awareness of them. On his journey across the Atlantic, he spoke openly to journalists of his hostility to what he saw as the selfish ambitions of the Allies and of his determination to fight against them. He also knew that he would face a battle in the Senate, and that such leading Republicans as Roosevelt (until his sudden death in January 1919) and Lodge were seeking to discredit him both at home and abroad. These circumstances reinforced Wilson's natural inclination toward solitary decision-making; the conference would involve making choices about his priorities that were too politically sensitive to be delegated. His overriding goal, as his negotiating partners soon realized, was the creation of a league of nations that embodied the promise of permanent peace, thereby justifying America's sacrifices in the war.

Wilson was greeted by enormous and enthusiastic crowds in France, Britain, and Italy, and this reception strengthened his position (as Lansing, for one, came to recognize). It seemed to confirm the belief that Wilson shared with House and many progressive commentators that the ordinary people of Europe were behind him rather than their own governments. It helped him to make the establishment of a league of nations integral to the peace treaty an early item of business, and he chaired the commission which drew up the Covenant. This included, as Article 10, the mutual guarantee of political independence and territorial integrity that Wilson saw as "the king pin" of the new system of international security. Soon after he had presented this document to the full conference, Wilson returned briefly to the United States to deal with legislation before the Congress adjourned. While he was there, enough senators to block approval of a treaty signed Lodge's Round Robin declaring that the League was unacceptable in its present form. This weakened Wilson's position on his return to Paris, in part because he had to request amendments to the Covenant to meet some of the objections. In drawing up the peace treaty with Germany, he made concessions to French and British demands (particularly over reparations) that led to bitter criticism from many of those who had looked to him to produce a magnanimous peace. He regained some credit with liberals when he issued a public statement opposing Italian claims for the Dalmatian coast and Fiume. The angry reaction this provoked in Italy may have contributed to Wilson's allowing Japan to take over Germany's former concessions in the Chinese province of Shantung, even though he was well aware that this would be very unpopular in America; the League of Nations would hardly be credible if neither Italy nor Japan joined.

Wilson's actions in Paris have often been criticized by historians, as they were by contemporary observers such as John Maynard Keynes and William C. Bullitt. Yet interpretations that lay great stress on his personal weaknesses as a negotiator or his possible health problems tend to overlook the limits of his options. The Italian case showed that public opinion in the Allied countries would not in fact back him against their own governments' claims and demands. He knew that Congress would not approve significant reconstruction loans, or even the reduction of the war debts, and so he could not offer the Allies such inducements. To withdraw from the conference would be to achieve none of his objectives, and even to threaten to do so risked further diminishing European confidence in the solidity of an American security guarantee. Moreover, when he did implicitly make such a threat, by summoning his ship, he was warned that this created a poor impression at home. In negotiations in which his bargaining position was so constrained, Wilson's priorities were to maintain the credibility of the League of Nations and to present the Senate with a treaty that it would be difficult to oppose. In response to the protests of one of his liberal admirers, he pointed out that the German treaty had been well received in America, where most apparently favored a "hard" rather than "soft" peace with the defeated enemy.

Defeat at Home

When Wilson presented the treaty to the Senate, a sole Republican joined in the applause. Although American membership of the League of Nations had been endorsed by most newspaper editors and had the support of many Republicans, including ex-President Taft, Lodge had united his colleagues behind a demand for "reservations" that excluded Article 10 and generally asserted America's continued freedom of action. During July and August 1919, Wilson held private meetings with individual senators and an open session with the whole Foreign Relations Committee in an unsuccessful effort to secure the necessary two-thirds majority for approval of the treaty without reservations. In September, he embarked on a nationwide speaking tour to develop public support for the treaty and the League. This had no significant effect on the Senate, but the 10,000-mile journey involving over thirty major speeches did prove too much for the President's fragile health. The trip was aborted after he collapsed in Pueblo, Colorado; he suffered a major stroke on October 2 shortly after his return to Washington. The severity of Wilson's disablement was, however, concealed by his close circle, and he continued in office as consideration of the treaty moved to the Senate floor.

Although proposed amendments to the treaty were defeated, the Republican majority endorsed Lodge's set of reservations, which included one declaring that the United States assumed "no obligation" under Article 10 to employ force unless Congress so decided "in any particular case." Declaring this "a nullification of the Treaty," Wilson from his sickbed told Senate Democrats that the reservations were unacceptable. Consequently, in votes in November 1919, the treaty failed to secure even a simple majority, either with or without the reservations. Wilson evidently now hoped to make the issue a winning one for the Democrats in the 1920 elections, but pressure for compromise built up within the party as well as from other supporters of the League at home and abroad. In a further vote in March 1920, about half the Senate Democrats accepted the Lodge reservations, but enough remained loyal to Wilson to block ratification.

Wilson's intransigence was thus responsible for keeping the United States out of the League of Nations that he had done so much to create. This has led scholars to favor psychological or medical explanations for his apparently irrational behavior. The stroke certainly affected the president's mental equilibrium, and there is evidence that he had been suffering symptoms of cardiovascular disease since the spring. His disablement also isolated Wilson and encouraged him to retain an unreal belief in the extent of popular enthusiasm for the League. Yet it may be doubted whether even a healthy Wilson would have accepted the Lodge reservation to Article 10, which undermined the credibility of the new system of collective security that he saw the League of Nations as embodying. (In declaring that Congress had "the sole power" to "authorize the employment of the military or naval forces of the United States," the reservation also restricted the president's prerogatives as commander-in-chief.)

In the last eighteen months of his period of office, Wilson remained incapable of conducting much business, and several of his actions seemed to reflect the effects of his stroke. He became yet more intransigent over the Fiume dispute. In February 1920, he forced Lansing's resignation because the latter had been calling cabinet meetings on his own authority. (Lansing's private reservations about the treaty had earlier been damagingly publicized by Bullitt.) In August 1920, Lansing's successor, Bainbridge Colby issued a note setting out at length the reasons why the United States could not recognize the Soviet government in Russia—the last significant foreign policy action of the Wilson administration. The election of 1920 demonstrated how far the League as well as Wilson himself had lost popular support. The Democratic nominees, James M. Cox and Franklin D. Roosevelt, found it prudent to qualify their initial commitment to the League as the campaign progressed, and were nonetheless buried in one of the largest landslides in American electoral history. Retiring to a house on S Street in Washington, D.C., Wilson died in February 1924.

Legacy

No other president's legacy has been as often invoked or as much argued over as Wilson's. This is not only because he was the president who led America's first major intervention in world politics but also because of the way that he justified that intervention, and the principles and program that he enunciated.

For the first twenty years after his death, Wilson was central in the long debate over whether the United States should assume responsibilities beyond the western hemisphere. In the 1920s and 1930s, as the nation followed an increasingly isolationist course, it was only a dedicated minority who remained loyal to Wilson's memory and ideals. However, World War II saw his rehabilitation with a wider public as it seemed to vindicate his warnings during his 1919 speaking tour that the United States would be drawn into another and more terrible war if it did not join the League of Nations. A lavish film biography, *Wilson,* was produced by Hollywood in 1944 to drive this lesson home. It was not, however, only isolationists who were critical of Wilson and his legacy. He was the main target of the "realist" writers of the 1940s and 1950s such as Walter Lippmann, Hans J. Morgenthau, and George F. Kennan, for what they saw as a moralistic and utopian approach to international relations, and a neglect of power factors and the necessity of basing policy on a strict sense of national interest.

Notwithstanding such criticism, Wilson's rhetoric and programs have been echoed by many later presidents. In part, this reflects the complex character of his legacy. Franklin Roosevelt's "Four Freedoms," Jimmy Carter's emphasis on human rights, and George H. W. Bush's invocation of a "new world order" have all been viewed as "Wilsonian." In seeking to promote democracy abroad, Ronald Reagan and George W. Bush have been described as Wilson's heirs, despite their administrations' skepticism about the United Nations. The policy of containment, the lodestar for U.S. administrations during the four decades of the Cold War, has been seen by some historians as the apotheosis of Wilsonianism, and by others as its antithesis. The former can cite the ideological and universal character of the commitment in the Truman Doctrine of 1947 and the assumption of American leadership. The latter point to the reliance on particular alliances, often with authoritarian regimes, to maintain the balance of power.

Protean though Wilsonianism is, the constant element is the appeal to values and principles that are seen as universally applicable. That the United States has a responsibility to uphold and embody such principles has been central to the republic's ideology from its foundation. But whereas the mission had traditionally been viewed as an exemplary one, Wilson transformed it into the justification for an active and extensive involvement in world politics. In so doing, he developed a rationale for overseas interventions and commitments that later experience suggests is an essential element if these are to enjoy the support of the American people.

John Thompson

Chronology

1913

February 9: General Victoriano Huerta overthrows Madero government in Mexico.

March 4: Wilson inaugurated as president.

May 2: Wilson recognizes republican government of Yüan Shi-K'ai in China.

1914

April 21: United States occupies and blockades Veracruz, Mexico.

June 15: Congress repeals Panama Canal toll exemptions.

July 15: Huerta flees Mexico; Constitutionalist government in Mexico City.

August 2–4: World War I begins in Europe.

August 6: Ellen Wilson dies.

August 18: Wilson's appeal to Americans to be neutral "in thought as well as in action."

December 8: Annual message STET rejects calls for military and naval "preparedness."

December 28: U.S. note of protest to Britain over blockade practices.

1915

February 4: German declaration of war zone around British Isles in which submarine warfare will be conducted.

February 10: Strict Accountability Note to Germany.

March 28: Sinking of *Falaba*—one American (Leon C. Thrasher) killed.

May 7: Sinking of *Lusitania*—1,200 deaths, including 128 Americans.

May 13: First *Lusitania* note.

June 7: W. J. Bryan resigns as secretary of state rather than sign second *Lusitania* note—succeeded by Robert Lansing.

July 21: Third *Lusitania* note: Wilson asks secretaries of war and the Navy to draw up programs for "adequate national defense."

July 28: U.S. military intervention in Haiti.

August 19: Sinking of *Arabic*—forty-eight deaths, including two Americans.

August 29: Wilson agrees to allow Britain and France to raise loan on U.S. market.

September 8: *Arabic* pledge—Germany promises no more liners will be sunk.

October 6: De facto recognition of Carranza government in Mexico.

November 4: Wilson publicly calls for preparedness.

December 18: Wilson's marriage to Edith Bolling Galt.

1916

February 22: House-Grey memorandum signed.

February 24: Wilson letter to Senator Stone calling for defeat of congressional resolutions warning Americans not to travel on armed belligerent ships.

March 9: Pancho Villa raid on Columbus, New Mexico.

March 15: Punitive military expedition under Pershing enters Mexico.

March 24: Sinking of *Sussex*—about eighty killed or injured, four Americans injured.

May 4: *Sussex* pledge—conditional German undertaking to follow rules of cruiser warfare against merchant ships.

May 15: Military intervention in Dominican Republic.

May 27: Addressing the League to Enforce Peace, Wilson declares U.S. willingness to join a postwar league of nations.

August 29: Navy Act, authorizing large building program, signed.

September 8: Revenue Act including provision for retaliatory action against nations infringing U.S. neutral rights.

November 7: Wilson reelected as president.

November 27: Wilson strengthens Federal Reserve Board warning against purchase of foreign Treasury bills.

November 29: U.S. occupies Santo Domingo.

December 18: Wilson sends note asking European belligerents to state peace terms.

1917

January 22: In address to Senate, Wilson calls for "a peace without victory."

January 31: German announcement of unrestricted submarine warfare.

February 3: Breaking of diplomatic relations with Germany.

February 26: Wilson requests congressional authority to arm merchant ships.

February 28: Zimmermann Telegram.

March 15: Abdication of Tsar in first Russian Revolution.

March 18: News reaches Washington of sinking of three American ships by German submarines.

April 2: Wilson's War Address to Congress.

April 6: U.S. declaration of war on Germany.

May 18: Selective Service Act signed.

August 27: Wilson's reply to Pope Benedict XV's call for peace.

November 5: Bolshevik Revolution in Russia.

1918

January 8: Wilson's Fourteen Points Address to Congress.

March 3: Treaty of Brest-Litovsk taking Russia out of the war.

March 21: Launching of German offensive on western front.

April 6: Wilson's speech calling for "Force without stint or limit."

July 17: U.S. forces sent to North Russia.

August 3: U.S. forces sent to Vladivostok, Siberia.

September 27: Wilson speech in New York insisting that League of Nations must be incorporated in peace treaty.

October 6: German note to Wilson asking for peace on basis of Fourteen Points.

November 5: In congressional elections, Republicans win control of both houses.

November 11: Signing of Armistice ending World War I.

December 4: Wilson sails from New York for Europe.

1919

January 18: Paris Peace Conference convenes.

February 14: Wilson presents draft of League of Nations Covenant to Conference.

February 14: Wilson sails for the United States.

March 3: Lodge's Round Robin signed by more than one-third of Senate.

March 13: Wilson returns to France.

May 7: Draft peace treaty presented to Germans.

June 28: Treaty of Versailles signed.

July 8: Wilson arrives back in the United States.

July 10: Wilson's speech to Senate presenting Versailles Treaty.

August 19: Wilson's meeting with Senate Foreign Relations Committee.

September 2–28: Wilson's speaking trip in support of treaty; cut short after collapse following speech in Pueblo, Colorado.

October 2: Wilson suffers paralytic stroke.

November 6: Lodge's Fourteen Reservations proposed.

November 19: In Senate votes, Treaty of Versailles defeated both with and without Lodge reservations.

1920

January 8: Wilson calls for 1920 election to be "a great and solemn referendum" on membership the League of Nations.

February 13: Lansing resigns as secretary of state; Bainbridge Colby appointed.

March 19: Treaty including Lodge Reservations fails to obtain necessary two-thirds majority in the Senate after Wilson had asked his followers to vote against it.

August 10: Colby note declaring policy of nonrecognition of Soviet government.

November 2: Republican Warren G. Harding elected president in a landslide.

1921

March 4: Harding inauguration; Wilson leaves White House.

References and Further Reading

Ambrosius, Lloyd E. *Wilsonian Statecraft: Theory and Practice of Liberal Internationalism during World War I.* Wilmington, DE: Scholarly Resources Books, 1991.

Cooper, John Milton, Jr. *Breaking the Heart of the World: Woodrow Wilson and the Fight for the League of Nations.* Cambridge: Cambridge University Press, 2001.

Heckscher, August. *Woodrow Wilson.* New York: Scribner, 1991.

Knock, Thomas J. *To End All Wars: Woodrow Wilson and the Quest for a New World Order.* New York: Princeton University Press, 1995.

Link, Arthur S. *Woodrow Wilson: Revolution, War, and Peace.* Arlington Heights, IL: H. Davidson, 1979.

Link, Arthur S. *Wilson: The Struggle for Neutrality 1914–1915.* Princeton, NJ: Princeton University Press, 1960.

Link, Arthur S. *Wilson: Confusions and Crises 1915–1916.* Princeton, NJ: Princeton University Press, 1964.

Link, Arthur S. *Wilson: Campaigns for Progressivism and Peace 1916–1917.* Princeton, NJ: Princeton University Press, 1965.

Thompson, John A. *Woodrow Wilson: A Profile in Power.* New York: Longman, 2002.

Warren Gamaliel Harding (1921–1923)

Early Life and Political Career

Warren Gamaliel Harding was born on November 2, 1865, in Blooming Grove (at the time, Corsica) Ohio, the oldest of the eight children of George Harding and Phoebe Elizabeth Harding, a former farmer and horse trader who had become physician. In 1879, Warren attended Ohio Central College where he joined the college band, edited the school yearbook, and enjoyed debating. Upon graduation, Harding moved to Marion, briefly taught school, studied law, and administered the finances of the Citizens' Cornet Band. In 1884, he bought *The Marion Star*, a failing local newspaper, where Harding met and eventually married the divorcee Florence Kling De Wolfe, the daughter of a Marion banking and real estate family, whose wealth and influence became a factor in forging both the commercial success of *The Star* and Harding's political career.

At this point, Harding was in most respects a promising candidate: an active citizen in local church, civic and business affairs, and the owner-editor of a print medium through which he could exert influence on any number of public issues. Moreover, he had a personal amiability and charm that was an asset in the divided and often raucous Ohio Republican Party. Harding was an energetic campaigner and a talented, if often voluble, public speaker. He attracted the attention of Harry Daugherty, a lobbyist and party manager who, on their first encounter, reportedly thought that Harding would make a fine president. With Daugherty's help Harding won the state lieutenant governorship in 1904 but failed in two successive attempts to win the governorship. He might well have abandoned politics entirely in the wake of these defeats had Dougherty and Mrs. Harding not intervened.

The Seventeenth Amendment, providing for the election rather than the appointment of the U.S. Senate, had come into effect in 1913. Daugherty approached Harding about running for a seat in the spring of 1914, when Senator Theodore E. Burton announced that he would not seek the Republican nomination. Harding's father-in-law Amos Kling had not supported Harding's political advancement, but after her father's death in 1913 Florence encouraged her husband to seek the Senate seat. Harding ran against former Senator Joseph B. Foraker and businessman Ralph Cole. He disliked the system of direct primaries, because he thought that pitting Republicans against each other damaged party solidarity, and his campaign was calculated to attack only

Warren Gamaliel Harding, opposed to Wilson's League of Nations, returned the country to isolationism. (Library of Congress)

Democrats, particularly President Woodrow Wilson. Harding won the primary, was endorsed by former President William Howard Taft, and was handily elected as the junior senator for the state of Ohio.

The power of the institution had diminished during the strong presidencies of Theodore Roosevelt and Woodrow Wilson. Senators were expected to keep a low profile and fulfill only the insignificant tasks they were assigned. Moreover, the Democrats had a fifty-six to forty majority in the chamber. It is revealing, therefore, that Harding found the Senate "a very pleasant place" yet was present for only 46 percent of the roll call votes. In 1915, he began an affair with Nan Britton, a twenty-year-old girl from Marion who later accused him of having fathered her daughter in one of the more damaging incidents of what became a scandal-ridden career. Still, Harding's Senate star rose. After six months in office he had his first opportunity for national notice when he asked to be the keynote speaker at the Republican Presidential Convention of 1916.

By virtue of his undeviating partisan loyalty, Harding had the respect of both the progressive and conservative Republican factions. With his strong speaking voice and his willingness to let the party bosses set policy, he was a benefit to many and a threat to very few. The Republicans opposed President Wilson on the issue of removing protective tariffs because they believed it would result in an increase in direct taxation. As war broke out in Europe they were in tune with the president's declarations on American neutrality, because they rightly thought that the United States had inadequate means of defense. As the administration's position on the war gravitated toward support for the Entente powers, Republicans opposed the foreign entanglement implied by Wilson's proposal to establish a League of Nations to secure the postwar peace. In the 1919 elections, the Republicans gained control of the Senate, and Harding secured a position on the Foreign Relations Committee from which he could champion the party position. He was chosen to respond to Wilson's Columbus, Ohio, speech on the League at an informal conference at the White House.

The Voice of Isolationism

President Wilson's stroke strengthened the probability of a Republican succession to his presidency. The country's economy suffered from a postwar flu of inflation and then slid quickly toward recession. The Senate was divided over the League and few Americans supported an assertive diplomacy after the country's first involvement in a major European war. General Leonard Wood of Illinois, Governor Frank O. Lowden of Illinois, and Californian Senator Hiram Johnson were all seeking the nomination. Ohio wanted Harding to seek the Republican candidacy, but state law prevented anyone from simultaneously running for two offices. Daugherty arranged a two-part resolution by the Republican State Central and Advisory Committees that enabled Harding to seek both the Senate and the White House. He was entitled to renomination for the Senate without opposition and was not required to file for reelection until June 12, 1920, at which time balloting for the presidential nomination was likely to be finished. Harding announced that he was running for president on December 17, 1919, with Daugherty as his campaign manager. He campaigned for nomination as a compromise candidate for the Senate on the assumption that the two front-runners would deadlock; he charted a similar strategy for the presidential primary—carefully mediating between Republican factions in order to widen his base of support.

There were nine candidates for the GOP nomination at the Chicago Convention in 1920, but the leading contenders were General Leonard Wood, a former Rough Rider and friend of Theodore Roosevelt; Illinois Governor Frank Lowden; and progressive candidate Senator Hiram Johnson of California.

Harding needed the support of the Ohio delegation but he was challenged by Wood for the state's forty-eight convention delegates. Ohio was a critical state in presidential elections, having produced seven presidents and four vice presidents. Wood represented Roosevelt progressivism and Harding championed isolationist Americanism. On April 27, 1920, Harding narrowly won the Ohio primary but did not win any Indiana delegates. Mrs. Harding prevented her husband from withdrawing from the race, while Daugherty asked the delegates to make Harding either their second or third choice in the event of a deadlock. Harding received enough support to guarantee him the position as the default nominee; among the candidates he had the smallest number of dedicated enemies. Harding's reputation as an emollient and mediator in the Senate had paid the ultimate dividend. So weakened were the Democrats of 1920 by the confusion about how to replace their faltering leader that the Republican nomination struggle was possibly more important than the presidential ballot itself.

Harding was perfectly in tune with his times. Whereas party heavyweights struck a popular chord with the formulation that "we ask only to live our life in our own way, in friendship and sympathy with all, in alliance with none," Harding offered a plush weave of isolationism and complacency. "America's greatest present need," he intoned before his nomination "is not heroics, but healing; not nostrums, but normalcy; not revolution, but restoration; not agitation but adjustment; not surgery, but serenity; not the dramatic, but the dispassionate; not experiment, but equipoise; not submergence in internationality, but sustainment in triumphant nationality." If, as William Gibbs McAdoo claimed, Harding's speeches were "an army of pompous phrases moving across the landscape in search of an idea," in 1920 they were what the nation wanted to hear. Harding ran his presidential campaign from the front porch of his house in Marion. The Democratic nominee, James Cox, and his running mate, Franklin Delano Roosevelt, began their traveling campaign with a meeting at the White House with President Wilson to no avail. Harding won the largest landslide in Republican history with 60 percent of the popular vote and 36 to 11 states in the Electoral College; Republican seats in the Senate jumped to 59 against 37 Democrats.

Strong Cabinet, Ambivalent Policy

"Well, Warren Harding," the new First Lady is reported to have asked, "I have got you the Presidency; what are you going to do with it?" The best evidence is that Harding was not altogether sure. Inaugurated on March 4, 1921, he had been elected largely on his slogan that promised a return to "normalcy." He fulfilled the expectation of the Republican platform by refusing to join the League of Nations, but he conceded that the United States was militarily available to defend other countries if necessary. Even this degree of foreign involvement did not sit well with the American people who had strong isolationist feelings following the war.

Harding, in fact, appreciated that the United States could not return to the comfortable habits of the pre-1914 era. Although he rejected much of Wilson's prescription for peace, he mostly agreed with his diagnosis of the ills of the old international order that had brought war. Additionally, he believed that American principles backed by economic power had a critical role to play in reconstituting European affairs. Aware of his own limitations, he appointed two of the best minds in American public life to guide his foreign policy. Secretary of State Charles Evan Hughes, a former governor of New York and Republican presidential nominee in 1916, maintained that the United States should establish a Pax Americana based on mutual respect, reason, and, more substantively, arms limitations. Secretary of Commerce Herbert Hoover shared Hughes's outlook and brought to the administration a rare combination of intellect and organizational acumen acquired in amassing a personal fortune in international business and in serving both with the Wilson administration during the war and at the Versailles peace negotiations. To the Treasury Harding appointed Andrew Mellon, in the president's own words "the ubiquitous financier of the universe," who under Harding successors Coolidge and Hoover became one of the greatest Treasury secretaries.

Money was at the core of Harding's diplomacy. Although critics charged that Wall Street was running the country, Hughes and Hoover attempted the reverse by informing American bankers that money should not go to the Soviet Union and also by using the war debts of European governments to leverage cooperation from them. There was enormous leverage available. Whereas at the start of the war the United States was indebted to other countries for a total of $3.7 billion, at war's end other countries owed the United States a total of $12.5 billion. Mellon asked Congress for the authority to negotiate separate debt payments with each country, the result of which was the creation of the World War Debt Commission with Mellon as its chairman. The commission's first major agreement was concluded with Britain in June 1923, and became the template for agreements with other war allies. In August 1921 Russia agreed to permit the American Relief Administration (ARA), under Hoover's control, to provide food for its starving population; when Hoover's critics charged the administration with aiding Bolshevism, the secretary of commerce responded that when 20 million people were starving, "whatever their politics, they shall be fed." To the humiliation of Soviet authorities, the ARA insisted on the authority to distribute food and medicine to those most in need, and by December

1921, some $66 million in assistance had been donated by the world's greatest capitalist power to the first victims of the Soviet experiment.

This was not isolationism in the pure sense of the word. Hughes and Hoover were rightly committed to the vitality of the international economy as the strongest foundation for international peace. Hoover in particular was troubled by the specter of economic misery and revolution as a threat to individual liberty abroad. The attempt to influence events from afar, rather, was the politically sustainable alternative to the discarded ideas of collective security and institutionalized engagement of the late President Wilson. At the time, Hoover was one of a very few who guessed at the enormity of the dangers a foreign policy of half-measures might have to face.

Naval Power and National Security

Harding was acutely aware at least of the financial cost of global military competition. This awareness, enhanced by Hoover's concern for the burden of defense spending on fiscal resources and Hughes preoccupation with the emergence of Japanese power in Asia and the Pacific, was the source of the administration's greatest diplomatic initiative: the Washington Naval Conference of 1921–1922. Harding and Hughes agreed that the United States should open the conference with the drama of calling for radical reductions in arms. The state of war with Germany, Austria, and Hungary was officially ended, and Armistice Day ceremonies took place at Arlington, VA, on November 11, 1921. Harding used the occasion to deliver a speech on the horrors of modern war as "cruel, deliberate, scientific destruction" with dignitaries from Japan, China, Italy, France, Great Britain, Belgium, Netherlands, and Portugal in attendance. The following morning he opened the conference's first plenary session by drawing the delegates' attention to "a world staggering with debt" from the conflict only recently concluded and called them "with high faith" to the business of the conference. Thereafter, the conference was in the able hands of Secretary Hughes.

The United States aimed specifically at reducing the size of the British and Japanese navies. Representing a Pacific power with an abiding interest in the future of China, Hughes was apprehensive at Japan's growing regional preeminence, marked by a spectacular naval victory over Russia at Tsushima in 1905 and now enhanced by the fact that both Russia and China were in throes of revolutionary upheaval. In January 1921, the U.S. Navy's Orange War Plan cited Japan as the most probable adversary in a future war and stressed the need for a U.S. Navy "second to none," capable of offensive action in the western Pacific and home waters of Japan. The situation was complicated by the Anglo-Japanese Treaty of 1902. Although Britain had signed the treaty in part to enlist Japanese strength in containing Russia, its terms stipulated that the signatories would come to each other's aid in the event of war with a third power—meaning that, in principle, the United States could find itself at war against the combined fleets of Britain and Japan. Beyond an international commitment to limit naval construction, Hughes was therefore determined that the 1902 treaty be broken.

He accomplished both objectives. The boldness of his disarmament proposals set the conference on course for a major agreement when Hughes offered to scrap 30 major warships, built or under construction, totaling 846,000 tons of displacement. He then told the stunned British and Japanese delegations that they should reduce their own fleets by 583,000 and 450,000 tons of capital ships respectively. Ultimately, the conference agreed that the American and British fleets would henceforth limit themselves to 500,000 tons each. Japan accepted 300,000 tons, while France and Italy were limited to 175,000 tons each. Altogether the United States, Britain, and Japan were to scrap or cancel construction of 78 capital ships totaling 1,878,043 tons. Hughes proposed further a 10-year "holiday" on capital ship construction; thereafter any vessel in service for a minimum of 20 years could be replaced but no new ship could exceed 35,000 tons displacement. The conference ended on February 6, 1922, with the conclusion of six treaties: the Five-Power Naval Limitation Treaty that ended the Anglo-Japanese treaty of 1902; a Five-Power Treaty on Submarine and Gas Warfare; a Four-Power Treaty on Pacific Ocean Possessions; a Nine-Power Treaty to Protect the "Open Door" to China; a Sino-Japanese Treaty on Shantung; and a Six-Power Treaty on Cable Rights in Former German Islands.

The Nine-Power Treaty rendered the Lansing-Ishii Agreement between the United States and Japan dating to 1917 redundant. In January 1923, the two countries agreed on its abrogation.

The Senate consented to each of the Washington treaties that involved the country directly, but it placed a restriction on the Four-Power Treaty. This stipulated that the United States had made no commitment to alliances or similar arrangements for common defense and required further that the president would need congressional approval to respond to any act of aggression in East Asia. On February 11, 1922, the administration signed an additional treaty with Japan dealing specifically with Yap, a former German possession occupied by Japan but located on sea-cable routes linking Hawaii with the Philippines. Henceforth, American citizens were to enjoy equal cable, radio, and residential rights with the Japanese on Yap, in return for which Washington recognized Japan's mandate to control over all former German islands in the Pacific north of the equator.

Japan demonstrated good faith by returning Kiaochow to China under the terms of the Shantung Treaty. Hughes

succeeded in holding Japan to its word with American economic power. Due to a postwar crisis in its economy, Japan was hard pressed to generate capital for its military and economic designs in Korea and Manchuria. Capital was made available by New York banks in return for Japan's adherence to Open Door principles in China. The American military protested that the Washington treaties recognized Japanese superiority in Asia and were troubled further by the American concession not to fortify U.S. bases in the Philippines, Guam, and Alaska. But Harding and Hughes were satisfied that enormous sums of money had been saved by the Washington naval reductions and limitations; that Britain had been reduced as a Pacific power although the United States and Japan had reached an understanding on the profitable development of China; that Japan's options were limited by its dependence on the New York money market; and that the United States had surrendered very little of its future freedom of action in return.

Beggaring the Future

The postwar economy was meanwhile in the grip of deflation, tight credit, and domestic firms carrying heavy inventories due in part to drop in foreign trade.

European currencies were fluctuating against the dollar, making it difficult for American manufacturers to predict demand. Europe's weak currencies made European goods so inexpensive in the United States that pressure mounted for tariff protection for domestic producers. The recovery of the European economies was nonetheless critical, Hughes observed, because "the prosperity of the United States largely depends upon economic settlements which may be made in Europe." This was especially true in the case of Germany, for two reasons. First, the size and centrality of the German economy meant that there could be no European recovery without a German recovery. Second, the German government had been presented at the Paris Peace Conference with a staggering $33 billion reparations bill that the French government in particular hoped would so weaken Germany that France would be safe from attack for generations. The reparations burden suffocated the German economy and worsened the prospects of national and continental recovery.

It also had wider implications. In April 1922, Germany signed the Treaty of Rapallo with the Soviet Union that ended at a stroke all Soviet claims for reparations in exchange for property seized during the war. Moscow also secretly permitted Germany to train soldiers with heavy weapons on Russian territory in violation of Versailles restrictions on German rearmament. France saw the treaty as accommodating the revival of German militarism. Both France and Britain relied on German reparations payments to pay off their own war debts to the United States. Thus, whenever Washington proposed a reduction of the German reparation bill to facilitate the economic recovery and political stabilization of the Weimar Republic, London and Paris demanded that the United States reduce their war debts too. Rather than forgive Allied war debts, the administration preferred to encourage American banks to make large loans to the German government with which it could restore its economy while paying down its reparations bill. In other words, American banks loaned money to Germany that was returned to the United States in the form of British and French war debt payments.

Congress undermined European recovery further with the passage in September 1922 of the Fordney-McCumber Tariff Act. The legislation reversed the prewar trend of tariff reduction undertaken by the Underwood Tariff of 1913 and raised rates 25 percent beyond those of the Payne-Aldrich Tariff of 1908. European governments could not pay their debts if they could not sell goods in the American market. Congressional protectionism thus worked like a cancer on the free market Harding, Hughes, and Hoover counted on to nurture a global economy. Late in 1922, Benito Mussolini became prime minister of Italy, a position from which he consolidated a dictatorship by 1926. Amid the economic and political chaos in Germany, Adolf Hitler's Nazi Party made its first tentative forays into electoral politics, while nationalist thugs assassinated moderate politicians like Matthias Erzberger and Walter Rathenau who attempted to honor the country's reparation commitments. When Germany finally defaulted on the payments in the form of coal deliveries in late 1922, France and Belgium sent troops into the Ruhr Valley in January 1923 to take over its mines and extract the reparations directly. Both Britain and the United States protested the French action, but the Harding administration went further by withdrawing the last American troops from the Rhineland in a demonstration of disapproval as well as by demanding that France pay its outstanding debt to the United States. When the French franc collapsed, Paris was at Washington's mercy.

The episode had two important aspects. Britain and the United States were reacting to French heavy-handedness in dealing with a young German democracy struggling to finds its feet. For its part, the French government felt compelled to take a tough line with Germany in part because its former allies withheld their support and seemed to want to dissociate themselves with the Versailles settlement. The withdrawal of the American troops from Germany severed the last security link between the United States and Europe dating to the war. While the condemnation of France was a first small measure of appeasement, the troop withdrawal inaugurated the isolationism that determined American policy toward Europe until the early 1940s.

On December 26, 1922, the Allied powers had jointly declared that Germany had defaulted on its payments and pondered military action. Because Secretary Hughes had hoped to prevent such a move, he proposed prior to the French Ruhr occupation that a group of American bankers

and businessmen study Germany's reparation problems for the purpose of formulating a realistic plan of payment. He designated Charles G. Dawes and Owen D. Young as unofficial delegates. The report they ultimately produced was the basis of the Dawes Plan of 1924 for rescheduling Germany's debt, stabilizing its currency, and securing French withdrawal. Although Hughes rejected the argument that German reparations and European debts were inextricably linked, he recognized that there could be no durable peace in Europe without a solution for the reparation-debt problem. The cancellation of all war debt and reparations might have been the most effective stimulation for European recovery, but the administration would have faced a domestic political backlash to any such move. In reality, the United States reduced significantly the outstanding obligations of thirteen European countries, but Hoover was never wholly candid with the American public about the concession he judged critical to any comprehensive settlement. In time the Dawes Plan would do a good deal to alleviate the problem, but President Harding would not be around to take any credit.

Legacy

Harding died suddenly, apparently of an embolism, in San Francisco on a return trip from Alaska. Thereafter his presidency was damaged by the Teapot Dome affair, the most serious high-level scandal of American government until the Watergate hearings on misdeeds of the Nixon administration. The Teapot Dome was the name of an underground geological dome in Salt Creek, Wyoming, containing oil. In 1912 the Taft administration had made the oil field a federal oil reserve, and in the final month of the Wilson presidency in 1920, Congress had directed the U.S. Navy to administer the reserve for the benefit of national security. Harding's modest contribution to the affair came shortly after his inauguration when, on the advice of Navy Secretary Edwin Denby and Interior Secretary Albert Fall, he issued an executive order transferring authority over the Teapot Dome from the Navy to the Department of Interior. Prior to the Washington Naval Conference, the Navy had an interest in the oil reserves for its Pacific fleet—above all because its battleships would soon be using oil for fuel rather than coal. The transfer entered the realm of scandal when conservationists pressured Congress to investigate the administration of the reserve and Senate hearings revealed that Fall had leased the Teapot Dome to private oil developers without competitive bidding. It came to light that the leases were a reward for "loans" made to Fall, and the Senate's investigation led to criminal proceedings against the oil developers and to the conviction of Fall for accepting bribes.

The fact that Harding himself had done nothing wrong became irrelevant when Harry Daugherty, his political manager from Ohio now heading the Justice Department, was eased from his post by President Coolidge and was himself subsequently indicted but acquitted. Harding's reputation was so soiled along with that of the lesser and eminently corruptible members of his cabinet that the trashing of his political and personal life became something of a cottage industry for journalists and historians for many years afterward.

None of this has any relevance to his foreign policy, the legacy of which is as significant for what it did not attempt as much as for what it did. With the nation's approval, Harding drew back from the bold course struck by his visionary predecessor; in style and substance his administration set the prevailing tone of American diplomacy for the next decade.

Laura Cameron

Chronology

1921

January 7: U.S. Navy's Orange War Plan approved.

April 27: Allied Reparations Committee demands $33B from Germany.

June 7: Romania and Yugoslavia form Little Entente.

November 12: Washington Naval Conference convenes.

1922

February 6: Washington Naval Conference ends.

February 11: United States and Japan settle Yap Island dispute.

February 22: Britain terminates protectorate of Egypt.

March 3: Fascist coup topples Fiume government in Italy.

April 10: Genoa Conference convenes.

April 16: Germany and Russia sign Treaty of Rapallo.

September 21: Congress passes Fordney-McCumber Tariff.

October 27: Fascist March on Rome.

October 31: Benito Mussolini forms a cabinet of Fascists and Nationalists in Italy.

December 6: Irish Free State proclaimed.

December 30: Union of Soviet Socialist Republics (USSR) established.

1923

January 11: French and Belgian troops occupy the Ruhr.

June 19: Britain accepts plan to repay U.S. loans.

July 14: Treaty of Lausanne establishes Allied peace with Turkey.

August 2: President Harding dies, Calvin Coolidge sworn in as president.

September 27: Britain thwarts Italian invasion of Corfu.

October 29: Turkey becomes a republic.

References and Further Reading

Dean, John. *Warren G. Harding.* New York: Henry Holt, 2004.

Feis, Herbert. *The Diplomacy of the Dollar, 1919–1923.* Hamden, CT: Archon Books, 1965.

Iriye, Akira. *After Imperialism: The Search for a New Order in the Far East, 1921–1931.* Chicago: Imprint Publications, 1990.

Leffler, Melvyn. *The Elusive Quest: America's Pursuit of European Stability and French Security, 1919–1933.* Chapel Hill, NC: University of North Carolina Press, 1979.

Russell, Francis. *The Shadow of Blooming Grove: Warren G. Harding in His Times.* New York: McGraw Hill, 1968.

Calvin Coolidge (1923–1929)

Early Life and Political Career

Calvin Coolidge was born on July 4, 1872, in the small Vermont town of Plymouth Notch, the only son of John and Victoria Coolidge. Coolidge grew up in the modest luxury afforded by his father's thriving shopkeeping business and attended the one-room school near where he lived. Coolidge received an early and firsthand political education from his father, who was not merely a prosperous shopkeeper but also an active politician who had served three terms in the state house and one in the state senate. The young Coolidge imbibed his father's love of politics and a strong New England sense of civic responsibility. By 1886 he had learned all that the Notch school could offer him and transferred to the Black River Academy in Ludlow to complete his high school education.

Coolidge graduated from Black River Academy in the spring of 1890 and took the train to Massachusetts to sit for the entrance examination for Amherst College. He contracted a bad cold, however, and did not complete the examination. In 1891, Coolidge returned to Black River Academy for postgraduate study, and in the spring term he attended St. Johnsbury Academy where he received his college entrance certificate to Amherst.

Coolidge was a studious if nondescript student at Amherst. He began to blossom in his junior and senior years as he focused his studies on history and philosophy and came under the influence of two scholars of national renown: historian Anton Morse and philosopher Charles Garman. During these years, Coolidge also became adept at public speaking and achieved a degree of social prominence on campus. He was elected the Grove Orator for his commencement class, and he gave his address with considerable aplomb. Coolidge and the other seventy-five members of the Amherst class of 1895 received their bachelor's diplomas on June 26. He then informed his father of his decision to read law in a law office in Northampton, a small city near Amherst.

Coolidge began his apprenticeship as a law clerk in the offices of John C. Hammond and Henry P. Field, both alumni of Amherst. Coolidge's addition to the law firm proved beneficial for all concerned. Coolidge was thereby apprenticed to men of substance in the community. In 1896, Coolidge handed out ballots for Field in his run for mayor of Northampton. Field won the election and Hammond was chosen as district attorney. Coolidge made his mark in

Calvin Coolidge was a passive administrator of American foreign policy. (Library of Congress)

Republican circles in Northampton with his point-by-point defense of the gold standard in response to an article by the former Democratic mayor of Northampton in the *Daily Hampshire Gazette* advocating William Jennings Bryan's doctrine of free silver. In 1897, shortly after graduating from his legal apprenticeship, Coolidge was recruited to the lower ranks of the Northampton Republican hierarchy with his selection to represent Ward Two in the Republican city committee, which was responsible for choosing the party's nominees for municipal offices. In 1898, he won his first election to public office as city councilman from his ward.

The next year, Coolidge declined renomination and instead ran for city solicitor and won. It was a desirable office for a young lawyer and politician. The duties were not too onerous, and the position gave Coolidge greater experience as a lawyer plus additional exposure to the practical workings of government. In 1903, he was appointed to the coveted sinecure position of clerk of the courts for Hampshire County. In 1904, he advanced further in the party hierarchy, when he was selected as chairman of the Republican city committee. In 1905, Coolidge met his first and only loss as a candidate for public office when he was defeated for a seat on the school board. That same year, he married Grace Goodhue, a teacher at the Clarke School for the Deaf. Coolidge was not out of public office for long; in 1906, he ran for the state legislature and served two one-year terms.

In his first year in the Massachusetts legislature, Coolidge was appointed to two minor committees: mercantile affairs and constitutional amendments. His politics in the legislature, like that of the Republican majority, was tinged with progressivism. During his two terms he voted for a six-day workweek, limits on the working hours of women and children, female suffrage, direct elections for the U.S. Senate, pensions for firemen's families, and half fares for school children on street cars. Coolidge retired from the legislature in 1908 after two terms and returned to Northampton to shore up his law practice while developing his political base in Hampshire County. In 1909, he was the Republican nominee for mayor of Northampton and was elected by a slender margin of 187 votes. His administration expanded and improved the fire and police departments, raised teachers' salaries, improved sidewalks and streets, and still managed to lower the tax rate and cut the city's debt by half. After two terms as mayor Coolidge decided in 1911 to run for the state senate, timing his effort to coincide with Hampshire County's turn at the senate seat.

Coolidge served on the agriculture and railroads committees in the state senate where he forged alliances with other politicos from western Massachusetts, particularly Murray Crane and Frank W. Stearns. In 1913, Coolidge was elected president of the senate after the incumbent lost his bid for reelection, having antagonized the suffragettes with his opposition to women's suffrage. As senate president, Coolidge was the state's ranking Republican officeholder. Teddy Roosevelt's bid for the presidency in 1912 through the Bull Moose Party had split the Republican Party in Massachusetts and handed the Democrats control of both the governorship and the lieutenant governorship. In 1918, Coolidge ran for the governorship against Democratic candidate Richard Long, a wealthy amateur who financed his own campaign. The campaign was more difficult than Coolidge had anticipated, and former presidents Teddy Roosevelt and William Howard Taft were enlisted to help campaign for the Republican ticket. It was a close election with Coolidge beating Long by only 16,000 votes.

As governor, Coolidge was quick to pass measures for the benefit of soldiers returning from the war in Europe, one of which was to give veterans preference in public appointments.

He instituted a new budget system that had been arranged previously by constitutional amendment. In 1919, Coolidge vetoed the "Salary Grab Bill," which increased the remuneration of legislators by 50 percent. Both houses voted to override his veto and passed the bill, but Coolidge received credit from the public for attempting to stop the measure. In 1920, Coolidge vetoed a bill that permitted the sale of beer and wine in violation of the Eighteenth Amendment and warned the bill's supporters that "there can be no constitutional instruction to do an unconstitutional act." Coolidge's final major accomplishment as governor was the consolidation of the state's 118 government departments into just 18.

In 1920, Frank Stearns started a campaign to build up support for Coolidge for president. Coolidge had gained national prominence for his decisive handling of the Boston police strike, but he could not draw sufficient support for first place on the ticket. The GOP Senate clique secured the nomination of Warren G. Harding for president and wanted to name Senator Irvine Lenroot of Wisconsin for the vice presidency. Lenroot declined. When another senator, Hiram Johnson of California also declined, Wallace McCamant, the former member of the Oregon Supreme Court and a delegate from that state, nominated the governor of Massachusetts for the vice presidency to the approval of the delegates at the Chicago convention. On November 2, 1920, Warren Harding's birthday, Harding and Coolidge were elected in a landslide, receiving 16 million votes against the 9 million votes for the Democratic ticket of Governor James M. Cox of Ohio and Franklin D. Roosevelt. The Electoral College vote was even more lopsided, with Harding and Coolidge winning 37 states and 404 electoral votes.

Coolidge settled into his duties as vice president, presiding over the Senate in an unobtrusive manner and attending to his other incidental duties faithfully. Harding had promised Coolidge a role in his administration and in fact did make him party to presidential deliberations. When Congress adjourned in March 1923, Coolidge looked forward to a long vacation to revive his sagging morale; the conventional wisdom was that he did not have much of a future in national politics. But when word of Harding's sudden death on August 2 finally reached Coolidge at the family farm in Plymouth Notch, his first thought was "I believe I can swing it." At 2:47 A.M. August 3, John Coolidge, who happened to be a public notary, administered the oath of office to his son, and Calvin Coolidge became the thirtieth president of the United States.

A Course for Continuity

During the 1920 presidential campaign, Harding asserted that "America's present need is not heroics but healing, not nostrums but normalcy." One of the central issues of the election was American membership in the League of Nations.

Wilson's project of international peace and harmony based on universal principles of justice and world government was too radical for Harding. Neither he nor Secretary of State Charles Evan Hughes were willing to expend precious political capital by picking a fight with Senator Henry Cabot Lodge and the irreconcilables over what was deemed a doomed cause. The Harding administration, however, did establish a policy of informal cooperation with the League. Hughes authorized the American minister to Switzerland to establish direct contacts with League officials and to convey informally, through back channels, the American perspective on various matters. The United States also participated in League humanitarian initiatives like the control of anthrax in cattle and the suppression of opium, prostitutes, and obscene material. Under Harding and Hughes, the United States quietly participated ad hoc in League activities that furthered America's interest while rejecting active membership. Both Harding and Hughes, however, were unambiguous in their support of American participation in the World Court, which had been established in 1922 under the auspices of the League. The irreconcilables led by Lodge, William Borah of Idaho, and Hiram Johnson of California, saw American membership in the World Court as the first step toward American membership in the League, and engaged in parliamentary delay tactics to deny a vote during Harding's tenure in office.

Although Harding differed with his predecessor's approach to the League and global peace initiatives, he continued to adhere to Wilson's hard-line policies on war debts and reparations and the refusal to grant diplomatic recognition to Bolshevik Russia. Any possibility of reviewing the administration's policy on recognition of Russia was dashed by Harding's sudden death.

When Coolidge assumed the presidency in August 1923, he had no experience in foreign affairs, and he depended heavily on his secretaries of state, Hughes and later Frank B. Kellogg. He had traveled only once outside the United States—his honeymoon in Montreal—and often gave the impression of a Vermont boy who had never strayed from the farm. Coolidge once shocked the wife of the British ambassador, probably quite deliberately, by telling her that he would never visit Europe since everything that he wished to learn could be found in America. Beneath the image of Yankee provincialism, however, Coolidge did have certain convictions regarding foreign affairs. He was against war as not merely wasteful of human life but also deeply disruptive of the social relations of all levels of society. War was also expensive, and for a president committed to thrift, it was necessary to take measures to avoid conflict and reduce expenditures on armaments. Coolidge also believed that international debt was deeply unsettling for the relations among states and that justly incurred debts had to be repaid to maintain confidence among states. Thus, the general thrust of Coolidge's foreign policy goals dovetailed nicely with a continuation of his predecessor's policies on not merely war debts and arms limitation, but also on the League of Nations, the World Court, and nonrecognition of Russia.

Nonrecognition of the Soviet Union

In 1923, there appeared to be a softening in the policies of the Soviet regime. The New Economic Program permitted small-scale rudimentary capitalism; the government sought to expand commercial ties; and there was a relaxation in the Communist propaganda directed against the United States and other countries. These events spurred the proponents of recognition like Senator Borah to lobby the administration to consider the possibility of recognizing the Soviet regime. Coolidge felt the pressure for recognition, and in his 1923 State of the Union message, he adopted a conciliatory stance toward Moscow. He stated that his administration would consider recognition provided the Soviet regime ended its revolutionary propaganda directed at the United States, paid for confiscated property, and recognized repudiated debts. Instead of accepting Coolidge's conditions unconditionally, the Soviet Commissar for Foreign Affairs Grigori Chicherin saw them instead as the starting point for negotiating outstanding differences between the two countries. Hughes ruled out any possibility of negotiations until the Soviets first fulfilled the conditions. He believed that Moscow could unilaterally lay the foundation for the resumption of diplomatic relations by implementing them; that it chose not to do so was proof of Soviet insincerity and perfidy. Hughes's hard-line position on nonrecognition carried the day and was continued by his successor, Frank Kellogg. Diplomatic relations with the Soviet Union were not resumed until 1933.

Hemispheric Interests

The Latin America policy of the Coolidge administration was directed at securing American commercial and financial interests in the hemisphere, withdrawing from interventions in the Caribbean and Central America, and concentrating on pressing issues involving Mexico and Nicaragua. The war had displaced Europe and established the United States as the principal source for investment and trade. Between 1919 and 1927, Latin American countries borrowed $200 million from their prewar European creditors and over $1.2 billion from the United States, while American exports to Latin America grew from $348 million in 1913 to nearly $1 billion when Coolidge left office. In the Caribbean, the U.S. Marines remained in occupation of Haiti where they had been since 1915, but withdrew from the Dominican Republic in 1924. In Cuba, General Gerardo Machado turned himself into a dictator.

The administration's goal in Mexico was to secure a stable investment climate for the large American interests there. Relations between the United States and Mexico had been strained by the Mexican revolution and the military interventions of the Wilson administration. The revolutionary governments of Mexico were determined to take back the concessions previously granted by the Diaz regime, with indemnities if necessary. The Mexican constitution of 1917 vested ownership of subsoil mineral rights in the Mexican nation and threatened the $1.5 billion in American-owned land, mineral rights, and oil properties. The Harding administration asserted that the Mexican constitution violated the principle of "prompt, adequate, and effective compensation" established in international law. Crisis was averted in 1923 when President Alvaro Obregón negotiated the Bucerelli agreements, whereby, in exchange for formal diplomatic recognition, Mexico acknowledged the property rights of American oil companies that had acquired lands prior to 1917.

In 1925, however, relations with Mexico were plunged into crisis anew when the Mexican Congress, acting at the behest of the new President Plutarco Elías Calles, passed two laws designed to affect to public ownership. The first law limited oil rights to fifteen years and required renewal of the rights or the forfeiture of those rights. The other law allowed foreigners to own land if they waived all rights to resort to their own governments for protection of their property in cases of violation of contract; this was the so-called Calvo clause, which would allow the Mexican government to nationalize American businesses with impunity. The ambassador to Mexico, James Rockwell Sheffield, counseled a hard-line American response, and Assistant Secretary of State Robert E. Olds made the sensational but unsubstantiated charge that Bolshevism had taken hold in Mexico and was spreading toward the Panama Canal. Calles's decision to intervene in the affairs in Nicaragua strengthened the hand of the hard-liners in the administration. On April 25, 1927, at the United Press Association dinner, Coolidge announced what was quickly dubbed the Coolidge Doctrine, asserting that "the person and property of a citizen are a part of the general domain of the Nation, even when abroad."

The Coolidge Doctrine was a rebuke to Calles, the Mexican Congress, and the Calvo clause, but Coolidge indicated simultaneously that he did not want any "controversy" with Mexico. He replaced Sheffield with Dwight Morrow, his Amherst classmate and a former partner at J. P. Morgan and Company. Morrow went to Mexico determined to change relations with Mexico for the better and he succeeded, quickly establishing a friendly and respectful working relationship with Calles. Morrow found a loophole in the 1917 constitution that stated that no laws should be retroactive, and Calles promised that the Mexican Supreme Court would help settle the matter. Under pressure from Calles, the court handed down a decision on November 17, 1927, striking down the Petroleum Law as unconstitutional

and permitting American oil companies that had started development prior to 1917 to retain ownership rights. Coolidge was so impressed with Morrow's handling of the Mexican crisis that he later recommended him as secretary of state to Herbert Hoover.

The other flashpoint in Latin America was Nicaragua, where the United States had a strategic interest in a possible alternative isthmian canal. In 1925, former president Emiliano Chamorro staged a coup and seized power. In the spring of 1926, revolution flared up on the east coast of Nicaragua and U.S. Marines were dispatched with orders to quell the fighting. By 1927, however, the fighting had spread to the west coast and Chamorro had been replaced by Adolfo Díaz, who was supported and recognized by the administration. To complicate matters further for Coolidge and Kellogg, Calles recognized Díaz's rival Juan Sacasa and supported his uprising against the government in Managua. Coolidge dispatched Henry L. Stimson, William Howard Taft's secretary of war, to negotiate a settlement and forestall a revolution in Nicaragua. Stimson devised a plan in which Díaz would remain in power for the time being and the United States would supervise elections in 1928 so as to guarantee fairness and a modicum of stability. All parties, with the exception of the revolutionary Augusto C. Sandino, agreed to abide by the terms of Stimson's plan. The 1928 election was won by the liberal candidate José Moncada.

The administration's Latin American policy marked a step backward from Harding's policy of "Good Neighborliness." Faced with crises in the region, Coolidge and Kellogg had sought to improvise policy on the fly and found it convenient to fall back on Teddy Roosevelt's policy of "Big Stick" intervention in the affairs of Latin American republics. In 1928, Undersecretary of State J. Reuben Clark drafted a memorandum rejecting any right for the United States to intervene in Latin America under the Monroe Doctrine but did not categorically rule out intervention. Coolidge sought to repair American relations with the Latin American republics in his address to the Havana Pan-American Conference in 1928, but any goodwill was lost when Hughes, the American representative, refused to endorse a motion renouncing the right of intervention under all conditions. American relations with the Latin American republics reached their nadir in the interwar period under Coolidge and Kellogg.

They Hired the Money

The question of war debts absorbed a considerable amount of time and energy for the Coolidge administration and was a constant source of irritation in relations with European states. The United States had loaned over $10 billion to its erstwhile allies and expected to be repaid. Coolidge may or may not have said, "They hired the money, didn't they?" but he was supported by the American public in his refusal to acquiesce to debt cancellation and determination to see that the war debts were repaid. The issue was complicated by its connection to the matter of reparations, which the former Allied powers expected from Germany. Woodrow Wilson had initiated the policy of denying any connection between debts and reparations, and his successors did the same thing in spite of the opposition of the Europeans, who portrayed the United States as "Uncle Shylock." From the American perspective, cancellation or even substantial reduction in the debts was impossible; it would cause a domestic financial panic, place an undue burden on American taxpayers—all anathema to a Republican administration committed to reducing taxes and the domestic debt.

The reparations situation reached a crisis point in 1923 when France and Belgium invaded the Ruhr in retaliation for German default on payments. The administration intervened in an attempt to reduce tensions, with Hughes proposing that the problem be studied by a commission of experts who would establish the amount that Germany was to pay and the conditions for payment. The French government, weakened by a run on the French franc, consented to an international conference on reparations to be held in Paris in January 1924. Coolidge appointed three American financiers, Charles G. Dawes, Henry M. Robinson, and Owen D. Young, to the committee of experts. The committee revised the amount owed by Germany for reparation payments, and in March 1924 the Dawes Plan was accepted by all parties. It scaled down German payments to 2.5 billion marks to be paid over fifty years and evacuated French troops from the Ruhr. Germany's economic and financial recovery, however, was underwritten by loans provided by American banks. The $2.5 billion in loans provided to Germany corresponded to the amount that the country owed in reparation payments, which in turn corresponded to the war debt payments that the United States received from its former allies. Prescient observers noted that the cycling of reparations and debt payments made no economic sense and was a disaster in the making, but in the heady days of "Coolidge prosperity," their warnings went unheeded.

Organizing the Peace

Latin America, recognition of the Soviet Union, and war debts and reparations paled in significance next to the central foreign policy problem facing the administration: the organization of international peace. With the end of the war there was a general belief that there was a need for an institutional arrangement that would prevent a reoccurrence of August 1914, yet the emphatic rejection of Woodrow Wilson's League of Nations and his plans for peace through world government meant that the administration had to find alternatives.

The first possibility was the World Court. The purpose of the court was mainly to support and advance the rule of law in the world and was in consonant with long-held American beliefs that peace needed to be bolstered by the rule of law. Harding and Hughes had been supportive of American membership of the World Court, and Coolidge felt bound by his predecessor's commitment to press for adherence. He also felt committed to represent the wishes of the people on this matter; he viewed his election as president in 1924 as a mandate from the people to proceed with American membership. Coolidge might also have been more confident with moving forward on membership after the election in light of the death of Henry Cabot Lodge, the most intransigent opponent of American involvement in the court. For a while, it appeared that Coolidge's initiative would pass smoothly, as the House of Representatives approved membership overwhelmingly by a vote of 302 to 28. However, Senator Borah, now chairman of the Senate Foreign Relations Committee with Lodge's passing, rallied the irreconcilables and railed against membership in the court as a backdoor for American entry into the League.

Sensing the mounting opposition to adherence in the Senate, Coolidge started to distance himself from the proposal. He indicated a willingness to accept four reservations that many senators insisted on attaching to the approval of the court protocol: the United States would not be considered to have assumed any obligations to the League; it would have an equal voice in the selection of judges; Congress would determine American financial obligations to the court; and the court's statute could not be amended without American consent. The irreconcilables prevailed further on Coolidge to accept a fifth reservation: the court could not, without American consent, hand down an advisory opinion on any matter involving the United States.

By his acceptance of the five reservations, Coolidge had signaled that he was unwilling to go far in fighting for the World Court; he had to consider support for the rest of his program in Congress and especially his reliance on Borah for supporting the administration on tax and budgetary matters. The supporters of the court nonetheless managed to overcome a filibuster by the irreconcilables and on January 26, 1926, the Senate agreed to adherence to the court with the five reservations by a vote of 76 to 17. The assent of the World Court's other forty-eight member-states to the first four American reservations was promptly secured, but they rejected the reservation on advisory opinions. In September 1926, twenty-one member-states offered to open negotiation on that reservation, but Coolidge took umbrage at their audacity and rejected the offer. There was nothing to negotiate; the court's members could take the American reservation on advisory opinions or they could leave it. Coolidge was unwilling to jeopardize his legislative agenda by getting involved in a prolonged fight with the Senate over the court.

The second possibility for organizing peace was through arms limitations. There was considerable public support for arms limitation, and Coolidge believed in it personally as a cure for war. Arms limitations had the additional appeal of economizing on public expenditures—a virtue that was not lost on the parsimonious president. His immediate goal was to concentrate on limitations on naval vessels, building on the success of the Washington Conference with limitations on ground weapons to come at a later date when conditions were more favorable. In the fall of 1926, Coolidge decided that the time was ripe for a major international initiative on arms limitations, so he sent out feelers to the other major powers expressing a willingness to consider extending the ratios of the Washington Conference to other classes of naval vessels. Coolidge received what he took to be favorable responses from the other powers. On February 10, 1927, he therefore formally proposed to Britain, Japan, France, and Italy a new naval arms limitation conference to be held in Geneva.

The Geneva Naval Conference opened on June 20, 1927, with France and Italy declining to attend because of their growing naval rivalry in the Mediterranean. It became immediately apparent that there was also no consensus among the United States, Britain, and Japan as to what restrictions should be imposed, and, to complicate matters further, there was dissension between the diplomats and naval officers of each of the three powers. The conference eventually foundered on Anglo-American distrust and naval rivalry. The Americans and British could not come to an agreement on limits on cruiser tonnages and types. The Americans viewed the British demand for a minimum of 600,000 tons as an extension rather than a limitation on cruisers, and the British regarded it as the minimum necessary for the Royal Navy to fulfill its imperial obligations. Neither could the two countries agree on limits to cruisers types. The Royal Navy favored a large fleet of light cruisers that could enforce maritime belligerent rights, including blockade, whereas the United States Navy placed an emphasis on heavy cruisers that were useful as commerce raiders and essential in breaking blockades. Underlying this technical debate was the fact that the British wanted more light cruisers to establish blockades, while the Americans wanted heavy cruisers to break blockades—possibly British blockades. For their part, the Japanese were perfectly happy to sit back and let the Americans and British fight it out. As a consequence, the conference ended without achieving any limitations on naval armaments. Coolidge was chagrined by the outcome; he had been embarrassed internationally and domestically, and believed that his pet project for world peace had been scuttled by British perfidy. When France and Britain concluded the Anglo-French naval agreement of July 31, 1928—which permitted them to build the vessels they wanted while sharply limiting the classes of warships that the United States wanted—Coolidge authorized a massive naval buildup. One of his last acts before leaving office was to sign into law the Naval Construction Act of February 1929, which authorized the construction of fifteen heavy cruisers and an aircraft carrier.

The third possibility for organizing international peace was to outlaw war, an idea that became the Kellogg-Briand Pact of 1928. Coolidge had been flirting with the advocates of outlawry since 1923; by promising consideration of their plans he had skillfully strung them along and gained their political support. That situation would probably have continued to the end of his term in office were it not for France. In 1927, one of America's leading pacifists, Professor James T. Shotwell of Columbia University, planted the idea of outlawry in the mind of French Foreign Minister Aristide Briand. Briand was an astute diplomat and was not taken in by the earnestness or naïveté of Shotwell, but he saw in the idea the potential to bring the United States into his European diplomatic calculations. A bilateral treaty renouncing war between France and the United States would at the very least reduce the ill will that had developed between the two countries and might even yield an American guarantee for Europe's territorial boundaries. If the two countries renounced war, France could gain moral leverage in calling on American assistance in any future war with Germany, or at a minimum permit it to push American neutrality to the limit without bringing the United States into war against France. Briand thus calculated that France could not lose by pursuing the outlawry idea.

Briand acted on April 6, 1927, the tenth anniversary of America's entrance into the war. In an address directed at the American people, Briand pledged France's willingness to join with the United States to outlaw war as an instrument of national policy. By circumventing normal diplomatic channels and addressing himself directly to the American people, the Frenchman forced the administration to consider the idea of outlawry seriously. Coolidge and Kellogg were irritated by Briand's display of public diplomacy, but they could not afford to ignore his proposal given the surge in public sentiment in favor of it. They tried to stall for time, but by December were worried that they could no longer resist the pressure to adopt the French proposal. Seizing on a suggestion by Senator Borah that the legal abolition of war be made multilateral, Kellogg outmaneuvered Briand with a counterproposal that France and the United States invite all the nations of the world to accede to a multilateral peace pact. Now it was the French government's turn to stall for time. Kellogg's proposal threatened Briand's plan for drawing the United States to France's side in case of war with Germany; if implemented, a multilateral pact outlawing war would throw up a legal barrier against any preventive war and make any hostile gesture by France deeply embarrassing. While Briand sought a way out of this dilemma, Kellogg became increasingly enamored of his own plan. He circulated his proposal among other powers and received favorable responses from Germany, Italy, and Japan. Faced with positive international reaction, Briand caved to Kellogg's proposal for a multilateral agreement. He had been hoisted by his own petard; by advocating outlawry so long and so well he could not back out now. On August 27, 1928, fifteen other nations joined France and the United States in signing the Kellogg-Briand Pact in Paris.

Unlike his secretary of state, Coolidge was not particularly enthused about the pact. He had acquiesced to it as a means of easing the pressure on him to do something for world peace. He hoped that the pact would not cause too much trouble and might actually do some good, but was doubtful. He nonetheless became somewhat more enthusiastic about the Kellogg-Briand Pact as the 1928 presidential election campaign got underway. With the pact his administration had managed to "out-covenant" even Woodrow Wilson, make up for some of the disappointment of the World Court and the Geneva Conference episodes, and permitted his chosen successor, Herbert Hoover, to run on a platform of peace and accomplishment. Coolidge campaigned for Senate ratification of the Kellogg-Briand Pact but also cautioned about the limits of what had been accomplished. He warned that perpetual peace had not magically replaced war just because a treaty had been signed; genuine peace would come about if the people of the nations enforced the pact by acting against aggressors and by preventing their own governments from undertaking aggression. Coolidge viewed the pact as offering the world a chance, albeit a slim one, to seize the peace, and he was willing to take that chance. On January 15, 1929, the Senate ratified the Kellogg-Briand Pact by a vote of 85 to 1 and on January 17, in a ceremony in the East Room of the White House, Coolidge signed America's instrument of ratification.

Legacy

Coolidge proved less able to "swing it" in foreign affairs than in domestic politics. He was fundamentally uninterested in the international arena and relied heavily on his able secretaries of state, Charles Evan Hughes and Frank B. Kellogg. His administration was content in general to continue pursuing the conservative internationalist policies of his predecessor. With the exception of the Geneva Naval Conference initiative, Coolidge was prepared to react to international events rather than initiate grand foreign policy plans.

Furthermore, his administration was prepared to defer to public opinion and to be led by it. Public opinion, however, proved to be a weak foundation upon which to construct a viable foreign policy because in the following decade public opinion gyrated wildly as the center in international politics buckled under the predations of both Communist and fascist regimes. The signal diplomatic accomplishment of Coolidge's administration, the Kellogg-Briand Pact, faded in its luster and came to be derided as a byword for international do-goodism and naïveté. Critics of the administration's foreign policy have charged Coolidge

with being unwilling to push harder for American membership in the League of Nations and the World Court, thereby contributing to the national isolationist impulse. The issue of the League and the World Court were, however, deeply entrenched in the domestic politics of the era. It constituted the "third rail" of politics of the day, and it is hard to see how, given his temperament and outlook on foreign affairs, Coolidge could have been expected to triumph over the irreconcilables who had successfully broken Woodrow Wilson and later intimidated even Franklin Roosevelt.

Adrian U-jin Ang

Chronology

1923
August 3: Coolidge sworn-in as president.

1924
September 1: Dawes Plan established for payment of German reparations.

October 25: Zinoviev letter incident damages Anglo-Russian relations.

November 4: President Coolidge reelected.

November 9: Nazi beer hall putsch in Munich defeated.

1925
June 27: Geneva Protocol signed.

October 5–16: Locarno Conference, Treaty of Locarno signed.

1926
September 8: Germany admitted to League of Nations.

November 11: Coolidge announces that United States will not join the World Court.

December 25: Taisho Emperor dies in Japan, Showa regime under Hirohito begins.

1927
April 12: Nationalist forces in China begin purge of Communists.

April 25: Coolidge Doctrine announced.

May 11: Henry L. Stimson concludes Treaty of Tipitata ending fighting in Nicaragua

June 20: Geneva Naval Limitations Conference convenes.

July 31: Anglo-French Naval Agreement signed.

November 11: France and Yugoslavia sign Treaty of Understanding.

1928
May 3: Japanese and Chinese forces clash in Shantung.

July 25: United States recognizes Nationalist government of Chiang Kaishek.

August 27: United States signs Kellogg-Briand Pact with thirteen other nations.

November 6: Herbert Hoover is elected president, Charles Curtis is vice president.

References and Further Reading

Cohen, Warren I. *Empire Without Tears: America's Foreign Relations, 1921–1933.* Philadelphia: Temple University Press, 1987.

Ellis, L. Ethan. *Republican Foreign Policy: 1921–1933.* New Brunswick, NJ: Rutgers University Press, 1968.

Ferrell, Robert H. 1998. *The Presidency of Calvin Coolidge.* Lawrence, KS: University Press of Kansas. 1998.

Johnson, Robert David. *The Peace Progressives and American Foreign Relations.* Cambridge, MA: Harvard University Press, 1995.

McCoy, Donald R. *Calvin Coolidge: The Quiet Presidency.* New York: MacMillan, 1967.

Rhodes, Benjamin D. *United States Foreign Policy in the Interwar Period, 1918–1941: The Golden Age of American Diplomatic and Military Complacency.* Westport, CT: Praeger, 2001.

Herbert Clark Hoover (1929–1933)

Early Life and Political Career

Born in West Branch, Iowa, on August 10, 1874, Herbert Clark Hoover spent much of his adolescence in Oregon after the premature deaths of his father (1880) and mother (1883). There followed a brief period of familial instability in which the nine-year-old Herbert and his two siblings, Theodore and Mary, were transferred among various relatives who shared the burden of caring for the three orphans. In September 1884, a month after his tenth birthday, Herbert was sent to Newberg, Oregon, to live with his maternal uncle, Dr. Henry John Minthorn. Soon after his arrival in Newberg he enrolled at the Friends Pacific Academy, a Quaker institution that was in part founded and directed by his uncle, a prominent local Quaker and respected physician. Although the boy was not inclined to absorb the spiritual tenets of Quakerism, he nevertheless inculcated the strong social ethos of his family's religious traditions. Quakerism thus permeated his youth and continued to pervade, inform, and sustain his conception of public service throughout his later life. In 1888, Hoover left the Academy when the Minthorn family relocated to Salem, Oregon, some 20 miles away. In Salem, his uncle established a land settlement business, the Oregon Land Company. For the next two years Hoover worked for his uncle as an "assistant bookkeeper," a task he performed diligently while attending night classes at the local business college.

In 1891, eager to continue his education, Hoover seized the opportunity to enter the newly established Leland Stanford Junior University in Palo Alto, California. He did so much to the chagrin of his pious Quaker uncle, who had made arrangements for Hoover to matriculate at one of two prominent Quaker institutions. At Stanford, Hoover majored in geology. He flourished at college, combining high academic distinction with a successful business acumen that allowed him to finance his education without incurring any debt. He spent summers with the United States Geological Survey in Arkansas and California, where he demonstrated a striking proficiency in mining and engineering as well as an abiding affection for nature and support for conservation. When Hoover graduated from Stanford in May 1895, he was already well equipped and prepared to employ his considerable knowledge and early geological experience in the mining industry. Graduation brought little immediate opportunity to apply his skills, however, as the

A serious and highly intelligent leader, Herbert Clark Hoover's foreign policy was overwhelmed by the Great Depression. (Library of Congress)

United States was still mired in the great economic depression and labor crisis of the mid-1890s. Hoover spent an interlude toiling in the depths of the Reward gold mine in Nevada City, California. This was followed by a less strenuous year in a management position working under a San Francisco mining engineer. Notwithstanding these initial disappointments, real opportunity arrived in February 1897, as Hoover took a position with a London mining concern, Bewick, Moreing and Company. The firm dispatched him to western Australia to manage one of its gold mines. He remained abroad for the next two years, honing his administrative and engineering skills and establishing an international reputation within the industry that would ultimately take him around the world as a leading mining expert.

In 1899, Hoover resigned his position with Bewick, Moreing and Company and returned briefly to the United

States. During his time stateside he married his college sweetheart, Louise "Lou" Henry, a fellow Stanford geology major. The wedding took place in Monterey, California. The next day the couple left not for a honeymoon but on a three-year assignment to China, where Hoover assumed a position offered by the Qing government as a technical consultant. His assignment—to assist in the development of China's natural resources—was interrupted by the outbreak of the antiforeigner and anti-Qing Boxer Rebellion in early 1900. The Hoovers soon found themselves engulfed by the ferocious defense of Tientsin where the beleaguered Western Legations and foreign families awaited the arrival of an international military expedition. Along with other Westerners, Americans came under fire from the Boxers who surrounded the city. Hoover's experiences in Tientsin, which included directing the construction of part of the Legation defenses and coordinating distribution of essential provisions, furnished invaluable lessons from which he would continue to draw in later public service in Belgium and Russia after World War I.

Once the Western Legations were relieved, the Hoovers departed China. Hoover returned to his old firm, becoming a junior partner at Bewick, Moreing and Company. For the next seven years he traveled the world as a consultant. When not accompanying her husband, Lou Hoover maintained their home in London. In 1903, they celebrated the birth of their first son, Herbert Clark Jr. In 1907, a second son, Allan Henry, was born. In July 1908, Hoover resigned his position with Bewick, Moreing and Company to found his own mining consultancy company, and soon established a lucrative international network of offices, with clients in Russia, Mexico, India, South Africa, the United States, and Europe. His fortune and reputation grew over the next six years. In 1909, he published his first book, *Principles of Mining*. He was named a trustee of his alma mater, Stanford University, in 1912. That same year, the Hoovers were jointly awarded a gold medal by the Mining and Metallurgical Society of America for their translation of Georgius Agricola's momentous 1556 scientific treatise, *De re metallica*.

In August 1914, the outbreak of World War I in Europe wrenched Hoover from the relative comfort of his burgeoning business interests. Nevertheless, when called to public service in a period of international crisis, he reacted with characteristic enthusiasm and vigor. During the previous decade Hoover had established a justifiably eminent international reputation as a highly efficient and talented administrator, and numerous wartime governments did not hesitate to assign him the prodigious tasks of wartime relief management. Hoover was in London when Germany declared war on France on August 3, 1914. The call from his own government came immediately. That same day, Walter Hines Page, American ambassador to Great Britain, asked Hoover to implement and administer the activities of the American Relief Committee established to facilitate the repatriation of some 120,000 Americans trapped in various European countries by the outbreak of hostilities.

In October 1914, again at the behest of Page, and this time in concert with the French and Belgian ambassadors to Great Britain, Hoover was called on to organize the Commission for Relief in Belgium (CRB). This proved to be a vast undertaking pregnant with difficult diplomatic considerations. Yet Hoover confidently negotiated these problems and almost single-handedly directed the Commission with great success. Funded by both government subsidy and private donations, the CRB dispensed an enormous quantity of food aid to Belgian and French citizens in German-occupied territory. The CRB functioned almost as a quasi-state (it even possessed its own flag, currency, and fleet). As a result of his leadership of the CRB, Hoover's reputation as a profoundly effective and indomitable administrator grew apace. When the United States declared war on Germany on April 6, 1917, Hoover relinquished control of the CRB to the neutral Spanish and Dutch and returned to the United States. From there he continued to exercise considerable influence over the CRB's activities.

Hoover was also keen to make a contribution to the Allied war effort. On August 10, 1917, Woodrow Wilson appointed him head of the United States Food Administration. In his new position, Hoover was responsible for the organization and distribution of food supplies in the United States under the terms of the Lever Act of 1917. He was also in charge of foreign food assistance for those Allied nations whose citizens and armies were dependent on the United States for much of their sustenance. Again, Hoover rose to the challenge. In January 1918, he instigated his famous food conservation campaign for "Meatless Tuesdays" and "Wheatless Mondays." Six months later the Sugar Equalization Board introduced sugar rationing in the United States.

During the last year of the Great War Herbert Hoover was foremost among Republicans who supported President Wilson's wartime pronouncements on the nature of the postwar international system to be constructed at the expected Peace Conference. He expressed support for the president's policies in a letter published during the crucial midterm elections of 1918. Following the Armistice that terminated the Great War on November 11, Hoover resumed his role as administrator of international relief in Paris. His international obligations expanded when the Paris Peace Conference convened in January 1919. From January to June 1919, Hoover served as a member of the Supreme Economic Council and as an economic adviser to the United States delegation in Paris, while also serving on various boards and councils committed to the reconstruction of Europe's devastated economic infrastructure. Also in 1919, his relentless energy found expression in the establishment of the Hoover Institution on War, Revolution, and Peace at Stanford University.

His governmental and nongovernmental service continued unabated following the conclusion of the Peace

Conference. Indeed, the years 1921–1923 represent a period of frenetic activity for Hoover in the United States and abroad. At home, he served as Vice Chairman of the Second Industrial Conference (convened by President Wilson in December 1919 to investigate management-labor conflict in the United States). He chaired a presidential Conference on Unemployment from 1921–1922. Abroad, he remained the Director General of the American Relief Administration (ARA) until 1923 while also serving as Chairman of the European Children's Fund. At the ARA he was singularly responsible for alleviating malnutrition in liberated Belgium. He followed that success with famine relief to the Soviet Union from 1921–1924, without regard for the political and ideological reservations of his critics. Specialist historians conclude that ARA relief may have saved as many as 30 million Soviet lives (and therefore, probably also the Bolshevik regime). In 1920, he founded the Belgian-American Educational Foundation, of which he remained Chairman until 1961. Throughout this tumultuous time, he continued to campaign for the adoption of the League of Nations in the United States, although he accepted the reservations of its American critics and agreed that some modification of the Covenant was necessary.

It was during this period that Hoover began actively cultivating a political career, aiming from the start for the top position. He made a short-lived run for the Republican Party nomination for president in 1920, aborting his effort when he finished behind Hiram Johnson in the Iowa primary. Hoover did not remain outside politics for long, however. In 1921, President Warren G. Harding appointed him secretary of commerce, a position he retained during the successor administration of Calvin Coolidge. In this role, Hoover worked assiduously to rationalize the nation's economic infrastructure. Hoover initiated innumerable conferences, committees, and associations during his tenure at Commerce, dealing with everything from aviation to radio, national parks to highways. His all-encompassing desire for order and efficiency prompted wags to suggest that the secretary of commerce was moonlighting as the "undersecretary of everything else." Even though his efforts to consolidate and organize the economy generated opposition within other government agencies and among private interest groups, his record as secretary of commerce was nevertheless imposing and his initiatives prolific.

One problem whose solution eluded him (and others) during this period was the question of war debts and reparations. To his credit, Hoover did encourage the intervention of American bankers in the European reparations crisis. Instead, the Dawes Plan of 1924, along with the Young Plan of 1929, bore the imprint of his corporatist philosophy regarding the appropriate relationship between government and business even as Hoover occasionally vacillated over the relative merits of American war debt repayment demands. His emphasis on American commercial expansion almost

certainly exacerbated the balance-of-payments crisis faced by the recovering economies of Europe.

His political stock continued to rise. Despite never having held lower elective office Hoover won the Republican Party's nomination for president on the first ballot at the 1928 Convention held in Kansas City. His extraordinary record of public service made him a near-unanimous choice for a party enjoying almost unparalleled electoral dominance during the 1920s, in a country grown tired of Wilsonian high idealism and looking instead for a high achiever and pragmatist. Hoover's rationalist approach to politics appealed to many lingering progressives who once supported Wilson. After eight years of overseeing economic revival and prosperity at Commerce, Hoover was enormously popular. In the 1928 election, he overwhelmingly defeated the Democratic nominee, Alfred Smith, by an Electoral College vote of 444 to 87.

The Coolidge Legacy: Isolated Internationalism

American foreign policy was relatively inconsequential as an issue in the election of 1928. The Republicans faced few substantial challenges, and the campaign tended to pivot around the merits of domestic social issues such as Prohibition. Also prominent were fears about the potentially subversive impact, as some saw it, of Alfred Smith's Catholicism. The relative absence of foreign policy issues during the campaign reflected the settled, minimalist international role of the United States during the 1920s. The United States was by no means entirely absent from the world stage. It was active on international economic issues and in the world disarmament movement, notably hosting the Washington Naval Disarmament conference in 1922. Yet, for the most part the United States charted a distinctly isolationist course under Harding and Coolidge. It had rejected membership in the League of Nations under Wilson. Under his Republican successors, it withdrew from all oversight responsibilities for the peace settlement and remained aloof from the effort to construct new international organizations to tame the nationalist passions and militarist traditions of the Old World. The last American troops were withdrawn from the Rhineland in 1923 after the French occupied the Ruhr, and the United States pulled out of the Rhineland Commission. During the 1920s, the United States had no official presence on the Reparations Commission despite the critical linkage of that problem to Allied war debt repayments. American failure to deal with the interrelated problems of reparations, war debts, and reconstruction loans contributed much to friction among the Western democracies, the breakdown of social order in Germany, and the outbreak of the Depression.

Despite Coolidge's general detachment from world affairs and Hoover's core, personal internationalism, there were continuities between their conduct of foreign policy. Eschewal of membership in the League did not preclude the

United States from pursuing the ideals of codified disarmament, for example. In 1927, the Coolidge administration tried and failed to extend the limited tonnage ratios of the 1922 Washington Naval Conference to cruiser-class naval vessels. Hoover, too, upheld the American commitment to the disarmament process. He affirmed his commitment to the Kellogg-Briand Pact, negotiated and signed in 1928 and consented to by the Senate in January, 1929. In his Inaugural Address delivered on March 4, 1929, Hoover explicitly linked the two themes of peace and disarmament, declaring that the Kellogg-Briand Pact "should pave the way to greater limitation of armament, the offer of which we sincerely extend to the world." There was less enthusiasm for, or success in, the long-standing debate over United States joining the Permanent Court of International Justice (the so-called World Court, predecessor to the International Court of Justice). This body was a central instrument of the League machinery dedicated to peace through international binding arbitration, and therefore an extension of prewar Republican and progressive foreign policy traditions. Despite opposition to the League of Nations, both Harding and Coolidge expressed support for adherence to the Court—albeit with reservations. They were blocked by a minority of irreconcilable isolationist senators. Hoover also endorsed membership in the Court, asserting in his Inaugural Address that it embodied American ideals and concluding: "The way should, and I believe will, be found by which we may take our proper place in a movement so fundamental to the progress of peace." Like his predecessors, Hoover tried but failed to persuade the Senate to consent to membership in the Court.

Foreign Policy: Disarmament, Depression, and Denial

Hoover's vast international experience surpassed that of perhaps any president before him. His widespread business associations, experience with international relief efforts, and participation in various nongovernmental organizations seemed to auger an increased American engagement in world affairs. The idealistic rhetoric of his Inaugural Address reinforced the claim that Hoover would not forsake an activist American foreign policy. He boldly asserted that American ideals should be a positive influence in the world, and that American engagement rather than isolation would contribute to world peace "not by mere declaration but by taking a practical part in supporting all useful international undertakings." The ultimate goal of his administration, Hoover affirmed, was to "advance the reign of justice and reason toward the extinction of force." In rhetoric, at least, there was little to distinguish him from Woodrow Wilson.

Hoover did not, of course, foresee the profound and dramatic changes in world politics that flowed from the global economic crisis that began in October 1929. The financial crisis that began with a catastrophic stock market crash and snowballed into a global economic depression dominated the rest of his presidency. More than any other issue, it shaped the historical reputation of his administration, in many ways quite unfairly, and obscured his many personal accomplishments as a public servant. The impact of global economic collapse brought home to Americans and the world the long neglected, and persistently denied, interconnections among war debts, reparations, and emergency loans to Weimar Germany. Yet Hoover was slow to understand this. He spent most of the next four years in search of a domestic remedy for America's economic plight while foreign policy concerns languished on his list of priorities. In country after country, including the United States, misguided efforts were pursued that sought to solve with national tariffs and spending measures an economic crisis that was fundamentally international at root and which demanded international solutions. Failure to comprehend this basic fact was the most serious error Hoover made as president. The fact that he was not alone in making it militates partly against the blame that accrued to him for a collapse long in the making that reached critical mass during his watch, but it does not erase his responsibility for then pursuing policies that seriously aggravated the underlying problem.

Latin America: Discarding the Big Stick

After decades of U.S.–Latin American antagonism, Hoover was eager to assuage the suspicions that encumbered hemispheric relations. Almost immediately after his victory in November 1928, he embarked on an unprecedented seven-week tour of Central and South America. From November 19, 1928, to January 6, 1929, Hoover visited ten different countries, including Argentina, Nicaragua, Peru, Chile, and Brazil. During the trip he made numerous speeches announcing his intention to abstain from intervention in Latin America. He gave the opening speech of the tour in Amapala, Honduras, in which he introduced the concept of the "good neighbor" to U.S.–Latin American relations. Despite that term's later association with Franklin D. Roosevelt, it was in fact Herbert Hoover who first invoked the analogy and shifted American policy away from hemispheric intervention when he declared that the United States had "a desire to maintain not only the cordial relations of governments with each other but also the relations of good neighbors." It was also during this trip that Hoover announced his intention to withdraw American troops from Nicaragua and Haiti. Though he received a mixed reception in some countries, most notably in Argentina, Hoover's trip was a milestone in the history of U.S.–Latin American relations. He reiterated his good neighbor policy in his Inaugural Address, proclaiming that in regard to Latin America the United States wanted "only for the maintenance of their independence, the growth of their stability and their prosperity."

Undersecretary of State J. Reuben Clark formulated the basis of this new approach in December 1928. Clark condemned the use of the Monroe Doctrine as a cover for U.S. intervention in Latin America, and effectively advocated renunciation of the Roosevelt Corollary to the Monroe Doctrine, which had been the basis for U.S. foreign policy in the region since 1904. Hoover published this previously secret memorandum in 1930 and remained committed to the spirit of the document throughout his term in office. He did not intervene when internal discord threatened the governments of Mexico and Cuba, and on January 2, 1933, the last contingent of U.S. marines left Nicaragua. The final withdrawal of American troops from Haiti, promised by Hoover, was delayed until 1934 due to the reluctance of the Haitian legislature to see them depart. Hoover and Secretary of State Henry L. Stimson made it clear that any Latin American government that could demonstrate a reasonable degree of stability would receive the recognition of the United States. Woodrow Wilson's policy of withholding recognition on moral grounds was displaced by a return to traditional international practice of extending *de jure* recognition to *de facto* governments.

Asia: The Stimson Doctrine of Nonrecognition

From 1925, the Nationalist government led by Chiang Kai-shek endeavored to unite China under the control of the Kuomintang. Coolidge pursued an ambiguous policy toward this development since American business interests feared that investments might be placed in jeopardy if the United States responded too vigorously. By the summer of 1928, the Nationalist government had seized control of Beijing. Despite the Leninist roots of the Kuomintang and Chiang's conduct of the "Shanghai massacre" of the urban cadres of the Chinese Communist party, he was supported by the Soviet Union. On the other hand, traditional Chinese-Russian tensions continued over control of Manchuria. In September 1929, skirmishes broke out between Soviet and Chinese troops along the northern frontier. Soviet pressure on China provoked the ire of Stimson and Hoover. Stimson especially feared that the Sino-Soviet conflict would undermine the Kellogg-Briand Pact, which had only been in force since July 24, 1929. Although neither China nor the Soviet Union were among the signatories of the Pact, Stimson attempted to invoke the treaty *vis-à-vis* both countries. The Soviets rejected this attempt at diplomatic intervention by a country that did not even recognize the Soviet government. Besides, Soviet troops were already in the process of withdrawal for reasons that had nothing to do with the Stimson initiative.

Long the subject of outside imperialist fantasies, Manchuria remained a flashpoint, and a potentially more serious issue soon arose there that threatened to draw the United States into an Asian conflict. Since the Japanese victory over Russia in 1905, Japan's military had reserved the right to station troops along the South Manchuria Railway. On September 18, 1931, a portion of the railroad near Mukden mysteriously exploded. The Japanese military insisted the explosion was the work of Chinese bandits and the Kwantung Army—Japan's military force in Manchuria that increasingly acted independent of Tokyo's wishes and policy—used the incident as a pretext for offensive operations against Chinese Nationalist forces along the railroad. Facing little initial resistance, the Japanese expanded their control throughout all Manchuria. China protested to the League of Nations, bringing that feckless organization to face the gravest challenge yet to its *raison d'être*: the concept of "collective security." The initial response of the League was to pass a resolution advising China and Japan to return to the *status quo ante*. In the United States, public opinion largely favored the Chinese, although Hoover and Stimson were reluctant to alienate Japan. The crippling effects of the Depression and indifference to the fate of distant Manchuria exacerbated the aversion of the international community to act forcefully against Japan. Nowhere was this mood more obvious than in the United States. As a signatory of the Kellogg-Briand Pact and the Nine Power Pact of 1922, the United States sought to use what little leverage those agreements afforded on an issue the Japanese knew Americans cared too little about to do more than talk. Ultimately, faced with the unpleasant prospect of potentially aggravating the crisis and the reality that his country was in no position to do anything more practical, Stimson announced the anemic policy that the United States would lend its "moral support" to the resolution passed by the League.

On December 10, 1931, with the approval of Japan and China, the League created a Commission of Inquiry led by the Earl of Lytton to ascertain the validity of each side's claims. One month later, in direct and angry defiance of the League, the Kwantung Army strengthened its grip on Manchuria. Stimson resolved to act, with more words. On January 7, 1932, he announced to Japan and China that the United States would refuse to "admit the legality of any situation de facto, nor does it intend to recognize any treaty or agreement entered into between those Governments." The Americans, in concert with the British, were finally moved to act more forcefully when the Imperial Japanese Navy bombarded the Chinese sectors of the international city of Shanghai in January 1932. Hoover dispatched U.S. troops and Navy ships to the city to protect the lives of foreign nationals. Nevertheless, the weak Hoover-Stimson policy of nonrecognition did not stop Japan from consolidating its Manchurian acquisitions. On February 18, 1932, Japan announced establishment of the puppet state of Manchukuo, on whose throne they placed the deposed Qing boy-emperor, Henry Pu Yi (aka Hsuan T'ung). Like most other countries, the United States never recognized Puu Yi's claim to be the K'ang Te (Kangde) Emperor of Manchukuo.

Arms Limitation and Disarmament

Since before World War I, the cause of international disarmament attracted a diverse and passionate array of nongovernmental activists and some diplomatic support. In the aftermath of World War I, the governments of the major industrial powers grew increasingly predisposed toward the ideal of arms limitation as a restraint on war. Many in the United States were horrified by the senseless slaughter of World War I while others were inspired by the idealistic rhetoric of Woodrow Wilson, by the Quakers, or the ideal schemes of international lawyers. Still others sought to lighten the financial burden of arms production. Hoover was interested in disarmament for moral as well as financial and idealistic reasons. In a period of rapid economic decline and diplomatic discord, Hoover joined in a broad international effort at disarmament. The successful Washington Naval Conference seemed to provide a model for the negotiated reduction of the world's principal navies. In 1927, the Coolidge administration had sought to revive the disarmament effort in Geneva. Although this attempt to limit the production of cruisers ultimately failed, Hoover revitalized the disarmament process in January 1930. The foremost naval powers of Great Britain, France, Italy, Japan, and the United States all attended the new conference, which began on January 21 in London. A principle source of disagreement surfaced almost immediately, derived from the unequal tonnage ratios established at the Washington Naval Conference eight years before. Japanese foreign policy had become increasingly assertive in the years following the ratification of the Washington Treaties and the Japanese Navy was no longer satisfied with the 5:5:3 ratio established in Washington, which reduced the permissible tonnage of their auxiliary ships *vis-à-vis* Great Britain and the United States.

A new formula was devised at the London Conference in response to Japanese grievances. The new ratio of 10:10:7 allowed Japan a slight increase in aggregate naval tonnage (although once all categories of vessel had been accounted for the actual Japanese ratio was actually 6.975). Italy and France declined to accept any modifications of the ratios agreed to at Washington. All five powers did agree, however, to continue ratios on capital ship production (weighing over 10,000 tons) as agreed in the Washington Treaties. The London Conference ended on April 22, 1930. The Senate was happy to approve any agreement that cut expenditures and consented to ratification of the London Treaties on July 21, by a vote of 58 to 9. Two years later, in February 1932, the World Disarmament Conference opened in Geneva. Although American involvement was limited, Hoover proposed a blanket one-third reduction on all armaments (his

original proposal, resisted by Stimson, had called for a 40 percent reduction). He also expressed his desire to see the eradication of bombers and tanks. These proposals were never implemented, and the conference never achieved any substantive arms limitations. Hitler's victory in the German elections of 1933 effectively ended the initiative when he immediately withdrew Germany from further participation. With that, the entire post–World War I disarmament movement ended in a whimper as the Great Powers shifted, one after another, toward rearmament and preparation for another world war.

The Great Depression: American Protectionism and War Debts

The U.S. stock market crash of October 29, 1929, was unquestionably the pivotal event of the Hoover presidency, and this had a paradoxical effect on U.S. foreign policy. The international repercussions of the economic downturn this event triggered were immense. U.S. investments, loans, and trade flows were essential to the functioning of the global economy in the aftermath of World War I. Since the implementation of the Dawes Plan in 1924, the United States effectively underwrote the German economy, which in turn financed the cycle of European reparations and war debt repayments. Private American investment abroad declined dramatically in the aftermath of the crash and much of the capital that had impelled European economic recovery was withdrawn to the United States as banks called in bad loans and global liquidity dried up. Given the American role in facilitating the operation of international finance and commerce, many commentators and analysts argued for greater American leadership in the effort to ameliorate the global depression. In fact, in an effort to protect domestic manufacturers and farmers, Congress instituted an inordinately restrictive tariff on imported goods. Instead of vetoing the bill, Hoover signed the 1930 Hawley-Smoot Tariff Act on June 17, 1930. It would prove one of the most damaging legislative acts in American history. The tariff led to reciprocal beggar-thy-neighbor retaliatory tariffs, a downward spiral in world trade, and further constrictions of international liquidity. All of that deepened the international depression as America's former trading partners were excluded from vital U.S. markets and replied with measures-in-kind.

In 1931, Hoover made a bold effort to break out of this vicious cycle and to alleviate the financial crisis which threatened to completely destroy the economies of Europe. In the spring of 1931, it appeared that Germany was on the verge of bankruptcy. The lingering French fear of German militarism precluded efforts to form a customs union with Austria, which was in any case forbidden by terms of the Versailles Treaty, and a number of Austrian banks faced extinction. On June 20, 1931, to bring some relief to the beleaguered European treasuries, Hoover announced a one-year moratorium on the payment of intergovernmental reparations and war debt payments. The edict was to take effect almost immediately, on July 1, 1931. Congress deferred to the president, but the nationalist-inclined legislature insisted that this in no way implied the permanent annulment of European war debts. This was a welcome gesture of economic goodwill and American leadership, but the underlying crisis remained and was aggravated by bad tariff policies. As expiration of this temporary reprieve approached, the European powers met in Lausanne to assess the future of German reparations. The Hoover administration declined to attend. To the annoyance of Hoover, Germany and her creditors reached an agreement in the absence of the United States. Under the terms of this accord, 90 percent of Germany's reparations obligations would be forgiven if the United States reciprocated by forgiving the war debt obligations of Germany's creditors. Hoover responded firmly that no such agreement was acceptable to his government. That effectively ended American leadership on the two key economic issues of the day, and allowed the international crisis to spiral out of control, ultimately into catastrophe.

Legacy

Herbert Hoover has the dubious honor of joining such presidents as William Taft and John Quincy Adams, for whom the presidency was to a large extent a blight on an otherwise exemplary career in public service. Hoover was unquestionably a man of vision, integrity, and great ability. But ultimately, his rhetoric promised more than he could deliver, and he failed the great test of leadership: he could not make the hard decisions that solve unforgiving problems born of national and international crises. Like so many who occupied the highest office, Hoover's intentions were thwarted by events beyond his control. The Depression ruined his presidency. The foreign policy implications of economic disaster that contributed to political radicalization and rabid militarism in several Great Powers—Italy, Germany, Japan, and the Soviet Union—continued to resonate throughout the 1930s and set the stage for the tragedy of the 1940s. It was not until the United States entered World War II that the U.S. economy revived. Similarly, Japan's unchecked and unbalanced aggression against China escalated in the 1930s. The Stimson Doctrine of non-recognition had no more discernible impact on Japanese imperialism than FDR's later "moral embargo" would have on Italian and German aggression in Europe. The American imperative remained the avoidance of conflict with Japan, until the attack on Pearl Harbor drew the United States into the Pacific War and four days later into the European war when Germany and Italy declared war on the United States. Disarmament remained a foreign policy chimera pursued at the expense of real national interests in rearmament and preparedness measures needed to face down fascism. As the threat of Adolf Hitler's Germany loomed over Europe, the superficial disarmament gains of the 1920s were exposed as actually contrary to the prospect of achieving peace through strengthened deterrence by a genuine league of armed democracies. Ironically, it was this impending threat of conflict that consolidated Hoover's most successful foreign policy initiative: improvement of relations with Latin America. Franklin Roosevelt's embrace of the Good Neighbor policy ensured that when war finally broke out in September 1939, most of the countries of the Western Hemisphere would remain allied to the United States.

After his term ended in 1933, Hoover continued to be a dynamic presence in national affairs and to some extent internationally. His exceptional organizational talents were again fully employed in numerous relief efforts during World War II. In later life, he moved harder to the right, advocating full-throated isolationism before, and again after, World War II. He was ever independent of mind, however, as he made evident in early and initially unpopular public criticism of President Harry Truman's approval of atomic bomb attacks on Japan in 1945. Hoover remained active in international relief and reconstruction efforts in the aftermath of World War II. With the onset of the Cold War in the late 1940s, he was moved to opine on the peril of the Soviet Union, but otherwise offered no effective advice on how to confront that threat. His long life of public service and remarkable personal humanitarianism finally ended on October 20, 1964, when Hoover died at the age of 90. He was buried in his hometown of West Branch, Iowa.

David Atkinson

Chronology

1929

February 28: United States revokes Roosevelt Corollary to the Monroe Doctrine.

August 31: Hague Economic Conference ratifies Young Plan for German reparations.

October 29: U.S. stock market crashes, onset of the Great Depression.

December 2: United States invokes Kellogg-Briand Pact to prevent Sino-Soviet war.

1930

February 6: Austrian and Italy sign friendship treaty.

April 22: London Naval Conference decides Naval Limitation Treaty.

November 14: Japanese prime minister Yuko Hamaguchi is assassinated.

1931

June 17: Congress approves Smoot-Hawley Tariff.

June 20: Hoover offers to postpone all debt owed to the United States.

September 18: Mukden incident, Japan occupies Manchuria.

December 9: Spain declares a republic, dissolves monarchy.

December 10: League of Nations approves Lytton Commission.

1932

January 7: United States declares Hoover-Stimson Doctrine against Japanese Manchurian occupation.

January 28: Japanese troops land in Shanghai.

February 2: Disarmament conference convenes at Geneva.

February 29: Britain imposes protective tariffs.

May 15: Japanese premier Ki Inukai assassinated, de facto military government established.

November 8: Franklin Roosevelt is elected president, John Garner is vice president.

References and Further Reading

Best, Gary Dean. *The Politics of American Individualism: Herbert Hoover in Transition, 1918–1921.* Westport, CT: Greenwood, 1975.

Burner, David. *Herbert Hoover: A Public Life.* New York: Alfred A. Knopf, 1979.

Costigliola, Frank. *Awkward Dominion: American Political, Economic and Cultural Relations With Europe, 1919–1933.* Ithaca, NY: Cornell University Press, 1985.

Fausold, Martin L. *The Presidency of Herbert C. Hoover.* Lawrence, KS: University Press of Kansas, 1985.

Iriye, Akira. *The Cambridge History of American Foreign Relations: Volume II1: The Globalizing of America, 1913–1945.* New York: Cambridge University Press, 1993.

O'Brien, Patrick G. *Herbert Hoover: A Bibliography.* Westport, CT: Greenwood Press, 1993.

Robinson, Edgar Eugene, and Vaughn Davis Bornet. *Herbert Hoover: President of the United States.* Stanford, CA: Stanford University Press, 1975.

Smith, Gene. *The Shattered Dream: Herbert Hoover and the Great Depression.* New York: McGraw-Hill Companies, 1984.

Smith, Richard Norton. *An Uncommon Man: The Triumph of Herbert Hoover.* New York: Simon and Schuster, 1984.

Wilson, Joan Hoff. *Herbert Hoover: Forgotten Progressive.* Boston: Little, Brown, 1975.

Franklin Delano Roosevelt (1933–1945)

Early Life and Political Career

On January 30, 1882, Franklin Delano Roosevelt was born into a life of privilege, the only son of Sara Delano Roosevelt and James Roosevelt. Franklin was not allowed to attend public school until he was fourteen. He was instead educated in the style of the privileged: by tutors and through extended trips to Europe. He was schooled for several years in Germany, where he became fluent in German. He subsequently submitted to the disciplined regimen of Groton Academy, where he successfully competed in debate, tried boxing, and strove to be among the best academically. At Harvard he did well in courses dealing with language, history, politics, and geography. He knew the world quite well; he had traveled broadly and was a serious stamp collector. He was also an avid reader of naval history, which stood him in good stead when he became undersecretary of the Navy and president.

He liked to present the image of a family background of service to the community, but this image certainly bore no relationship to the reality of his family. If that was a Roosevelt trait, it came from his cousin Theodore, whose career Franklin closely emulated. He told friends early on that he planned to become an assemblyman, assistant secretary of the Navy, and president like his Republican relative. During his college years, Franklin met and fell in love with a distant cousin, Eleanor Roosevelt, and in 1905 married her over the objections of his mother. Cousin Theodore himself, President of the United States, gave the bride away. Franklin learned from Eleanor a genuine concern for the less fortunate. This, and her determined support through his bout with polio, cultivated the convictions and fired the metal that later made him a great national leader.

He ran successfully for the New York state senate in 1910 and was appointed assistant secretary of the Navy by President Woodrow Wilson. He lost his race for vice president in 1920, but won the New York governorship in 1928 and 1930. Still, serious political reformers and intellectuals such as Francis Perkins and Walter Lippmann discounted Roosevelt's future, seeing him as a pleasant and ambitious, but not deep, fellow who aspired to office beyond his abilities. The assessment was accurate at that point in Roosevelt's life. What changed him fundamentally was his battle back from near death and seemingly permanent invalid status after he contracted polio in 1921 during a vacation at the family home on Campobello Island, New Brunswick. The

Franklin Delano Roosevelt was a pragmatic idealist who hated war yet waged it so successfully against Germany and Japan that the United States emerged from WWII the first among nations. *(Library of Congress)*

trial of the next two years in particular deepened his character. Confronted by the knowledge that he would never walk again without assistance, he faced the world with the unshakeable optimism that took him back into public office and later guided the nation through its own infirmities.

In 1928, Roosevelt began to show his new stature, winning the governorship of New York state and performing well as governor. There was a great battle for the Democratic Party nomination in 1932, as it was assumed that almost any Democrat could defeat Republican President Herbert Hoover, who was blamed for everything that went wrong during the Depression. The nomination was swung to Roosevelt by a man who later became his most bitter foe, William Randolph Hearst, who controlled the California delegation and the Hearst newspaper empire. Roosevelt was only able to gain Hearst's endorsement by publicly repudiating the League of Nations, insuring there would be no internationalist orientation of the platform in the election. Still, he managed to meet Hearst's demand without alienating the Wilson wing of the party by saying he no longer supported joining the League because it was not the League that Woodrow Wilson had envisioned.

While it may be true that any Democrat could have defeated Hoover in 1932, Roosevelt did so more easily than almost any one else could have. There were several reasons for this. Roosevelt, for one thing, had gained not only public sympathy, but admiration for his winning battle with the effects of polio. He also impressed the voters with his innovative style, beginning with his decision to fly to Chicago to accept the Democratic nomination instead of following precedent and waiting to be informed of it. Lastly, his attitude in overcoming, or at least ignoring, his handicap and his general good humor made him an attractive candidate.

The Perception of Threats, 1932–1933

Roosevelt's concern with foreign policy issues in the face of economic depression and the isolationist orientation of the nation and Congress resulted in part from his clear and far-sighted perception of threats to the national interest. Aggression was already underway in Asia by Japan, which invaded Manchuria in 1931 and was threatening China. Adolf Hitler's Nazi Party emerged as the largest in the Reichstag, and Hitler was consequently chosen by Hindenburg as chancellor on January 30, 1933. Intent on blocking Japanese expansionism in Asia and preventing a return to war in Europe caused by German revanchism, Roosevelt responded positively to Soviet feelers designed to reestablish normal diplomatic relations with Russia, which had been severed during the Bolshevik Revolution in 1918. He also explored British views on blocking Japanese access to international credit. The need to put pressure on the Japanese by such means was only increased when Japan, rejecting the condemnation of the seizure of Manchuria by the League of Nations, withdrew from the League in May of 1933.

Roosevelt's foreign policy was also a response to fundamental threats to security and prosperity from the absence of agreement on international stabilization of currencies and on forgiving war debts and reparations payments dating to the peace settlement of 1919. Roosevelt was beginning to appreciate that there was an essential linkage between international economic policy and trade and domestic recovery from the Great Depression. One of Roosevelt's efforts to confront the deflationary effects of the Great Depression was to abandon the gold standard (on April 19, 1933) as the sole basis of support for U.S. currency. He did so with the intent and result of devaluing the dollar overseas and thereby increasing the price of commodities, silver, and stocks. This action was alarming to the British and French, who hoped instead for an agreement on international stabilization of currencies. The London Economic Conference was convened in search of agreement to cooperate on currency stabilization and to deal with the crisis in international war debts and reparations payments, but it proved an abysmal failure.

Discovering the Limits of Diplomacy

On July 15, 1933, Germany, Italy, Britain, and France signed the Four Power Pact. Benito Mussolini initiated the discussions leading to this agreement, which signaled the end of the League of Nations. Mussolini did not like the influence exerted in the League by small nations, and the Pact was intended to work outside the framework of the League. Roosevelt thought the Pact was a step in the direction of promoting international cooperation on questions of economic crisis and arms limitation, but it had no real effect except to further the process of weakening the League.

The process accelerated when, on October 14, 1933, Germany announced that it would withdraw from the League as well as the Geneva Disarmament Conference. Hitler achieved an unexpected objective with this action, since Germany's rearmament program and the ultimate failure of the conference itself kept pressure on Britain and France. Roosevelt had believed that if the conference could succeed, it would provide a real relief of the economic problems facing not only the United States, but Britain and France as well.

Roosevelt carefully prepared the domestic ground for his initiative toward the Soviet Union, then made approaches to the Soviet commissar for foreign affairs, Maxim Litvinov, inviting him to come to the United States. He told Litvinov that among the motives for cooperation between the two nations, putting a curb on Germany was in the forefront. This was certainly a surprise to Litvinov, who, until his visit to the United States, had found little support for his campaign to confront the German menace. The new relationship between the two countries had little immediate impact in curbing Japan or Germany, but Roosevelt's ability to bring it about in the face of U.S. isolationism was still an achievement. There was some doubt about how effective the relationship would be in thwarting Japan's expansionist goals in the Far East; certainly, in the end, it served Soviet interests more directly than U.S. interests.

The Russians played the American card by confronting Japanese incursions along the Siberian border with Manchuria and by demanding compensation for the Russian-owned Chinese Eastern Railway there. The Japanese were convinced that there was a secret arrangement between the Russians and the Americans, which caused them to back down from overt aggression in Siberia. The impact on Germany was far less promising, as Nazi leaders were unimpressed by the resumption of formal Soviet-U.S. relations. Hopes that recognition would help alleviate the Depression by increased Soviet purchases in the United States also did not materialize.

Roosevelt turned to hemispheric affairs upon his inauguration, beginning, in his words, a new "policy of the good neighbor." His first success came at the Montevideo Conference on Intercontinental Affairs, which culminated in the agreement of December 26, 1933. The president was worried that too many concessions to the free-trade philosophy advocated by Secretary of State Cordell Hull might hinder domestic economic recovery, but Hull convinced him that trade agreements would be beneficial and that he could cultivate a new attitude toward the United States among Latin American leaders. After Hull's return to Washington, Roosevelt lauded the new approach, promising that the day of American direct intervention in Latin America was over.

Behind the initiative was a concern about possible foreign—especially German—footholds in the Western Hemisphere. The Depression had hit Latin economies hard, as normal markets for agricultural products in Europe dried up. Hitler tried to gain influence by promising to take up the slack if Germany received favorable treatment in reciprocity and influence. After some failed attempts at exerting economic controls, the U.S. answer was the creation of the Export-Import Bank. Acting under authority granted in the National Recovery Act and the Reconstruction Finance Corporation, the bank was established February 2, 1934, to finance foreign trade via short-term credits for agricultural exports and longer-term credits in support of manufactured products, plus loans to U.S. exporters where foreign credits were insufficient to match dollar obligations.

National recovery and national security were tied together in Roosevelt's support of the Naval Act of March 27, 1934. This act sought to bring the United States Navy up to treaty strength. Roosevelt tried to deal with two objectives at once, hoping that naval expansion would relieve unemployment and promote security through credible naval defense of the Western Hemisphere. The best evidence that a much larger navy might be needed came when the Japanese Foreign Office announced, on April 17, 1934, that Japan would pursue an exclusive sphere of influence in Asia. Cordell Hull responded by denouncing the new Japanese policy as a violation of existing treaties with other powers that guaranteed noninterference in trade and/or possessions. Roosevelt did not want direct confrontation at this juncture; he still had hopes of getting a continuing naval limitation arrangement at the Naval Conference which was to meet in London in 1935.

These hopes seemed doomed in advance when on December 26, 1934, Japan announced it was giving the required two-years notice that it would no longer abide by the agreement established by the Washington Naval Conference of 1922, which limited Japan to a fleet inferior to the United States and Great Britain. Washington and London went ahead with preparations for the 1935 conference without Japan.

Pessimism about events unfolding in Europe deepened as well. Hitler's first attempt to promote a Nazi coup in Vienna and then annex Austria to the "Third Reich" failed in July 1934. However, in a plebiscite held in January 1935, the Saar region voted overwhelmingly for reunion with Germany. In March, Hitler announced the expansion of the German army to thirty-six divisions. Italy and Yugoslavia joined Britain and France at a meeting in Stresa, Italy, and announced their collective opposition to Hitler's challenge to the Versailles Treaty system. Roosevelt wrote to Colonel Edward House, Wilson's old advisor, that he would consider supporting the "Stresa Front" powers if they announced an effective blockade of Germany. However, nothing came of the Stresa initiative.

Neutrality and Isolation

U.S. public and congressional opinion sought ways to ensure that the United States would not be drawn into a conflict in Europe or Asia. Where Roosevelt foresaw war and decided to enhance U.S. security by aiding the potential victims of Axis aggression, Congress responded by passing legislation aimed at keeping the United States neutral in any conflict. When Roosevelt and Secretary Hull sought congressional authorization to embargo trade with aggressors, Congress chose to hamstring their effort with an act to prohibit trade with *any* belligerent.

Mussolini ordered an Italian invasion of Ethiopia on October 3, 1935. The League again proved ineffective. The weakness of U.S. neutrality laws became instantly evident. As Ethiopia had no navy and few resources, prohibiting the purchase and delivery of military supplies only hurt the Ethiopian cause and did no harm to Italy, which could simply ignore the ineffective "moral" embargo called for by Roosevelt and Hull. Nevertheless, on October 5, Roosevelt embargoed delivery of war supplies to both belligerents, warning that any who traded with the warring parties did so at their own risk. Americans were also warned not to travel on belligerent ships, a provision of the Neutrality Act inserted in remembrance of the sinking of the *Lusitania* and other passenger liners prior to U.S. entry into World War I.

Roosevelt approached the London Naval Conference in December 1935 with two alternative outcomes in mind. If he could get Japan to agree to new limitations on its navy, he would be hailed as a successful statesman. If he failed, he would still get credit for trying to avoid a naval arms race, and he would also have a valid reason to augment U.S. defenses in the face of a potential foe. As expected, Japan resisted British and U.S. proposals to at least continue the limitations set forth in two previous conferences. A naval arms race was on. The problem was how much the United

States and Great Britain could afford to spend on naval expansion. They had to decide which ships were most needed to augment the best defense schemes. After the Japanese left the conference on January 15, 1936, the British, U.S., and French delegates signed a naval treaty on March 25, committing them to maintaining naval parity in coordination with whatever Japan did to increase the size and strength of its navy. Roosevelt was thus finally able to persuade Congress of the need to expand the Navy, even as it passed additional neutrality legislation in 1936 and 1937.

On March 7, 1936, Hitler sent German troops to occupy the Rhineland, a clear violation of the Treaty of Versailles. France called on Britain to join in forcing Hitler to withdraw. Britain and Italy joined France in protesting Hitler's action, but they refused a more forceful response, thus leaving France impotent to oppose Germany's move. The French government also appealed to Roosevelt. Given the isolationist mood of the country, the fact that it was in the midst of a reelection campaign, and British and Italian reluctance to take concrete steps, Roosevelt refused. He did approve Treasury Secretary of Henry Morgenthau's plan to punish Germany by leveling special duties on German imports subsidized by the Nazi government. Cordell Hull protested that this action would antagonize Germany, but Roosevelt countered that it was the least he could do to slow down German aggression.

When Italian troops occupied Addis Ababa on May 5, 1936, Mussolini announced that Ethiopia's annexation was complete. The League call for sanctions had proved impotent, effectively ending any possibility that the League could act to halt aggression. Meanwhile, Leon Blum became the new prime minister of France in the mid-year elections of 1936 as the leader of the left-of-center Popular Front, which campaigned on promises of internal social reform and opposition to the new German militarism.

The prospect for collective security in Europe was decisively dimmed by the response to the Spanish Civil War. Blum was at first determined to aid the Popular Front government in Spain against Franco's forces, which were backed by Germany and Italy. When, in July 1936, José Giral, prime minister of the Popular Front government in Madrid, requested aid from France against the military uprising led by Franco, Blum agreed to send aircraft and artillery. He came under pressure from British prime minister Stanley Baldwin and foreign secretary Anthony Eden, and from right-wing members of his own government, to alter this position. London urged restraint and offered only moral condemnation of the rebels and a strict neutrality policy, and France was forced to adopt a neutrality policy as well. When Hitler and Mussolini sent troops and military equipment to support Franco's forces and the Soviet Union sent massive aid to the Republic, the neutrality policy of all the democratic governments was in shambles.

Roosevelt's reelection in 1936 gave him new leeway in foreign policy. That he now had more room to maneuver could be seen in the provisions of the third Neutrality Act of May 1, 1937. The main change in the act extended the mandatory embargo provisions to civil conflicts when the president deemed arms exports might endanger or threaten the peace of the United States. The president could not get the discretionary powers he wanted in the application of neutrality, but he was able to get Congress to agree to a "cash-and-carry" provision in the new act. This provision allowed "other goods" besides arms to be purchased by belligerents if they paid cash, transferred ownership in advance, and carried them on their own vessels. It was designed to facilitate aid to Britain and France in case of a war with Germany or Italy, as they were the only countries with sufficient naval strength and carrying capacity to take advantage of this loophole.

Neville Chamberlain, British prime minister from May 28, 1937, believed that an accommodation with the dictators was possible. Whereas Roosevelt assumed from Hitler's rise to power that he was out to destroy democratic states, most British Conservatives thought Hitler and Mussolini boorish, but not beyond the limits of ordinary statesmen with whom they could strike a deal. Therefore, appeasement was the cornerstone of Chamberlain's diplomacy in Europe from the outset of his government.

At the time, the situation in the Far East was deteriorating even more rapidly. The war plans of Japan assumed that China was too weak to effectively protest the conquest of Manchuria and that war would come with the Soviet Union, not China. When the Chinese Nationalist government refused to recognize the conquest of Manchuria, it took only an "incident" to shift Japanese plans, making the Chinese the primary enemy. The incident occurred on July 7, 1937, when Japanese troops near the Marco Polo Bridge clashed with Chinese troops, who refused to move away from the area and permit the Japanese to enter the city of Wanping to search for a "missing" Japanese soldier. In response, the Japanese began artillery fire into the city, killing at least 200 Chinese. Over the next six weeks, as the conflict expanded, orders came from Tokyo to attack Nanjing, and an undeclared war was in progress in China.

Secretary of State Hull merely preached to other nations that they should follow the U.S. example of international good conduct. At a July 16 press conference he told reporters that the United States hoped to bring pressure on both conflicting powers to reach an amicable settlement and cease hostilities. In contrast, Roosevelt acted to aid China. A provision of the neutrality legislation allowed him discretionary powers to define when the law could be applied. He warned government shippers that they should not carry weapons to either belligerent and warned private shippers that they carried arms or other supplies at their own risk. As Japan was the only power with a shipping capacity that could blockade China, this approach in essence aided the Chinese by preventing material from flowing to Japan.

Roosevelt crossed the country giving a series of addresses more and more openly in favor of some action to block Japanese aggression. He had more than Japan in mind, as he was worried about the general disintegration of the peace in the face of mounting belligerence by Germany and Italy as well. As the reaction to his speeches seemed positive, he decided to call for a policy of "quarantining" aggressors as though they were the carriers of a contagious disease. It was not until some time later that he defined a quarantine to include blockading the ports of an aggressor nation.

The Japanese fired on both a U.S. and a British vessel on the Yangtze River December 12, 1937. Newspapers across the country and isolationist congressmen demanded that the United States withdraw its ships from area where conflict was in progress. The U.S. response was to demand an apology and indemnity from Japan to the survivors and the families of those who had been killed. The British, more accurately Foreign Secretary Anthony Eden, wanted joint action or even a naval demonstration, but the United States chose separate protest over joint response. It was nonetheless this incident that caused Roosevelt to seek coordinated naval plans with the British in case of a future war with either Germany or Japan.

On February 20, 1938, Hitler announced he would defend all German minorities outside the Reich. Konrad Henlein, leader of German nationalists in the Sudetenland region of Czechoslovakia, then put forth the Carlsbad Program calling for full equality and full autonomy for the Sudeten Germans. The Czech premier Milan Hodža rejected Henlein's demands. Henlein promptly declared that the only solution was for Sudetenland to be annexed to Germany, and the stage was set for confrontation between Prague and Berlin. Roosevelt and Hull initially resisted involvement and encouraged Britain and France to defend Czech sovereignty, as the isolationist climate in the United States prohibited anything more than an offer of moral support. After Hitler sent an ultimatum to the Czechs that they must surrender the Sudetenland by October 1, Roosevelt urged the European governments to continue searching for a negotiated settlement. When Hitler rejected the appeal, Roosevelt first asked Mussolini to exert his influence and then appealed directly to Hitler with a proposal for an international conference to deal with the Sudeten and "correlated" issues. The United States, however, was to assume no responsibility in the negotiations. Britain and France had already assured Hitler that, if he came to the conference table, they would agree to most of his demands.

Hitler, Mussolini, Chamberlain, and Premier Edouard Daladier of France met in Munich to discuss a settlement of the Czech crisis. The Czechs and the Soviets had a defensive alliance, which Litvinov claimed that Moscow would honor. The Soviets and the French also had a defensive alliance, which would come into effect if either was threatened by Germany. In theory, this meant that if France stood up to Germany, it could count on Soviet assistance against any German retaliatory action. The French government was inclined to accept this risk only if Britain joined them. The British cabinet met, considered the circumstances, and warned Paris that if France got in a war over the Czech crisis by angering Germany, it would be on its own. Only an unprovoked attack by Germany on France would lead to a British intervention. Meanwhile, the Poles made it clear that if the Soviets attempted to go to the aid of the Czechs through Polish territory, they would face the Polish army.

After Chamberlain returned from Munich holding up an agreement that had brought "peace in our time" by giving Hitler most of what he wanted—10,000 square miles of territory and 3,500,000 new citizens for the Third Reich—Roosevelt sent a telegram containing just two words: "good man." Privately he expressed his real reaction. He concluded that Chamberlain could not be trusted in any circumstance, and was prepared to accept peace with Germany at any price. He told his cabinet that rather than preserving peace, Chamberlain had instead sold out the Czechs.

Beginning with a press conference on April 20, 1938, Roosevelt tried to get Americans to understand that dangers to national security need not be directed against the United States itself. He maintained that the neutrality legislation had to be altered because it played into the hands of aggressors. The United States was obviously committed to defending the Philippines in the Pacific, but he also posed the prospect of a fascist power supporting a revolution in Mexico. America's defense perimeters, in other words, included the whole Western Hemisphere and all approaches to the United States. A reporter said that defending so huge an area would be an impossible task, to which Roosevelt responded that one would obviously have to defeat one enemy before taking on another. He thus began to state the case for his Europe-first strategy, at the same time advertising his plan for a two-ocean navy. In this fashion he gradually built public support for expanded defense spending, which in the next budget led to the largest peacetime expenditure for military equipment and support in U.S. history. When Roosevelt called for the production of 20,000 warplanes a year, military planners objected that he was placing too much emphasis in one area when others were equally needy. He acquiesced and cut aircraft production back to 6,000 planes, but held to the conviction that a future conflict would demand an unprecedented commitment to airpower.

Preparing for War across Two Oceans

In his State of the Union address of January 4, 1939, Roosevelt warned that the country could no longer believe it was safe from attack. As the democratic powers of the world were surrounded by dictatorships determined to destroy their freedoms, the United States could not ignore the accelerating erosion of the peace. He affirmed that the United States would stand against any attempt to harm a nation in the Western Hemisphere. He cautioned that the weapons of modern warfare were so advanced that the nation could not rely on arming itself only after war was declared. The new menaces required the United States to aid the victims of aggression, which in turn required amendments to the neutrality legislation. The same afternoon of this address he told those who attended his news conference that the needs of defense would require an expenditure of more than $1 billion in 1939 and $1.12 billion in 1940, mostly for new battleships.

On March 15,1939, Hitler charged that the Czechs were not living up to agreements about turning over German areas of population to the Reich and announced protectorates over Bohemia, Slovakia, and Moravia. Hungary and Poland then accelerated Czechoslovakia's dismemberment by annexing territories adjacent to their own borders. Chamberlain's statement that the Czechs would some day thank him for saving them for a better day came back to haunt him, as protests were registered and ignored concerning the promises Hitler had made to preserve the remainder of the Czech nation when the Sudeten region was annexed. The U.S. response came swiftly. The United States would not recognize the German occupation of Czechoslovakia, and Czech assets in the United States would be turned over to a government in exile. Unable to defeat both rebel forces and their German and Italian allies, meanwhile, the Spanish government surrendered to the rebels March 28, 1939.

On March 31, 1939, British and French leaders pledged to aid Poland in case of a German attack. Technically, this meant an end to appeasement. Some members of the British cabinet, including Foreign Secretary Lord Halifax, thought it was time to heal the breach with the Soviet Union, but Prime Minister Chamberlain thought the Soviets were at least as much of a menace to Britain and civilization as Hitler. The folly of the Chamberlain government was to make a commitment to defend Poland and yet refuse the offer of an alliance with the Soviet Union.

The U.S. fleet was on maneuvers in the Caribbean and at the New York World's Fair when Japan took over the Spratly Islands and Hainan in February and March of 1939 respectively. Roosevelt hoped to deter the Japanese by moving the fleet to a Hawaiian base from April 15, 1939, to implicitly support the Royal Navy in the Pacific. The occupation of Hainan off the Chinese coast was a matter of great concern to the British, as it enabled the Japanese navy to block the route to Singapore. On April 15, 1939, Roosevelt called on Hitler and Mussolini, demanding guarantees against an Axis attack on any of thirty-one "threatened" nations. Hitler lampooned Roosevelt's appeal in the Reichstag, where the assembled representatives roared with laughter as he repeated all the arguments the U.S. isolationists had used for years to show why Roosevelt should mind his own business.

Despite the arguments of Chamberlain and others—who saw the Soviet Union as a greater threat than Germany and were convinced that there was no danger of an agreement between the Soviets, who hated the Germans and Hitler—Roosevelt resisted all pressures to break with the Soviet Union. When Litvinov was removed as Soviet foreign minister and replaced by Vyacheslav Molotov, it was clear to informed observers that a major shift in Soviet policy would be forthcoming. On August 23, 1939, the Nazi-Soviet Pact was announced, stunning the world with the naked expediency of the two great ideological enemies. Roosevelt immediately came under even stronger pressure to sever relations with Moscow. He had no choice but to lump Stalin together with the "other dictators," a judgement about Stalin's aims in 1929 that has been justified by subsequent historical research and discoveries.

World War II

On September 1, 1939, German troops crossed the Polish border. On September 3, Britain and France declared war on Germany. Roosevelt had no choice but to declare that the neutrality acts were immediately in force. He flatly stated that, though he was required to declare formal legal neutrality, he had no intention of asking the American people to remain neutral in thought or sentiment. He also stated that he would seek revision of the neutrality laws to make it possible to aid victims of aggression.

Though he was faced with strong isolationist opposition, Roosevelt was able to persuade Congress that revision of the neutrality laws was imperative, and the new act passed in early November. Roosevelt argued during the debate that continuing to allow Britain and France to purchase surplus military equipment through the cash-and-carry provision and eliminating the arms embargo provisions would allow Britain and France to fight against forces that sought to destroy democracy. He enlisted notable Republicans in this campaign, such as former presidential candidate Alf Landon and his running mate Frank Knox, as well as Hoover's former secretary of state, Henry L. Stimson. The degree to which the mood of the Congress changed after the Nazi invasion of Poland was illustrated by the fact that the new act passed the Senate 63 to 30 and the House 243 to 18. The new bill lifted the arms embargo, designated areas where U.S. vessels should not go, and prohibited loans except short-term credits to belligerents.

In early October the Soviet Union demanded military bases on Finnish soil. In essence, yielding to this demand would have ceded the Karelian Isthmus portion of Finland to the Soviet Union. The Finns asked the United States to offer its good offices in getting the Soviets to withdraw this unreasonable demand. The Soviets refused the request on

October 11 and again on November 29 and invaded Finland on that date. The attack on the Finnish republic brought forth renewed demands for Roosevelt to sever relations with the Soviet Union, understanding that the main enemy remained Nazi Germany.

On April 9, 1940, Hitler made his next move. He simultaneously invaded Norway and Denmark. The Danes offered little resistance, and a brief struggle by the Norwegians was overcome by a combined German air and land assault, forcing Norway to capitulate. Hitler then launched attacks on the Netherlands, Belgium, and Luxembourg on the road to Paris on May 10, 1940. On that day, Winston Churchill replaced Neville Chamberlain as prime minister of Great Britain and the Western democracies together plunged into a fight for survival against the invading Germans. On May 16, 1940, Roosevelt asked Congress to finance production of 50,000 aircraft a year and upgrade the regular army to the tune of $1.18 billion. Congress actually appropriated $1.3 billion. Two weeks later he requested an increase. Congress voted a further $1.7 billion, expanded the regular army from 285,000 to 375,000 men, and gave Roosevelt authority to call up the National Guard. Emboldened by the changed political atmosphere, Roosevelt attacked the isolationists who had for years thwarted his campaign for military preparedness. At the University of Virginia commencement, he charged that isolationists had contended that the United States could be an island of sanity in a warring world, but that peoples suffering Nazi aggression would plead otherwise. The latest act of perfidy, he told his audience, was the Italian attack on Southern France, as Mussolini hastened not to "miss the bus" of Axis conquests.

Many observers, including the defeatist U.S. ambassador to Great Britain, Joseph P. Kennedy, concluded that with the surrender of France, Britain could not stand alone against Germany and Italy. Roosevelt, however, intended to give all-out aid to Britain. He ordered the Joint Army–Navy Board to assume Britain would survive the onslaught through the winter of 1940 and to alter American war plans to include an active alliance with Britain. On June 3 Roosevelt ordered that half of all U.S. production of military aircraft and munitions should go to Britain. He pushed Congress to appropriate funds for a two-ocean navy; on July 20, 1940, he received authorization to equip the navy with additional seven battleships, six heavy cruisers, 19 aircraft carriers, 60 cruisers, 150 destroyers, and 140 submarines. With these additions, the United States was to have the largest fleet in the world.

Roosevelt came under pressure from some congressmen to give comparable aid to China and to stop any shipment of essential materials to the Japanese. Henry Morgenthau was among those who wanted to aid China in any way possible, and on July 25 he encouraged the president to embargo shipments of oil and scrap metal. Hull and Undersecretary of State Sumner Welles argued that, since the Axis forces had won on the continent of Europe, it was not an appropriate time to provoke Japan to hostile action with a full embargo. They persuaded Roosevelt to impose only a partial embargo, but months later he changed his mind and ordered the cessation of shipments of all scrap iron and steel to any foreign power except Great Britain.

Toward an Atlantic Alliance

Churchill was desperate to get additional U.S. support, especially in thwarting the German submarine attacks against merchant shipping carrying vital war materials across the Atlantic. Churchill appealed to Roosevelt to give him destroyers to escort merchant convoys. Roosevelt came up with the idea of exchanging "over aged" destroyers for "crucial" British defensive bases in the Western Hemisphere. After carefully judging the public response as favorable to the bargain, he announced the destroyers-for-bases deal on September 3. The destroyers were not all that useful to the British, but the deal did what it was intended to do; it brought Anglo-American cooperation in the war effort closer to reality.

During August 1940, Roosevelt was reluctant to support any legislation for a military draft. He was in the midst of a reelection campaign against Wendell Wilkie, and he feared that open support for the draft would play into the hands of the isolationists. Yet when both a Republican isolationist senator and a conservative Democratic senator expressed support for the idea of selective service, he encouraged public debate of the issue. When Wilkie then came out for a draft on grounds of national defense, Roosevelt felt more comfortable in giving his support, though he was careful to base that support on the needs of national defense as well. On September 16, he signed the Selective Service Act into law to be operable for one year. Still, Wilkie charged that the president was consciously leading the nation to war. Democratic advisors urged the president to do something to counter this attack as Wilkie's ratings in the polls began to climb. The need to counter Wilkie led to the statement that was later to come back to haunt Roosevelt: In a speech given in Boston, he said that he had noted before and would say it "again, again, and again: your boys are not going to be sent into any foreign wars." The isolationists charged later that Roosevelt lied in these assurances. The truth is that he thought that the United States was going to be attacked, and if he led the country into war then, it would by definition not be a "foreign" war. Whether people believed Roosevelt or not, Wilkie won only 10 states and 82 out of 531 electoral votes, reflecting an apparently overwhelming approval of Roosevelt's leadership in a time of crisis.

While the cash-and-carry program proved effective in gaining congressional support, by the end of 1940, the British treasury was in serious trouble. Churchill knew he needed U.S. financial aid in addition to war material. Roosevelt's response came in a fireside chat (as Roosevelt called his radio talks) of December 29, 1940. He had already decided that new means of providing aid to Britain were necessary and approved the Lend-Lease Program; to build support for this extension of wartime credit to the British, he deployed the analogy of lending a fire hose to a neighbor whose house is on fire. He told the radio audience that if Britain burned down, the Western Hemisphere would be laid bare before antidemocratic forces bent on the destruction of everything Americans believed in. It was one of the most successful arguments he ever made.

On January 6, 1941, Roosevelt announced his intention to ask Congress to lend aid to all nations combating the Axis aggressors. He couched this appeal in idealistic terms, speaking of the need to defeat those who would destroy the basic freedoms of the democratic nations, which he defined as the freedom of speech, freedom of religion, freedom from want, and freedom from fear. After the speech, one of his first acts was to authorize the dispatch of U.S. officers as observers to lay the groundwork for subsequent military coordination. Staff meetings of U.S., British, and Canadian officers in Washington were arranged for later that month. By late March, a plan, ABC-1, marked Germany as the primary enemy and assumed changes in the Rainbow 5 Navy War Plan due to the aggressive moves Japan was making in the Pacific. In the event of a war in the Pacific, operations there were to be defensive until victory in Europe was assured. Congress began debating the Lend-Lease Act on January 10. Sponsors of the bill dubbed it H.R. 1776 (a new declaration of independence), but gave it the official name, "An Act to Further Promote the Defense of the United States and For Other Purposes." It authorized the president to dispose of defense materials to countries whose defense was deemed "vital to the defense of the United States" and authorized the president to decide if repayment would be in kind or property or any other thing he might deem appropriate. It passed Congress on March 1, authorizing initial expenditures of $7 billion. On May 6, Roosevelt added China to the nations authorized to receive Lend-Lease aid.

Hitler's invasion of the USSR on June 22, 1941, came as no surprise to the Americans or the Russian section of the British Foreign Office. The only person who seemed shocked was Josef Stalin, even though the Americans, the British, and his own secret agent in Japan, Richard Sorge, had warned him it was coming. One ironic result of Hitler's decision was that it persuaded Churchill, who had opposed an alliance with the Soviets during the earlier negotiations, to welcome them now with open arms as allies. On June 23, Secretary of State Welles told the press that aid to the Soviets was vital to defeat Germany and protect the Western Hemisphere. An agreement to provide aid under the Lend-Lease Act was not signed until June 11, 1942.

The Atlantic Charter

Roosevelt now sought close ties with Churchill. Both leaders felt that they needed to assure their own peoples and the rest of the world that the current war was being fought for higher goals than simply winning. They met on board a warship in Placentia Bay, Newfoundland, August 9–12, 1941. There they drafted the Atlantic Charter, a joint statement of principles that ultimately became the official foundation of Allied war objectives. The Charter pledged that there would be no territorial acquisitions at the expense of other peoples. It also reiterated a commitment to the national self-determination of peoples and the right of all peoples to choose their own governments. Roosevelt also wanted open trade and uninhibited access to raw materials for all peoples, but when Churchill countered that there were certain obligations the British had to the Commonwealth nations on preferential duties, Roosevelt compromised. Roosevelt especially wanted some wording guaranteeing basic human rights as he saw them, and so a statement was included that there should be freedom from want and fear. Churchill was persuaded to alter a traditional British reservation and guarantee freedom of the seas. Finally, they agreed on the establishment at the end of the war of a "permanent peace structure" and the disarmament of the aggressors.

On September 6, Roosevelt issued an order to the Navy patrols to "shoot on sight" any German submarine they encountered—this because a German submarine fired at the destroyer *Greer*. What he did not report was that the *Greer* was tracking and reporting to British aircraft the location of the submarine and had dropped depth charges trying to destroy it. On October 17, the destroyer *Kearny* went to the aid of a British convoy under attack and attempted to drop a depth charge on one of the U-boats, whereupon the U-boat fired three torpedoes—one of which hit the ship and killed eleven seamen. Roosevelt called it an unprovoked attack and said there was no question as to who had fired the first shot in this undeclared naval war. Congressional and public opinion began to swing behind the campaign to aid Britain and protect convoys when on October 20 a German submarine attacked the destroyer *Reuben James* doing escort duty on a convoy off Iceland. It was shortly after this that Hitler ordered his submarines to avoid firing at destroyers because it was difficult, from a U-boat, to distinguish between U.S. and British destroyers. He did not wish to give the U.S. president the cause Woodrow Wilson had had for taking the United States into the war against Germany in 1917.

The End of Neutrality

On November 6, Roosevelt announced that the Soviet Union was to be included in the Lend-Lease Program, after he was able to persuade Congress and the public that it was vital to U.S. security to keep the Soviet Union in the war. At this point, Roosevelt thought he had enough support to also ask Congress to end the restrictions of the Neutrality Act. Still, he was cautious in his approach, first appealing to Congress only to eliminate section 6 of the Act, forbidding the arming of U.S. merchant vessels. Secretary Hull told the Congress that sections 2 and 3 should go as well, the former preventing U.S. vessels from going to belligerent ports and the latter excluding U.S. merchant vessels from belligerent waters. When Congress came to vote on Roosevelt's request on November 17, it passed by a small (212–194) majority.

Meanwhile, U.S. code breakers informed the high command and the president that Japan was about to move aggressively in the Pacific. On November 27, all units in the Pacific were given notice that an "aggressive move by Japan is expected within the next few days" and that everyone should expect an attack. The best intelligence was that attacks would be directed against the Philippines, Thailand, the Kra Peninsula, or Borneo. Though he did not believe it would do any good, Roosevelt made one last appeal to avoid conflict in a message to Emperor Hirohito on December 6. The note said that the only way to ensure peace was for Japan to withdraw her troops from China and Indochina, so that negotiations could then follow. There was no answer from Japan until dawn of December 7, when Japanese aircraft bombed U.S. Navy warships, airfields, and supply facilities at Pearl Harbor in Hawaii.

The Japanese command planned and executed the attack brilliantly, but it blundered badly in the assumptions made regarding the U.S. response. Part of Japan's strategic plan was to cripple the U.S. fighting capacity so that Japan could gain the industrial resources from conquered areas, making up for deficiencies in oil and other commodities before the Americans could launch an effective counteroffensive.

This plan assumed not only the destruction of the battleships at Pearl Harbor but also of the vessels that could carry the war to Japan's home waters—the great fleet carriers. But the carriers were all out on maneuvers when the attack occurred and so escaped unharmed. In addition, Japan misjudged the public reaction to the attack. Pacifist and isolationist sentiments in the United States were immediately replaced by profound anger and a determination to retaliate. Hull and Roosevelt had received an intercepted message from Japan instructing Ambassador Nomura to meet with Hull at exactly 1 p.m. to announce the break in relations with the United States. The message did not say where the attack would take place and did not tell Nomura to declare war on the United States. Thus Nomura had no idea that the attack had already occurred when he met with Hull. When Nomura walked into Hull's office and presented him with a prepared text, Hull read the note and told Nomura that in fifty years of public service, he had "never seen a document that was more crowded with infamous falsehoods and distortions."

On December 8, President Roosevelt addressed Congress with his famous "day of infamy" speech, calling for acknowledgement that a state of war now existed with the Empire of Japan. He secured a congressional declaration of war against Japan with only one dissenting vote, that of the philosophical pacifist, Jeanette Rankin of Wyoming. Some advisors wanted Roosevelt to also declare war on Germany and Italy, but he thought it impolitic at the time. He was saved from the decision on December 11, when Hitler and Mussolini jointly declared war on the United States. On January 1, 1942, Roosevelt gave the name to the alliance of anti-Axis states: The United Nations. (In 1945, the victorious allies would lend this name to the new postwar international organization set up at the behest of Roosevelt.)

Winston Churchill and Roosevelt spent the period from December 21 to January 14 planning war strategy in a meeting called the Arcadia Conference. While Churchill thought of it as merely a meeting for war strategy, Roosevelt saw it as something more. He was concerned about U.S. reaction to simply fighting to win, so he asked for pledges to carry forth the principles enunciated in the Four Freedoms Declaration made to Congress on January 7, 1941. The Four Freedoms speech—the freedom of speech and expression, the freedom of religion, the freedom from want, the freedom from fear—was a succinct statement of the things Americans were prepared to fight for, and therefore of the principles the United States intended as the basis for a reconstitution of international relations after an Allied victory. Once Roosevelt received the pledges he sought, both he and Churchill then got down to the essential task of planning wartime strategy. First, Roosevelt had to pacify those in his military and political structure who wanted to focus on defeating Japan. The ABC-1 Plan underlay the emerging strategy, which meant a defensive war in the Pacific until the main European objective was achieved. What also emerged was a war council. There were disagreements over its composition and location, but Roosevelt held fast in insisting the center would be in Washington, D.C., and that, while there would be an Anglo-American partnership, the Americans would be the senior partners. An Anglo-American Combined Chiefs of Staff was established, as well as Boards for Production Assignments, Raw Materials, Munitions Allocations, Shipping, Production, Resources, and Food.

On February 19, 1942, Roosevelt authorized the relocation of 110,000 Japanese-Americans from the West Coast to internment camps inland. This action came partly as a result of the Army's expressed concern over what had happened in Hawaii, where U.S. intelligence reports contended, not without some evidence, that residents loyal to Japan had provided information that aided in the Pearl Harbor assault. It was also the result of long-standing local prejudices.

Roosevelt was worried that the Pearl Harbor attack and the series of Japanese successes that followed it would lower morale unless he could do something to illustrate that the war was being brought home to Japan. When he conceived the plan of attacking with land bombers, some people in the military command thought it too risky, but Lt. Colonel James H. Doolittle thought he could do it if he could select his own crew. Roosevelt gave his approval. Of the sixteen planes, all but one dropped their bombs on either designated or alternate targets, and all of those aimed at Tokyo made it. Roosevelt was exceptionally pleased when intercepted Japanese messages told of the shock, surprise, and chaos the raid caused. Most significant, the Doolittle raid immediately influenced Japanese strategy. Some Japanese leaders had been promoting an attack on Australia as a prelude to an assault on India and occupation of Madagascar, and perhaps linkage with the Germans at Suez, crushing the British Empire. But now planning shifted to an offensive against Midway Island, intended to draw out the American carriers and destroy them. The stage was thus set for the decisive Battle of Midway. When the Japanese then attacked Midway Island, they lost four fleet carriers against the U.S. loss of one fleet carrier and a destroyer. At a stroke, the U.S. Navy had permanently altered the balance of naval forces in the Pacific war.

Taking the Offensive

After much debate over where the contact between U.S. forces and the German army would come, Roosevelt finally acceded to Churchill's argument that an assault on North Africa was the safest approach and could tie down German forces in an area where they could not affect the war in Europe. In other words, it would take some pressure off the Soviets. Roosevelt ordered the go-ahead for the North African operation, code-named Torch. He was concerned about mounting pressure to focus on defeating Japan and wanted U.S. forces engaged against Germany as the first real step in Europe. He wrote Churchill that this was a turning point in the war, as they were now partners, shoulder-to-shoulder. Yet Roosevelt found it hard to argue with the strategy—adopted by Admiral King and supported by General Douglas MacArthur—of making selective assaults in the Pacific based on strategic locations. The idea was to begin moving toward Japan by "island hopping," and it used U.S. forces relatively sparingly, as Japanese outposts were bypassed and their supply lines cut off. One of the first operations was launched against Guadalcanal, which could be a staging area for missions against the Japanese home islands. The battle raged until the Japanese withdrew February 9, 1943.

Churchill wished to talk with Stalin directly about the second front which Stalin wanted opened in Western Europe, and which would be delayed by the adventure in North Africa and later, in Italy in 1943. The prime minister was concerned lest Stalin think the British were neglecting the needs of the Red Army. Averell Harriman represented Roosevelt at these meetings, where it was no easy task to persuade the ever-suspicious Stalin that an attack in North Africa could help the Soviets when the German army was deep in Russian territory. In fact, this proved to be the case.

Roosevelt and Churchill exchanged messages in December 1942 concerning a conference of the Big Three to determine the next stage of the war. They urged Stalin to attend, but he refused to leave Soviet territory during the last stages of the Stalingrad campaign, which played such a key role in destroying the myth of the invincibility of the German army. Stalin was convinced that Churchill and Roosevelt would seek from him an agreement that the attack on the mainland of Europe could not occur in 1943. The Americans were of two minds on this issue; General Marshall wanted an attack on France to take precedence over Churchill's proposed strike at the "soft underbelly" of Europe through Sicily and the Balkans. The shorter route across the Mediterranean, drawing German defenses in that direction, made sense to Roosevelt and only made Stalin more suspicious of the real intentions of his allies. The British were fearful that the U.S. efforts in the Pacific would draw resources from the European campaign, but Roosevelt assured Churchill at Casablanca that the way they were proceeding would keep Japan on the defensive. Admiral King and the Joint Chiefs of Staff persuaded the British that U.S. strategy was sound, and they promised no diversion of resources from the preparation for the attacks on Sicily, Italy, and the opening of the "second front" in France in 1944.

After Casablanca, Roosevelt sided with his military advisers in insisting that there be no diminution of the effort to build the forces needed for a frontal assault on the Continent, originally scheduled for May 1, 1944. Churchill finally received Roosevelt's grudging support for an Anglo-American invasion of Italy, but only after promising Marshall that a full-scale effort would proceed to gather the forces and equipment in Great Britain for the cross-channel invasion of France. At the first Quebec Conference in August 1943, Roosevelt again insisted on invading France at the earliest possible date, deflecting British efforts to delay.

Planning the Postwar International Order

At Cairo, in November 1934, Roosevelt assured nationalist Chinese leader Chiang Kai-shek that the United States would ensure that all territory Japan had seized since 1931 would be returned to China, including Manchuria. Roosevelt and Churchill were well aware that the Soviet Union needed a territorial incentive to enter the war against Japan; Chiang agreed that Sakhalin Island and the Kurile Island chain would be ceded to Russia, along with free access to the port at Dairen. These concessions were negotiated in the context of a delay of the planned Allied campaign in Burma until 1944. Thereafter, Churchill, Roosevelt, and Stalin finally met face to face in Tehran, from November 28 to December 7, 1943. Stalin accepted China as one of the "Big Four," but he proposed a division of post-war responsibilities that excluded China from decisions in Europe. Such a division was in keeping with Churchill's desire to have a regional arrangement among the victorious Great Powers instead of a single international security organization. Roosevelt realized that military facts on the ground would leave the Soviet Union in control of much of Eastern Europe. Still, he argued for the right of the Baltic republics to hold plebiscites on a return to the sovereign independence they enjoyed before their annexation by the Soviet Union under terms of the Nazi-Soviet Pact. Stalin asserted adamantly that plebiscites had already been held and that these republics would remain under Soviet control. The president and prime minister also asked Stalin to restore relations with the Polish government-in-exile in London, but no final agreement was made regarding the postwar status of Poland. Ultimately, Stalin refused recognition to the "London Poles" in favor of imposing the Communist "Lublin Poles," whom he completely controlled, as the government of postwar Poland.

The major decision taken at Tehran was to launch the invasion of Europe by the Western powers in 1944. Stalin wanted a specific commitment on the invasion of France and was reluctant to agree on other issues as long as Churchill seemed to be holding back on setting a firm date for the invasion. When Churchill finally consented to a spring invasion, Stalin agreed to discuss coordinating Soviet military operations to coincide with Operation Overlord, the official codename for the Allied invasion of Hitler's "Fortress Europe." He also promised Soviet entry into the war in the Pacific upon the defeat and surrender of Germany. Roosevelt was adamant about the establishment of an international security organization, and finally Stalin, and then Churchill, gave in on this demand, though without resolving key issues of structure and membership. Churchill insisted that Austria should be treated as the first victim of German aggression rather than the cradle of Nazism. His plan to have Allied zones of occupation in Austria prevailed, which probably saved Austria from Soviet control. Churchill and Roosevelt lamented Finland's decision to ally with Germany and agreed that Helsinki must make territorial concessions to the Soviet Union in the Karelian Peninsula. However, they insisted that Finland should not be annexed by the Soviet Union, which had attacked it in an unprovoked war of aggression during the "Winter War" of 1939–1940. The Soviets were determined that Germany should be occupied, pay heavy reparations, and never again pose a security threat to the Soviet Union; they also insisted that France had not made a sufficient contribution to Allied victory to warrant a role in the occupation of Germany. Roosevelt, deeply and personally antagonistic toward Free French leader Charles de Gaulle, was initially opposed to French participation in postwar occupation of Germany, but he was brought around to support

a role for France by Churchill. Germany would be divided administratively, but the Allies agreed that it should be considered a single political unit under their occupation and control. (There was no intent or decision to divide Germany politically or permanently; its eventual partition was a result of the early Cold War, rather than any wartime decision made by the Allied leaders.) Regarding Poland, Churchill and Stalin proposed that there should be a substantial shift of the Polish border in the west so that the Soviets could retain those parts of eastern Poland they had seized in 1939. Final discussions of Polish borders were left for future settlement at the Yalta Conference in 1945. Roosevelt and Churchill left Tehran believing they had moved the wartime alliance in the direction of a reasonable and reasoned postwar structure, in principle aligned with the ideals of the "Four Freedoms"; Stalin left knowing that he had confirmed, in principle, Allied acceptance of the coming *de facto* Soviet control of most of the non-Russian territories he coveted beyond the Soviet Unions prewar western borders.

At the Second Quebec Conference, September 16, 1944, Roosevelt and Churchill clarified their earlier agreement to divide Germany into occupation zones. Roosevelt initially supported a plan proposed by Secretary of Agriculture Henry Morgenthau to eliminate industrial production in Germany and turn the country into a pastoral nation incapable of waging a future industrialized war of aggression. However, Roosevelt abandoned this fanciful idea when it became clear that a pastoralized Germany would not only be unable to pay reparations, but would be dependent on American reconstruction aid and a drag on the postwar world economy. At this stage, Roosevelt's thinking vacillated between punishing Germany and rehabilitating it.

From August to October, 1944, representatives of the Big Four met at Dumbarton Oaks, a suburb of Washington, to draw up plans for an international organization. The U.S. delegation made a pitch for an organization concerned with both security and economic and social cooperation. The Soviets feared that such an organization would penetrate their buffer zone in Eastern Europe and expose their internal weaknesses. They argued that there should be a separate Security Council dominated by the Big Four. They also complained that if the British Empire was granted votes for the Commonwealth nations, the Soviet Union should have votes for all fifteen Soviet Socialist Republics. Roosevelt appealed directly to Stalin to put off the membership issue until the organization was established. The participants finally agreed there should be a General Assembly and a Secretariat for the new United Nations. They also agreed there should be a Security Council, but could not settle the matter of the veto powers of the Big Four.

On October 21, Roosevelt recalled General Joseph Stilwell from China, with the hope that his replacement might be better able to persuade Chiang to engage the

British prime minister Winston Churchill (left), U.S. president Franklin D. Roosevelt (center), and Soviet leader Josef Stalin (right) at the Yalta Conference in February 1945. (Franklin D. Roosevelt Library)

Japanese instead of building his army to fight the Communists. When Stilwell's replacement was equally unsuccessful, Roosevelt finally abandoned his long held hope that the Nationalist Chinese would play a major role in the defeat of Japan. Instead, he accepted that a bloody Allied invasion of the Japanese home islands would be necessary, and turned to Soviet entry into the Asian land war as a means of drawing off Japanese divisions, thereby limiting American casualties. In February 1945, Roosevelt, Stalin, and Churchill met at Yalta, the Soviet resort and port on the Black Sea. Churchill and Roosevelt were concerned that their stated opposition had not stopped the Soviets from recognizing the Soviet-created Lublin Committee ("Lublin Poles") as the legitimate government of Poland, following the severe dispute between Moscow and the "London Poles" recognized by Great Britain and the United States. Roosevelt's primary objective at Yalta was to finalize Allied commitments for the United Nations, as he proposed the

new postwar security organization be called, after the wartime alliance which founded it. Failure to participate in the League of Nations, he argued, had set the nation, and indeed the world, on course for the next war. Controversy continues among historians as to the degree to which Roosevelt suffered illusions about what the Soviet leader planned for the areas of Europe occupied by the Red Army. Critics maintain that Roosevelt failed to correctly gauge the character and intentions of Stalin's regime, while admirers argue that all he and Churchill could do was to get Moscow to agree to elections—a promise Stalin was likely to betray—and otherwise seek to ameliorate an inevitable Sovietization of Eastern Europe.

On Poland, Roosevelt got Stalin to accept expansion of the Lublin government to include democratic leaders from the London Poles and other Polish expatriates, but Stalin would not accept "equal" treatment of all these factions, insisting that the Lublin Poles be preeminent. Roosevelt was willing to accept border revisions ceding to the Soviet Union areas of eastern Poland in return for an expansion of Polish territory on the west, at Germany's expense. On the rest of Eastern Europe, he essentially had to accept a modified deal on "spheres of influence" that Churchill and Stalin had already adopted at a meeting in Moscow in October 1944, in which the British and Soviet leaders assigned percentages to each other's future levels of influence in various nations to be liberated from the Nazis. As for Germany, after some argument, Stalin said that the French could have an occupation zone only if the Americans or British wanted to share theirs with them. Additionally, the Soviets asked for $10 billion in reparations from Germany. It was decided to let the Allied Reparations Commission deal with the problem, with the instruction that reparations should not exceed $20 billion and that half should go to the Soviet Union, whose people and economy had suffered the most devastation during the war. In return for his promise to enter the war against Japan three months after Germany's formal surrender, Stalin wanted the restoration of what the Soviet Union lost to Japan at the end of the Russo-Japanese War in 1905. He was assured that he would receive all of Sakhalin Island, in addition to the Kuriles, Dairen, and Port Arthur, and restoration of the Manchurian Railway. There was no mention of Outer Mongolia, which the Red Army would in fact occupy later in the year. Another compromise concerned the voting arrangements within the U.N. Security Council. They finally agreed on a rotating membership for lesser powers on the Security Council, with permanent membership for the "Big Four," later supplemented by the addition of France. Roosevelt believed he had been successful at Yalta. The fact was that the Soviet Union already occupied Eastern Europe and East Germany; short of war, there was little Roosevelt and Churchill could do to free those territories from Soviet control. Thrusting the war-weary British and U.S. publics into a new conflict with their wartime ally seemed inconceivable.

Over the following months, the final horrific acts of World War II were played out. On February 14, 1945, U.S. and British bombers attacked Dresden, Germany, with firebombs, killing some 35,000 people. Strategic planners decided that the destruction of Japanese morale was absolutely essential to the termination of the war, so in March, similar destruction was visited upon Tokyo, in fire bombings by the USAF that killed 83,793 and injured 40,918. On February 19, 1945, the invasion of Iwo Jima, a small island 750 miles from Japan, began. Five weeks of extremely fierce fighting followed; 6,000 U.S. Marines died in this campaign against a fanatical defense that took the lives of nearly all the 21,000 Japanese defenders. On April 1, 1945, the Marines began the invasion of Okinawa. This was considered to be an important objective; air bases on Okinawa were only 325 miles from the main cities of Japan. The battle raged viciously, characterized by intensive flame throwing assaults on Japanese positions. The level of Japanese resistance played a role in later convincing President Truman to order the use of the atomic bomb.

Legacy

On April 12, 1945, Roosevelt wrote to Stalin to say that he hoped that when their armies met in Germany, it would be a prelude to the final disintegration of the Nazi armies. The message was not delivered until April 13, and in the intervening hours Roosevelt suffered a cerebral hemorrhage and died. Harry Truman, who had been largely ignored by Roosevelt (a major error of judgment, given the state of his health) where wartime decision-making was concerned, was virtually struck dumb by the weight of responsibility thrust upon him by the president's death. What he inherited was the immediate and pressing responsibility for ending the greatest conflict in history, a second major war still underway in Asia, and growing doubt about the future of the Soviet-U.S. relationship and hence the shape of the postwar peace. But he also inherited from Roosevelt a mighty pending victory over fascism and a level of power and influence, economic, political, cultural, and military, unprecedented in American or modern world history.

For those who admired his leadership, Roosevelt's legacy encouraged strong U.S. involvement in international affairs, an ongoing attempt to bring the rule of law into those affairs through the United Nations, but even more importantly, an abiding awareness that U.S. engagement and military and economic power were essential to preservation of world order, international security, and increasing prosperity and fairness.

Edward M. Bennett

Chronology

1933

January 30: Adolf Hitler becomes Chancellor of Germany.

February 24: Japan quits League of Nations.

April 19: United States abandons gold standard.

July 15: Britain, France, Germany, and Italy agree on Four Power Pact.

October 14: Germany quits League and Geneva Disarmament Conference.

November 17: United States and Soviet Union normalize relations.

1934

February 2: Export-Import Bank established.

March 27: Vinson Naval Act authorizes new ship and plane construction.

July 25: Attempted Nazi coup in Vienna fails.

December 29: Japan announces it will abandon 1922 Washington Naval Treaty.

1935

March 16: Hitler announces increase in size of German armed forces.

May 2: France and Soviet Union form defensive alliance.

May 16: Czechoslovakia and Soviet Union form defensive alliance.

June 18: Anglo-German Naval Agreement signed.

August 31: First Neutrality Act passes Congress.

October 3: Italy invades Ethiopia.

October 5: United States embargoes arms to Italy.

October 11: League of Nations sanctions Italy.

1936

January 15: Japan withdraws from London Naval Conference.

February 29: Second Neutrality Act passes Congress.

March 2: United States abolishes protectorate in Panama.

March 7: Germany denounces Treaty of Locarno, occupies Rhineland.

May 5: Italian conquest of Ethiopia completed.

June 5: Popular Front government elected in France.

July 17: Spanish Civil War begins.

September 25: United States, Britain, and France agree on currency stabilization.

October 25: Germany and Italy sign Anti-Comintern Pact.

November 3: Roosevelt reelected.

November 18: Germany and Italy recognize Franco regime in Spain.

November 25: Germany and Japan sign Anti-Comintern Pact.

December 23: Pan-American Peace Conference concludes.

1937

May 1: Third Neutrality Act passes Congress.

May 28: Neville Chamberlain becomes British prime minister, diplomacy of appeasement begins.

July 7: Japanese and Chinese troops clash at Marco Polo Bridge.

October 5: Roosevelt gives Quarantine Speech.

October 6: League of Nations condemns Japan for aggression in China.

December 12: U.S. gunboat *Panay* is sunk by Japanese aircraft; HMS *Ladybird* is also fired on.

December 23: Roosevelt orders naval staff talks with Britain.

1938

January 10: Ludlow Resolution passed by House.

March 13: Germany annexes Austria.

March 28: Japanese install puppet Chinese government in Nanjing.

April 16: Anglo-Italian Pact agreed.

May 17: Congress approves 20 percent increase in naval construction.

May 20: Britain and France back Czech government against Nazi secessionists.

September 12: Czech Crisis breaks out.

September 29: Anglo-French appeasement diplomacy at Munich Conference resolves Czech Crisis.

October 28: French Popular Front government collapses.

October 11: Roosevelt calls for production of 20,000 aircraft per year.

November 15: "Crystal Night" brings violent attacks on Jews all over Germany.

November 17: United States, Britain, and Canada sign Reciprocal Trade Agreements Pact.

1939

March 15: Germany declares protectorate over Bohemia, Moravia, and Slovakia.

March 28: Spanish Civil War ends with Franco victorious.

March 31: Britain and France pledge aid to Poland.

April 3: United States recognizes Nationalist Spain.

April 7: Italy invades Albania.

April 28: Germany denounces Anglo-German Naval Pact of 1935.

May 17: Britain announces proposal for independent Palestine.

August 23: Germany and Russia sign Non-Aggression Pact.

September 1: Germany invades Poland.

September 3: Britain and France declare war on Germany; World War II begins.

September 5: Roosevelt declares U.S. neutrality.

September 17: Soviet forces invade Eastern Poland.

November 4: Roosevelt signs Fourth Neutrality Act.

November 29: Soviet forces invade Finland.

1940

March 12: Finland accepts Soviet peace terms.

April 9: Germany invades Norway, occupies Denmark.

May 10: Germany invades Belgium, Luxemburg, and Netherlands.

May 10: Winston Churchill becomes British prime minister.

May 12: Germany invades France.

June 3: United States begins sale of surplus equipment to Allies.

June 17: France surrenders to Germany.

June 28: Alien Registration Act passed.

July 20: Roosevelt signs $4 billion Navy appropriation.

August 8: Battle of Britain begins.

August 18: United States and Canada sign Ogdensburg Agreement.

September 16: Roosevelt signs Selective Service and Training Act.

September 27: Japan signs tripartite pact with Germany and Italy.

November 5: Roosevelt is reelected a second time.

December 29: Roosevelt delivers "Arsenal of Democracy" speech.

1941

January 6: Roosevelt cites Four Freedoms in State of the Union speech.

March 11: Congress approves Lend-Lease Act.

April 9: United States and Denmark agree to U.S. bases in Greenland.

April 13: Japan and Soviet Union sign nonaggression pact.

May 6: Lend-Lease is extended to China.

May 27: Roosevelt announces unlimited national emergency.

June 22: Operation Barbarossa: Germany invades the Soviet Union.

July 26: United States freezes Japanese assets

August 12: Roosevelt and Churchill sign Atlantic Charter.

August 17: United States warns Japan against further aggression in Asia.

October 17: German U-boat attacks USS *Kearny.*

October 30: German U-boat attacks USS *Reuben James.*

November 6: Lend-Lease Program is extended to Soviet Union.

November 17: Neutrality Acts are repealed.

November 27: War warning is sent to U.S. forces in Pacific and Asia.

December 7: Japanese aircraft attack U.S. facilities at Pearl Harbor.

December 8: United States declares war on Japan.

December 10–25: Japanese forces attack the Philippines and occupy Guam, Wake Island, Hong Kong.

December 11: Germany and Italy declare war on United States.

1942

January 1: United Nations Declaration signed.

February 19: Roosevelt authorizes relocation and internment of Japanese Americans on the West Coast.

April 18: U.S. bombers attack Tokyo.

May 7: U.S. Navy wins Battle of the Coral Sea.

June 1: Roosevelt promises Moscow a second front by the end of 1942.

June 6: U.S. Navy wins Battle of Midway.

June 13: Office of Strategic Services (OSS) is established.

August 7: U.S. forces land at Guadalcanal.

September 13: Battle of Stalingrad begins.

November 8: Operation Torch: Anglo-American invasion of North Africa begins.

November 19: Soviet counteroffensive against Germany begins.

1943

January 24: Churchill, Roosevelt, Charles de Gaulle, and Henri Giraud meet at Casablanca Conference.

January 31: German forces surrender at Stalingrad.

May 13: Axis armies in North Africa surrender.

July 10: Anglo-American forces invade Sicily.

August 11–24: First Quebec Conference.

September 3–9: Anglo-American forces land in Italy.

November 7: Soviet forces retake Kiev.

November 22–26: Churchill, Roosevelt, and Chiang Kai-shek (Jiang Jieshi) meet at First Cairo Conference.

December 2–7: Tehran Conference of Churchill, Roosevelt, and Stalin.

December 6: Cairo Declaration.

1944

January 11: Anglo-American strategic bombing of Germany begins.

January 22: U.S. forces land at Anzio, Italy.

March 26: Soviet forces invade Romania.

June 6: Operation Overlord: U.S., British, and Canadian armies invade France in Normandy.

July 11: United States recognizes de Gaulle as leader of Free French.

July 2: Bretton Woods Conference establishes International Monetary Fund and World Bank.

August 15: Allied forces land in southern France.

September 12: U.S. forces enter Germany.

September 16: Second Quebec Conference.

October 7: Dumbarton Oaks Conference founds the United Nations Organization.

October 18: Second Moscow Conference ends.

October 20: U.S. forces invade the Philippines at Leyte Gulf.

November 7: Roosevelt reelected for a fourth term.

December 16–26: German army defeated in Battle of the Bulge.

1945

January 17: Soviet army captures Warsaw.

February 4–11: Churchill, Roosevelt, and Stalin meet at Yalta Conference.

February 14: RAF and USAF bomb Dresden.

March 9–10: USAF firebombs Tokyo.

March 17: U.S. Marines capture Iwo Jima.

April 12: President Roosevelt dies; Harry S. Truman sworn in as president.

References and Further Reading

Bennett, Edward M. *Franklin D. Roosevelt and the Search for Security: American-Soviet Relations, 1933–1939.* Wilmington, DE: Scholarly Resources, 1985.

Bennett, Edward M. *Franklin D. Roosevelt and the Search for Victory: American-Soviet Relations, 1939–1945.* Wilmington, DE: Scholarly Resources, 1990.

Bennett, Edward M. *Separated by a Common Language: Franklin Delano Roosevelt and Anglo-American Relations, 1933–1939: The Roosevelt-Chamberlain Rivalry.* Lincoln, NE: iUniverse, Inc. 2002.

Black, Conrad. *Franklin Delano Roosevelt: Champion of Freedom.* New York: Public Affairs Press, 2003.

Dallek, Robert. *Franklin D. Roosevelt and American Foreign Policy.* New York: Oxford University Press, 1979.

Goodwin, Doris Kearns. *No Ordinary Time: Franklin and Eleanor Roosevelt: The Home Front in World War II.* New York: Simon and Schuster, 1995.

Larrabee, Eric. *Commander in Chief: Franklin Delano Roosevelt, His Lieutenants and Their War.* New York: Harper and Row, 1987.

Miller, Nathan. *FDR: An Intimate History.* New York: Doubleday, 1983.

Morgan, Ted. *FDR: A Biography.* New York: Simon and Schuster, 1985.

Harry S. Truman (1945–1953)

Early Life and Political Career

Harry S. Truman was born on May 8, 1884 in Lamar, Missouri, the oldest of three children of John Anderson and Martha Ellen Young. The family moved to Independence, about 10 miles east of Kansas City, in 1890, drawn by both the economic opportunities and the excellent school system the growing railroad center provided. By then, young Harry had been diagnosed with severe myopia, and on entering first grade in 1892 he was fitted with thick eyeglasses whose fragility and high cost forced him to forego the roughhouse sports and activities other boys typically enjoyed. Truman found other outlets. His mother encouraged him to take piano lessons, and Harry showed considerable musical talent, practicing diligently and developing into an accomplished pianist whose love of classical music lasted his entire life. He also was an avid reader, his favorite subject being history, and took full advantage of the Independence public library. When Harry was twelve, his mother gave him a four-volume set of Charles F. Horne's *Great Men and Famous Women*, which he pored over with great care. Truman also enjoyed the books of fellow-Missourian Mark Twain. Although he received a sound education in Independence and was a good student—the best student among his classmates was Charlie Ross, later President Harry Truman's press secretary—Truman did not go to college because business reversals his father had suffered made further education unaffordable by the time Harry graduated from high school in 1901. Another college option was foreclosed when young Truman was unable to apply for admission to the United States Military Academy at West Point because of his poor eyesight.

Truman worked at a series of clerical jobs after high school before joining with his father in 1906 to run his grandmother's farm near the town of Grandview, about 20 miles from Kansas City. He would work on the 600-acre farm until World War I. Meanwhile, the year before, he had taken what turned out to be an important step when he enlisted in the Missouri National Guard, serving until 1911. The connections he made in the guard and later in the army played a crucial role in helping him start his political career. In 1908, Truman became a Mason and remained a member for the rest of his life.

When the United States entered World War I in 1917, Truman was thirty-three years old. He nonetheless took it as

Harry S. Truman was a pivotal president in U.S. foreign policy. Never short on courage and decisiveness, he ended WWII in the Pacific with nuclear weapons and later committed American policy to the containment of Soviet communism. (U.S. Army, courtesy Harry S. Truman Library)

his patriotic duty to serve and rejoined the National Guard. After his unit was mobilized into the regular army, Truman, by now a captain, was put in command of Battery D of the 129th Field Artillery. The unit fought on the front lines in France in several major battles during the last months of the war, and Truman, who as a boy had been told to avoid fights because of his expensive glasses, discovered not only that he had considerable physical courage under fire but that he was an able commander of men. His men deeply respected the officer they called "Captain Harry," and he maintained ties with them until the end of his life. He remained in the Army Reserve after the war, eventually rising to the rank of colonel. (Truman tried to return to active duty after the outbreak of World War II, by which time he was a senator, but was told by Army Chief of Staff General George C. Marshall that he was "too damn old.")

On returning home in 1919, Truman married Elizabeth (Bess) Wallace, his childhood sweetheart, whom he first met in Sunday school when he was six. The Trumans had one daughter, Margaret, who later would write biographies of both of her parents. Along with an army buddy, Truman opened a men's clothing store in Kansas City. The partners did well until the severe economic turndown of 1921–1922, when their business shared the fate of many others and failed. Because Truman was unwilling to declare bankruptcy, his business failure left him with debts that took him a decade to pay back. Meanwhile, in 1922, an army friend brought him to the attention of Thomas J. Pendergast, the boss of the Democratic Party political machine in Kansas City. Pendergast needed a candidate for judge of Jackson County, which included Independence as well as Kansas City. Despite the title, the position actually was not judicial but executive: Jackson County was administered by three judges, one of whom was the presiding judge. With the backing of the Pendergast machine, Truman was elected judge, representing the eastern part of the county in 1922 and, after a defeat for reelection in 1924, in 1926 and 1930 was elected to consecutive terms as the court's presiding judge. Truman was an honest and effective public servant. He worked hard to improve public services and was especially known for his role in securing funding for building a network of modern roads throughout the county. He became increasingly aware of the particular problems of disadvantaged groups among his constituents, including African Americans. This in turn fueled his belief that the government had to provide assistance for people who were in need through no fault of their own, and made him a strong supporter of the New Deal policies of the Roosevelt administration from 1933 onward. At the same time, while attempting to serve the people of Jackson County, Truman had to tolerate the corruption of others associated with the Pendergast machine, from his benefactor, Tom Pendergast, on down. This, historians agree, he managed to do without compromising himself.

Truman's political career took a giant step forward in 1934 when Pendergast once again found himself in need of a candidate, this time for one of Missouri's seats in the U.S. Senate. Truman was anxious to seek higher office. With the help of Pendergast's machine, he was elected, and in 1935, took office as Missouri's junior senator. The backing of a corrupt political machine had its downside, as some people in Washington uncharitably referred to Truman as the "senator from Pendergast." Still, during his first term he established a reputation as a hard worker, good colleague, and loyal New Dealer, playing a significant role in the passage of two major pieces of legislation: the Civil Aeronautics Act of 1938 and the Transportation Act of 1940. After surviving a hard-fought reelection campaign in 1940, Truman made his mark in the Senate, in the wider Washington political community, and nationally during his second term. The issue on which he focused was national defense. Following the thinking of Woodrow Wilson, a president he greatly admired, Truman strongly rejected isolationism and believed the United States had to play an active role in international affairs. He also believed that this was impossible unless the country had a strong military. At the same time, with both Europe and Asia already engulfed by World War II, Truman was concerned that the United States was not using its limited resources, and the people's tax dollars, to prepare its military forces as effectively as possible. In early 1941, the Senate, on his initiative, established a Special Committee to Investigate the National Defense Program. Under Truman's chairmanship, during the next several years the committee was credited with saving the country billions of dollars by ferreting out waste and inefficiency in various aspects of the war effort. As a result, in 1944 when Democratic Party leaders sought an alternative to Vice President Henry Wallace—who was viewed as too left-wing and lacking in practical political skills—they turned to Truman, who reluctantly agreed to what in effect was a smoke-filled-room draft. Roosevelt's reelection elevated Truman to the vice presidency in January 1945. He would serve in that office less than three months. On April 12, 1945, Franklin D. Roosevelt died and Harry S. Truman, who had never sought the office, became the thirty-third president of the United States.

The Roosevelt Legacy: A Winning Weapon and a Fraying Postwar Policy

A few days after taking office Truman reportedly commented, "I know nothing about foreign affairs, and I must acquaint myself with them at once." Whatever the accuracy of the first part of that statement, the urgency expressed in the second part was beyond question, as Truman became president at a time when extremely difficult foreign policy decisions had to be made and there was very little time to make them. The great immediate question of the era—the outcome of the war—had been decided: the Allies were going to triumph over both Germany in Europe and Japan in the Pacific. Indeed, by April 12, 1945, German resistance was collapsing, leaving the Nazis less than a month away from total defeat. Japan's position was hopeless, even as its leaders, blinded to reality by a fanatical nationalist faith, were preparing for a final, titanic battle to defend the Japanese home islands and save their emperor-worship system of government against an Allied assault expected to begin in the late fall. But many key questions about the postwar world remained unanswered. At the Yalta Conference in February 1945, in Roosevelt's last major foreign policy initiative, the United States, Britain, and the Soviet Union had formulated plans for the postwar division of Germany into occupation zones. They had reached partial agreement on the difficult issue of Poland's postwar borders and signed the "Declaration on Liberated Europe," which presumably mandated free elections and democratic governments in Eastern Europe. The uneasy partners—relations between the two Western capitalist democracies on the one hand and their totalitarian socialist partner on the other had been tense throughout the war—also had agreed that the Soviet Union would enter the war against Japan after Germany's defeat (in return for considerable territorial and economic concessions in the Far East) and settled some important issues regarding the formation of an international peacekeeping organization to be called the United Nations. But many details, large and small, had not been worked out, and in the Yalta agreements even more than in most international agreements, the devil was in the details.

In Europe, the most vexing of these details involved the ultimate disposition of Germany and the nature of the governments in Poland and the other countries of Eastern Europe that the fortunes of war were going to leave under Soviet military occupation. In Asia, the urgent first order of business was to bring about the final defeat of Japan. That was expected to entail invading Japan proper, with the United States bearing the primary burden of that invasion. Another undecided issue was precisely when the Soviet Union would enter the war against Japan. However, with regard to the war against Japan, there was a potential wild card in the deck of available options. Since 1941, the United States had been developing a top-secret weapon of unparalleled power, the atomic bomb, which had been intended for use against Nazi Germany but, it turned out, would not be ready before Germany's surrender. If the new weapon worked (and that question would not be answered until July 1945) the next questions were how and when—not if—it would be used. Given the growing intensity of Japanese resistance and the enormous casualties American forces were suffering as they approached Japan's home islands, America's top policy makers quite reasonably assumed that only a Japanese surrender could prevent the atomic bomb from becoming the latest new weapon developed during the war to be rushed into combat as soon as possible in order to secure victory.

The new president also carried the burden of securing a durable postwar peace. Throughout the war, President Roosevelt and his top advisors had assumed cooperative arrangements could be worked out with the Soviet Union to help manage postwar international affairs. Much of this cooperation was expected to take place under the auspices of the still-to-be-founded United Nations. But by the spring of 1945, as Moscow increasingly violated the Yalta agreements with a campaign of repression and intimidation against non-Communists in Eastern Europe, justifiable concerns about Soviet intentions and fears about Moscow's expansionism and power on the continent of Europe began

to erode those optimistic assumptions. Roosevelt was among those concerned with Soviet behavior and intentions. All of these problems, and more, now descended on Roosevelt's successor; no wonder the day after he was sworn in Truman told a group of reporters he felt as if "the moon, the stars, and all the planets had fallen on me."

Ending World War II

Truman came into office committed to continuing Roosevelt's policies, foreign as well as domestic, and during the remainder of 1945 that is what he tried to do. Like Roosevelt, the new president was a strong believer in the United Nations and understood full well the organization would be stillborn unless the Soviet Union participated in a constructive way. Truman also was aware of Roosevelt's hardening attitude toward the Soviet Union during the last weeks of his life, an attitude the new president shared. At the same time, Truman held Roosevelt's naïve confidence that he could deal with Soviet dictator Joseph Stalin by using personal diplomacy and by being a tough but fair bargainer willing to compromise as long as the other side demonstrated commensurate flexibility. Both Truman and James F. Byrnes, who became secretary of state in July, believed they could use the same methods of horse trading and compromise that had served them so well in the Senate in their dealings with Stalin. Their confidence turned out to have been misconceived. Once Germany surrendered on May 8, 1945, Stalin vigorously and ruthlessly worked to entrench Soviet power in areas occupied by his Red Army, and the Grand Alliance, bereft of the anti-Nazi glue that had held it together during the war, quickly began to fall apart.

Truman's first venture in dealing with the Soviets did not go well. In a meeting in late April 1945 with Foreign Minister Vyacheslav Molotov, who was on his way to the founding conference of the United Nations in San Francisco, Truman scolded his Soviet visitor in undiplomatically blunt language for Moscow's failure to adhere to the Yalta agreements in Eastern Europe. The president then quickly backtracked, however. At the end of May, he sent Harry Hopkins, one of his predecessor's closest confidants, to Moscow for a series of meetings with Stalin to make it clear to the Soviet dictator that Washington wanted to preserve the wartime alliance and was prepared to allow the Soviets considerable leeway in Eastern Europe in order to do so. That stance included recognizing the Soviet-installed, Communist-dominated government of Poland, once the Soviets made cosmetic changes by including a few non-Communists in the Warsaw cabinet, all of which was done by early July. Further, over British Prime Minister Winston Churchill's strong objections, Truman ordered American troops to withdraw from territory in central Germany that, under the Yalta agreements, belonged to the Soviet occupation zone in Germany (he also withdrew U.S. troops from

Czechoslovakia), a decision that duly was implemented in late June. For Truman, Soviet participation in the United Nations and Stalin's willingness to enter the war against Japan took precedence over how much territory Moscow controlled in Germany and Eastern Europe.

The Potsdam Conference

All of this was a prelude to getting together with Stalin and Churchill to deal with immediate postwar problems in Europe and ending the war against Japan. The meeting took place from July 17 to August 2 in the Berlin suburb of Potsdam. The conference began well enough. Truman was upbeat after his first meeting with Stalin, confident that he had made a good impression on the Soviet dictator and would be able to make satisfactory deals with him. By then, the president had received news that an atomic bomb had been successfully tested in the desert of New Mexico, although crucial details about the bomb's power were not yet available. Thereafter, matters became increasingly tense and acrimonious as the conferees differed on issues such as the German-Polish border, Stalin's demand for $10 billion in reparations from Germany, and freedom of navigation on European waterways. Important agreements nonetheless were reached, including on the matters of Poland's borders and the specific timing of Moscow's entry into the war against Japan. However, the acrimony of many of the discussions, the difficulties in reaching agreements, and the failure to settle several pressing issues made it clear that while the United States and Britain on the one hand and the Soviet Union on the other had avoided an open split, their Grand Alliance was crumbling.

The Potsdam Conference took place quite literally at the dawn of the atomic age. On July 21, five days after being informed that the atomic bomb had been tested successfully, Truman received details about its awesome power. It was welcome news; Washington's need for Soviet troops to fight Japan, while still important, was now less urgent, and Truman dealt with Stalin more assertively during subsequent negotiations. That, however, was as far as it went: there was no attempt at Potsdam to intimidate the Soviets into making concessions on any issue by brandishing the bomb. In fact, it was not specifically mentioned. The main American-British goal seems to have been to let Stalin know about the new weapon in an unthreatening way so as not to disrupt the ongoing negotiations, and at the same time to give him as little information about its revolutionary technology as possible. Therefore, at the close of business on July 24, Truman casually mentioned to Stalin that the United States had developed a weapon of "unusual destructive force." Unknown to Truman, this was no surprise to Stalin: Soviet spies had penetrated the Manhattan Project, as the program to develop the bomb was called, and had been providing Moscow with a steady stream of information about

the bomb's development. Stalin asked no questions, which puzzled Truman, replying instead that he hoped the weapon would be used against the Japanese. Two days later, the United States, Britain, and China (not the Soviet Union, which still officially was neutral in the Pacific War) issued the Potsdam Declaration, warning Tokyo to immediately surrender unconditionally or face "prompt and utter destruction." The Potsdam Declaration did not mention the atomic bomb, primarily because its shock value when used against a Japanese target was considered one of the key factors that hopefully would convince Tokyo to surrender on Allied terms.

The Bombing of Hiroshima

Indeed, aside from working out postwar arrangements regarding Europe with Stalin, Truman's other major concern at Potsdam was to finalize American plans for ending the war with Japan. He therefore was very pleased with Stalin's specific commitment to enter the Pacific War on August 15. That left the matter of when to use the bomb. The final decision to use atomic weapons against Japan is generally considered the most controversial of Truman's presidency. A reasonable examination of the situation the America's leaders faced in late July and early August 1945 makes it clear why that decision was made.

By the summer of 1945, Japan had been dealt a string of defeats in the Pacific. While Tokyo still had a formidable army of several million men to defend the home islands, its navy and air force had been almost completely destroyed. The home islands were subject to an effective blockade by the American Navy and their cities exposed to constant and destructive bombardment by U.S. B-29 bombers. Still, the Japanese had refused to surrender, even after a devastating firebomb raid on Tokyo in March destroyed almost 16 square miles of the city. By the summer, every sign pointed to a determination to fight to the bitter end. In particular, because the United States had broken the Japanese diplomatic code, Truman was privy to crucial top-secret communications, including those between Japan's foreign minister and Tokyo's ambassador to Moscow. These intelligence revelations, known as the MAGIC intercepts, clearly indicated not only that the military leaders who controlled the Japanese government were unwilling even to consider unconditional surrender—which had been official Allied policy since 1943—but that they would reject any terms minimally consistent with Allied war aims.

American intelligence also was reading Japanese military messages. These ULTRA intercepts revealed a massive military buildup on Kyushu, Japan's southernmost main island, precisely where American forces were planning to land when the invasion began on November 1, 1945. (The second stage of the American plan called for a landing near Tokyo in early 1946.) Evidence that emerged from Japanese documents and testimony after the war has confirmed the American judgment of the summer of 1945 that a Japanese surrender was not forthcoming and that, barring an unforeseen development, an invasion of the home islands would be necessary to end the war. Indeed, that judgment was confirmed two days after the Potsdam Declaration, when Japan's prime minister rejected the declaration at a news conference, using language that implied contempt as well as rejection. Ironically, the Potsdam Declaration, while formally demanding unconditional surrender, in fact included terms that mitigated that demand. For example, it guaranteed that the occupation of Japan would be temporary and that the Japanese people would be allowed to choose their own form of government, assurances that Germany, which was forced to surrender without any terms whatsoever, did not receive.

Inextricably linked to the projected invasion of Japan was the question of what the cost would be in American casualties. This was Truman's most important concern when on June 18, 1945 he met with his top civilian and military advisors to discuss the invasion. Although the president ended up approving the first stage of the invasion, he did so without obtaining specific estimates from his military commanders who were present, including General George C. Marshall, the Army chief of staff. Projections floating around Washington at the time varied greatly, ranging as high as 500,000 or more. In fact, it was one such high projection, albeit from a civilian source (former President Herbert Hoover), that had caused Truman to call the June 18 meeting in the first place. In any event, any internal projections the military made through June quickly became outdated as ULTRA intercepts during July and early August revealed that the Japanese buildup on Kyushu meant that invading Allied forces would face approximately twice as many Japanese troops as had been expected in mid-June. To this was added the reality of the horrendous casualties American troops had suffered fighting against the Japanese, especially between February and June 1945, in the battles of Iwo Jima and Okinawa, and Japan's deadly use during the Okinawa campaign of suicide kamikaze planes to attack U.S. naval vessels, a tactic that made Okinawa the most costly battle in the history of the United States Navy.

It was against this background that Truman gave the final authorization during the Potsdam Conference to use atomic bombs against Japan. In the end, it took two atomic bombs—one dropped on Hiroshima on August 6 and the other on Nagasaki on August 9—to convince the Japanese to surrender. Japan insisted on one condition on offering to surrender: that the emperor remain on his throne. That condition was accepted in Washington, although not without debate and with the important proviso that the emperor would be subject to the Allied commander in charge of the occupation. The Japan government, although not without a heated debate of its own, accepted the American terms

on August 14, and the formal surrender took place on September 2, finally ending World War II.

The Origins of Containment, 1945–1947

In negotiations with the Soviets prior to, during, and after the Potsdam Conference and in using the atomic bomb to end World War II, Truman essentially followed the foreign policy he inherited from Roosevelt. He expected to continue in Roosevelt's foreign policy footsteps after the war, an approach that included maintaining as much as possible a working relationship with the Soviet Union. The problem was this wartime hope ran up against the reality of postwar Soviet expansionism. Moscow was determined to control Eastern Europe, either directly or indirectly, depending on the country, and to expand its influence in Western Europe and in strategically important areas like the Middle East. As Foreign Minister Molotov, the man directly responsible for implementing Stalin's foreign policy at the time, recalled many years later, "My task as the minister of foreign affairs was to expand the borders of the Fatherland." He added with satisfaction, "And it seems that Stalin and I coped with this task quite well."

As these aims became clearer in Washington, relations with Moscow deteriorated quickly, becoming increasingly tense during the second half of 1945 and adversarial in 1946. Truman and his advisors had to reevaluate the new security threats the United States faced and formulate a totally new foreign policy to deal with them, a task made more complicated by the lingering uncertainty about Stalin's ultimate plans in Europe and grave doubts regarding the stability of the countries of Western Europe. That policy evolved over several years and came to be called *containment*. Albeit with tactical adjustments, containment remained Washington's foreign policy for the duration of the Cold War, the forty-five-year period of Soviet-American rivalry that followed World War II. It was the most important and durable initiative of the Truman administration and the one on which Truman's reputation as a president ultimately rests.

The policy of containment began to emerge, both in terms of actions and statements, during 1946. In January, after a series of frustrating foreign ministers' meetings, Truman informed Secretary of State Byrnes that he was "tired of babying the Soviets." The president demonstrated his new, tougher outlook shortly thereafter when the government of Iran went to the U.N. Security Council to protest the continued Soviet occupation of its northern provinces, a presence that violated a wartime treaty. Moscow was using its troops to promote a secessionist movement in northern Iran and to put pressure on Tehran for oil concessions. A strong American protest to Moscow and steady pressure from Washington brought about a Soviet withdrawal in May. The United States stood firm again when in the summer, Stalin, reiterating a complaint he had made at Yalta, demanded that Turkey grant the Soviet Union joint control of the Dardanelles, the straits that link the Black and Mediterranean seas. The demand immediately produced a serious Soviet-American confrontation. American officials saw this as the first step in a Soviet campaign to win naval bases in Turkey and possibly turn that country into a Soviet satellite. Truman responded by ordering a powerful naval task force built around the newly commissioned aircraft carrier *Franklin D. Roosevelt* to the area. By the fall of 1946, the Soviets had backed down and the crisis was over.

Meanwhile, the early months of 1946 echoed with harsh words from several quarters. In February, Stalin delivered a militant speech in which he stated that capitalism and communism were incompatible and that the Soviet Union therefore had to begin a military buildup. The speech unnerved many American officials, among them Supreme Court Justice William O. Douglas (one of the people party leaders had considered for the vice presidential spot on the Democratic ticket that ultimately went to Truman) who called Stalin's speech a declaration of World War III. The next salvo in the verbal war came from Winston Churchill, now a private British citizen after his party's electoral defeat the previous July. At Truman's invitation, Churchill came to Fulton, Missouri, in early March, where, with the president sitting just behind him on the speaker's platform, he issued a dramatic warning about Soviet expansionism that included the famous phrase "an iron curtain has descended across the Continent." Most important from an American policy perspective was an 8,000-word telegram written by George F. Kennan, the State Department's leading Soviet specialist, who was stationed in the American embassy in Moscow. Responding to a request from Washington for an analysis of Stalin's speech, Kennan's so-called Long Telegram painted a picture of a formidable and dangerous adversary. Kennan called the Soviet Union a police state, expansionist by its very nature, that needed foreign enemies to justify its harsh rule. Soviet expansionism and paranoia were rooted both in anticapitalist Marxist dogma dating from the Bolshevik Revolution of 1917 and in an older centuries-long Russian sense of insecurity. Kennan warned that the Soviet Union would continue its expansionist policies and try to undermine the capitalist states of Western Europe, activities that posed a serious threat to American security. While avoiding specific policy proposals, he argued that the Soviet Union was "impervious to the logic of reason" but "highly sensitive to the logic of force." The good news, and there was not much, was that the Soviet Union was considerably weaker than the United States and its allies which, if they maintained "cohesion, firmness, and vigor," could influence Moscow's behavior.

Kennan's Long Telegram quickly made the rounds among top administration officials. His analysis seemed to confirm what Truman and his advisors were seeing and thinking and to validate a tougher stand against the Soviets. In July 1947, revised and updated, the Long Telegram made its public debut in the journal *Foreign Affairs* as "Sources of Soviet Conduct" and included a policy recommendation: "a long-term, patient but firm and vigilant containment of Russian expansive tendencies." If implemented correctly, Kennan added, over time, containment would force the "break-up or the gradual mellowing of Soviet power."

The Truman Doctrine

By the time "Sources of Soviet Conduct" was published, the first building block of containment, the Truman Doctrine was already in place, largely because of a crisis in Greece. Greece, on the southern tip of the Balkan peninsula, actually was far from the epicenter of the Soviet-American confrontation in the center of Europe. Washington's urgent interest in Greece began in February 1947 when the British informed Truman and his new secretary of state, George Marshall, that they could no longer afford to support the conservative Greek government in its struggle against Communist guerrillas. The British, exhausted by their six-year-long war effort against Germany, also told Washington they could no longer supply Turkey, Greece's immediate neighbor to the east, with financial aid.

Truman and Marshall believed that without outside support, the Greek government would fall to the Communist insurgents, whose on-and-off efforts to seize control of Greece dated from 1943, when the country was still under German occupation. The Greek regime, to be sure, was corrupt and had limited public support. Its main virtue in the eyes of the West was that it was staunchly anti-communist. Washington feared that a Communist victory in Greece would destabilize France and Italy, whose Communist parties were very strong and potentially capable of coming to power via elections. Furthermore, a Communist takeover would permit the expansion of Soviet power into the Mediterranean region and thereby threaten the vital sea routes to the oil-rich Middle East. It also would destabilize Turkey and Iran, both of which bordered on the Soviet Union and formed a "northern tier" protecting the rest of the Middle East from Moscow's ambitions. In short, the Truman administration was convinced that the collapse of Greece would have serious and far-ranging implications damaging to American security.

Washington blamed Moscow for providing the outside aid that was essential to sustaining the Communist insurgency inside Greece. That assessment was not quite correct, but it was close enough. The main source of outside aid to the insurgency was coming from the Communist regime of Yugoslavia, which was led by Joseph Broz Tito, a loyal Stalin ally but also an independent actor able to follow his own agenda. Tito's desire to spread his power across the Balkan peninsula by supporting the Greek Communists was at odds with Stalin's agenda. In fact, Stalin was worried that direct support of the Greek insurgency might provoke a Western reaction that could threaten the Soviet position elsewhere in Eastern Europe. He therefore was at odds with his Yugoslav ally lest Tito's ambitions in the Balkans cause Moscow problems with the Western powers. That does not mean, however, that the Soviet Union did not help the Greek Communists. Instead, after World War II ended, Stalin played the role of cautious but alert opportunist, secretly providing limited aid via several Eastern European puppets. Moscow thereby avoided incriminating behavior while keeping alive the possibility that the Greek Communists might be able to come to power largely by their own efforts.

Truman's problem was how to respond. Demobilization left the United States with a skeleton force of inexperienced draftees in Europe, and the defense budget had been cut to the bone. The Republican-controlled Congress was loath to spend more money, especially if that meant raising taxes, to meet what Truman might consider new and urgent needs. The American public, just settling down to peacetime life after a long war, was reverting to its traditional isolationism and was uninterested in problems in Europe.

That public indifference helps to explain the intensity of Truman's speech to a joint session of Congress on March 12, 1947. He asked for $400 million in aid for Greece and Turkey, the latter country being included in the aid package because it had been the object of several Soviet threats since 1945. Truman told Congress and the American people that Greece and Turkey were just the tip of the iceberg: the real issue was the struggle between free and totalitarian societies. No democratic country, including the United States, could be safe in a world dominated by dictatorships. That is why the national interest demanded that the United States "support free peoples who are resisting attempted subjugation by armed minorities or outside pressures." This commitment became known as the Truman Doctrine.

The bill authorizing aid to Greece and Turkey was signed into law on May 15, 1947. For the first time in its history, the United States had become involved in the internal affairs of a European country in peacetime. This was an important step in the transformation of American foreign policy from one that was fundamentally isolationist to one that was fundamentally internationalist in its outlook.

The Truman Doctrine was crucial in turning the tide against the Communist insurgency in Greece. In early 1948 the firm American response convinced Stalin, as he told the Yugoslavs, that it was time to "fold up" the insurgency in Greece since the "balance of forces" was unfavorable to the Communist side and he did not want to risk a stronger American reaction that might jeopardize other Soviet interests. The Yugoslavs nonetheless continued to help their Greek comrades, and hard fighting continued for more than another year, but by the fall of 1949, the insurgency was defeated. Meanwhile, aid to Turkey, including training of 19,000

military personnel by 1950, greatly strengthened that country's armed forces, and correspondingly lessened the fears expressed in 1947 of a Soviet military invasion.

Initially, the Truman Doctrine amounted to much less than it suggested. Although Truman's wording in theory implied a worldwide commitment, that certainly was not his intent, as administration officials repeatedly stressed in congressional hearings. In practice, the program provided only piecemeal and limited assistance for two countries on the fringe of Europe. There were no funds, nor was there a coherent strategy, to provide meaningful support for the major countries of Western Europe, the key area of American concern abroad, much less any place further afield. Only additional and dramatically larger commitments could give a viable shape and structure to the new American policy that ultimately would be known as containment.

The Marshall Plan

It turned out those commitments were not long in coming. They were made in Western Europe, whose historical position as a leading center of industrial and military power, Washington policy makers agreed, made it vital to the national security of the United States. (In 1948, Kennan listed five such world power centers, two of which, Great Britain and Germany, were in Europe. The other three were the United States, the Soviet Union, and Japan.) The problem was that despite two years of peace and extensive American loans, the countries of Western Europe were not recovering from the devastation of the war. The bitterly cold winter of 1946–1947 had crippled the British economy, leaving millions unemployed, cold, and hungry. Conditions were no better in France and Italy, and far worse in the Western occupation zones in Germany, where economic hardship was driving people to desperation. The demoralization in Western Europe was creating ideal conditions for Communist propaganda; in France the Communist Party was winning one-fourth of the vote, in Italy one-third. In addition, the Europeans could no longer afford to buy American products, which boded ill for the U.S. economy.

The Truman administration's response was the European Recovery Program, better known as the Marshall Plan. The secretary of state announced the plan during a speech at Harvard University early in June of 1947. It called for the United States to give, not loan, the countries of Western Europe a large sum of money to help them rebuild their economies. Marshall did not specify what his plan would cost, but it was going to be expensive. The original European request, announced after a sixteen-nation conference in September, was $22 billion over four years, a staggering sum about 50 percent higher than the annual American defense budget at the time. Another controversial aspect of the Marshall Plan was its inclusion of Germany (that is, the western part under Allied control) because, as

Marshall and others stressed, Germany's industrial infrastructure and its critical place in Western Europe's overall economy meant there could be no European recovery without a German recovery. Congress therefore at first balked, even though Truman quickly lowered the funding request to just under $17 billion. It took a Soviet-sponsored coup in Czechoslovakia in February 1948, which overthrew that country's democratic government and replaced it with a Communist dictatorship, to sufficiently highlight the Soviet threat to Western Europe. Within a matter of weeks Britain, France, and the Benelux countries (Belgium, the Netherlands, and Luxembourg) signed a defensive military treaty called the Brussels Pact. At the end of March, Congress passed the Marshall Plan.

Between 1948 and 1952, the Marshall Plan's termination date, the United States provided more than $13 billion in aid to Western European countries, almost $12 billion in grants and the rest in loans, a sum equal to about $100 billion in 2005 dollars. Along with providing funds for reconstruction, machinery, and other needs, the Marshall Plan encouraged economic cooperation among the recipients. By 1952, Western Europe had completed a remarkable economic recovery. Industrial production exceeded its prewar levels by 40 percent, while agricultural production was 20 percent higher than before the war. Because the sixteen nations receiving help spent their aid to buy necessary goods from the United States, as required by the Marshall Plan regulations, and because Europe's recovery increased the ability of its people to purchase additional American products, the Marshall Plan also contributed to American economic growth and prosperity.

The Marshall Plan was an essential complement to and extension of the Truman Doctrine; as the president later put it, the two programs were "two halves of the same walnut." Although some historians have pointed out that Western Europe's recovery probably began before Marshall Plan aid started having its impact in mid-1948, it seems fair to say that the plan, at a minimum, played a central role in promoting and speeding that recovery and also was crucial in checking the growth of Communist influence in Western Europe. That certainly was the assessment of Ernest Bevin, Britain's foreign minister at the time, who called the plan "a lifeline to a sinking man." It may not quite have measured up to Winston Churchill's effusive assessment of being "the most unsordid act in history," but most Europeans at the time clearly appreciated America's generosity, and it arguably was the most successful American policy initiative of the Cold War.

The Berlin Blockade and the Formation of NATO

The Soviets reacted angrily and aggressively to the Marshall Plan, a stance that proved to be an important link in the chain of events that soon added a new dimension to containment: a military alliance called the North Atlantic Treaty Organization (NATO). Moscow's response actually grew out of a series of steps, foremost among them being the Marshall Plan that the United States and its European allies were taking on the continent. The Soviet Union wanted Western Europe to remain economically weak, inasmuch as a weak Europe strengthened the Soviet position on the continent. The Marshall Plan was a massive American commitment to make Western Europe economically strong. But there was more. A fundamental premise of Soviet foreign policy was to keep Germany weak. Yet the Western powers, led by the United States, were including Germany in the Marshall Plan and, in the wake of constant failures to reach agreement with Moscow about Germany's future as a whole, were taking steps toward combining their zones into a unified, economically powerful, non-communist state. Furthermore, by early 1948, Stalin was quarreling with Yugoslavia's Tito, who, unlike the other Communist leaders of the Soviet satellite states of Eastern Europe, had come to power on his own and therefore was an independent force. In June, that quarrel produced a split in the Communist world. Denounced by Stalin, Yugoslavia in effect defected from the Communist bloc and became one of the first avowedly neutral states in the intensifying Cold War. The split, to be sure, was the result of Stalin's blunders, but in his paranoid eyes real blame lay with the evil machinations of the United States.

Stalin reacted to all of this in several ways. He tightened his grip on the satellite states of Eastern Europe with a series of bloody purges. Further west, he ordered the French and Italian Communist parties to foment strikes and to undermine the economies of their countries. The Soviet dictator's main target, and therefore the scene of his most forceful countermove, was Germany. He did not want to see Germany—and the Western democracies controlled the industrial heartland and thus the most important part of that country—cast its lot with the Americans and the West. If Moscow could demonstrate to the Europeans that Washington would not stand firm under real pressure, the Germans might decide to rely less on the United States and cut the best deal they could with the Soviet Union. Discrediting American resolve also might weaken Western Europe's transatlantic ties.

Stalin's lever for forcing American influence out of Europe was the Berlin Blockade. Its purpose was to drive the United States, Britain, and France out of the city. The Western powers were vulnerable because Berlin, and therefore their occupation zones, was entirely surrounded by Soviet-controlled territory. On June 24, 1948, the Soviets banned all overland and river traffic into Berlin. They technically were within their rights, insofar as the Potsdam agreements did not guarantee the Western powers access routes to their zones in Berlin. Truman's response nonetheless was unequivocal: "We are going to stay, period," he told his advisors. The question was how to do so without using force and risking a war to reach the Western-controlled zones of Berlin. The answer was the remarkable Berlin Airlift, which for eleven months supplied a city of 2.5 million people with the necessities of life, from coal and machinery to blankets, eggs, and powdered milk. Unwilling himself to risk war by interfering with the West's massive air armada, Stalin finally lifted the blockade on May 12, 1949.

By then, from Moscow's point of view, the damage had been done. What the blockade made clear to leaders in Washington and Western Europe was that military security, and the stability only it could provide, was an unavoidable prerequisite for economic recovery. Actually, the insight that Western Europe needed military security in the face of a growing Soviet threat was not new. Europeans, and especially the British, had been pushing for Western military agreements to provide security against Moscow since 1947. Ernest Bevin, Britain's foreign minister, had taken a leading role in getting the United States to issue the Truman Doctrine. At virtually the same time, he had negotiated a mutual defense agreement, the Treaty of Dunkirk, between his country and France and, in March 1948, again played a pivotal role in negotiating the Brussels Pact, which added the Benelux countries to that European defense agreement. The outlook in London was shared in Paris. Indeed, the Soviet-sponsored Communist coup in Czechoslovakia, which had taken place the month before, had so unnerved the French that their foreign minister had called on the United States to join an anti-Soviet military alliance. For its part, the United States Senate, with strong White House backing, had officially endorsed the Brussels Pact and the establishment of similar defense agreements in the Vandenberg Resolution, which was named after Republican Senator Arthur H. Vandenberg, a leading supporter of a bipartisan foreign policy based on standing up to the Soviet threat.

The culmination of these developments was the establishment of the North Atlantic Treaty Organization (NATO), which came into being on April 4, 1949, even as negotiations to end the Berlin Blockade continued. The United States, Britain, France, Canada and eight other European countries were its charter members. They pledged to provide each other "continuous self-help and mutual aid" and affirmed that an attack against one "shall be considered an attack against them all." Within a few years, NATO had fifteen members, including the Federal Republic of Germany, which was formally set up as an independent state just days before the Berlin Blockade officially ended.

Despite opposition from isolationists, the Senate officially endorsed the NATO treaty on July 21, 1949. NATO was a landmark in several ways. It was a devastating defeat for Soviet policy in Europe. It promoted Western European economic and political integration. At the same time, it signaled the unnatural division of Europe as a whole into a democratic, capitalist west and a Communist east and was a major step in the institutionalization of the Cold War. NATO also marked a fundamental change in American foreign policy: for the first time in this nation's history, it entered a military alliance in peacetime. A country that since its founding had relied on two oceans for safety had concluded that in the modern world, Europe was now its first line of defense.

While the precise extent of Washington's contribution of soldiers and military resources to NATO still remained undetermined, after 1949 containment took on an increasingly military character. In addition, containment had become a multilateral enterprise, which in turn meant that the defense of the United States, contrary to the advice of George Washington, was inextricably intertwined with that of allies thousands of miles from its shores.

The Soviet Atomic Bomb, Communist Victory of China, and NSC-68.

Two other events in 1949 played major roles in the evolution of containment. On August 29, the Soviet Union tested its first atomic bomb, a development that shocked Washington and most of the American people. Suddenly the monopoly the United States had enjoyed in atomic weaponry was over years before most prognosticators had expected. (In fact, information from Klaus Fuchs and other Soviet spies probably speeded up Soviet development of an atomic bomb by about two years.) Meanwhile, another huge bomb, this one political, was going off in China, where Communist forces were about to complete their victory in a three-year civil war against the rival Nationalists. The United States had supported the Nationalists, at first in late 1945 and 1946 by trying to head off a civil war by bringing the two sides together in a coalition government, and then by providing military aid to the Nationalists. Altogether, between 1945 and 1949 Washington provided the Chinese Nationalists with about $3 billion in aid, most of which was squandered by a regime that was both hopelessly inept and thoroughly corrupt. By 1949 the Communists had won the civil war. Nationalist leader Chiang Kai-shek and the remnants of his regime found shelter on Taiwan, a large island about 110 miles from the mainland, while Communist leader Mao Zedong consolidated his control over the rest of the country. On October 1 Mao announced the founding of the People's Republic of China. In a stroke, about one-fourth of the world's population had moved into the Communist camp.

President Truman's response, in January 1950, was to order a reevaluation of America's defense posture. At the same time, in a meeting that lasted only seven minutes, Truman ordered a speedup of research on thermonuclear (fusion) weapons, or hydrogen bombs, which potentially were far more powerful—with explosive power measured in millions rather than thousands of tons of TNT—than Hiroshima-type fission bombs. Truman acted despite criticism from scientists and others who feared that such a decision would lead to a disastrous arms race with the Soviet Union, and quite possibly an apocalyptic nuclear war. In retrospect, Truman made the correct decision, since the Soviet Union already was well into the race, having made a commitment to developing a hydrogen bomb in 1946. By 1948—a year before its first successful test of a fission bomb—the Soviets had a basic design concept for a thermonuclear bomb, and priority research began in November 1949, only a few months after testing their first atomic bomb.

Several months after requesting the defense evaluation, Truman got his answer in the form of a top-secret document known as NSC-68 (National Security Council Paper Number 68). NSC-68 warned that the Soviet Union was relentlessly expansionistic and predicted that the future would bring "an indefinite period of tension and danger." The United States had to take a global view of its security needs and be prepared to respond to Soviet or Communist expansion anywhere in the world. In other words, containment should become a global policy. Because the Soviets now had atomic weapons, the United States would have to build more atomic bombs of its own and develop hydrogen bombs as well. NSC-68 also said the United States had to build up its conventional warfare capability. This, argued NSC-68, would reduce the danger of nuclear war because it would lessen America's reliance on atomic weapons in meeting a variety of Soviet threats or expansionist probes. The downside of the military buildup was that it would be very expensive. The State Department estimated that the NSC-68 recommendations would cost at least $35 billion and perhaps as much as $50 billion per year (an amount NSC-68 said the country could afford), compared to about $15 billion the Truman administration had been planning to spend annually in the coming years.

It was anybody's guess how the administration could convince Congress to foot that huge bill. However, on the Korean peninsula thousands of miles away from Washington events were about to unfold that soon would make most of the NSC-68 recommendations a reality.

The Korean War

The Korean War exploded out of a smoldering unsolved problem left over from the end of World War II. In September 1945, for the purpose of taking the surrender of occupying Japanese troops, the Korean peninsula was divided, supposedly temporarily, at the 38th parallel, with Soviet forces in the north and American forces in the south. However, the Soviets thwarted reunification by installing a Communist dictatorship headed by Kim Il-Sung. In the

south, American-sponsored elections in 1948 were won by Syngman Rhee, whose main virtue was his staunch anti-communism, rather than any commitment to democracy. American troops left Korea the next year. By then, the Truman administration, based on the president's assessment of what the country could afford, struggled to keep the American defense budget in the range of $13 to $14 billion despite increasing commitments and needs. This left important sections of the military establishment starved for resources and available forces were stretched dangerously thin. This lack of preparedness became all too clear when U.S. troops suddenly were called on to fight in 1950.

The Korean War began on June 25, 1950, when Kim Il-Sung's Soviet-equipped army invaded South Korea. Kim acted with direct Soviet support, mainly because Stalin did not believe the United States would intervene in a conflict in a country presumably not vital to American interests. Indeed, public statements by leading American officials during early 1950, including a speech by Secretary of State Dean Acheson, had placed the Korean peninsula outside of what those officials called America's defense perimeter. The Soviets were shocked when the United States, using the United Nations Security Council as its vehicle, reacted immediately and within days sent soldiers to bolster the crumbling South Korean defenses. But for Truman and his top advisors, a lot more was at stake than South Korea, especially in light of the appeasement that had preceded World War II in both Europe and Asia. They assumed, correctly, that the Soviet Union was behind the North Korean attack. They saw the attack on South Korea as a direct threat to Japan, just across the Korea Strait, and, perhaps even more important, as a test of America's resolve to defend its interests worldwide, from Asia to the Middle East to Europe. Indeed, the administration feared the entire principle of collective security as embodied by the United Nations was in jeopardy if the United States failed to respond forcefully and sufficiently to such overt aggression.

The president did not go to Congress for a declaration of war, a decision that generally is regarded as a serious mistake. American forces sent to defend South Korea, commanded by World War II hero General Douglas MacArthur, officially fought under the United Nations flag, that status coming from resolutions of the Security Council calling for the defense of South Korea. The stated U.N. goal was to repel the aggressors and restore the former border at the 38th parallel. At first, the war went badly; poorly equipped and trained American and South Korean forces retreated to the southeastern corner of the peninsula around the port of Pusan. There they made a successful stand until September, when MacArthur launched a brilliantly conceived counterattack behind North Korean lines at the port of Inchon. The North Korean army, caught in a vise, was defeated easily and fled north of the 38th parallel. At that point, the Truman

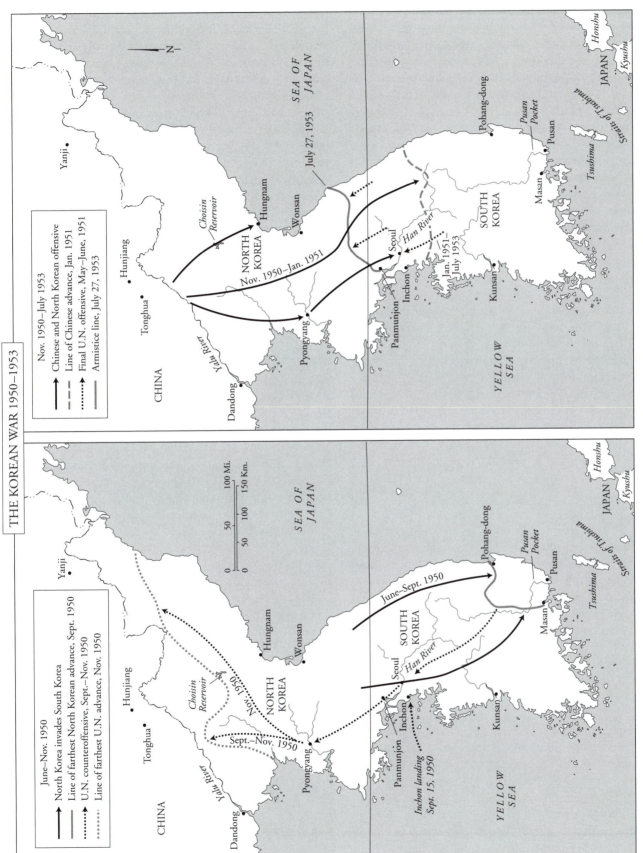

THE KOREAN WAR 1950–1953

Nov. 1950–July 1953

→ Chinese and North Korean offensive
– – – Line of Chinese advance, Jan. 1951
····· Final U.N. offensive, May–June, 1951
—— Armistice line, July 27, 1953

Yanji

CHINA

Tonghua

Hunjiang

Dandong

Yalu River

NORTH KOREA

Choisin Reservoir

Hungnam

Wonsan

Nov. 1950–Jan. 1951

Pyongyang

Panmunjon

Inchon

Seoul

Han River

Jan. 1951–July 1953

Kunsan

SOUTH KOREA

Masan

Pusan
Pusan Pocket

Pohang-dong

July 27, 1953

SEA OF JAPAN

YELLOW SEA

Straits of Tsushima

Tsushima

JAPAN

Honshu

Kyushu

June–Nov. 1950

→ North Korea invades South Korea
—— Line of farthest North Korean advance, Sept. 1950
····· U.N. counteroffensive, Sept.–Nov. 1950
········ Line of farthest U.N. advance, Nov. 1950

Yanji

CHINA

Tonghua

Hunjiang

Dandong

Yalu River

Nov. 1950

NORTH KOREA

Choisin Reservoir

Hungnam

Wonsan

Sept.–Nov. 1950

Pyongyang

Panmunjon

Inchon

Inchon landing Sept. 15, 1950

Seoul

Han River

SOUTH KOREA

June–Sept. 1950

Kunsan

Masan

Pusan
Pusan Pocket

Pohang-dong

SEA OF JAPAN

YELLOW SEA

Straits of Tsushima

Tsushima

JAPAN

Honshu

Kyushu

0   50   100 Mi.
0   50   100   150 Km.

The Korean War ended in a stalemate, but also intensified the Cold War generally. It did more than any single event to transform NATO from a loose alliance to a potent military pact committed to a forward defense of Western Europe.

administration made the fateful decision to expand the original war aims and cross the former border between the two Koreas to unify the country. Warnings that China would intervene were ignored, largely on MacArthur's assurances, with disastrous results. In late November the Chinese intervened with hundreds of thousands of troops, catching MacArthur flatfooted, and pushed U.N. forces back below the 38th parallel.

When China intervened, the Truman administration, worried that any expansion of the war or a direct attack on Chinese territory might bring the Soviet Union into the struggle, returned to the original limited aim of restoring the border between the two Koreas at the 38th parallel. At the same time, to avoid any confrontation that might bring Moscow into the war, U.N. forces were barred from direct attacks on Communist bases and supply routes located on Chinese territory. MacArthur was furious, and when he publicly disagreed with and then criticized administration policy in April 1951, Truman fired the popular general. While this further undermined Truman's sagging popularity at home, the president by his action reaffirmed the Constitutional principle that the military was subject to civilian authority: that civilian authorities, not the military, made and implemented foreign policy. Eventually, the fighting stabilized near the 38th parallel in a stalemate that lasted until an armistice finally was signed in July 1953, a half year after Truman left office. By then, the war, which cost more than 54,000 American lives, had led to an American military buildup that matched the recommendations contained in NSC-68.

Legacy

The Korean War badly tarnished Truman's second term. It was one of the main reasons for his extremely low popularity ratings—31 percent in January 1953—when he left office. Indeed, even before the Korean War Truman lived in the White House under the shadow of President Roosevelt, with whom he frequently was compared unfavorably. During his last year in office, Truman took some comfort that in the long run he might expect a more favorable judgment in the court of history than he was getting at the time from the American people. As he put it, "It isn't polls or public opinion alone of the moment that counts. It is right and wrong, and leadership." One noted writer of history at the time agreed, and he took the opportunity to tell that to Truman personally. Thus, in early 1952, Winston Churchill admitted that back in 1945 he had held Truman in "very low regard." That said, Churchill continued: "I misjudged you badly. Since then, you, more than any other man, have saved Western Civilization." And, indeed, over the years, judgments of the Missouri native who never sought the presidency have headed steadily upward. A decade after Truman left office, he was ranked as a "near-great" president, and

ninth best overall, in a poll of seventy-five professional historians, just below an elite group of five presidents—Lincoln, Washington, Franklin Roosevelt, Wilson, and Jefferson—who were rated as "great." By the time of his death in 1972, the so-called common and ordinary qualities that had made Truman an object of disrespect while in office had turned him into something of an American hero: a man who truly was one of the people, who had represented them honestly and well, and who symbolized America's ability to produce leaders, often from ordinary and modest backgrounds, capable of guiding this country through perilous times. In a number of polls of experts conducted over the next three decades, Truman consistently was ranked as between the seventh and ninth best president overall and just as consistently was found among the "near-great" presidents when that category was used to group them.

To some extent, that positive reassessment of Truman, both by the public and by professional historians, reflects his domestic efforts under what he called the Fair Deal to extend the social and economic reforms of Roosevelt's New Deal and to combat racial discrimination against African Americans and promote civil rights. It likewise derives in part from the understanding that he had the courage to do what he believed was right, even under difficult circumstances. A prime example is his support for the creation of the state of Israel, which took place under United Nations auspices in 1948. Truman supported Israel's establishment amid a storm of tumultuous international debate and then extended the new and insecure country diplomatic recognition in the face of strong domestic and foreign opposition and against the advice of several of his top diplomatic and military advisors, among them Secretary of State Marshall. In the end, the president was convinced that he had both done the right thing and acted in a manner consistent with American interests, as was his sworn duty.

Truman's reputation as president rests primarily on the continuing reevaluation of his foreign policy of containment. That evaluation has become increasingly positive for a variety of reasons, including the emergence of documents from the archives of the former Soviet Union confirming Moscow's expansionist designs in Europe after World War II, its intent to build thermonuclear weapons well before the United States decided to do the same, its crucial role in enabling North Korea to launch the Korean War, and the utterly brutal and murderous nature of the Soviet regime under Stalin. These recent revelations have added compelling new support to the thesis that the Cold War originated as a result of expansionist Soviet policies and was not simply a struggle for hegemony between two nuclear superpowers. Instead it was a contest between two opposing ways of life, one based on totalitarian socialism, which denies human beings their most basic freedoms, and the other on democratic capitalism, which, whatever its flaws, is based on the recognition of those freedoms. When viewed against that background, containment, notwithstanding its cost and the fact that its implementation involved many mistakes, including some by the Truman administration, emerges as a vital contribution to protecting the United States and the American way of life under difficult circumstances. Sam Rayburn, for many years the speaker of the House of Representatives and a Truman friend of long standing, reportedly once said that Harry Truman was "Right on all the big things, wrong on most of the little ones." Containment, it is fair to say, was one of those big things.

Chronology   *Michael Kort*

1945
April 25: San Francisco Conference of the United Nations convenes.

May 7: German Army signs unconditional surrender.

June 5: European Advisory Commission determines the division of Germany.

June 26: United Nations Charter is signed.

July 16–August 2: Churchill (then Attlee), Stalin, and Truman meet at Potsdam Conference.

August 6: United States drops atomic bomb on Hiroshima.

August 8: Soviet Union declares war on Japan.

August 9: United States drops atomic bomb on Nagasaki.

August 15: Japan surrenders unconditionally.

September 2: Ho Chi Minh declares Vietnam's independence from France.

November 14: The International Military Tribunal at Nuremberg begins.

November 17: U.S. efforts to mediate between Chinese Nationalists and Communists fail.

November 27: George Marshall begins mission to China.

1946
January 10: First session of UN convenes in London.

January 27: Local elections held in U.S. zone of Germany.

February 24: Juan Perón elected president of Argentina.

March 5: Churchill delivers "iron curtain" speech in Fulton, Missouri.

April 14: Chinese civil war reignites.

May 3: Gen. Clay stops Soviet reparations pillage of Western occupations zone of Germany.

June 3: Japanese war crimes trials begin.

July 1: United States conducts nuclear tests at Bikini Atoll.

July 4: Philippine's are given independence.

August 31: Britain and France agree to evacuate Syria.

October 1: Nuremberg Tribunal hands down verdicts.

October 13: French Fourth Republic established.

November 19: Soviet puppet government confirmed in Romania.

December 2: Britain and United States fuse occupation zones in Germany.

1947
January 29: United States abandons Chinese mediations.

March 12: President Truman declares Truman Doctrine in Congress.

May 25: George Kennan appointed Director of State Department's Policy Planning.

June 5: Secretary of State Marshall proposes economic aid for Europe.

July 26: National Security Act passes Congress.

August 15: India and Pakistan gain independence from Britain.

November 29: UN General Assembly approves plan to partition Palestine.

1948
February 25: Communist coup topples Benes˘ government in Czechoslovakia.

March 17: Treaty of Brussels signed, West European defense alliance formed.

March 20: Four-Power Council in Germany breaks up.

March 28: General Agreement on Tariffs and Trade (GATT) signed; International Trade Organization (ITO) created.

April 16: Organization for European Economic Cooperation (OEEC) formed.

May 2: Organization of American States (OAS) formed.

May 7: Congress of Europe convenes at The Hague.

May 14: The state of Israel is established.

June 24: Soviet Union blockades Berlin, United States Berlin airlift begins.

November 2: Truman reelected president.

December 9–10: UN adopts the Universal Declaration of Human Rights.

1949
April 4: North Atlantic Treaty Organization (NATO) is formed.

May 8: Federal Republic of Germany is constituted in Western zones of occupation.

May 11: Berlin blockade lifted by four-power accord.

May 15: Communists gain control of Hungarian government.

June 14: France installs Emperor Bao Dai in Vietnam.

July 16: Chinese Nationalist forces retreat to Formosa.

August 10: Department of Defense established.

August 22: Joint Chiefs of Staff sanction first-use of nuclear weapons.

August 29: Soviet Union tests its first nuclear weapon.

October 1: Mao Tse-tung proclaims the People's Republic of China.

October 7: German Democratic Republic established in Soviet occupation zone.

December 28: NSC48/1 cites Southeast Asia as a vital interest of the United States.

1950

January 12: Secretary of State Dean Acheson outlines perimeter strategy for Asia.

January 21: Alger Hiss convicted of perjury.

January 24: Klaus Fuchs confesses to espionage for the Soviet Union.

February 7: United States recognizes Bao Dai government in Vietnam.

February 9: Senator Joseph McCarthy charges that 205 Communists hold State Department positions.

April 14: NSC-68 recommends increased defense spending.

May 9: Schuman Plan proposes six-nation single market for European coal and steel.

June 5: Truman approves $3 billion for European Recovery Program.

June 25: North Korea invades South Korea.

September 15: U.S. forces land at Inchon, North Koreans thrown back.

October 7: UN passes resolution for unity of the Koreas.

November 26: Chinese Communist forces launch counteroffensive.

1951

April 5: Julius and Ethel Rosenberg sentenced to death.

April 10: President Truman dismisses General MacArthur.

May 2: West Germany joins Council of Europe.

May 4: United States and Iceland agree to NATO bases in Iceland.

July 8: Korean truce negotiations begin.

August 30: United States and Philippines sign mutual defense treaty.

September 8: United States and Japan sign mutual security treaty.

September 20: Greece and Turkey join NATO.

1952

February 2: Great Britain tests a nuclear weapon.

February 6: Elizabeth II is coronated Queen of the United Kingdom.

March 10: Batista military coup in Cuba.

May 27: European Defense Community (EDC) created.

July 1: Schuman Plan goes into effect.

November 5: Dwight D. Eisenhower is elected president, Richard M. Nixon is vice president.

References and Further Reading

Donovan, Robert J. *Tumultuous Years: The Presidency of Harry S. Truman.* New York: Norton, 1982.

Ferrell, Robert H. *Harry S. Truman: A Life.* Columbia, MO, and London: University of Missouri Press, 1995.

Ferrell, Robert H., ed. *Off the Record: The Private Papers of Harry S. Truman.* New York: Harper and Row, 1980.

Frank, Richard B. *Downfall: The End of the Imperial Japanese Empire.* New York: Random House, 1999.

Gaddis, John Lewis. *We Now Know: Rethinking Cold War History.* Oxford: Clarendon, 1997.

Hanby, Alonzo L. *Man of the People: A Life of Harry S. Truman.* New York and Oxford: Oxford University Press, 1995.

Jones, Randall B., and Howard Wood. *Dawning of the Cold War: The United States' Quest for Order.* Chicago: Ivan R. Dee, 1991.

Kirkendall, Richard S., ed. *The Truman Encyclopedia.* Boston: G. K. Hall, 1989.

Kuniholm, Bruce R. *The Origins of the Cold War in the Near East: Great Power Conflict and Diplomacy in Iran, Turkey, and Greece.* Princeton, NJ: Princeton University Press, 1980.

Leffler, Melvyn P. *The Specter of Communism: The United States and the Origins of the Cold War, 1917–1953.* New York: Hill and Wang, 1994.

Mastny, Vojtech. *The Cold War and Soviet Insecurity: The Stalin Years.* New York and Oxford: Oxford University Press, 1996.

McCullough, David. *Truman.* New York: Simon and Schuster, 1992.

Thomas, Hugh. *Armed Truce: The Beginnings of the Cold War, 1945–1946.* New York: Atheneum, 1987.

Truman Harry S. *Memoirs,* Vol. 1, *Year of Decisions.* Vol. 2, *Years of Trial and Hope.* Garden City, NY: Doubleday, 1955, 1956.

Dwight David Eisenhower (1953–1961)

Early Life and Military Career

Dwight David Eisenhower was born on October 14, 1890, in Denison, Texas. His family moved to Abilene, Kansas, the following year. A creamery there employed his stern father as an engineer. Eisenhower's mother was a devout Christian of pacifist orientation. She reared her six sons in a household imbued with biblical and New Testament commitments. Despite her abhorrence of war, she did not object to Eisenhower's winning an appointment to attend the United States Military Academy (West Point).

Eisenhower compiled a satisfactory record at West Point. He graduated in the middle of his 1915 class ("the class the stars fell on") with an army commission as second lieutenant in the infantry. He married Mamie Geneva Doud in July 1916. She gave birth to a son, Doud Dwight, in September 1917. He died of scarlet fever in January 1921. The grief stricken couple had a second son, John Sheldon Doud, born in August 1922.

Competence marked Eisenhower's early army resume, but showed no clear sign of future distinction. Eisenhower, to his chagrin, did not see military action in World War I. His wartime assignments were to stateside training camps. They included a tank school in Camp Colt, Pennsylvania, where he developed an appreciation for the offensive potential of armor.

Eisenhower's postwar career featured staff work rather than troop command. During 1922–1925, he served on the staff of General Fox Connor, presiding officer in the Panama Canal Zone. Eisenhower's stints as a student at the Command and General Staff School at Fort Leavenworth, Kansas (1925–1926) and the Army War College in Washington, D.C. (1927–1928), alternated with his assignments to the War Monuments Commission. They entailed his writing a guide to French battlefields where U.S. doughboys had fought in 1917–1918. More staff positions followed. These peaked in January 1933 with his posting as personal military assistant to the Army Chief of Staff, General Douglas MacArthur. Eisenhower chafed under this imperious and ambitious soldier but stayed with him, even through his Philippines career until late 1939. Eisenhower thereupon returned to the United States and took command of an infantry battalion at Fort Lewis, Washington. He then served as the Third Army's chief of staff in Fort Sam Houston, Texas. His impressive performance as coordinator in the Third Army's mammoth

Dwight David Eisenhower waged the Cold War at a lower human and financial cost. (Library of Congress)

Louisiana maneuvers of 1941 earned him notice in Washington, D.C. Only a colonel in that fateful year, Eisenhower's fortunes began to rise.

General George Marshall, Army chief of staff, directed Eisenhower to lead the War Plans Division in 1942 with the rank of major general. He was next named in June to command U.S. forces in Europe and sent to London. Promotions and broader responsibilities followed in rapid succession. Eisenhower had earned five stars by the war's end. He had organized the Allied landings in North Africa in November 1942 and was the senior Allied officer responsible for the triumphant cross-Channel invasion in June 1944. His charm, diplomatic skill, and unswerving dedication to mission and careful planning won him the confidence of Franklin Delano Roosevelt and Winston Churchill plus the cooperation of such prima donnas as General George Patton and Field Marshall Bernard Montgomery. President Harry Truman selected Eisenhower to be army chief of staff following the end of hostilities in 1945.

Approached by both Democrats and Republicans interested in having him run for president in 1948, Eisenhower demurred. He insisted that neither partisan affiliation nor political ambition was consistent with his army obligations or position as chief of staff. He served subsequently in 1948–1949 in two remarkably unlike positions: temporary head of the newly organized Joint Chiefs of Staff and president of venerable Columbia University. He subsequently was chosen to command and organize the military side of NATO and remained there until his retirement from the military in 1952. That same year, he accepted the Republican nomination for president. The war hero enjoyed a thumping victory over his rival, Adlai Stevenson, thereby ending the Democrats' White House incumbency of twenty years.

Containment

Eisenhower inherited the Cold War from a beleaguered Truman government. It relinquished power in the midst of a protracted, costly, and increasingly unpopular Korean War. Anti-Communist fundamentalists of the Joseph McCarthy ilk had, meanwhile, sparked widespread unease about the loyalty and integrity of administration officials, including the secretary of state, Dean Acheson. Acheson had, with other personages—including Truman, Marshall, James Forrestal, Paul Nitze, and George Kennan—built the U.S. side of the Cold War order, which obtained from 1946 to the collapse of European communism in 1989 and the 1991 implosion of Soviet power. American strategy as devised by the Truman government pivoted on the notion of containment. A somewhat loose concept, it was premised on the idea that Soviet influence—political and military—should not expand beyond the geographical limits reached by the Red Army in 1945. Ideally, Soviet control of Eastern Europe could be eroded; the several states therein ultimately dislodged from Moscow's grip.

The Marshall Plan, unveiled in 1947, and the founding of NATO in 1949 were key components of containment. They aimed to rehabilitate Western Europe as a political-economic entity and to protect against it purported Soviet ambition. Thus defined, containment as it was applied in Western Europe succeeded, evidenced by the area's mounting prosperity and stability in the early 1950s. But the Truman record in East Asia was highly susceptible to criticism. Communists came to power in China in 1949 after a grueling civil war that toppled America's wartime ally, Chiang Kai-shek. He and his battered forces took refuge on the island of Taiwan. Mao Zedong declared that revolutionary China would henceforth lean toward the USSR in its contest against U.S.-led imperialism. Observers on both sides of the ideological divide held that the balance of power in Asia had swung dramatically to Soviet advantage. That

same year Soviet scientists exploded an atomic bomb—well before many Western experts thought possible—and thus broke the U.S. monopoly on such weaponry. Next, in June 1950, North Korean forces launched a stunning offensive against South Korea, presumably with Sino-Soviet connivance, concluded Washington officials. American intervention, legitimized by UN endorsement and material support, saved the Seoul regime. Despite subsequent mastery at Inchon (September 1950) and invasion of North Korea, the U.S./UN forces under General MacArthur could not retain the offensive. By the time Eisenhower took the oath of president, the Korean fighting was locked in stalemate. Negotiations to resolve the conflict had become harrowing and inconclusive. The U.S. defense budget meanwhile soared. Additionally, the government had elected to accelerate the arms race by creating a new and more destructive thing, the hydrogen bomb.

Republican spokesmen during the hard fought 1952 election campaign—prominently John Foster Dulles—castigated containment as feckless and immoral. They hoped to replace it with dynamic "rollback" and "liberation" in Eastern Europe. Eisenhower also pledged that were he elected president that he would go to Korea, implying that he would somehow find a way out of the military impasse. President-elect Eisenhower did visit Korea in late November/early December 1952. The war, however, dragged on for another half year, until the armistice signing of July 1953 at Panmunjon.

Waging Cold War

Contrary to his fond hopes, Eisenhower had not ended the Cold War by the time he left office in 1961. The testing of enormous nuclear devices by the Soviets and Americans throughout the 1950s underscored this point. While popular anxieties intensified about a possible third world war, William Faulkner posed the question that rendered infinities of destruction meaningful: "When will I be blown up?" Still, Eisenhower did manage in his presidential tenure to prevent the Cold War from spiraling out of control, not a mean feat, especially when compared to the extravagant arms-building program and war fought by his predecessor.

Eisenhower's waging of the Cold War on the home front also had some merit. Regarding the odious McCarthy, the president decided not to dignify him by direct challenge. It would only elevate the senator's moral standing, casting him as a David to the presidential Goliath, and would risk offending the right wing of the GOP, whom Eisenhower could not afford to alienate. He chose to ignore the rascal and let his own antics bring about his downfall. The denouement came none too soon in the 1954 Army-McCarthy hearings. They were followed by the Senate's censure of McCarthy, ending his rampage but not before damaging the careers of many honorable people, including members of the Foreign Service.

The Cold War analysis that Eisenhower conveyed to Americans was not helped by his famously garbled syntax. According to critics, it reflected the qualities of a muddled mind. Yet, in fact, Eisenhower understood well the moral and material costs of the Cold War, on which subject he was twice eloquent. The first occasion arose soon after the death of Joseph Stalin and a demarche by his Kremlin survivors to review outstanding East-West problems. Eisenhower lamented the dangers of a continued Cold War in his speech, "The Chance for Peace" (April 6, 1953):

> The worst to be feared and the best to be expected can be simply stated.
>
> The worst is atomic war.
>
> The best would be this: a life of perpetual fear and tension; a burden of arms draining the wealth and the labor of all peoples; a wasting of strength that defies the American system or the Soviet system or any system to achieve true abundance and happiness for the peoples of this earth.
>
> Every gun that is made, every warship launched, every rocket fired signifies, in the final sense, a theft from those who hunger and are not fed, those who are cold and are not clothed.
>
> This world in arms is not spending money alone.
>
> It is spending the sweat of its laborers, the genius of its scientists, the hopes of its children.
>
> The cost of one modern heavy bomber is this: a modern brick school in more than 30 cities.
>
> It is two electric power plants, each serving a town of 60,000 population.
>
> It is two fine, fully equipped hospitals . . .
>
> We pay for a single fighter plane with a half million bushels of wheat.
>
> We pay for a single destroyer with new homes that could have housed more than 8,000 people . . .
>
> This is not a way of life at all, in any true sense. Under the cloud of threatening war, it is humanity hanging from a cross of iron.

Eisenhower made his second memorable statement on the Cold War in his Farewell Address (January 17, 1961). It reflected his concern about the harm inflicted on civil liberties by McCarthy, loyalty boards, and congressional investigating committees. He also expressed unhappiness with the distorting effects of heavy defense spending on the U.S.

economy. He concluded his warning against the untoward influence of a "military-industrial complex" and the threat to traditional freedoms posed by a garrison state with this hopefulness: "America knows that this world of ours, ever growing smaller, must avoid becoming a community of dreadful fear and hate, and be, instead, a proud confederation of mutual trust and respect."

In the eight-year interval between these two speeches, Eisenhower pursued a moderate foreign policy. It certainly did not inaugurate a new era of "mutual trust," but did resist the temptations of renewed isolation (exemplified by the Robert Taft wing of the GOP) and the thrill of crusade (per John Kennedy/Lyndon Johnson in Vietnam).

The USSR and Europe

Eisenhower and Secretary of State Dulles, one of the more capable foreign policy teams in U.S. history, tried to decrease the intensity of Cold War confrontation in Europe while not jeopardizing U.S./NATO positions of strength. To this end, Eisenhower took a number of steps. He proposed Atoms for Peace in December 1953 at the United Nations, a program to foster international cooperation in nuclear technology with applications for peaceful purposes. This modest attempt at arms control failed as Soviet leaders discerned defects in it, including encouragement of nuclear proliferation.

The July 1955 Geneva Conference was the site where Eisenhower launched his Open Skies scheme, a type of verification regime to monitor Soviet and U.S. missile/nuclear facilities. Each side would allow the other to conduct high level aerial surveillance. Nikita Khrushchev balked, lest the Americans discovered the paltriness of Soviet strategic forces and other vulnerabilities in the unevenly developed USSR. The conference itself—the first meeting since World War Two between top American and Soviet leaders—did not produce any resolution to outstanding East-West questions: divided Europe, Germany's future, arms race. Still, the tone of Soviet-U.S. relations improved slightly, palpable in the so-called spirit of Geneva. It proved short-lived.

The Hungarian uprising of October-November 1956 was crushed by Soviet armed forces lest the reformist regime of Imre Nagy succeed in establishing a society antithetical to proletarian rule and withdrawing his country from the Warsaw Pact. Eisenhower did not want to precipitate a third world war by authorizing U.S./NATO action on behalf of the Budapest resistance; he thereby gave the lie to earlier talk about "rollback" and "liberation." Washington officialdom was nevertheless appalled by Soviet severity and resultant carnage. In various forums, notably the United Nations, administration figures condemned Soviet brutality, which culminated in Nagy's incarceration (and later execution).

The October 1957 success of Sputnik heightened American anxiety about Moscow's intentions. Presumably, if the Soviets could send a missile into outer space, they could equip one with a nuclear warhead capable of striking U.S. territory or that of Washington's European allies. A year later Khrushchev increased tensions centered on Berlin when he issued an ultimatum to the Western occupying powers (Britain, France, United States): they should agree to the city becoming demilitarized and free. If not, he would permit East German authorities to assume control of all communication lines to the city's Western sector. The United States, meanwhile, rejected a Soviet proposal to ban permanently the testing of atomic bombs.

The gathering gloom caused by Hungary, Sputnik, Berlin, and the arms race was briefly dispelled in September 1959 when flamboyant Khrushchev made a whirlwind tour of the United States. His most important stop was at Camp David where he conferred with Eisenhower. Pundits hailed the meeting as signifying the start of a brighter era ("spirit of Camp David"). Plans afterward materialized for an East-West summit conference in Paris to be held in May 1960. This meeting collapsed in acrimony and embarrassed Eisenhower, however. The Soviets downed a U-2 spy plane as it traversed the USSR's airspace just days before the meeting convened. The president's failure to apologize allowed Khrushchev to condemn U.S. recklessness and then to dissolve the Paris conference. Not until after the November elections produced a new U.S. president, Khrushchev opined, would he have any chance of finding an authentic partner for negotiations.

Cold War in East Asia

Although Europe remained the cockpit of the Cold War, East Asia presented problems in abundance to Eisenhower. Singly or cumulatively, they could have led to a wide war. The Korean truce sprang from several sources. Important among them was uncertainty in the Kremlin, epitomized by the struggle for succession to Stalin's mantle. This awkwardness argued for relaxing international tensions, especially a Korean respite. The war, moreover, had exhausted China, whose forces may have suffered a million fatalities and distracted from Mao's urgent reconstruction programs. Finally, Eisenhower intimated that the United States would use atomic weapons against Chinese targets should Korean negotiations continue to sputter. Bereft of reliable Soviet support, burdened with mounting battlefield sacrifices, and threatened with possible devastation, the Sino-North Korean delegation agreed to an armistice.

Eisenhower did not hesitate after Korea to rattle America's nuclear sabers to impress Mao and did so with this conviction in mind: the Soviet Union would not risk a war with the United States for the sake of China. Dulles's massive retaliation doctrine, with its promise of responding instantly by means and places of American choosing, must also have undercut any Soviet enthusiasm for coming to

China's rescue against the militarily superior United States. Very likely, Eisenhower and Dulles felt, the Sino-Soviet alliance was riven by cracks that Moscow-Beijing refrains on socialist solidarity could not fix.

Skirmishing between Mao's China and Chiang's Taiwan over the offshore islands—Quemoy and Matsu—occurred in 1954–1955 and in 1958. On both occasions, the administration communicated, indirectly and subtly but with chilling clarity, that the United States would in extremis use nuclear weapons to preserve Taiwan's security. As predicted, the Soviets did not hurry to China's side or otherwise indicate a willingness to bolster Mao in emergency. Consequently, in 1955 and 1958, the Chinese backed down from confrontation with the United States and Taiwan, themselves bound in a defense pact, solemnized December 1954.

The crumbling of France's Southeast Asian empire occasioned Eisenhower's other Far Eastern problem. Despite the pleas of Paris, Eisenhower chose not to deploy U.S. soldiers or bombers to relieve French forces under siege at Dien Bien Phu in May 1954. He instead confirmed via Dulles—at the July Geneva conference—the end of French rule in Indochina and allowed for the independence of Laos and Cambodia. As for Vietnam, it was divided at the 17th parallel between a Communist north and a Nationalist south. An internationally supervised election was scheduled for 1956, but never took place. South Vietnam became an American client and recipient of material and other support during the remaining years of Eisenhower's presidency. Determined not to dispatch large numbers of troops to the Asian mainland, Eisenhower nevertheless invested U.S. prestige and aid in South Vietnam. He warned that its succumbing to communism would trigger the failure of pro-Western governments throughout Asia (domino theory). This prospect of Sino-Soviet expansion later misled Kennedy and Johnson into thinking that vital U.S. interests were at stake in Vietnam, an impoverished country unconnected to the world balance of power.

Cold War in the Middle East

Three dramatic episodes punctuated Eisenhower's Middle Eastern policy. These involved Iran in August 1953, Suez in October-November 1956, Lebanon in July 1958. Eisenhower authorized the CIA to help create turmoil—in tandem with British intelligence operatives—in Iran. The CIA's aim was to undermine the regime of Prime Minister Mohammed Mossadegh. He had nationalized the Anglo-Iranian Oil Company in 1951, and afterward acted to reduce the power of the Shah, Mohammed Reza Pahlavi. The Iranian army and police forces mounted a coup against Mossadegh. They restored the Shah to full power. Very likely the coup would have failed in the absence of covert CIA support. American policy benefited in the short-term from the Shah's restoration. He brought Iran into the pro-Western Baghdad Pact in 1955. A secularist and modernizer, he made Iran into a regional power and a reliable ally of the United States. But nationalist, militant, and religiously motivated Iranians—of the kind that swept Ayatollah Khomeini to power in 1979—never forgave the overthrow of Mossadegh and they loathed the Shah's U.S. ties. Eisenhower acquired, through CIA action, an advantage for the West in a crucial and volatile part of the world, but he also sowed the seeds for future Iranian-U.S. suspicion and estrangement.

The Suez crisis began in late July 1956, when Egypt's President Gamal Abdel Nasser nationalized the canal to the dismay of Anglo-French stockholders. He hoped to use revenues generated by canal traffic to finance the ambitious Aswan dam project. In league with Israel, Anglo-French forces attacked Egypt in late October with the aim of recovering control of Suez and its operations. Israeli forces concentrated on capturing the Gaza strip and Sinai. Khrushchev responded with threats to expel the Anglo-French-Israeli invasion by direct force, which, he suggested, might entail nuclear attacks on British and French cities. He also made preparations to send Red Army units to Suez to assist his Egyptian ally.

The Western/Israeli war on Egypt infuriated Eisenhower. The allies had not given Washington advance notice of their plans. This regional conflict could also have quickly expanded into a broader war. The invasion, moreover, seemed likely to push Egypt (and perhaps other Arab or Muslim countries) into the Soviets' orbit. Finally, canal fighting deflected world attention from the Hungarian drama and seemed to confirm anew that colonialist reflexes still dominated Western thought. Even while he prepared to counter a Soviet move into the Suez area with U.S. forces, Eisenhower publicly condemned the Anglo-French-Israeli governments. He pressed them to suspend military operations against Egypt. At the United Nations, the Soviet delegation joined the American in excoriating the invaders, a remarkable and rare instance of Moscow-Washington cooperation. Under U.S. pressure, the Anglo-French powers withdrew their forces in November; the Israelis did likewise, though they delayed in Sinai until 1957.

In London, Anthony Eden's government fell soon after the Suez crisis. Frenchmen, Charles de Gaulle among them, concluded that the American guarantee was not worth much and contemplated the desirability of loosening Paris's ties to Washington-dominated NATO. In the meantime, Eisenhower's siding with the underdog did not pay high dividends to the United States. Rather, the action of two of its closest allies was read in Egypt as further evidence of Western enmity; the differences between London and Paris on the one hand versus Washington on the other were presumably ones of degree not of kind. Egypt continued to drift away from the West, despite Eisenhower's strenuous efforts, and became increasingly receptive to Soviet blandishments.

However censorious of Anglo-French misdeeds in Egypt, Eisenhower was not restrained in employing stiff measures for U.S. purposes in the Middle East. Under cover of the so-called Eisenhower Doctrine, which pledged aid to victims of Soviet (or other) aggression in the Middle East, he sent Marines to Lebanon to shore up the weakening position of President Camile Chamoun. This Christian leader and his party were under pressure from Islamists, allegedly backed by the United Arab Republic (Egypt plus Syria and Yemen). Behind it loomed Soviet power and machinations according to Washington officials. The U.S. intervention did forestall civil war and helped buttress a fragile government friendly to the United States. The putative Soviet connection to Lebanese turmoil was a canard, however. It merely dignified Eisenhower's intervention in the internal affairs of another country, itself remote to the main Soviet-U.S. contest.

Cold War in the Americas

In line with longstanding Washington tradition, Eisenhower sought to uphold a version of stability in the Americas compatible with U.S. economic-security interests. His administration perceived two particularly urgent problems, one centered in Guatemala, the other in Cuba.

Jacobo Arbenz was the reform-minded president of Guatemala during 1950–1954. He took initiatives, notably in land redistribution, which alarmed both the country's property owners and military establishment. Arbenz also struck U.S. officialdom as a radical whose example might inspire leftists elsewhere in Central and South America. Even worse, Eisenhower and Dulles believed, he could easily become a dupe to local Communists and become a tool of Soviet power in the New World. Eisenhower had the CIA cooperate closely with rebellious elements of the Guatemalan army, led by Colonel Carlos Castillo Armas (operating out of Honduras). They and their CIA backers overthrew Arbenz's regime in June 1954 and inaugurated another period of reaction in the troubled country.

Eisenhower's government at first welcomed the deposing of the Cuban despot, Fulgencio Batista, in January 1959 by Fidel Castro's revolutionary army. Castro himself made a goodwill tour of the United States in April, meeting with members of Congress, Vice President Nixon, and the newly appointed secretary of state, Christian Herter. Despite this promising start, Cuban-U.S. relations quickly deteriorated.

From Eisenhower's standpoint, by spring 1960, Castro had squandered America's goodwill that originally gravitated to him. He got too cozy with the USSR and Mao's China. Washington became especially unsettled as he entered into agreements with these two countries that involved Cuba's accepting credits, trade deals, and security pledges. Also, Communists within Castro's ruling coalition assumed prominent government positions while far-reaching domestic innovations were implemented, along with tough measures against dissenters. Cuban-U.S. relations were severed in early January 1961 amidst mutual recriminations and denunciations. The CIA had also concocted a plan to help Cuban refugees bring down Castro's regime, later disastrously undertaken by Kennedy in April 1961 in the Bay of Pigs invasion.

Legacy

The United States emerged from the 1950s in sturdy shape. The GNP had gone up with only slight inflation. The West European economies, closely aligned to the United States, continued to expand and prosper. Oil interests were intact in the Middle East. NATO had not only survived Suez, but the alliance's power had also been augmented by the inclusion of West Germany in 1955. American naval and air bases were secure throughout the Pacific. Even if the government was spending only two-thirds of the amount on military procurements that Democrats and restive officers in the Joint Chiefs of Staff recommended, the military prowess of the United States in 1961 was far greater than the USSR's. As John Kennedy discovered upon coming to office, a missile gap certainly existed. But it was one in which the United States enjoyed vast advantage. Success in the 1962 Cuban missile crisis stemmed from Eisenhower's careful cultivation of robust strategic and naval forces in the 1950s.

Eisenhower also deserves praise for his perceptive warning about the military-industrial complex and the need to limit its political influence. His anxiety about the effects on civil life and liberties of a militarized society was also earnest and apt.

A veteran soldier with firsthand experience of the disasters of war, he understood the complicated relationship between using military instruments and achieving sound diplomatic goals. And he tried intently—and to a degree succeeded—in lowering Cold War tensions that had so anguished the world during the final years of Truman's presidency.

Despite political campaign rhetoric about the alleged deficiencies of containment, Eisenhower did not depart from Truman's course in Europe and was not about to provoke wide war by invading the Soviet sphere of influence. When cracks appeared in Moscow's East European empire in 1953 and in 1956, Eisenhower abstained from intervening. He was content to register sharp protests; prudence did not allow more.

In the Third World, by contrast, a U.S. policy of interventionism was readily apparent during the 1950s through events in Iran (1953), Guatemala (1954), Quemoy and Matsu (1954, 1958), Lebanon (1958), support of the French in Indochina, and (after 1954) of the Vietnamese

government in Saigon. Eisenhower's ingrained caution enabled the United States to maneuver through these crises without suffering immediate damage. American armies were nowhere engaged in combat by 1961, a considerable achievement when compared with Eisenhower's successors. Although uttered in another context, these words of Eisenhower's in 1956 might have been usefully heeded by the later architects of U.S. war in Vietnam: "I don't see the point in getting into a fight to which there can be no satisfactory end, and in which the whole world believes you are playing the part of the bully."

David Mayers

Chronology

1953
March 5: Death of Stalin.

June 17–18: Soviet troops crush anti-Communist riots by workers in East Berlin.

July 27: Korean War armistice signed.

August 8: Soviet Union tests hydrogen bomb.

August 19: Government of Mohammed Mossadegh in Iran is toppled in Ango-American aided coup.

October 30: NSC-162 outlines Eisenhower's "New Look" defense policy.

September 15: Soviet Union provides massive economic aid to China.

1954
January 12: Secretary of State John Foster Dulles outlines doctrine of "massive retaliation."

January 26: Senate ratifies mutual security treaty with South Korea.

March 1: United States tests 15 megaton hydrogen weapon at Bikini Atoll.

March 14: Vietminh forces attack French garrison at Dien Bien Phu.

April 26: Geneva Conference on Korea and Vietnam convenes.

May 7: French garrison at Dien Bien Phu falls.

May 19: United States and Pakistan sign mutual defense pact.

June 9: Arbenz-Guzmán regime in Guatemala overthrown in CIA-aided coup.

June 15: Ngo Dinh Diem becomes premier of French-sponsored Vietnamese government.

July 20: Geneva Conference approves settlement of Indochina conflict.

August 30: French parliament rejects EDC.

September 8: Southeast Asia Treaty Organization (SEATO) established.

October 23: United States offers aid to Diem government in Vietnam.

December 1: United States and Nationalist China sign mutual defense pact.

December 2: U.S. Senate censures Joseph McCarthy.

1955

January 25: Congress authorizes U.S. defense of Formosa and the Pescadores.

February 12: United States agrees to train South Vietnamese army.

February 18: Turkey and Iraq sign Baghdad Pact.

April 18–27: Bandung Conference of twenty-nine African and Asian nations held.

May 9: West Germany admitted to NATO.

May 14: Eight East European nations form Warsaw Pact under Soviet leadership.

July 18–24: Geneva four-power summit conference.

July 22: West German parliament approves rearmament.

September 16: Military coup topples Perón government in Argentina. 1956.

1956

January 28: Eisenhower rejects Soviet friendship proposal.

February 14: Soviet Premier Nikita Khrushchev attacks Stalin's crimes, advocates peaceful coexistence.

April 17: Khrushchev claims Soviet leadership in nuclear weapons.

May 9: United States refuses to supply Israel with arms.

July 19: United States cancels aid to Egypt for Aswân High Dam.

July 26: Egypt nationalizes Suez Canal Company.

October 23–Nov. 4: Hungarian uprising crushed by Soviet tanks and troops.

October 29–Nov. 6: Suez Crisis.

November 6: Eisenhower reelected president.

1957

January 5: President explains Eisenhower Doctrine to Congress.

March 13: Jordan gains independence from Britain.

March 24: Anglo-American meeting at Bermuda.

March 25: Treaty of Rome is signed, European Common Market founded.

May 15: Britain tests its first hydrogen bomb.

August 26: Soviet Union announces successful test of intercontinental ballistic missile.

October 5: Soviet Union orbits Sputnik, the first artificial earth satellite, with a live dog.

November 7: Gaither Report is presented to the National Security Council.

December 5: Sukarno government of Indonesia expels all Dutch nationals.

December 17: First U.S. intercontinental ballistic missile, Atlas, successfully tested.

December 19: NATO Paris summit meeting.

1958

January 23: Venezuelan government overthrown by junta.

January 31: First US earth satellite launched.

February 1: Egypt and Syria form United Arab Republic.

March 27: Khrushchev consolidates power in Soviet Union.

April 28–May 14: Vice President Nixon met with anti-American sentiment in Latin American tour.

May 31: General Charles de Gaulle heads emergency government in France.

June 1: Charles de Gaulle becomes French premier amid turmoil centered on Algerian crisis.

July 14: Army coup ousts King Faisal II in Iraq.

July 15: U.S. Marines go ashore in Lebanon to quell unrest allegedly connected to Islamic rebels backed by USSR.

August 3: USS *Nautilus* completes crossing of North Pole.

August 23: China bombards Quemoy and Matsu.

September 28: French Fifth Republic established.

October 7: Coup in Pakistan establishes military control.

October 23: Soviet Union finances Aswân High Dam.

October 29: Start of reign of Pope John XXIII.

October 31: Geneva Nuclear Test Ban Conference.

November 10–December 14: 1958 Berlin Crisis.

November 27: Khrushchev vows to give East German authorities control of communication lines to West Berlin, precipitating a new Berlin crisis.

1959

January 1: Cuban Batista government falls to forces led by Fidel Castro.

January 3: Alaska becomes forty-ninth state.

March 5: United States signs defense pacts with Iran, Pakistan, and Turkey.

March 13–31: China invades and annexes Tibet.

June 29: Canadian-American St. Lawrence Seaway opens.

July 12: United States protests Castro's Cuban land reform.

July 24: Nixon-Khrushchev kitchen debate.

August 21: Hawaii becomes fiftieth state.

September 15: Khrushchev tours United States.

1960

February 13: Soviet Union and Cuba sign economic agreement.

February 13: France tests its first nuclear weapon.

May 5: U-2 Affair—U.S. spy plane shot down over Soviet Union.

May 27: Military coup in Turkey.

June 27: Communist countries withdraw from Geneva disarmament talks.

June 30: Belgium gives independence to Congo.

July 1: Soviet Union shoots down U.S. plane over Barents Sea.

July 6: Castro nationalizes all U.S. property in Cuba.

July 20: first Polaris missile launch.

September 10: Organization for Petroleum Exporting Countries (OPEC) is formed.

October 19: United States embargoes all exports to China.

November 8: John F. Kennedy is elected president, Lyndon Johnson is vice president.

December 20: National Liberation Front (NLF) formed in South Vietnam.

1961

January 3: United States cuts diplomatic relations with Cuba.

January 6: Soviet Union announces support for wars of national liberation.

January 17: Eisenhower's farewell speech warns of "military industrial complex."

References and Further Reading

Ambrose, Stephen. *Eisenhower: Soldier, General of the Army, President-Elect, 1890–1952.* New York: Simon and Schuster, 1983.

Ambrose, Stephen. *Eisenhower: The President.* New York: Simon and Schuster, 1984.

Brendon, Piers. *Ike: His Life and Times.* New York: Harper and Row, 1986.

Burk, Robert. *Dwight D. Eisenhower: Hero and Politician.* Boston: Twayne, 1986.

Chandler, Alfred, and Louis Galambos, eds. *The Papers of Dwight D. Eisenhower.* Baltimore: Johns Hopkins University Press, series, 1970–2001.

Cook, Blanche Wiesen. *The Declassified Eisenhower: A Startling Appraisal of the Eisenhower Presidency.* New York: Penguin, 1984.

Divine, Robert. *Eisenhower and the Cold War.* New York: Oxford University Press, 1981.

Eisenhower, Dwight. *Mandate for Change, 1953–1956.* Garden City, NY: Doubleday, 1963.

Eisenhower, Dwight. *Waging Peace, 1956–1961.* Garden City, NY: Doubleday, 1965.

Eisenhower, Dwight. *Stories I Tell to Friends.* Garden City, NY: Doubleday, 1967.

Eisenhower, John. *Strictly Personal.* Garden City, NY: Doubleday, 1974.

Eisenhower, Milton. *The President Is Calling.* Garden City, NY: Doubleday, 1974.

Ferrell, Robert, ed. *The Eisenhower Diaries.* New York: W. W. Norton, 1981.

Greenstein, Fred. *The Hidden-Hand Presidency: Eisenhower as Leader.* New York: Basic Books, 1982.

Griffith, Robert, ed. *Ike's Letters to a Friend, 1941–1958.* Lawrence, KS: University Press of Kansas, 1984.

Lee, R. Alton. *Dwight D. Eisenhower: Soldier and Statesman.* Chicago: Nelson-Hall, 1981.

Lyon, Peter. *Eisenhower: Portrait of a Hero.* Boston: Little, Brown, 1974.

Melanson, Richard, and David Mayers, eds. *Reevaluating Eisenhower: American Foreign Policy in the 1950s.* Urbana, IL: University of Illinois Press, 1987.

Pach, Chester, and Elmo Richardson. *The Presidency of Dwight D. Eisenhower.* Lawrence, KS: University Press of Kansas, 1991.

Parmet, Herbert. *Eisenhower and the American Crusades.* New York: Macmillan, 1972.

Public Papers of the Presidents of the United States: Dwight D. Eisenhower, 8 vols. Washington: Government Printing Office, series.

John Fitzgerald Kennedy (1961–1963)

Early Life and Political Career

John Fitzgerald Kennedy was born in Brookline, Massachusetts on May 29, 1917, the second oldest of Joseph Patrick and Rose Fitzgerald Kennedy's nine children. As a child, the future president suffered from poor health, contracting a range of illnesses including scarlet fever. He attended the Choate private boarding school for adolescent boys in Connecticut. He was not one of its best students, but was known for his daily subscription to the *New York Times*. In 1936, John graduated from Choate and enrolled at Harvard. The following year his father was appointed ambassador to Great Britain, a position he held until 1940. Because of his father's position, John became very interested in history, government, and current events. His interest and understanding of foreign affairs was fueled and influenced by extensive international travel. In the summer of 1937, at the age of twenty, he traveled across Europe. In 1939, the future president spent seven months traveling through Eastern Europe, the Soviet Union, the Balkans, and the Middle East. By the time World War II began, Kennedy was a senior at Harvard. Drawing on his experiences in Europe, he wrote his senior thesis on Great Britain's lack of preparedness for war. The thesis was later published as a book titled *Why England Slept.*

After graduating in 1940, Kennedy joined the U.S. Navy as a Lieutenant commanding a patrol torpedo boat, PT-109, in the South Pacific. During a night patrol on August 2, 1943, a Japanese destroyer rammed PT-109 killing several of the crew and cutting Kennedy's boat in two. Kennedy found one of his severely wounded shipmates and saved him by clenching a strap from the wounded sailors life-vest in his teeth and towing the crewman to where the rest of the crew was clinging to a piece of the boat. Kennedy's heroic leadership earned him the Navy and Marine Corps Medal.

As the end of the war neared, Kennedy contemplated his future career. He considered becoming a teacher or a writer and spent a couple years as a reporter. He covered the founding conference of the United Nations in San Francisco, the British general elections, and the Potsdam Conference. His life changed when his father convinced him to run for Congress. In 1946, drawing on his good looks, charisma, family connections, and status as a war hero, Kennedy won the Eleventh Congressional District of Massachusetts.

John Fitzgerald Kennedy committed the nation to "pay any price, bear any burden" in the defense of liberty. (John F. Kennedy Library)

Kennedy spent six years, 1946–1952, in the House of Representatives and took stands on issues very different from those of his father, an isolationist opposed to American involvement in World War II and the Cold War. Kennedy voted to support the Truman Doctrine, the Marshall Plan, and the creation of the North Atlantic Treaty Organization (NATO). He continued his education in foreign affairs, visiting Israel, India, Indochina, and Japan. In 1952, Kennedy was elected to the U.S. Senate in an upset victory over the Republican incumbent Henry Cabot Lodge, Jr. During his first term as senator, he lobbied successfully for a place on the powerful Foreign Relations Committee. Drawing upon his experience abroad, Kennedy endeavored to revise U.S. policy toward the Third World. Specifically, he attempted to get his Senate colleagues to understand the growing role of nationalism in foreign affairs. His focus on nationalism led him to oppose military intervention to assist the French in Vietnam, to advocate independence for Algeria and, ironically, to initially support Fidel Castro's revolution in Cuba.

In 1956, Kennedy was considered for the Democratic vice presidential nomination, and barely missed being selected. Four years later, the Democratic Party chose him as its nominee for president. Kennedy selected the Texan Lyndon Baines Johnson as his running mate, despite their fierce clashes during the primary elections.

The Kennedy/Johnson ticket ran against Republican nominee Richard Nixon, and his running mate Henry Cabot Lodge, Jr. The dominant foreign policy issues of the campaign involved U.S.-Soviet Cold War competition: the status of Soviet ballistic missile production, the Space Race, and developments in Cuba.

Throughout the campaign, Kennedy continuously accused the Republicans of doing nothing about the Cuban dictator Fidel Castro and suggested that, if he were elected, he would do something, possibly even involving force. The election was very close and rife with controversy, but in the end, the forty-three year-old Kennedy became the youngest man elected president in U.S. history.

The Eisenhower Record

Eisenhower's presidency had been dominated by the Cold War and efforts to rebalance American foreign policy from the perceived excesses of the Truman administration. Eisenhower was an anti-communist who believed in moderation and in the doctrine of containment, both of which guided much of his foreign policy. He was enamored with covert operations and saw psychological operations and CIA-assisted coups as cost-effective and plausibly deniable ways of dealing with difficult situations. He approved the CIA-backed toppling of Mohammed Mosaddegh's government in Tehran in 1953 and Jacobo Arbenz's in Guatemala the following year. These seemingly low-risk, low-cost successes led Eisenhower, in March 1960, to approve a CIA plan to recruit and train Cuban forces to overthrow the Castro regime.

Europe was the source of a series of crises. Some were interalliance squabbles resulting from Eisenhower's humiliation of the British and French for their intervention in the Suez in 1956 and the conflict over the deployment of U.S. nuclear weapons on West German territory. Additionally, there was a series of East-West crises: the integration of West Germany into NATO in 1955, Soviet repression of the Hungarian uprising in 1956, and Soviet Premier Nikita Khrushchev's negation of the Potsdam agreements on the status of Berlin in 1958. An attempt to address these issues at a spring 1960 summit in Paris ended when Khrushchev refused to attend after the Soviets shot down an American U-2 spy plane.

Eisenhower's policy in Asia focused on containment without risking war. He used American naval power to help defend the Nationalist Chinese strongholds Quemoy and Matsu, two small islands off the coast of the People's Republic of China, from potential Communist aggression in 1954–1955. He formed the South East Asia Treaty Organization (SEATO) that incorporated the United States, Australia, Britain, France, New Zealand, Pakistan, the Philippines, and Thailand to extend protection to Cambodia, Laos, and the Republic of Vietnam. Although Eisenhower did little to assist the French in Indochina, he did initiate the first direct American role in Vietnam by increasing financial aid and sending military advisors to the South Vietnamese republic. It was the first small step on the slippery slope of America's longest war.

Throughout his presidency, Eisenhower resisted calls for a large-scale military buildup and, during the numerous flare-ups in American-Soviet relations, rejected any suggestions of expanding U.S. military strength in preparations for a ground war in Europe. His moderation on the issue of military spending led to him being accused of permitting a "missile gap" and "bomber gap" to develop to the advantage of the Soviet Union. Although U-2 flights and other intelligence convinced Eisenhower there was no such gap, this did not prevent the Kennedy from using the issue to his advantage in the 1960 presidential campaign.

A Short, Intense Learning Process

As a senator, Kennedy had been bored by domestic policy; he believed his presidency would make its mark above all in the arena of international affairs. While he was anti-communist and valued the importance of military power, his views were tempered by an optimistic view of human nature and the possibilities for peace. In his inaugural address, he made it clear that the tone of his presidency would be one of energy and action. The speech is remembered principally for it nationalistic call to duty and for intervention around the world.

"And so, my fellow Americans: ask not what your country can do for you," he urged, "ask what you can do for your country." Americans, Kennedy stated, were prepared "to pay any price, bear any burden, meet any hardship, support any friend, oppose any foe to assure the survival and success of liberty."

Kennedy nonetheless believed it was possible to negotiate with the Soviet Union and that the two superpowers could coexist peacefully. Kennedy interpreted Khrushchev's liberalization and de-Stalinization policies as evidence the Soviet premier was open to slowing or even halting the arms race. To pursue his belief, Kennedy proposed a meeting with Khrushchev to discuss arms control. Khrushchev interpreted Kennedy's willingness to negotiate as a sign of weakness. This encouraged the Soviets to behave more aggressively in Europe during the Berlin Crisis of 1961 and in Latin America during the Cuban Missile Crisis in 1962.

Khrushchev's misreading of Kennedy's intentions forced the president to return to the containment policies of his predecessors. Kennedy's only success in negotiating with the Soviets was the 1963 Limited Nuclear Test Ban Treaty, outlawing atmospheric nuclear weapons tests.

In 1960, Kennedy had campaigned hard on the claim the Soviets had more Intercontinental Ballistic Missiles (ICBMs) than the United States possessed, the so-called "missile gap." Although once in office he quickly learned that Eisenhower had in fact kept the United States well ahead in the arms race, events led Kennedy to increase military spending, leading ultimately to a sevenfold increase in the American missile arsenal and an even greater advantage over the Soviet Union.

This build-up was leavened by a strong belief in the ability of nonmilitary power to improve the world and was coupled with Kennedy's understanding of the problems in the post-colonial countries. These tenets necessitated a new American emphasis on monetary aid and economic assistance in the Third World. The obligation of the United States, according to Kennedy, was not simply to help developing countries economically but to spread democracy as well. In his first thirty days as president Kennedy initiated several programs intended to shift U.S policy away from military assistance toward economic development. These included the Food for Peace program, the Peace Corps, and the Alliance for Progress.

The first of these programs, Food for Peace, was created on January 24, 1961. For the most part, Kennedy simply changed the name and expanded an Eisenhower administration program, which used the American agricultural surplus to facilitate economic development. The second program, the Peace Corps was an initiative close to the president's heart. Kennedy initially introduced the program in 1960, while campaigning for the college student vote at the University of Michigan. Critics of the program described it as a haven for draft dodgers and doubted that college volunteers possessed the skills to be of much assistance. Nevertheless, Kennedy was devoted to the program and in one of his first acts as president on March 1, 1961 he signed the executive order creating the Peace Corps. The idea of sending young American volunteers abroad to assist lesser-developed nations was not merely idealistic; the program was intended to have secondary strategic benefits. Kennedy saw the Peace Corps as part of an information campaign to counter the perceptions of "Yankee imperialism," create a positive image of the United States in the Third World, and serve the broader anti-communist strategy.

The third program, the Alliance for Progress, created on March 13, 1961, was a long-term economic assistance program to create a political and economic environment favorable to Western capitalism. The so-called Marshall Plan for Latin America was a result of American concerns that the region was vulnerable to Communist expansion. The conditions for the aid from the United States to Latin American, including land and tax reform and more democratic governance, were not popular with Latin American leaders. The program withered away in the late 1960s.

The Bay of Pigs

In 1959, revolutionary forces led by Fidel Castro overthrew the U.S.-aligned Batista government of Cuba, establishing a communist regime 90 miles off the coast of Florida. The existence of a communist country so close to the United States, able and willing to export revolution to vulnerable Latin American states, was a grave strategic threat. In the zero-sum world of the Cold War, the Soviet Union's gain was the free world's loss, and the Eisenhower administration began to look at options to deal with the threat. The original plan, dating to January 18, 1960, was for a small group of exiles trained by the CIA on a coffee plantation in Guatemala to sneak onto the island to assist the anti-Castro underground. The idea was modeled on the successful 1954 CIA-engineered coup in Guatemala.

The president-elect first heard of the project on November 18, 1960, ten days after his election. Kennedy shared both the previous administration's assumption that revolutionary Cuba might serve as a model for other Latin American countries and its affinity for covert operations. Although Kennedy felt it inappropriate and premature to commit to the outgoing administration's policies until he had full responsibility, he was interested.

The first ninety days of the Kennedy administration were a whir of activities: requests to Congress for legislation, meetings with foreign leaders, and numerous policy initiatives. During this frenzy of administrative activity the CIA's plans for invading Cuba continued, along with training the exiles, with little oversight from Kennedy. The original plan had evolved from a small group of less than thirty CIA-trained exiles working with the Cuban underground to a brigade-sized amphibious assault force of 1,500 men intended to trigger a popular uprising that would swell the ranks of the anti-Castro forces. As Kennedy entered his second month of office, momentum behind the plan grew. In March, the Guatemalan president stated he wanted the Cubans out of his country by the end of April. Additionally, the question of what to do with the brigade if the operation was cancelled was on everyone's mind. It was also getting increasingly difficult to keep the CIA's efforts out of the media. Finally, to cancel the project would have opened Kennedy to the criticism that he was not doing enough to fight communism.

On March 15, 1961, Kennedy reluctantly approved the plan on the condition no U.S. military units would be directly involved lest he look like an aggressor with the impending launch of his Alliance for Progress initiative. He insisted the United States would not get involved militarily regardless of the outcome and demanded the plan allow him to cancel the mission up to twenty-four hours prior to its launch. He was assured by both the military and the CIA that American support would remain covert. Even if the invasion went poorly, his advisors told him confidently, the brigade could always melt away into the mountains and fight a guerilla war.

When the newly elected president, a Pulitzer Prize winning man-of-action surrounded by some of best intellects of the time, was presented with a plan approved by the CIA's covert operations specialists, how could he refuse? Although Kennedy always had some doubts, the winds of fate seemed to drive him toward approving the plan. The combination of an arrogant CIA and a young, talented, self-assured president, confident of his many skills, led the country into one of its biggest Cold War blunders.

The operation was a disaster. The training of the exiles had been an open secret in Latin America. Knowing that Washington was planning something, Castro had been purchasing Soviet weapons to improve his military. The location for the invasion, the Bay of Pigs, could hardly have been a worse choice. Castro frequently vacationed there and was very popular in the region, so there was no popular uprising to assist the invaders. The landing site was surrounded by swamps, and the closest mountains to hide in were over 80 miles away. In less than three days, Castro's military defeated the invaders, taking the survivors prisoner. In December 1962 Castro released the 1,113 captured exiles in exchange for $53 million in food and medicine raised by private donation in the United States. Despite this outcome, Kennedy never gave up trying to topple Castro.

The blowback from the Bay of Pigs, combined with Kennedy's hopes for some type of covert operation finally to rid him of Castro, pushed Cuba closer to the Soviet Union. Khrushchev gladly offered to provide Cuba with military and economic assistance. The Soviets were looking for a Latin American ally and Kennedy's efforts provided an opening.

The Berlin Wall

After the Bay of Pigs debacle, Kennedy looked for an opportunity to demonstrate his grasp of foreign affairs. The June 4, 1961 Vienna summit with Khrushchev provided it. For Kennedy, the summit was a chance to reach out to Moscow on arms control issues. Additionally, he warned that neither side should try to upset the balance of power. The Soviet leader's agenda focused on a solution to the question of a divided Germany and Berlin, and he also made it clear he would continue to support "wars of national liberation." During the summit, Khrushchev was very forceful and

pushed the new president hard on numerous issues. Khrushchev warned Kennedy that the USSR was considering signing a separate peace agreement with East Germany, allowing the Soviet satellite to cut off transportation routes to West Berlin. He went on to threaten that if the United States responded militarily, the Soviets would reply in kind. Although Kennedy was unyielding on the German issue, he left the summit with the impression Khrushchev considered him a weak and inexperienced novice who could be pushed around and intimidated. Indeed, news footage of the summit revealed nervousness in Kennedy, which stood in stark contrast to Khrushchev's calm and paternalistic demeanor.

Upon returning from the summit Kennedy increased military spending dramatically, activated 250,000 reservists, asked Congress to expand the country's military by 25 percent, and began to talk tough. Additionally, he discussed options with key NATO allies leading both France and West Germany to increase their military investments in the transatlantic alliance. "If we don't meet our commitments in Berlin," Kennedy warned, "it will mean the destruction of NATO. . . . All Europe is at stake in West Berlin." Kennedy continued his saber rattling rhetoric, stating, that "We do not want to fight, but we have fought before. And others in earlier times have made the same dangerous mistake of assuming that the West was too selfish and too soft and too divided to resist invasions of freedom in other lands." As the rhetoric heated up throughout the summer, relations with the Soviets chilled dramatically.

Although the threat to close off Berlin did not materialize, the Soviet response to Kennedy's tough talk took the Western alliance by surprise. On the night of August 13, 1961, the East Germans built a wall dividing Berlin, guarded by heavily armed soldiers ordered to shoot-to-kill anyone trying to leave the Communist portion of the city. The vast exodus of East German refugees, which was averaging over 1,000 per day, abruptly stopped. The Kennedy administration, along with the rest of the leaders of the free world, did little more than publicly condemn the erection of the wall. Part of the reason for the languid response was Kennedy's hope and belief he could establish cordial relations and negotiate with the Soviets. Reacting too aggressively would complicate his diplomatic objectives. Additionally, the wall was a highly visible example of Soviet repression and provided a continuing source of superb propaganda. Over time Kennedy was able to ease tensions through negotiations, but in doing so, further weakened NATO by angering the political leadership in France and West Germany, who saw him equivocating on the German reunification issue.

Over the next two years Kennedy's optimistic views on cooperation with the Soviet leadership evolved and he became increasingly skeptical. Part of his new hardened approach to the Soviet Union involved a visit to Rudolf Wilde Platz in West Berlin on June 26, 1963, where Kennedy gave one of his most famous speeches. The speech was intended to assure Europeans and the citizens of West Berlin of America's commitment to their freedom. In making his point, Kennedy spoke one of his many unforgettable lines, saying that "All free men, wherever they may live, are citizens of Berlin, and, therefore, as a free man, I take pride in the words *Ich bin ein Berliner.*" On the other side of the wall, East Berliners applauded Kennedy's speech, sending an unmistakable message to their Communist leaders. Kennedy used the Berlin Wall as an example of the popular dislike of communism, observing that "Freedom has many difficulties and democracy is not perfect, but we have never had to put a wall up to keep our people in."

Although the wall remained and the situation in Germany was a stalemate, Khrushchev was not pleased with the global strategic situation. He angrily asked his advisors, "Why [do] Americans have so many bases around the Soviet Union and we have no bases near the United States?"

The Cuban Missile Crisis

In July 1962, a routine U-2 flight detected an unusually heavy concentration of Soviet ships in the waters around Cuba. Additionally, reconnaissance showed an extraordinarily large Soviet troop buildup on the island and the presence of surface-to-air missile (SAM) installations. The following month, further U-2 reconnaissance discovered the construction of more missile sites. On October 14, photographs proved there were nuclear-capable medium-range missiles on launching pads, and the Soviets were constructing intermediate range ballistic missile (IRBM) installations. Two days later, Kennedy convened a special group of top advisors, later to be known as the ExComm (Executive Committee), to address the situation. Kennedy, drawing on his Harvard thesis experience, made clear his own interpretation that "the 1930s taught us a clear lesson: aggressive conduct, if allowed to go unchecked and unchallenged ultimately leads to war."

Although a number of options were discussed, two seemed to have the best possibility of getting the missiles removed without starting a nuclear war. The first option was a naval blockade, later called *quarantine* due to the fact in international law a blockade is an act of war. The second option was a "surgical" air strike to destroy the missile sites. Attorney General Robert Kennedy was opposed to a Pearl Harbor–type preemptive strike. The president, he said, did "not want to be known as another Tojo."

On October 20, Kennedy chose the naval quarantine, in part because it allowed both superpowers more options. In a dramatic television address on October 22, he made public the presence of Soviet offensive missiles in Cuba and announced the naval quarantine of Cuba until the missiles were removed and warned that, if any missiles were fired at the United States, he would respond against the Soviet

Union. The NATO allies endorsed the president's position, and the Organization of American States unanimously supported the quarantine. Kennedy ordered, for the first time in history, U.S. Strategic Air Command to full-war readiness, and hundreds of nuclear-armed B-47, B-52 and B-58 bombers were on maximum alert and in the air continuously.

On October 24, twelve of the twenty-five Soviet ships then steaming for Cuba turned back and two days later, in one of history's many ironies, sailors from the U.S. destroyer *Joseph P. Kennedy* boarded a Soviet-chartered freighter bound for Cuba and found no missiles on board. With the Soviet ships changing course, it seemed the crisis was abating, but the most dangerous moments were still ahead.

On October 26, Kennedy received an impassioned rambling letter from Khrushchev proposing the removal of the missiles in exchange for a public U.S. guarantee never to invade Cuba. The following day a U-2 was shot down by a SAM over Cuba, killing the pilot, and reports came in that Soviet technicians had moved the warheads closer to the missiles, possibly preparing for a strike, while a second, much more strongly worded letter arrived from Khrushchev. This letter demanded that the American Jupiter missiles in Turkey be removed in return for dismantling the Soviet missiles in Cuba. Although Kennedy had planned on removing the outdated missiles, linking them to the Cuban situation would appear to give Khrushchev a major public victory.

An exhausted ExComm met to discuss the development and a bitter meeting ensued over how to proceed with the growing crisis and two different letters. Robert Kennedy suggested answering the first letter and ignoring the second. Later that evening Robert Kennedy met with the Soviet Ambassador, stating the president would not publicly connect the removal of the Jupiter missiles in Turkey with removal of the Soviet missiles in Cuba, but he assured him the missiles would be removed shortly after the crisis had passed. Thus on October 28, just two days before the United States was to have launched air strikes against the missiles, Kennedy announced that Moscow had agreed to crate up the weapons and remove them from Cuba.

Although the European allies were publicly supportive of the United States during the crisis, behind the scenes it strained the alliance by demonstrating that the Europeans were impotent bystanders. Additionally, the Turkish government was not pleased that Kennedy had bartered away their Jupiter missiles—although Turkey owned the missiles, the United States owned the warheads—without consultation. French President De Gaulle saw the episode as more proof of America's willingness to act in its own interest and arrogantly ignore Europe's. He decided the best way to give France a real voice in international affairs was to create its own *force de frappe* of nuclear weapons. Britain and other

NATO partners had similar, although more muted, views of the crisis.

Kennedy's image as a steely negotiator grew as a result of his handling of the crisis. There were also several more important repercussions. The crisis exposed the Soviet Union's nuclear inferiority and led to a massive military buildup. It contributed to Khrushchev's ousting and encouraged both governments toward more indirect and less dangerous competition in the Third World. Finally, acknowledging the role communication played in averting a superpower nuclear exchange, the two countries established a Washington-Moscow "hot line" for future crisis management.

The Slippery Slope in Indochina

At the time of Kennedy's election, there were about 700 American military advisors in Vietnam; by the end of 1963 there were nearly 17,000. Although supportive of protecting South Vietnam's independence from communist North Vietnam, Kennedy remembered his visit to Vietnam a decade earlier and the fate of the French colonial regime, so he refused on several occasions to send U.S. combat troops. He saw the conflict as South Vietnam's to win or lose; the United States could only assist.

By 1963, a Buddhist rebellion and the televised self-immolation of a monk suggested to the Kennedy administration that South Vietnamese President Ngo Dinh Diem lacked the confidence of his people and was unlikely to be able to quell the insurrection. The U.S. Ambassador to South Vietnam, Kennedy's old political rival Henry Cabot Lodge Jr., learned that the country's top generals no longer had confidence in Diem and were planning a coup. Authorized by Kennedy, Lodge informed the generals they would receive American assistance if they succeeded, but no assistance if they failed. On November 1, 1963, the Vietnamese generals staged a successful coup, later killing Diem. Suddenly, the United States was nearly irreversibly committed to the future of South Vietnam's new government.

On November 22, 1963, barely three weeks after Diem's murder, President Kennedy was assassinated. He was in Dallas to deliver a speech arguing that the United States was "the watchman on the wall of freedom" and that assistance to nations can be "painful, risky and costly, as is true in Southeast Asia today. But we dare not weary of the task."

Legacy

Kennedy's legacy is a mixture of success and failure, of optimistic hopes for negotiated compromises and hard-nosed, realist reassessments. He will be remembered for his strong leadership in successfully steering the United States through the Cuban Missile Crisis as well as for his weighty bequest to his successor, Lyndon Johnson, of Vietnam's rapidly deteriorating circumstance.

Shaped by the crisis over the Berlin Wall and the Cuban Missile Crisis, and troubled by the long-term dangers of nuclear weapons development and proliferation, Kennedy was also an active advocate of arms control, including the Partial Test Ban Treaty, which prohibited atomic testing in the atmosphere. When Kennedy signed the treaty into law, he considered it to be one of his administration's greatest accomplishments.

Kennedy's presidency generally was rife with important events, speeches, and policies, but the Peace Corps is one of his most significant legacies. Although it has evolved greatly since its inception, the Peace Corps has achieved a great deal of its promise. It has not been without controversy. Throughout its existence there have been accusations that the program was a cover for agents of the Central Intelligence Agency. Additionally, some host governments have tried to use the volunteers as leverage in political disputes with the United States. Overall, the program must be measured by a different criterion than simply the accomplishments made in the target country. Over the years, thousands of Peace Corps volunteers have influenced U.S. foreign policy in many ways. Many volunteers remain in international development work, securing employment with the Foreign Service, the Agency for International Development, universities, and myriad international and nongovernment organizations.

Craig Cobane

Chronology

1961

January 20: President Kennedy's inaugural pledges that the United States will "bear any burden."

March 1: Kennedy creates the Peace Corps by executive order.

March 13: Alliance for Progress with Latin America initiated.

April 17: Bay of Pigs Invasion, U.S.-backed Cuban rebels defeated.

May 25: Kennedy sets national goal of a manned moon mission by the end of the decade.

June 4: U.S.-Soviet summit conference in Vienna, Khrushchev confrontational over Berlin.

August 13: Soviets begin construction of the Berlin Wall; Berlin Crisis begins.

August 31: Moscow announces resumption of nuclear testing.

October 22–28: Berlin crisis climaxes and ends with agreement on access to the city.

November 22: United States sends first combat-support troops to South Vietnam.

December 2: Castro announces official goal of a communist Cuba.

1962

February 20: Lt. Col. John Glenn launched into earth orbit.

April 25: United States resumes nuclear testing.

July 4: Kennedy offers multilateral nuclear defense for European allies.

July 23: Geneva Conference guarantees independence and neutrality of Laos.

October 20: Chinese and Indian border forces clash.

October 22: Kennedy informs nation of Soviet missiles in Cuba; Cuban Missile Crisis begins.

October 24–28: Cuban Missile Crisis climaxes and ends with personal letters between Kennedy and Khrushchev.

December 17: United States gives aid to UN to fight Katanga secessionists.

1963

January 14: De Gaulle announces French veto of Britain's application to join the EEC.

May 8: Buddhist monks begin demonstrations and self-immolations to protest Diem government in Saigon.

May 22: NATO foreign ministers approve a multilateral nuclear strike force.

June 14: Beijing denounces Moscow's "revisionist" communism.

June 20: United States and Soviet Union agree to establish a diplomatic "hot line."

June 26: Kennedy visits West Berlin and pledges U.S. support.

August 5: United States, Soviet Union, and Britain sign Limited Nuclear Test Ban Treaty.

November 1–2: Military coup ousts Diem government in South Vietnam.

November 22: President Kennedy assassinated, Lyndon Baines Johnson sworn in as president.

References and Further Reading

Allison, Graham. *The Essence of Decision: Explaining the Cuban Missile Crisis.* Boston: Little, Brown, 1971.

Beschloss, Michael. *The Crisis Years: Kennedy and Khrushchev, 1960–1963.* New York: Edward Burlingame, 1991.

Fischer, Fritz. *Making Them Like Us: Peace Corps Volunteers in the 1960s.* Washington, DC: Smithsonian Institution Press, 1998.

Freedman, Lawrence. *Kennedy's Wars: Berlin, Cuba, Laos and Vietnam.* New York: Oxford University Press, 2000.

Kennedy, Robert. *The Thirteen Days: A Memoir of the Cuban Missile Crisis.* New York: W. W. Norton, 1969.

Maga, Timothy P. *John F. Kennedy and New Frontier Diplomacy, 1961–1963.* Malabar: Krieger Publishing, 1994.

Martin, Edwin M. *Kennedy and Latin America.* Lanham: MD University Press of America, 1994.

Nash, Philip. *The Other Missiles of October: Eisenhower, Kennedy and the Jupiters, 1957–1963.* Chapel Hill, NC: University of North Carolina Press, 1997.

Paterson, Thomas G., ed. *Kennedy's Quest for Victory.* New York: Oxford University Press, 1989.

Schlesinger, Arthur M. Jr. *A Thousand Days: John F. Kennedy in the White House.* Boston: Houghton Mifflin, 1965.

Lyndon Baines Johnson (1963–1969)

Early Life and Political Career

Born in 1908 in Stonewall, Gillespie County, Texas, Lyndon Baines Johnson was the eldest of the five children reared by Samuel Ealy Johnson Jr. and Rebekah Baines in the rural poverty of the West Texas hill country. He worked his way through Southwest Texas State Teachers College, developing a life-long sympathy for the underdog based partly on his own experience but more forcefully on the abject deprivation of the Mexican-American elementary pupils in his charge. As a teacher, Johnson was tireless in the pursuit of high standards and intensely demanding both of himself and his students—a trait that figured prominently in his congressional career and ultimately in his approach to the presidential office.

Johnson's apprenticeship in national politics began as private secretary to Congressman Richard M. Kleberg of Corpus Christi during the final months of the Hoover administration, 1929–1933. In 1934, Johnson married Claudia Alta "Lady Bird" Taylor of a prominent East Texas family and acquired thereby an astute promoter of his political ambitions with the financial means to assist. With $10,000 borrowed by Lady Bird, Johnson ran for the seat of the Tenth Congressional District of Texas in 1937 and won handily on a platform of robust support for the national New Deal programs of President Franklin Roosevelt, including his controversial "court packing" approach to the Supreme Court's opposition to those programs. The election was formative in two ways. Unqualified loyalty to Roosevelt was rewarded with the president's personal interest in Johnson's political advancement and interventions on his behalf by administration officials such as Thomas Corcoran, Harry Hopkins, and Harold Ickes, while House Majority Leader Sam Rayburn made Johnson a political protégé and personal friend. Identification with New Deal policies meanwhile gave Johnson the firm belief in active and beneficent government typical of New Deal Democrats, and admiration of Roosevelt's wartime leadership convinced him of the importance of centralized Oval Office control of foreign policy.

Johnson served briefly as a U.S. Navy lieutenant in the South Pacific during World War II, winning a Silver Star. Initially unsuccessful in pursuit of a Senate seat in 1941, he was elected in 1948 and began one of the great political careers in the history of the chamber. In 1953, he became

Lyndon Baines Johnson, a president of extraordinary energy, led the nation to landmark civil rights reform yet also deepened the American involvement in Vietnam with disastrous consequences. (Yoichi R. Okamoto/LBJ Library Collection)

the youngest ever Senate Minority Leader, then Majority Leader when the Democrats won control of the chamber the following year. Johnson combined strong partisan support for New Deal liberalism with a talent for accommodating conflicting partisan interests and extraordinary energy in pursuit of legislative results. When, in 1957, he shepherded the first civil rights law through the Senate in eighty-two years, he was compared to Henry Clay, the "Great Compromiser" of the nineteenth century. Considered by many the most successful Majority Leader in history, Johnson brought vast political experience, manic vitality, personal charm, and ruthless determination to the office of the presidency.

Civil Rights and Southeast Asia

Johnson's assumption of presidential powers as a consequence of the Kennedy assassination imposed certain limitations on his policy options. Equally, national circumstance in November 1963 presented opportunities to a politician with Johnson's legislative skills and a New Deal Democrat with experience in using government to promote social change.

On arrival in the Oval Office, Johnson moved quickly to exploit the sense of national loss, first by saying "let us continue" to a joint session of Congress and then applying his legislative experience as a caretaker of Kennedy's programs and policies, in the process calling in the many political debts accumulated in Congress over the previous decade. Significant international events during his early months in office included the independence of the British colony of Kenya, the dissolution of the Federation of Rhodesia and Nyasaland, a military coup in Brazil, and the resolution of the crisis in Panama in which Johnson agreed to review demands to revise the Panama Canal Treaty to provide for the rights of Panamanians in the canal zone. In Europe, President Charles de Gaulle announced in April 1964 that French naval staff officers would no longer serve under NATO command, thereby initiating a process of increasing French independence within the Atlantic Alliance; in Africa Moise Tshombe became premier of the Congo in July 1964 and was given American assistance in the form of CIA-recruited Cuban exiles flying U.S. aircraft against Congolese rebels, some of whom were assisted by the People's Republic of China.

It was nonetheless a domestic cause—the most sweeping civil rights reforms on behalf of black Americans since Reconstruction—that claimed top spot among Johnson's personal priorities. The modern era of the civil rights movement, inaugurated with the Supreme Court's *Brown v. The Board of Education* decision of 1954, had, under the leadership the Reverend Martin Luther King Jr., developed a following large enough to command the attention of the Kennedy administration. At the time of Kennedy's premature death, however, very little civil rights reform had been accomplished. Johnson moved quickly to put legislative substance behind the rhetorical inspiration of Kennedy's civil rights pronouncements. The Civil Rights Act of 1964, in fact, became Johnson's greatest legislative achievement, indeed, an enviable legislative legacy by any moral or political measure. However, it required so much effort in congressional coalition-building to override a filibuster by senators from southern segregationist states that Johnson was at pains to avoid any threat to the bill that might have resulted from disturbing the national consensus on foreign policy, above all in the commitment to the defense of South Vietnam.

In the summer of 1964, in fact, a principal threat to Johnson's bid to secure an electoral mandate in his own right in the presidential election in November was the attack of the Republican nominee, Arizona Senator Barry Goldwater, on the New Deal record of public policy dating to the 1930s along with the Cold War policy of containment. Goldwater's presidential campaign cut so sharply across the prevailing national consensus on foreign policy, most especially in his insistence that containment was a passive and defensive strategy, that his chances of defeating Johnson ranged from the remote to the impossible. Johnson's political instincts nonetheless prompted him to seek the maximum electoral insurance by way of a campaign portraying Goldwater as a bellicose demagogue who might start a nuclear war in his pursuit of total victory over the Soviet Union while demonstrating his administration's own toughness in the containment of Communist insurgency in South Vietnam.

Continuity and Crisis in Vietnam

Three factors are critical to understanding the foreign policy of the Johnson administration. The first is that Johnson finished Kennedy's term in office and was able to function with an electoral mandate in his own right only after his landslide victory over Goldwater in November 1964. He therefore sought support for his leadership initially by continuing with Kennedy's foreign and domestic policies. The second factor was Johnson's personal preoccupation with domestic policy, in particular his historic civil rights legislation and Great Society legislation, set against comparative disinterest in—and ignorance of—international affairs. The final and possibly most important factors were the extraordinary political skills developed during congressional career dating to the late 1930s, which enabled Johnson to secure broad, bipartisan support for his most ambitious initiatives at home and abroad. In combination, these factors led to a deepening of the American military involvement in Vietnam so that by 1968, the conflict eclipsed Johnson's domestic achievements, destroyed political support for his leadership, and plunged the nation into the first stage of a constitutional crisis that climaxed during the succeeding administration of Richard M. Nixon.

Intensified involvement in Vietnam began with passage of the Southeast Asia Resolution, commonly known as the Gulf of Tonkin Resolution, on August 7, 1964. The resolution was occasioned by reported attacks on the U.S. Navy destroyers *Maddox* and *Turner Joy* in the Gulf of Tonkin by North Vietnamese gunboats. The presence of the *Maddox* off the North Vietnamese coast was itself part of Plan 34a, authorized by Johnson in February 1964, for covert measures to pressure Hanoi to withdraw its forces from South Vietnam. These included U-2 flights over North Vietnam; American assistance for South Vietnamese commando raids in the North to destroy road and rail links, bridges, and coastal defenses; raids by American aircraft disguised with Laotian air force markings; and destroyer patrols to gather intelligence on North Vietnamese radar and coastal defense installations. On August 2 and 4, the U.S. destroyers reported torpedo attacks by North Vietnamese gunboats, although the reliability of the August 4 report was later questioned. Johnson's response was immediate and unequivocal. In a television broadcast that interrupted regular programming nationwide, he announced to the public that "unprovoked" attacks on U.S. Navy vessels required prompt reprisals. In an interpretation of the Tonkin events crafted to change public perceptions of the Vietnamese conflict, he claimed that Communist subversion of South Vietnam had now been joined by aggression on the high seas against the United States. Johnson additionally pounced on the opportunity afforded by the Tonkin incidents, real and imagined, to put Congress on record in support of presidential prerogative henceforth to conduct Vietnam policy with broad discretionary latitude. Congress obliged in the Tonkin Resolution (H.J. Res 1145), declaring that it "approves and supports the determination of the President, as Commander in Chief, to take all necessary measures to repel any armed attack against the forces of the United States and to prevent further aggression." It stated further that the United States was prepared "as the President determines, to take all necessary steps, including the use of armed force to assist any member or protocol state of the Southeast Asia Collective Defense Treaty requesting assistance in defense of its freedom."

It is important to note that in this, Johnson acted according to his political instincts, mindful in an election year to appear resolute, but also that he enjoyed unalloyed support both for immediate military action and for executive authority to wage war from Kennedy administration appointees such as Secretary of Defense Robert McNamara and Secretary of State Dean Rusk. The presence of McNamara and Rusk in Johnson's cabinet meant that his ability to alter the course of U.S. policy in Vietnam established under Kennedy was limited, most especially during the period between Kennedy's assassination and Johnson's victory over Goldwater in the presidential election of 1964. For a caretaker president to have contemplated withdrawal would have precipitated conflict within the cabinet and possibly one or more major resignations. McNamara advised an immediate and vigorous response to the Tonkin incident and testified to Congress on the authenticity of the attack reports. Rusk had a necessarily broader view of foreign policy. He held that American international credibility depended on a demonstrated willingness to persevere in Vietnam and thus advocated a limited yet open-ended military effort with an outcome similar to Korea—stalemate, negotiations, and armistice—in mind. Additionally, Rusk

took the president's constitutional duty as commander-in-chief literally, regarded Congress as a body to be manipulated to accept the executive's interpretation of the national interest, and withheld or circulated information on the administration's actions in Vietnam in accord with this principle. He believed that in Korea, President Truman had erred in failing to secure from Congress an open declaration of support for his administration's aims and that the Tonkin Resolution provided *a priori* sanction to Johnson under domestic and international law to escalate the American military effort as he judged appropriate. The counsel of McNamara and especially Rusk nonetheless did not contradict Johnson's own earlier advice to Kennedy. Returning from a vice presidential trip to South Vietnam in May 1961, Johnson had told Kennedy that the future of Southeast Asia hinged on Vietnam and that "we must decide whether to help these countries to the best of our ability or to throw in the towel in the area and pull back our defenses to San Francisco and a 'Fortress America' concept." Johnson's stark interpretation of the policy alternatives was thus in harmony with Rusk's view of the stakes in Vietnam before the Kennedy assassination propelled him into the White House.

Rolling Thunder

With reelection secure and the Tonkin Resolution passed, Johnson was free to prosecute war in Vietnam according to executive convenience. So long as the United States was committed to the defense of South Vietnam, this authority was both necessary and perilous—necessary because South Vietnam was clearly incapable of defending itself and perilous because its corrupt and increasingly anarchic leadership showed little interest in developing such a capability. In early 1965, reports by Maxwell Taylor, U.S. ambassador to Saigon, and John McNaughton, an assistant to McNamara, explained to the administration that the new ruling military junta brought to power in a coup and headed by Nguyen Khanh, Nguyen Cao Ky, and Nguyen Van Thieu was corrupt beyond repair and paid little heed to American advice. Only if the United States assumed control of the South Vietnamese military cause was there any prospect of improvement. So it was that 1965 became the year in which the conflict was transformed from a Vietnamese war with American support for one side into a war between the United States and North Vietnam. On February 7, 1965, Vietcong guerillas staged a mortar attack on a U.S. Army barracks at Pleiku, killing 8 Americans and wounding more than 100. Johnson ordered retaliatory air attacks under the code name Fleming Dart II from U.S. Navy carriers against the North Vietnamese barracks at Dong Hui and a communications center at Vinh Lui.

The retaliation for Pleiku was the first act in a broader campaign of graduated escalation in the bombing of North

Vietnamese targets designed to demonstrate that American military actions would not be purely reactive and defensive. Beginning on March 19, 1965, Operation Rolling Thunder air attacks against North Vietnamese targets were conducted two or three times each week for the next three years, accounting in total for 309,996 raids and 408,599 tons of explosive. Another, more critical threshold was crossed on March 8, 1965, when Johnson dispatched 3,500 marines to defend the American air base near the coastal city of Da Nang at the request of General William Westmorland, prompting Ambassador Taylor to observe that the policy of avoiding the deployment of ground combat forces to Vietnam had now been reversed. The administration had moved the United States from a policy of support for South Vietnamese counter-insurgency to an American ground war against North Vietnam, which was conducted not for the purpose of defeating the enemy but rather for defeating the enemy's campaign to conquer South Vietnam.

Dissent at Home and Abroad

The first large protests against U.S. involvement in Vietnam emerged in March 1965. They often took the form of university campus "teach-ins" in which faculty and students criticized Johnson's conduct of the war, in particular Rolling Thunder, but also the order of his administration's priorities. On the domestic front, Johnson sought to add to his historic triumph by passing the Civil Rights Bill of 1965 with its broader program of legislation promoting social justice, racial equality, and economic reform under the rubric of the Great Society. The inevitable competition for fiscal resources between "guns or butter" programs moved the protesters to charge that Johnson was beggaring laudable progressive initiatives at home to pay for conflict of uncertain length and in pursuit of elusive goals in Southeast Asia. Johnson was sensitive to and resentful of this criticism, above all for the personal reason that his domestic achievements were his claim as the greatest reformer since Franklin Roosevelt, but also because of the political calculation that the perception of failure in Vietnam would make him vulnerable to attack from conservative Republicans. Because any explicit commitment to a wider war in Vietnam could elicit opposition from both quarters, university campuses and Congress, Johnson and his advisors were, in 1965, essentially taking the United States in the direction of a full-scale conventional war without acknowledging publicly the size of the commitment.

On December 24, 1965, Johnson ordered a pause in the bombing of North Vietnam based on the hope, in part encouraged by Soviet Ambassador Anatoly Dobrynin, that Moscow and other Warsaw Pact governments might be able to talk Hanoi into serious negotiations for a peaceful end of hostilities. A joint Hungarian, Polish, and Soviet delegation visited Hanoi during the pause but failed to convince Hanoi

to negotiate. The administration therefore resumed bombing on January 31, 1966. In the meantime, Senator J. William Fulbright (D-Arkansas), whose congressional support had been vital to the passage of the Tonkin Resolution, used his chairmanship of the Senate Foreign Relations Committee to convene televised hearings on Johnson's Vietnam policy. When George Kennan, a principal architect of the Truman administration's Cold War diplomacy and intellectual father of the concept of containment, testified to the effect that a communist Vietnam would represent neither a security threat to the United States and its allies nor a strategic benefit to the Soviet Union or the People's Republic of China, he gave a new legitimacy to dissent against the war. While Kennan opposed any precipitant withdrawal, he maintained that the United States was unlikely to prevail in a contest of attrition with North Vietnam and that the administration's war effort was causing it to neglect important interests elsewhere. Reinforced by the critical dissent of other foreign policy analysts such as Walter Lippmann and Hans Morgenthau, Kennan's remarks served to cultivate articulate opposition to the war within the Democratic Party. In February 1966, President Charles de Gaulle withdrew France from NATO's integrated command. Although the move was in fact an expression of opposition to the idea of a NATO multilateral force (MLF) dating to the Kennedy administration, it tended to confirm the charge that Johnson had made Vietnam a first-order priority at the price of neglecting Europe, the primary theater of the Cold War.

The rest of 1966 featured a combination of diplomacy by the administration to counter mounting domestic criticism of its Vietnam policy with an increased military effort. In late October, Johnson attended the Manila Conference hosted by President Ferdinand Marcos of the Philippines. Included were representatives from Washington and Saigon as well as from all other governments contributing troops to the South Vietnamese cause: Australia, New Zealand, South Korea, and Thailand. The conference concluded with a statement, included partly at the urging of Soviet Foreign Minster Andrei Gromyko, that the allied nations sought no permanent presence in South Vietnam and would withdraw within six months of the restoration of peace. In November, Johnson stabilized the Rolling Thunder attacks and deployed an additional 70,000 troops to South Vietnam, yet declined to call up military reserves. The same year also witnessed the emergence of two developments of major import to international affairs and U.S. foreign policy over the coming decades. In August 18, Mao Zedong launched the Great Proletarian Cultural Revolution, plunging China into a decade of near-anarchy dominated by purges of the Communist Party and People's Liberation Army and a level of arbitrary violence committed by Red Guard youths, which brought the country close to civil war. Also, in August and November, Israeli forces clashed with Syria and Jordan after Israel retaliated against Arab guerilla forces and the

Palestinian al-Fatah for conducting raids against Israel from their territory and that of Lebanon. Israel was censured in the United Nations, and Johnson sent military aid to Jordan, but the fighting merely presaged the Six-Day War of June the following year.

The Intensification of Ground Combat

In 1967, the Johnson administration lost confidence that the United States could eventually prevail in Vietnam, the final act of which was the resignation of Secretary of Defense Robert McNamara. The same year saw improvements in American relations with the Soviet Union. Additionally, deep divisions began to appear within the Democratic Party over the lack of tangible progress toward either victory or peace in Vietnam. In the 1966 congressional elections, Republicans registered considerable gains in both houses; only two years after Johnson's crushing defeat of Barry Goldwater; this measure of electoral decline only heightened the concern of vulnerable or ambitious Democrats to distance themselves from Johnson's foreign policy, which was now all but consumed by Vietnam. Early in the year, McNamara testified to the Senate Armed Services Committee that the Soviet Union's strategic missile capability was developing faster than expected and recommended that the United States seek talks with Moscow to limit the deployment by either superpower of an antiballistic missile (ABM) system. On January 27, the United States and the Soviet Union, along with 58 other countries, signed the Outer Space Treaty, prohibiting the use of space for military purposes. In February, British prime minister Harold Wilson's attempts to get the participants of the 1954 Geneva talks on Vietnam to reconvene were exhausted, and Johnson ordered a resumption of bombing with a new list of North Vietnamese targets after having held to a temporary truce and writing personally to Ho Ch Minh requesting direct talks.

The United States was by now pouring a million tons of supplies into Vietnam each month to support its troops there—close to 100 pounds a day for each American—but the situation in the South Vietnamese republic continued to deteriorate. In March 1967, Johnson was presented with a copy of a new Vietnamese constitution modeled roughly after the American presidential system, but the Vietnamese economy was hobbled by black markets and government corruption. The relationship between the South Vietnamese Army and the rural population was so poisoned by corruption that the Vietcong was able to replenish its manpower quickly by recruiting locally. In the face of substantial evidence that the continued bombing of North Vietnam had not diminished the capacity of its forces to wage war in the south and that large numbers of American combat forces were no substitute for a responsible government in Saigon, Defense Secretary McNamara concluded in May 1967 that

the cost of the war exceeded any legitimate objective that might be achieved. He issued a memorandum stating that the administration no longer had any attractive policy actions in Vietnam, on the one hand because the military forces committed there had hitherto done little more than to stave off the fall of South Vietnam, and on the other because the war was becoming progressively less popular with the American public. He recommended that the administration enter a new phase in which the U.S. military prevent a Communist victory while a greater effort was committed to establishing a broad-based representative government in Saigon capable of implementing economic and social reforms to win the population's loyalty. Without this, what he called "the rot in the fabric" would continue.

McNamara's revisionism clashed with the view of General Westmorland and the Joint Chiefs of Staff, for whom 100,000 additional troops was the minimum short-term requirement of continuing a war of attrition in which, they reasoned, North Vietnam would eventually be unable to replace its losses. In some instances the administration's strategists applied bizarre theories of "forced urbanization" to hasten the day when the Vietcong's rural sources of recruitment would dry up. Operation Cedar Falls involved 30,000 U.S. troops against Communist strongholds in Binh Duong province near the Cambodian border. The province's villages were bombed, its rice fields denuded, and its surrounding jungles defoliated before the infantry swept the region with tanks and bulldozers to destroy enemy bunkers and tunnels. Some 7,000 inhabitants were forced off the land and into the cities. While their ensuing urban poverty aggravated the instability of South Vietnamese society, North Vietnamese and Vietcong forces quickly reestablished themselves in the province once the American troops had left. Yet Johnson tended to defer to the comparatively optimistic reports from those military and civilian advisors who echoed what they knew to be his hopes. He increasingly came to identify his congressional critics and the antiwar protesters as personal enemies and unwitting accomplices of the North Vietnamese. Johnson sought simultaneously both to give Westmorland the additional troops he demanded for military results and to avoid the public alarm that would result from calling up reserves. He was at this point somewhat delusional in that he professed to be encouraged by the progress being made in Vietnam while keeping from the public the size of Westmorland's new troop requests. He was fearful above all of a collapse of public support for the war and did not trust a public informed of the realities in Vietnam to continue to back him.

War in the Middle East

In the spring of 1967, the administration's attention shifted temporarily from Southeast Asia to the Middle East, when

Israel's relations with its Arab neighbors lurched toward war. Responding to Syrian radio broadcasts that he had failed to support brother Arab states in their conflict with Israel, on May 14, Egyptian President Gamel Abdel Nasser mobilized his army and moved troops into the Sinai Desert. Four days later he asked UN peacekeeping forces to leave the Gaza Strip and Sharm el Sheikh at the mouth of the Gulf of Aqaba where they had been since the Suez Crisis of 1956. He then announced that the Strait of Tiran would be closed to all shipping headed for the state of Israel, and on May 29 concluded a mutual defense pact with Jordan. As Israeli military leaders lobbied Prime Minister Levi Eshkol for a preemptive strike against Egypt, Johnson pleaded with both countries to keep the peace. On May 31, he asked the UN Security Council for a resolution calling on all parties to resolve the dispute diplomatically. Johnson was attempting to organize a multinational naval force to keep the port of Aqaba open and to persuade the UN to adopt a resolution on the right of innocent passage in the Strait of Tiran, when Israeli forces struck on June 5 against the coalition of Arab states. Israeli troops overran the Gaza Strip and the Sinai peninsula, captured the West Bank of the Jordan River and East Jerusalem from Jordanian forces, and seized the Golan Heights on the Syrian border, before Israel agreed to a cease-fire on June 11. The UN Security Council had passed Resolution 234 calling for a cease-fire on June 6. Jordan and Egypt had agreed immediately, Syria on June 10.

The Six Day War occasioned the first use of the Moscow-Washington "hot line" since its establishment by Kennedy and Khrushchev after the 1962 Cuban Missile Crisis. Johnson and Soviet Premier Alexei Kosygin agreed to work for a cease-fire, the United States with Israel, the Soviet Union with Egypt and Syria. Although the administration sought assurances from Tel Aviv that any conquered territories beyond the armistice line of 1949 would be evacuated, Israel declared the 1949 borders invalid and refused to evacuate the occupied territories in the absence of peace agreements with the Arab states guaranteeing Israel's security. Over 100,000 Palestinians fled from Israel and the West Bank to Jordan. Washington supported a UN resolution condemning Israel for the annexation of East Jerusalem, but the Johnson administration refrained from pressuring Tel Aviv to abandon the conquered territories and in December 1967 sold Israel fifty F-4 Phantom jets. The administration's tilt in favor of Israel opened a new phase in American involvement in the Middle East. Thereafter, the United States replaced France as the principal arms supplier to the Jewish state, which it increasingly viewed as an ally against Soviet influence in the region, while Moscow sought to exploit Arab resentment at American support for Israel to court favor with radical Arab states. With the withdrawal of all British forces from the remnants of its empire "east of Suez" between 1968 and 1971, the presence of the United States and its support for Israel assumed ever greater importance in shaping events in the region.

Indirectly, the Six Day War also brought about an informal summit meeting between Johnson and Soviet Premier Kosygin when the Soviet leader visited the UN to support the Arab cause. They met at Glassboro State College for two days of talks that achieved nothing of substance but were noteworthy for the relaxed and amiable atmosphere, differences not withstanding. The meeting could be regarded as a first installment on the superpower détente developed during the Nixon presidency, especially in light of the fact that on June 17 China tested its first hydrogen bomb and relations between the two major Communist powers soured noticeably in the following years.

The McNamara Resignation

Such developments were, however, of no benefit or use to Johnson as he returned his attention to Vietnam. McNamara's rethinking of basic strategy was criticized by the Joint Chiefs as defeatist, and they recruited Senator John Stennis (D-Mississippi), Chair of the Senate Armed Services Committee, as the congressional spokesmen for an alternative view. Stennis arranged closed hearings in August 1967 to investigate attempts by "unskilled civilian amateurs" to shackle the military in its prosecution of the war. Specifically, Chief of Staff General Earle G. Wheeler and U.S. Commander Pacific Vice Admiral U.S.C. Sharp Jr. blamed the ineffectiveness of the bombing on target restrictions imposed by the administration, in particular those against bombing either Hanoi or Haiphong, the harbor through which North Vietnam was supplied by the Soviet Union. McNamara defended his own interpretation of the situation at the hearings—that enemy operations in South Vietnam could not be stopped by any air bombardment short of the annihilation of North Vietnam and its people—but the report's verdict was in effect that the nation's civilian leadership should get out of the way of the "systematic, timely and hard-hitting actions" that were now indispensable. In the meantime, the political situation in South Vietnam continued to deteriorate. In September 1967, Nguyen Van Thieu was elected to the country's presidency in a ballot widely considered to be a fraud from ballot box stuffing by Thieu's organization. Thieu subsequently imprisoned losing candidates who accused him of having cheated; thus his government enjoyed no more popular legitimacy than that of Ngo Dinh Diem could claim during the Kennedy administration.

The war thus entered a pivotal phase in which circumstances were beginning to tilt against the United States. This was reflected in Johnson's failed attempt, also in September 1967, through French intermediaries and Harvard Professor Henry A. Kissinger to get North Vietnam to enter into meaningful negotiations in return for a halt in U.S. bombing raids. In November, Johnson arranged a consultation with a representative delegation of "wise men," experienced elder statesmen among foreign policy and national security experts, which included such architects of early Cold War policy as Dean Acheson and Clark Clifford. Their advice was that the administration should "stay the course" in Vietnam; its effect was to undermine McNamara's memorandum of the preceding May, especially his advice to end Rolling Thunder, and his position within the administration as secretary of defense. McNamara's resignation therefore followed on November 28, although he agreed to stay on until March 1968 when Clark Clifford succeeded him at the Pentagon.

The administration's determination to demonstrate resolve and optimism was momentarily vindicated in January 1968 when North Vietnamese forces attacked an American base at Khesanh near the Laotian border. The attack was anticipated by U.S. intelligence so that General Westmorland was able to deploy additional troops to the sector and draft plans for hitting North Vietnamese forces with a massive aerial bombardment. He also initiated a study on the feasibility of using tactical nuclear weapons in the imminent engagement but was vetoed by a directive from Washington for fear that news of such a study would intensify antiwar protests in the United States. Westmorland's preparation for the kind of decisive confrontation he had long sought with North Vietnamese regulars nonetheless paid impressive dividends. North Vietnamese forces suffered 10,000 deaths in exchange for fewer than 500 U.S. Marines killed. This outcome encouraged General Westmorland to draft an optimistic year-end report, stressing the heavy losses incurred by the enemy and forecasting an exhaustion of North Vietnam's capacity to continue the struggle. In response to the battle at Khesanh, both administration officials and the press made repeated and misleading comparisons of the American victory with the defeat inflicted on French forces at Dien Bien Phu in 1954.

The Tet Offensive

The shock to the administration was therefore that much more profound when at the end of January 1968 North Vietnam launched an offensive in South Vietnam during the first days of Tet, the Vietnamese New Year, on a scale entirely unanticipated by the U.S. command. Beginning on January 30, more than 84,000 Vietcong and North Vietnamese troops launched coordinated attacks on forty-four provincial capitals, sixty-four district capitals, and five major cities in South Vietnam. In the capital city of Saigon, Vietcong commandos attacked the compound of the U.S. embassy, initiating a fire fight that lasted six hours and resulted in the deaths of five American soldiers. General Westmorland's headquarters and the South Vietnamese general staff offices were also attacked. Though taken by surprise—by the scale and ferocity if not the fact of the offensive—U.S. and South Vietnamese forces responded coolly and effectively to the attacks, bringing to bear superior firepower to inflict massive casualties on the enemy and gain the upper hand in only two weeks of fighting. Some 50,000 Vietcong and North Vietnamese regulars perished, while the South Vietnamese and American forces suffered losses of 4,000 and 2,000 respectively. In the ancient imperial city of Hue, the fighting continued for three weeks with some of the most brutal combat of the war, taking 500 Americans, 5,000 Vietcong, and countless civilian casualties.

The Tet Offensive was in every respect a military fiasco for North Vietnam, not only because the change in tactics from guerrilla to conventional warfare was ill-suited to the experience and weaponry of North Vietnamese forces but also because a variety of tactical errors were committed in the offensive's execution. The expectation that South Vietnam's populace would rise up against its own government was, despite that government's obvious corruption, misplaced altogether. Moreover, North Vietnamese and Vietcong troops were profoundly depressed both at the numbers of their losses and their failure to achieve and hold most of their objectives. Still, the accurate claim of Westmorland's command in Saigon that the enemy had suffered a major defeat in the field could not compensate for a decisive defeat in the court of public opinion. The fact that in spite of the presence of more than 500,000 U.S. troops the Vietcong was, in 1968, still able to stage coordinated attacks throughout South Vietnam was itself a psychological blow. That the administration had worked through the second half of 1967 to convince the public that North Vietnamese strength was on the wane doubled the impact of the shock and transformed dismay into widespread fury—at an apparently endless struggle of attrition on the other side of the world; at the administration's optimistic assertions and calculated deceits; and at the president himself as the chief architect of a national humiliation. In the six weeks after Tet, Johnson's public approval rating dipped from 48 to 36 percent.

Crisis in the Democratic Party

Opposition to the war on college campuses that had begun in response to the bombing campaign of 1965 acquired a new urgency and aggressiveness, not least of all because Johnson's demand for ever more troops required the deployment of large numbers of draftees. Tet also occasioned more vocal opposition to the war, along with more personal attacks on Johnson's credibility and integrity among influential business leaders, press and television commentators, university faculty, and clergymen—not to mention celebrities whose appetite for attention eclipsed their knowledge of or interest in foreign policy. Congressional critics of

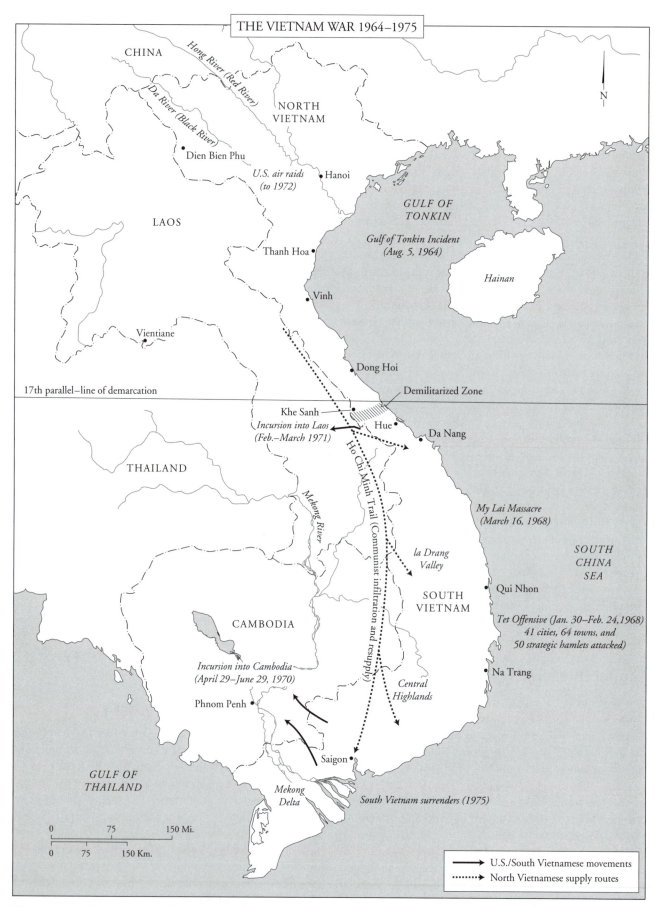

THE VIETNAM WAR 1964–1975

CHINA

Hong River (Red River)

Da River (Black River)

NORTH VIETNAM

• Dien Bien Phu

U.S. air raids (to 1972)

• Hanoi

GULF OF TONKIN

Gulf of Tonkin Incident (Aug. 5, 1964)

Hainan

LAOS

Thanh Hoa •

• Vinh

Vientiane •

• Dong Hoi

17th parallel–line of demarcation

Demilitarized Zone

Khe Sanh

Incursion into Laos (Feb.–March 1971)

Hue •

• Da Nang

THAILAND

Mekong River

Ho Chi Minh Trail (Communist infiltration and resupply)

My Lai Massacre (March 16, 1968)

la Drang Valley

SOUTH CHINA SEA

• Qui Nhon

SOUTH VIETNAM

Tet Offensive (Jan. 30–Feb. 24, 1968) 41 cities, 64 towns, and 50 strategic hamlets attacked)

CAMBODIA

Incursion into Cambodia (April 29–June 29, 1970)

Phnom Penh •

Central Highlands

• Na Trang

Saigon •

GULF OF THAILAND

Mekong Delta

South Vietnam surrenders (1975)

N

0   75   150 Mi.

0   75   150 Km.

→ U.S./South Vietnamese movements

┄┄► North Vietnamese supply routes

The experience of the Korean War became a major factor in the refusal of American civilian leadership to launch an offensive of ground forces into North Vietnam. This condemned the United States to a defensive and reactive strategy.

Johnson's Vietnam policy going back to 1965–1966 now felt vindicated in their mounting skepticism over the very prudence of the American commitment. Others, such as Senator Eugene McCarthy (D-Minnesota) and Senator Robert Kennedy (D-New York), saw in the public's heightened anger over Vietnam an electoral opportunity to run for the presidency in the name of peace and against "Johnson's War." On March 12, 1968, McCarthy nearly defeated Johnson in the New Hampshire Democratic primary, tallying 42.2 percent of the vote against Johnson's 49.5. Scenting blood in the water, Kennedy announced his candidacy for the presidency just four days later.

In addition to a rapidly deteriorating situation at home, Johnson was now faced with stark alternatives in Vietnam. Returning from a trip to assess the situation there in late February, Joint Chiefs Chairman General Earle Wheeler maintained that the United States would need an additional 206,000 troops to regain the initiative. This would have brought the total of American troops in Vietnam to 710,000 and would have required the call-up of 280,000 civilian reservists. The rumor of the request in the press provoked a flurry in resolution-drafting, often among hitherto hawkish supporters of the president, to get Congress on the record opposing the dispatch of any additional troops. Senator Fulbright, stiffened by hearings into the misrepresentation of intelligence reports at the time of Gulf of Tonkin incident, rose to question Johnson's authority to commit additional troops on the grounds that the Tonkin Resolution had been based on deception and was therefore null and void. The alternative to further military escalation, a diplomatic settlement to end the fighting, had through 1966 and 1967 been repeatedly vetoed by Hanoi's preconditions for serious negotiations: an end to all bombing of North Vietnam, the withdrawal of U.S. ground troops from South Vietnam, and the resignation of the Thieu-Ky government in Saigon in favor of a coalition with Communist participation. The fiscal constraints on choice were now truly daunting. The national balance-of-payments crisis arising from the concurrent costs of Johnson's domestic programs and the expense of the war prompted international speculation against the U.S. dollar that in turn affected the budgets of other Western economies whose currencies were pegged to the dollar.

Resignation and Succession

On March 25–26, Johnson therefore chaired another meeting of the wise men and was now confronted with advice contrary to what he received the previous November. The very advisors who had supported a continued war of attrition on that occasion now counseled a change in strategy to reemphasize counter-insurgency operations. Even his new secretary of defense, Clark Clifford, agreed with the departing McNamara. Faced with a negative verdict from the most experienced foreign policy authorities available—as well as the unacceptable troop demands from the Pentagon and impossible diplomatic demands from Hanoi—Johnson announced in a televised address on March 31 that he would not be seeking a second term in the Oval Office. Signaling his continuing willingness to negotiate an end to hostilities, he reiterated his call for Hanoi to enter peace talks even as he pledged a continued determination to stand by South Vietnam and noted the deployment of an additional 30,000 troops.

With Johnson's decision against running for reelection in November 1968, the conduct of foreign policy entered a "lame duck" period as the race among candidates to succeed him intensified and the president's capacity to dominate national political debate waned. In May, North Vietnam finally agreed to negotiations, not about terms for peace with South Vietnam but about the conditions for opening negotiations. The first session was held in Paris on May 13, with Averell Harriman representing the United States and Xuan Thuy representing North Vietnam. Meanwhile, the United States experienced in the summer of 1968 a sense of national crisis created by the sense of failure in Vietnam and heightened conflict over Johnson's domestic programs. Two events in particular symbolized the troubled spirit of national political life: the assassination on April 4 of civil rights leader Dr. Martin Luther King Jr. by James Earl Ray, and the assassination on June 5 of Democratic presidential aspirant Senator Robert F. Kennedy by Palestinian extremist Sirhan Bishara Sirhan. King had become a public critic of the administration's Vietnam policy, notwithstanding Johnson's historic civil rights legislation, because the war's cost competed with social programs for fiscal resources. Kennedy, who was at the time of his shooting the leading contender for the Democratic presidential nomination, had expressed strong support for Israel's position in the Middle East conflict, a matter of growing importance to the foreign policy of coming administrations, Republican and Democratic.

The First Measure of Superpower Détente

In the midst of this turmoil, the administration was modestly compensated for its efforts to stabilize relations with the Soviet Union with the signing on July 1, 1968 of the Nuclear Non-Proliferation Treaty as the conclusion to negotiations dating back to 1963. The nuclear powers—the United States, the Soviet Union, Britain, and later France and China—pledged to work for nuclear arms control and disarmament. At his Glassboro meeting with Soviet Premier Alexei Kosygin in June 1967, Johnson had broached the idea of negotiations on antiballistic missile (ABM) and intercontinental ballistic missile (ICBM) systems. A year later Kosygin advised Johnson that Moscow was prepared to negotiate ABM and ICBM limitations. Johnson was scheduled to travel to Moscow to inaugurate talks beginning in October 15, 1968, but on August 20 the forces of the Soviet Red Army, accompanied by troops from the Bulgarian, East German, Hungarian, and Polish Warsaw Pact allies, invaded Czechoslovakia to oust the government of Alexander Dubček in Prague and reverse its liberal economic and political reforms. Dubček was not initially removed from office but was compelled to report to Moscow to accept the Moscow Protocol according to which communist orthodoxy was restored in his country. Gustav Husak replaced him as first secretary of the Czech Communist Party in May 1970. In the meantime, Moscow formalized the reasoning behind the invasion with the announcement of the so-called Brezhnev Doctrine, which declared the right of the Soviet Union to intervene in any state within the Soviet sphere of influence where Moscow deemed the socialism and the leading role of the Communist Party to be threatened by "counter-revolutionary" forces. The United Nations Security Council condemned the Soviet action, with the notable support of China, but the invasion otherwise received only a muted international response. Although Johnson's trip to Moscow was cancelled and the ABM/ICBM negotiations delayed for Johnson's successor to pursue, the administration was restrained in its reaction both by the awareness that it might need help from Moscow in getting North Vietnam to negotiate in good faith and by a desire to use further arms negotiations to improve bilateral relations.

The Nixon Alternative

On August 8, Richard Nixon received the Republican nomination for the presidency, partly on the strength of his criticism of Johnson for failing to use American power more decisively in Vietnam, but partly also because of his pledge to employ more robust diplomacy, possibly involving Moscow in search of settlement. Nixon's chances of election were improved substantially by the spectacle of the Democratic convention in the last week in August, during which deep internal divisions over Vietnam spilled into the streets of the host city of Chicago. Some 11,900 Chicago police along with 7,500 Illinois National Guard and 1,000 FBI and Secret Service agents were deployed to protect delegates from radical new left groups such as the Students for a Democratic Society (SDS) and the Youth International Party, otherwise referred to as Yippies. Ultimately, a highly fractious convention nominated Johnson's vice president, Hubert Humphrey, but not before a minority led by Senator George McGovern and Senator Edward Kennedy issued a statement calling for an unconditional end to the war and a coalition government for South Vietnam that would include the Vietcong. Conservative Democrats from the South who had been already partly alienated by Johnson's

civil rights legislation of 1964–1965 now broke with the Democratic Party altogether and rallied to George Wallace, the segregationist governor of Alabama, when he formed the American Independent Party.

Between May and October 1968 the American and North Vietnamese delegations in Paris conducted secret talks to arrange a cease-fire in Vietnam. To end his presidency on a positive note Johnson agreed to halt the bombing of North Vietnam in return for an agreement from Hanoi that the Thieu government would have a direct role in negotiations. The outcome of the compromise was less than perfect. No cease-fire was agreed, and the negotiations were to proceed even as the fighting continued. Still, Johnson ordered an end to all bombing, consistent with Hanoi's demand. At this point, the weak link in Washington's goals for Vietnam going back to the Kennedy administration again stymied even this morsel of progress: two days after the bombing had stopped the Thieu government announced that it would not sit down to negotiate with representatives of the Vietcong. It later emerged that Republican presidential nominee, Richard Nixon, had in fact contacted the Thieu government through Anna Chan Chennault, widow of the WWII hero General Claire Chennault, to urge him to boycott the talks with the promise of better treatment from a Republican administration.

It was not his appetite for manipulative intrigue but rather the divisions within the Democratic Party, however, that won Nixon the presidency in November. Governor Wallace's candidacy cut deeply into the Democratic base in the South, taking 9,901,151 votes and permitting Nixon an easy electoral college victory over Humphrey despite his last-minute surge in the polls. Johnson retired from office, physically and emotionally exhausted. His historic contribution to civil rights was unassailable, but many of his Great Society programs were under attack from the left and the right while his gargantuan efforts in Vietnam had come to utter failure. Indeed, they constituted a national tragedy that poisoned the spirit of American politics through the presidencies of Richard Nixon and Gerald Ford. Johnson published *The Vantage Point*, a memoir of his administration and useful discussion of the nature of presidential leadership, in 1971 and died a maligned and misunderstood man in 1973.

Legacy

Johnson's legacy to U.S. foreign policy was therefore almost entirely negative. Indeed, the enormous yet militarily incoherent effort his administration had undertaken in Vietnam between the Tonkin Resolution and Johnson's decision against running for reelection in 1968 had the effect within the Western alliance of undermining confidence both in the prudence of American leadership and in the potency of American power. More damaging still were the divisions within American society itself caused by the demonstrated failure of Johnson's policy in Vietnam, its distortion of foreign policy priorities, its human and financial cost, and the resultant erosion of support for Johnson's domestic programs. As a politician interested above all in domestic social reform, Johnson had attempted to insulate his Great Society programs from the competing demands of the Cold War by managing—rather than prosecuting—a regional hot war in Vietnam. It is no exaggeration to say that the war destroyed his presidency.

The damage did not end there. By 1968, the Democratic Party, since 1932 the dominant electoral force of national politics, had lost its image among the American public as the more legitimate custodian of American diplomacy. It was torn internally by a power struggle involving the New Deal/Cold War Democrats of Johnson's generation, authentic congressional critics of the Vietnam war such as George McGovern and Frank Church, hastily-reconstructed Cold Warriors such as Robert Kennedy, and an insurgent generation of "new left" activists within the Democratic Party and on the campuses.

Additionally, Johnson's skilled presidential leadership in securing congressional support for his Vietnam policy in 1964–1965 had by 1967 degenerated into the habit of defending the escalating American commitment with half-truths and deception regarding the balance sheet of military success and failure. The consequent erosion of trust between Johnson's White House and Congress was not partisan in nature and featured mounting criticism from within the Democratic majority. Beginning with the hearings convened by Senator William Fulbright, congressional inquiry into Johnson's conduct of Vietnam policy turned into a more general attack by the legislative branch on executive prerogative in foreign policy that evolved into institutional warfare while Johnson was in power and into constitutional crisis under his successor, Richard M. Nixon.

The irony for Johnson was that he had inherited from Kennedy a diplomatic commitment to the sovereignty of South Vietnam in which American resolve and international credibility were thought to be at stake. In pursuit of this largely symbolic rather than strategic goal, Johnson radically deepened an American commitment that Kennedy had only begun to militarize at the time his assassination but which Johnson felt bound to continue. As Johnson sought to insulate his presidency from a backlash that might endanger his domestic reforms by managing a conflict rather than prosecuting a war, his administration's credibility was in the end terminally wounded. In the final year of Johnson's presidency, Pentagon estimates of the number of troops required to force Hanoi to negotiate a peace exceeded 700,000, an absurdly large force in light of the limited policy objectives.

On the positive side, superpower relations stabilized and improved during the Johnson years, a fact evidenced in part by Johnson's Glassboro summit with Alexei Kosygin and the sobriety the superpowers brought to their relations during the 1967 Six Day War. This change, which prefigured the superpower détente of the Nixon administration, had as much to do with change inside the Soviet Union and with deteriorating Sino-Soviet relations as with American efforts. Still, the fact that Washington could achieve a more relaxed disposition in its continuing confrontation with Soviet communism even as unexamined Cold War strategy led to humiliation and defeat in Vietnam testified as to the extent to which the Cold War struggle had evolved since the Cuban Missile Crisis.

Carl Cavanagh Hodge

Chronology

1963
November 22: President Kennedy assassinated, Lyndon Baines Johnson is president.

December 12: Kenya gains independence from Britain.

December 26: Secretary McNamara calls South Vietnam unstable.

1964
February 11: Fighting breaks out between Greeks and Turks on Cyprus.

March 31: Military coup in Brazil.

April 28: France withdraws from NATO's integrated command.

August 2–7: Gulf of Tonkin incidents, Congress passes Southeast Asia Resolution.

October 14: Soviet Presidium ousts Khrushchev, Alexei Kosygin is premier.

1965
February 6: Vietcong attacks U.S. forces at Pleiku.

March 19: Operation Rolling Thunder begins.

April 28: Johnson sends U.S. marines to the Dominican Republic.

June 12: Nguyen Van Thieu and Nguyen Cao Ky take control of South Vietnamese government.

October 14: Defense Department announces major draft call-up.

1966
January 19: Indira Gandhi becomes prime minister of India.

January 28: Congressional hearings on Tonkin resolution begin.

August 18: Cultural Revolution in China begins.

October 25: Manila Conference.

November 13: Israeli reprisal attacks against Jordan for Palestinian raids.

1967

January 26: Defense Secretary McNamara brief Congress on nuclear doctrine of Mutual Assured Destruction.

February 14: British attempt to reconvene Geneva Conference on Vietnam fails.

May 23: Johnson protests Egyptian blockade of Gulf of Aqaba.

June 5: Israel attacks Egypt, Iraq, Syria, and Jordan: Six Day War begins.

June 17: China tests first hydrogen bomb.

June 25: Johnson meets Soviet Premier Kosygin at Glassboro, Pennsylvania.

November 28: Defense Secretary McNamara resigns.

November 30: Senator Eugene McCarthy announces candidacy for presidency on peace platform.

1968

January 16: Britain withdraws its forces from Persian Gulf region.

January 26: General Westmorland issues favorable report on Vietnam.

January 30: North Vietnam's Tet Offensive begins.

March 12: Johnson barely wins New Hampshire Democratic primary.

March 16: Senator Robert Kennedy announces presidential candidacy.

March 31: Johnson announces bombing halt, offer to negotiate with Hanoi, decision not to run for reelection.

April 4: Martin Luther King Jr. assassinated.

June 5: Robert F. Kennedy assassinated.

July 1: Nuclear Non-Proliferation Treaty signed with Britain, Soviet Union and fifty other countries.

August 20: Warsaw Pact forces invade Czechoslovakia and topple Dubček government.

October 31: U.S. and North Vietnam agree to conduct peace negotiations.

November 5: Richard Nixon elected president.

References and Further Reading

Evans, Rowland, and Robert Novak. *Lyndon Johnson: The Exercise of Power.* New York: New American Library, 1966.

Dallek, Robert. *Flawed Giant: Lyndon Johnson and His Times, 1961–1973.* New York: Oxford University Press, 1998.

Divine, Robert. *The Johnson Years,* 3 vols. Lawrence, KS: University Press of Kansas, 1987–1994.

Gelb, Leslie. *The Irony of Vietnam: The System Worked.* Washington DC: Brookings, 1979.

Herring George C. *America's Longest War: The United States and Vietnam 1950–1975.* Boston: McGraw-Hill, 2002.

Johnson, Lyndon Baines. *The Vantage Point: Perspectives on the Presidency, 1963–1969.* New York: Popular Library, 1971.

Karnow, Stanley. *Vietnam, A History.* New York: Viking, 1983.

Leuchtenberg, William E. *In the Shadow of FDR: Harry Truman to Ronald Reagan.* Ithaca, NY: Cornell University Press, 1983.

Mann, Robert. *A Grand Delusion: America's Descent into Vietnam.* New York: Basic Books, 2001.

Moise, Edwin E. *Tonkin Gulf and the Escalation of the Vietnam War.* Chapel Hill, NC: University of North Carolina Press, 1996.

Oren, Michael. *Six Days of War: June 1967 and the Making of the Modern Middle East.* New York: Presidio, 2003.

Richard Milhous Nixon (1969–1974)

Early Life and Political Career

Richard Milhous Nixon was born in Yorba Linda, Orange County, California, on January 9, 1913, the second of the five sons of Francis A. and Hannah Milhous Nixon. The family moved to Whittier, California, when Nixon was nine years of age. There Nixon's father ran a grocery store and gas station while Nixon attended local public schools and at age seventeen entered Whittier College, a small Quaker academy dating to 1887. In this, the influence of his mother, a serious woman who brooked neither extravagance nor frivolous pursuit and insisted that her sons acquire a college education, was probably critical. At any rate, Nixon was a serious and competitive high school and college student, socially awkward and bookish yet skillful in argument and formal debate.

On graduation from Whittier in 1934, Nixon won a scholarship to Duke University Law School, where he subjected himself to a particularly spartan living and study regimen, partly due to the modest financial means that required he retain his scholarship and partly due to a personal drive that left him indifferent to creature comforts. After his bar exams, Nixon returned in 1937 to Whittier to work for the law firm of Wingert & Bewley, becoming a partner in 1939 with primary responsibility for cross-examination in trials. In August 1942, Nixon joined the U.S. Navy as a lieutenant and served with Naval Air Transport in New Caledonia and Bougainville in the Solomon Islands. In 1944 he was ordered back to the United States and finished the war winding up contracts with Glenn L. Martin and Bell Aircraft, work for which he received a meritorious service citation from the secretary of the Navy.

Nixon's political career was launched immediately after the war, when in September 1945, Herman Perry, a banker and community leader in Whittier, invited him to run as a Republican for California's 12th congressional district. Nixon won the Republican nomination and then defeated the incumbent Jerry Voorhis, a New Deal Democrat, on a platform of support for small business against unnecessary government regulation of the economy. The campaign established two precedents that followed Nixon for the rest of his political career: he was a zealous anti-communist and he was ruthless in electoral combat.

This reputation was strengthened once Congress convened in 1947, under Republican control for the first time since the 1930s, when Nixon gained a seat on the House

Richard Milhous Nixon wound down the war in Vietnam, established détente with Moscow, and opened relations with China, yet was destroyed by the Watergate scandal and his own efforts to contain it. (Library of Congress)

Committee on Education and Labor as well as the House Un-American Activities Committee (HUAC). Nixon helped draft the 1947 Taft-Hartley Act; defied public opinion in his home district to cultivate bipartisan support for General George Marshall's European Recovery Program; and assumed a prominent role in HUAC in assembling a case against Alger Hiss, a former State Department official and president of the Carnegie Endowment for Peace under investigation for prewar activities with the Communist Party. The Hiss case gave Nixon national prominence, a fact he was quick to exploit when he sought a Senate seat the same year. The campaign against his Democratic opponent Helen Gahagan Douglas became a more sophisticated version of that against Voorhis. When Nixon challenged

Douglas to deny that Communism's threat to the United States was the central issue of the campaign, she took the bait. Against the evidence of the conquest of mainland China by Communist forces in the fall of 1949; the Soviet test of a nuclear weapon the same year; Nixon's successful prosecution of Hiss; and the subsequent prosecutions of Klaus Fuchs, Harry Gold, David Greenglass, and Ethel and Julius Rosenberg, Douglas's response was imprudent. It became fatal when in the middle of the campaign Communist North Korea invaded South Korea. Nixon accused the Truman administration of an inept foreign policy and associated Douglas with its failures. He defeated her with the largest plurality of any Senate winner in 1950.

In 1952, Nixon was selected as the vice-presidential running mate for the Republican nominee for the Oval Office, General Dwight D. Eisenhower. After Eisenhower's landslide victory over the Democratic nominee, Adlai Stevenson, Nixon spent the next eight years as a particularly active vice president. He established a studied expertise in foreign affairs supplemented by numerous trips abroad as an ambassador for the administration, the most storied among them being a 1959 visit to Moscow in which he debated before assembled journalists the relative merits of the American and Soviet systems with Soviet Premier Nikita Khrushchev. His experience as vice president put Nixon in an unassailable position for the Republican nomination in the 1960 presidential election year, but he nonetheless lost the election by only 112,803 votes to the Democratic nominee, John F. Kennedy.

Nixon returned to California and in 1962 made a run for governor against the Democratic incumbent Edmund Brown in which he was roundly trounced. He went to work for Mudge, Stern, Baldwin & Todd, a Wall Street law firm, yet stayed in close contact with ambitious Republicans, endorsing Barry Goldwater for the presidency in 1964 and shoring up the morale of congressional Republicans who, like Goldwater, lost spectacularly in the landslide reelection of President Johnson that year. By 1968 Nixon's patient partisan loyalty had earned him wide reciprocal support among Republicans who sought a presidential candidate more centrist than the conservative wing of the party, now led by California Governor Ronald Reagan, and the Northeastern liberal wing, led by New York Governor Nelson Rockefeller. He therefore won on the first ballot of the 1968 party convention and faced a Democratic Party torn internally over the mismanagement of the Vietnam War. A conservative with impeccable Cold Warrior credentials, the first task of his presidency would have to be the termination of the nation's greatest foreign policy misadventure since the articulation of the Truman Doctrine.

National Acrimony

Nixon was elected in November 1968 by a popular vote margin over Vice President Hubert Humphrey only slightly larger than that of John F. Kennedy over Nixon in 1960. The national circumstances of his election, moreover, were grim. The American people were deeply divided over the failure to prevail militarily or diplomatically in Vietnam as well as over the costs of the Johnson administration's domestic programs. The inflation rate ran at 4.3 percent, the highest since the Korean War, while interest rates were at their highest levels since the Civil War.

An acceptable end to the Vietnam conflict was far and away the strongest point of contention. In the two and a half months between Nixon's election and inauguration, American GIs were killed at a rate of 300 each week while peace talks with North Vietnam bogged down in wrangling over the shape of the negotiating table. Demonstrators burning American flags and declaring Nixon a war criminal marred the inauguration parade; Nixon's limousine was at one point pelted by stones, beer cans, and bottles. The general public looked to the new administration to resolve the greatest national crisis since World War II, yet Congress sought simultaneously to recover some of the terrain it had conceded to Nixon's predecessor beginning with the Tonkin Resolution by limiting executive prerogative in the conduct of foreign affairs. During his briefings of the president-elect, Johnson advised the utmost secrecy in the determination of executive policy, warning in particular that unauthorized leaks of the internal discussions could be terminal to Nixon's ability to formulate and implement ideas coherently.

Nixon was in many respects especially well-equipped to bring about radical change in American foreign relations. He arrived in office both with the experience accumulated during eight years as vice-president in the Eisenhower administration and with a number of ideas developed in the meantime on how to restructure American foreign relations. He believed that the Soviet Union had achieved strategic parity with the United States and that the military superiority Washington had enjoyed during the 1950s and 1960s could not be restored. Equally, he maintained that the United States could accept and acknowledge strategic parity yet continue to contain Soviet power by minimizing direct confrontation and balancing other states and factors against it. Détente—an abatement of hostility and relaxation of tensions with Soviet Union—was to be the centerpiece of a new relationship with Moscow. Nixon's reputation as a Republican with impeccable anti-communist credentials meant that he would face far less domestic opposition to his initiatives from the political right than Democrats such as Kennedy and Johnson could have hoped for.

The Nixon Doctrine

In an address to Congress in February of 1970, Nixon pledged that "the United States will participate in the defense and development of its allies and friends," yet cautioned that "America cannot—and will not—conceive all the plans, design all the programs, execute all the decisions, and undertake all the defense of the free nations of the world. We will help where it makes a real difference and is in our interest." In Vietnam, a turning point in the conduct of Cold War foreign policy had been reached. Since the articulation of the Truman Doctrine the national dilemma had been to bridge the gap between the formal commitments implied by containment and the resources required to sustain them. Nixon had decided to stop trying with the methods Kennedy and Johnson had employed. The Nixon Doctrine represented a renunciation of Kennedy's inaugural promise to bear *any* burden and fight *any* foe to ensure the survival and success of liberty. Nixon sought instead to meet the fundamental foreign policy goals set forth by Truman with a much greater emphasis on the diplomatic over the military tools of statecraft—to achieve the goals of containment more economically, in financial and human terms, by adjusting American diplomacy to new realities.

The administration sought first to consult regularly with traditional European allies, whose perceptions and concerns Johnson had neglected as his administration was overwhelmed by Vietnam. Nixon visited the NATO Council in Brussels, as well as London, Bonn, West Berlin, Rome, Vatican City, and Paris. He then complemented fence-mending with NATO allies by creating a new strategic bargaining chip with the Soviet Union. In re-approaching the strategic arms limitation talks (SALT) sought by Johnson prior to the Soviet invasion of Czechoslovakia in August 1968, Nixon asked Congress for funding to build an antiballistic missile (ABM) system. The Soviet Union was already constructing ABM defenses around Moscow, which, Nixon argued, would give the Kremlin a first-strike capacity against the United States by protecting Soviet population centers against American retaliation for a nuclear attack. Nixon defended the ABM as essentially an arms-control initiative, in part by pointing out that the system would defend American missile sights rather than population centers but also by announcing that Secretary of Defense Laird would be trimming $2.5 billion from the Johnson defense budget, the first such cut in eight years.

Nixon and his national security advisor, Henry Kissinger, used "linkage," a forthright emphasis of the interrelatedness of issues, in their overall approach to détente. Kissinger held that linkage was integral to the attempt to bring conceptual order to foreign policy and free the United States from the danger of oscillating between overextension and isolation. In application, it involved offers of trade opportunities to the Soviet Union, or the withdrawal of the same, in return for Kremlin cooperation in arms control. The leverage acquired over Soviet policy in the cultivation of certain common interests with the United States would incrementally domesticate the Kremlin leadership into an acceptance of world order in which adherence to a code of conduct

reduced confrontation and made Soviet behavior more predictable.

Orderly Retreat from Vietnam

Turning to Vietnam, Nixon initially set aside this stress on stabilization and authorized an extension of American bombing sorties to include targets in Cambodia, mostly North Vietnamese and Vietcong bases thought to account for as many as 40,000 troops supplied through the port of Sihanoukville on the Gulf of Siam. The Joint Chiefs of Staff had long recommended such bombings, but President Johnson had been unable to secure permission from Cambodian leader Prince Norodom Sihanouk for operations on the territory of a neutral country. The military value of the bombings was disputed by the CIA and the State Department, but a good part of Nixon's motivation was diplomatic. He would have preferred a strategic bombing of North Vietnam but did not want to disrupt peace discussions; the strikes in Cambodia were thus an indirect signal to Hanoi of his readiness to resort to tough measures. The administration went to elaborate pains to keep the bombings secret, to avoid both a new provocation to antiwar sentiment in the American public and possible international objection to raids on a country whose neutrality the United States officially recognized. This involved "dual reporting" of bombing raids by the Pentagon, in which B-52s would take off to attack Vietnamese targets but have their mission redirected toward Cambodia in mid-flight. Bombs that fell "officially" on Vietnam were in fact dropped on Cambodia. The Cambodian raids were not acknowledged until 1973, when the revelation helped to fuel congressional interest in Nixon's impeachment.

In the meantime, they accomplished two things. Their secrecy was calculated to avert protests against Sihanouk, who not only remained silent but also furnished American forces with intelligence on Vietnamese Communist bases in Cambodia. Hanoi also held its tongue, because any diplomatic protest would have confirmed its illicit deployment of troops in a neutral country. In May of 1969, Nixon spoke to the nation on television, proposing a cease-fire, the withdrawal of American and North Vietnamese troops, the exchange of prisoners of war, and an international commission to conduct free elections in South Vietnam. This represented the administration's opening bargaining position for negotiations in Paris. Hanoi rejected it outright. Nixon nonetheless announced together with South Vietnamese President Nguyen Van Thieu the "Vietnamization" of the war effort and the withdrawal of the first 25,000 U.S. troops in June 1969. When Nixon attempted to apply linkage to superpower relations over Vietnam, insisting that the Soviet leadership exert pressure on Hanoi to be more forthcoming in Paris, Soviet Ambassador Anatoly Dobrynin said that

Moscow wished to improve relations with the United States regardless of events in Vietnam, rightly guessing that Nixon wanted the same. Secretary of Defense Melvin Laird pressed for a timetable to reduce U.S. forces in Vietnam from their peak of 543,482 in April 1969 to 206,000 by the end of 1971. Laird factored anticipated troop reductions into the Pentagon's budgetary procedure, thus making it difficult to interrupt them without violating Nixon's commitment to lower defense costs.

Kissinger, however, was adamantly opposed to a hasty "de-escalation" and argued that a strong U.S. presence in Vietnam remained one of Nixon's important bargaining chips. Still, the administration beat Laird's timetable, withdrawing another 60,000 troops in December 1969; cutting to 280,000 by the end of 1970; and reaching a total troop strength of 140,000 in December 1971. With the troop reductions, Nixon hoped that the antiwar fury on university campuses would decline, a goal he sought to pursue further by phasing out the Selective Service System dating to the late 1940s. He also asked Congress to draft nineteen-year-old men first to reduce the period of draft eligibility from seven years to one. The changes meant that most men over nineteen no longer feared the draft, and the intensity of student opposition to the war declined significantly.

On July 29, 1969, the lunar module *Eagle* landed on the surface of the moon, thus meeting President Kennedy's challenge of May 1961 to accomplish the task by the end of the decade. The summer and fall of 1969 were otherwise full of evidence that an era was ending: Charles de Gaulle resigned from the French presidency in June; Ho Chi Minh died in September after answering a letter from Nixon rejecting entirely Washington's interpretation of the conflict between North and South Vietnam; and, Willi Brandt, former Mayor of West Berlin became Chancellor of West Germany on October 21. In August, Kissinger began secret negotiations with North Vietnamese representative Xuan Thuy in Paris, while the United States and the Soviet Union convened SALT negotiations in Helsinki in November, the U.S. Senate having approved construction of an ABM system in August. In November 1969, it was made public that U.S. troops under the command of Lieutenant William L. Calley had shot 450 unarmed South Vietnamese civilians. Though Nixon condemned the atrocity and expressed concern that it not discredit American servicemen fulfilling an honorable mission in Vietnam, the news hardened the zeal of the war's most dedicated opponents in the United States that the administration end "immoral" American involvement in Vietnam as quickly as possible.

The gradualness of Nixon's withdrawal from Vietnam, combined with his resort to rearguard military measures covering an orderly retreat, meant that his diplomatic triumphs elsewhere were constantly troubled by tense and often confrontational relations with Congress. Explicit opposition to the U.S. involvement in Southeast Asia was vastly more popular in a Democratic legislature now dealing with a Republican president than it had been during Johnson's term. Congress was also determined to reclaim the authority in foreign policy it had been surrendering to the executive branch since the Kennedy administration. The year 1970 therefore saw the administration successfully manage a crisis in the Middle East and astutely support significant changes in West Germany's relationship with the Warsaw Pact. It also witnessed the use of covert action and overt force in defense of American interests abroad that deepened the rift between the White House and Congress.

The principal rift centered on administration actions related to withdrawal from Vietnam. In March 1970, while vacationing in France, Prince Sihanouk was overthrown by his prime minister, Lon Nol. North Vietnamese and Vietcong troops and their allies in the Cambodian Khmer Rouge were pushing back the Cambodian army, while South Vietnamese army units crossed the border accompanied by U.S. advisors—contrary to Pentagon orders against violating Cambodian neutrality. On April 14, Lon Nol broadcast an appeal for outside help, a step Nixon had been preparing to take even prior to Sihanouk's ouster. A clear demonstration of U.S. power and determination, Nixon believed, would at the very least drive Hanoi toward more flexibility at the negotiations in Paris. As Communist forces closed on the Cambodian capital, Phnom Penh, and General Abrams cautioned him that the remaining American troops in South Vietnam would be imperiled unless enemy sanctuaries in Cambodia were eliminated, Nixon announced on April 30, 1970, that a joint U.S.-ARVN "incursion" of Cambodia by 20,000 troops was underway. The invasion killed some 2,000 enemy troops, cleared 16,000 acres of jungle, and destroyed 8,000 bunkers. It reduced North Vietnamese operations in Cambodia significantly but its impact on operations in South Vietnam was transitory.

The Climax of the Antiwar Movement

Among domestic opponents of the Vietnam War the reaction was visceral, as was Nixon's own response to the reaction. Having soothed student opposition to the war by ending the draft, he now faced the biggest protests to date. That held at Kent State University on May 4 was the most consequential. Governor John Rhodes likened the demonstrators to "brown shirts" and ordered 750 National Guardsmen to the Kent State campus when an Army ROTC building was burned down. Nervous Guardsmen fired at unarmed students, killing four and wounding nine. Over 448 colleges and universities experienced protests over the following weeks; some 100,000 protestors marched in Washington. Nixon rejected outright any criticism of his authority and readiness as commander-in-chief to strike back anywhere at enemy forces attacking American troops but referred additionally to dissident students as "bums burning down campuses" and interpreted the shooting as the almost inevitable outcome of dissent turning into violence. His television address to the nation on the Cambodian operation predicted that, in the absence of American strength and resolve, "the forces of totalitarianism and anarchy will threaten free nations and free institutions throughout the world," implying that the nation's enemies overseas were aided and abetted by the administration's critics at home.

The Senate's reaction to Cambodia was to restrict the president's capacity to wage war. The Foreign Relations Committee adopted nine to one an amendment to a military appropriations bill, the Cooper-Church Amendment, that would withhold funds for Cambodian operations after June 30, the deadline announced by Nixon for having all U.S. combat units out of the country. It also rejected a proposal authorizing Nixon to send troops back into Cambodia to protect Americans in Vietnam and voted down a proposal that would have permitted him to aid other states, such as Thailand, to help Cambodia in the future. Yet the Senate also rejected the McGovern-Hatfield "end the war" amendment to cut off all funding for operation in Vietnam after December 31, 1971, unless Congress declared war. Nixon argued that he had not started, but rather had inherited, the Vietnamese war and maintained that his responsibilities as commander-in-chief to American servicemen fighting it overrode any legal or constitutional objections to his methods.

The Cooper-Church amendment ultimately passed the full Senate by fifty-nine to thirty-seven—after six weeks of debate that made it almost irrelevant. Congress was in reality interested in opposing Nixon symbolically but wary of the political cost of extracting the nation from Vietnam on any terms other than his. A Gallup poll revealed that 50 percent of the public approved of the president's decision to go into Cambodia while 39 percent opposed it, a weak constituency for Nixon's policy but a losing one for its opposition.

Crisis Management in the Middle East

Meanwhile, conditions in the Middle East were deteriorating rapidly. Since March 1969, Secretary of State William Rogers had been discussing possible solutions to the Arab-Israeli conflict with Moscow. The Rogers Plan included a demilitarized Sinai with a guarantee of Israel's security in the Strait of Tiran; Israeli withdrawal from occupied territory, followed by Arab-Israeli negotiations on the details of peace; and separate discussions to settle the status of the Gaza Strip. Egypt balked at direct negotiations because it would appear to acknowledge Israel's right to exist, whereupon Moscow also withdrew its support for the plan. Rogers never had the full backing of either Nixon or Kissinger. The first half of 1970 witnessed sporadic skirmishing along Israel's border with Egypt, Jordan, and Syria. Both Moscow and Washington increased the supply of arms

to their respective regional clients, but the Soviet Union supplied Egypt with air defense combat personnel as well as the usual arms and equipment. Additionally, Moscow warned the administration that unless pressure was brought to bear on Israel to withdraw speedily from occupied territories in accordance with U.N. resolutions, the Soviet Union would be "forced" to supply her Arab neighbors with the means to rebuff "the arrogant aggressor." Similar messages were sent to Prime Minister Harold Wilson of Great Britain and Georges Pompidou, who had succeeded de Gaulle as president of France in June 1969. Moscow's message was in fact a diplomatic maneuver to justify a military reinforcement already underway.

In June 1970, King Hussein of Jordan, whose country had become a haven for Palestinian refugees after the Arab-Israeli war of 1948–1949, took measures to prevent Palestinians from launching raids on Israel from Jordanian territory, angering the Popular Front for the Liberation of Palestine (PFLP) and the Palestine Liberation Organization (PLO) headed by Yasser Arafat. A Palestinian uprising began on June 9 in which the PFLP and the PLO *fedayeen* took American hostages and killed an American military attaché in retaliation for U.S. support for Israel. Hussein responded with force and secured the release of the hostages. Nixon then decided to venture a new peace initiative, the Rogers Plan II, aimed at an Egyptian-Jordanian-Israeli cease-fire. This was accomplished and went into effect on August 7. To scuttle the fragile peace, the PFLP highjacked three international airliners and demanded the release of Palestinians held in Israeli, British, Swiss, and West German jails. At this point Nixon announced that he was delivering eighteen Phantom jets to Israel and made preparations for possible U.S. intervention by ordering the U.S. Sixth Fleet to the Eastern Mediterranean and sending air transport and combat aircraft to a base at Incirlik in Turkey.

As King Hussein deployed tanks to take over the Palestinian camps in Jordan to force the PFLP and PLO out of his country, Syria and Iraq threatened to oppose him. Syria moved a tank column into Jordanian territory. Nixon then told the press on September 17 that the United States would intervene with Israel in defense of Hussein if Syria or Iraq moved against him. On September 20, Hussein asked for Israeli support to launch an offensive against Syria and the Palestinians, and Israeli Prime Minister Golda Meir immediately looked in turn for American guarantees. Two days later, Nixon put U.S. troops on alert and agreed to protect Israel from Egypt and the Soviet Union if Meir helped Hussein maintain his authority. The United States and the Soviet Union were closer to war than at any time since the Cuban Missile Crisis of 1962. By September 23, Hussein's army had turned back the Syrians—possibly aided by Soviet pressure on Damascus to back down—and reasserted Jordanian control. The radical Palestinian organizations moved into Lebanon to regroup.

Superpower Détente and German Ostpolitik

The closing weeks of 1970 witnessed events with far-reaching consequences in South America and Europe. In September Salvador Allende emerged as the leading candidate in a three-way election for the presidency of Chile with a 36.3 percent plurality. Since 1962, the CIA had been funneling aid to Allende's opponents, but Nixon now ordered CIA Director Richard Helms to make a major effort to prevent Allende's accession to power with bribes to Chilean congressmen who under Chile's constitution were now responsible for choosing the president. This effort failed when the Chilean Congress picked Allende on October 24. At this point, CIA activities in Chile gravitated to a new level that contributed to the coup against Allende two years later.

In August 1970, West German Chancellor Willi Brandt and Soviet Chairman Alexei Kosygin signed a treaty recognizing the political status quo in Europe. Bonn thus technically renounced the goal of reuniting the two Germanys. Then, in early December, Brandt and Polish Premier Józef Cyrankiewicz signed a treaty recognizing the Oder-Neisse line as the German-Polish border, thereby making official German acceptance of the Yalta compromise of 1944–1945, which awarded formerly German territory to Poland. The treaty was integral to Brandt's pursuit of Ostpolitik—Eastern Policy, aimed at improving relations with the Soviet Union and the Warsaw Pact—and aimed at more normal diplomatic relations with the Warsaw Pact nations and the Soviet Union. Ostpolitik was largely in tune with Nixon's policy of superpower détente even if the administration was nervous about possible Soviet ambitions to lure Bonn toward a neutralist position to undermine NATO. The year ended with the administration, partly at the prompting of the European allies, persuading the Israeli government to resume peace talks with Egypt through U.N. mediator Gunnar Jarring.

The year 1971 was pivotal both to Nixon's détente diplomacy in Europe and to a related effort to balance American relations between the two Communist nuclear powers, the Soviet Union and the People's Republic of China. Although the Soviet intervention in Czechoslovakia in August 1968 had made most West European governments wary of new initiatives with Moscow, unofficial East-West contacts in Europe grew. Additionally, Moscow had been eager since the spring of 1969 to convene a European security conference that would legitimize the political status quo on the Continent. While Moscow initially opposed the participation of non-European states, at the June 1970 meeting of Warsaw Pact governments, the Soviets announced a willingness to accept the participation of the United States and Canada. The bilateral Ostpolitik of the West German government was thus supplemented by the gravitation of NATO and the Warsaw Pact toward a Conference on Security and Cooperation in Europe (CSCE), which ultimately convened in Helsinki in November 1972, as well as talks on Mutual and Balanced Force Reductions (MBFR), which began on January 31, 1973. In the meantime, West Germany's bilateral treaties with Moscow and other Warsaw Pact governments were supplemented by a Quadripartite Agreement on Berlin—involving Britain, France, the United States, and the Soviet Union—signed on September 3, 1971. The agreement acknowledged the legitimacy of East Germany by the Western powers yet facilitated access by West Berliners to the East Berlin and East Germany for visits of up to thirty days, reduced Berlin's potential as a flashpoint for superpower crises, and improved the negotiating climate for the CSCE and MBFR talks.

Both Nixon and Brandt employed economic diplomacy in furthering the goals of détente and Ostpolitik. Because the Soviet Union had more to gain from trade and investment opportunities, the Western democracies were in a position to employ linkage by offering or withdrawing economic privileges in return for revised Soviet behavior in other areas. Over time, however, a differentiation in the American and West German perception of trade with the Soviets developed. While Nixon as well the presidents who followed him were willing to view trade *primarily* as a political lever on Soviet behavior, some sectors of West German industry came to view investment opportunities in Eastern Europe and the Soviet Union, traditionally natural markets for German goods, as a benefit in their own right. For his part, Nixon was often castigated on the domestic front for trading with the Soviet Union in order to influence its *foreign* policy by critics who wanted trade used as a lever on Soviet *domestic* policy. Moreover, détente generally, and trade with Soviet Union specifically, served to cultivate an unlikely alliance of domestic political opponents of the administration. Liberals thought that trade should be used to challenge Soviet human rights abuses such as highly restrictive emigration policies, particularly for Soviet Jews; conservatives took offense at the administration's willingness to violate the traditional ban on commercial contacts with Communist countries. When, in April 1973, Nixon sought congressional approval for most-favored-nation (MFN) trade status for the Soviet Union, liberal and conservative opposition to what critics saw as Nixon's amoral Realpolitik demonstrated the fragility of domestic support for an innovative foreign policy.

The China Diplomacy

This problem encouraged Nixon to centralize control of foreign policy initiatives as much as possible in the White House. As early as 1967 he had published an article in *Foreign Affairs* in which he advocated "pulling China back

President Richard Nixon meets with Chinese Communist Party chairman Mao Zedong during his historic 1972 China trip. (National Archives)

into the world community" and had established indirect contact with Beijing through France, Pakistan, and Romania. Washington and Beijing had thus been conducting discreet discussions on renewing normal diplomatic relations for some time, when in April 1971 an American table tennis team attending a tournament in Japan was invited by their Chinese counterparts to visit China. The subsequent warm reception of the American players in Beijing by Premier Chou En-lai prompted Nixon to respond immediately to Chou's express wish for friendship between "our two peoples" with the announcement that he would be ending travel restrictions to China along with other changes that required neither negotiation nor congressional approval. The establishment of cordial relations with the second Communist power was a critical piece of the Nixon Doctrine.

In announcing his ABM decision, Nixon had cited the need to defend the United States against a possible nuclear attack from China and observed additionally that the Soviet Union "would be just as reluctant as we would" to leave itself naked against a potential Chinese threat. Moscow had so mismanaged its relations with Beijing during the 1960s that in the spring and summer of 1969 a series of fighting clashes along the Ussuri River border took bilateral relations between them to a new low. This kind of comment therefore struck a nerve in Moscow. Nixon sought to widen the rift between Beijing and Moscow to establish a triangular relationship to American advantage. If Beijing were open to the idea of a new relationship, ideological differences notwithstanding, Nixon was free to define relations on national terms and play on Soviet insecurities about the rival Communist power. Teasing historic Russian fears of encirclement through Sino-American rapprochement might move Moscow to ponder the gap between its own ambitions and capabilities and become more cooperative on new arms-control agreements, European security, and Middle Eastern affairs.

But Nixon wanted maximum control over the circumstance and optics of his China diplomacy. He therefore dispatched Kissinger to a secret meeting with Chou En-lai and went to great lengths to keep other parties, including Secretary of State Rogers, as uninformed as possible about the administration's evolving plans. Kissinger and Chou established an extensive agenda of change for Sino-American relations and accepted a formal invitation for Nixon to visit Beijing.

On July 15, Nixon then announced to a surprised television and radio audience that he would be visiting China—overturning a U.S. policy dating to 1949—early in 1972. In February of that year Nixon and Kissinger flew to Beijing for talks with Chairman Mao Zedong and Premier Chou En-lai. Television reports carried many of the visit's formal events live into American homes while the substance of the Sino-American diplomacy was negotiated to produce the Shanghai Communiqué, a ten-point charter for future diplomatic relations. China stated that it would have no full diplomatic relations with the United States as long as Washington recognized Taiwan.

Nixon promised a gradual withdrawal of American forces from Taiwan and agreed that there was one China of which Taiwan was part, thus inaugurating the One China policy. In October 1971, the People's Republic of China was admitted to the United Nations and the nationalist government in Taiwan expelled. Nixon announced that the United States would be in favor of giving Beijing a permanent seat on the Security Council. Japan and the West European allies generally approved of Nixon's China policy and the visit but were dismayed at neither being consulted nor informed in advance at such a radical change to the terrain of international affairs. The apparent suddenness of the visit, however, appealed to Nixon's and Kissinger's taste for secrecy followed by bold *faits accomplis,* as well as their preference for working outside the normal protocol channels and diplomatic apparatus of the State Department. The Shanghai Communiqué was drafted without the knowledge or consent of Secretary of State Rogers.

Holding the Initiative

Nixon's determination to make a new start with China was complicated by regional crises that he and Kissinger viewed from an inappropriately Cold War perspective. The Third Indo-Pakistani War in 1971 is an example. The secession of East Pakistan from West Pakistan and Indian support for it—ultimately the creation of the sovereign state of Bangladesh in December 1971—was the flashpoint of a conflict in which Nixon sought to "tilt toward Pakistan" partly because he sought Pakistani help in his China diplomacy but also due to personal animosity, entirely reciprocated, toward Indian Prime Minister Indirah Gandhi. Gandhi, fearful of a U.S.-China-Pakistan alignment, countered with

the Soviet-Indian Friendship Treaty. The Nixon administration overreacted, claiming in the face of contradictory evidence that India wanted to destroy West Pakistan and warning Moscow to stay out of a conflict in which it showed no sign of intervention. India triumphed militarily, oversaw Bangladeshi independence, took 2,500 square miles of territory from West Pakistan as damages, and held 93,000 Pakistanis as prisoners of war until 1973. The war shifted the South Asian regional balance of power decisively in India's favor and created a new state, neither of which the administration could prevent. Too eager in this instance to look tough, the administration ended up looking foolish.

Nixon's penchant for unilateral action extended to economic diplomacy. A foreign trade imbalance had been growing since the late 1960s, and European governments had wanted the United States to devalue the gold price of the dollar from the rate of $35.00 per ounce at which it had been fixed since 1933. In 1971, the U.S. trade surplus disappeared for the first time in the twentieth century, symbolizing the economic maturity of the West European and Japanese economies. On August 15, 1971, Nixon suspended the dollar's gold convertibility, imposed a domestic wage-price freeze, and imposed a temporary 10-percent surcharge on imports, thereby ending both dollar-gold convertibility and the Bretton Woods monetary system established in 1944. The trade surcharge in particular shocked the major trading partners of the United States. Secretary of the Treasury John Connally was a strong advocate of restrictive measures as a stick to remove subsidies and non-tariff barriers against imported American goods. For his part, Nixon wanted American allies—now regarded by many Americans as the ungrateful beneficiaries of trade and monetary norms skewed against the United States—to bear a greater share of the liquidity, adjustment, and trade burdens of a revamped international system. George Schultz, his secretary of labor, favored floating exchange rates—a principle Nixon came to accept at a conference held with French President Georges Pompidou on the Portuguese Azores, where Pompidou unofficially represented the Western European perspective on the crisis. The Azores Pact was later ratified by the Group of Ten, consisting of France and the other European governments, as well as Canada and Japan, in the Smithsonian Agreement of December 1971.

The preference of Nixon and Kissinger for centralizing the agenda of foreign policy in the White House was a rational reaction to the experience of the Johnson administration. Johnson had found that the leakage of confidential information made it increasingly difficult to conduct foreign policy, and to influence the American public's perception of it, at a time of deepening crisis over Vietnam. Equally, however, Nixon and Kissinger shared a taste for centralized authority and internal secrecy which, when compromised, drove them to overreact. The publication in June 1971 by the *New York Times* of a multivolume document record of U.S.

involvement in Vietnam, 1945–1968, with classified papers, thereafter universally referred to as the *Pentagon Papers*, demonstrated this. Because the papers revealed how the Kennedy and Johnson administrations had deliberately obscured their policies on Vietnam to the public, Nixon was more troubled about the publication of classified documents in principle than worried over any danger to his own administration. Kissinger, by contrast, was humiliated and enraged, in part because the papers had been leaked by Daniel Ellsberg who had worked as a consultant on Kissinger's NSC staff and in part because Kissinger placed a premium on secrecy in preparing the ground for high-level initiatives such as the breakthrough on SALT negotiations with Moscow and Nixon's visit to China, the latter still in the planning phase when the *Pentagon Papers* story broke. Kissinger's argument that "some idiot can publish all of the diplomatic secrets of this country" and "could destroy our ability to conduct foreign policy" prompted Nixon to take action. He established a "Plumbers Unit" in the White House to put an end to leaks of classified material. The unit undertook a variety of clandestine operations over the next two years—many of them illegal, absurd, and beneath the dignity of a government—to neutralize Nixon's political enemies, real and imaginary.

The Vietnamese Truce

Nixon's week-long visit to China in February 1972, was an unqualified diplomatic success, demonstrating his capacity for coming to terms with changed international realities. The trip was also a political success, orchestrated and publicized to serve as the unofficial launch of Nixon's reelection campaign. Over the following months, however, the desire to show some progress in Vietnam was temporarily of equal importance. In March 1972, North Vietnam began an "Easter Offensive" in South Vietnam, attacking at a time when only 6,000 U.S. combat troops remained in the country. Because South Vietnamese forces were now required to bear the primary burden of ground combat, General Abrams tasked B-52 bombers based in Guam with providing the critical component of American support. Air strikes against the densely populated southern delta region near Saigon in particular destroyed many peasant villages and homes, yet were also credited more generally with helping to reverse the military tide when South Vietnamese counterattacks began to push back.

The use of air power, including bombing raids against targets previously off-limits to U.S. aircraft, was now in fact vital in applying pressure on Hanoi for a final diplomatic settlement of the conflict. On April 4, Nixon renewed B-52 raids on North Vietnam for the first time since President Johnson's halt of Rolling Thunder. He simultaneously dispatched Kissinger to Moscow for secret talks with Brezhnev both to sound out the Kremlin's reaction to intensified U.S.

military action against North Vietnam and to elicit Soviet support for a breakthrough in Kissinger's negotiations with the North Vietnamese in Paris. The results of the meeting were twofold. Kissinger learned that for Moscow, events in Vietnam could not trump the priority of superpower détente. Nixon thus felt confident when in May he ordered Linebacker I, the renewal of large-scale bombing of North Vietnam, along with the mining of the harbor of Haiphong with some 11,000 mines in coastal areas and inland waterways, an action urged by the Joint Chiefs of Staff since 1965. The action produced only mild protests from Moscow and Beijing. Kissinger meanwhile informed Brezhnev that the United States would accept a cease-fire, which left in place the 100,000 North Vietnamese troops in the South as of March 30. Brezhnev forwarded Kissinger's proposal to Hanoi and arranged for a renewal of the Paris talks. On July 19, Kissinger and North Vietnamese representative Le Duc Tho resumed negotiations.

By the summer of 1972, Nixon had therefore done much to deliver on his pledge of 1968 to extract the United States from Vietnam. In July, Kissinger and Le Duc Tho began their final round of truce negotiations and by mid-October had worked out a draft agreement. Although Kissinger's announcement on October 26 that "peace is at hand" was not fully accurate—South Vietnamese President Nguyen Van Thieu, whose agreement Nixon considered important to a "peace with honor," refused his consent—the progress of Vietnamization and the Paris negotiations put Nixon in strong position for reelection in November. It was made stronger still by the Democratic Party's nomination of Senator George McGovern for the presidency. Internal conflict within the party brought on by the failure of the Johnson administration in Vietnam favored the activists who supported McGovern on a platform well to the left of the electoral mainstream. On November 7, 1972, Nixon won reelection with 520 electoral votes against McGovern's 17. Because Nixon's electoral triumph over the McGovern challenge had been a near certainty, the bizarre and often illegal measures taken by executive branch staff in the Committee to Re-Elect the President were a tribute to the administration's obsession with destroying its political enemies. These included a bungled burglary of the offices of the Democratic National Committee in the Watergate apartment complex on June 17, 1972, a minor incident that had little influence on the election but which, when investigated along with other White House activities over the two years following, led ultimately to Nixon's impeachment and resignation in August 1974.

Having settled the matter of reelection, Nixon turned his attention to Thieu's objections to the draft treaty worked out by Kissinger in Paris. Thieu was nonetheless unmoved by a personal letter in which Nixon cautioned that South Vietnam was in no position to gamble away American and international sympathy. Bolstered by an ultimatum threatening force, Kissinger attempted simultaneously to secure Le Duc Tho's agreement to treaty revisions included to placate Thieu but had little success. On December 18, 1972, the administration consequently proceeded with Linebacker II, the "Christmas bombing" of North Vietnam in which the U.S. Air Force was freed from many of its previous target restrictions. In more than 3,000 sorties spread over eleven days, B-52 and other aircraft struck at transportation and communications facilities primarily in a 60-mile populated corridor between Hanoi and Haiphong—the most concentrated air assault of the war. Although the public response to the bombing was muted and congressional reaction split mostly along partisan lines, the *New York Times* accused the administration of "stone age barbarism" while antiwar activists visiting North Vietnam urged the mayor of Hanoi to claim a death toll of 10,000. He refused. The official North Vietnamese figures for civilian deaths were 1,318 for Hanoi and 305 for Haiphong. In fact, Hanoi's reporting of the destruction was in this respect more accurate than American newspaper, television, and radio reports that referred fallaciously to the "carpet bombing" of North Vietnam. The B-52s were instructed to spare civilians and for the most part succeeded in striking their targets with precision.

When Congress reconvened in January 1973, many members spoke of their readiness to cut off funding for the war, while the international press accused Nixon of "terror attacks." Still, the bombing achieved its purpose. Le Duc Tho resumed his discussions with Kissinger on January 8. Thieu accepted an agreement that hardly differed from that of the previous October when Nixon threatened to cut a deal with Hanoi without South Vietnamese consent. On January 27, two separate treaties were signed in Paris, one between North Vietnam and the United States, the other a four-power agreement that added the Republic of South Vietnam and the Provisional Revolutionary Government (the name given after 1969 to the National Liberation Front, the political organization of Communists in South Vietnam). The agreements declared the 17th parallel separating North and South not a border between states, as in the 1954 Geneva Treaty, but a "provisional boundary" until such time as Vietnam could be united into one state. By the end of March, the last American soldier had left Vietnam with the exception of some 2,300 troops missing in action. Of the 2.5 million U.S. service personnel who had served there, more than 50,000 were killed and 300,000 wounded.

The Besieged Presidency

With signing of the truce agreements Nixon's presidency went into its final phase. Although SALT I was signed in May 1972, the pursuit of his priorities for a second term—further progress on SALT with Moscow, exchanges with China, a Middle East settlement, the resolution of trade issues with Europe—became more difficult as his administration was forced to commit ever more time and energy into containing the political damage inflicted by the congressional and press investigation of Watergate. On May 17 1973, the Senate Watergate hearings began. Nixon's renewed bombing of targets in Cambodia, where the North Vietnamese continued to support Laotian Communists and the Khmer Rouge, was a constant source of further friction with Congress due to the latter's prohibition against such raids other than to protect American troops in Vietnam. When Congress voted in a supplemental appropriations bill to cut off funding for the raids, Nixon vetoed the bill; in July and August the Senate Armed Services Committee disclosed its findings on the administration's secret bombing sorties in Cambodia in 1969 and 1970.

In October 1973, the Senate version of the War Powers Act was approved but immediately vetoed by Nixon. This time, however, both houses of Congress mustered the two-thirds majority needed to override the veto in early November. The act imposed a sixty-day limit on the president's deployment of U.S. forces to hostilities abroad failing an extension authorized by Congress. It constituted the most serious congressional attempt to limit executive war-making powers since the neutrality acts of the 1930s, although it was motivated above all by the Vietnam experience dating to President Johnson's manipulation of Congress in securing the Gulf of Tonkin Resolution in 1965. Nixon ignored it. Neither he nor any succeeding president has accepted the act's express limitation on the executive's constitutional authority as commander-in-chief. Still, the episode was symptomatic of Nixon's progressive isolation. On September 11, 1973, a military coup ousted Chilean President Salvador Allende and replaced his government with an openly oppressive junta led by General Augusto Pinochet Ugarte. When a Senate committee later discovered that the administration used the CIA to undermine popular support for Allende, much of the press coverage implied that CIA activities in Chile had been inaugurated by Nixon. Meanwhile, Henry Kissinger was confirmed in his promotion from national security advisor to secretary of state after the resignation of William Rogers. In line with Nixon's preference for tight central control of foreign policy, Kissinger had eclipsed Rogers as an architect of U.S. diplomacy from the outset. Kissinger was also more popular with the press than Nixon and received gentle treatment in his congressional confirmation hearings, despite his deep involvement in decisions like the CIA's Chilean activities over which many in Congress and the press feigned shock and dismay.

The Yom Kippur War

On October 6, 1973, Israel was attacked simultaneously by Egyptian and Syrian forces while Jordan mobilized its army to tie down Israeli forces deployed near the Jordanian border. This Fourth Arab-Israeli War, popularly known as the Yom Kippur War, lasted nineteen days and witnessed the largest tank battle since WWII. In the first week of fighting Kissinger avoided sending Israel equipment and sought a cease-fire resolution in the United Nations.

At a high cost in casualties and material, Israel eventually reversed early Arab gains, aided in large part by a massive airlift of U.S. shells, tanks, and aircraft authorized by Nixon, after some hesitation, on October 13. A true cease-fire was not achieved until October 25, at which time the Soviet Union urged that a joint Soviet-American force go to Egypt to maintain the peace and warned that without American cooperation Moscow might choose to act unilaterally.

Nixon ordered a global alert of most U.S. forces, raised the Defense Condition of the U.S. Army to Level 3 (Def Con 3), and set U.S. forces in the Mediterranean at Def Con 2, one step short of war. He then informed Moscow that there was no need for a joint Soviet-American force and that the United States would not accept unilateral Soviet action. United Nations Security Council Resolution 340, providing for a cease-fire and a small-powers U.N. force to police it, passed 14–0 and was accepted by the belligerents. Among NATO allies in Western Europe, the principal theater of any general war between the United States and the Soviet Union, there was considerable annoyance at the administration's failure to advise and consult on its actions, but equally there was little European appreciation of the fact that such a war would likely make the United States itself into a battleground.

Kissinger thereupon became a pivotal figure in arranging the discussions among Israeli, Egyptian, and Jordanian representatives that took place in Geneva on December 21, and constituted the first in a series of negotiations that returned borders in the Middle East to their condition as of October 5, 1973. In early January of 1974, he began a process of negotiation and consultation between the Israeli and Egyptian governments, the beginning of "shuttle diplomacy," that led to the disengagement of their armies and a five-point plan for peace in the Suez region including American aerial surveillance of the area. In the meantime, an accompanying consequence of the Yom Kippur War was the announcement of a 10-percent cut in oil production followed by an oil embargo, on behalf of Egypt and Syria, by the United Arab Emirates, Saudi Arabia, Kuwait, Libya, and Algeria against the United States, Western Europe, and Japan in an effort to shake up their diplomatic position on the Middle East. Other OPEC states such as Iran, Nigeria, and Venezuela did not join the embargo but imposed steep prices. The economies of the targeted countries were hit hard, but those of developing states suffered much more fundamental damage. In a televised address, Nixon told Americans that they would have to roll back their consumption of fossil fuels for heating and transportation and asked

Congress for $10 billion for Project Independence to achieve national oil self-sufficiency by 1980. In February 1974, a conference in Washington to work out a joint Western strategy on oil supplies and prices was unsuccessful due to the preference of some European states, especially France, for arranging separate deals with Arab oil exporters. The oil embargo was lifted officially on March 17.

Legacy

The year 1974 otherwise accounted for three foreign policy initiatives that remained incomplete in Nixon's administration. Whereas in March 1973 the United States had vetoed a UN Security Council Resolution favoring restoration of Panamanian sovereignty to the Panama Canal Zone, Kissinger visited Panama on February 1974 and signed a statement of principles for negotiations on the canal issue—negotiations completed in 1977 under the Carter administration. In June, Nixon met with Egyptian President Anwar Sadat in Cairo and signed a statement of Principles of Relations and Cooperation in which the United States pledged to help Egypt with its effort to develop nuclear power and otherwise aimed to replace the Soviet Union as Cairo's principal superpower benefactor and possibly take Egypt out of the Arab coalition of states contesting Israel's right to exist. This change was completed, again by Carter, in the Camp David Accords of 1978. In late June and early July Nixon visited Brussels for NATO talks and went to Moscow to discuss SALT II agreements with Premier Brezhnev. The ABM agreement was amended to restrict the signatories to one rather than two ABM sites, and a Threshold Test Ban Treaty was signed restricting nuclear tests to weapons with less than a 150 kiloton yield. Aside from a symbolic renewal of détente little was otherwise accomplished; the SALT II agreement died in December 1979 with the Soviet invasion of Afghanistan.

By this time, Nixon's presidency had been terminally weakened by revelations of the extent of the Watergate illegalities and Nixon's role in them. On July 30, the House Judiciary Committee voted three articles of impeachment against him, and on August 8 Nixon announced his resignation from office, making Gerald Ford the thirty-eighth president of the United States. In the five years and eight months in which the United States and the office of the presidency had been under enormous strain, Nixon had accomplished a great deal. He had effectively ended the most wasteful war in the nation's history by withdrawing from Vietnam and had neutralized some of the social strife over the war by eliminating the military draft. He had established a more pragmatic working relationship with the Soviet Union through détente and support for German Ostpolitik. By ending the diplomatic isolation of China, he had added a whole new dimension to the national commitment to contain and defeat communism while placing the containment of the Soviet Union specifically on a more cost-effective footing. He had prevailed diplomatically in the most dangerous Middle East crisis to date and begun the work of reconciling Egypt and Israel. In the process he had insisted on a level of presidential control and secrecy he considered imperative in the circumstances of the national crisis he had inherited. Much of the national frustration and rage of the time came unfairly to focus on the figure of Richard Nixon, but his reaction to criticism and opposition was so frequently excessive that he failed to win over his dedicated critics by virtue of his achievements and alienated many political allies with frequent demonstrations of a petty vengefulness that evolved into criminal activity. Nixon, a highly intelligent and studied foreign policy leader, was ultimately driven from office in disgrace—a polarizing figure of folkloric dimensions, too soon condemned in anger or excused in defense.

Carl Cavanagh Hodge

Chronology

1969

March 14: Nixon asks Congress for antiballistic (ABM) missile system.

May 14: Nixon makes first peace offer to Hanoi.

June 8: Announcement of first Vietnam troop withdrawals.

July 20: U.S. astronauts make first moon landing.

August 4: Paris peace negotiations begin.

October 21: Willy Brandt elected West German chancellor.

November 17: SALT negotiations begin.

November 25: Nuclear Non-Proliferation Treaty ratified.

1970

February 18: Nixon Doctrine unveiled to Congress.

April 29: U.S.-ARVN forces invade Cambodia.

May 4: Kent State demonstration, shooting death of four students.

June 22: Senate repeals Tonkin Resolution.

August 7: United States brokers Middle East cease-fire.

September 6–22: Jordanian crisis.

December 7: West Germany and Poland sign reconciliation treaty.

1971

March 16: United States proposes Middle East peace plan.

May 3: Massive antiwar demonstration in Washington, D.C.

June 13: New York Times begins to publish Pentagon Papers.

July 9: National Security Advisor Henry Kissinger consults with Chinese Foreign Minister, Chou En-Lai.

August 12: West Germany and Soviet Union sign borders treaty.

August 15: Nixon announces new economic policy.

September 3: Quadripartite agreement on Berlin.

December 3–17: India-Pakistan war.

1972

February 17–28: Nixon visits China.

March 30: North Vietnam launches offensive in South Vietnam.

April 4: United States renews B-52 bombing of North Vietnam.

May 8: Nixon orders mining of Haiphong Harbor, renews large-scale B-52 attacks.

May 22–30: Nixon and Brezhnev sign SALTI and ABM treaties.

June 17: Watergate burglary of Democratic National Headquarters.

September 5: Palestinian terrorists take hostages at Munich Olympic Games.

November 7: Nixon reelected.

December 16: Kissinger announces peace talk impasse.

December 18: United States begins "Christmas bombing" raids on North Vietnam.

1973

January 27: Vietnamese truce agreements signed in Paris.

March 29: Last U.S. combat troops leave Vietnam.

May 17: Senate Watergate hearings begin.

June 16: Soviet leader Leonid Brezhnev begins summit meeting with Nixon.

June 30: Selective Service expires.

September 11: Military coup in Chile ousts President Salvatore Allende.

September 21: Henry Kissinger becomes secretary of state.

October 6: Yom Kippur War begins.

October 16: Arab states announce oil embargo.

October 25: Middle East cease-fire, Nixon puts U.S. forces on alert.

1974

March 17: End of Arab oil embargo.

May 18: India explodes nuclear device.

June 27–July 3: Nixon visits Moscow.

July 20: Turkey invades Cyprus.

July 30: House Judiciary Committee votes articles of impeachment against President Nixon.

August 8: Nixon announces resignation, effective August 9; Gerald R. Ford Jr. sworn in as president.

References and Further Reading

Ambrose, Stephen E. *Nixon: The Education of a Politician, 1913–1962.* New York: Simon and Schuster, 1988.

Ambrose, Stephen E. *Nixon: The Triumph of a Politician, 1962–1972.* New York: Simon and Schuster, 1989.

Ambrose, Stephen E. *Nixon: Ruin and Recovery, 1973–1990.* New York: Simon and Schuster, 1991.

Garthoff, Raymond. *Détente and Confrontation: American-Soviet Relations from Nixon to Reagan.* Washington, DC: Brookings, 1994.

Hoff, Joan. *Nixon Reconsidered.* New York: Basic Books, 1994.

Karnow, Stanley. *Vietnam, A History.* New York: Viking, 1991.

Kissinger, Henry. *White House Years.* Boston: Little, Brown, 1979.

Litwak, Robert S. *Détente and the Nixon Doctrine.* New York: Cambridge University Press, 1984.

Nixon, Richard. *RN: The Memoirs of Richard Nixon.* New York: Simon and Schuster, 1979.

Safire, William. *Before the Fall: An Inside View of the Pre-Watergate White House.* New York: Belmont Tower, 1975.

Gerald Rudolph Ford (1974–1977)

Early Life and Political Career

Gerald Rudolph Ford was born Leslie Lynch King in Omaha, Nebraska, on July 14, 1913. His mother Dorothy divorced his father and moved to Grand Rapids, Michigan, where she married Gerald R. Ford on February 1, 1916. Though never formally adopted by his stepfather, the future president took his name and became Gerald Rudolph Ford, Jr. Known as Junior or Jerry, the boy worked in his stepfather's paint business, applied himself in school, and became an Eagle Scout. But his real métier was on the gridiron, and he won an athletic scholarship to attend the University of Michigan where he became an All-American center. Upon graduation, Ford left for Yale and served as an assistant on the Bulldog football team and as head boxing coach. In 1938, he won probationary acceptance to Yale Law School, soon was invited to be a full-time student, and graduated in 1941 in the top third of his class.

Ford returned to Michigan and opened a small law office in Grand Rapids with a college fraternity brother, Philip Buchen, who would later become a close political advisor. But World War II cut that venture short, and he enlisted in the Navy in April 1942 as an ensign. Barely escaping death during a typhoon that rocked the USS *Monterey* in December 1944, Ford received ten battle stars before his discharge as a lieutenant in December 1945.

Returning again to Grand Rapids, Ford decided to mount a primary election challenge against the incumbent four-term congressman, an isolationist Republican, Bartel Jonkman, who was a member of the House Foreign Affairs Committee. By touting his war record and his commitment to internationalism, Ford upset Jonkman and then breezed to victory in November 1946. This election also brought both Richard Nixon and John Kennedy to Washington as House freshmen. Ford would be repeatedly returned to office by his fifth district constituents in landslides over the ensuing three decades.

Representative Ford quickly established himself as a Capitol Hill insider joining the Chowder and Marching

Gerald Rudolph Ford was burdened by the Nixon legacy and his own non-elected status. (Library of Congress)

Club in 1949, a group of junior Republicans led by Nixon. Ford strongly supported him in 1952 when the new California senator's name was being mentioned as a running mate for Dwight Eisenhower. They remained political allies, and Nixon even considered Ford briefly for his presidential ticket in 1960. Meanwhile, Ford's unwavering loyalty to the Republican Party eventually reaped benefits, and in January 1965, with the assistance of the so-called Young Turks, he narrowly defeated the long-serving House minority leader, Charles Halleck, to become one of the two most powerful Republicans in Congress. In this position, Ford

This essay represents the views of the author alone and not those of the National Defense University, the Department of Defense, or the United States Government

worked very hard to thwart President Johnson's Great Society initiatives, while strongly urging him to pursue a more aggressive military strategy in Vietnam. For his part, Johnson famously dismissed Ford as someone who had played football once too often without a helmet. It was a barb against Ford's intellect that would bedevil him throughout his political career and would be echoed by others in Washington.

The election of 1968 brought Ford's old friend Richard Nixon to the presidency, and the House minority leader acted as the loyal foot soldier, dutifully deferring to a president intent on centralizing power in the White House. Yet Ford carried out his diminished duties without public complaint, and when Vice President Spiro Agnew, facing prosecution for income tax evasion, resigned on October 10, 1973, Nixon nominated Ford to serve as Agnew's successor. He did so largely because Ford, who had made few enemies despite the maelstrom of the Watergate hearings and investigations, was the only Republican likely to be confirmed by a heavily Democratic Congress in open revolt against Nixon. Despite protesting during his confirmation hearings that he believed Nixon to be innocent of any misconduct, both houses voted by huge majorities to elevate Gerald Ford to the vice presidency under the terms of the Twenty-fifth Amendment. On December 6, he took the oath of office and humbly told Congress that he was "a Ford, not a Lincoln."

But another constitutional crisis loomed as the release of secretly taped White House conversations between Nixon and his inner circle prompted Congress to begin impeachment proceedings. Though Ford remained loyal to the president as the noose slowly tightened, he did launch public attacks on the White House staff for betraying the trust of the public. On July 24, 1974, the Supreme Court ordered the immediate release of tapes to the Watergate Special Prosecutor and the relevant congressional committees that Nixon had claimed were protected by "executive privilege." Among them was the infamous "smoking gun" that showed that Nixon had indeed attempted to obstruct justice shortly after the Watergate burglary in June 1972. With impeachment and conviction now inevitable, Nixon became the first president to resign from office, and Gerald Ford was sworn in on August 9, 1974, as Air Force One returned Nixon and his family to San Clemente, California. In his unprecedented Inaugural Address delivered from the White House, the new president declared that "Our long national nightmare is over. Our constitution works. Our great republic is a government of laws and not of men."

The Nixon Legacy: Watergate, Vietnam, and Détente

It proved easier to proclaim that the nightmare was over than it was to restore the public's faith in the presidency, for Nixon's actions had deeply disillusioned millions of Americans at the same time that large numbers blamed the media and the liberal political establishment for his downfall. With Nixon literally in exile in California and reportedly under a suicide watch, Ford, with a minimum of consultation with his advisers, issued a presidential pardon to Nixon exactly one month after taking office, sparing the disgraced president the ignominy of federal prosecution and the country the travails of a trial. This rather precipitous action promptly ended Ford's honeymoon with the American public, and his approval rating plummeted from 70 to 50 percent. It would remain at or slightly below this level for most of the remainder of his short presidency. Many years later, polls confirmed that a large majority eventually came to agree with Ford that pardoning Nixon was the best thing for the country.

President Ford also moved quickly to deal with another deeply divisive issue—Vietnam War draft resisters, evaders, and deserters. Largely reviled by the public, Nixon had vowed never to forgive or forget their disservice to the nation. Nor did Ford sympathize with those who urged him to grant a blanket amnesty, but under the prodding of the press, some of his top advisers, and his family, he began to appreciate that he needed to try and heal these wounds. Consequently, on August 18, Ford unveiled before the annual convention of the Veterans of Foreign Wars a rather complicated clemency program that supporters called "earned reentry" and critics dubbed "shamnesty" in contrast to his gentle treatment of Nixon. Eventually, federal clemency boards disposed of nearly 20,000 cases in a variety of ways ranging from outright pardons to prison sentences, yet the program did little to mollify the public.

The Paris Accords that ostensibly settled the Vietnam War in January 1973 had allowed almost 150,000 North Vietnamese troops to remain in the South. President Thieu considered the Accords to be a sellout and was only partially satisfied after Nixon had offered assurances that the United States would take any action necessary to prevent a Communist victory. Yet in June, Congress signaled its intention to end all American involvement by passing the Case-Church amendment, effectively cutting off funding for South Vietnam and Cambodia. Thus, Ford inherited a very delicate situation from Nixon but appeared determined to carry out his predecessor's promises to Thieu.

Gerald Ford had always considered himself to be an internationalist and had been a strong supporter of the Nixon-Kissinger strategy of détente that sought to ease tensions with the Soviet Union through a carrot and stick diplomacy while ignoring its domestic behavior. Yet while it appeared to remain reasonably popular with the American public, liberal and conservative elites had begun to chastise the policy for quite different reasons. When faced with a nomination challenge from Ronald Reagan in 1976, Ford would banish the word from his vocabulary and replace it with the more muscular "peace through strength."

President Ford immediately realized that it would be extremely difficult to implement Richard Nixon's main foreign policy objectives, not simply because the international landscape was in flux, but also because he faced an angry Congress (or, at least the Democratic majority) seeking to avenge the humiliations that Nixon had allegedly inflicted on it and aiming to play a major role in setting American foreign policy. And that majority swelled in the elections of 1974 that brought forty-three more Democrats to the House and an additional three to the Senate. Moreover, conservative Republicans began to increasingly criticize the initiatives of Secretary of State and National Security Advisor Henry Kissinger.

CIA Besieged

Widespread accusations of past CIA misconduct had begun to surface in the wake of the Watergate break-in when it was revealed that several of the burglars had former ties to the Agency. Under mounting congressional and media pressure, Nixon fired Richard Helms, the Director of Central Intelligence (DCI), and replaced him with James R. Schlesinger, the first person to hold this position without previous CIA experience. In May 1973, shortly before resigning to become the secretary of defense, he asked his deputy (and successor) William Colby to compile a dossier of all past illegal CIA covert domestic and international activities. The ensuing report, portions of which were leaked to the press in June 1974, proved to be a bombshell that catalogued efforts to overthrow governments, assassinate foreign leaders, and spy on American citizens.

Apparently Ford was surprised by the report and, fearing congressional wrath, established a presidential commission chaired by Vice President Nelson Rockefeller on January 4, 1975, to inquire into domestic CIA activities. But the Rockefeller Commission angered critics of the CIA by holding closed meetings, limiting the scope of its inquiry, and issuing a rather tepid final report in June that merely slapped the wrist of the Agency and recommended that an Executive Order be issued forbidding it from collecting information about U.S. citizens. (The National Security Act of 1947 that had created the CIA had, in fact, previously prohibited these activities.) Ford welcomed the findings, but the Senate had already created a special committee, under the chairmanship of Frank Church (D-ID), to investigate the Agency, including the allegations of assassinations of foreign leaders. Church led an extremely aggressive effort, which congressional Republicans castigated as "grandstanding," to publicize CIA wrongdoing. The Ford administration resisted this committee's demands for material that it considered protected by "executive privilege," but Colby undercut this strategy by

agreeing to provide Church with copious amounts of information, including evidence of assassination plots. Ford beseeched Church to not release this material, but the Idaho senator refused, and when the Senate declined to vote out "Alleged Assassination Plots Involving Foreign Leaders," Church defied his colleagues and did so anyway. In December 1975, after months of piecemeal releases of the full committee report, the entire report was published, recommending almost 200 reforms, including the creation of permanent oversight committees in both houses. An outraged Ford fired Colby and named George H. W. Bush, the U.S. envoy to China, as his replacement. In early 1976, he also unveiled a series of intelligence reforms, including the creation of an Intelligence Oversight Board, that increased executive supervision of clandestine operations while forbidding others, such as foreign assassinations. But Republicans sought revenge against Church for what they believed to be demagoguery, and they successfully targeted him for defeat in his 1980 reelection bid.

Covert Intervention in Angola

As the Ford administration fended off demands for a drastic overhaul of the CIA, events in Angola pushed it to employ the Agency in an attempt to prevent Marxists from coming to power in this soon-to-be-independent Portuguese colony in southwest Africa. On April 25, 1974, a group of leftist military officers overthrew the dictatorship of Marcello Caetano and soon announced that they would dissolve Portugal's overseas empire. The Nixon administration had been a staunch supporter of Caetano, and his removal caused great concern, particularly in regard to the mineral-rich colony of Angola, which was on the verge of civil war. In January 1975, the new Portuguese government set Angolan elections for November 11, thus precipitating a fierce three way armed struggle among the Soviet/Cuban backed MPLA, and two factions supported by Washington, the FNLA led by Holden Roberto (and also favored by China and Zaire) and UNITA under the nominal control of Jonas Sivimbi. The Ford administration, without notifying Congress, quickly committed $300,000 to the FNLA that was used to begin an offensive against the MPLA. The latter group obtained Soviet aid and Cuban troops and soon launched a fierce counterattack. On July 14, 1975, upon the recommendation of Henry Kissinger, Ford approved $14 million for Operation FEATURE, followed less than a month later by another $10.7 million. Yet this assistance, as well as a South African military incursion probably coordinated with the CIA, failed to prevent the MPLA from entering the capital city of Luanda and declaring itself the government of the new independent state of Angola. The administration, which had told Congress nothing about this operation, now embraced UNITA in the continuing civil war. But details of

FEATURE soon leaked to the press, and congressional hearings were held just as the Church committee's work was reaching a climax. In December, the so-called Clark amendment, named after Senator Dick Clark (D-IA), cutting off all funding for the Angolan rebels, passed both houses by veto-proof margins.

With defeat all but certain in Angola, Ford and Kissinger turned their attention to Rhodesia, which had been ruled by the white minority regime of Ian Smith since it broke away from Britain in 1965. The administration feared that the Soviet Union and Cuba planned to support the black rebels there and create another Marxist government in southern Africa. Thus Kissinger quite unexpectedly became an advocate for a democratically elected Rhodesian government and began a vigorous round of negotiations aimed at convincing the Smith regime to hold elections under universal suffrage. But this effort was stymied because of the intransigence of the white minority South African government, and Ford's term ended with Smith still in control. Nevertheless, he attempted to capitalize on Kissinger's diplomacy in his nomination fight against Ronald Reagan in 1976 after the California governor suggested that the United States send "advisors" to Rhodesia to prop up the regime.

Final Defeat in South Vietnam and Cambodia

Beginning with President Eisenhower, successive American administrations had been committed to the defense of South Vietnam, yet a massive, sustained military effort had failed to achieve victory over the Communist government of North Vietnam. The Republic of Vietnam (South Vietnam) remained largely a protectorate of the United States, unable to function without the influx of aid. On January 27, 1973, the Paris Accords formally ended America's direct participation in the war. Nixon proclaimed that he had achieved his goal of "peace with honor" and assured President Thieu that massive American military and economic assistance would prevent the North from overrunning the South. But critics, citing the continued presence of almost 150,000 Communist troops in the South, claimed that the Accords had merely bought Nixon a "decent interval" between American withdrawal and South Vietnam's collapse. More than forty years later, debate still rages within the United States over "who lost Vietnam." In their respective memoirs both Nixon and Kissinger blame Congress for failing to provide the aid that could allegedly have saved the Saigon government. But most scholars argue that the ultimate cause of Thieu's defeat was his inability to achieve legitimacy for his regime and to create a viable independent state. Yet almost all agree that the collapse of the South occurred more quickly than even the North Vietnamese had anticipated.

In theory, Gerald Ford could have taken the advice of one Republican senator who urged that "we declare victory and come home," but the new president's instincts, as well as the strong advice he received from Kissinger, who remained both secretary of state and national security advisor, removed that option. Consequently, one of Ford's first presidential decisions was to assure Thieu that he intended to honor the commitments made by Nixon—commitments that involved substantial amounts of military and economic aid and a pledge to preserve the independence of the Republic of Vietnam. He did so despite overwhelming public and congressional opposition. In fact, Congress had appropriated $725 million for South Vietnam and Cambodia but then refused to release the bulk of the money. Undeterred, in January 1975 Ford asked for supplemental assistance for both countries, as well as $6 billion in postwar reconstruction aid, and reassured Thieu that more help would be forthcoming. Ford even sent the Army Chief of Staff General Fred Weyland, to Saigon on a fact-finding mission. Weyland returned with an urgent request to resume U.S. bombing of Communist forces in the South. But Congress rejected the administration's requests, implying that the time had come to cut America's losses and redirect its priorities.

The end came swiftly. On April 17, 1975, the Cambodian capital of Phnom Penh fell to Khmer Rouge forces hours after U.S. helicopters evacuated almost 300 people. Under the leadership of the genocidal Pol Pot, the new government forcibly emptied major Cambodian cities and instituted a "Killing Fields" rampage that eventually claimed the lives of millions of Cambodians. Meanwhile, Republic of Vietnam forces (ARVN) were in full retreat, Thieu resigned, and Communist troops were poised to enter Saigon, culminating an offensive that had begun in January. Ford, though not Kissinger, finally realized that the endgame had come. On April 23, Ford gave a speech that had not been cleared by Kissinger in which he claimed that now America "could regain the sense of pride that existed before Vietnam. But it cannot be achieved by refighting a war that is finished as far as America is concerned." Six days later the United States evacuated 5,600 Vietnamese and 1,400 Americans from the U.S. embassy. Television cameras showed desperate people being forcibly pushed from the runners of the evacuation craft. South Vietnamese pilots ditched their planes off shore and were rescued by American sailors. Saigon was quickly named Ho Chi Minh City as the nation was forcibly unified under Communist control. America's twenty-year effort to defend the South had failed, but not before creating an atmosphere of domestic divisiveness not seen since the Civil War.

The *Mayaguez* Incident

Since the 1950s, American policymakers had argued that defeat in Southeast Asia would call into question U.S. global credibility among both foes and allies. The double defeat in April 1975 persuaded Kissinger that the United States needed to take decisive international actions lest the Soviet Union, Cuba, and China be emboldened by America's misfortunes. Such an opportunity occurred on May 12, 1975, when the American merchant vessel, SS *Mayaguez*, carrying nonlethal Defense Department cargo, was boarded by Cambodian troops in what the United States considered international waters. Initial intelligence reports proved murky, for both the whereabouts of the ship and the location of the crew were unclear. Yet many of Ford's senior advisors feared that if decisive action were not taken, the *Mayaguez* could become another *Pueblo,* the U.S. reconnaissance ship captured in 1968 by North Korea whose crew was held for thirteen months on spy charges.

That affair had proven to be a major embarrassment for the Johnson administration, and Ford officials were determined to avoid another debacle. But Kissinger immediately realized that a skillful handling of the *Mayaguez* "crisis" could begin to restore America's tarnished image. Hence, despite the objections of Secretary of Defense Schlesinger and the Joint Chiefs of Staff, who merely wished to rescue the crew, Kissinger persuaded Ford that Cambodia should also be punished for its actions. Believing that the *Mayaguez* and its men had been transported to the island of Koh Tang, located about 50 miles off the coast of Cambodia near Vietnam, the president ordered the aircraft carrier USS *Coral Sea* to sail to the area with an amphibious assault unit, and airlifted a battalion of 1,100 Marines from Okinawa to U-Tapao air force base in Thailand. On May 15, Ford ordered the Air Force to begin bombing the Cambodian mainland. Soon thereafter the USS *Holt,* with seventy Marines, boarded the *Mayaguez* by force but found it deserted. Meanwhile, eight helicopters attacked Koh Tang, but Khmer Rouge forces, apparently dug in with the expectation of a Vietnamese landing on this contested island, downed four of the choppers and damaged three others. At least sixty Marines were stranded on the island. Fourteen hours later a rescue mission extracted all but three of them at about the same time the *Mayaguez* crew of thirty was being freed from a small fishing vessel approximately 40 miles away from Koh Tang, apparently through the intervention of China. When the operation ceased, forty-one Marines had been killed on Koh Tang and twenty-three Air Force personnel had lost their lives while being transported to U-Tapao. U.S. officials reckoned that about sixty Khmer Rouge soldiers had been killed in combat. Despite these somewhat mixed results, the public and Congress hailed the mission as an important victory, and Ford's approval rating increased by 11 percent. The president was pleased with the outcome, not only because he had reasserted American military muscle, but because he had refused to inform Congress of his plans until the operation had been concluded, thus depriving it of the chance to invoke the War Powers Resolution. One leading scholar noted that Kissinger had told Ford at the beginning of the incident that he had the chance to "look ferocious."

The Turkish Invasion of Cyprus

Although sharing membership in the North Atlantic Treaty Organization (NATO), Greece and Turkey also harbored long-standing animosities that the United States had tried to diffuse. A major source of tension concerned Cyprus, an island nation granted independence by Britain in 1957, that contained a ruling Greek majority and a hostile Turkish minority. In 1967, a military coup in Athens toppled the elected government of Andreas Papandreou and severely strained relations with Washington. On June 15, 1974, this junta supported the overthrow of the Cypriot leader, Archbishop Makarios III by a Greek nationalist, Nikos Sampson, who announced the immediate absorption of the island by Greece. In July, Turkey invaded and forced 200,000 Greek Cypriots to flee south to the Greek majority. This ethnic faction soon rioted, attacked the American embassy in Nicosia, and killed the U.S. ambassador. The Ford administration decided to support Turkey, largely because of the geostrategic significance of that nation as a neighbor of the Soviet Union and the host of several important U.S. military installations. Yet the Greek-American lobby constituted a potent domestic political force, and it pressured Congress to cut off all military aid to Turkey. Congress twice narrowly failed to override Ford's veto but eventually forced the president to end assistance by February 5, 1975. Ankara retaliated by closing all U.S. military and intelligence installations and all but one NATO air base. They did not reopen until the embargo was lifted three years later. A resurgent Congress had effectively changed American foreign policy and had seemingly altered the balance of executive-legislative relations.

The Arab-Israeli Conundrum

The Arab-Israeli conflict had bedeviled U.S. presidents since Truman recognized Israel in 1948, but the wars of 1967 and 1973 had made its resolution appear even more urgent. During the latter conflict, that had been initiated by Egypt, the Nixon administration, fearing another overwhelming Israeli victory would make regional peace more difficult to achieve, had been slow to resupply an increasingly desperate Tel Aviv and then had forced the Israelis to accept a cease-fire before they had a chance to annihilate the Egyptian Army in the Sinai peninsula. But Nixon and Kissinger also angered the Soviets by preventing them from coming to the aid of Cairo. In the aftermath of the 1973 "Yom Kippur" war, they sensed an opportunity to restart the "peace process" in light of Egypt's somewhat better showing on the battlefield. Thus began the first round of Kissinger's "shuttle diplomacy" that eventually led to the disengagement of Israeli and Egyptian forces in the Sinai and the disengagement of Syrian and Israeli troops on the Golan Heights.

President Ford decided that the next step should be the normalization of relations between Israel and Jordan, seemingly the most moderate of the Arab frontline states, yet still smarting from the loss of the West Bank to Israel during the 1967 Six Day war. But as the new Israeli government dallied, the Arab League designated the Palestinian Liberation Organization (PLO), under the erratic leadership of Yassir Arafat, as the entity that would negotiate a West Bank agreement. This decision effectively ended any hope for a quick settlement of this dispute, so the administration refocused its attention on Egypt. Kissinger embarked on a second round of shuttle diplomacy in an effort to persuade Israel to further withdraw from the Sinai, including two key oil fields, in exchange for an Egyptian pledge to terminate its state of belligerency with Tel Aviv. But when the Israelis balked, Ford intervened in March 1975 with an exceedingly blunt letter to Israel's leadership—a ploy that had the unintended consequence of scuttling the negotiations. An angry Ford announced that he would "reassess" U.S. policy in the Middle East.

For its part, the Israeli government felt betrayed, as did the powerful American-Israel Public Affairs Committee (AIPAC), which encouraged Congress to protest. In May, seventy-five senators wrote to Ford asking him to support Israel's request for over $2.5 billion in aid and to oppose further territorial concessions. The president blamed Israel for this letter and decided to undertake his own diplomatic mission in early June, meeting first with Anwar Sadat of Egypt and then with Yitzhak Rabin of Israel. Impressed with Sadat's reasonableness, Ford made his suggestions the basis for the Sinai II Accord that was signed in Washington on September 4. According to its terms, the Israelis returned two strategic passes and one of the contested oil fields to Egypt, while Sadat agreed to reopen the Suez Canal to non-military Israeli vessels. The U.S. also pledged an additional $1.5 billion in military aid to Tel Aviv and secretly promised to not negotiate with the PLO until it recognized the existence of the Jewish state. Yet relations with Israel remained strained, and no further diplomatic breakthroughs occurred until after Ford left office.

The Decline of Détente

In 1969, Richard Nixon had not only inherited a stalemated war in Vietnam from an administration apparently imprisoned in a "more of the same" mentality, but he also felt himself burdened by a foreign policy that had seriously ossified

during the previous decade. In part, this paralysis stemmed from the obsessive attention that President Johnson had paid to Vietnam, while critical issues like Soviet-American relations and the Arab-Israeli conflict were largely submerged. But there remained a deeper problem. Both Nixon and Kissinger believed that the *structure* of international relations had changed significantly since the political bulwarks of American foreign policy like NATO had been established in the late 1940s. Because of the outcome of World War II, the United States had briefly exerted inordinate international influence. That unique moment had inevitably given way to an environment characterized by the growth of Soviet military power to parity, the remarkable economic recovery of Western Europe and Japan, and the fragmentation of monolithic communism. The United States, however, had failed to devise a strategy to deal effectively with this new international landscape. A crude anti-communism remained the wellspring of an American foreign policy that had become lost in an obsession with crisis management. The results had been drift and incoherence in place of strategy and design.

Neither Nixon nor Kissinger celebrated the relative decline of American power. Had they been in office at an earlier time both surely would have eagerly pursued global containment. As it was, however, they thought these changing systemic circumstances required the United States to adapt. The Nixon-Kissinger grand design entailed the creation of a stable, ultimately multipolar international structure cemented by a shared sense of Great Power legitimacy. Most essentially, this structure would maintain and stabilize the nuclear peace by making the status quo palatable to the major powers. Soviet-American rivalry would be muted, though not eliminated, by regulating the nuclear arms race and by preventing regional disputes from escalating into dangerous direct confrontations. The Soviet Union, which, according to the old Cold War paradigm, constituted an implacable, world-revolutionary foe, would now be viewed more traditionally as an ambitious, opportunistic rival that shared certain interests with the United States. This conservative, largely nonideological design additionally insisted that the United States refrain from imposing its domestic order on the international framework. That is, the United States had to construct an unbreachable barrier between the universal claims of its internal political values and the sense of limits required by the new international equilibrium. Ideology would no longer constitute the litmus test of foreign policy. The United States, according to this vision, could continue to assert its global primacy by adroitly manipulating the balance.

The Nixon-Kissinger strategy for realizing their grand design involved three main components. First, they recognized that little could be done so long as the Vietnam War sapped American power and poisoned the domestic political atmosphere. The war had to be terminated, but if not done correctly, a U.S. withdrawal could actually inhibit the emergence of a stable international equilibrium by raising serious questions about American resolve and credibility. Domestically, a precipitous pullout would trigger bitter recriminations, ugly insinuations about who lost Vietnam, and a public unwillingness to support further American global activism.

Second, it was imperative to establish more normal relations with the People's Republic of China and to begin to integrate it into the international system. Normalization possessed potential benefits. Closer Sino-American ties would at the very least obligate Moscow to devote greater military resources to its extremely lengthy border with China, thus reducing somewhat the Soviet threat to NATO. They would also heighten the diplomatic isolation of North Vietnam and encourage it to accept a compromise settlement of the war.

And third, the central feature—Soviet-American relations—required additional stability. For the United States to flourish in a "post-hegemonic" world, effective means had to be found to contain the expansionistic tendencies of the Soviet Union. The most extreme, though least likely, threat, Nixon and Kissinger thought, came from the Soviet nuclear arsenal. With its achievement of nuclear parity, however, Moscow might now be willing to regulate the arms race and strengthen deterrence. And it was in U.S. interests to prevent the Soviets from seeking to gain the credible perception of nuclear superiority. But Nixon and Kissinger fretted even more about the consequences of a highly armed Soviet Union engaged in provocative, bullying, erratic international behavior, whether in Berlin, the Middle East, Cuba, or some other area of tension. These actions could easily provoke a superpower confrontation that might escalate into a nuclear crisis. To reduce the likelihood of nuclear war, Nixon and Kissinger wished to involve the Soviets in realistic negotiations designed, ultimately, to institutionalize deterrence. So critical was this issue that they were willing to detach it from other Soviet-American disputes.

On the other hand, to persuade the Soviet Union to reduce regional tensions and to accept the legitimacy of the international order, they sought to enmesh Moscow in a complex web of incentives and punishments woven in Washington. As inducements to limit Soviet geopolitical ambitions, the United States could offer technology, grain, credits, and other desired economic benefits. In addition, recognition of the Soviet Union as a genuine superpower, and acquiescence in the legality of existing European boundaries, as well as Moscow's dominant position in Eastern Europe, could further diminish American-Soviet tensions. In exchange, Nixon and Kissinger had reasonable hopes for a Berlin settlement that guaranteed Western access to the city; Moscow's assistance in helping the United States to withdraw gracefully from Vietnam; and a Soviet

willingness to manage Third World crises. But if the Kremlin reverted to its imperialist ways the United States would move swiftly to withdraw economic favors, diminish Moscow's new international status through symbolic actions, and resist Soviet designs on the geopolitical periphery. Indeed, depending on the circumstances, these rewards and punishments might be meted out simultaneously. As Kissinger later noted, the basic issue was "whether we will use them or they will use us."

In important respects, therefore, the Nixon-Kissinger reformulation departed from the Cold War policy of global anti-communist containment. Their grand design envisioned the emergence of a stable, multipolar balance chiefly managed by the United States and animated by a shared sense of international legitimacy. The strategy entailed a reduction of U.S.-Soviet tension by engaging on a variety of issues as well as a Sino-American rapprochement; and the tactics demanded that the United States be free to act swiftly and adroitly, and perhaps even with amorality and deceit. The Nixon-Kissinger approach, like its Cold War predecessor, identified the Soviet Union as the primary threat to international peace, but attempted to restrain it through a complex mix of incentives, rewards, and Soviet *self*-containment.

Yet by the time Ford assumed the presidency in August 1974, détente had come under attack by domestic critics on both the Left and the Right. Nixon and Kissinger had been aware from the beginning that the Right would find it difficult to accept the premises of détente but felt that because of Nixon's own long-standing anti-communist reputation, it would have little choice but to at least tolerate this new approach. But as the process of détente unfolded and produced tangible superpower agreements, conservative critics, led at first by Senator Henry Jackson (D-WA) and his aide Richard Perle, and then increasingly among Republicans by Ronald Reagan, Nixon and Kissinger were thrown on the defensive. These critics contended that the Soviet Union was blatantly exploiting détente to achieve global military domination. As early as the summer of 1972, Jackson began criticizing the "asymmetries" of the Strategic Arms Limitation Treaty (SALT) that allowed the Soviets to maintain a larger ICBM force than the United States (although the United States had more bombers and nuclear warheads). He convinced the Senate to pass a resolution that demanded that any SALT II treaty would have to address these concerns about numerical imbalances. In the autumn of 1972, Jackson, with the cosponsorship in the House of Charles Vanik (D-OH), introduced an amendment to the omnibus trade bill that would have made the granting of Most Favored Nation (MFN) status to Moscow contingent on the liberalization of its Jewish emigration policy. Strongly backed by AIPAC, the amendment sought to link the reform of the Soviet domestic system to any future economic carrots from the United States. Kissinger strongly objected to this misapplication of linkage and argued that its passage would merely encourage Moscow to clamp down even more on its Jewish population. The trade bill remained before Congress when Ford became president. On August 14, 1974, he persuaded the Soviet ambassador Anatoly Dobrynin that Moscow needed to increase further its annual quota of Jewish émigrés to 55,000. Initially, Jackson appeared mollified by this new figure, but in October he demanded that the number be raised to at least 60,000, which provoked the Soviets to formally protest to Kissinger and to warn that they would ignore any requirements for additional Jewish emigration. The Senate, nevertheless, passed the bill 88–0 on December 13, and in January 1975, the Soviets carried out their threat, thereby depriving themselves of MFN status while removing a linchpin of détente.

Shortly before the Senate acted on the trade bill Ford traveled to Vladivostok, Siberia, to meet the Soviet leader, Leonid Brezhnev. The SALT I agreement was due to expire in October 1977, and Ford wanted to negotiate a framework for its extension, but his desire to do so unleashed a dispute between Kissinger and Secretary of Defense Schlesinger. Whereas Kissinger was willing to grant the Soviets a numerical edge in land-based ICBMs as long as the United States kept its lead in total warheads because of its more numerous bombers and submarine launched missiles, Schlesinger insisted that land-based parity had to be achieved. Probably in order to placate conservative critics of détente, who had sided with the secretary of defense, Ford adopted Schlesinger's position. At their Vladivostock summit Brezhnev and Ford agreed on a framework for a SALT II treaty that allowed each side to possess 2,400 strategic delivery systems of which 1,320 could carry multiple warheads. Only bombers that carried missiles with a range exceeding 600 kilometers would count against the 2,400 total. Because the result was to *increase* the total strategic delivery systems, liberals were quick to condemn it as an invitation to a new arms race, but the more damaging criticism came from the right. Henry Jackson and his allies attacked the agreement, because it did not treat the Soviet TU–22M (Backfire) bomber as a strategic (i.e., intercontinental) weapon. A nasty debate then ensued over the capabilities of an airplane that Kissinger considered obsolete, but the ultimate result was to convince Ford to postpone the completion of a SALT II treaty until after the 1976 presidential election lest it become a major issue in his nomination fight against Ronald Reagan.

Other conservative critics of détente further sought to corner Ford by asking him to meet with the renowned Soviet dissident and Nobel Prize–winning author, Aleksandr Solzhenitsyn. Senator Strom Thurmond (R-SC) and Senator Jesse Helms (R-NC) backed a move to declare him an honorary U.S. citizen and suggested that the president invite Solzhenitsyn to the White House on June 30, 1975, shortly before a scheduled Soviet-American summit

in Helsinki. Ford, who detested the Russian, demurred, thus bringing down the wrath of the right. But when Ford then invited him to visit after the conclusion of the summit, Solzhenitsyn claimed that his busy schedule would prevent him from coming to Washington. The damage had been done, and the episode returned to haunt Ford in his struggles against both Reagan and Jimmy Carter.

President Ford attempted to win back conservatives by bowing to their demands in early 1976 that he appoint a so-called Team B to review the findings of a CIA assessment of the Soviet military buildup that they had found overly optimistic. Predictably this group of hardliners revised the original figures upward, and Ford accepted its report. But he did not follow the advice of conservatives who advised him to reject the work of the Conference on Security and Cooperation in Europe that had been meeting since 1973 with thirty-three nations participating. Instead he traveled to Finland in late July and early August 1975 to sign the Helsinki Accords, the Conference's "Final Act." In essence, the Soviets won from the West long-sought recognition of the post–World War II Eastern European borders but were forced to accept "Basket Three," which, in effect, urged greater respect for human rights throughout Europe and ultimately spawned a number of democratic groups in the Soviet satellite states. While in Helsinki, Ford failed to persuade Brezhnev to reclassify the Backfire bomber as the right had urged. Yet conservatives ignored both "Basket Three" and Ford's acceptance of their Backfire position and seized instead on the European borders agreement, likening it to another Yalta.

Liberals, on the other hand, generally applauded détente but found other reasons to dislike the Ford-Kissinger approach to foreign policy. At the root of their criticism lay the conviction that the world had changed more than Ford and Kissinger were willing to admit. Thus liberals argued that American foreign policy, in its extreme focus on the Soviet Union, had proven insensitive to a host of global developments. While they acknowledged the desirability of stable superpower relations, they contended that American foreign policy had become anachronistic. Impressed by the power of Third World nationalism—from North Vietnam's resiliency to the Organization of Petroleum Exporting Countries (OPEC)—liberals claimed that U.S. foreign policy needed a new agenda that reflected the growing importance of so-called North-South relations. They castigated Kissinger's contemptuous dismissal of Third World demands for a New International Economic Order that would have redistributed wealth from the rich nations to the impoverished ones, his apparent satisfaction with the status quo in South Africa, and his very belated involvement in the Zimbabwe negotiations to end white rule in Rhodesia. Moreover, liberal critics grew increasingly vocal about the Ford-Kissinger practice of selling large-scale arms to friendly tyrants in states such as Iran, Nicaragua, and the

Philippines. They also charged that Kissinger's geopolitical machinations had inevitably neglected the emergence of pressing international economic issues. The recently formed Trilateral Commission chastised Kissinger for ignoring relations with Western Europe and Japan and suggested that resource shortages, global inflation, ecological damage, and similar "transnational phenomena" required the United States to manage the growing interdependence of the globe. As the 1976 election approached, liberal critics announced their desire for a more reform-minded, less Machiavellian, more moral, and multilateral American foreign policy.

Foreign Policy and the 1976 Election

Gerald Ford's foreign policy team was an awkward amalgam of people inherited from the Nixon administration and advisors chosen by the new president. This system produced personal and bureaucratic rivalries that Ford found increasingly intolerable. Moreover, the once invincible Henry Kissinger now appeared to be a political liability as Ford prepared for a bruising nomination fight against Governor Reagan. Thus on November 2, 1975, he announced a massive shakeup of his foreign policy apparatus. Never wholly comfortable with Kissinger's dual roles as national security advisor and secretary of state, Ford relieved him of his National Security Council job and replaced him with Brent Scowcroft, a retired Air Force Lieutenant General with a PhD from Columbia University, who had been serving as Kissinger's deputy at the NSC and who had impressed Ford during the *Mayaguez* incident and the evacuation of Saigon. He also fired Secretary of Defense James Schlesinger, who the president considered insufferably arrogant, and named Donald Rumsfeld, a friend of Ford since their House days, as his successor. Finally, the president asked for the resignation of William Colby as director of Central Intelligence, primarily as punishment for his perceived insubordination during the Church investigations. George Bush, the envoy to Beijing and another old House colleague, became the new head of the CIA. And, on the same day, Vice President Rockefeller, long a villain in the eyes of conservatives, announced that he would not serve in a second Ford term.

The Ford-Reagan nomination battle proved to be unprecedented in the modern history of the Republican Party for its ferocity, closeness, and length, and the California governor made Ford's foreign policy record a centerpiece of his challenge. He hammered Kissinger for a détente policy that he claimed was little more than Soviet appeasement, citing the Helsinki Accords and Ford's refusal to meet with Solzhenitsyn as shameful episodes. He also seized on erroneous newspaper reports that State Department Counselor Helmut Sonnenfeldt had spoken of a permanent "organic union" between Moscow and its East European satellites. These attacks proved telling, for not only did Ford stop using the term "détente," but he agreed to a "Morality in Foreign Policy" plank in the Republican platform that essentially denounced the Kissinger approach. Moreover, the president leaked to the media reports that Kissinger would be replaced if Ford were reelected.

Perhaps even more damaging, however, was Reagan's attacks of Ford's Panama Canal policy. The U.S. possession of the Canal and the 10-mile zone that flanked it had always rankled Latin Americans as symbols of American duplicity and imperialism. In January 1964, rioting broke out in the Canal Zone; it claimed the lives of four U.S. soldiers and twenty-three Panamanians. President Johnson decided to renegotiate the terms of the 1903 treaty that had granted to the United States permanent control of the Canal and the Zone. But the issue also proved deeply emotional to Americans—especially those vocal U.S. citizens who lived in the zone—and in March 1974, Senators Strom Thurmond and John McClellan (D-AR) introduced a resolution with thirty-six of their colleagues that opposed any treaty that would surrender U.S. sovereignty over the Canal Zone. Ford sought a compromise that would eventually turn over the Panama Canal to the Panamanians but reserve to the United States the right to defend it. But this formula did not placate Senator Jesse Helms, who urged Reagan's political advisors to turn it into a major campaign issue. By doing so, Reagan defeated Ford in the North Carolina primary on March 23, 1976, and created panic within the president's camp. Nevertheless, Ford survived, largely by ridiculing Reagan's plan to privatize the Social Security system, and eked out an 1,187–1,070 victory at the Kansas City convention in August.

Foreign policy played a much less prominent role in the 1976 general election. The Democrats had nominated Jimmy Carter, a former one-term governor of Georgia, who emerged from their New York City convention in July with a twenty-point lead in the polls. Carter's campaign focused on the economy—simultaneous recession and inflation (stagflation)—and unveiled a "misery index" that allegedly showed how much worse off Americans had become under the Republicans. But Carter did castigate Kissinger for his "Lone Ranger" tactics, the Helsinki "sell-out," and Ford's dealings with Solzhenitsyn, and vowed to restore morality and trust to American foreign policy. In response, Ford tried to persuade the electorate that his experience made him more worthy of election than his unproven opponent. Yet that claim was called into question during the second presidential debate when the president, quite inexplicably, contended that Poland was not within the Soviet sphere of domination. A surprised Carter capitalized on the gaffe, but Ford did not retract the statement for several days. Overall, however, Carter ran a rather cautious and lackluster campaign, and Ford closed on him rapidly in the polls, especially after promising a large tax cut, losing in November by only 2 percent of the popular vote. An 8,000-vote swing in Hawaii and Ohio would have given him the election.

Legacy

Gerald Ford had the misfortune of succeeding a disgraced president in an especially divisive domestic atmosphere. The legacy of Watergate, the sensational CIA revelations, the impending defeat in Southeast Asia, and the growing contentiousness of détente combined to place Ford on the defensive, and he was never quite able to recover. Nevertheless, his contributions to American foreign policy were not insignificant. The Sinai II agreement indirectly led to the conclusion of the Camp David Accords in 1978; his willingness to renegotiate the Hay-Bunau Treaty laid the basis for the Panama Canal treaties that were ratified under President Carter; the Helsinki Accords eventually helped give rise to opposition groups in Eastern Europe, spawning dissidents who would one day play important leadership roles after the demise of the Soviet Union; Ford's initial refusal to meet Aleksandr Solzhenitsyn demonstrated a certain degree of courage; Kissinger's efforts to end Ian Smith's rule in Rhodesia paved the way for the creation of Zimbabwe, even though its leader, Robert Mugabe, ultimately proved to be a tyrant. On the other hand, some of Ford's foreign policy decisions proved less constructive: he misled President Thieu into believing that American aid would save him; his behavior during the *Mayaguez* incident contained more than a dash of political opportunism; his handling of the Colby report on CIA abuses appeared clumsy and defensive; his covert intervention in Angola, which aligned the United States with South Africa, was counterproductive; and his repeated capitulations to conservative critics of détente in order to win the Republican nomination were not his finest moments.

But President Ford had little room to maneuver, because both the liberal left and the conservative right relentlessly narrowed his options. Congress's demand to "codetermine" American foreign relations made it more difficult to conduct a coherent policy, while critics in his own party forced him to adopt positions that violated his convictions. Fundamentally, Ford was a centrist internationalist, but the radical bifurcation of the country in the 1970s made it exceedingly difficult to govern from the middle.

Richard Melanson

Chronology

1974

October 18: President Ford signs legislation threatening to cut off aid to Turkey.

November 24: Ford and Brezhnev meet in Vladivostock and agree to place a ceiling on offensive nuclear weapons.

December 20: Congress refuses Soviet Union most favored nation status and restricts trade pending change in Soviet Jewish emigration policy.

1975

January 8: Twenty nations agree to recycle petrodollars to avoid a global recession.

January 22: Ford approves the Geneva Protocol of 1925 and the 1972 Biological Weapons Convention.

April 12: Fighting erupts in Lebanon between Christians and Muslims.

April 13: Fighting erupts between the Christian militia and Palestinians in Lebanon.

April 17: Cambodia falls to the forces of the Khmer Rouge.

April 25: Portugal holds its first free elections in fifty years.

April 29: Saigon falls to North Vietnamese forces, last U.S. helicopter evacuates U.S. embassy.

May 12–15: Mayaguez Incident, U.S. cargo ship seized by Cambodia and recovered by U.S. marines.

June 5: Egypt reopens Suez Canal, closed since 1967 to international shipping.

June 10: Rockefeller Commission recommends reform of CIA.

July 1: Vietnam officially is reunified.

July 24: House rejects Ford's request to lift Turkish arms embargo.

August 1: Thirty-five nations sign Helsinki Accords.

September 1: Egypt and Israel sign an agreement on buffer zones in the Sinai.

November 10: UN General Assembly condemns Zionism as a form of racism.

November 21: Senate Church Committee reports on CIA efforts to assassinate foreign leaders.

December 1–5: Ford makes a five-day visit to China.

1976

January 27: Congress rejects Ford's request for aid to anti-communist forces in Angola.

March 1: Ford announces he will no longer use the word *détente.*

March 18: India Prime accuses the CIA of trying to undermine its government, U.S. stops aid.

May 28: United States and the Soviet Union sign a treaty limiting the size of underground nuclear tests.

June 16: U.S. ambassador to Lebanon, Francis E. Meloy, Jr. is assassinated.

July 4: Israeli commandos free Jewish hostages in Entebbe, Uganda.

August 18: Two U.S. Army officers killed in Panmunjon, Korea.

September 9: Mao Zedong dies.

November 2: James Earl Carter is elected president, Walter F. Mondale is vice president.

November 11: United States vetoes UN membership for Vietnam.

December 1: United States abstains as Angola joins the UN.

References and Further Reading

Cannon, James. *Time and Chance: Gerald Ford's Appointment with History.* Ann Arbor: University of Michigan Press, 1994.

Dietz, Terry. *Republicans and Vietnam, 1961–1986.* Westport, CT: Greenwood, 1986.

Ford, Gerald R. *A Time to Heal: The Autobiography of Gerald R. Ford.* New York: Harper and Row, 1979.

Greene, John Robert. *The Presidency of Gerald R. Ford.* Lawrence, KS: University Press of Kansas, 1995.

Jesperson, T. Christopher. "Kissinger, Ford, and Congress: The Very Bitter End in Vietnam." *Pacific Historical Review* 71/3 (2002): 439–473.

Kissinger, Henry. *Years of Renewal: The Concluding Volume of His Memoirs.* New York: Simon and Schuster, 1999.

Maresca, John. *To Helsink.* Durham, NC: Duke University Press, 1987.

Noer, Thomas J. "International Credibility and Political Survival: The Ford Administration's Intervention in Angola." *Presidential Studies Quarterly,* 23/4: 771–786.

Quandt, William B. *Decade of Decisions: American Policy Toward the Arab-Israeli Conflict, 1967–1976.* Berkeley: University of California Press, 1977.

Wettenhahn, Ralph. *The Last Battle: The Mayaguez Incident and the End of the Vietnam War.* New York: Carroll and Graf, 2001.

James Earl Carter, Jr. (1977–1981)

Early Life and Political Career

James Earl Carter, Jr. took a different path to the top than his predecessors. He was the first president since Eisenhower not to have previously served in any national office or decision-making position, in either the executive branch or Congress. And unlike Eisenhower, who had distinguished himself in a brilliant military career, Carter was known only as a former governor of his native Georgia. After an unsuccessful run for governor in 1966, he was elected in 1970 and gradually made his mark during his four-year tenure as an effective and progressive administrator. Though he had been campaigning for his party's presidential nomination since 1975, Carter was still largely unknown at the national level during the presidential primaries of 1976—hence the famous question of that campaign "Jimmy Who?"

At first, Carter was not taken entirely seriously; commentators felt his successful stewardship of the family peanut farm would not suffice to convince Americans of his qualifications to lead. But Carter's character gradually won over the public. Americans came to respect his integrity, confidence, moral integrity, and Christian values. The publication of his autobiography *Why Not the Best?* during the election campaign attracted considerable attention and interest, for it articulated a political vision that differed sharply from that of the Washington elite. The contrast between Carter's ideas and those of the "Establishment" helped propel him to the presidency, not beholden to special interests and not tied to any particular philosophy.

The electorate viewed Jimmy Carter's election in November 1976 as a break with the policies of Nixon and Ford. His idealism and moral message ran counter to what was seen as the overly realistic, not to say Machiavellian, approach of his Republican predecessors. The memory of the Watergate scandal and Ford's presidential pardon of Nixon was still fresh. Americans hoped that Carter would restore to the presidency the integrity and dignity that they associated with the office. However, Carter's triumph was short-lived. International developments thwarted the president's natural inclinations, forced him to backtrack on his original positions, and to rethink some of his principles.

Early Success

Carter enjoyed high levels of popularity during his first weeks in the White House. His positive and determined

James Earl Carter, Jr., a president in difficult times, was ultimately overwhelmed by them. (Library of Congress)

approach contrasted sharply with Nixon's imperial style. During his first two years in office, Carter scored a number of foreign policy successes, such as the Panama Canal Treaty, the Camp David Accords between Israel and Egypt, and the normalization of relations with the People's Republic of China, all of which testified to his undeniable negotiating skills and perseverance.

But while Carter's tenacity often paid off, it sometimes led to setbacks, as in the Iran hostage crisis. Carter subscribed to an ideal of excellence that induced him to search for the optimal decision at all times and to balk at compromise. As he himself acknowledged, "I can tell you with complete candor that we didn't assess the adverse political consequences of pursuing our goals." His goal was to govern on the basis of expertise, not by opinion polls. Over time, however, Carter grew more sensitive to the public mood and by the end of his term, he appeared much more hesitant in dealing with international crises.

With no guiding principle other than the will to apply moral precepts to specific circumstances, Carter's foreign policy was driven by the need to respond to international events, particularly the crises in Iran, Nicaragua, and Afghanistan in 1979. Carter tried to take a firm line, but his grip on the levers of power was shaky. Gradually, he lost his magic touch and fell victim to the quirks of his personality and his style. When he took office, he seemed at home in the role of president. By the end of his term, the sheen had long worn off.

Panama and Camp David

The agreements between Egypt and Israel reached at Camp David in 1978, which led to the signing of a peace treaty between the two countries the following year, were Carter's most important diplomatic achievements as president. However, his brilliant performance in peacemaking did not produce a consistent long-term foreign policy. Multiple advocacy, a managed process of internal debate designed to weigh accepted premises against countervailing arguments, was not really practiced in the Carter White House, and the

administration gradually sank into disarray. Differences of opinion and divergent perceptions within the administration did not prevent it from scoring some initial successes elsewhere, such as the 1977 treaty that restored full Panamanian sovereignty over the canal, which until then had been under U.S. administration.

On these issues, consensus among the administration's top policy-makers led to successful outcomes. In both cases, the management process operated effectively and the president was personally involved to an unprecedented degree. The decisions garnered the support of everyone involved in the process, and all the top officials were satisfied with the operation of the machinery of the National Security Council, although National Security Advisor Zbigniew Brzezinski took a backseat role. Carter surely would have liked these two major successes to be a harbinger of things to come during his presidency, but foreign policy-making came unglued over the thorny question of U.S.-Soviet relations, a problem that, along with Iran, undermined the administration's credibility.

The SALT Treaties

The first issue that caused trouble for the new administration arose in the Strategic Arms Limitation Talks (SALT) arms control negotiations with the Soviet Union. Secretary

President Jimmy Carter signs the Camp David Peace Treaty on March 26, 1979. Carter's partners in this historic peace agreement were Egyptian president Anwar Sadat (seated to Carter's right) and Israeli prime minister Menachem Begin (on Carter's left). (Jimmy Carter Library)

of State Cyrus Vance and Paul Warnke, director of the Arms Control and Disarmament Agency, tried with the president's support to alter dramatically the agreement-in-principle reached by Ford and Brezhnev in Vladivostok in 1974. Meanwhile, National Security Advisor Zbigniew Brzezinski was skeptical about the possibility of revising the previously negotiated arms ceilings. In March 1977, Carter sent Vance to Moscow to propose deep cuts: instead of 2,400 land-based and submarine-based missiles, each side could have 1,800 missiles, of which 1,100, instead of 1,320, could be armed with multiple warheads. Showing scant regard for Brezhnev's sensibilities, Vance publicly announced the details of his offer before his arrival in Moscow. The Kremlin wanted to hold to the Vladivostok agreement and rebuffed the idea of substantial reductions. The American proposal turned into a diplomatic fiasco, and negotiations dragged on until June 1979, when Carter and Brezhnev finally signed the SALT II Treaty in Vienna. In the end, SALT II was not significantly different from the Vladivostok agreement; it allowed 2,250 missiles on each side, 1,320 of which could carry multiple warheads.

Alexander Moens has suggested that throughout the decision-making process that led to the deep-cuts proposal, Carter received inadequate warning about the feasibility of the plans. Brzezinski kept his misgivings about Vance's proposal to himself and supported the consensus in favor of deep cuts in a spirit of collegiality. He also wanted to give the Soviets a chance and, most importantly, to keep open the possibility of an agreement different from the one negotiated by Henry Kissinger. However, he did tell his staff he had doubts. "It was unlikely the Soviets would agree to that," he wrote in his memoirs. "At best the Soviets will accept modest reductions."

Brzezinski was proved correct by the failure of Vance's initiative in March 1977, after which Brzezinski was able to take charge of the talks and controlled the Special Coordinating Committee's instructions to Warnke and his successor Ralph Earle. Looking back at the episode, William Hyland, who was still a member of Brzezinski's staff at the time, had no doubt that it was badly handled by everyone. The president did not realize the risks involved in making a spectacular offer, and announcing it publicly to boot. At the time, no one spoke out against his idealist vision or Carter's impatience to push through deep cuts. Although some had serious doubts, they kept silent. Later, the national security advisor's realism on the SALT negotiations and his pessimism about Soviet conduct led the administration to link the arms control talks closely with the evolution of geopolitical relations between the two superpowers.

Ethiopia

The administration's image problems worsened between January and March 1978, when Soviet and Cuban support helped the Marxist regime in Ethiopia recapture the Ogaden Desert, which had been invaded by Somalia in July 1977. The assistance provided by the Soviet Union and Cuba was part of their policy of support for revolutionary movements that had taken power in Africa, such as the governments of Mozambique and Angola. The large-scale airlift organized by Moscow and the presence of approximately 20,000 Cuban troops and advisors in Ethiopia was a matter of serious concern to Brzezinski, who saw the "offensive" as a threat to the stability of East-West relations. At two February meetings of the Special Coordinating Committee, Brzezinski suggested that Carter send U.S. aircraft carriers to positions off the coast of Somalia and authorize the transfer of arms from American allies in the region to the Somali government.

The Ogaden conflict crystallized for the first time the differences of opinion within the Carter administration about the implications of Soviet conduct. Brzezinski's view was that Moscow's attitude was jeopardizing détente and that superpower relations in general and the arms talks in particular ought to be linked to problems in other areas, such as the Horn of Africa. The national security advisor supported a clear, direct response, while Vance, backed in this case by Defense Secretary Harold Brown, was opposed and favored instead a political and diplomatic search for a regional solution. Brzezinski was alone among senior officials in advocating a hard line. At the NSC (National Security Council) meeting on February 23, the other officials in attendance convinced the president to take a hands-off stand on the Ogaden. Carter announced the position at a press conference at the beginning of March. However, Brzezinski continued to argue that Soviet actions in Ethiopia were incompatible with the code of détente and would complicate the SALT talks. He later went so far as to declare that the SALT negotiations lay buried in the sands of Ogaden.

Carter seemed unsure what course to take with Moscow. Unable to choose between the contradictory recommendations from Brzezinski and Vance, he decided to split the difference. In a speech delivered in Annapolis on June 7, he tried to reconcile the two approaches by supporting both a firm policy toward the Soviet Union and superpower détente. The speech received poor reviews in the press, which criticized Carter for sending a confused message. Correspondent James Fallows later commented that Carter had assembled the speech by stapling Vance's memo to Brzezinski's without addressing the tensions between them. The speech revealed a president with muddled perceptions and objectives. He had made the decision not to intervene in the Ogaden, but his attitude toward Moscow remained ambivalent.

The Neutron Bomb

As early as 1978, the neutron bomb issue underscored the lack of coordination in the Carter White House. In August 1977, the president authorized research into the "neutron bomb," an enhanced radiation weapon designed to destroy life with a massive shower of neutrons and other short-term radiation but featuring sharply reduced blast effects. The interdepartmental studies were all planned through NSC mechanisms. However, in April 1978, Carter decided to cancel the project when he realized, late in the day, that no NATO government had agreed to deploy the bomb if it were produced. The turnaround caused considerable embarrassment and confusion for both the Washington government and major NATO allies. Brzezinski and his staff had underestimated Carter's reluctance to authorize the building of the bomb without clear support from the allies, and they did a poor job of informing the military brass of the political factors that might influence the president's final decision.

From Cuba to Afghanistan

The sudden rediscovery of the presence of a Soviet brigade in Cuba in August 1979 led to a series of inept decisions and political miscues that did nothing to help the administration's efforts to push the SALT II treaty through Congress. The intelligence services, particularly the Pentagon's National Security Agency, had forgotten that 3,000 Soviet soldiers had been stationed in Cuba since 1962 to conduct training exercises with the Cuban army.

The national security advisor quickly concluded that the "Cuban brigade crisis" was a serious matter. After its existence was made public by Senators Richard Stone of Florida and Frank Church of Idaho, both Democrats, Brzezinski treated it as a diplomatic test between Washington and Moscow. In December, Carter decided to assemble a committee of senior statesmen, including McGeorge Bundy, Dean Rusk, George Ball, Clark Clifford, Henry Kissinger, Brent Scowcroft, and William Rogers to study the problem. Not surprisingly, they concluded that the American reaction had been out of proportion to the situation, which in any event was not new. The brigade, they found, posed no threat to the United States.

Once again, the impression created was that of an incompetent administration. For this, Brzezinski had to accept his share of the blame. He and his staff were closely supervising the operations of the CIA and its director. They should have been able to better weigh the information provided by the intelligence services before concluding that there was a serious threat. In the end, Carter delivered a speech on October 1 in which he downplayed the crisis for the American public and acknowledged that the brigade could legitimately stay in Cuba. Brzezinski later admitted in his memoirs that he should not have permitted the crisis to be handled in such an unwieldy manner.

Carter has acknowledged in a television interview that the invasion of Afghanistan on December 25, 1979, radically altered his perception of the Soviet Union, an admission that made him seem naive. Until then, the president had vacillated interminably on matters related to East-West relations, leaning sometimes toward Brzezinski, sometimes toward Vance. Bereft of any consistent principle, U.S. diplomacy was hostage to bureaucratic infighting, particularly on the issue of technology exports to the Soviet Union. Brzezinski and Carter's political aides wanted to impose sanctions on Moscow in response to the invasion, while the State, Commerce, and Treasury departments opposed the idea, pointing to the achievements of détente.

Although the administration had appeared more divided than ever throughout 1979, the invasion of Afghanistan closed the rift. From that point on, Brzezinski had the president's ear. He told Carter, that "before you are a President Wilson, you have to be for a few years a President Truman." Carter acted tough, imposing a series of sanctions including an embargo on wheat exports, suspending the SALT ratification process, and declaring a doctrine of reprisal in the event of any Soviet intervention in the Persian Gulf. But the international setbacks suffered by the United States fed a mood of public frustration—a mood deepened by the Iran hostage crisis—and created an increasingly negative impression of the president's leadership.

The Fall of the Shah of Iran

Fourteen months after Carter declared, during a visit to Teheran in December 1977, that Iran was an "island of stability" in the region, the Shah, Muhammad Reza Pahlavi, who had been in power since 1941, was overthrown and a fundamentalist Islamic regime led by the Ayatollah Ruhollah Khomeini took power. American policy during this tumultuous period in Iran was a major factor in subsequent problems with Khomeini later during the hostage crisis. Carter's team was initially caught off guard and then failed to formulate a coherent response to the fall of the Shah. The rivalry between Brzezinski and Vance permeated the smallest details of the decision-making process, and the administration's attitude toward the Shah constantly waxed hot and cold. The 1979 hostage crisis also highlighted serious cognitive failures and administrative weaknesses on the part of the policymakers, and revealed poor management of the decision-making process by the national security advisor.

All the signs of an impending crisis were recognizable as early as 1977. It was increasingly clear that the Shah's regime was opposed by most Iranians and many mullahs, who were dissatisfied with their country's pro-Western and particularly pro-American political and economic policies. As well, the fierce repression practiced for many years by the Shah's secret police, the SAVAK, had helped turn the public against the dictatorial Pahlavi regime. These were the factors that led to the outbreak of protests, concentrated in Qom, Iran's religious capital. Street demonstrations there in January 1978 set off the series of events that brought Khomeini to power a year later.

As protests spread across Iran, the demonstrations were brutally repressed. To stem the surging popular and religious opposition movement, the Shah declared martial law on August 11. On August 19, a fire in an Abadan movie theater killed 477 people. The government accused the religious opposition of starting the blaze in order to stoke opposition to the regime, while the mullahs suspected the SAVAK of responsibility. Though the Shah had appointed a new prime minister and a reform-minded cabinet on September 3, open opposition continued to grow. On September 8, the army drove 20,000 demonstrators out of Jaleh Square in Teheran, killing hundreds in the process. That event sparked the Islamic revolution, gradually engineered by Khomeini from exile in Iraq and then France. The opposition riposted by staging work stoppages across Iran.

As the demonstrations grew more frequent and violent, the Shah had to choose between harsher repression and concessions. Wavering and visibly shaken, he tried unsuccessfully to wield both the carrot and the stick. On December 29, he appointed one of his opponents, Shapour Bakhtiar, prime minister. At the same time, he ordered the army to enforce martial law. More bloodshed ensued. On December 31, 170 people were killed in the city of Mashad. On the same day, the Shah announced his intention to leave the country temporarily for medical reasons. On January 12, Khomeini announced his return to Iran. On January 16, the Shah relinquished power and flew to Cairo. On January 27, millions of Iranians took to the streets of Teheran to demonstrate in support of Khomeini, who finally returned to the country on February 1. In the days that followed, Islamic revolutionary forces seized control of the levers of power and the army swung its support behind the Ayatollah's new regime after the top military leadership had fled the country. Khomeini's anti-American positions intensified and ten months later, the United States became the revolutionaries' target.

Was there something the Carter administration could have done in the months preceding the fall of the Shah to preserve the American ties with Iran and safeguard its traditional diplomatic interests? In several ways, the NSC's decision-making machinery and the actions of the national security advisor prevented the Carter team from recognizing at an earlier date the imminent danger of the Shah's overthrow and the urgent need to adjust the goals of American diplomacy. The commonly accepted interpretation is that the United States could not have headed off the revolution. However, an in-depth analysis of the American response between January 1978 and January 1979 suggests that Washington should not have been surprised by the events and could have assessed them differently.

On November 11, 1978, the president sent his advisors a memo written by Brzezinski expressing dissatisfaction with the failure of the intelligence community to warn the administration of the crisis. This charge was in fact unfounded. A number of agencies, including the State Department's Bureau of Intelligence and Research (INR), had been attempting for some time to draw the NSC's attention to the Shah's precarious position. For example, on January 29, 1978, the INR sent the director of central intelligence and the national security advisor a memo in which its analysts stated that traditional Islamic opponents were in their strongest positions and time was not on the side of the Shah. Subsequently, the INR issued a series of warnings on the political fragility of the Shah's regime, noting the growing influence of religious fundamentalism and the tensions caused by the Shah's economic policies. On September 1, the INR expressed doubt that the Shah could keep the army's support and predicted that he would be forced to step down by 1985. On October 29, the forecast was revised to question the Shah's ability to survive in power over the next eighteen to twenty-four months. At that point, in fact, the Shah had only eleven weeks left, but the INR had accurately appraised the instability of his regime. On November 2, the Bureau reported that only drastic measures could stave off a descent into chaos and on December 5, it suggested that the Shah abdicate and leave the country. The matter was no longer whether he should leave but a question of when and how, the INR analysts concluded. On December 26, they recommended that the United States open a dialogue with the opposition to facilitate the handover of power in Teheran. However, the INR reports were not taken seriously.

The president and his closest advisors refused to contemplate the prospect of the overthrow of the Shah. According to David Newsom, undersecretary of state for political affairs, this mistake was not due to any failure on the part of the intelligence services but rather to the unwillingness of people in high places either to accept the full implications of available intelligence or to know what to do about it if they did accept it. Stansfield Turner, director of central intelligence, ignored similar reports from the CIA, while Brzezinski did not bring the INR's warnings to the attention of the NSC or the president. By refusing to circulate or discuss the memo, perhaps just confining it to the Friday foreign policy breakfasts, Brzezinski possibly prevented the administration from having an open and timely debate on the crisis. Given his rivalry with Vance and his staunch support for the Shah, it is not surprising that the national security advisor disregarded the information he received. He also ignored studies by his deputy, General Odom, which arrived at the same conclusions as the INR. As a result, it was not until November 2, 1978, that Brzezinski called the first NSC interdepartmental meeting on the situation in Iran. Meanwhile, Vance too had refused up to that point to credit the gloomy forecasts from his intelligence bureau. This attitude was dominant within the circle of senior policy-makers.

As in the hostage crisis, which broke out one year later, Carter was not exposed to information and options that would have made him aware of the problem at an earlier date and enabled him to steer the American response more effectively. The national security advisor therefore bears a heavy burden of responsibility for the failure of presidential decision-making in response to the fall of the Shah.

The Iran Hostage Crisis

The taking of American hostages in Iran was the gravest problem Carter faced during his four years in the White House. The crisis broke out on November 4, 1979, when Iranian students stormed the embassy of the United States in Teheran with the support of the revolutionary government of the Ayatollah Khomeini. The fate of the 60 hostages absorbed the full energies of the White House for the next 444 days.

The Iranian hostage crisis can be divided into several phases, marked by numerous reversals and false hopes. As events unfolded, Carter lost credibility with the American people, and the lengthy detention of the hostages hamstrung his campaign for reelection against the Republican presidential nominee, Ronald Reagan, in November 1980. Ultimately, the hostages were released on January 20, 1981, the day Reagan was sworn in. Carter and his advisors were preoccupied with every twist and turn in the hostage affair. By making the crisis his personal priority for more than a year and achieving no results, the president gave an impression of paralysis.

Carter had made the mistake of caving in to pressure from Brzezinski and his political advisors to let the Shah come to the United States for medical treatment. At that time, Carter asked, "What are you guys going to advise me to do if they overrun our embassy and take our people hostage?" He then authorized the national security advisor to meet with the Iranian prime minister in Algiers, at a time when Iran was still in a state of ferment and the credibility of revolutionary spokesmen was uncertain. Those decisions were among the events that triggered the crisis of November 4.

Over the following five months, Carter wavered between advice from Vance, who advocated a diplomatic and humanitarian approach, and Brzezinski, who focused on defending the national interest and was prepared to contemplate the use of force. The NSA made its position clear: Teheran should be bombed if the hostages were killed. Uncertain which way to turn, Carter found the worst of both worlds by keeping a great glare of publicity on the hostages while apparently doing nothing about them. He finally realized that he should have taken a firmer line from the beginning of the crisis and decided, in April 1980, to launch a military rescue operation. Operation Eagle Claw turned into a greater fiasco than the Bay of Pigs and had to be abandoned within hours. It was planned by a small group at the Pentagon and the NSC, dominated by Brzezinski, on the basis of information in official reports.

The planning of the operation was cumbersome and poorly coordinated. Those who doubted its feasibility were shut out of the process. No disagreement was tolerated. The only difficulty Brzezinski raised was the question of how many people would die in the operation. Key factors, such as the effect of desert sandstorms on military equipment, were overlooked. Military experts subsequently criticized the resources provided to the rescue mission. Vance was consulted only at the last minute, on April 15, and his objections were not really considered, because the operation had already been approved. He resigned on April 17.

Already perceived as indecisive, Carter came to be seen as weaker still because of his administration's inability to act effectively. In the last months of the crisis, the president tried again, unsuccessfully, to follow the diplomatic track initially recommended by Vance and then doggedly pursued by Deputy Secretary of State Warren Christopher.

Legacy

Americans elected Carter in the hope of bringing integrity and dignity back to the Oval Office. Once elected, however, Carter's honeymoon with the American people was brief. International events threw a wrench into his plans, and Carter had no choice but to abandon some of his principles and redefine his original positions. At the end of his term, Carter reversed his approach to diplomacy but was too late to prevent a stinging electoral defeat at the hands of Ronald Reagan in November, 1980.

The Carter administration is an object lesson in how decision-making problems and weak leadership can have a disastrous effect on the conduct of foreign policy. Jimmy Carter wanted to run a hands-on presidency and make all decisions with his advisors. His collegial, democratic approach to decision-making was similar to that of the Kennedy White House and seemed to work during his first two years in office. However, the process ran aground in the administration's last two years. During that period, in the absence of clear, consistent presidential leadership, Carter's advisors—particularly Zbigniew Brzezinski and his NSC staff—waged a corrosive bureaucratic battle against the State Department. But Brzezinski was never able to entirely eclipse the secretary of state as his predecessors in the Kennedy, Johnson, and Nixon administrations had done. By the end of Carter's presidency, the national security advisor dominated the decision-making process, but at that point, the damage was too widespread for the public perception of weak leadership to change.

Carter could not have foreseen the events that would transpire in the international arena over the following four years. But it must also be acknowledged that the failures of decision-making in the Carter White House itself were largely responsible for the foreign policy setbacks he suffered. That did not prevent him from persevering along the same idealistic path after leaving office, and in 2002 Carter was awarded the Nobel Peace Prize in recognition of his efforts to settle international disputes and his work to promote democracy, human rights, and development.

Charles-Philippe David

Chronology

1977

February 17: President Carter sends a personal letter of support to Soviet dissident Andrey Sakharov.

May 17: Likud leader, Menachem Begin, is elected prime minister of Israel.

June 15: Spain conducts its first democratic election in forty years; Adolfo Suarez is prime minister.

July 1: Carter cancels the B-1 bomber program.

August 8: War breaks out between Ethiopia and Somalia.

September 7: United States and Panama sign treaties governing the future of the Panama Canal.

November 15: Israeli Prime Minister Menachem Begin invites Egyptian President Anwar Sadat to visit Israel.

December 2: Radical Arab leaders oppose Egypt's peace diplomacy with Israel.

December 14: In Cairo, U.S., Egyptian, and Israeli representatives discuss peace.

1978

March 10: Palestinian terrorists launch an amphibious raid on Israel.

March 14: Israel attacks Palestinian bases in southern Lebanon.

April 7: President Carter postpones production of the neutron bomb.

April 27: Military coup ousts Daoud regime in Afghanistan.

May 16: Ethiopia invades Eritrea.

June 16: United States and Panama exchange ratification of Panama Canal treaties.

July 18: Soviet Union sentences dissident Anatoly Sharansky to thirteen years in prison; United States protests.

September 17: Egypt and Israel sign Camp David Accords brokered by Carter.

September 23: Radical Arab states denounce Camp David Accords.

November 26–27: A twenty-four-hour strike protests the rule of the Shah of Iran.

December 3: Vietnam invades Cambodia.

December 15: United States and China establish normal diplomatic relations; United States terminates Mutual Defense Treaty with Taiwan.

1979

January 7: Vietnamese and Kampuchean forces capture Phnom Penh.

January 16: Forced from power, the Shah of Iran flees to Egypt.

February 1: The Ayatollah Khomeini forms a provisional Iranian government.

February 17: China launches punitive invasion of Vietnam.

March 26: Begin and Sadat sign Israeli-Egyptian peace treaty.

April 10: Carter signs the Taiwan Relations Act.

May 3: Margaret Thatcher is elected prime minister of Britain.

June 18: Carter and Brezhnev sign SALT II.

July 17: Nicaraguan dictator Anastasio Somoza is forced from power.

July 20: UN resolution calls on Israel to end West Bank settlement construction.

August 6: United States offers to deploy Pershing II and Cruise missiles in NATO countries.

November 4: U.S. embassy in Iran is stormed by radical students; 52 hostages are taken.

November 20: Guerrillas hostile to the Saudi government storm the Grand Mosque in Mecca.

December 28: Soviet forces invade Afghanistan.

1980

January 2: Carter asks Senate to delay ratification of SALT II.

January 4: Carter announces sanctions against the Soviet Union.

January 14: UN demands Soviet withdrawal from Afghanistan.

January 23: Carter cites the Persian Gulf a vital interest of the United States, the Carter Doctrine.

February 23: UN commission arrives in Iran to settle hostage crisis.

April 7: United States severs diplomatic relations with Iran.

April 25: Mission to rescue hostages in Teheran is aborted.

June 16: United States warns West Germany about Soviet attempt to freeze U.S. missile deployments.

June 25: Congress approves Carter's request to revive selective service system.

July 1: West German Chancellor Helmut Schmidt visits Moscow to discuss détente.

July 19: United States and fifty-eight other states boycott Moscow Olympics.

August 13: Polish dock workers strike in the Gdansk shipyard.

September 4: Iraq invades Iran; Iran-Iraq war begins.

November 8: Ronald Regan is elected president; George H.W. Bush is vice president.

References and Further Reading

Brzezinski, Zbigniew. *Power and Principle: Memoirs of the National Security Adviser, 1977–1981.* New York: Farrar, Straus and Giroux, 1983.

Carter, Jimmy. *Keeping Faith: Memoirs of a President.* New York, Bantam, 1982.

David, Charles-Philippe, et al. *Foreign Policy Failure in the White House: Reappraising the Fall of the Shah and the Iran-Contra Affair.* Lanham, MD: University Press of America, 1993.

Garrison, Jean. *Games Advisers Play: Foreign Policy in the Nixon and Carter Administrations.* College Station, TX: Texas A&M University Press, 1999.

Kaufman, Burton. *The Presidency of James Earl Carter.* Lawrence, KS: University Press of Kansas, 1993.

Moens, Alexander. *Foreign Policy Under Carter: Testing Multiple Advocacy Decision-Making.* Boulder, CO: Westview, 1990.

Skidmore, David. *Reversing Course: Carter's Foreign Policy, Domestic Politics, and the Failure of Reform.* Nashville, TN: Vanderbilt University Press, 1996.

Strong, Robert, *Working the World: Jimmy Carter and the Making of American Foreign Policy.* Baton Rouge, LA: Louisiana State University Press, 2000.

Vance, Cyrus. *Hard Choices: Critical Years in America's Foreign Policy.* New York: Simon and Schuster, 1983.

Ronald Wilson Reagan (1981–1989)

Early Life and Political Career

Ronald Wilson Reagan was born on February 6, 1911, in Tampico, Illinois, the second son of Nelle and John Reagan. The Reagan family moved many times as John Reagan sought employment, but settled in Dixon, Illinois long enough for Ronald Reagan to consider it home. Reagan attended high school in Dixon and then entered Eureka College on a needy-student scholarship, where he studied economics and sociology, became involved in student politics, played football, and acted in school plays. When Reagan graduated from college in 1932, the Great Depression was at its nadir and unemployment in the United States exceeded 26 percent. Reagan found a job as a sports announcer and became a familiar voice around the Midwest calling baseball games. In 1937, Reagan was covering the Chicago Cubs and volunteered to follow the team to their spring training camp in California; while in Los Angeles he won a screen test and a seven-year contract with Warner Brothers that paid $200 weekly.

Reagan moved to Hollywood and was cast in a number of forgettable B-movies; A-list stardom eluded him. That changed in 1940, when Reagan gave his best performance in *King's Row*, and also won the part of George Gipp, "The Gipper," in *Knute Rockne, All American*. The Japanese attack on Pearl Harbor, however, halted the momentum of Reagan's acting career. He was an officer in the U.S. Cavalry reserves and was called up for active service three months after Pearl Harbor at Fort Mason, outside San Francisco. Commissioned as a second lieutenant, Reagan served as a liaison officer in charge of loading convoys with troops.

After the war, Reagan returned to a Hollywood roiled by political turmoil. In September 1946, a strike was called by Herb Sorrell, the head of the Conference of Studio Unions. Sorrell was a secret member of the Communist Party, a contact for Soviet intelligence, and had a history of leading violent strikes in the Bay Area in the 1930s. Sorrell sought to use the strike to gain control of the major unions in Hollywood. As a member of the Screen Actors Guild (SAG), Reagan was part of a group tasked with deciding whether the actors ought to cross the picket lines. Reagan's group held that the strike ought not to be honored, a position endorsed by the SAG membership by a vote of 2,748 to 509. The strikes persisted, however, and Reagan received anonymous death

Ronald Wilson Reagan first recommitted the United States to the original principles of the Cold War struggle against the Soviet Union and then hastened its peaceful conclusion with his policies. (Library of Congress)

threats. The strikes eventually fizzled and Sorrell ceased to be a political force in Hollywood.

Reagan was now a political force in Hollywood. He was nominated by Gene Kelly to be president of SAG and was elected resoundingly. In September 1947, Reagan received a subpoena to appear before the House Un-American Committee (HUAC), which was investigating communism in Hollywood. Reagan testified under oath that Hollywood was capable of taking care of its own affairs and did not welcome federal intervention in the matter. Reagan was a firm opponent of communism but he was determined to oppose blacklists and protect those unfairly accused of harboring Communist sympathies. Shortly after Reagan was elected president of SAG, his first wife, Jane Wyman, filed for divorce. His continued work on behalf of actors threatened with blacklisting put him in touch with a young contract actress, Nancy Davis. Ronald Reagan and Nancy Davis were married on March 4, 1952.

Reagan's movie career was effectively over, but in 1952 General Electric approached Reagan with an offer to host a weekly Sunday-night drama series called *General Electric Theater*. His contract with GE included a clause that required him to travel as the company's goodwill ambassador. In his speeches, Reagan spoke of the blessings of democracy and warned of the perils of big government. As a New Deal Democrat and a staunch anti-communist, he had been a keen supporter of Harry Truman's policy of containment and his conduct of the Korean War. But by 1952, Reagan was concerned about the Democratic Party's drift in its resolution to combat communism. The Party's presidential candidate, the cerebral Adlai Stevenson, failed to inspire much confidence. Instead Reagan supported the Republican candidacy of General Dwight D. Eisenhower, who was pro-business and a moderate conservative.

In 1960, Reagan registered as a Republican and a conservative. He insisted that he had not left the Democratic Party; it had left him when it embraced higher taxes, increased government intervention, an antibusiness bias, and what Reagan considered to be a weak foreign policy. In early 1962, Reagan gave a speech before the Phoenix Chamber of Commerce to an audience that included Arizona Senator Barry Goldwater, leader of the conservative wing of the Republican Party. In 1964, Goldwater approached Reagan to become the co-chair of his presidential campaign in California. Reagan stumped around California for Goldwater but also taped a speech in which he attacked the policy of containment and peaceful coexistence with the Soviet Union for providing only a choice "between fight and surrender" and promised a "rendezvous with destiny" for those who would fight for American freedoms. The speech prompted liberals to label Reagan a "right-wing extremist" but among his supporters it quickly became known as "The Speech" and it resulted in over $8 million flowing into the coffers of Goldwater's embattled presidential campaign.

The Pursuit of the Presidency

Barry Goldwater lost the 1964 election to Lyndon Johnson in a landslide, but the GOP was being reborn as a conservative party, and Reagan was its rising new star. A group of California businessmen approached Reagan to run for governor of California against the incumbent, Pat Brown. Reagan defeated Brown by over a million votes with 58 percent of the total. Although he campaigned to lower taxes and decrease the size of government, Reagan found upon assuming office that the state was virtually bankrupt. He instituted austerity measures in the state government and

raised taxes despite campaign promises. Reagan's record was nonetheless generally conservative. Nowhere was this more evident than in his tough stance against student radicals on California campuses. Even while governor of California, Reagan kept a close eye on foreign affairs and the politics of the Cold War, observing events in Vietnam especially closely. Within nine months of becoming governor, Reagan led a movement within the Governors' Association to withdraw support for the Johnson administration's conduct of the war. While Johnson clung to the hope of a negotiated settlement, Reagan believed that a decisive military victory was still possible. His views on Vietnam also put him at odds with the putative Republican presidential candidate of 1968, Richard Nixon, who believed that a détente with the Soviet Union would prompt Moscow to help negotiate a settlement to end the war.

Reagan had supported Nixon's presidential campaign in 1960 and his run at the California governorship in 1962, but he now had serious doubts about what sort of president Nixon would be. Those doubts prompted Reagan to make a late insurgent campaign for the Republican presidential nomination in 1968. The campaign went nowhere, as Nixon had locked up the necessary number of primary delegates. Nixon viewed Reagan as both a potential ally and a threat; Reagan had a sizable constituency within the GOP and was poised strategically on the right to threaten Nixon if his foreign policy moved too far to the left. Nixon therefore sought to bring the California governor on board for one of his boldest diplomatic moves: the opening of relations with mainland China. While conservatives like Goldwater lambasted Nixon for "selling out" to the Communists, Reagan appreciated the strategic implications of reaching out to China and further separating it diplomatically from the Soviet Union. In October 1971, Reagan made a trip to Asia as Nixon's personal envoy to reassure worried American allies that the United States remained a dependable ally in spite of the diplomatic overture to Beijing.

While Reagan agreed with Nixon on China, he disagreed with the administration's détente toward the Soviet Union. Reagan was unaware of the secret negotiations between Henry Kissinger and Anatoly Dobrynin that culminated in the Strategic Arms Limitation (SALT I) agreement and Antiballistic Missile Treaty (ABM treaty) signed by Nixon and Leonid Brezhnev in Moscow on May 26, 1972. Nixon and Kissinger believed that American technological superiority would allow the United States to retain strategic nuclear parity with the Soviet Union, whereas the Kremlin leadership believed it had attained a position of strategic superiority. Reagan was opposed to both SALT I and the ABM treaty, but out of deference to Nixon did not make his criticisms public. In July 1972, Nixon tapped Reagan once again as his personal envoy to Western Europe to reassure worried leaders there. Reagan reassured the Europeans, but in private he complained that Nixon had given up too much to the Soviets. When Nixon resigned over Watergate, Reagan went public with his criticisms of SALT I and the ABM treaty, arguing that the United States was falling behind in the arms race.

In 1974, Reagan's second term as governor ended and he returned to private life. He turned down Gerald Ford's offer to join his cabinet. Reagan liked Ford personally but opposed his foreign and domestic policies. Reagan decided to enter the 1976 presidential primary campaign, running as an outsider against the Washington establishment. In the New Hampshire primary he lost to Ford by a mere 1,500 votes out of a total of 108,000 votes, a symbolic victory in that he had come extremely close to defeating the sitting president, but lost the next five primaries. Reagan then won a surprising upset victory in North Carolina in part by making Ford's foreign policy record a campaign issue, hammering Ford for signing the 1975 Helsinki Accords, and accusing him of accepting the Soviet enslavement of the nations behind the Iron Curtain in exchange for vague and meaningless promises of better Soviet behavior. He also attacked Ford's policy of "parity and sufficiency" in the arms race and called instead for the restoration of "military superiority."

When the Republican convention met in mid-August, neither Ford nor Reagan had secured a majority of the delegates. Ford won on the first ballot with 1,187 votes, a slim majority of only 117 votes for an incumbent president. Reagan was disappointed by the outcome of the primaries yet endorsed Ford and campaigned hard for him. At the head of a divided Republican Party, Ford faced the Democratic nominee, the former governor of Georgia, Jimmy Carter. The polls showed that it was a close race, and Ford ended up losing with 48 percent of the popular vote and 240 electoral votes against Carter's 50.1 percent and 297 electoral votes.

The Carter Legacy

During the 1976 presidential campaign, Carter had made it a point of attacking the "Nixon-Kissinger-Ford" foreign policy for its lack of consonance with deeply held American values. Détente was premised on maintaining a global balance of power, and Carter believed that this emphasis on power at the expense of morality and American values had led to the agony of Vietnam. Carter intended to forge a new consensus in foreign policy that took into account the political legacies of Vietnam and Watergate—disaffection with a militarized foreign policy, skepticism about the universal applicability of liberal democratic-capitalist values and institutions, declining American preeminence and prestige, and eroded public trust in American governmental institutions. Carter's predecessors had accepted to varying degrees a view of the Cold War based on the centrality of the Soviet threat, but Carter sought to free American foreign policy from what he considered an "inordinate fear of communism" and focus it instead on a new paradigm of human rights.

In his inaugural address Carter made human rights the centerpiece of his foreign policy. Human rights diplomacy had the potential of forging a consensus among liberals and conservatives, but it also featured inherent problems of definition and consistency as well as the age-old dilemma of reconciling ideals and interest. In April 1977, Secretary of State Cyrus Vance noted that there were three key types of human rights: a right not be brutalized or tortured by the state, economic rights, and broad civil and political freedoms. Vance made it clear that civil and political rights would receive the least emphasis as the administration had no wish to interfere in the internal affairs of sovereign states. Still, this did not prevent Carter from reducing or eliminating economic and military aid to American allies in Latin America such as Argentina, Bolivia, Chile, Nicaragua, and El Salvador for alleged human rights abuses; the administration's human rights coordinator, Warren Christopher, considered those countries to be governed by "retrogressive fascists." Carter proved more reticent when it came to the Soviet Union and its satellites. In a September 1977 meeting with Soviet Foreign Minister Andrei Gromyko, Carter did not raise the subject of Soviet human rights abuses and even told his interlocutor that his human rights initiative did not really extend to the Soviet Union. Carter did campaign on behalf of individual Soviet dissidents—something his predecessors were unwilling to do—but he was at pains to make it clear that his efforts should not be permitted to jeopardize U.S.-Soviet relations.

By the latter part of 1979, the Carter administration had nonetheless essentially abandoned human rights, world order politics, and accommodation with the Soviets, and fallen back instead on containment as the guiding principle of its foreign policy. Détente appeared not to have satiated the Soviets' expansionist impulses, and communism was advancing globally. In Southeast Asia, Vietnam, Laos, and Cambodia had all fallen to Communist regimes. In southern Africa, Angola and Mozambique had fallen into the Soviet orbit—with the aid of tens of thousands of Cuban troops. In the Horn of Africa, Mengistu Haile Mariam aligned Ethiopia with the Communist bloc, and a pro-Soviet faction seized power in South Yemen. In the Caribbean Maurice Bishop's Cuban-backed New Jewel Movement took power.

Three events of 1979 sent the Carter administration into full-crisis mode: the Iranian Revolution and the subsequent hostage crisis, the overthrow of the Somoza regime in Nicaragua, and the Soviet invasion of Afghanistan. The Shah was a long-standing American ally and Carter had overlooked the dismal human rights record of his secret police because Iran had become an important source of oil as well as the principal market for American arms exports.

The overthrow of the Shah and the installation of the fundamentalist and fanatically anti-American Khomeini regime disrupted oil supplies and compounded domestic economic dislocation. The subsequent taking of fifty-two American hostages by Islamic militants and the failed rescue attempt merely added to the sense of panic and impotence in the administration. In Nicaragua, the removal of Anastasio Somoza was facilitated by the United States, which had cut off aid and called formally for his removal, but Carter was unsure about whether to conciliate or oppose the new Sandinista-dominated regime. By 1980, however, the administration accused the Sandinistas of fomenting revolution throughout the hemisphere, diverted covert funds for the destabilization of their regime, and resumed "non-lethal" aid to the right-wing regime in neighboring El Salvador. The Soviet invasion of Afghanistan represented the first extensive use of direct Soviet power outside of Eastern Europe and prompted the president to promulgate the Carter Doctrine, warning that any attempt by an outside power to gain control of the Persian Gulf would be met by American force if necessary. In addition, Carter announced a series of anti-Soviet measures that included the suspension of grain sales, an American boycott of the Olympic Games in Moscow, the withdrawal of SALT II from Senate consideration, and a significant increase in defense spending.

During the 1980 presidential campaign, Reagan attacked Carter's domestic record, famously stating that "recession is when your neighbor loses his job, depression is when you lose your job, and recovery is when Jimmy Carter loses his job." Reagan also ridiculed Carter on foreign affairs, decrying the naïveté of his human rights policy and world order politics that had sapped the West's willingness to stand up to Soviet aggression. Reagan ran on a platform that called for peace through strength. A peaceful world would be obtained through the renewal of American power and a reassertion of the nation's place as the leader of the "free world." Reagan called for military and technological superiority over the Soviets and a "roll back" of the expansion of communism. The message struck a chord in an electorate disillusioned with Carter's handling of domestic and foreign crises. It elected him president in a landslide, with 50.7 percent of the popular vote and 489 electoral votes against Carter's 41 percent and 49 electoral votes.

Peace through Strength

Reagan had been an early and forceful advocate of American military superiority. Carter had proposed increased defense spending in his last year in office, but the defense budget had been cut steadily and substantially since the end of the Vietnam War, resulting in a hollowed-out military plagued with morale problems. Reagan expanded on Carter's proposed increase, setting a real annual increase of 7 percent in military expenditures over the objections of his Budget

Director David Stockman. It would be the largest peacetime military buildup to date, pushing defense appropriations from $134 billion in 1980 to $253 billion in 1985 when it leveled off. The administration's goal was to recover American military effectiveness after years of neglect, as well as part of a grand strategy of pricing the Soviets out of superpower competition.

Reagan increased the number of active divisions in the Army, the number of tactical fighter wings in the Air Force, and the number of ships in the Navy. He also secured increases in military pay and benefits in a successful effort to fill recruitment quotas and restore morale. The key component, however, was the modernization of the American nuclear arsenal. This consisted of plans to deploy the new land-based MX (Peacekeeper) ICBM system to complement aging Minutemen and Titan missiles; B-1B bombers to replace the aging fleet of B-52s; and D-5 Trident II submarine-launched ballistic missiles (SLBMs) to replace the Navy's obsolescent Polaris and Poseidon missiles.

Nuclear modernization was designed to restore the perception of strategic balance in the face of Soviet modernization in the 1970s, make possible an American counterforce strategy aimed at Soviet military forces rather than the civilian population, and to recover negotiating leverage in arms talks. The program came under immediate attack from the antinuclear weapons movement, which argued that the nuclear buildup would merely provoke the Soviets into hostility, making arms control more difficult and conflict more likely. At its peak, the "nuclear freeze" movement claimed millions of sympathizers and was successful in lobbying the Democrat-controlled House of Representatives to pass a nonbinding nuclear freeze resolution in 1983. Opposition to the nuclear buildup was not confined to the United States. In October 1983, nearly 2 million people took to the streets in London, Paris, Rome, and other European cities to oppose the deployment of American Pershing II and Tomahawk cruise missiles in Western Europe to counter the threat of Soviet SS-20s. A majority in Congress nonetheless voted to proceed with the modernization program, and American missiles were deployed on schedule in Western Europe in 1983. Prime Minister Margaret Thatcher of Britain, who had strongly supported Reagan, was reelected the same year. Chancellor Helmut Schmidt of West Germany lost a parliamentary vote of no-confidence in part because of opposition to the missile deployments from within his own center-left coalition government, but Schmidt was replaced by a center-right coalition led by Helmut Kohl, who carried through on Schmidt's commitment to the deployments.

Strengthening Alliances

Reagan's refusal to back down from the deployment of American missiles to counter Soviet SS-20s was instrumental in preserving NATO, the cornerstone of the American international security system. His approach to foreign policy was guided by the "Munich paradigm" rather than the "Vietnam paradigm"; unlike Carter, he was more concerned with the dangers inherent in appeasement than with the hazards of assertiveness. Reagan believed it necessary to be firm on the issue of missile deployment since it was essential to convince the Soviets that they would fail in any attempt to "Finlandize" Western Europe. The test of the missile deployment crisis served to restore and strengthen the bonds of NATO. Despite the direst predictions of his critics, Reagan's policies did not destroy the Western alliance; on the contrary, as Margaret Thatcher noted, Reagan "strengthened not only America's defenses, but also the will of America's allies."

In Asia, the administration moved to strengthen the long-standing American alliance with Japan. Reagan withstood strong domestic pressure to engage in a trade war with Japan over its protectionist practices and managed to persuade the government of Prime Minister Yasuhiro Nakasone to undertake the unpopular and controversial task of increasing Japanese military spending to shoulder a greater share of the burden in protecting vital sea lanes of communications in Northeast Asia. Reagan also viewed the maintenance of Sino-American ties as a key to balancing Soviet power, having been an early supporter of normalizing ties with China. Both nations were opposed to Soviet expansionism, and China could be counted on to tie down nearly fifty Soviet divisions in Siberia that might otherwise be deployed in Europe. Despite its inclination to support Taiwan, the administration moved to strengthen diplomatic, economic, and military ties with China.

The Reagan Doctrine

Before taking office, Reagan told Richard V. Allen, who later served as his national security advisor, that "my idea of American policy toward the Soviet Union is simple. It is this: 'we win and they lose.'" Reagan had been critical of the traditional containment policy because it placed the United States and its allies permanently on the defensive. He sought a new policy wherein cracks in the Soviet empire could be exploited to accelerate the collapse of what he considered an inherently weak system. The framework for this approach was established between 1982 and 1983 in three national security decision directives. The first, NSDD-32, outlined an American policy to "neutralize" Soviet control behind the Iron Curtain by supporting underground movements and psychological operations against the Communist regimes. The second, NSDD-66, outlined a strategy of economic warfare against the Soviets, while NSDD-75 declared that although the United States sought the roll-back of Soviet influence globally, the ultimate policy objective was a change in the Soviet system itself.

In a speech at Notre Dame University, Reagan promised that the West would not merely contain communism; it would "transcend" it. Addressing the British Parliament in June 1982, Reagan castigated the Soviet system and called for a new "crusade for freedom" to leave "Marxism-Leninism on the ash heap of history." In March 1983, Reagan addressed the National Association of Evangelicals in Orlando and told his audience that the Soviet Union constituted an "evil empire" and was "the focus of evil in the modern world." The worldview that Reagan articulated in these speeches was dubbed the "Reagan Doctrine" by columnist Charles Krauthammer. The Reagan Doctrine was immediately attacked by the Western intellectual class as "simplistic" and "dangerous" but the president was unfazed. The rhetorical and ideological offensive against the Soviet Union was designed to restore the moral context of the Cold War: to remind the American people and their allies of the fundamental purpose behind their struggles and sacrifice, which had been blurred by détente and Carter's human rights policies. By casting that struggle in Manichean terms of good and evil, Reagan sought also to strip the Soviet dictatorship of any legitimacy and to strengthen the resolve of those resisting the "evil empire" behind the Iron Curtain.

The Strategic Defense Initiative

On March 23, 1983, Reagan announced that the United States would develop a ballistic missile defense system under the name Strategic Defense Initiative (SDI). Domestic critics of the program pointed variously to the technological difficulties of developing a system of lasers or projectiles to shoot down incoming missiles, the prohibitive costs of the system, the inability of the system to provide comprehensive protection from a missile attack, and the destabilizing effect SDI would have on the strategic balance of terror that the ABM treaty had sought to preserve. Fundamental to Reagan's advocacy of SDI was his long-standing moral aversion to the prevailing doctrine of "mutual assured destruction" (MAD). Reagan asked, "Is there either logic or morality in believing that if one side threatens to kill tens of millions of our people, our only recourse is to threaten killing tens of millions of theirs?" Moral anguish, however, was not the sole reason for proceeding with SDI. The Soviets were known to be working on ballistic missile defense and had maintained and upgraded the one antiballistic missile site outside Moscow permitted by the ABM treaty. Thus, SDI was also driven by the strategic consideration of preventing the Soviets from beating the United States in developing an effective missile defense system. Lastly, SDI was also attractive in view of the diminished credibility of extended deterrence resulting from the increased vulnerability of American land-based ICBMs.

The Soviet leadership denounced the announcement of the SDI in hysterical and apoplectic tones. Even if SDI was based on fantasy and junk science, as its critics claimed, the Soviets comprehended its potential in altering the strategic environment in favor of the United States. Reagan was changing the game entirely, threatening to render obsolete the massive Soviet investment in ICBMs and forcing Moscow into a ruinous new arms race that the economic backwardness of their economy could not sustain. This led them to launch a propaganda campaign accusing Reagan of threatening the militarization of space; when propaganda failed, they turned to arms control in an attempt to eliminate SDI. The climax of the Soviet campaign to eliminate SDI through negotiation occurred at the Reykjavik summit in October 1986, where Mikhail Gorbachev offered an unverifiable elimination of all nuclear weapons in exchange for the termination of SDI. Reagan rejected Gorbachev's offer yet still managed to achieve his goal of arms reduction at the Washington Summit of December 1987.

Economic Warfare

The NSDD-66 document of 1982 outlined a policy of economic warfare based on an understanding of the fundamental weakness of the Soviet economy and a determination to exploit it. Reagan's defense buildup was perceived by the Soviets as a particularly effective form of economic warfare. In an effort to counter it, in 1981 the Politiburo ordered a 45 percent increase in military expenditures over five years and two years later ordered an additional 10 percent increase. This massive shift in resources weighed heavily on a faltering economy as civilian consumption shrank to less than 50 percent of Soviet GNP as the military's share rose to 27 percent. Reagan thus achieved the goal of hamstringing an already weak Soviet economy. This in turn would weaken the Soviets globally as fewer resources were available to maintain its empire. Kremlin leaders understood that the administration's pursuit of SDI threatened the Soviet economy with ruin. The economic noose was tightening in other ways as well. The Coordinating Committee for Multilateral Export Controls (COCOM), became more aggressive in restricting Western technology transfers to the Soviet Union, and the Saudi decision at American behest to increase oil production on a large scale reduced global oil prices and wiped away tens of billions in hard currency earnings that were desperately needed. At the same time, the American economy was in the midst of an expansion that cast serious doubt on hitherto confident Soviet predictions of its collapse.

Roll-back, Covert Operations, and Democracy

The Reagan Doctrine's provision of covert support for rebel groups engaged in guerilla warfare against Soviet-imposed or Soviet-backed regimes was pursued to realize three strategic objectives as outlined in NSDD-75. In the short-term, the objectives of providing aid to rebel forces were to halt further communist advances by placing the Soviets and their allies on the defensive and to deter future adventurism by making it clear that such moves would risk incurring heavy losses. In the medium-term, the American objective was to secure a victory in one or more countries to signal to communist and non-communists regimes alike that, contrary to the Brezhnev Doctrine, communism was not the wave of the future and its advances were not irreversible. The long-term objective was to use the aforementioned successes and the political pressure resulting from them to break the global strategic deadlock in favor of the United States.

In his State of the Union address in February 1985, Reagan enunciated an affirmation and an enlargement of the Truman Doctrine, extending it to include support for rebels against communist regimes and not merely regimes under pressure from communist forces. The address made public what was already established administration policy. On entering office, the administration expanded on the Carter administration's program of covert military assistance to the Afghan mujahadeen. In 1981 Reagan authorized a major covert operation aimed at providing assistance to the armed opponents of the Sandinista regime in Nicaragua. The program of aiding the Contras, however, enjoyed less support in Congress than that of aiding the Afghan mujahadeen, with Congress changing its collective mind on numerous occasions and placing numerous restrictions on covert operations. The administration's reaction to congressional restrictions on covert operations against the Sandinista regime was to increase the public rhetoric against Communist regimes, but also to flout the law and lie to Congress, which culminated in the Iran-Contra scandal.

While the Afghan operation was the largest and the Nicaraguan operation was the most controversial, they were not the only covert operations mounted by the administration. In 1985, the administration secured from Congress $5 million in covert aid to the non-Communist resistance in Cambodia and the repeal of the 1976 Clark Amendment that had prohibited assistance to the pro-Western UNITA rebels fighting the Cuban-backed Angolan regime. American covert operations reached even into the heart of the Soviet empire. Reagan and Pope John Paul II had arrived at a "quiet alliance" whose principal aim was to bring an end to communism in Europe. Working through an intricate network that encompassed the Catholic Church and the AFL-CIO, the administration covertly supplied the Solidarity labor movement in Poland with money and communications equipment that helped it survive underground when the Communist regime declared martial law in 1982.

The Reagan Doctrine provoked great controversy. The intellectual foundation of doctrine had been provided by Reagan's UN Ambassador Jeane J. Kirkpatrick, a former Democrat and political science professor at Georgetown

University. In a 1979 *Commentary* magazine article titled "Dictatorships and Double Standards," Kirkpatrick argued that not only were traditional authoritarian governments less repressive than totalitarian regimes, they were corrigible and capable of liberalization. Hence, an American policy consonant with vital geopolitical interests and a commitment to freedom and democracy should operate on the premise that there would be a greater likelihood of progressive liberalization and democratization in Argentina, Brazil, El Salvador, Chile, Taiwan, South Korea, than in Cuba, Nicaragua, North Korea, China, and Angola. Thus, it was not surprising that much of the criticism of the Reagan Doctrine was directed at its overreliance on the anti-communist credentials of pro-American governments and rebels while overlooking their human rights abuses and other unsavory practices.

Reagan was influenced by Kirkpatrick's thesis in formulating a campaign for a broad expansion of democracy globally that would serve as a companion to the international offensive against the Soviet Union. The "campaign for democracy" was announced by Reagan in his 1982 speech to the British Parliament, and the next year the National Endowment for Democracy (NED) was established. The NED disbursed funds to diverse organizations such as the Free Trade Union Institute, which was affiliated with the AFL-CIO, the National Chamber Foundation, affiliated with the U.S. Chamber of Commerce, the Republican and Democratic Parties' International Affairs Divisions, as well as other private organizations. Despite its relatively small budget, the NED assisted with poll watching in emerging democracies, assisted free labor union movements, and trained Third World political leaders in the practices of democracy. The administration also took a more direct approach to encouraging democracy in authoritarian regimes by helping oust pro-American allies like Ferdinand Marcos in the Philippines and "Baby Doc" Duvalier in Haiti. The administration promoted economic freedom abroad, arguing that capitalism provided the best means of achieving international economic development. With the American economy recovering and expanding as a result of massive tax cuts and deregulation, talk of a redistributionist "New International Economic Order" faded while the American free-enterprise model gained adherents globally.

Direct Military Action

Under Reagan, the United States employed military force in multiple ways, ranging from engagements against Libya for its sponsorship of terrorism to the re-flagging of Kuwaiti oil tankers in the Persian Gulf to ward off Iranian attacks. Despite the attempts by his political opponents to portray him as a "trigger-happy cowboy," Reagan was restrained in his use of American military power. He committed U.S. forces to ten missions abroad, compared with twenty under George H. W.

Bush and nearly sixty under Bill Clinton. Reagan's prudence was underscored by Secretary of Defense Caspar Weinberger's doctrine of never deploying U.S. military forces without clear goals, public and congressional support, and an "exit strategy." When Reagan decided to use military force, however, it was calculated to achieve maximum effect. The most important direct military action in his administration was the invasion of Grenada on October 25, 1983.

Grenada had been ruled since 1979 by a communist dictator Maurice Bishop, whose New Jewel Movement had seized power in a coup. On October 13, 1983, Bishop was overthrown and subsequently murdered by a rival faction within the movement who believed him to be insufficiently dedicated to revolutionary principles. The island had been under the political-military orbit of Cuba and the Soviet Union, and there were several thousand Cubans in Grenada working on the construction of a ten thousand foot runway, which could be used for Cuban and Soviet military planes. American military analysts believed that Grenada posed a strategic threat as the third point in a triangle (the other points were Cuba and Nicaragua) that enveloped the Caribbean through which U.S. reinforcements for NATO would have to pass in time of war. There were also concerns for the safety of approximately 1,000 American medical students on the island. On October 22, Reagan gave his approval for the invasion of the island. The next day he received news that a suicide bomber had crashed an explosive-filled truck into the U.S. Marines barracks in Beirut, killing 241 marines and wounding hundreds more. Reagan was urged to cancel the Grenada operation to avoid the inevitable political outcry over casualties and the possibility of another foreign policy debacle. He nonetheless proceeded with it.

On the morning of October 25, approximately 2,000 U.S. troops along with units from six Caribbean states stormed Grenada. They met fierce initial resistance from units of the Grenadian army and well-armed Cuban "construction workers," but U.S. military forces prevailed in three days and the Revolutionary Military Council was overthrown with minimal American casualties. The international and domestic outcry against the invasion, however, was intense. The UN voted to condemn the invasion and even Margaret Thatcher, Reagan's closest and staunchest ally, strongly protested the invasion of a Commonwealth country. At home, the reaction to the invasion was even more strident: there were calls for Reagan's resignation; editorials and some members of Congress insinuated that he had ordered the invasion to divert public attention from the Beirut massacre. A handful of Democratic members even submitted a resolution calling for Reagan's impeachment. Criticism subsided somewhat when U.S. military forces found large stockpiles of military equipment and documents detailing the deposed regime's secret pacts with other communist countries as well as its plans to turn the island into a military base for the Soviets. The captured documents also revealed plans to take American medical students hostage and identified Cuban "construction workers" as military advisors.

Grenada was a small-scale military operation, but its political consequences were enormous. For the first time since the Vietnam War, the United States had committed ground forces abroad in a combat assignment, sustained casualties, and prevailed with the support of the American public. The Grenada operation helped begin the process of exorcising the demons of Vietnam from the American psyche. It represented the first time since the end of the Second World War that a Communist takeover of a country had been reversed through direct military action.

Diplomacy

The administration adopted a more hardheaded approach to arms control negotiations than its predecessors. It viewed arms control as a means of enhancing American national security. Any arms control agreement that failed to secure that end was considered worse than no agreement at all. Further, Reagan believed that the Cold War was a struggle between freedom on the one hand and totalitarianism on the other, not the product of some misunderstanding between morally equivalent superpowers. From his perspective, the arms race was a symptom rather than the cause of the Cold War; the source of the problem was communism itself and Soviet aggression. Thus, while he was committed publicly to peace, he was determined not to pursue arms control for its own sake.

Reagan's stance on arms control was evident at the Reykjavik summit in October 1986 with Gorbachev. Gorbachev agreed in principle with Reagan's "zero-option" of trading the elimination of Pershing II missiles in Western Europe for all Soviet SS-20s, which would remove intermediate-range nuclear missiles entirely from the European theater. Gorbachev also pledged to reduce the Soviet strategic arsenal by half, in conformity with Reagan's START proposal. The Soviet leader included a nonnegotiable condition, however; he wanted the elimination of SDI. Reagan refused to contemplate the cancellation of SDI, and the talks collapsed. He was excoriated in the press and by liberal politicians for sacrificing what appeared to be a very good arms control agreement for his pet project. But in December 1987, Gorbachev dropped his demand that the United States abandon SDI and visited Washington to sign the Intermediate-range Nuclear Forces (INF) Treaty.

If the left had been hostile to Reagan's strategic plan to undermine Soviet power, the right was now suspicious of his pursuit of arms control. The consensus on the right was that Reagan was walking into a trap and would be outmaneuvered by the wily Gorbachev. The INF Treaty, however,

turned out to the first stage of Gorbachev's surrender in the Cold War. He agreed to negotiations for the reduction in strategic nuclear missiles. The START I Treaty would be signed in 1991. Gorbachev also agreed to deep unilateral cuts in Soviet forces stationed in Eastern Europe. In May 1988, Soviet forces started withdrawing from Afghanistan. Further, Soviet advisors left Ethiopia, and, at Moscow's prodding, Cuban troops were withdrawn from Angola. In Southeast Asia, Gorbachev agreed to have Vietnam withdraw 50,000 soldiers from Cambodia.

Legacy

In her eulogy of Reagan, Margaret Thatcher called him "the Great Liberator." The Soviet empire in Eastern Europe started to collapse shortly after Reagan left office. Beginning with Poland, Soviet satellite regimes collapsed one after another and on November 9, 1989, the Berlin Wall—for so long the symbol of the Cold War—was pulled down. Within another two years, the "evil empire" itself ceased to exist. Many of Reagan's opponents—who had proclaimed the moral equivalence of the United States and the Soviet Union, who had turned a blind eye to the suffering caused by totalitarian communism, who had insisted on the permanence of Soviet power, who had accused Reagan of being a war-monger for seeking to halt and roll-back Soviet advances, who derided the president for being delusional in his fantasies of ultimate victory in the Cold War—now rushed forward to proclaim the "inevitability" of Soviet collapse.

Reagan deserves a large measure of credit for helping the West triumph in the Cold War. This is not to say that he single-handedly brought about the demise of the Soviet empire; he was supported in the enterprise by the Pope, Thatcher, Lech Walesa, Vaclav Havel, and other dissidents who kept faith behind the Iron Curtain. When Reagan left office, the Cold War had essentially been won, and the Soviet Union—indeed the whole Soviet system in Central and Eastern Europe—was about to be thrown on the "ash heap of history" as he predicted. When he entered office, the outcome of the struggle had been in doubt, with the United States on the defensive and its allies wavering in the face of seemingly inexorable Soviet advances. There was nothing "inevitable" about the outcome of the Cold War. The United States could have responded to the Soviet advances of the 1970s by accommodating itself passively to that new reality under the guise of "peaceful coexistence." It would not be too great a stretch of the imagination to envision a different outcome to the Cold War with another president who did not rebuild American nuclear and conventional forces, who did not engage in ideological warfare against the Soviets, who did not seek to roll-back Soviet advances, who did not wage a campaign of economic warfare, who did not support rebels groups fighting Communist regimes, who did not initiate research in SDI,

President Ronald Reagan delivers a speech at the Brandenburg Gate in West Berlin on June 12, 1987, calling upon Soviet leader Mikhail Gorbachev to tear down the Berlin Wall. (Ronald Reagan Library)

and who did not believe in the inevitable triumph of the Free World. Instead it was Reagan who, in the words of Margaret Thatcher, "sought to mend America's wounded spirit, to restore the strength of the free world, and to free the slaves of communism."

Adrian U-jin Ang

Chronology

1981

January 20: American hostages in Iran freed hours after President Reagan takes oath of office.

February 18: President Reagan promotes lower taxes, welfare cuts, increased defense spending.

February 24: Military coup attempt in Spain fails.

February 25: United States vetoes UN human rights report critical of American allies.

March 2: United States increases aid to El Salvadoran government.

March 3: United States announces it will honor SALT I and SALT II treaties.

March 9: Reagan rejects Soviet proposal to freeze medium-range missile deployments in Europe.

March 30: Reagan wounded in failed assassination attempt.

April 1: United States suspends aid to Nicaragua.

April 12: Columbia, first space shuttle, is launched.

April 24: United States ends grain embargo against Soviet Union.

April 24: United States announces creation of a Persian Gulf Command to implement the Carter Doctrine.

May 10: François Mitterrand elected president of France.

June 7: Israeli jets destroy Iraqi nuclear reactor.

July 29: Iranian president Bani-Sadr ousted, Muslim radicals monopolize power.

August 9: United States resumes production of neutron bomb.

August 19: U.S. Navy jets shoot down two Libyan jets.

October 2: Reagan announces MX missile and B-1 bomber programs.

October 24: Large-scale antinuclear rallies in Western Europe.

November 18: Reagan advocates "zero option" for long-range nuclear forces.

November 23: Reagan authorizes CIA to aid antigovernment Contras in Nicaragua.

November 30: Geneva missile talks begin.

December 13: Polish government declares martial law.

December 14: Israel annexes Golan Heights.

December 23: United States imposes sanctions on Soviet Union to protest Polish martial law.

1982

January 19: Japan and European allies reject economic sanctions against Poland and Soviet Union.

January 26: United States links superpower arms negotiations to resolution of Polish crisis.

March 10: United States embargoes trade with Libya.

March 25: Argentine commandos seize South Georgia Island.

April 2: Argentina invades British-owned Falkland Islands, Falkland Islands War begins.

April 30: United States announces support for Britain in Falklands War.

April 25: Israel returns Sinai to Egypt.

April 28: UN General Assembly condemns Israel and U.S. support for Israel.

May 5: Hungary joins the International Monetary Fund (IMF).

May 9: Reagan proposes Strategic Arms Reduction Talks (START) with the Soviet Union.

June 6: Israel invades Southern Lebanon.

June 14: Argentine forces on Falklands surrender, Falkland Islands War ends.

June 27–August 6: U.S. diplomat Philip Habib negotiates cease-fire in Lebanon.

June 29: START talks begin in Geneva.

August 20: United States orchestrates debt payment plan for Mexico.

September 1: Reagan sends U.S. Marines to Lebanon to join French and Italian peacekeepers.

October 8: Polish government bans trade unions.

November 10: Soviet president Leonid Brezhnev dies, Yuri Andropov succeeds him.

December 21: Reagan signs the Boland Amendment, barring funds for the overthrow of the Nicaraguan government.

1983

January 20: France and West Germany reaffirm support for NATO and INF deployments.

March 6: West German Chancellor Helmut Kohl reelected.

March 8: President Reagan delivers "Evil Empire" speech.

March 23: Reagan unveils his Strategic Defense Initiative (SDI).

March 30: United States proposes INF limitations, Moscow rejects proposals.

April 18: Terrorists bomb U.S. embassy in Beirut, sixty-three killed.

May 3: Congress bans covert aid to Nicaraguan contras.

July 5: United States imposes tariffs on specialty steels.

July 21: Polish government ends martial law.

July 28: House votes to cut off covert aid to Contras.

August 21: Philippine opposition leader Benigno Aquino assassinated.

August 26: Soviet Union offers to destroy SS-20 missiles withdrawn from Europe.

September 1: Soviet aircraft shoots down South Korean passenger jet.

September 26: Reagan makes new INF proposal, Soviet Union rejects it.

October 23: Suicide truck bomb destroys U.S. Marine barrack in Beirut, 241 killed.

October 25: U.S. forces invade Grenada, Thatcher government in Britain outraged.

November 23: U.S.-Soviet arms control talks collapse.

December 4: U.S. and Syrian forces clash in Lebanon.

1984

January 13: EEC retaliates against U.S. steel tariffs.

January 16: Reagan offers new flexibility in arms control talks.

February 9: Soviet President Andropov dies, Konstantin Chernenko replaces him.

February 15: U.S. General Leamon Hunt assassinated in Rome.

April 3: Secretary of State George Schultz advocates preemptive action against terrorists.

April 4: U.S. mining of Nicaraguan ports revealed.

April 26–May 1: Reagan makes five day visit to China.

May 7: Soviet Union boycotts Los Angeles Olympic games.

May 10: Danish parliament refuses deployment of NATO INF missiles.

June 20: Nunn Amendment to reduce American troops in Europe is defeated.

June 25: United States and Nicaragua conduct peace talks in Mexico.

September 1: Nicaragua shoots down Contra helicopter, two Americans killed.

September 20: Bomb attack on U.S. embassy annex in Aukur, northeast of Beirut, twenty-four killed.

September 24: Reagan urges new superpower arms talks.

October 12: IRA bomb attack attempts assassination of British Prime Minister Thatcher.

October 12: Boland Amendment II prohibits U.S. aid to Contras.

October 23: Philippine government officials accused of Aquino assassination.

October 31: Indian Prime Minister Indira Gandhi assassinated by Sikh bodyguards.

November 6: President Reagan reelected.

November 22: United States and Soviet Union announce new arms to begin Jan.7.

November 26: United States and Iraq reestablish diplomatic relations.

1985

January 2: Reagan urges Japan to open markets.

January 10: United States and EEC set quotas for steel pipes and tubes.

March 10: Soviet chairman Chernenko dies, Mikhail S, Gorbachev succeeds him.

April 7: Gorbachev announces moratorium on intermediate-range missile deployments.

April 24: House rejects aid request for Contras.

May 1: Reagan slaps trade embargo on Nicaragua.

May 5: Reagan visits Bitburg military cemetery in Germany.

June 11: Gorbachev advocates reform of the Soviet economy.

July 8: Reagan charges Iran, Libya, North Korea, Cuba, and Nicaragua with supporting terrorism.

August 30: Polish Solidarity leader, Lech Walesa calls for negotiations with government.

September 9: United States imposes limited trade sanctions on South Africa.

October 1: Israeli jet destroy PLO headquarters in Tunis.

October 7: Palestinian terrorists hijack cruise ship Achille Lauro, kill one American.

October 10: U.S. Navy jet intercept plane carrying Achille Lauro hijackers.

November 1: Netherlands announces it will accept U.S. medium-range missiles.

1986

January 28: Space shuttle *Challenger* explodes.

February 25: Widespread protests of election fraud forces President Ferdinand Marcos to flee the Philippines, Corazon Aquino becomes president.

March 27: West Germany agrees to cooperate in SDI research.

April 5: Terrorist bomb explodes in West Berlin night club, Reagan blames Libya.

April 14: U.S. planes bomb five targets in Libya.

April 26: Chernobyl power plant in Ukraine has worst nuclear accident in history.

August 30: American correspondent Nicholas Daniloff arrested in Moscow.

October 4: Nicaragua shoots down U.S. plane.

October 5: London *Times* reports that Israel possesses nuclear weapons.

October 11–12: Reagan and Gorbachev discuss massive arms reductions at Reykjavík but conclude nothing.

November 3: Lebanese magazine reveals that U.S. had arms-for-hostages deal with Iran, Iran-Contra scandal begins.

1987

January 25: Chancellor Kohl reelected in West Germany.

February 2: Filipinos approve new constitution.

February 19: United States lifts sanctions on Poland.

February 26: Tower Commission Report blames Iran-Contra on Reagan's casual leadership style.

February 28: Gorbachev offers to eliminate INF forces in Europe.

March 3: Secretary of State Schultz visits China and discusses economic reform.

April 1: British Prime Minister Thatcher visits Moscow.

April 13: Schultz and Soviet Foreign Minister Eduard Shevardnadze discuss INF reductions.

May 19: U.S. flags Kuwaiti oil tankers in Persian Gulf.

May 29: Young West German, Mathias Rust, lands Cessna in Red Square, Soviet air defense fails.

June 11: Thatcher elected to third term.

August 23: Baltic Soviet republics have demonstrations for independence.

August 28: Failed coup against Aquino government in Philippines

September 7: East German leader Eric Honecker visits West Germany.

October 3: United States and Canada sign historic Free Trade Agreement, eliminating tariffs.

October 19: Iranian missile strikes U.S.-flagged tanker, U.S. warships shell Iranian oil rig.

December 2: Contras begin peace talks with Nicaraguan government.

December 8: At Washington summit Reagan and Gorbachev sign INF Treaty.

December 9: Palestinian Intifada begins in West Bank and Gaza Strip.

December 14: United States and Israel sign ten-year alliance agreement.

1988

February 4: United States indicts Panamanian General Manuel Noriega for drug trafficking.

February 17: U.S. Army Lt.Col. in Lebanon is kidnapped by pro-Iranian Shiites.

March 23: Contras and Nicaraguan government sign truce agreement.

April 14: Soviet Union signs Geneva accord for withdrawal from Afghanistan.

April 18: U.S. and Iranian navies tangle in Persian Gulf.

May 8: French President François Mitterrand reelected.

July 3: Cruiser USS *Vincennes* shoots down Iranian passenger jet in Persian Gulf.

July 11: Nicaragua expels U.S. ambassador.

August 14: Soviet Union completes withdrawal of 100,000 troops from Afghanistan.

October 5: Chilean dictator Augusto Pinochet ousted in plebiscite.

November 8: George H. W. Bush elected president, J. Danforth Quayle is vice president.

November 8: Protests in Serb province of Kosovo oppose policies of Belgrade government.

December 6: In UN address Gorbachev pledges to reduce Soviet forces by 500,000 men.

1989

January 15: The last Soviet troops leave Afghanistan.

References and Further Reading

Brown, Seyom. *The Faces of Power: Constancy and Change in United States Foreign Policy from Truman to Clinton.* New York: Columbia University Press, 1994.

Brownlee, W. Elliot, and Hugh Davis Graham, eds. *The Reagan Presidency: Pragmatic Conservatism and Its Legacies.* Lawrence, KS: University Press of Kansas, 2003.

Busch, Andrew E. *Ronald Reagan and the Politics of Freedom.* New York: Rowan and Littlefield, 2001.

D'Souza, Dinesh. *Ronald Reagan: How an Ordinary Man Became an Extraordinary Leader.* New York: Touchstone, 1997.

Gaddis, John Lewis. *The United States and the End of the Cold War: Implications, Reconsiderations, Provocations.* Oxford: Oxford University Press, 1982.

Gaddis, John Lewis. *We Now Know: Rethinking Cold War History.* Oxford: Oxford University Press, 1998.

Morris, Edmund. *Dutch: A Memoir of Ronald Reagan.* New York: Random House, 1999.

Noonan, Peggy. *When Character Was King: A Story of Ronald Reagan.* New York: Viking, 2001.

Reagan, Ronald. *An American Life.* New York: Simon and Schuster, 1990.

Tygiel, Jules. *Ronald Reagan and the Triumph of American Conservatism.* New York: Longman, 2004.

—— George Herbert Walker Bush (1989–1993) ——

Early Life and Political Career

George Herbert Walker Bush was born on June 12, 1924, in Milton, Massachusetts, the second child of Prescott and Dorothy Walker Bush. His father, a graduate of Yale, had been a successful investment banker at Brown Brothers, Harriman in New York City, while his mother had also been raised in very comfortable surroundings in Kennebunkport, Maine, and St. Louis. George attended the Greenwich (CT) Country Day School before being sent to boarding school at the Phillips Academy in Andover, Massachusetts, beginning in the ninth grade. He excelled at this very prestigious prep school, serving as senior class president and captain of the baseball and soccer teams. Bush had already been accepted at Yale when the Japanese attacked Pearl Harbor, and he enlisted in the Navy on his eighteenth birthday. A year later, he became one of that service's youngest pilots and was involved in extensive combat in the Pacific. On September 2, 1944, his plane was shot down, some of his crew was killed, and he narrowly escaped capture at sea. When he was discharged on September 18, 1945, Lieutenant Bush had flown fifty-eight missions and won the Distinguished Flying Cross.

He enrolled at Yale for the fall semester of 1945 in an accelerated program that allowed him to graduate in 1948. Bush again performed exceptionally well, being elected to Phi Beta Kappa and the Skull and Bones Club, a secret honor society, where Bush met several young men who would remain life-long friends. He also starred at first base on the Eli baseball team.

Rather than follow his father to Wall Street, the new graduate, backed with a $300,000 family stake, moved to Odessa, Texas to sell oil-drilling equipment. Yet he continued to summer at the family retreat in Kennebunkport and evinced a number of liberal-to-moderate social positions including membership in Planned Parenthood. In 1959, Bush became president of a subsidiary of the oil company he helped found and moved to Houston. Prescott had been elected to the U.S. Senate in 1952 as a moderate Republican, and soon after his arrival, George accepted the chairman-

George Herbert Walker Bush, elected as the Soviet empire in Europe was about to collapse, handled the tranformation and unification of Europe with skill and tact, and simultaneously led a grand coalition of states in the Gulf War of 1990–1991. (George Bush Library)

ship of the moribund Harris County Republican Party. He joined the Council on Foreign Relations, a bastion of internationalism, in order to learn more about foreign policy, and decided to seek elective office. In 1964, Bush ran for the Senate against the very liberal Democrat Ralph Yarborough but could muster only 43 percent of the vote as he fell victim to the Lyndon Johnson landslide over Barry Goldwater. But two years later Bush won a House seat and was reelected in 1968. In 1970, President Nixon asked him to again

---

challenge Yarborough. The incumbent, however, was upset in the Democratic primary by the much more conservative Lloyd Bentsen, who proceeded to trounce Bush in the general election.

Bush was soon rewarded for his loyalty by being picked by Nixon to serve as the U.S. Permanent Representative to the United Nations. After Nixon was reelected in 1972, he asked Bush to chair the Republican National Committee, which was attempting to survive the Watergate scandal. Three years later Gerald Ford passed him over as vice president despite the fact that a canvass of Republican state chairmen favored him for the position. Instead, Bush was named U.S. envoy to China and in November 1975, succeeded William Colby as director of Central Intelligence at a time of enormous turbulence at the CIA.

On May 1, 1979, George Bush announced that he would seek the presidency. At first, he attempted to run as a Ford moderate, but backers of Ronald Reagan quickly denounced him as a liberal, eastern elitist. To placate the Right, he resigned from the Council on Foreign Relations, as well as the Trilateral Commission, an august group founded by the banker David Rockefeller, committed to improving relations with Western Europe and Japan. Bush also tried to distance himself from his earlier positions on population control and women's rights issues. After squeaking past Reagan in the Iowa caucuses, he was beaten in the New Hampshire primary and dropped out of the race in May. But despite being distrusted by many of Reagan's advisors, the Republican nominee asked Bush to join his ticket as the vice presidential candidate.

Quite predictably, Bush proved to be an exceedingly loyal and generally deferential vice president. He traveled extensively, played a major role in persuading European allies to allow the deployment of a new U.S. nuclear missile, and was not directly implicated in the Iran-Contra scandal in which the profits made on secret arms sales to Iran were illegally funneled to the anti-communist forces in Nicaragua. It came as little surprise that in October 1987, he announced that he would again seek the Republican nomination for president.

In 1988, he won that nomination rather easily and faced Massachusetts Governor Michael Dukakis in November. Running a very negative, personal campaign in which substantive issues were rarely discussed, Bush roared from behind after the Republican Party convention in August to swamp his opponent in the general election.

From Cold War to Détente II

Ronald Reagan had assumed the presidency in 1981 as an anti-communist hardliner who had accused Jimmy Carter of conducting a foreign policy indistinguishable from appeasement. Under his watch, the U.S. defense budget soared, at least during his first term; significant aid was given to friendly groups trying to overthrow Marxist governments in Asia, Africa, and Latin America; he used his formidable rhetorical skills to brand the Soviet Union an "evil empire" and to call upon Soviet leader Mikhail Gorbachev to "tear down" the Berlin Wall. Yet by the time he left office, many observers believed that the Cold War had all but ended. Significant strategic arms agreements had been signed, Gorbachev appeared determined to reform the Soviet domestic system, and Soviet-American relations had reached unprecedented degrees of cordiality. Indeed, many of Reagan's conservative supporters believed that he had grown naïve about the Russian leader's alleged true intentions. Even Vice President Bush appeared somewhat uneasy about the rapid improvement in Soviet-American relations.

From Status Quo Plus to a New World Order

President Bush took office during a period of seismic international change. From July to December 1989, Poland, Hungary, East Germany, Czechoslovakia, Bulgaria, and Romania ousted Communist dictators and replaced them with governments more or less committed to democratic politics and market economic reforms. In 1990, the process of German reunification began, and by December of the following year the Soviet Union had ceased to exist. In early 1991, the United States led a multinational coalition that quickly drove Iraq from Kuwait, a tiny nation that it had invaded the previous August. As a result of these events, America stood as the world's sole superpower, and some commentators announced that it now enjoyed a unique "unipolar moment" of uncontested preeminence. The normally cautious Bush proclaimed a "new world order" of international cooperation.

An Early Test: Manuel Noriega

Noriega, the Panamanian strongman since 1985, had received more than $330,000 in payments from the CIA and the Defense Department for a variety of services including facilitating the transfer of money from the sale of U.S. arms to Iran to the Nicaraguan Contras. But he was also a major drug trafficker and had allegedly passed secrets to Cuba. In January 1988, the Reagan administration demanded his resignation, and when he demurred, a federal court indicted him on the drug charges. In May 1989, Noriega refused to recognize the newly elected Panamanian president, Guillermo Endara, and ordered his "Dignity Battalions" to publicly assault him. This widely televised event prompted President Bush to order the Joint Chiefs of Staff to devise a plan—initially code-named BLUE SPOON—to overthrow Noriega. The United States began sending additional troops to Panama to increase pressure on him. In early October, an abortive military coup was staged, apparently without the full knowledge of Washington. Its leader was captured and executed by Noriega's forces, but the Bush administration came under heavy criticism in Congress and the press for its clumsy behavior during the incident. The president, who took enormous pride in his foreign policy experience and acumen, berated his inner circle for its poor performance.

Then, on December 16, two incidents occurred that gave Washington the pretext to invade Panama. Noriega's troops killed a U.S. soldier attempting to escape a rioting crowd, and an American naval officer and his wife were detained and beaten by Panamanian forces before being released. Four days later, immediately after Endara was sworn in as president, Operation Just Cause—the renamed mission—began with a paratroop assault on Panama City. In the ensuing brief fight, twenty-three Americans were killed and 394 wounded. Noriega eluded capture and received asylum at the home of the papal nuncio but surrendered on January 3, 1990, after being subjected to nonstop loud, recorded music played by U.S. psychological warfare experts. In April 1992, an American jury found him guilty on eight charges, and he was sent to a federal prison in Illinois. Several Latin American governments condemned these unilateral actions as tantamount to "kidnapping," but the Bush Administration portrayed "Operation Just Cause" as necessary to restore democracy to Panama. By the end of 1989, Bush's approval ratings topped 75 percent—the highest first-year level since John F. Kennedy.

Ending the Cold War

The Bush administration would have been comfortable in continuing to manage the Cold War in a cautious and prudent manner. The president, proud of his credentials and determined to make foreign policy his principal activity, created an inner circle of largely like-minded "professional buddies"—Secretary of State James Baker, National Security Advisor Brent Scowcroft and his deputy (later CIA director) Robert Gates, Defense Secretary Richard Cheney, and, several months later, General Colin Powell as chairman of the Joint Chiefs of Staff. None of them initially shared Ronald Reagan's enthusiasm for Mikhail Gorbachev, nor his belief that the Cold War had ended. They entered office fully prepared to continue the tradition of containing the Soviet Union.

Scowcroft, in particular, viewed some of Reagan's arms control proposals as reckless and myopic. Firm advocates of deterrence, the Bush team rejected Reagan's nuclear abolitionism—most evident at the 1986 Iceland summit where he apparently thought about full mutual nuclear disarmament—and worried that the momentum of the Strategic Arms Limitation Talks (START) could, if not slowed, produce a treaty that denuclearized United States defenses.

Furthermore, these officials wished to shorten the wild swings that had allegedly characterized the American public's approach to East-West relations since the early 1970s. They believed that Reagan had exacerbated this tendency by first helping to initiate a second Cold War and then by prematurely announcing its demise. The Bush administration desired, instead, a superpower relationship immune to exaggerated fears and unfulfilled hopes. Yet this task was made even more difficult by the ongoing drama in the Soviet Union and Eastern Europe. Not since Harry Truman had anyone assumed the presidency at a time of comparable international flux, and Bush's first challenge was simply to make sense out of these upheavals. But by late 1989 a host of questions still needed to be answered: What kind of Soviet Union would Gorbachev's pursuit of internal reform produce? Should the United States wish him well? How attainable were his goals? What would be the new status of Eastern Europe? Could and should NATO survive if the Soviet threat disappeared or was drastically diminished? What would be the role of the United States in a post–Cold War environment?

Senior administration officials, comfortable with the regularities of the Cold War, were hard-pressed to discern Gorbachev's motives, predict the results of his initiatives, or evaluate the implications for Soviet-American relations. Placed on the defensive by Gorbachev's enormous international popularity ("Gorby fever"), the administration at first seemed almost annoyed with the Soviet leader. But in April 1989 when Richard Cheney "guessed" that Gorbachev would fail in his reform efforts and be replaced by a reactionary, Bush publicly disagreed with his defense secretary.

In part to slow down the momentum begun by the Reagan-Gorbachev rapprochement, and, in part, to buy time, president-elect Bush had ordered a top-level strategic policy review. By April 1989, this review had yielded an approach to the Soviet Union called "status quo plus," provisionally concluding that the process of change in the Soviet Union was likely to continue for several years, even if Gorbachev were replaced. It counseled the president to carefully broaden the superpower dialogue to include regional issues like Africa, as well as functional topics such as terrorism and chemical weapons.

The Bush team spent most of 1989 attempting to shape a strategy for a world turning upside down. The imminent end of the Cold War era proved positively unsettling to some old hands who had grown almost fond of its predictability. In September, Deputy Secretary of State Lawrence Eagleburger voiced these sentiments in a Georgetown University address suggesting that "the process of reform in the Soviet bloc and the relaxation of Soviet control over Eastern Europe" were "bringing long-suppressed ethnic antagonisms and national rivalries to the surface, and putting the German question back on the international agenda." The waning of the Soviet-American duopoly had produced a nascent multipolar world that would not necessarily be "a safer place than the Cold War era . . . given the existence and proliferation of weapons of mass destruction."

Building pressure on Bush from Western European governments and congressional Democrats to engage Gorbachev seriously forced the administration to move beyond "status quo plus." Borrowing a phrase from Michael Dukakis, Baker privately argued that "testing Gorbachev" sounded appropriately skeptical and hard-headed to American ears, and the inner circle agreed that regional conflicts from Afghanistan through Angola to Central America would provide good "tests." Gorbachev, though apparently offended by the condescending tone of the phrase, moved to end Soviet support for several Third World clients, including Cuba. Nevertheless, only a few weeks before the fall of the Berlin Wall in November, Brent Scowcroft told a senior official that "It would be dumb if we decided the Cold War is over, or that the Soviets aren't a threat anymore, or that we don't need NATO and we can use our defense budget to straighten out our domestic economic order."

Certainly the administration's response to the pro-democracy movement in China smacked of Cold War geopolitics. As student demonstrations mounted in size and intensity during the spring of 1989 the Bush team openly worried about the stability of the Chinese government. Fearing the removal of a strategic counterweight to Moscow, but at a time when the Soviet empire was collapsing, President Bush pursued a policy that disappointed many congressional Democrats. When Chinese troops brutally crushed the Tiananmen Square demonstrators in early June, Bush cited the importance of the Sino-American relationship and merely "deplored" the massacre. His secret dispatch of Scowcroft and Eagleburger to Beijing in December designed to improve relations provoked an angry congressional response. But Bush remained undeterred, vetoing a bill designed to grant permanent residency to Chinese students studying in the United States and vowing to extend China's most favored nation (MFN) trading status into 1991.

Secretary Baker, in particular, however, believed that Gorbachev had passed his "tests," and that it was now time to further improve the relationship. He urged Bush to meet Gorbachev soon. The president, who had been avoiding such a meeting for almost a year, reluctantly agreed but insisted that it not be called a "summit." In fact, their "non-summit" in Malta in early December 1989 proved pivotal in inaugurating the final phase of Soviet-American relations, one that Baker soon referred to as a "partnership." Bush decided at Malta that Gorbachev would be a reliable partner. He seemed almost like a Western European politician to the president, and Bush sympathized with Gorbachev's domestic political predicament.

From then until the abortive coup launched against Gorbachev by hard-line Communists in August 1991, the Bush administration attempted to realize five strategic objectives designed to ease the transition to a post–Cold War world: (1) to encourage Gorbachev on the path of political and economic reforms; (2) to lock in arms control agreements favorable to the United States in case Gorbachev fell to reactionaries; (3) to maintain the territorial and administrative integrity of the Soviet Union; (4) to insist that a reunified Germany be a member of NATO and the European Community (by 1991, the European Union); and (5) to achieve a stable and democratic Eastern Europe.

Some senior Bush officials like Robert Gates and Vice President Dan Quayle worried that an economically and politically reformed Soviet Union might still pose a threat to the United States, especially if its military capabilities remained intact. Consequently, they were not sure they wanted Gorbachev to succeed, and even Baker, perhaps the administration's biggest fan of Gorbachev, opposed direct economic assistance to Moscow for fear that it would be wasted and might even be used to prop up the Soviet military-industrial complex. Gorbachev denied any interest in "charity," but his increasingly desperate domestic situation intensified his pleas for loans and for admittance to the so-called Group of Seven (comprised of the world's leading industrial democracies), the International Monetary Fund, and World Bank on the grounds that membership would mollify his opponents. Bush, who had experienced Gorbachev's economic illiteracy firsthand at Malta, resisted this pressure, though steps were taken to grant the Soviets observer status in these institutions. Furthermore, the administration made MFN for the Soviets dependent on their passage of liberal emigration laws and refused to approve credit guarantees for $1 billion in agricultural purchases until December 1990. Even then the commodity credits were delayed for months, MFN status was further postponed, and Gorbachev was actively discouraged from attending the July 1991 Group of Seven (G-7) summit in London.

This balancing act of wishing Gorbachev well while refusing to provide much material help was pursued, in part, because of the situation in the Baltic. The United States had never officially recognized the Soviet absorption of the three Baltic republics in 1940, and when Lithuania declared its independence in March 1990, followed by Latvia two months later, Bush came under considerable domestic pressure to acknowledge their sovereignty. During the remainder of 1990, the Soviets tried to intimidate these new governments, and in January 1991 their troops seized parliamentary buildings in Vilnius, Lithuania, and fired on civilians there and in Riga, Latvia. President Bush repeatedly warned Gorbachev to find a peaceful solution but declined to do more for fear of provoking the violent disintegration of the Soviet Union. While Lithuanian leaders publicly accused the United States of appeasement,

Gorbachev implored Bush to understand his exceedingly fragile domestic predicament. Faced with a choice between Lithuanian self-determination and Soviet stability, Bush opted for the latter and delayed recognition until September 1991, although he continued to chastise Gorbachev for his heavy-handedness.

The administration's refusal to offer significant economic assistance to Gorbachev went deeper than the Baltics dispute, because it could never abandon its suspicion that aid would be, at best, squandered. This understandable fear explains Bush's antipathy toward the "Grand Bargain," a scheme devised by Grigori Yavlinsky, a former deputy prime minister of the Russian Republic, and a small group of Harvard academics led by Graham Allison, dean of the Kennedy School of Government. It proposed that the G-7 offer, in specific phases, several kinds of economic assistance, beginning with food, medicine, and technical help, and ultimately progressing to the financing of infrastructure reconstruction. The aid, to be disbursed between 1991 and 1993, would have totaled as much as $60 billion. Allison, working at Harvard through a former Bush NSC staffer, Robert Blackwill, attempted to enlist the support of Undersecretary of State Robert Zoellick. But senior Bush officials found the plan risky and expensive, and the Soviet government hesitated to commit to the prescribed reforms. The Bush team decided to confine its support for Gorbachev to largely symbolic actions.

On December 25, 1991, the Soviet Union officially disbanded, although Russian Federation President Boris Yeltsin had for some time acted as the region's dominant political figure. Yeltsin appeared to be more serious about economic reform than Gorbachev, but the administration remained hesitant to provide much assistance. In March 1992, former president Richard Nixon publicly lambasted Bush's aid program as "a pathetically inadequate response in light of the opportunities and dangers" presented by the crisis in the former Soviet Union. In a memorandum circulated among foreign policy analysts Nixon recalled that "the hot-button issue in the 1950s was 'Who lost China?' If Yeltsin goes down, the question, 'Who lost Russia?' will be an infinitely more devastating issue in the 1990s." If Yeltsin failed, Nixon warned, "war could break out in the former Soviet Union as the new despots use force to restore the 'historical borders' of Russia"; the "new East European democracies would be imperiled . . . China's totalitarians would breathe a sigh of relief," and the new Russian leaders—in collaboration with Iraq, Syria, Libya, and North Korea—would threaten American interests "in hot spots around the world." The White House protested that it had previously proposed the addition of $645 million in aid to the former Soviet Union to supplement the $1.5 billion announced in late 1991 and blamed Congress for stalling on a $12 billion request to replenish the IMF. Stung by Nixon's characterization of his assistance program as "penny ante," President Bush argued that "there are certain fiscal financial constraints on what we can do, but we have a huge stake in the success of democracy in Russia and in the other CIS (Commonwealth of Independent States) countries."

The White House feared that any serious effort to increase assistance would further alienate a public whose historic animosity to foreign aid had recently grown even more pronounced and who already saw Bush as a president excessively interested in foreign policy. A 1989 survey, for example, found that fully half of the American public believed that foreign aid constituted the single largest item in the federal budget! Nevertheless, in the wake of Nixon's criticisms, a surprising number of senators and congressmen, including conservatives like Jesse Helms (R-NC) and Strom Thurmond (R-SC), strongly urged the White House to provide more leadership on this issue.

Second, President Bush tried to lock in arms control agreements with Gorbachev (and later Yeltsin) in case hard-liners came to power in Moscow. During the Nixon, Ford, Carter, and Reagan administrations, arms control negotiations had been at the core of Soviet-American relations. Protracted wrangling over seemingly arcane minutiae was common, symbolic of the reality that neither side really trusted the other. Even when agreements had occasionally been reached, American critics routinely claimed that the Soviets would subvert them anyway.

Although initially reluctant to unveil an arms control strategy, domestic pressure, as well as Gorbachev's penchant for announcing unilateral reductions, forced a reconsideration. The pace of two interminable negotiations quickened—Conventional Armed Forces in Europe (CFE) and Strategic Arms Reduction (START)—especially after Malta. By the time Bush left office in January 1993, CFE and START agreements had been reached with Gorbachev, and a START II pact had been concluded with Yeltsin. Together these treaties effectively ended the East-West military confrontation of almost a half-century. Yet because of the dizzying speed of political and economic change in the East, they were widely seen as little more than footnotes to the disintegration of Moscow's domination of Eastern Europe, the demoralization of the Red Army, and the disappearance of the Soviet Union. These agreements, however, were significant, for taken together they dramatically reduced conventional force sizes from the Urals to the Atlantic and ultimately diminished the number of strategic nuclear warheads from about 30,000 to fewer than 7,000. Moreover, the Bush administration eliminated long-standing United States manpower and weapons disadvantages with these understandings, although, to reiterate, they may in any event have soon disappeared. Finally, the decision to move quickly in 1990 and 1991 was partially vindicated by subsequent Soviet foot-dragging over treaty interpretation and implementation made worse by the August 1991 coup.

Third, since 1947, the goal of the strategy of containment had been to cause either the mellowing or collapse of the Soviet Union, but few American strategists had taken either possibility seriously. To the contrary, as the Cold War became an apparently permanent condition, United States policymakers focused on the more immediate problem of deterring a Soviet nuclear attack. Although the Nixon-Kissinger strategy of détente sought to modify Soviet behavior by enmeshing Moscow in a web of linked agreements and dependencies, even it did not envision a world without the Soviet Union. Some Reagan officials claimed retrospectively that their strategy had aimed to implode the Soviet empire, but even if true, there is little evidence to suggest that they had thought through the consequences of success. Gorbachev's political reforms, however, unleashed such powerful centrifugal forces that the Bush administration was forced to confront the likelihood of Soviet collapse. It decided to do what it could to prevent the violent breakup of the old adversary. In early 1991, Brent Scowcroft summarized the administration's strategic objective at a National Security Council meeting: "Our policy has to be based on our own national interest, and we have an interest in the stability of the Soviet Union. The instability of the USSR would be a threat to us. To peck away at the legitimacy of the regime . . . would not . . . promote stability." In particular, senior Bush officials worried that the excesses of "romantic nationalism" could lead to civil war which, in turn, could undermine the security of the Soviet nuclear arsenal. In other words, the Bush administration wanted Moscow to mellow but not collapse.

But apart from offering reassuring words to Gorbachev, the administration could (or would) do little to prevent disintegration. On August 1, 1991, Bush tried to help in a speech delivered to the Supreme Soviet of the Republic of the Ukraine. Bush had not been eager to visit the capital of an outlying republic, fearing his presence would undermine Gorbachev's efforts to maintain the unity of the Soviet Union, but the administration was under considerable domestic pressure to support the principle of national self-determination. With the onset of the 1992 presidential campaign only five months away, senior advisers convinced Bush to make some sort of gesture toward the republics. But the speech seemed designed primarily to bolster Gorbachev, for the president referred to his Kiev audience as "Soviet citizens," warmly praised Gorbachev's vision of the Soviet future, and made clear his lack of enthusiasm for Ukrainian secession. Promptly dubbed the "Chicken Kiev" speech by *New York Times* conservative columnist William Safire, Bush's remarks were, however, wholly consistent with his desire to preserve the Soviet Union.

Gorbachev, squeezed between Communist centralizers and secession-minded republics, wobbled back and forth. His offer of a "Union Treaty," granting significant power to the periphery, precipitated the hard-line coup which almost toppled him in August 1991. Soon afterward, Bush and most of his inner circle resigned themselves to the collapse of the Soviet Union but still hoped that the breakup would be peaceful. The administration now began to work with Yeltsin and the leaders of the other republics with nuclear weapons (Ukraine, Belarus, and Khazakhstan) to ensure the safety of their arsenals. In the end, Bush's goal of a reformed Soviet Union proved an oxymoron, and it was forced to confront the prospect of resurgent nationalism and pandemic instability in Eurasia.

Interestingly, however, in pursuing its fourth interim strategic objective, the administration showed no hesitancy in supporting German national self-determination, probably because it believed that reunification would lead to greater European stability. For decades, the declared American policy had been to encourage the creation of a unified German state so long as it remained closely tied to the West, but as the Cold War glacis froze Central Europe, American strategists largely stopped considering that prospect and quietly hoped for a perpetuation of the status quo. Even as East Germany collapsed in late 1989, with thousands of its citizens voting with their feet against a divided state by seeking refuge in the West, it seemed inconceivable that the nation would soon be reunified. These events surprised the administration and worried London and Paris. Rather than placing obstacles in the path of German reunification, however, the United States devised a negotiating framework designed to keep the new Germany anchored in NATO and the European Community (EC). Under this arrangement, the two Germanies first agreed on the terms of reunification after which the four occupying powers—Britain, France, the Soviet Union, and the United States—accepted the results. The administration worked to reassure British Prime Minister Margaret Thatcher and French President Francois Mitterrand that they need not fear a reunified Germany and pressed Moscow to acquiesce in NATO membership for it. Bush's strategic objective was achieved in July 1990 when West German Chancellor Helmut Kohl promised significant economic assistance to Moscow in exchange for Gorbachev's surrender on NATO.

The administration pursued its final transitional strategic objective—nurturing democratic governments in Eastern Europe—with considerably less boldness and creativity than it had demonstrated in handling German reunification. Nevertheless, it surely passed the modest test it set for itself: to do no damage. As one prominent scholar noted, the Bush administration could have erred in two directions. On the one hand, it could have loudly and ostentatiously celebrated the demise of the Warsaw Pact, thus embarrassing Gorbachev and perhaps endangering the remarkable peacefulness of the East European revolutions. At the other extreme, it might have negotiated the future of those nations with the Soviet Union out of fear that Gorbachev would otherwise use force to preserve the Pact. But by constantly reassuring Moscow that these revolutions need not imperil legitimate Soviet interests, the Bush administration helped events in Eastern Europe run their course.

In the aftermath of the incredible revolutions of 1989, as these fledgling democracies struggled to build viable political institutions and market economies, the administration's interest in them appeared to wane. In part, of course, the ongoing drama in the Soviet Union preoccupied it. Nonetheless, Bush and his advisers failed to appreciate that these Eastern European experiments might actually make the successful transformation from command to market economies. Consequently, it offered only meager amounts of assistance, though Congress modestly increased the size of the aid package. Instead, the administration encouraged the European Community to assume most of the burden.

War in the Persian Gulf

In 1980, Saddam Hussein's Iraq invaded Iran, believing that the Islamic Revolution engulfing its larger neighbor made Iraq vulnerable to attack. Despite this aggression, both the Carter and Reagan administrations supported Iraq, calculating that Iran posed the greater long-term threat to American interests in the region. When the war finally ended in 1988 with both adversaries exhausted, Iraq owed substantial sums to nations that had provided financial assistance during the hostilities. Saddam Hussein began to pressure Kuwait, a neighboring oil-rich, but tiny sheikdom, whose sovereignty Iraq had never acknowledged, to write off wartime loans, but was repeatedly rebuffed. Apparently believing that the United States would not intercede (based on a conversation with the American ambassador), Iraq invaded Kuwait on August 2, 1990, and quickly occupied this nation.

President Bush was under little international pressure to either contain Iraq or roll it back from Kuwait. The United States had no treaty obligations to fulfill, and with the end of the Cold War, little "credibility" at stake. In the first hours after the invasion, Arab regional leaders tried to persuade Saddam to withdraw, and though now more threatened by Iraq, Saudi Arabia's initial response was conciliatory. Only Margaret Thatcher immediately demanded action and probably played a crucial role in convincing Bush "to draw a line in the sand." But once prompted, Bush proved indefatigable in exploiting his characteristic brand of personal diplomacy and soon put together an unlikely coalition of emirs, dictators, and democrats. With the Soviet Union largely preoccupied with survival, the old Cold War game of superpower bidding by weak states for security assistance had been replaced by one in which only the United States could dispense security assurances in return for political support. Thus when Bush declared that "this aggression will not stand," and ordered troops to the region, American officials persuaded leading allies to financially underwrite most

of the expense. Crowning this multilateral effort was his deft use of the long paralyzed United Nations. Moving rapidly, the Security Council condemned the Iraqi invasion only hours after the attack and imposed broad economic sanctions just four days later. These were followed by a series of resolutions culminating in the authorization to use force to eject Iraq from Kuwait. Soon thereafter the European Community and Japan announced support for a trade embargo of Iraq; Saudi Arabia and Venezuela promised to help replace the oil lost from Iraq and Kuwait; and the Kuwaiti government-in-exile pledged to subsidize Turkey in exchange for closing its pipeline from Iraq.

Thus when President Bush delivered his first formal national address on the crisis on August 8, the international coalition had already begun to take shape, while domestic opinion remained largely unformed. Bush filled this vacuum with a presidential-driven policy that gradually won public support. In this speech, Bush articulated four principles to guide American policy in the Persian Gulf: (1) the immediate, unconditional, and complete withdrawal of all Iraqi forces from Kuwait; (2) the restoration of Kuwait's legitimate government; (3) the security and stability of the Persian Gulf; and (4) the protection of American citizens abroad. He further announced the deployment of the 82nd Airborne Division and two squadrons of F-15 fighters to Saudi Arabia. These goals would be frequently repeated throughout the crisis and would occasionally be joined by others. For example on August 15 he claimed that "our jobs, our way of life, our own freedom, and the freedom of friendly countries" were at stake. On September 11, Bush declared that the successful punishment of Iraqi aggression would usher in a "new world order," and as war seemed more and more likely, the president began to warn that Saddam was on the verge of acquiring nuclear weapons, an argument that proved especially effective in mobilizing domestic support.

Throughout the fall of 1990, the Bush administration faced several challenges: (1) Would economic sanctions alone force Saddam from Kuwait, and, if not, then when would armed force become necessary? (2) How could the Soviet Union be persuaded not to try and broker a compromise deal with its long-standing ally in Baghdad? (3) How could Israel be convinced to absorb potential Iraqi missile attacks for the sake of sustaining the fragile international coalition that contained several Arab states? (4) Would the American people tolerate substantial casualties if war did break out? (5) If the sanctions failed, should the president seek an authorization from Congress to use military force? These issues consumed Bush's inner circle for months as a series of diplomatic initiatives were launched to show Saddam Hussein that complete withdrawal from Kuwait was his only alternative.

Except for, perhaps, Baker and Powell, senior advisors believed that economic sanctions would fail and thus pursued a parallel strategy of military pressure. By the end of August, almost 80,000 troops had been deployed to Saudi Arabia as part of "Operation Desert Shield." Two months later, that number had risen to 230,000, including reservists. On October 31, Bush decided to increase coalition strength to 500,000 but waited until November 8, shortly after the off-year congressional elections to make the announcement, because the public's support of his Gulf policy had steadily eroded during the autumn. Large urban protests in the United States and Western Europe raised questions about Bush's real reasons for wanting Iraq to pull out of Kuwait, suggesting that cheap oil, not opposition to aggression, was the true motivation. Saddam Hussein, meanwhile, portrayed the crisis in terms of Zionist-American imperialism and called upon his Arab brothers to join him in the "mother of all battles."

Nevertheless, the international coalition held, and on November 29, 1990, the UN Security Council passed Resolution 678 that set January 15, 1991, as the deadline for complete Iraqi withdrawal. Secretary of State Baker, sensing that a final diplomatic gesture would help dampen antiwar sentiment in the United States, persuaded Bush to "go the extra mile." Thus on November 30, the president offered to dispatch Baker to Baghdad to talk with Saddam. Two weeks later the Iraqi leader agreed to send his foreign minister, Tariq Aziz, to Geneva to meet with the secretary of state. But at their January 9th meeting, no negotiations took place; rather, Baker delivered an ultimatum from the president that reiterated Bush's demands and seemingly made war inevitable.

Although President Bush believed that he had the constitutional authority to employ military force without congressional approval, he also wanted to maximize the legitimacy of his actions, so against the advice of Cheney and White House Counsel C. Boyden Gray, Bush asked Congress to support a resolution authorizing the use of force against Iraq. The ensuing debate was exceptionally edifying, but overwhelmingly partisan. On January 12 the Senate passed the Joint Resolution 52 to 47 with nine Democrats and two Republicans defecting, while the House favored it by 250–183. Three days later Bush signed National Security Directive 54 that initiated Operation Desert Storm.

On January 16, 1991, the air war, timed to coincide with live coverage on the networks' evening news shows, commenced with massive bombardments of Baghdad. A 100-hour land war began on February 24, and ended with the remnants of the Iraqi forces fleeing toward the southern city of Basra on the so-called "Highway of Death." Bush, not wanting to destroy the allied coalition by going after Saddam and fearing that the breakup of Iraq would create a dangerous regional power vacuum, ordered a halt to the carnage. Apparently believing that Saddam's rule was ending, Shiites in the south and Kurds in the north staged separate uprisings but were brutally suppressed by Saddam's

helicopter gunships. While Bush's domestic popularity soared to an unprecedented 91 percent in the aftermath of Operation Desert Storm, a majority concluded by mid-1991 that it had been a mistake to leave Saddam Hussein in power.

This war proved incontrovertibly that U.S. military power dwarfed that of any other nation. One commentator opined that America had achieved "a unipolar moment." But how would the Bush administration capitalize on this unique situation?

A New World Political Order

Although President Bush quickly dropped this phrase from his public discourse after the some journalists pointed out that Hitler had used the same words to describe his global aims, the administration labored to define America's role in the post–Cold War world. In effect, this America was to function as a kind of benevolent hegemon, protecting the growing "zone of democratic peace" against regional outlaws, terrorists, nuclear proliferators, and other threats to order. It would do so in concert with others, if possible, and unilaterally, if necessary. But as the 1992 presidential campaign approached, and as the public evinced a growing concern about the domestic economy, George Bush showed a reticence to further elaborate his potentially controversial grand design. He had originally scheduled four foreign policy speeches for June 1991 in which he was expected to define further the new world order but then decided to use these occasions to attack the Great Society programs of the 1960s, condemn "political correctness" on college campuses, and malign Congress for allegedly practicing partisanship in foreign affairs. Apparently, the president's staff feared that public debate over a new world order would prove a distraction. And so, after the summer of 1991 he confined his foreign policy statements to rhetorical celebrations of the Gulf victory and no longer spoke of his hopes for a post–Cold War world.

Within the administration, especially in the office of the undersecretary of Defense for Policy, work proceeded to plan for a new world order. These efforts had begun shortly after the Gulf War ended as small Pentagon study groups examined alternative strategic objectives, tried to identify the regional implications of the Cold War's demise, and reevaluated the size and composition of the American nuclear arsenal as well as the appropriate number of conventional forces. The early fruits of these labors were leaked to the *New York Times* in February and March 1992 in the form of drafts of two planning documents. In the first, the Pentagon argued that United States military forces in the post–Cold War era required funding sufficient to allow it to fight at least two major regional conflicts simultaneously, while standing ready to repel an attack on Europe by a resurgent Russia. The document listed seven "illustrative scenarios" that the United States should be prepared to deter or resolve: (1) an Iraqi invasion of Kuwait and Saudi Arabia; (2) a North Korean attack on South Korea; (3) the simultaneous occurrence of both; (4) a Russian assault on Lithuania through Poland with the help of Belarus; (5) a coup in the Philippines threatening 5,000 American residents; (6) a Panamanian coup endangering access to the Panama Canal; and (7) the emergence of a new expansionist superpower.

A related series of studies, coordinated primarily by Zalmay Khalilzad, assistant deputy undersecretary for policy planning, produced a second (leaked) document. Khalilzad's group focused explicitly on America's role in the post–Cold War world. It examined and rejected three strategic options for the United States: isolationism, collective security, and balance-of-power. It did so because isolationism failed to acknowledge America's vital overseas interests; because collective security entrusted the protection of this nation's interests to others; and because balance-of-power systems historically had always resulted in major war. This planning group instead preferred "global leadership," an option that appeared to capture much of Bush's new world order. "Global leadership" presumed America's continuing international preeminence and argued that it should actively prevent the emergence of a bipolar or multipolar world. By using existing security arrangements to ensure the safety of its allies, the United States would view as potentially hostile any state with sufficient human and technological resources to dominate Europe, East Asia, or the Middle East. This strategy recognized that by early in the next century Germany and Russia might threaten Europe; Japan, Russia, and eventually China might threaten East Asia; and the domination of either region would consequently imperil the Middle East. Yet its architects did not consider the strategy to be anti-German or anti-Japanese. While they did fear the emergence of an unstable semi-democratic Russia, Khalilzad and his colleagues argued that the United States could preserve German and Japanese friendship by nurturing existing security arrangements. Thus these two states would presumably have no incentive to challenge American preeminence, for their interests would be cared for by Washington. Khalilzad's draft also alluded to "ad hoc assemblies" of states that would, at times, supplant permanent alliances to help achieve U.S. goals. Moreover, it suggested that this nation could be confronted by "the question of whether to take military steps to prevent the development or use of weapons of mass destruction." Notably missing from the global leadership strategy was any significant role for the United Nations.

Despite its apparent fidelity to Bush's new world order, this document, "Defense Planning Guidance, 1994–1999" (DPG), deeply embarrassed the administration. Senior Pentagon officials quickly disavowed it, even though Undersecretary for Policy Paul Wolfowitz and probably

Richard Cheney had known of it for some time. They did so because it offended important United States allies and threatened to unleash a potentially divisive domestic debate about America's role in the post–Cold War world. A revised version of the DPG was written by I. Lewis "Scooter" Libby and leaked to the press in May 1992. It appeared to support a strategy more seriously committed to multilateral institutions, but, in fact, now envisioned that the United States would build up its military capabilities to such an extent that there could never be a rival. America would develop such enormous superiority in military power and technology that other countries would realize it would be self-defeating to try to compete.

A New World Economic Order

The new world order also featured a foreign economic component, and responsibility for its articulation largely fell to the Office of the Undersecretary of State for Economic Affairs Robert Zoellick. It did so because senior Treasury and Commerce officials tended to eschew grand strategy in favor of a case-by-case approach, while Zoellick, who enjoyed the full confidence of Secretary Baker, had earned a reputation as one of the administration's few genuine conceptualizers. Like the DPG, Zoellick's strategy began with the assumption of American global preeminence and noted that this nation's economy accounted for 22 percent of the world's gross product.

From Zoellick's perspective, the United States could best serve its economic interest by acting as the primary catalyst for a series of integrative economic structures that would substantially increase global prosperity. By spurring economic growth, these structures would encourage further democratization of political systems, which, in turn, would bring to (or keep in) power leaders committed to even greater regional economic integration. The United States could play a key role in sustaining this accelerating cycle of trade liberalization, democratization, and economic integration.

Indeed, the Reagan administration had begun this regional process in 1987 with the conclusion of a Free Trade Agreement with Canada. The election in Mexico of Carlos Salinas de Gortari the following year raised the possibility of extending this trade zone to that country, and in the summer of 1990, negotiations for a North American Free Trade Agreement began. Despite vigorous opposition from some U.S. unions and a number of conservative commentators, a treaty was signed on December 17, 1992.

Ultimately the Bush administration wished to design a "new world order of trade" strategy designed to link American economic and geopolitical goals and interests, though his reelection defeat in 1992 meant that much of it would be implemented by Bill Clinton. First, it sought to deepen the economic and security interactions between the

United States and its major traditional allies—Western Europe and Japan. Through a variety of bilateral, regional, and global trade agreements, these long-standing relationships would be further solidified. Economic liberalization between the United States and the European Union, for example, would proceed apace with NATO's evolution.

Second, the United States would reach out to a second tier of potential partners in Latin America, East Asia, and Eastern Europe to develop increasingly dense institutional linkages. Devices such as NAFTA, the Enterprise for the Americas Initiative (which envisioned a hemispheric free trade zone), and the Asia-Pacific Economic Cooperation (APEC) forum (largely a "talking shop" but possessing institutional possibilities) represented obvious examples of this notion. These developing institutions would gradually develop habits of cooperation that could, in times of crisis, be drawn on to build ad hoc security coalitions *under American leadership*. They might also prove useful in helping to settle such regional issues as, for example, Argentina's decision to stop the purchase of Iranian missiles and to sign a nuclear nonproliferation agreement with Brazil. While the Bush administration did not regard these arrangements as "trading blocs," it did recognize that they could serve as useful levers to encourage states in other regions to liberalize their trade policies or to increase pressure for concessions in the multilateral negotiations.

And third, even farther on the periphery, loomed Russia, China, and the Middle East. Zoellick advised that over time, the United States should seek to demonstrate to them the benefits of their peaceful integration into the system as well. Like its Defense Department counterpart the administration's foreign economic strategy asserted the indispensability of American global leadership. It strongly supported the voluntary creation of a series of regional economic integrative institutions in which the United States would act as the common linchpin. In Zoellick's strategy, as in Khalilzad's, all roads ultimately led to Washington.

The Arab-Israeli Puzzle

Presidents had long been expected both domestically and in the region to involve themselves in the so-called Arab-Israeli "peace process" despite the intractability of the issues. Yet after Nixon, Carter, and Reagan's rather peripatetic diplomacy, George Bush, at least initially, favored an incrementalist approach designed to put the burden of peace-making on Israel and the Arab nations. Nevertheless, he and Baker assembled a Middle East negotiating team of Dennis Ross, Richard Haass, Daniel Kurtzer, and Aaron Miller drawn from the State Department and the staff of the National Security Council. These experts, as well as Bush, Baker, Cheney, and Deputy Secretary of State Lawrence Eagleburger, had long been sympathetic to Israel, but believed that its current government, led by the Likud

Party's Yitzhak Shamir, had proven especially rigid. The major impediments concerned the rapid expansion of Israeli settlements in territories taken in the 1967 War, now fueled by large numbers of Soviet Jews, and Tel Aviv's refusal to bargain with the Palestinian Liberation Organization (PLO), which it considered to be a terrorist group.

Soon after taking office, the Bush administration solicited Shamir and Israeli Defense Minister Yitzhak Rabin, a member of the opposition Labor Party, for ideas about how to revive the peace process. When they failed to respond, the administration, despite its early misgivings, waded into the conflict. In May 1989, Baker angered Israel and the American Israel Public Affairs Committee (AIPAC), its most powerful domestic lobbying organization, by envisioning an agreement that would call for "territorial withdrawal." At the same time, the administration wished to convince the PLO to sanction talks with Israel conducted by Palestinians who were not members of the PLO leadership, despite that group's assertion that it constituted "the sole, legitimate representative of the Palestinian people." In March 1990, President Bush further enraged Tel Aviv by criticizing Israeli settlements in East Jerusalem, the first time an American president had done so. Shamir responded by reshuffling his cabinet to produce an even more hard-line government shorn of Labor Party participation.

But relations with the PLO were simultaneously deteriorating. In February 1990, Iraqi strongman Saddam Hussein told an Arab gathering that it must oppose what he claimed to be an effort by the United States and Israel to rule the Middle East. These comments were well received by the PLO whose leader, the unpredictable Yassir Arafat, even threatened to move his headquarters from Tunis to Baghdad. Relations further worsened when a Palestinian commando unit attempted to land on a beach near Tel Aviv. On June 20, after several more provocations, Bush announced a halt to the dialogue with the PLO. Six weeks later, Iraq invaded Kuwait, with Arafat openly siding with Saddam Hussein.

As was noted earlier, President Bush worked hard to sustain the unwieldy international coalition against Iraq, and on October 1, as a symbol of his commitment to achieving an Arab-Israeli settlement, he promised to refocus his efforts on the peace process after Saddam had withdrawn from Kuwait.

Victory in the Gulf War directly led to the administration's most ambitious attempt to restart the peace process. Impressed by the cooperation with the United States demonstrated by Egypt, Saudi Arabia, and Syria during Operation Desert Storm; aware that Arafat's support of Saddam Hussein, as well as the decline of the Soviet Union, left him without a patron; and impressed that Shamir did not retaliate when Iraq fired SCUD missiles at Israel during the war, Bush and Baker decided that the time was ripe for a fresh approach. Consequently, Baker undertook an elaborate series of Middle East trips reminiscent of Henry Kissinger's shuttle diplomacy during the Nixon-Ford years to try and convene a regional peace conference. Interestingly, the chief obstacles remained the same as before the Gulf War: the composition of the Palestinian delegation and the issue of Israeli withdrawal from the occupied territories. But these were compounded by Tel Aviv's request for a $10 billion loan guarantee spread over five years to help pay for the settlement of additional immigrants from the Soviet Union, many of whom would live in the occupied territories.

Secretary Baker finessed a compromise to the first problem by suggesting a joint Palestinian-Jordanian delegation with the stipulation that the Palestinians be residents of the occupied territories (which allegedly contained more "moderates" than those who lived abroad). But he allowed the PLO to pick the representatives. This formula mollified Shamir, who refused to deal directly with the PLO, but also placated Arafat. He then wrote letters to the leaders of Israel, Syria, Saudi Arabia, Jordan, and Egypt inviting them to attend a peace conference in Madrid. The Arab states quickly agreed, but Shamir conditioned his acceptance by rejecting any prior commitment to withdraw from the West Bank, East Jerusalem, the Gaza Strip, and the Golan Heights.

With Bush and Gorbachev serving as cochairs, the first session of the Madrid conference was held on October 30, 1991. Almost wholly ceremonial, the administration viewed it as a catalyst to restart the long stalled Middle East peace process. But as one observer noted, Baker apparently wished the United States to play the role of convener rather than mediator, which reflected the initial inclinations of Ross and Haass. Four subsequent meetings were held in Washington from December 1991 through April 1992 as well as additional gatherings in Rome, but the administration continued to refuse to put a peace plan on the table. In June 1992, Shamir's Likud Party lost to Rabin's Labor Party in an electoral landslide. Bush greeted this victory by lending support to the earlier Israeli request for the large loan guarantee, as Rabin appeared to be more flexible on the settlements issue. But no substantive progress could be achieved through the Madrid mechanism, and the reoccurrence of serious Palestinian-Israeli violence in the fall of 1992 effectively ended the administration's peace efforts.

The Disintegration of Yugoslavia

The United States had supported the territorial integrity and political unity of multiethnic Yugoslavia since World War II. Marshal Tito's secession from the Soviet empire in the late 1940s served American interests, so Washington consistently overlooked his often repressive rule. Tito's death in 1980 put his fragile and complex political edifice in jeopardy, yet Yugoslavia limped along for another decade.

Then, prompted in part by the democratic revolutions sweeping Eastern Europe, it began to violently disintegrate as Slobodan Milosevic, president of the Serbian republic within Yugoslavia, abandoned his communist ideology in favor of an aggressive Serb nationalism. The Bush administration supported the Yugoslav federal government of Ante Markovic, who, like the leaders of other former Communist states, pledged his commitment to democratic politics and market reforms. It also tried to persuade the republics of Slovenia and Croatia to remain in the Yugoslav federation. In the fall of 1990, the Bush administration notified NATO of an impending crisis there, but, in part distracted by events in the Gulf, it deferred to its European allies' wish to handle the problem as a symbol of their new political maturity. Though Secretary Baker, in a well-publicized speech in Belgrade in the spring of 1991, pleaded for unity, he seemed to be aiming his remarks primarily at the restive Soviet republics, for the administration had become resigned to a Yugoslav breakup. Moreover, he acknowledged at about the same time that "we don't have a dog in this [i.e., Yugoslav] fight." In June 1991, Slovenia and Croatia declared their independence, but ethnic Serbs, trapped in Croatia, with assistance from elements of the Serbian army in Belgrade, took up arms against the new Zagreb government. A ghastly ethnic war ensued. In December, Germany formally recognized both new governments. The European Union and the United States soon followed. Meanwhile Macedonia had seceded from the federation, and, after holding a referendum that was boycotted by ethnic Serbs, Bosnia-Herzegovina also withdrew in February 1992. The Bush administration—no longer constrained by events in the now defunct Soviet Union—quickly recognized the new Muslim-dominated Sarajevo government despite the near certainty that Milosevic would violently oppose it. War now engulfed Bosnia as Serbs, Croats, and Muslims battled one another in the most vicious fighting in Europe since World War II. The Bush administration, the United Nations, and the European Union applied economic sanctions against Belgrade for its support of the Bosnian Serbs, provided humanitarian assistance to the Muslims, and instituted an arms embargo against all the combatants despite the fact that the Serbs had most of the weapons. Washington also lent tacit support to a Bosnian peace plan devised by former Secretary of State Cyrus Vance and former British Foreign Secretary David Owen (representing the United Nations and the European Union respectively) that would have broken Bosnia into ten semiautonomous (and tiny) ethnic enclaves. This compromise proved unacceptable to the warring sides. As the fighting escalated, the Bush administration refused to contribute American personnel to a large United Nations peacekeeping force under continual harassment from Serb troops, and placed Bosnian air operations under the joint control of NATO and the UN Security Council, thus seriously undermining American moral and military authority and leverage. Moreover, it appeared uninterested in reports that the Bosnian Serbs had committed genocide as part of their "ethnic cleansing" program.

Flush from victory in the Gulf War, the Bush administration feared that military intervention in Yugoslavia could rapidly become another Vietnam "quagmire" as U.S. forces bogged down in the same difficult terrain that the Germans had encountered during World War II. Moreover, it did not believe that vital national interests were at stake and so could not count on sustained domestic support. Thus, in contrast to his adept handling of German reunification and Iraqi aggression, President Bush stumbled in Yugoslavia and bequeathed the Balkan imbroglio to his successor, Bill Clinton.

Humanitarian Intervention in Somalia

Another humanitarian crisis, in the Muslim East African nation of Somalia, unfolded almost simultaneously, and the Bush administration came under significant domestic pressure to alleviate the suffering caused by a severe famine. Television pictures of starving Somali infants and children began to appear during the summer of 1992 with Bush in the midst of his reelection campaign. Members of Congress such as the Black Caucus, but also Senator Nancy Kassebaum (R-KS), argued that the United States had a moral responsibility to intervene. The Reagan administration had given military aid to the anti-communist government of Siad Barre but had lost interest in Somalia with the termination of the Cold War. Barre had been overthrown in 1991 with several regional warlords attempting to gain effective political control of a chaotic situation. Indeed, these warlords had decided to manipulate the distribution of food as a means to achieve power. On August 14, President Bush decided to begin an emergency food airlift and to offer to transport 500 Pakistani troops under UN command to the capital of Mogadishu. But most of the food fell into the hands of the warring militias who used it for political purposes. In September, 2,500 U.S. Marines arrived off the coast to try and protect the UN soldiers, but this action provoked the ire of Mohamed Farrah Aidid, perhaps the strongest of the warlords and a long-time enemy of UN Secretary General Boutros Boutros-Ghali.

The situation continued to deteriorate throughout the autumn, but Bush did not reassess American policy until after his electoral defeat. Then on November 25, 1992, he decided to mount a large-scale military intervention, dubbed "Operation Restore Hope," that would involve about 30,000 ground troops. Its announced purpose was to ensure that starving Somalis received the food that the warlords had been intercepting and manipulating. According to Acting Secretary of State Eagleburger, the administration decided to act in Somalia rather than in the Balkans because the risks were lower, not because American interests were more substantial. President Bush evidently believed that U.S. forces

would begin to withdraw before Clinton's inauguration on January 20, 1993, but this timetable proved to be extremely unrealistic. First, the administration had difficulty deciding whether American forces should disarm the militias or simply attempt to deliver food. Disarmament would involve taking sides and thus placing these forces at risk, but the mere delivery of food to areas controlled by the warlords meant that the supplies could be manipulated, and the "famine" would return as soon as the troops left. Second, the administration never fully debated whether the famine was primarily a natural or a man-made disaster. If the latter, then it would be very difficult to avoid becoming entangled in the intricacies of Somali politics—a prospect that Bush abhorred. As it turned out, no troop withdrawals could be made before Bush left office, and President Clinton inherited, as in Bosnia, an exceedingly volatile and complex situation.

Foreign Policy and the 1992 Election

With the disappearance of the Soviet Union and with the United States apparently in the midst of its "unipolar" moment, many Americans lost interest in international affairs. George Bush, the quintessential foreign policy president, faced an electorate that worried about a nagging recession, relatively high unemployment, and fears that countries like Mexico were "stealing" good jobs from hardworking Americans. As Bush began his reelection bid in early 1992, his considerable foreign policy accomplishments seemed to be liabilities, and he tried to convince the public that he genuinely cared about domestic issues.

Bush, moreover, had alienated many conservative Republicans who accused him of abandoning Reagan's social and economic agendas. Most galling to them was Bush's decision in November 1990 to renege on his 1988 campaign promise not to raise taxes despite enormous federal budget deficits. Patrick Buchanan, a former Nixon speechwriter, conservative columnist, and television pundit, posed Bush's chief challenge in the Republican primaries, blasting NAFTA and Operation Desert Storm. Essentially an anti-immigration isolationist, Buchanan failed to win any primary elections but also refused to drop out of the race, forcing Bush to expend valuable resources and distracting his attention from his main challengers, Bill Clinton and Ross Perot.

Perot, a billionaire Texas businessman, announced his independent candidacy on CNN's *Larry King Live* on February 20, 1992. His rather quixotic campaign focused on the federal deficit—which Perot promised to eliminate—and his opposition to NAFTA—which he likened to "a great sucking sound" of jobs leaving the United States for Mexico. After showing well in the early polls, he quit the race in late summer in the face of a strong Clinton run but reentered on October 1 in time to participate in the three presidential debates.

Arkansas Governor Bill Clinton positioned himself as a centrist Democrat determined to reinvigorate the economy through a combination of federal investments, tax cuts, and improved public education. Although he devoted little attention to foreign policy during the campaign, Clinton did castigate Bush for coddling the "butchers of Beijing" and pledged to oppose granting China permanent most favored nation trading status, called on the president to lift the arms embargo against Bosnia and to order air strikes of Serb positions, contended that more should be done to help starving Somalis, criticized Bush for his policy of forcibly returning fleeing Haitian refugees to their island homeland, and suggested that the United Nations be given additional peacekeeping and peacemaking responsibilities. Eventually, he lent his support to NAFTA but warned that workers' rights and environmental concerns needed to be addressed.

Notwithstanding this rhetoric, however, foreign policy played the smallest role in the 1992 election of any since the Great Depression. Bush failed to overcome perceptions that he simply did not care much about domestic issues and won only 38 percent of the vote. Perot garnered 19 percent, an exceedingly strong showing for a third party candidate, while Clinton received 43 percent as well as an Electoral College landslide.

Legacy

George H. W. Bush, by background, training, and temperament very comfortable with the verities of the Cold War, probably would have preferred to pursue a strategy of Soviet containment. Indeed, he spent much of 1989 attempting to slow down the momentum of the Reagan-Gorbachev express. But at the Malta meeting in December of that year, Bush concluded that he could do business with Gorbachev and decided to initiate a set of strategic objectives designed to ease the transition to a post–Cold War world. Among these goals was German reunification, and the administration orchestrated that process with adroitness, patience, imagination, and aplomb.

After continuing to pursue Ronald Reagan's policy of détente with Iraq in an effort to balance the power of Iran, Bush appeared startled by Saddam Hussein's invasion of Kuwait in August 1990. Yet by creating and leading an unlikely international coalition and then by carefully cultivating domestic support for military action in the Persian Gulf, Bush performed masterfully, and a grateful American public made him the most popular president since the advent of approval ratings.

But from this pinnacle of February 1991, Bush stumbled badly. Instead of engaging in a national debate over America's role in his new world order, he retreated into merely celebrating and re-celebrating the victory in Operation Desert Storm. Furthermore, the administration

ceded leadership in the Yugoslav cauldron to the European Union, shrank from doing much to assist the new post-communist governments in Eastern Europe, and appeared reluctant to genuinely assist Boris Yeltsin.

In large part, this timidity was driven by Bush's perceptions of the 1992 presidential campaign. Dogged by the widespread view that he cared little for domestic issues and plagued by a recession that lingered longer than expected, President Bush came to regard his foreign policy accomplishments and aspirations as impediments to his reelection chances.

Nevertheless, this transitional president bequeathed to his immediate successors a set of global priorities for the world's sole superpower. That agenda featured efforts to retard the proliferation of weapons of mass destruction, the further expansion of free trade areas with the United States serving as the fulcrum, primary reliance on American military power to provide "regional stability" in East Asia and the Middle East, perhaps a greater inclination to involve international organizations in U.S. initiatives, and the assertion that the new "democratic peace" depended on American global leadership.

Richard Melanson

Chronology

1989

February 6: Polish government agrees to talks with opposition.

March 26: Multiparty elections in the Soviet Union end over seven decades of Communist Party monopoly.

April 15: In China student pro-democracy demonstrations begin.

April 25: Soviet Union begins withdrawal of troops from Eastern Europe.

May 4: Hungary opens its border with Austria, thousands of East Germans flee to the West.

May 25: Soviet Congress of People's Deputies elects Gorbachev president of the Supreme Soviet.

June 3–4: Chinese army attacks student demonstrators in Tiananmen Square, hundreds are killed.

June 5: President Bush protests repression in China, imposes sanctions.

July 13–19: G-7 summit leaders offer financial aid to Poland and Hungary.

August 17: Gorbachev proposes autonomy for Soviet republics.

October 6: Gorbachev advises East Germany to reform its government.

October 18: Hungarian National Assembly ends Communist Party monopoly.

November 9: East German border with West Germany opens, destruction of Berlin Wall begins.

November 28: Mass demonstrations in Prague; Communist Party agrees to share power with oppostition Civic Forum.

December 1–3: Bush and Gorbachev discuss trade and arms control in Malta.

December 19: East and West Germany agree to plan for reunification.

December 20: United States invades Panama toppling Noriega regime.

December 20: Gorbachev opposes Lithuanian independence.

December 22–25: Romanian President Nicolae Ceausescu is overthrown and summarily shot.

December 28: Elections in Czechoslovakia end Communist rule.

1990

January 23: Yugoslavia dissolves League of Communists.

February 2: South African government legalizes the African National Congress (ANC).

February 12: 2+4 Plan for German reunification is established.

February 25: Violeta Chamorro wins Nicaraguan elections, ousting Sandinista regime.

February 25–27: United States urges European Community to cope with Yugoslav crisis.

March 18: East German elections endorse speedy reunification.

May 29: Boris Yeltsin is elected president of the Russian Federation.

June 9: Reformers win Czechoslovakian parliamentary elections.

July 5: In Yugoslavia the Serb Republic assumes direct control over the province of Kosovo.

August 2: Iraq invades Kuwait; United States and Soviet Union condemn Iraq's aggression.

August 6: Bush deploys U.S. forces to Saudi Arabia in Operation Desert Shield.

August 25: UN Security Council authorizes naval and air blockades of Iraq.

September 12: 2+4 talks adopt a treaty, Settlement with Respect to Germany, for German reunification.

September 20: East and West Germany are officially reunified.

November 29: UN Security Council authorizes "all necessary means" to end Iraqi occupation of Kuwait.

December 2: Germany hold first elections since reunification; Chancellor Kohl's Christian Democrats win.

1991

January 12: Congress authorizes military force against Iraq.

January 16: Operation Desert Storm begins; twenty-eight-nation coalition begins the liberation of Kuwait.

February 23–28: One hundred-hour ground offensive against Iraqi forces in Kuwait ends in Iraqi defeat.

March 3: Iraqi military signs UN cease-fire terms.

March 6: In a speech to Congress Bush heralds "new world order."

March 6: Uprisings by Shiites and Kurds in Iraq are crushed.

April 18: Iraq accepts cease-fire terms of UNSC Resolution 687.

May 29: Bush vows to ban all weapons of mass destruction (WMD) from the Middle East.

July 31: Bush and Gorbachev sign START I Treaty.

August 16: Baghdad rejects UN oil-for-food program.

August 19: Attempted coup against Soviet President Gorbachev is defeated.

August 20: Three Soviet Baltic republics declare independence.

September 7: Croatia and Slovenia declare independence from Yugoslavia.

September 25: UN Security Council embargoes arms sales to Yugoslavia.

November 8: NATO approves post–Cold War strategic concepts.

December 8: Three former Soviet republics form the Commonwealth of Independent States (CIS).

December 23: Germany recognizes independence of Croatia and Slovenia.

1992

January 31: UN Security Council plans higher profile in preventive diplomacy and peacekeeping.

February 5: UN Security Council reinstates economic sanctions against Iraq.

March 17: UN fails to stop fighting between Armenia and Azerbaijan.

March 26: Germany suspends all arms deliveries to Turkey.

April 6: United States and European Community recognize Bosnia-Herzogovina.

April 24: UN sends observers to Somalia to monitor cease-fire.

May: France and Germany agree to 35,000 member joint military force under NATO.

May 23: United States agrees with Russia, Belarus, Kazakhstan, and Ukraine to abide by START I.

June 2: UN sends peacekeeping force to Sarajevo.

July 3: Croats in Bosnia proclaim an independent state.

July 16: Germany's central bank raises interest rates.

August 6: United States seeks humanitarian aid for Sarajevo, rejects military action.

August 27: EC-UN conference fails to end fighting in Bosnia.

September: Britain withdraws from EMS due to Sterling's crash against the Deutschmark.

October 3: United States airlifts food and medicine to Sarajevo.

November 3: William Clinton is elected president; Albert Gore Jr. is vice president.

November 25: Czechoslovakian assembly votes for separate Czech and Slovak republics.

December 3: UN approves U.S.-led humanitarian mission to Somalia.

December 17: United States, Canada, and Mexico sign North American Free Trade Agreement (NAFTA).

December 17: Germany provides Russia with debt-relief and housing finance.

1993
January 3: United States and Russia sign START II Treaty.

References and Further Reading

Baker, James A., III, with Thomas M. DeFrank. *The Politics of Diplomacy: Revolution, War, and Peace.* New York: Putnam, 1995.

Beschloss, Michael, and Strobe Talbott. *At the Highest Levels: The Inside Story of the End of the Cold War.* Boston: Little, Brown, 1993.

Bush, George, and Brent Scowcroft. *A World Transformed.* New York: Random House, 1998.

Gow, James. *Triumph of the Lack of Will: International Diplomacy and the Yugoslav War.* New York: Columbia University Press, 1997.

Greene, John Robert. *The Presidency of George Bush.* Lawrence, KS: University Press of Kansas, 2000.

Hirsch, John L., and Robert B. Oakley. *Somalia and Operation Restore Hope: Reflections on Peacemaking and Peacekeeping.* Washington, DC: United States Institute of Peace, 1995.

Hurst, Steven. *The Foreign Policy of the Bush Administration: In Search of a New World Order.* London and New York: Cassell, 1999.

Quandt, William B. *Peace Process.* Washington, DC: Brookings Institution, 2001.

Tucker, Robert W., and David C. Hendrickson. *The Imperial Temptation: The New World Order and America's Purpose.* New York: Council on Foreign Relations, 1992.

Woodward, Bob. *The Commanders.* New York: Simon and Schuster, 1991.

Zelikow, Philip, and Condoleezza Rice. *Germany Unified and Europe Transformed: A Study in Statecraft.* Cambridge: Harvard University Press, 1995.

William Jefferson Clinton (1993–2001)

Early Life and Political Career

On August 19, 1946, William Jefferson Blythe III was born in Hope, Arkansas, three months after his father died in a fatal car accident. He was named after his father, William Jefferson Blythe Jr., who worked as a salesman and frequently traveled. When William was four-years-old his mother was remarried to Roger Clinton of Hot Springs, Arkansas, the city in which he grew up. As a member of Boys Nation in high school, Clinton visited Washington, D.C., where he met President John F. Kennedy in the White House Rose Garden. From that point forward, Clinton was drawn to the city and fascinated by politics.

After graduating from high school, he enrolled in an undergraduate program at Georgetown University and worked for Senator J. William Fulbright. In 1968, the young Clinton won a Rhodes Scholarship, which took him to Oxford University. After returning from England, Clinton enrolled in law school at Yale University and graduated in 1973. After graduation, Clinton decided to return to Arkansas and teach law at the University of Arkansas. Only one year later, in 1974, Clinton ran for office in the House of Representatives against the Republican John Paul Hammerschmidt, but lost the election. In 1975, Clinton married Hillary Rodham, also a graduate from Yale University Law School and his former classmate. In 1980, the Clintons' only child, Chelsea, was born.

Clinton's political career started in 1976 when he was elected attorney general of Arkansas. This was only a stepping stone to higher office. Two years later, he was elected governor of Arkansas, the youngest governor in American history. His tenure in office only lasted for one term due to unpopular policies such as a vehicle tax and difficulties with the public-image of his spouse, who seemed to many to be too liberal for a small, southern state. Clinton was defeated in a bid for re-election in 1980. However, in 1982 he regained the governorship. With his wife assuming a more traditional public role, including adopting his surname, socially conservative Arkansas re-elected Clinton five times. He thus served as governor until he decided to run for president in 1992. After securing the Democratic Party nomination, Governor Clinton defeated President George H. W. Bush in November 1992. Clinton won 43.3 percent of the popular vote against Bush's 37.7 percent, with a third-party candidate, H. Ross Perot, taking 19 percent, a significant

William Jefferson Clinton was the first president of the post-Cold War era. (Library of Congress)

portion of which would likely have gone to Bush in a two-way race.

Clinton's first years in office looked very promising. It helped him greatly that the Democrats retained majorities in both houses of the U.S. Congress. However, this "honeymoon period" only lasted for about two years. After the election in 1994, the Republicans recovered and won the majority of both houses. The opposition in both houses made life for the Democratic president difficult in the years to come. Clinton and Vice President Albert Gore represented a new generation in American politics. Both were young, dynamic, striving for the highest office, and were born after World War II. This 'new political generation' wave was also evident in Europe in the mid-1990s when majorities in elections in European capitals went to center-left wing parties. On both sides of the Atlantic, third way politics advocating a middle road between defeated communism and unfettered capitalism held rhetorical sway and political office. Clinton was considered a moderate politician and worked domestically to reform the education and health care systems, to save the environment, and to register private guns.

The Globalization President

Clinton was the first president who was faced with a post-Cold War environment. He argued that the United States needed to find a new foreign policy paradigm to meet the challenges of the twenty-first century. What was needed, he argued, was a "new vision" for the country "to meet a new set of opportunities and threats." Clinton, then governor of Arkansas and on the presidential campaign, argued that the incumbent Bush administration was "rudderless, reactive, and erratic," while the country needed positive leadership that was based on American values. Following the victory of American-led forces in the Persian Gulf War of 1991, Bush had enjoyed unprecedented public approval ratings. But between the Gulf War and the peaceful revolutions in the former Soviet Union and Eastern European countries, Bush's presidency had been consumed with foreign policy and largely neglected domestic politics. Bush, moreover, was seen mainly as a problem-solver rather than a visionary president. A coherent post-Cold War foreign policy had not been developed.

President Clinton proposed a rhetorically new foreign policy that was supposedly based on traditional American values and principles. This foreign policy outlook promised to leave behind the Cold War emphasis on national security. Rather, economics, the promotion of democracy around the world, and "saving the environment" stood at the forefront in Washington. Moreover, domestic and foreign policy would be tied together again. Clinton said that "we must tear down the wall in our thinking between domestic and foreign policy." The administration believed that the United States would be able to retain global leadership only if its economy was strong.

Unlike Bush, who had come to the Oval Office with vast experience in foreign policy, Clinton carried neither foreign policy baggage nor expertise into office from previous assignments in government. In addition to the inexperience common to presidents who formerly were governors, Clinton was faced with several foreign policy disadvantages. The dissolution of the Soviet Union took away the threat it posed during the Cold War and left the U.S. military without a clear enemy. As a result, the administration had to reconcile and reconsider its foreign and defense policy to try to find answers for a post-Cold War era. Furthermore, the American public was unsupportive of ambitious foreign policy initiatives; it very much wanted to keep the troops home and saw little purpose in renewed American engagement in the world. However, this change also permitted Clinton a larger margin of error in shaping foreign policy. When Clinton entered the White House, he was mostly uninterested in foreign policy and concentrated on domestic issues.

The mantra of his presidential campaign, "it's the economy, stupid!," showed where the president intended to direct his attention. Clinton left foreign policy issues to National Security Advisor Anthony Lake, and told him to keep foreign policy from becoming a problem politically. In fact, the administration's policy in early 1993 was to keep foreign policy off the presidential radar as much as possible. Clinton showed greater interest in domestic issues such as educational and health care reforms. Therefore, it is not a surprise that during the first term, the administration struggled to formulate a coherent policy that explained to the American people what the United States would strive to accomplish in the international arena. Weak coordination between the White House and the National Security Council Staff did not help to solve this dilemma either. The chief problem was the lack of a strong leader in the national security team that could bind divergent views together. In addition, most of Clinton's foreign policy team had already served under President Carter and was therefore seen as less than innovative. Even though the performance of the National Security Council improved during the 1990s, the foreign policy of the administration was still unsteady. Critics such as Republican Senator John McCain from Arizona frequently condemned the administration publicly for its lack of strategic coherence and its failure to identify key American interests.

Clinton's foreign policy in the first term was largely concerned with opening foreign markets for American products and liberalizing trading systems isolated from the international market. Warren Christopher told the Senate during his confirmation hearings as Clinton's secretary of state that three principles should guide American foreign policy: attaining economic security, reorganizing the U.S. military, and promoting democracy abroad. The first item Christopher discussed during the confirmation hearings was the need to use the international economic system to promote greater prosperity for the American people. During his campaign in 1992, Governor Clinton had declared that the United States must overcome obstructions between domestic and foreign policy; this was the "single grand concept" of Clinton's approach and could be labeled the "strategy of enlargement," replacing the long-term policy of containment. Presidential candidate Clinton had said that "our first foreign priority and our first domestic priority are one and the same: reviving our economy"; in office Clinton issued several key domestic initiatives to achieve this goal. The administration sought to make American workers and companies more productive to better compete in the global marketplace. This policy was combined with an effort to reduce federal budget deficits and ensure that the United States would be a more reliable trading partner. The creation of the National Economic Council (NEC), which was seen as the economic equivalent of the NSC, underlined the importance of economic affairs during Clinton's first term. This new organization ensured that economic interests and issues were woven into the overall foreign policy making process. Economic advisors gained importance and enjoyed close access to the inner circle of power. In addition, other offices and branches of government dealing with economic issues—such as the United States Trade Representative and the State Department's Office of the Coordinator for Business Affairs—shared foreign policy responsibilities.

Additionally, Clinton moved ahead quickly to complete the free trade agreement negotiations with Canada and Mexico. With respect to tariffs, the North American Free Trade Agreement (NAFTA) stated that all tariffs on goods produced by the three countries and sold among them should be eliminated. The agreement also applied to foreign investment and outlined that all foreign investment should be treated as a national investment. As well, copyrights, industrial designs, and trademarks were provided protection under the NAFTA charter. The House of Representatives and the Senate passed the NAFTA agreement in 1993 with the help of Republican votes. The congressional victory was praised as an important foreign policy success. Additional side agreements were reached after substantial opposition to NAFTA arose from the Democratic Party, sections of the American public, and labor unions. These groups feared that free trade deals would eliminate domestic jobs and undermine environmental standards. By late 1993, it became clear that this liberal internationalism was moving toward a transformation. Liberal internationalism was mixed with the policy of enlargement or democratic engagement. The president and his national security advisor committed the administration to not only increase the number of market democracies and market economies, but also to increase the number of free societies around the globe as a fundamental goal for American foreign policy.

In 1994, the Clinton administration successfully completed the negotiations of the Uruguay Round of the General Agreement on Tariffs and Trade (GATT) regulating global trade, replaced in January 1995 by the World Trade Organization (WTO). As was the case with the NAFTA agreement, the Uruguay Round demanded vigorous congressional lobbying to pass both the House and the Senate; in the end, it was approved by a two-thirds majority. The changes in the GATT agreement called for an 85 percent reduction of general tariffs and for the first time brought agriculture, services, and intellectual property under GATT. Agricultural subsidies were to be reduced by 36 percent worldwide and agricultural products exported with the financial support of the government would be cut by 21 percent. Also, quotas on textiles imported by developed countries from underdeveloped countries were to be eliminated after ten years.

After concluding the Uruguay Round, the administration moved ahead in promoting economic liberalism and supported the notion that the Asia-Pacific Economic Cooperation (APEC) forum should establish a free trade agreement among its member countries by 2010. Despite Clinton's appetite for multilateral free trade agreements, he went forward in negotiating various bilateral free trade agreements with other states to foster American economic security. In January 1994, the White House drafted a list with ten countries the United States identified as emerging markets: Brazil, China, India, Indonesia, Mexico, Poland, South Africa, South Korea, and Turkey. The long-term goal was to enhance access to these growing markets. These countries were attractive to the United States because they had started to reform their economies and therefore promised opportunities for American investments and exports. One country stood out in particular: China. A country with more than a billion people became the natural target for an expansive trade agenda. The administration therefore sought to enhance reciprocal trade and investment opportunities, despite China's discouraging record of human rights violations, with a long-term strategy of bringing China into the international system and thereby encouraging a transformation of its political system. In China's case in particular, economic policy, and above all trade policy, *became* foreign policy.

This approach was grounded ideologically in Wilsonian liberal internationalism, a foreign policy stressing the importance of economic liberalism and the vitality of democratic governments beyond American shores. It seemed especially well-suited to a world in which the phenomenon of "globalization"—the expansion of commerce from national and regional settings to an evermore global format, facilitated by revolutionary changes in communications—accelerated in the post-Cold War international environment of the 1990s. It was periodically backed by the willingness of the administration to use military force for humanitarian purposes in political crises abroad. During the Haiti crisis in 1994 the Clinton administration threatened to invade the country and finally convinced the rebels to retreat voluntarily to restore President Jean-Bertrand Aristide's power. This reduced bloodshed on the doorstep of American territory and reduced the number refugees fleeing to the United States. Simultaneously the administration restructured and downsized the U.S. military while maintaining an effective defense for the United States. All services were affected by these cuts. The military had to become smaller, more efficient, more mobile, and capable of facing a greater variety of threats in a more fluid and unpredictable security environment.

Selective Engagement

During his second term in particular, President Clinton became more involved personally in foreign policy and his foreign policy team was shuffled around. Secretary of State Christopher was replaced by the more eloquent and outspoken Ambassdor to the United Nations Madeleine Albright. Albright was better able to communicate foreign policy initiatives to the American people and Congress. Clinton also decided to change the secretary of defense and appointed the retiring Republican Senator William Cohen to this senior cabinet position. Cohen was highly experienced in the defense field before he came to the new job. This appointment was also intended to build bridges with the Republicans to shape bipartisan foreign and defense policies, indirectly acknowledging the Republican majority in Congress. The new foreign policy team functioned more solidly. Last, Clinton's foreign policy made a shift from political idealism to realism in the second term.

This shift began shortly before the 1996 presidential election campaign, a contest again dominated largely by domestic issues. The nation was at peace with no imminent threat from overseas lurking around. In a climate of economic boom, Clinton scored an easy reelection victory over his Republican opponent, Senator Bob Dole, who also showed little interest in foreign policy issues. The changing international environment of the mid 1990s nonetheless demanded a closer definition of foreign policy priorities. Contributing to these changes were American military involvements in Somalia, Haiti, and Bosnia. Authorized by the United Nations Security Council, President Bush had sent U.S. military forces to Somalia in December 1992 in Operation Restore Hope to provide humanitarian assistance. Initially, the Clinton administration sought to expand the mission and included a nation-building objective to restore order and good government. American forces were deployed to protect the international community's aid supplies.

However, this nation-building ambition was abandoned when eighteen U.S. Rangers were killed on October 4, 1993, during a firefight with the forces of the local warlord Mohamed Aidid. Clinton disagreed in principle with UN Secretary General Boutros Boutros-Ghali about the need for ground forces to prevent a humanitarian catastrophe, but the killing of twenty-four Pakistani peacekeepers on June 5 nevertheless prompted a massive American response. During a mission to capture Aideed, U.S. forces were trapped in a fire fight, and the bodies of the fatally wounded were mutilated and dragged through downtown Mogadishu before the cameras of television journalists. Public protest in the United States was so intense that it forced Clinton to withdraw U.S. forces. By 1995 the entire United Nations mission in Somalia had collapsed.

Some critics accused the administration of a "social work" foreign policy. In Bosnia, the administration was slow to develop policies that would support the Western countries in their efforts to stop the ethnic cleansing, although Clinton was able in November 1995 to broker the Dayton Accords and subsequently deployed 20,000 U.S. troops to underwrite the peace. The new international developments required alternative foreign policy initiatives that went beyond economic liberalism. The administration reached a crossroads where it had to decide either to engage in the world and face these challenges or to retract to a more isolationist stance. The Clinton administration decided to pursue the former path but with important qualifications. In May 1994, the Somalia debacle prompted Clinton to issue Presidential Decision Directive 25 (PDD), a review of U.S. involvement in peacekeeping operations. The directive acknowledged that peacekeeping operations could be a "very important and useful tool of American foreign policy," but asserted that "our purpose is to use peacekeeping selectively and more effectively than has been done in the past." This made official a fundamental shift in foreign policy away from the idealist notion of spreading democracy and free markets around the world toward a policy that looked out for American national interests in the world.

As a consequence, Clinton decided not to get involved in the conflict in Rwanda in 1994—indeed to use Washington's influence to limit United Nations involvement to stop the genocidal frenzy of killing in the country—and to instead concentrate its foreign policy crisis-management on the war in the Balkans. The policy review, according to Clinton, can "help us make those hard choices about where and when the international community can get involved; where and when we can take part with the international community . . . and where and when we can make, thus, a positive difference." Consequently, the primary purpose of the American military was to "fight and win wars," while PDD 25 was a compass the administration used to further a humanitarian agenda without overstretching American forces. It also meant that working with the UN in peacekeeping missions was only feasible when the mission was considered in the national interest of the United States.

This approach to foreign policy can be labeled "selective engagement." Senior government officials made clear in a variety of speeches that the United States reserved the right to act unilaterally or multilaterally on a case-by-case basis. In 1993, Clinton had already authorized the unilateral use of force in Presidential Decision Directive 39, a document dealing specifically with terrorism that served notice that the United States intended to "seek to identify groups or states that sponsor such terrorists, isolate them and extract a heavy price for their actions." Based on PDD-39, Clinton bombed a chemical facility in Sudan suspected to be producing weapons of mass destruction. Anthony Lake said in a speech at John Hopkins University in September 1993 that "only one overriding factor can determine whether the U.S.

should act multilaterally or unilaterally, and this is America's interests." Moreover, Washington was not afraid to use force to reach these goals. Secretary of State Madeleine Albright argued in a speech at the National War College in September 1993 that "when diplomacy fails, we have both the capacity to use force effectively and the will to do so when necessary." The bombing of the World Trade Center in February 1993 and the release of sarin gas on a Tokyo subway alerted the administration. Albright explained that the United States intended to pursue arms control and nonproliferation while adopting hard-line policies against international crime, terror, and drug trafficking. In addition, protecting Americans at home required new military capabilities such as a national missile defense system that would be able to destroy incoming missiles launched by states that are hostile to the United States.

The policy of selective engagement called for strengthening the community of major market democracies and fostering new democracies and market economies—where possible especially in states of special strategic significance. It was also intended to counter aggression and support the liberalization of states hostile to democracy. It featured a humanitarian element, not only by providing aid but also by working to help democracy and market economies take root in regions of greatest humanitarian concern. Warren Christopher outlined the administration's foreign policy goals in an address to the Kennedy School of Government and cited the specific regional threats the United States faced. Christopher identified troubled hot spots in Bosnia, Central and Eastern Europe, Russia, Haiti, Cyprus, Angola, Burundi, Peru, and Ecuador that could pose a threat to national security. The transnational threats were identified as the proliferation of weapons of mass destruction, terrorism, international crime, and environmental damage.

At this point, the strategy of enlargement was no longer the focal point in the administration's diplomacy. Even though the theoretical change in policy took place by the end of Clinton's first term, it was fully implemented during his second term in office. By May 1997, the new National Security Strategy for a New Century reinforced the changes already underway, saying that the United States should "enhance our security with effective diplomacy and with military forces that are ready to fight and win, to bolster America's economic prosperity and to promote democracy abroad." In short, the new NSS reestablished the hierarchy of policy issues; economic policy was downgraded, whereas military capacity gained preeminence. This can be interpreted as a shift back toward a more realist approach, including the preemptive, unilateral use of force if American national interests were in danger.

Selective engagement did not call for an isolationist foreign policy. Quite the contrary, it demanded that the United States remain engaged in world affairs. However, decisions to get involved were to be based more closely on national interests. The White House was able to get consent for the Chemical Weapons Convention from the Senate but was refused consent for the Comprehensive Test Ban Treaty (CTBT). Moreover, the National Missile Defense Act was signed by the president in 1999. It was the same year in which the president delivered the State of the Union address endorsing bigger defense budgets and an increased role for the military. This was a decisive step insofar as it broke with the strategy of enlargement in particular. Further, the United States reserved the right to act unilaterally should it decide to use force.

The NSS outlined a policy platform that would make the United States less committed to change the international system through the expansion of market economies and more focused on stabilizing relations with other states. Thus, the administration put more emphasis on managing conflicts rather than eliminating them quickly with military force. The emphasis was on stabilizing the international order and preserving the status quo rather than trying to reform the system itself. This view was enforced by Congress, which after the election of 1994, was controlled by the Republican Party. Generally speaking, the significant shift that took place during Clinton's second term was that the defense of the United States homeland returned as the main priority of foreign policy. Homeland defense, international commerce, and peace and stability were the cornerstones of Clinton's diplomacy during the second half of his first term.

NATO and European Security

Clinton's renewed interest in international security during his second term was also felt in the North Atlantic Treaty Organization (NATO). In the latter half of 1994, the Clinton administration approved the notion of NATO expansion by offering Eastern European countries a membership in the alliance. This quite naturally raised concerns in Moscow. NATO implemented the "Partnership for Peace" (PfP) program, which could be seen as a junior membership agreement for former states from Central and Eastern Europe. These countries would be guided toward a closer relationship with NATO. However, in some countries, the PfP agreement, which foresaw a bilateral friendship with NATO rather than a membership, was not particularly welcomed. In addition, domestic politics as well as heavy lobbying convinced the administration in Washington to finally offer full membership to Poland, Hungary, and the Czech Republic during the NATO Madrid Summit in July 1997. By calling for a greater European share in the transatlantic burden, the Clinton administration insisted that the Europeans should improve their defense budgets to alleviate the direct American costs of transatlantic defense. At the same time, the Europeans developed a European Security and Defense Identity (ESDI) that called for greater European autonomy within the NATO framework.

The war in the Balkans perfectly demonstrated the selectivity of Clinton's foreign policy. In early 1999, it became clear that the bitter war between the Kosovo Liberation Army (KLA) and the Yugoslav Army could develop into an ethnic cleansing of Albanians living in Kosovo who made up 80 percent of the population in the province. On March 23, 1999, the UN High Commissioner for Refugees special envoy to the region counted about 260,000 internally displaced persons within Kosovo and more than 100,000 refugees in the region. Also, it was in the interest of the United States to stop the violations against humanity in spite of European paralysis in conflict management. Without a clear mandate from the United Nations Security Council, the administration therefore launched a NATO air campaign, Operation Allied Force, against Serbia to end ethnic cleansing in the province of Kosovo on March 24, 1999. The campaign lasted for seventy-eight days. Clinton justified American involvement by arguing that this war could possibly destabilize the entire European continent as well as the NATO alliance. However, the operation in the Balkans was limited to air combat due to the fear of American casualties. The bombs dropped on Yugoslavia were an effort to pressure its president, Slobodan Milosevic, to agree to four principles: termination of all military activities and killings, a complete withdrawal of the Serbian military, the return of all refugees, and a political future for Kosovo built on the Rambouillet Accords.

The Middle East

Clinton pursued the strategy of dual containment with regard to Iran and Iraq. Washington tried to shore up diplomatic support from neighboring countries to contain these countries. Nonetheless, Clinton was quick to use air power to force Iraq's compliance with the UN endorsed no fly zone in Northern Iraq. Further, the administration got heavily involved in producing a peace settlement between Israel and the Palestinians in the Oslo Accords of 1993 and the Wye River Accords of 1998 because Clinton saw the dispute as a threat to regional security in the entire Middle East region. The administration also managed to successfully negotiate peace agreements between Israel and Jordan. Both the Israeli-Palestinian conflict and the containment of Iran and Iraq, however, remained unfinished business for the administration of George W. Bush after Clinton left the White House.

Legacy

William Clinton left behind a distinct legacy that shaped U.S. foreign policy for almost a decade. Probably the most distinguished legacy the president achieved was a continuous commitment to world affairs. After the end of the Cold War in 1989, there were voices in the United States that

called for a return to isolationism. Sending U.S. soldiers to rebuild failed states was not thought to be a foreign policy objective as vital to American interests as the half-century commitment to contain communism. Clinton maintained American internationalism by reaching out for markets, signing more than 230 free trade agreements, and promoting democracy around the globe. On this basis, NAFTA as well as the Uruguay GATT were reached. Also, Clinton continued to commit about 100,000 troops to the European continent as well as Asia. He thereby managed to place economic policies at the top of the foreign policy agenda. The administration reshaped the foreign policy establishment by highlighting the importance of global economic initiatives to ensure American prosperity and freedom.

Clinton also redefined the threats facing America after the end of the Cold War, ranging from terrorism to weapons of mass destruction as well as regional conflicts, but developed a clear and concise strategy on how to meet these challenges. The Clinton years left the public with the idea of a president being more involved in foreign policy issues by the end of his second term than any other president before him. The fast track authority Clinton received for the negotiation of the free trade agreements underlines an increased executive involvement in foreign policies. As a result, the administration left office with an imperative for greater involvement of the executive in foreign policy. With regard to Europe, Washington enlarged NATO's sphere of influence by pushing the Alliance to go out of its area, a theme of American alliance leadership that was continued after Clinton by the administration of George W. Bush.

There are a few areas where Clinton's policies failed. One of the strategies that ran out of breath in Washington was the "strategy of enlargement," which did not gain much support at home. Yet Clinton was wise enough to listen to domestic opinions and lobbies; any other action might have resulted in a major isolationist backlash. This is mainly because the American public wanted to cash in the peace dividend after the end of the Cold War. Americans saw no rationale for continuous American involvement on a European continent that had just experienced a peaceful revolution. The necessity for the American commitment to European security by deploying military forces, as well diplomatic dedication to NATO, were seen as outdated.

Consequently, the Clinton administration came to office with a strong prospect for promoting democracy and human rights around the world. As is often the case in foreign policy, unanticipated events tend to dominate the foreign policy agenda so that campaign promises are sometimes are hard to keep. It can be argued that this was the case in terms of promoting democracy. The war on the Balkans as well as the crises in Iraq, Somalia, Rwanda, and Haiti demanded the fullest attention of policy makers in Washington and distracted them from their promises. Economic interests always trumped human rights concerns during Clinton's tenure, as the China example clearly showed. Moreover, from a Republican point of view it can be argued that the Clinton administration was too friendly in the bilateral relationship with Russia. After the Soviet empire dissolved, the central theme in Russian foreign policy had been to restore multipolarity to the international system by calling for a balance to American hegemony. To this end, Russia aligned itself with China and Iran, to which it also sold weapons systems. These countries remained the two most difficult strategic opponents of the United States, and the Clinton administration did little during its two terms to ensure American dominance.

After 1998, Clinton's presidency was largely overshadowed by the Monica Lewinsky scandal. As a result of the allegations that he had sexual contact with a former intern in the White House, Congress started an impeachment process, a complicated procedure to discharge the president from office. In the end, Clinton was acquitted by the Senate, and the attempt to remove him from office failed. He apologized to the American people for his misbehavior. Despite these allegations and his lies to the American people, he continued to enjoy unprecedented popularity. The Lewinsky affair was an unfortunate distraction, as major foreign policy challenges of the future were in evidence in 1998. On August 7, bombs exploded at U.S. embassies in Nairobi, Kenya, and Dar-es-Salaam, Tanzania. Intelligence sources reported that that al Qaeda terrorist organization of Osama bin Laden had been responsible for these and other attacks on American assets abroad. Clinton ordered the U.S. Navy to launch retaliatory cruise missile strikes against al Qaeda training camps in Afghanistan and a pharmaceutical plant in Sudan suspected of manufacturing chemical weapons. The strikes were not very effective, but they presaged things to come not long after Clinton left office. So too did North Korea's test of a ballistic missile on August 31. Both al Qaeda and North Korea were destined to exert a profound impact on the foreign policy of George W. Bush.

Ben Zyla

Chronology

1993

January 27: Haiti refuses UN human rights observers.

February 27: Radical Islamist terrorists bomb the World Trade Center in New York.

February 28: United States drops food and medical supplies to Bosnian Muslims.

April 19: Fighting breaks out between Muslims and Croats in Bosnia.

May 1: UN and NATO reject President Clinton's lift-and-strike proposal for Bosnia.

May 28: United States renews Chinese most favored nation status.

June 16: Rival Bosnian factions reject Vance-Owen Peace Plan.

June 21: U.S. Supreme Court authorizes forcible return of Haitian refugees.

June 26: United States launches missile attack against Iraqi intelligence headquarters.

August 18: U.S. State Department designates Sudan a terrorist state.

August 25: United States imposes trade sanctions on Pakistan and China.

September 13: Israel and the Palestinian Liberation Organization sign the Oslo Accords.

September 27: Clinton asks UN to limit peacekeeping but to promote free trade.

October 3: U.S. Delta and Army Ranger troops attacked by Somali guerillas.

October 6: Clinton orders U.S. troops out of Somalia.

October 22: NATO adopts Partnership for Peace program.

November 1: The Maastricht Treaty on European Union comes into effect.

1994

January 1: Mexican rebels seize towns in the state of Chiapas.

February 3: United States ends trade embargo against Vietnam.

February 28: NATO jets shoot down Serb aircraft over Bosnia.

March 29–April 11: NATO aircraft bomb Serb artillery positions in Bosnia.

April 30: United States ends restrictions on arms sales to Taiwan.

May 13: Five-nation Contact Group issues peace plan for Bosnia.

June 8: United States agrees to help humanitarian mission in Rwanda.

July 31: UN approves U.S.-led intervention in Haiti.

August 10: United States and North Korea agree to inspections of North Korean nuclear facilities.

October 4: Clinton attempts to revive Northern Ireland peace talks.

October 26: Israel and Jordan sign a peace treaty.

November 21–28: Lack of NATO unity permits Serbs to continue aggression in Bosnia.

December 1: Senate approves World Trade Treaty, World Trade Organization (WTO) is created.

December 9: Russian forces seal the border of Chechnya.

December 27: Russia uses massive force against rebels in Chechnya.

1995

January 20: Russia prematurely declares victory in Chechnya.

January 31: U.S. Treasury intervenes in Mexico's financial crisis.

March 20: Bosnian cease-fire is broken.

March 20: Japanese terrorist cult releases nerve agent in Tokyo subway: 8 die and 4,700 are injured.

April 18: Fighting in Rwanda intensifies.

May 1: United States imposes trade embargo on Iran for assisting terrorism and seeking nuclear weapons.

June 16: China recalls its ambassador from Washington.

July 11: Serb atrocities in Srebrenica provoke international outrage.

July 30: Russian signs peace accord with Chechen rebels.

September 5–28: NATO conducts air raids against Serb military installations.

September 5: French nuclear tests at Mururoa Atoll provoke international protest.

September 5: NATO develops plans to admit new members.

September 24: Israel and Palestinian representatives sign Oslo II Accord.

November 4: Israeli Prime Minister Yitzhak Rabin is assassinated.

November 14: Terrorist bomb kills five Americans in Riyadh, Saudi Arabia.

November 21: Clinton signs Dayton Peace Accord with Serb, Croat, and Bosnian leaders.

1996

January 28: Russian forces launch new offensive in Chechnya.

March 7–25: China conducts missile tests in Taiwan Strait; Clinton reinforces U.S. naval forces in the region.

March 12: Clinton signs Helms-Burton Act restricting third nation trade with Cuba.

March 13: President Yeltsin orders an end to Russian war in Chechnya.

April 3: U.S. Secretary of Commerce Ron Brown dies in a plane crash in Croatia.

April 24: Clinton signs antiterrorist legislation.

May 6: New constitution ends apartheid in South Africa, establishes electoral democracy.

June 25: Terrorist bomb destroys apartment block in Dhahran, Saudi Arabia; nineteen Americans killed.

June 29: Refah Party heads new coalition in Turkey.

July 3: Yeltsin reelected president of Russia.

August 9: Rebels recapture Grozny, capital of Chechnya.

September 14: Elections in Bosnia confirm ethnic divisions.

September 24: Opening of Jerusalem tunnel provokes fighting between Israel and Palestinians.

September 27: Taliban extremists capture Kabul and impose Draconian version of Islamic law in Afghanistan.

October 17: Rwandan crisis erupts anew.

November 6: President Clinton is reelected.

November 25: UN Security Council approves oil-for-food program for Iraq.

December 11: NATO approves plan to admit Poland, Hungary, and Czech Republic.

1997

February 19: Deng Xiaoping dies; Ziang Zemin becomes leader of China.

March 7: United States vetoes UN condemnation of Israel's settlements east of Jerusalem.

May 1: Tony Blair is elected prime minister of Great Britain.

May 18: Rebel forces oust regime of Mobuto Sese Seko in Zaire (Congo).

May 23: Moderate cleric Muhammad Khatami is elected president of Iran.

May 27: NATO and Russia sign *Founding Act*.

May 31: Russia and Ukraine sign friendship treaty.

June 22: Russia is admitted to the G-7 group, which becomes the G-8.

July 8: Poland, Hungary, and the Czech Republic are invited to join NATO.

August 7: United States, China, North Korea, and South Korea hold talks.

September 17: United States refuses to sign international landmine treaty.

September 26: NATO-Russia Joint Council begins operations.

October 24: Onset of Asian financial crisis.

October 27-November 10: Iraq orders UNSCOM inspectors to leave, Clinton threatens bombing.

December 11: Kyoto Protocol on greenhouse gases is signed by 150 nations; United States, among others, declines to sign.

December 18: Clinton cautions that U.S. troops will stay in Bosnia indefinitely.

1998

January 21: Clinton affair with White House intern Monica Lewinsky; affair revealed to public.

February 13: UN Secretary General Kofi Annan reaches weapons inspection compromise with Iraq.

February 28–March 10: Serb police and paramilitaries slaughter Kosovar civilians.

March 5: United States imposes sanctions on Yugoslavia (Serbia).

March 23: Clinton makes eleven-day visit to Africa, announces "African renaissance" is underway.

April 10: Britain and the Republic of Ireland reach agreement on Northern Ireland.

April 19: Thirty-four nations agree to negotiate free trade in the Western Hemisphere.

April 30: Defense Department approves a plan to develop a national missile defense system.

May 21: Indonesian President Suharto is forced to resign.

May 11–13: India conducts five underground nuclear tests; Pakistan reciprocates with five nuclear test explosions. United States imposes sanctions on both countries

July 14: Congress eases sanctions on India and Pakistan.

August 7: Terrorist bombs explode at U.S. embassies in Kenya and Tanzania.

August 17: Clinton admits affair with Monica Lewinsky.

August 20: In retaliation for African bombings, Clinton fires cruise missiles into terrorist training camps in Afghanistan; separate cruise missile attack destroys pharmacuetical plant in Khartoum, Sudan. August 31: North Korea successfully tests long-range ballistic missile.

September 27: Gerhard Schröder is elected chancellor of Germany.

October 8: House of Representatives votes to hold impeachment hearings about President Clinton.

October 23: Clinton brokers Israel-Palestinian Wye River Accords.

October 31: Iraq ends UNSCOM inspections.

December 16: Anglo-American aircraft launch punitive raids in Iraq.

December 18: House of Representatives approves two articles of impeachment against President Clinton.

December 21: Israeli coalition collapses without approval of Wye River Accords.

December 22: U.S.-EU trade dispute erupts over banana exports

1999

January 1: The EU's Euro currency goes into effect on stock and bond markets.

February 12: Senate acquits Clinton of impeachment charges.

March 1: Serb forces begin "ethnic cleansing" of Muslims in Kosovo.

March 21: U.S.-EU trade dispute widens.

March 23: NATO authorizes air strikes against Yugoslavia (Serbia).

May 7: U.S. aircraft accidentally bomb Chinese embassy in Belgrade, based on outdated CIA map.

June 10: Belgrade accepts NATO's terms after seventy-eight days of bombing, culminating in a shift to targeting of civilian infrastructure inside Serbia.

July 22: China outlaws Falun Gong religious sect.

September 4: Israel and Palestinians agree on tentative peace plan.

September 11: Clinton and Ziang agree on Chin's membership in the World Trade Organization (WTO).

October 12: Coup ousts Pakistani Prime Minister Nawaz Sharif, General Pervez Musharraf assumes power.

October 13: U.S. Senate rejects Comprehensive Test Ban Treaty.

December 1: Antiglobalization demonstrations and riots mar WTO meeting in Seattle.

December 31: Vladimir Putin named acting president of Russia

2000

January 1: Panama gains full control of the Panama Canal.

February 21: Russian troops recapture Grozny.

March 13: United States eases sanctions on Iran.

March 15: U.S. troops stop Albanian raids into Serbia.

March 26: Vladimir Putin is elected president of Russia.

April 14–21: Russia ratifies SALT II and CTBT treaties.

May 24: House approves Normal Trade Relations (NTR) with China.

May 24: Israel precipitously withdraws from Southern Lebanon; Lebanese Christian militias collapse; Hezbollah siezes border territory.

June 3: Clinton visits Moscow, urges Putin to negotiate revised ABM treaty.

July 2: Vicente Fox is elected president of Mexico, breaking seventy-one years of PRI rule.

July 11–25: Israeli and Palestinian leader fail to reach peace agreement at Camp David.

August 12: Russian nuclear submarine *Kursk* sinks, 116 lives are lost.

September 1: Clinton postpones development of missile defense system.

September 24: Vojislav Kostunica wins Yugoslav presidential election.

September 28: Violence erupts in Jerusalem after Ariel Sharon visits the Temple Mount.

October 6: Protests in Belgrade force Milos̆evic to concede Yugoslav election.

October 12: USS *Cole* is damaged by a suicide boat while visiting yemen.

November 7: U.S. presidential election results in disputed vote in Florida.

December 12: U.S. Supreme Court orders end to selective election recount in four Florida counties, George W. Bush is president-elect; Richard Cheney is vice president-elect.

December 18: National Intelligence Report cites increasing terrorist threat until 2015.

2001

January 20: Clinton leaves office; George W. Bush is president; Richard Cheney is vice president.

References and Further Reading

Art, Robert J. "Geopolitics Updated: The Strategy of Selective Engagement," *International Security,* 23/3 (1998/99): 341–72.

Brinkley, Douglas. "Democratic Enlargement: The Clinton Doctrine," *Foreign Policy,* 106 (1997): 111–27.

Campbell, Colin, and Bert A. Rockman (eds.) *The Clinton Legacy.* New York: Chatham House, 2000.

Christopher, Warren. *In the Stream of History.* Stanford, CA: Stanford University Press, 1998.

Clinton, Bill. *My Life.* New York: Alfred A. Knopf, 2004.

Daalder, Ivo H., and Michael E. O'Hanlon. *Winning Ugly: NATO's War to Save Kosovo.* Washington, DC: Brookings, 2000.

Hayland, William G. *Clinton's World: Remaking American Foreign Policy.* Westport, CT: Praeger, 1999.

Holbrooke, Richard C. *To End a War: From Sarajevo to Dayton and Beyond.* New York: Random House, 1998.

Lieber, Robert J., ed. *Eagle Adrift: American Foreign Policy at the End of the Century.* New York: Longman, 1997.

Lippman, Thomas W. *Madeleine Albright and the New American Diplomacy.* Boulder, CO: Westview, 2000.

Mandelbaum, Michael. "Foreign Policy as Social Work," *Foreign Affairs,* 75/1 (1996): 16–32.

Stephen Schlesinger, "The End of Idealism," *World Politics Journal,* 24/4 (1998/99): 36–40.

George Walker Bush (2001–)

Early Life and Political Career

George Walker Bush was born in 1946 in New Haven, Connecticut, but his formative years were spent in Midland, Texas. His father, George Herbert Walker Bush, who in 1988 became the forty-first president of the United States, left for the Southwest after finishing at Yale University and eventually settled in Midland to start his own oil company, Zapata Oil. In the ensuing ten years in Midland, George W. Bush led the life of an average American kid in a small-sized city. Bush imbibed the strong Bush-Walker family values, the hard-working and risk-taking business values of the oil town, and the small town characteristics of semi-rural Texas.

When his family moved to Houston and soon thereafter sent Bush to private school in Andover, Massachusetts, a sense of belonging and certainty about those 1950s small "c" conservative values grew strong in Bush's life. At the Phillips Academy and at Yale University, Bush clung to his Texas identity. He never wavered on conservative values; as a result did not connect with the counterculture of the 1960s and avoided public debates about Vietnam or social issues. Instead, he socialized and partied, becoming a famous cheerleader at Phillips Academy and fraternity president at Yale.

In addition to his low-key conservatism, Bush early on showed another key feature: people skills. Like many born politicos, he had a capacity to relate to all kinds of people. With coaching from his father, who began his political career in Houston after Bush's grandfather, Prescott Bush, stepped down from the U.S. Senate, Bush learned to remember people, their names, and a few key facts about them. But, unlike his father, he had a charismatic and jovial bond with people, was unusually at ease with himself, and extraordinarily confident and extroverted.

Bush's genuine connection with people was matched by his keen interest in political campaigns. He began working in his father's campaigns for the U.S. House and Senate but also worked in other races in Florida and Alabama. By the time Bush ran for the White House in 1999, he had worked in at least eleven elections from the lowest positions on the team to de facto cochair in the presidential campaign of 1988 with the famous Lee Atwater.

After his graduation from Yale, Bush kept one eye on the political landscape even though he did not start a successful political career until 1994. Several commentators have called

George Walker Bush was the architect of the most radical changes to U.S. foreign policy since Truman. (White House)

the late 1960s and early 1970s Bush's nomadic years. He flew fighter jets or trained for the Texas Air National Guard on the weekends and held several short-term jobs, but nothing seemed to set him on a definite course. It was not until Bush's admission to Harvard Business School that a sense of direction emerged. Upon graduation, he set out for Midland to look for oil as his father had done some twenty years earlier. But even then he made an unsuccessful run for the U.S. House in 1978, revealing an enduring attraction to political office. Bush spent nearly ten years in the oil exploration business. Although he was an excellent salesman and attracted many investors, his various companies never hit a "gusher."

Bush married Laura Welch, a Midland girl, in 1977, and they had twin girls in 1981. At the start of his oil career, OPEC (Organization of the Petroleum Exporting

Countries) had driven up the prices of crude to unprecedented levels, but in the mid-1980s oil prices fell steeply. The stress of business, the demands of his new family, and the tension generated by his bouts of social drinking were factors in Bush's religious awakening in the mid 1980s. While he never explained his turn as a born again experience, Bush did stop drinking, began reading the scriptures daily, and attended a Christian Bible fellowship. The old faith values of his youth became personal. From then on, Bush's 1950s beliefs were grounded in a conservative Christian affirmation of these values. Still, he never became a conventional evangelical player in American politics; rather, he developed a unique blend of equal rights for faith, whose key purpose was to get people of faith accepted as equals in the making of American public policy. This new blend would form the background to his so-called "compassionate conservatism."

Bush's investment of nearly all his money in the Texas Rangers baseball team in 1989 was arguably even riskier than his investments in oil. The team had been losing for some twenty years. But the team's good fortune, aided by Bush's public relations and managerial skills, turned around his business career and gave him the platform from which to launch his bid for political office. When his father retired after a loss to Bill Clinton in the presidential election of 1992, Bush gathered all his political campaign experience and secured the services of Karl Rove, an ambitious political consultant brought to work for the Republican National Committee in Washington by Lee Atwater, to challenge the popular Democratic governor of Texas, Ann Richards.

The 1994 race against Richards prefigured features of Bush's subsequent political career. He was badly underestimated yet turned low expectations to his advantage by following two tactics that paid off handsomely. First, he developed a handful of big public policy issues, such as education and tort reform, and campaigned consistently on them, defining them in terms of values. Second, Bush stayed "on message" with an extraordinary amount of personal discipline that ultimately led to victory.

The majority of observers were surprised again when Bush settled into the governor's mansion with a smooth and effective managerial style. Bush stayed focused on the campaign themes and devoted time to charming his main legislative opponent, Lieutenant-Governor Bob Bullock, into a cooperative and eventually a shared agenda. Bush gained a reputation as an effective governor. Achieving both education and juvenile justice reforms, he gained approval in both conservative and moderate wings of the Texas Republican Party. His social conservatism and his outreach to Latino voters produced inroads into a traditionally Democratic electoral constituency. Bush was reelected with a huge majority in 1998 and was considered by many an early favorite in the 2000 race for the White House. The 2000 presidential contest against Democratic nominee Vice President Albert Gore Jr. ended in a statistical dead heat and was finally won by Bush through the Electoral College vote, only after the U.S. Supreme Court intervened to stop all recounts in the tightly contested state of Florida.

Presidential Blueprint

Bush came to Washington in 2001 with a plan of three main components: values, strategy, and loyalty. From this blueprint, Bush completed one of the fastest presidential transitions in modern times, even though the actual time frame had been cut in half by the Florida electoral dispute. The blueprint stressed a domestic agenda with little room for foreign policy and dominated the White House until the terrorist attacks of September 11, 2001. Thereafter, the War on Terror flipped Bush's agenda upside down.

For Bush, all public policy was defined in terms of values. These were school reform, faith-based and community-based welfare reform, tax cuts, and military transformation. Bush's values were more than what Lee Atwater called "wedge issues"—broad ideas that separated Democrats from Republicans—and were meant to launch public policy programs in a radically different way than conventional liberal or big government programs in an overall domestic plan called Compassionate Conservatism. The strategy was to achieve traditionally liberal goals such as education and helping the destitute through conservative means, with equal opportunity for institutions of faith. This was to be accomplished without increasing the size of the federal government and incorporating more opportunity for individuals to control programs such as prescription drugs and Social Security. It was Bush's feeling that giving individuals greater responsibility, including more ownership in such areas as prescription drug programs and Social Security, would leave people better off. The third leg of the blueprint was that of loyalty to his system of decision making. The bar of loyalty was set unusually high in the Bush White House. Given the leak-prone and decentralized nature of American government, Bush concluded that only the tightest form of teamwork would give him a chance to set the agenda.

Equipped with confident values, a political strategy, and a loyal team of advisors, the Bush administration hit the ground running in January 2001. Tax cuts—including the elimination of the "marriage penalty" and doubling the child tax credit—already enjoyed support among a strong minority of conservative Democrats in the Senate. Bush's legislative strategy was based on speed and overwhelming momentum, so that the president who many thought had only a skimpy mandate bulldozed tax cuts larger than Reagan's through the Congress and did it twice as fast. Bush gained respect and a reputation as a capable president, succeeding against the low expectations of the "accidental candidate" who had come "ambling into history."

Given the challenge of getting legislation passed in Washington's system of checks and balances plagued by frequent bouts of gridlock, Bush's presidential blueprint served him remarkably well. Moreover, Bush stuck to his plan on key values and pushed through a variety of executive orders that effectively directed over $10 billion in funds to various faith-based and community initiatives. There was a cost to Bush's strategy, as it included no rationale for a single presidential veto with the result that more spending and overspending took place than Bush had planned or could afford for long. This weakened Bush's defense of his compassionate conservative agenda and complicated his legislative plans to reform Social Security early in his second term.

Foreign Policy Before September 11, 2001

The most important feature of Bush's foreign policy before September 11, 2001 was that it played second fiddle to the domestic agenda. Of all the administration's initiatives, only two were in foreign policy and were best described as security policies: building missile defense capability and transforming the military. Bush chose Donald Rumsfeld as his secretary of defense to oversee military reform at the Pentagon. The idea was to cut large Cold War-type weapons programs, such as the Crusader artillery system and the Comanche helicopter project, and to redirect the funding to leaner fighting forces. Bush wanted to shake a status quo mindset in the military that had largely been unchallenged in the 1990s. He sought reform both in strategy and capabilities. The administration also raised the threat assessment posed by hostile rogue states such as North Korea and weapons of mass destruction.

Military transformation created enormous bureaucratic and budgetary fights in the Pentagon and in Congress, but the fact that it was a value for Bush was evident from his speeches. In an early key address on national security at Charleston, South Carolina, in September 1999, he called "a strong, capable, and modern military," the "foundation of our peace." Swiftness, information, and stealth were the goals for transformed military power. The best way to keep the peace, Bush noted, was to redefine war on American terms.

While military transformation was largely a domestic fight, creating a capability to intercept missiles from North Korea or Iran included a crucial diplomatic component. In his inaugural address, Bush promised to build "defenses beyond challenge." As Rumsfeld and Deputy Secretary of Defense Paul Wolfowitz lobbied Congress to nearly double the funding for missile defense research and development, the administration had to find a way out of the Anti-Ballistic Missile Treaty signed with the Soviet Union by the Nixon administration in the 1970s that prohibited the United States from developing almost all forms of missile defense. Bush proceeded with a carefully constructed plan to charm Russian President Vladimir Putin into either fundamental revisions of the ABM treaty or its outright abrogation. Condoleezza Rice, Bush's national security advisor

and senior Russian specialist, made several special trips to Moscow to move the process along. When Bush praised Putin at their first meeting in Slovenia in June 2001, Western reporters criticized the new president for his naiveté. How could he look Putin in the eye and simply declare that he could trust him? But Bush had a reason to handle Putin with silk gloves. The Russian-American relationship Bush envisioned was one akin to the Anglo-French friendship in that both had nuclear weapons but posed no threat to each other. The White House simultaneously put pressure on Putin by asking Congress for the funding to build a "test-bed facility" for missile defense. There were also incentives. Both parties were willing to reduce their active nuclear weapon stockpiles to levels far below the most recent arms control agreement, and, when Putin insisted the deal be put into treaty form, Bush consented and signed the Moscow Treaty in May 2002. Putin resisted as long as he could but after the attacks of September 11, 2001, realized that whatever congressional hesitation remained about building missile defenses had evaporated. Putin agreed to react very mildly to Bush's announcement in December 2001, to abrogate the ABM treaty, calling it merely a "mistake."

The rest of Bush's early foreign policy was more complex than many appreciated at first. Bush developed a foreign policy vision during the 2000 campaign and worked a set of values into his vision for America in the world. He rejected the two dominant ways of looking at the world and how American foreign policy should fit in. He was not a traditional realist looking at the balances of interests among states and maneuvering U.S. foreign policy through a narrow channel of relative gains sought in the short-run; he was also not an international institutionalist, seeking new collaboration through regional or global organizations by means of global treaties as many European states had become. Bush's vision, that of sovereign states engaging in limited partnerships to achieve specific values, was both more traditional and more idealistic than either of these.

Bush's approach was not captured by the terms unilateral or multilateral and certainly not by the easy label "imperial." Bush was not a doctrinaire unilateralist. Speaking at the Reagan Library in November 1999, Bush said, "Let us reject the blinders of isolationism, just as we refuse the crown of empire." In fact, for Bush these are all "process words," which do not get to the core of things. Bush was best described as "mission-lateral" and "task-oriented."

The key for allies of the United States was whether they could have a real say in the mission and how it should be conducted. This became a point of major contention for President Jacques Chirac of France and Chancellor Gerhard Schroeder of Germany. Their complaint was that Bush's value missions essentially meant that he told them what to do and they had to follow. But that is not how it ultimately worked with British Prime Minister Tony Blair and the war in Iraq. Blair had real influence on the mission and the implementation of the policy. To explain this it is necessary to add a key piece of Bush's blueprint which he also used in foreign policy: loyalty. Loyalty among leaders meant complete frankness in private but no criticism in public. Blair appreciated this distinction, but Schroeder and Chirac did not. Leaving aside whether this was a weakness or strength on Bush's part, when he tried to include them as partners they felt slighted by the terms of Bush's inclusion.

Having a value-based and unified vision of international affairs meant that Bush had strong views about the major international problems he inherited. But his domestic priorities and tightly set agenda precluded concrete policies and implementation plans beyond missile defense. What emerged was an administration that knew what it did *not* want in foreign policy, yet was not ready to offer alternatives. Early assessments of Bush's foreign policy concluded that it looked like a "just say no" policy. Eventually, the administration got its alternatives on the table and demonstrated remarkable determination to stay on course.

South Korean President Kim Dae Jung fell victim to this when he came to Washington in early March 2001, hoping to persuade Bush to continue the Clinton administration's attempts to buy off North Korea's bad behavior on nuclear material and missiles. Bush was dead set against this type of "crime pays" policy and wanted to send the opposite signal. Bush did not stop the oil-or-food shipments going to North Korea under the terms of the Agreed Framework of 1994, but he clearly signaled that he did not trust North Korea and that inspections and verification of North Korea's nuclear activities had to be moved to the top of the agenda. The real collapse in the relationship—and the end of shipments—came when North Korea admitted in the summer of 2002 that it had been enriching uranium in complete violation of the spirit of the accords reached with Clinton.

On the Israeli-Palestinian issue there was a widespread assumption that Clinton had come so close to a settlement that Bush should try just a little bit harder to lean on Israeli and Palestinian leadership to get both parties over the last hump. Bush felt just the opposite. If after years of Clinton charm and pressure, the two still could not reach a deal, why would he continue down that path of diminishing returns? Moreover, the Israeli electorate had reacted strongly against more Israeli concessions by electing Ariel Sharon, whom Bush knew personally and respected. Putting the entire Oslo peace process logic on its head, Bush announced in 2002 that the Palestinians should first achieve responsible government that could contain suicide bombings against Israelis so that negotiations would be meaningful again. It was not a pro-Israeli policy, as some critics alleged. For the first time in history, in fact, an American president proclaimed that a real Palestinian state beside Israel would be part of the final outcome. The "Road Map" eventually became the de facto policy in 2004, as the result of the death

of Palestinian leader Yassir Arafat and the election of Mahmoud Abbas as the new Palestinian president. Not only did the Palestinian side make progress, but Sharon took the historic step of handing the entire Gaza strip back to the Palestinians.

As with North Korea and the Palestinian issues, the Clinton administration had been unable to finish the Kyoto Protocol negotiations on climate control or secure the key amendments to the International Criminal Court that the United States had demanded. Disingenuously, he signed the United States onto the Rome Statute on the last day of his administration. Democrats and Republicans knew that the Senate would never give its consent to either. "Kyoto is dead," Condoleezza Rice told European Union ambassadors at a luncheon in Washington early in 2001, "I am surprised you are surprised."

The approach came across as harsh to many leaders in Europe, South America, and Asia. Did Bush's foreign policy have to be so strident? Bush's foreign policy was usually on the back-burner and occasional bursts of attention sounded brash. It also did not help that some key advisors such as Defense Secretary Donald Rumsfeld possessed a rather brusque style, although his deputy, Paul Wolfowitz, was smooth, gentle, and persuasive. But Bush's ideas were so startlingly unconventional that they left many interlocutors rattled. The administration figured this out by May 2001. Bush's two trips to Europe that summer were attempts at making him listen to his counterparts, admitting that the time had come for dialogue. In fact, all Bush's trips to Europe were labeled sooner or later as "fence mending." But the Europeans were not as innocent as they liked to profess. Western European governments, with the help of Canada, had outsmarted the Clinton administration on a treaty banning the production and sale of antipersonnel mines. Then they outmaneuvered Washington on the International Criminal Court. They were working on a small-arms trafficking ban that again would leave the United States diplomatically isolated. And the governments were winning the diplomacy on Kyoto. Below the radar, they were pushing the Americans on the Comprehensive Nuclear Test Ban Treaty (CTBT) and on not abandoning the ABM treaty. This habit extended even to domestic policy, such as lecturing Washington on the immorality of the death penalty.

China was a different story. Speaking on values during the 2000 election campaign, Bush explained that Taiwan had become a constitutional democracy that deserved American protection. The future was not for Taiwan to be lowered by force into the category of semi-communism like the regime in Beijing. Instead, the future was for China to proceed along the trajectory of responsible and accountable government as set up in Taipei. Bush did not want to redirect the relationship with Beijing from cooperation to confrontation, but he wanted to make sure that the United States abided by respectable criteria for a positive relationship.

The collision between an American spy plane and a Chinese fighter jet in early April 2001 landed Bush his first real international crisis. In the aftermath of a harrowing emergency landing by the American plane on a Chinese island, Beijing took a hard line. Bush kept his cool and communicated the message via former Secretary of State Henry Kissinger that the crew could not be turned into hostages. They were returned unconditionally while Beijing allowed Washington to fudge a letter that featured no forthright admission of wrongdoing on the American side. It simply said that the United States was sorry that the collision had happened and that an unapproved landing on Chinese sovereign territory had taken place. Bush made no escalating demands on the aircraft, but allowed it to return much later and in crates. Significantly, the incident did not spill over into the Taiwan debate and seemed to earn Bush some respect in the eyes of the Chinese. Except for the hot spot in North Korea, the early trend for Bush's foreign policy in Asia was as positive as it was negative in Western Europe. By the end of Bush's first term, relations with both India and Pakistan had improved, a close alliance with Japan was renewed, and a respectful understanding with China preserved.

After September 11, 2001

The al Qaeda attacks on New York and Washington of September 11, 2001 did not change Bush's values, sense of political strategy, or his foreign policy vision, but it *did* change the agenda radically. Security and foreign policy now dominated policy with an extraordinary urgency. Before the attacks, Bush had not bothered "selling" his foreign policy, as he was preoccupied with domestic changes. But again, the administration did not take much time and effort to explain the big picture of what it was trying to do, with the difference that now it was too intense and high strung about getting it done.

In a very charged atmosphere after September 11, Bush made a series of decisions that set the direction for his War on Terror policy. During Operation Enduring Freedom, the invasion of Afghanistan to oust the Taliban regime in late 2001 and early 2002, Bush and his inner circle continued a fundamental revamp of the threat assessment, American objectives, and strategy. It was an atmosphere in which many expected further al Qaeda attacks. The nation was nervous about a string of anthrax letters killing people in different cities, and Bush had serious intelligence about the possibility of a "dirty" nuclear bomb being detonated in a major American city. Troops in the Afghan city of Kandahar found the blueprints and videos of al Qaeda trying to learn how to obtain or make weapons of mass destruction. Osama bin Laden instructed his followers that it was their sacred duty to use such weapons against the United States.

In the summer of 2002, as the administration was working out its regime change policy in Iraq, it added further

elements, including the ambitious design of reforming the entire Middle East. The centerpiece for this policy became the Anglo-American invasion of Iraq to topple the regime of Saddam Hussein. Operation Iraqi Freedom began on March 19, 2003, and proceeded until the fall of Baghdad on April 9. Again, in the fall of 2003, as Bush was besieged by a battering insurgency in Iraq, the White House refined and sharpened some of its ideas, especially the notion of freedom as the vaccine against terror and the need for a "soft power" component to help the region transform. What followed was a set of controversial and risky policies. Yet behind the risk was more strategy and more vision than people at first realized.

Bush and Secretary Rumsfeld had changed the threat assessment in the Quadrennial Defense Review in early 2001 from a document based on the specific *intent* of rogue states to one addressing the wider overall *capability* of such regimes. Bush now took a second look at the confluence of threats. What resulted was a very pessimistic and maximalist threat scenario. The new threat assessment combined the most hostile rogue states (Iraq being the only state that celebrated the terrorist acts of September 11), with the most devastating means (the use of weapons of mass destruction), and the most hostile actors (al Qaeda and like-minded groups topping the list). Given the capabilities that a combination of the three could muster, the United States had to be both preemptive and prepared to lower the burden of proof before acting in self-defense.

The maximum threat setting of the late fall of 2001 is a crucial backdrop to the changes that have since followed. Bush challenged the existing ideas about national security, imminent threat, war, and preventative war. Bush declared *war* on terror so as to open all avenues of action, giving the maximum flexibility the administration sought. Critics concluded that Bush was ignoring the root causes of terror and storming off quixotically all directions to battle the windmills of terror. He actually did the opposite and went to the root cause without saying so. He wiped out the conventional ideas of faceless and stateless terror. He imposed a strong face on the terrorists, identifying them as a branch of Islamic militants who took the religion of Islam out of context in order to further their narrow political aims. Al Qaeda and affiliates, Bush said, stand for a new type of armed totalitarian ideology that aims to win the hearts and minds of people in the region, seeks to capture a major religion, and ultimately wants to control the states of the Middle East. He later called this armed ideology or pseudoreligious tyranny, the heir to fascism and communism. Bush also declared war on the havens of terror, going after both the "rattlers and the ranchers," as he put it. It was the ranchers who could allow the terrorists to gather people or weapon ingredients, stay hidden, and thus avoid a return address.

The root cause of al Qaeda's brand of terrorism for Bush was not American foreign policy in Saudi Arabia or toward

Israel but more profoundly the prevalence of political repression and lack of economic opportunity in the Middle East. Thus, Bush set a new and ambitious goal for his overall policy: freedom and democracy for the entire Middle Eastern region. In setting the new goal, Bush rejected both an isolationist turn for American foreign policy and the status quo. Rather than waging a narrow war against certain terrorist groups and leaving the region otherwise to its own fortunes, Bush chose the riskiest option, believing that the right values of individual freedom and economic opportunity would bear him out in the long run. No doubt Bush was inspired by Ronald Reagan's hard stance against the "evil empire" in the early 1980s, which became a catalyst for political change in the Soviet Union and Eastern Europe. He did so by rejecting the status quo. Likewise, Bush had to inspire and empower Arab democrats.

There is a direct relationship between Bush slowly moving toward this enormously ambitious goal in his presidency after 9/11 and his domestic politics before the terrorist attacks. Compassionate conservatism was not about tinkering a bit with existing ideas about how to improve schools or deliver welfare. It was revolutionary in its dismissal of the status quo. The Western approach toward Arabs and Muslims, as defended by realists, would let them remain undemocratic and continue the soft bigotry of low expectations. By making the cause entirely political, Bush, the "faith president," embraced Islam and democracy at the same time and confounded the critics who feared he was embarking on a clash of civilizations. This led to a four-prong policy. The first prong was homeland defense. The Patriot Act brought together various aspects of intelligence and crime prosecution that previously had hitherto been "stovepiped," and it nearly wiped away the fine line between foreign and domestic operations. It removed legal prohibitions that had precedent in the fight against the Mafia and the "War on Drugs." The Department of Homeland Security, at first opposed by Bush because it would create a bigger government, was the symbol of the second leg of the first prong. This new department was to coordinate the efforts of all agencies involved in protecting the air, land, and sea approach of people coming to the United States and the combined tasks of preventing and responding to terrorist threats at home. The 9/11 Commission Report called for the reorganization of all the intelligence agencies reporting to a new director of national intelligence.

The second prong of Bush's new security policy was an international network of overt and covert intelligence operations against al Qaeda and like-minded groups. This was to be a multinational and ongoing series of intelligence, crime, and financial operations to capture al Qaeda operatives and prevent future attacks. Upward of sixty countries were to work with U.S. authorities on a variety of operations. Contrary to popular thought, the war in Iraq in 2003 did not halt this second prong. In fact, that same year, the

United States, in close cooperation with France, Germany, and Britain, set up the Proliferation Security Initiative that focused on intercepting weapons or weapon materials on the high seas destined for hostile rogues.

No doubt the riskiest and most controversial prong of Bush's policy was the invasion of Iraq. The Bush team concluded that the United States had to create an offensive front and that it should be in the heart of the cauldron, the Middle East—in effect, kicking in the door so the regimes in the entire region would accept that Washington meant business and adjust their own expectations and approach. Iraq was the ideal offensive front. It fostered enough anti-Western hostility to risk participation in the terrorist agenda, it had a track record in weapons of mass destruction, a recent history of territorial aggression, and it was diplomatically isolated. Saddam Hussein was the "rancher" to be removed. Regime change was the policy set by Bush in early February 2002. Bush was not doctrinaire about the method by which this could be realized. If real diplomatic pressure or covert intelligence operations could topple the regime and create a new government that would cooperate in the fight against terror and the removal of weapons of mass destruction, he would have welcomed it. There is no evidence that he or British Prime Minister Tony Blair were misleading about Iraq's possession of weapons of mass destruction. They simply accepted the 1998 report card by the last United Nations inspectors and the general consensus among Western intelligence agencies in the late 1990s that Hussein had chemical weapon stockpiles, was working on biological weapons, and wanted to have nuclear weapons. Tiny bits of intelligence confirming these suspicions seemed to be more than enough. In light of Hussein's record of serial aggression, Bush and Blair assumed the worst concerning his future intentions.

Toward the end of the buildup of diplomatic and military pressure against Saddam Hussein in late 2002, this story got more complicated. In early 2002, Blair insisted that the regime change decision had to be articulated in public foremost as a campaign against weapons of mass destruction. He needed that to keep his own Labour Party on board and to persuade the British public. Secretary of State Colin Powell's success in the summer of 2002 at persuading Bush to channel the endgame into a UN-led coercive diplomacy campaign further narrowed Bush's options. Now the public face of Bush's original decision to change the regime in Baghdad had to meet two tests: it had to be sufficient in terms of weapons of mass destruction, and it had to be sufficient inside the terms of UN Security Council Resolution 1441, passed on November 8, 2002.

In strict legal terms, Bush and Powell did not do badly concerning Resolution 1441. They built in two triggers to rule Saddam Hussein in violation of the measure and thus in material breach: failure to provide a complete disclosure and failure to provide unfettered access to the team led by

UN inspector Hans Blix. By mid-January 2003, Saddam had tripped both triggers. At the same time, the gap between the old assumption about Saddam's weapons of mass destruction and the minuscule findings of Blix turned the entire public relations blitz back on Blair and Bush. Why, critics asked, would we go with the narrow terms of 1441 if Saddam apparently no longer has weapons of mass destruction? And if he did not, the whole regime change decision unraveled. Bush and Blair resorted to bolstering their WMD argument and retreating to the narrow legal terms of 1441 as well as the pre-1441 arguments about how evil the regime of Saddam really was.

The Anglo-American invasion of Iraq, launched March 19, 2003, was executed in brilliant fashion. Rumsfeld managed to speed up his military transformation process during both the Afghanistan and Iraqi operations. Still, the diplomatic contention going into the final push for regime change created an atmosphere in which Bush and Blair were isolated in the insurgency war that followed. The aftermath of the campaign became a bloody battle with American casualties going far beyond what had been expected. Now American authorities were in a race to set up Iraqi governing structures while a potent mix of old Ba'athists, new Jihadist and stockpiles of conventional munitions literally blew away most opportunities to show progress.

The least understood prong of Bush's policy was the carrot to the whole enterprise of changing the Middle East. The first ideas of soft power showed up in the administration's Middle East Partnership Initiative in 2002. The plan was to fund teacher education programs, strengthen a free media sector, set up regional banks to provide loans for small businessmen, and help local nongovernmental organizations educate the public about elections and how to organize for them. In the Greater Middle East Initiative, which was leaked in 2003, Bush wanted to set aside some $1 billion for these civil society, democracy, and economic development projects. The plan was to launch the idea in the G-7 meetings and to get the other G-7 partners to add another billion dollars. The very negative reaction of Egypt and Saudi Arabia to the idea of nurturing democracy inside their borders clipped European enthusiasm for the project and forced the Americans to scale back. Watering down the plans in the G-7, however, did not mean backing off. In the fall of 2003, Bush intensified his drive for accountable government and economic opportunity in the Middle East. By 2005, the administration had spent nearly $300 million on these civil-society building projects, some with governments, others with the private sector or NGOs. After Bush's election victory in 2004, freedom in the Middle East became the central plank of his second-term foreign policy.

Legacy

The severity of the 9/11 attacks and urgency of a response would have caused serious changes by any president,

Republican or Democrat. However, the centrality of Bush's value approach and his personal propensity to take risks led to a revolution in American foreign policy. The United States went from what Henry Kissinger termed a status quo great power in the 1990s to a revolutionary great power in the first four years of the new century. The debate over how costly or beneficial this sudden change has been will go on for a long time. It is also too early to speculate whether Bush will continue in a revolutionary mode in his second term or if he will shift to a more reconciliatory posture. Reagan called the Soviet Union the "evil empire" in the early 1980s—just as Bush referred to Iraq, Iran, and North Korea as an "axis of evil" in his State of the Union address of January 29, 2002—and overthrew détente as practiced by Nixon and Carter. Despite pleas from Western Europe to be more realistic, Reagan insisted on demanding change in both the USSR and Eastern Europe. It was Mikhail Gorbachev who engaged Reagan on substantive change. As a result, Reagan's tone softened in his second term. The elimination of short-range nuclear weapons in Europe, and the beginning of political reform that turned into a tide of democracy, vindicated Reagan's controversial push for freedom. Bush, surely, was inspired by this example.

Bush's version of American internationalism, as he announced it in his speech at the Reagan Library in November 1999, was "idealism without illusions," or "realism in the service of American ideals." It is possible that his rejection of the conventional multilateralist world order as pursued by Western Europe in the 1990s in the form of Kyoto, the ICC, and various efforts at nonproliferation will lead to some form of new compromise between the two. The idea of "effective multilateralism" broached by Bush and adopted by the European Union's strategy document may be the beginning. The NATO alliance has been squeezed hard by the fallout of disagreement over Iraq. For Washington, the key issues are military transformation, the inclusion of Eastern Europe, the adaptation of the old Atlantic area to a global arena. For Europe, NATO has been an incubator for the European Security and Defense Policy.

Most likely, Bush's foreign policy will be made or unmade in the Middle East. The prolonged and devastating insurgency in Iraq made Bush very vulnerable in the 2004 presidential election. More so than Bush's reelection, the January 2005 elections in Iraq provided the most important signal that Bush might after all reach the goal he set out in 2002. Iraqi voters could have stayed home and signaled that they did not have any faith in the direction of Iraq as set by the Americans. But a turnout rate of some 60 percent of eligible voters, at the risk of life and limb, demonstrated that Iraqis wanted a new direction and were open to the path of representative government.

Meanwhile, the Palestinians had also conducted a respectful election and chosen as leader a man Bush had signaled as early as 2002 as someone he could work with.

Against all expectations, Afghanistan held a peaceful national election. Saudi Arabia took some baby steps toward municipal elections. President Hosni Mubarak agreed to modify the constitution to allow more open contest in Egypt. When Syrian intelligence operatives were suspected of killing a Lebanese former prime minister, Bush, in close cooperation with French President Jacques Chirac, put maximum pressure on Syria to remove its troops and agents from Lebanon, creating expectations that Lebanon may be the next nation in the region to inch closer to democratic freedom. All in all, Bush's language on freedom, dismissed as recently as his 2005 inaugural, began to gather some respect. Even vested critics of Bush began to flirt with the heresy that Bush's soaring rhetoric about ending tyranny in the Middle East might just be what the area needed. As in Eastern Europe, it will ultimately be Middle Eastern democrats who can take the catalyst offered by Bush and bring about political and economic reforms in the region. The hurdles they face are enormous.

Alexander Moens

Chronology

2001

February 6: Likud-led coalition elected in Israel, Ariel Sharon is prime minister.

February 16: United States and British aircraft strike Iraqi air defense installations.

February 18: FBI agent Robert Hanssen arrested for spying for the Soviet Union and Russia.

April 1–3: Mid-air collision between U.S. and Chinese aircraft over Hainan brings diplomatic crisis.

April 20–22: Leaders of western hemisphere nations discuss a Free Trade Area of the Americas (FTAA).

June 7: British Prime Minister Tony Blair reelected.

August 25–September 4: U.S. and British aircraft strike Iraqi air defenses.

September 11: Terrorist attacks in New York and Washington kill more than 3,500 people.

September 12: President Bush calls terrorist attacks "act of war"; NATO invokes Article V of North Atlantic Treaty.

September 20: British Prime Minister Blair pledges British support to joint session of Congress.

September 22: United States lifts sanctions against India.

September 26: U.S. embassy in Afghanistan stormed and burned.

October 7–18: U.S. and British air and missile strikes target Taliban regime and al Qaeda terrorists in Afghanistan.

October 19–20: U.S. troops conduct raids in Afghanistan.

November 1–13: Anglo-American and Northern Alliance forces advance to and capture Kabul, Afghanistan.

November 27–December 22: In Bonn, Germany, Afghan factions discuss a provisional post-Taliban government.

December 12: Bush announces that United States will abrogate the 1972 ABM Treaty.

2002

January 28: Afghan leader Hamid Karzai meets with President Bush in Washington.

February 20–21: Israeli forces conduct strikes terrorist bases in the West Bank and Gaza Strip.

March 2: U.S. and Afghan forces begin mop-up operations against Taliban and al Qaeda.

March 11–15: Twenty thousand Israeli troops sweep West Bank and Gaza.

March 29: Israeli forces enter Ramallah and surround headquarters of Yasser Arafat.

April 4: All large towns under Palestinian Authority, except Jericho, reoccupied by Israel.

April 8: Iraq announces halt to oil exports to protest Israeli operations.

May 5: President Jacques Chirac reelected in France.

May 6: United States announces that it will not cooperate with the International Criminal Court.

May 24: Bush and Russian Prime Minister Vladimir Putin sign the Treaty of Moscow.

June 1: Bush unveils preemptive strategic doctrine in West Point graduation speech.

June 14: U.S. and British aircraft strike Iraqi air defenses.

June 24: Bush calls for new Palestinian leadership, issues "road map" for Middle East peace.

August 25–26: U.S. aircraft strike Iraqi radar sites.

September 3: Blair announces Britain ready to join U.S. attack on Iraq.

September 10: Blair declares UN diplomacy vital.

September 12: Bush tells UN that Security Council resolutions will be enforced.

September 16: Iraq agrees to weapons inspections.

September 17: United States issues 2002 National Security Strategy of the United States.

October 10–11: Congress approves military force to disarm Iraq.

October 22: Bush declares regime change in Iraq "the states policy of our government."

November 8: UN Security Council approves Resolution 1441, calling on Iraq to disarm.

November 21: NATO invites Bulgaria, Estonia, Latvia, Lithuania, Romania, Slovakia, and Slovenia to join.

November 25: Bush signs legislation creating the Department of Homeland Security.

December 10: EU invites ten East European states to join.

2003

January 9: UN Iraq weapons inspections return mixed results.

January 21: United States warns Iraq that "time is running out."

January 28: Britain declares Iraq in material breach of UNSCR 1441.

January 29: Seven European states support US on Iraq.

February 5: Secretary of State Powell presents Iraq WMD evidence to UN.

February 10: France, Germany, and Russia issue joint declaration for continued weapons inspections.

February 17: EU calls on Iraq to disarm; France, Germany, and Russia refuse support for military action.

February 18: Canada rejects military action without UN support.

March 1: Iraq begins destroying 120 *al Samoud* missiles.

March 7: Weapons inspections reveal no revival of Iraqi nuclear program.

March 18: Australia pledges forces for Iraq war.

March 19: U.S. aircraft and missiles strike Baghdad.

March 20: Major air strikes begin; coalition grounds forces begin invasion of Iraq.

April 4: U.S. forces capture Saddam International Airport.

April 9: U.S. forces control Baghdad; British forces occupy Najaf.

April 11: Iraqi forces in North surrender; U.S. and Kurdish forces capture Mosul and Kirkuk.

May 22: UN lifts sanctions on Iraq.

May 23: United States and Japan warn North Korea against nuclear weapons development.

May 25: Israel backs U.S. Middle East "road map."

June 4: Bush meets Israeli and Palestinian leaders in Jordan.

June 18: United States presses Iran over nuclear weapons program.

July 17: In Britain, former weapons inspector David Kelly commits suicide.

July 21: Bush cites Iran and Syria for assisting terrorism.

July 22: Uday and Qusay Hussein killed by U.S. forces.

August 1: Hutton Inquiry into Kelly suicide begins.

August 7: Sporadic attacks on U.S. troops continue.

October 2: U.S.-led weapons inspections find no WMD in Iraq.

December 14: U.S. forces capture Saddam Hussein.

December 19: Libya pledges to scrap its WMD programs.

2004

January 19: One hundred thousand Iraqis demonstrate in support of Ayatollah Ali al-Sistani.

January 28: Hutton Inquiry Report clears Blair government of wrongdoing in Kelly suicide.

February 29–March 3: Rebels oust Aristide government in Haiti; U.S. and French troops intervene.

March 2: Terror bombs target Shiites in Baghdad and Kerbala.

March 11: Bomb attacks on commuter trains in Spain kill 191 people.

March 14: Socialist leader Jose Zapatero elected prime minister of Spain, pledges to withdraw Spanish troops from Iraq.

April 4–12: Bombings and insurgency on the rise in Iraq.

April 14: Bush endorses Israel's claim to part of the West Bank, rejects Palestinian "right of return."

April 19: U.S. forces surround insurgents in Falluja and Najaf.

April 29: U.S. soldiers accused of abusing Iraqi prisoners in Abu Ghraib prison.

May 22: Fahrenheit 9/11, a film critical of Bush Iraq policy, wins Palme d'Or at Cannes.

October 9: Afghanistan holds first democratic election.

November 3: Bush wins reelection with 51.6 percent of the vote.

References and Further Reading

Daalder, Ivo H., and James M. Lindsay. *America Unbound: The Bush Revolution in Foreign Policy.* Washington, DC: Brookings, 2003.

Ferguson, Niall. *Colossus: The Price of America's Empire.* New York: Penguin, 2004.

Gaddis, John Lewis. *Surprise, Security and the American Experience.* Cambridge, MA: Harvard University Press, 2004.

Keegan, John. *The Iraq War.* New York: Knopf, 2004.

Moens, Alexander. *The Foreign Policy of George W. Bush: Values, Strategy, Loyalty.* Aldershot, Hampshire: Ashgate, 2004.

Woodward, Bob. *Bush at War.* New York: Simon and Schuster, 2002.

Primary Source Documents

1. George Washington's Farewell Address, September 19, 1796

The first president's retirement from public life occasioned a speech, written mostly by Alexander Hamilton, in which he spoke of both the corrosive influence of factionalism in domestic affairs and of the appropriate posture for the young republic in international affairs. The injunction against permanent alliances in the excerpt below is considered by many to be the first article in the "isolationist" tradition of American foreign policy, a valid point if considered from the perspective of Washington's devout wish that the United States remain aloof of European power politics.

Observe good faith and justice toward all nations. Cultivate peace and harmony with all. Religion and morality enjoin this conduct. And can it be that good policy does not equally enjoin it? It will be worthy of a free, enlightened, and at no distant period a great nation to give to mankind the magnanimous and too novel example of a people always guided by an exalted justice and benevolence. Who can doubt that in the course of time and things the fruits of such a plan would richly repay any temporary advantages which might be lost by a steady adherence to it? Can it be that Providence has not connected the permanent felicity of a nation with its virtue? The experiment, at least, is recommended by every sentiment which ennobles human nature. Alas! is it rendered impossible by its vices?

In the execution of such a plan nothing is more essential than that permanent, inveterate antipathies against particular nations and passionate attachments for others should be excluded, and that in place of them just and amicable feelings toward all should be cultivated. The nation which indulges toward another an habitual hatred or an habitual fondness is in some degree a slave. It is a slave to its animosity or to its affection, either of which is sufficient to lead it astray from its duty and its interest. Antipathy in one nation against another disposes each more readily to offer insult and injury, to lay hold of slight causes of umbrage, and to be haughty and intractable when accidental or trifling occasions of dispute occur. . . .

So, likewise, a passionate attachment of one nation for another produces a variety of evils. Sympathy for the favorite nation, facilitating the illusion of an imaginary common interest in cases where no real common interest exists, and infusing into one the enmities of the other, betrays the former into a participation in the quarrels and wars of the latter without adequate inducement or justification. It leads also to concessions to the favorite nation of privileges denied to others, which is apt doubly to injure the nation making the concessions by unnecessarily parting with what ought to have been retained, and by exciting jealousy, ill will, and a disposition to retaliate in the parties from whom equal privileges are withheld; and it gives to ambitious, corrupted, or deluded citizens (who devote themselves to the favorite nation) facility to betray or sacrifice the interests of their own country without odium, sometimes even with popularity, gilding with the appearances of a virtuous sense of obligation, a commendable deference for public opinion, or a laudable zeal for public good the base or foolish compliances of ambition, corruption, or infatuation. . . .

Against the insidious wiles of foreign influence (I conjure you to believe me, fellow-citizens) the jealousy of a free people ought to be constantly awake, since history and experience prove that foreign influence is one of the most baneful foes of republican government. But that jealousy, to be useful, must be impartial, else it becomes the instrument of the very influence to be avoided, instead of a defense against it. Excessive partiality for one foreign nation and excessive dislike of another cause those whom they actuate to see danger only on one side, and serve to veil and even second the arts of influence on the other. Real patriots who may resist the intrigues of the favorite are liable to become suspected and odious, while its tools and dupes usurp the applause and confidence of the people to surrender their interests.

All primary source documents are excerpted from their original sources and no not necessarily reflect the original documents in their entirety.

The great rule of conduct for us in regard to foreign nations is, in extending our commercial relations to have with them as little political connection as possible. So far as we have already formed engagements let them be fulfilled with perfect good faith. Here let us stop. Europe has a set of primary interests which to us have none or a very remote relation. Hence she must be engaged in frequent controversies, the causes of which are essentially foreign to our concerns. Hence, therefore, it must be unwise in us to implicate ourselves by artificial ties in the ordinary vicissitudes of her politics or the ordinary combinations and collisions of her friendships or enmities.

Our detached and distant situation invites and enables us to pursue a different course. If we remain one people, under an efficient government, the period is not far off when we may defy material injury from external annoyance; when we may take such an attitude as will cause the neutrality we may at any time resolve upon to be scrupulously respected; when belligerent nations, under the impossibility of making acquisitions upon us, will not lightly hazard the giving us provocation; when we may choose peace or war, as our interest, guided by justice, shall counsel.

Why forego the advantages of so peculiar a situation? Why quit our own to stand upon foreign ground? Why, by interweaving our destiny with that of any part of Europe, entangle our peace and prosperity in the toils of European ambition, rivalship, interest, humor, or caprice?

It is our true policy to steer clear of permanent alliances with any portion of the foreign world; so far, I mean, as we are now at liberty to do it, for let me not be understood as capable of patronizing infidelity to existing engagements. I hold the maxim no less applicable to public than to private affairs that honesty is always the best policy. I repeat, therefore, let those engagements be observed in their genuine sense. But in my opinion it is unnecessary and would be unwise to extend them.

Taking care always to keep ourselves by suitable establishments on a respectable defensive posture, we may safely trust to temporary alliances for extraordinary emergencies. . . .

2. The Monroe Doctrine, December 2, 1823

The Monroe Doctrine was articulated by President James Monroe in his seventh annual message to the United States Congress, December 2, 1823. Drafted by Secretary of State John Quincy Adams, it was occasioned by the request of British Foreign Secretary George Canning for a joint declaration opposing intervention in Spanish America by any European alliance. The British request was motivated by the threat of the Holy Alliance to restore monarchy in the newly independent Latin American republics. Ostensibly directed at Russia, Spain, and France, Adams's concern that the United States deliver a unilateral statement against any and all

European interference in the Western Hemisphere resulted in a doctrine of precocious ambition that was in principle equally directed against Britain.

At the proposal of the Russian Imperial Government, made through the minister of the Emperor residing here, a full power and instructions have been transmitted to the minister of the United States at St. Petersburg to arrange by amicable negotiation the respective rights and interests of the two nations on the northwest coast of this continent. A similar proposal has been made by His Imperial Majesty to the Government of Great Britain, which has likewise been acceded to. The Government of the United States has been desirous by this friendly proceeding of manifesting the great value which they have invariably attached to the friendship of the Emperor and their solicitude to cultivate the best understanding with his Government. In the discussions to which this interest has given rise and in the arrangements by which they may terminate the occasion has been judged proper for asserting, as a principle in which the rights and interests of the United States are involved, that the American continents, by the free and independent condition which they have assumed and maintain, are henceforth not to be considered as subjects for future colonization by any European Powers. . . .

It was stated at the commencement of the last session that a great effort was then making in Spain and Portugal to improve the condition of the people of those countries, and that it appeared to be conducted with extraordinary moderation. It need scarcely be remarked that the results have been so far very different from what was then anticipated. Of events in that quarter of the globe, with which we have so much intercourse and from which we derive our origin, we have always been anxious and interested spectators. The citizens of the United States cherish sentiments the most friendly in favor of the liberty and happiness of their fellow men on that side of the Atlantic. In the wars of the European powers in matters relating to themselves we have never taken any part, nor does it comport with our policy to do so. It is only when our rights are invaded or seriously menaced that we resent injuries or make preparation for our defense. With the movements in this hemisphere we are of necessity more immediately connected, and by causes which must be obvious to all enlightened and impartial observers. The political system of the allied powers is essentially different in this respect from that of America. This difference proceeds from that which exists in their respective Governments; and to the defense of our own, which has been achieved by the loss of so much blood and treasure, and matured by the wisdom of their most enlightened citizens, and under which we have enjoyed unexampled felicity, this whole nation is devoted. We owe it, therefore, to candor and to the amicable relations existing between the United States and those powers to declare that we should consider any attempt on their part to extend their system to any portion of this hemisphere as dangerous to our peace and safety. With the existing colonies or dependencies of any European power we have not interfered and shall not interfere. But with the Governments who have declared their independence and maintain it, and whose independence we have, on great consideration and on just principles, acknowledged, we could not view any interposition for the purpose of oppressing them, or controlling in any other manner their destiny, by any European power in any other light than as the manifestation of an unfriendly disposition toward the United States. In the war between those new Governments and Spain we declared our neutrality at the time of their recognition, and to this we have adhered, and shall continue to adhere, provided no change shall occur which, in the judgement of the competent authorities of this Government, shall make a corresponding change on the part of the United States indispensable to their security.

The late events in Spain and Portugal shew that Europe is still unsettled. Of this important fact no stronger proof can be adduced than that the allied powers should have thought it proper, on any principle satisfactory to themselves, to have interposed by force in the internal concerns of Spain. To what extent such interposition may be carried, on the same principle, is a question in which all independent powers whose governments differ from theirs are interested, even those most remote, and surely none of them more so than the United States. Our policy in regard to Europe, which was adopted at an early stage of the wars which have so long agitated that quarter of the globe, nevertheless remains the same, which is, not to interfere in the internal concerns of any of its powers; to consider the government de facto as the legitimate government for us; to cultivate friendly relations with it, and to preserve those relations by a frank, firm, and manly policy, meeting in all instances the just claims of every power, submitting to injuries from none. But in regard to those continents circumstances are eminently and conspicuously different. It is impossible that the allied powers should extend their political system to any portion of either continent without endangering our peace and happiness; nor can anyone believe that our southern brethren, if left to themselves, would adopt it of their own accord. It is equally impossible, therefore, that we should behold such interposition in any form with indifference. If we look to the comparative strength and resources of Spain and those new Governments, and their distance from each other, it must be obvious that she can never subdue them. It is still the true policy of the United States to leave the parties to themselves, in hope that other powers will pursue the same course. . . .

3. John L. O'Sullivan on Manifest Destiny, 1839 and 1845

As the founding editor of The United States Magazine and Democratic Review, *a magazine espousing the territorial expansion of the United States in the 1840s, John O'Sullivan is widely credited with having coined the Manifest Destiny as an article of faith of the American national mission. O'Sullivan initially broached the issue in the article "The Great Nation of Futurity" in 1839, wherein he connected the American role in the world to the very origin and nature of the republic.*

The American people having derived their origin from many other nations, and the Declaration of National Independence being entirely based on the great principle of human equality, these facts demonstrate at once our disconnected position as regards any other nation; that we have, in reality, but little connection with the past history of any of them, and still less with all antiquity, its glories, or its crimes. On the contrary, our national birth was the beginning of a new history, the formation and progress of an untried political system, which separates us from the past and connects us with the future only; and so far as regards the entire development of the natural rights of man, in moral, political, and national life, we may confidently assume that our country is destined to be *the great nation* of futurity.

It is so destined, because the principle upon which a nation is organized fixes its destiny, and that of equality is perfect, is universal. It presides in all the operations of the physical world, and it is also the conscious law of the soul—the self-evident dictates of morality, which accurately defines the duty of man to man, and consequently man's rights as man. Besides, the truthful annals of any nation furnish abundant evidence, that its happiness, its greatness, its duration, were always proportioned to the democratic equality in its system of government. . . .

What friend of human liberty, civilization, and refinement, can cast his view over the past history of the monarchies and aristocracies of antiquity, and not deplore that they ever existed? What philanthropist can contemplate the oppressions, the cruelties, and injustice inflicted by them on the masses of mankind, and not turn with moral horror from the retrospect? America is destined for better deeds. It is our unparalleled glory that we have no reminiscences of battle fields, but in defence of humanity, of the oppressed of all nations, of the rights of conscience, the rights of personal enfranchisement. Our annals describe no scenes of horrid carnage, where men were led on by hundreds of thousands to slay one another, dupes and victims to emperors, kings, nobles, demons in the human form called heroes. We have had patriots to defend our homes, our liberties, but no aspirants to crowns or thrones; nor have the American people ever suffered themselves to be led on by wicked ambition to depopulate the land, to spread desolation far and wide, that a human being might be placed on a seat of supremacy.

We have no interest in the scenes of antiquity, only as lessons of avoidance of nearly all their examples. The expansive future is our arena, and for our history. We are entering on its untrodden space, with the truths of God in our minds, beneficent objects in our hearts, and with a clear conscience unsullied by the past. We are the nation of human progress, and who will, what can, set limits to our onward march? Providence is with us, and no earthly power can. We point to the everlasting truth on the first page of our national declaration, and we proclaim to the millions of other lands, that "the gates of hell"—the powers of aristocracy and monarchy—"shall not prevail against it." The far-reaching, the boundless future will be the era of American greatness. In its magnificent domain of space and time, the nation of many nations is destined to manifest to mankind the excellence of divine principles; to establish on earth the noblest temple ever dedicated to the worship of the Most High—the Sacred and the True. Its floor shall be a hemisphere—its roof the firmament of the star-studded heavens, and its congregation an Union of many Republics, comprising hundreds of happy millions, calling, owning no man master, but governed by God's natural and moral law of equality, the law of brotherhood—of "peace and good will amongst men. . . ."

Yes, we are the nation of progress, of individual freedom, of universal enfranchisement. Equality of rights is the cynosure of our union of States, the grand exemplar of the correlative equality of individuals; and while truth sheds its effulgence, we cannot retrograde, without dissolving the one and subverting the other. We must onward to the fulfilment of our mission—to the entire development of the principle of our organization—freedom of conscience, freedom of person, freedom of trade and business pursuits, universality of freedom and equality. This is our high destiny, and in nature's eternal, inevitable decree of cause and effect we must accomplish it. All this will be our future history, to establish on earth the moral dignity and salvation of man—the immutable truth and beneficence of God. For this blessed mission to the nations of the world, which are shut out from the life-giving light of truth, has America been chosen; and her high example shall smite unto death the tyranny of kings, hierarchs, and oligarchs, and carry the glad tidings of peace and good will where myriads now endure an existence scarcely more enviable than that of beasts of the field. Who, then, can doubt that our country is destined to be *the great nation* of futurity?

In 1845, O'Sullivan then turned specifically to the acquisition of Texas and California.

[I am] in favor of now elevating this question of the reception of Texas into the Union . . . up to its proper level of a high and broad nationality, it surely is to be found, found abundantly, in the manner in which other nations have undertaken to intrude themselves into it . . . in a spirit of hostile interference against us, for the avowed object of thwarting our policy and hampering our power, limiting our greatness and checking the fulfillment of our manifest destiny

to overspread the continent allotted by Providence for the free development of our yearly multiplying millions. . . .

It is wholly untrue, and unjust to ourselves, the pretense that the Annexation [of Texas] has been a measure of spoliation, unrightful and unrighteous—of military conquest . . .

California will, probably, next fall away from [the Federation of Mexico]. . . . Imbecile and distracted, Mexico never can exert any real governmental authority over such a country. . . . The Anglo-Saxon foot is already on [California's] borders. Already the advance guard of the irresistible army of Anglo-Saxon emigration has begun to pour down upon it, armed with the plow and the rifle, and marking its trail with schools and colleges, courts and representative halls, mills and meetinghouses. . . . [All this will happen] in the natural flow of events, the spontaneous workings of principles. . . . And [the Californians] will have a right to independence—to self-government—to the possession of the homes conquered from the wilderness by their own labors and dangers, sufferings and sacrifices—a better and a truer right than the artificial title of sovereignty in Mexico a thousand miles away. . . . The day is not distant when the Empires of the Atlantic and the Pacific would again flow together into one. . . .

4. Polk's War Message, May 11, 1846

In the case of the Mexican War more than any other project of territorial acquisition, American expansion was more a product of design than of destiny. President Polk's policy in Texas was to provoke Mexico militarily and then to misrepresent the circumstances of conflict in order to excite Congress into a declaration of war.

. . . In my message at the commencement of the present session I informed you that upon the earnest appeal both of the Congress and convention of Texas I had ordered an efficient military force to take a position between the Nueces and the Del Norte. This had become necessary to meet a threatened invasion of Texas by the Mexican forces, for which extensive military preparations had been made. The invasion was threatened solely because Texas had determined, in accordance with a solemn resolution of the Congress of the United States, to annex herself to our Union, and under these circumstances it was plainly our duty to extend our protection over her citizens and soil.

This force was concentrated at Corpus Christi, and remained there until after I had received such information from Mexico as rendered it probable, if not certain, that the Mexican Government would refuse to receive our envoy. Meantime Texas, by the final action of our Congress, had become an integral part of our Union. The Congress of Texas, by its act of December 19, 1836, had declared the Rio del Norte to be the boundary of that Republic. Its jurisdiction had been extended and exercised beyond the Nueces. The country between that river and the Del Norte had been represented in the Congress and in the convention of Texas, had thus taken part in the act of annexation itself, and is now included within one of our Congressional districts. Our own Congress had, moreover, with great unanimity, by the act approved December 31, 1845, recognized the country beyond the Nueces as a part of our territory by including it within our own revenue system, and a revenue officer to reside within that district has been appointed by and with the advice and consent of the Senate. It became, therefore, of urgent necessity to provide for the defense of that portion of our country. Accordingly, on the 13th of January last instructions were issued to the general in command of these troops to occupy the left bank of the Del Norte. This river, which is the southwestern boundary of the State of Texas, is an exposed frontier.

From this quarter invasion was threatened; upon it and in its immediate vicinity, in the judgment of high military experience, are the proper stations for the protecting forces of the Government. In addition to this important consideration, several others occurred to induce this movement. Among these are the facilities afforded by the ports at Brazos Santiago and the mouth of the Del Norte for the reception of supplies by sea, the stronger and more healthful military positions, the convenience for obtaining a ready and a more abundant supply of provisions, water, fuel, and forage, and the advantages which are afforded by the Del Norte in forwarding supplies to such posts as may be established in the interior and upon the Indian frontier.

The movement of the troops to the Del Norte was made by the commanding general under positive instructions to abstain from all aggressive acts toward Mexico or Mexican citizens and to regard the relations between that Republic and the United States as peaceful unless she should declare war or commit acts of hostility indicative of a state of war. He was specially directed to protect private property and respect personal rights.

The Army moved from Corpus Christi on the 11th of March, and on the 28th of that month arrived on the left bank of the Del Norte opposite to Matamoras, where it encamped on a commanding position, which has since been strengthened by the erection of fieldworks. A depot has also been established at Point Isabel, near the Brazos Santiago, 30 miles in the rear of the encampment. The selection of his position was necessarily confided to the judgment of the general in command.

The Mexican forces at Matamoras assumed a belligerent attitude, and on the 12th of April General Ampudia, then in command, notified General Taylor to break up his camp within twenty-four hours and to retire beyond the Nueces River, and in the event of his failure to comply with these demands announced that arms, and arms alone, must decide the question. But no open act of hostility was committed until the 24th of April. On that day General Arista, who had succeeded to the command of the Mexican forces, communicated to General Taylor that "he considered hostilities commenced and should prosecute them." A party of dragoons of 63 men and officers were on the same day dispatched from the American camp up the Rio del Norte, on its left bank, to ascertain whether the Mexican troops had crossed or were preparing to cross the river, "became engaged with a large body of these troops, and after a short affair, in which some 16 were killed and wounded, appear to have been surrounded and compelled to surrender." The grievous wrongs perpetrated by Mexico upon our citizens throughout a long period of years remain unredressed, and solemn treaties pledging her public faith for this redress have been disregarded. A government either unable or unwilling to enforce the execution of such treaties fails to perform one of its plainest duties.

Our commerce with Mexico has been almost annihilated. It was formerly highly beneficial to both nations, but our merchants have been deterred from prosecuting it by the system of outrage and extortion which the Mexican authorities have pursued against them, whilst their appeals through their own Government for indemnity have been made in vain. Our forbearance has gone to such an extreme as to be mistaken in its character. Had we acted with vigor in repelling the insults and redressing the injuries inflicted by Mexico at the commencement, we should doubtless have escaped all the difficulties in which we are now involved.

Instead of this, however, we have been exerting our best efforts to propitiate her good will. Upon the pretext that Texas, a nation as independent as herself, thought proper to unite its destinies with our own she has affected to believe that we have severed her rightful territory, and in official proclamations and manifestoes has repeatedly threatened to make war upon us for the purpose of reconquering Texas. In the meantime we have tried every effort at reconciliation. The cup of forbearance had been exhausted even before the recent information from the frontier of the Del Norte. But now, after reiterated menaces, Mexico has passed the boundary of the United States, has invaded our territory and shed American blood upon the American soil. She has proclaimed that hostilities have commenced, and that the two nations are now at war.

As war exists, and, notwithstanding all our efforts to avoid it, exists by the act of Mexico herself, we are called upon by every consideration of duty and patriotism to vindicate with decision the honor, the rights, and the interests of our country. . . .

5. Abraham Lincoln's First Inaugural Address, March 4, 1861

Lincoln's First Inaugural Address was given at an hour of maximum national crisis. A handful of Southern states had already seceded from the Union along with the federal government property within their borders. In it, Lincoln cited not the sin of slavery but the offense of secession as the causus belli of a civil war becoming ever more probable. Republicans commended the speech for its firmness and moderation. Confederates labeled it a declaration of war. In fact, it was an invitation to the Southern states to avoid war by acknowledging that by the oath of office Lincoln would not and could not accept their secession.

Fellow-Citizens of the United States: In compliance with a custom as old as the Government itself, I appear before you to address you briefly and to take in your presence the oath prescribed by the Constitution of the United States to be taken by the President "before he enters on the execution of this office."

I do not consider it necessary at present for me to discuss those matters of administration about which there is no special anxiety or excitement.

Apprehension seems to exist among the people of the Southern States that by the accession of a Republican Administration their property and their peace and personal security are to be endangered. There has never been any reasonable cause for such apprehension. Indeed, the most ample evidence to the contrary has all the while existed and been open to their inspection. It is found in nearly all the published speeches of him who now addresses you. I do but quote from one of those speeches when I declare that "I have no purpose, directly or indirectly, to interfere with the institution of slavery in the States where it exists. I believe I have no lawful right to do so, and I have no inclination to do so. . . ."

. . . I now reiterate these sentiments, and in doing so I only press upon the public attention the most conclusive evidence of which the case is susceptible that the property, peace, and security of no section are to be in any wise endangered by the now incoming Administration. I add, too, that all the protection which, consistently with the Constitution and the laws, can be given will be cheerfully given to all the States when lawfully demanded, for whatever cause—as cheerfully to one section as to another. . . .

. . . The Union is much older than the Constitution. It was formed, in fact, by the Articles of Association in 1774. It was matured and continued by the Declaration of Independence in 1776. It was further matured, and the faith of all the then thirteen States expressly plighted and engaged that it should be perpetual, by the Articles of Confederation in 1778. And finally, in 1787, one of the declared objects for ordaining and establishing the Constitution was "*to form a more perfect Union.*"

But if destruction of the Union by one or by a part only of the States be lawfully possible, the Union is less perfect than before the Constitution, having lost the vital element of perpetuity.

It follows from these views that no State upon its own mere motion can lawfully get out of the Union; that resolves and ordinances to that effect are legally void, and that acts of violence within any State or States against the authority of the United States are insurrectionary or revolutionary, according to circumstances. . . .

That there are persons in one section or another who seek to destroy the Union at all events and are glad of any pretext to do it I will neither affirm nor deny; but if there be such, I need address no word to them. To those, however, who really love the Union may I not speak?

Before entering upon so grave a matter as the destruction of our national fabric, with all its benefits, its memories, and its hopes, would it not be wise to ascertain precisely why we do it? Will you hazard so desperate a step while there is any possibility that any portion of the ills you fly from have no real existence? Will you, while the certain ills you fly to are greater than all the real ones you fly from, will you risk the commission of so fearful a mistake? . . .

Plainly the central idea of secession is the essence of anarchy. A majority held in restraint by constitutional checks and limitations, and always changing easily with deliberate changes of popular opinions and sentiments, is the only true sovereign of a free people. Whoever rejects it does of necessity fly to anarchy or to despotism. Unanimity is impossible. The rule of a minority, as a permanent arrangement, is wholly inadmissible; so that, rejecting the majority principle, anarchy or despotism in some form is all that is left. . . .

One section of our country believes slavery is right and ought to be extended, while the other believes it is wrong and ought not to be extended. This is the only substantial dispute. The fugitive-slave clause of the Constitution and the law for the suppression of the foreign slave trade are each as well enforced, perhaps, as any law can ever be in a community where the moral sense of the people imperfectly supports the law itself. The great body of the people abide by the dry legal obligation in both cases, and a few break over in each. This, I think, can not be perfectly cured, and it would be worse in both cases after the separation of the sections than before. The foreign slave trade, now imperfectly suppressed, would be ultimately revived without restriction in one section, while fugitive slaves, now only partially surrendered, would not be surrendered at all by the other.

Physically speaking, we cannot separate. We cannot remove our respective sections from each other nor build an impassable wall between them. A husband and wife may be divorced and go out of the presence and beyond the reach of each other, but the different parts of our country cannot do this. They cannot but remain face to face, and intercourse, either amicable or hostile, must continue between them. Is it possible, then, to make that intercourse more advantageous or more satisfactory after separation than before? Can aliens make treaties easier than friends can make laws? Can treaties be more faithfully enforced between aliens than laws can among friends? Suppose you go to war, you cannot fight always; and when, after much loss on both sides and no gain on either, you cease fighting, the identical old questions, as to terms of intercourse, are again upon you. . . .

My countrymen, one and all, think calmly and well upon this whole subject. Nothing valuable can be lost by taking time. If there be an object to hurry any of you in hot haste to a step which you would never take deliberately, that object will be frustrated by taking time; but no good object can be frustrated by it. Such of you as are now dissatisfied still have the old Constitution unimpaired, and, on the sensitive point, the laws of your own framing under it; while the new Administration will have no immediate power, if it would, to change either. If it were admitted that you who are dissatisfied hold the right side in the dispute, there still is no single good reason for precipitate action. Intelligence, patriotism, Christianity, and a firm reliance on Him who has never yet forsaken this favored land are still competent to adjust in the best way all our present difficulty.

In *your* hands, my dissatisfied fellow-countrymen, and not in mine, is the momentous issue of civil war. The Government will not assail you. You can have no conflict without being yourselves the aggressors. You have no oath registered in heaven to destroy the Government, while I shall have the most solemn one to "preserve, protect, and defend it."

I am loath to close. We are not enemies, but friends. We must not be enemies. Though passion may have strained it must not break our bonds of affection. The mystic chords of memory, stretching from every battlefield and patriot grave to every living heart and hearthstone all over this broad land, will yet swell the chorus of the Union, when again touched, as surely they will be, by the better angels of our nature.

6. William McKinley's War Message, 1898

The McKinley administration became the most expansionist since James Polk had taken the United States to war against Mexico, but its policy was vastly more consequential. McKinley did not want war but was driven to it by the multiple factors such as stopping an interminable revolutionary conflict in Cuba; protecting American property there; restoring business confidence; bellicose public and press opinion; and asserting American influence over all developments in the Caribbean. As a result of the war, the United States emerged as an imperial power both there and in the Pacific.

. . . The present revolution is but the successor of other similar insurrections which have occurred in Cuba against the dominion of Spain, extending over a period of nearly half a century, each of which, during its progress, has subjected the United States to great effort and expense in enforcing its neutrality laws, caused enormous losses to American trade and commerce, caused irritation, annoyance, and disturbance among our citizens, and, by the exercise of cruel, barbarous, and uncivilized practices of warfare, shocked the sensibilities and offended the humane sympathies of our people. . . .

In April 1896, the evils from which our country suffered through the Cuban war became so onerous that my predecessor made an effort to bring about a peace through the mediation of this government in any way that might tend to an honorable adjustment of the contest between Spain and her revolted colony, on the basis of some effective scheme of self-government for Cuba under the flag and sovereignty of Spain. It failed through the refusal of the Spanish government then in power to consider any form of mediation or, indeed, any plan of settlement which did not begin with the actual submission of the insurgents to the mother country, and then only on such terms as Spain herself might see fit to grant. The war continued unabated. The resistance of the insurgents was in nowise diminished. . . .

There remain the alternative forms of intervention to end the war, either as an impartial neutral by imposing a rational compromise between the contestants, or as the active ally of the one party or the other.

As to the first, it is not to be forgotten that during the last few months the relation of the United States has virtually been one of friendly intervention in many ways, each not of itself conclusive, but all tending to the exertion of a potential influence toward an ultimate pacific result, just and honorable to all interests concerned. The spirit of all our acts hitherto has been an earnest, unselfish desire for peace and prosperity in Cuba, untarnished by differences between us and Spain, and unstained by the blood of American citizens. The forcible intervention of the United States as a neutral to stop the war, according to the large dictates of humanity and following many historical precedents where neighboring states have interfered to check the hopeless sacrifices of life by internecine conflicts beyond their borders, is justifiable on rational grounds. It involves, however, hostile constraint upon both the parties to the contest as well to enforce a truce as to guide the eventual settlement.

The grounds for such intervention may be briefly summarized as follows:

First, in the cause of humanity and to put an end to the barbarities, bloodshed, starvation, and horrible miseries now existing there, and which the parties to the conflict are either unable or unwilling to stop or mitigate. It is no answer to say this is all in another country, belonging to another nation, and is therefore none of our business. It is specially our duty, for it is right at our door.

Second, we owe it to our citizens in Cuba to afford them that protection and indemnity for life and property which no government there can or will afford, and to that end to terminate the conditions that deprive them of legal protection.

Third, the right to intervene may be justified by the very serious injury to the commerce, trade, and business of our people, and by the wanton destruction of property and devastation of the island.

Fourth, and which is of the utmost importance, the present condition of affairs in Cuba is a constant menace to our peace, and entails upon this government an enormous expense. With such a conflict waged for years in an island so near us and with which our people have such trade and business relations; when the lives and liberty of our citizens are in constant danger and their property destroyed and themselves ruined; where our trading vessels are liable to seizure and are seized at our very door by warships of a foreign nation, the expeditions of filibustering that we are powerless to prevent altogether, and the irritating questions and entanglements thus arising — all these and others that I need not mention, with the resulting strained relations, are a constant menace to our peace, and compel us to keep on a semiwar footing with a nation with which we are at peace. . . .

In any event, the destruction of the *Maine*, by whatever exterior cause, is a patent and impressive proof of a state of things in Cuba that is intolerable. That condition is thus shown to be such that the Spanish government cannot assure safety and security to a vessel of the American Navy in the harbor of Havana on a mission of peace, and rightfully there. . . .

The long trial has proved that the object for which Spain has waged the war cannot be attained. The fire of insurrection may flame or may smolder with varying seasons, but it has not been, and it is plain that it cannot be, extinguished by present methods. The only hope of relief and repose from a condition which can no longer be endured is the enforced pacification of Cuba. In the name of humanity, in the name of civilization, in behalf of endangered American interests which give us the right and the duty to speak and to act, the war in Cuba must stop.

In view of these facts and of these considerations, I ask the Congress to authorize and empower the President to take measures to secure a full and final termination of hostilities between the government of Spain and the people of Cuba, and to secure in the island the establishment of a stable government, capable of maintaining order and observing its

international obligations, insuring peace and tranquillity and the security of its citizens as well as our own, and to use the military and naval forces of the United States as may be necessary for these purposes.

And in the interest of humanity and to aid in preserving the lives of the starving people of the island, I recommend that the distribution of food and supplies be continued, and that an appropriation be made out of the public Treasury to supplement the charity of our citizens.

The issue is now with the Congress. It is a solemn responsibility. I have exhausted every effort to relieve the intolerable condition of affairs which is at our doors. Prepared to execute every obligation imposed upon me by the Constitution and the law, I await your action.

Yesterday, and since the preparation of the foregoing message, official information was received by me that the latest decree of the queen regent of Spain directs General Blanco, in order to prepare and facilitate peace, to proclaim a suspension of hostilities, the duration and details of which have not yet been communicated to me.

This fact, with every other pertinent consideration, will, I am sure, have your just and careful attention in the solemn deliberations upon which you are about to enter. If this measure attains a successful result, then our aspirations as a Christian, peace-loving people will be realized. If it fails, it will be only another justification for our contemplated action.

7. The Roosevelt Corollary to the Monroe Doctrine. Theodore Roosevelt's annual message, December 6, 1904

Frequent revolutions in the smaller republics of the Caribbean and Central America heightened American concern over intervention by European powers to protect citizens and collect debts. In December 1904, this moved Roosevelt for the first time to supplement the Monroe Doctrine with a claim on behalf of a unique American police power in the region.

. . . It is not true that the United States feels any land hunger or entertains any projects as regards the other nations of the Western Hemisphere save such as are for their welfare. All that this country desires is to see the neighboring countries stable, orderly, and prosperous. Any country whose people conduct themselves well can count upon our hearty friendship. If a nation shows that it knows how to act with reasonable efficiency and decency in social and political matters, if it keeps order and pays its obligations, it need fear no interference from the United States. Chronic wrongdoing, or an impotence which results in a general loosening of the ties of civilized society, may in America, as elsewhere, ultimately require intervention by some civilized nation, and in the Western Hemisphere the adherence of the United States to the Monroe

Doctrine may force the United States, however reluctantly, in flagrant cases of such wrongdoing or impotence, to the exercise of an international police power. If every country washed by the Caribbean Sea would show the progress in stable and just civilization which with the aid of the Platt amendment Cuba has shown since our troops left the island, and which so many of the republics in both Americas are constantly and brilliantly showing, all question of interference by this Nation with their affairs would be at an end. Our interests and those of our southern neighbors are in reality identical. They have great natural riches, and if within their borders the law reign of law and justice obtains, prosperity is sure to come to them. While they thus obey the primary laws of civilized society they may rest assured that they will be treated by us in a spirit of cordial and helpful sympathy. We would interfere with them only in the last resort, and then only if it became evident that their inability or unwillingness to do justice at home and abroad had violated the rights of the United States or had invited foreign aggression to the detriment of the entire body of American nations. It is a mere truism to say that every nation, whether in America or anywhere else, which desires to maintain its freedom, its independence, must ultimately realize that the right of such independence cannot be separated from the responsibility of making good use of it.

In asserting the Monroe Doctrine, in taking such steps as we have taken in regard to Cuba, Venezuela, and Panama, and in endeavoring to circumscribe the theater of war in the Far East, and to secure the open door in China, we have acted in our own interest as well as in the interest of humanity at large. There are, however, cases in which, while our own interests are not greatly involved, strong appeal is made to our sympathies. . . . But in extreme cases action may be justifiable and proper. What form the action shall take must depend upon the circumstances of the case; that is, upon the degree of the atrocity and upon our power to remedy it. The cases in which we could interfere by force of arms as we interfered to put a stop to intolerable conditions in Cuba are necessarily very few. . . .

8. Woodrow Wilson's War Message, April 2, 1917

Informed by the German government that it intended to resume unrestricted submarine warfare, Wilson declared Germany an aggressor against all humanity and called upon Congress to take the United States into a conflict in order to change the very nature of international affairs.

Gentlemen of the Congress:

I have called the Congress into extraordinary session because there are serious, very serious, choices of policy to be made, and made immediately, which it was neither right nor constitutionally permissible that I should assume the responsibility of making.

On the third of February last I officially laid before you the extraordinary announcement of the Imperial German Government that on and after the first day of February it was its purpose to put aside all restraints of law or of humanity and use its submarines to sink every vessel that sought to approach either the ports of Great Britain and Ireland or the western coasts of Europe or any of the ports controlled by the enemies of Germany within the Mediterranean. That had seemed to be the object of the German submarine warfare earlier in the war, but since April of last year the Imperial Government had somewhat restrained the commanders of its undersea craft in conformity with its promise then given to us that passenger boats should not be sunk and that due warning would be given to all other vessels which its submarines might seek to destroy, when no resistance was offered or escape attempted, and care taken that their crews were given at least a fair chance to save their lives in their open boats. The precautions taken were meager and haphazard enough, as was proved in distressing instance after instance in the progress of the cruel and unmanly business, but a certain degree of restraint was observed. The new policy has swept every restriction aside. Vessels of every kind, whatever their flag, their character, their cargo, their destination, their errand, have been ruthlessly sent to the bottom without warning and without thought of help or mercy for those on board, the vessels of friendly neutrals along with those of belligerents. Even hospital ships and ships carrying relief to the sorely bereaved and stricken people of Belgium, though the latter were provided with safe-conduct through the proscribed areas by the German Government itself and were distinguished by unmistakable marks of identity, have been sunk with the same reckless lack of compassion or of principle. . . .

It is a war against all nations. American ships have been sunk, American lives taken, in ways which it has stirred us very deeply to learn of, but the ships and people of other neutral and friendly nations have been sunk and overwhelmed in the waters in the same way. There has been no discrimination. The challenge is to all mankind. Each nation must decide for itself how it will meet it. The choice we make for ourselves must be made with a moderation of counsel and a temperateness of judgment befitting our character and our motives as a nation. We must put excited feeling away. Our motive will not be revenge or the victorious assertion of the physical might of the nation, but only the vindication of right, of human right, of which we are only a single champion. . . .

With a profound sense of the solemn and even tragical character of the step I am taking and of the grave responsibilities which it involves, but in unhesitating obedience to what I deem my constitutional duty, I advise that the Congress declare the recent course of the Imperial German Government to be in fact nothing less than war against the Government and people of the United States; that it formally accept the status of belligerent which has thus been thrust upon it, and that it take immediate steps not only to put the country in a more thorough state of defense but also to exert all its power and employ all its resources to bring the Government of the German Empire to terms and end the war. . . .

. . . We have no quarrel with the German people. We have no feeling towards them but one of sympathy and friendship. It was not upon their impulse that their Government acted in entering this war. It was not with their previous knowledge or approval. It was a war determined upon as wars used to be determined upon in the old, unhappy days when peoples were nowhere consulted by their rulers and wars were provoked and waged in the interest of dynasties or of little groups of ambitious men who were accustomed to use their fellow men as pawns and tools. . . .

We are accepting this challenge of hostile purpose because we know that in such a government, following such methods, we can never have a friend; and that in the presence of its organized power, always lying in wait to accomplish we know not what purpose, there can be no assured security for the democratic governments of the world. We are now about to accept gauge of battle with this natural foe to liberty and shall, if necessary, spend the whole force of the nation to check and nullify its pretensions and its power. We are glad, now that we see the facts with no veil of false pretence about them, to fight thus for the ultimate peace of the world and for the liberation of its peoples, the German peoples included: for the rights of nations great and small and the privilege of men everywhere to choose their way of life and of obedience. The world must be made safe for democracy. Its peace must be planted upon the tested foundations of political liberty. We have no selfish ends to serve. We desire no conquest, no dominion. We seek no indemnities for ourselves, no material compensation for the sacrifices we shall freely make. We are but one of the champions of the rights of mankind. We shall be satisfied when those rights have been made as secure as the faith and the freedom of nations can make them. . . .

It is a distressing and oppressive duty, gentlemen of the Congress, which I have performed in thus addressing you. There are, it may be, many months of fiery trial and sacrifice ahead of us. It is a fearful thing to lead this great peaceful people into war, into the most terrible and disastrous of all wars, civilization itself seeming to be in the balance. But the right is more precious than peace, and we shall fight for the things which we have always carried nearest our hearts —for democracy, for the right of those who submit to authority to have a voice in their own governments, for the

rights and liberties of small nations, for a universal dominion of right by such a concert of free peoples as shall bring peace and safety to all nations and make the world itself at last free. To such a task we can dedicate our lives and our fortunes, everything that we are and everything that we have, with the pride of those who know that the day has come when America is privileged to spend her blood and her might for the principles that gave her birth and happiness and the peace which she has treasured. God helping her, she can do no other.

9. Woodrow Wilson's Fourteen Points, January 8, 1918

Speaking before a joint session of Congress, Wilson outlined a blueprint for European and international peace based on fourteen principles, all of which were applied in one form or another to the Treaty of Versailles and many of which influence international diplomacy to this day.

Gentlemen of the Congress:

Once more, as repeatedly before, the spokesmen of the Central Empires have indicated their desire to discuss the objects of the war and the possible basis of a general peace. Parleys have been in progress at Brest-Litovsk between Russian representatives and representatives of the Central Powers to which the attention of all the belligerents have been invited for the purpose of ascertaining whether it may be possible to extend these parleys into a general conference with regard to terms of peace and settlement. . . .

We entered this war because violations of right had occurred which touched us to the quick and made the life of our own people impossible unless they were corrected and the world secure once for all against their recurrence. What we demand in this war, therefore, is nothing peculiar to ourselves. It is that the world be made fit and safe to live in; and particularly that it be made safe for every peace-loving nation which, like our own, wishes to live its own life, determine its own institutions, be assured of justice and fair dealing by the other peoples of the world as against force and selfish aggression. All the peoples of the world are in effect partners in this interest, and for our own part we see very clearly that unless justice be done to others it will not be done to us. The program of the world's peace, therefore, is our program; and that program, the only possible program, as we see it, is this:

I. Open covenants of peace, openly arrived at, after which there shall be no private international understandings of any kind but diplomacy shall proceed always frankly and in the public view.

II. Absolute freedom of navigation upon the seas, outside territorial waters, alike in peace and in war, except as the seas may be closed in whole or in part by international action for the enforcement of international covenants.

III. The removal, so far as possible, of all economic barriers and the establishment of an equality of trade conditions among all the nations consenting to the peace and associating themselves for its maintenance.

IV. Adequate guarantees given and taken that national armaments will be reduced to the lowest point consistent with domestic safety.

V. A free, open-minded, and absolutely impartial adjustment of all colonial claims, based upon a strict observance of the principle that in determining all such questions of sovereignty the interests of the populations concerned must have equal weight with the equitable claims of the government whose title is to be determined.

VI. The evacuation of all Russian territory and such a settlement of all questions affecting Russia as will secure the best and freest cooperation of the other nations of the world in obtaining for her an unhampered and unembarrassed opportunity for the independent determination of her own political development and national policy and assure her of a sincere welcome into the society of free nations under institutions of her own choosing; and, more than a welcome, assistance also of every kind that she may need and may herself desire. The treatment accorded Russia by her sister nations in the months to come will be the acid test of their good will, of their comprehension of her needs as distinguished from their own interests, and of their intelligent and unselfish sympathy.

VII. Belgium, the whole world will agree, must be evacuated and restored, without any attempt to limit the sovereignty which she enjoys in common with all other free nations. No other single act will serve as this will serve to restore confidence among the nations in the laws which they have themselves set and determined for the government of their relations with one another. Without this healing act the whole structure and validity of international law is forever impaired.

VIII. All French territory should be freed and the invaded portions restored, and the wrong done to France by Prussia in 1871 in the matter of Alsace-Lorraine, which has unsettled the peace of the world for nearly fifty years, should be righted, in order that peace may once more be made secure in the interest of all.

IX. A readjustment of the frontiers of Italy should be effected along clearly recognizable lines of nationality.

X. The peoples of Austria-Hungary, whose place among the nations we wish to see safeguarded and assured, should be accorded the freest opportunity to autonomous development.

XI. Rumania, Serbia, and Montenegro should be evacuated; occupied territories restored; Serbia accorded free and secure access to the sea; and the relations of the several Balkan states to one another determined by friendly counsel along historically established lines of allegiance and nationality; and international guarantees of the political and economic independence and territorial integrity of the several Balkan states should be entered into.

XII. The Turkish portion of the present Ottoman Empire should be assured a secure sovereignty, but the other nationalities which are now under Turkish rule should be assured an undoubted security of life and an absolutely unmolested opportunity of autonomous development, and the Dardanelles should be permanently opened as a free passage to the ships and commerce of all nations under international guarantees.

XIII. An independent Polish state should be erected which should include the territories inhabited by indisputably Polish populations, which should be assured a free and secure access to the sea, and whose political and economic independence and territorial integrity should be guaranteed by international covenant.

XIV. A general association of nations must be formed under specific covenants for the purpose of affording mutual guarantees of political independence and territorial integrity to great and small states alike.

In regard to these essential rectifications of wrong and assertions of right we feel ourselves to be intimate partners of all the governments and peoples associated together against the Imperialists. We cannot be separated in interest or divided in purpose. We stand together until the end. For such arrangements and covenants we are willing to fight and to continue to fight until they are achieved; but only because we wish the right to prevail and desire a just and stable peace such as can be secured only by removing the chief provocations to war, which this program does remove. . . .

10. The Atlantic Charter, August 14, 1941

At a secret meeting aboard the cruiser USS Augusta off the coast of Newfoundland, President Roosevelt and Prime Minister Churchill issued a joint declaration on the purposes of the war against fascism, a war in which the United States was not yet officially engaged.

The President of the United States of America and the Prime Minister, Mr. Churchill, representing His Majesty's Government in the United Kingdom, being met together, deem it right to make known certain common principles in the national policies of their respective countries on which they base their hopes for a better future for the world.

1. Their countries seek no aggrandizement, territorial or other.

2. They desire to see no territorial changes that do not accord with the freely expressed wishes of the peoples concerned;

3. They respect the right of all peoples to choose the form of government under which they will live; and they wish to see sovereign rights and self government restored to those who have been forcibly deprived of them;

4. They will endeavor, with due respect for their existing obligations, to further the enjoyment by all States, great or small, victor or vanquished, of access, on equal terms, to the trade and to the raw materials of the world which are needed for their economic prosperity;

5. They desire to bring about the fullest collaboration between all nations in the economic field with the object of securing, for all, improved labor standards, economic advancement and social security;

6. After the final destruction of the Nazi tyranny, they hope to see established a peace which will afford to all nations the means of dwelling in safety within their own boundaries, and which will afford assurance that all the men in all the lands may live out their lives in freedom from fear and want;

7. Such a peace should enable all men to traverse the high seas and oceans without hindrance;

8. They believe that all of the nations of the world, for realistic as well as spiritual reasons must come to the abandonment of the use of force. Since no future peace can be maintained if land, sea or air armaments continue to be employed by nations which threaten, or may threaten, aggression outside of their frontiers, they believe, pending the establishment of a wider and permanent system of general security, that the disarmament of such nations is essential. They will likewise aid and encourage all other practicable measures which will lighten for peace-loving peoples the crushing burden of armaments.

Franklin D. Roosevelt

Winston S. Churchill

11. Franklin Roosevelt's War Message, December 8, 1941

Roosevelt asked Congress for a declaration of war against the Empire of Japan in response to the attack on Pearl Harbor.

Mr. Vice President, Mr. Speaker, members of the Senate and the House of Representatives:

Yesterday, December 7, 1941—a date which will live in infamy—the United States of America was suddenly and deliberately attacked by naval and air forces of the Empire of Japan.

The United States was at peace with that nation, and, at the solicitation of Japan, was still in conversation with its government and its Emperor looking toward the maintenance of peace in the Pacific.

Indeed, one hour after Japanese air squadrons had commenced bombing in the American island of Oahu, the Japanese Ambassador to the United States and his colleague delivered to our Secretary of State a formal reply to a recent American message. And, while this reply stated that it seemed useless to continue the existing diplomatic negotiations, it contained no threat or hint of war or of armed attack.

It will be recorded that the distance of Hawaii from Japan makes it obvious that the attack was deliberately planned many days or even weeks ago. During the intervening time the Japanese Government has deliberately sought to deceive the United States by false statements and expressions of hope for continued peace. The attack yesterday on the Hawaiian Islands has caused severe damage to American naval and military forces. I regret to tell you that very many American lives have been lost. In addition, American ships have been reported torpedoed on the high seas between San Francisco and Honolulu.

Yesterday the Japanese Government also launched an attack against Malaya.

Last night Japanese forces attacked Hong Kong.

Last night Japanese forces attacked Guam.

Last night Japanese forces attacked the Philippine Islands.

Last night the Japanese attacked Wake Island.

This morning the Japanese attacked Midway Island.

Japan has, therefore, undertaken a surprise offensive extending throughout the Pacific area. The facts of yesterday and today speak for themselves. The people of the United States have already formed their opinions and well understand the implications to the very life and safety of our nation.

As Commander-in-Chief of the army and navy I have directed that all measures be taken for our defense.

Always will we remember the character of the onslaught against us.

No matter how long it may take us to overcome this premeditated invasion, the American people, in their righteous might, will win through to absolute victory. I believe that I interpret the will of the Congress and of the people when I assert that we will not only defend ourselves to the uttermost but will make it very certain that this form of treachery shall never again endanger us.

Hostilities exist. There is no blinking at the fact that our people, our territory and our interests are in grave danger.

With confidence in our armed forces, with the unbounding determination of our people, we will gain the inevitable triumph. So help us God.

I ask that the Congress declare that since the unprovoked and dastardly attack by Japan on Sunday, December 7, a state of war has existed between the United States and the Japanese Empire.

12. The Truman Doctrine

On March 12, 1947, President Truman addressed a joint session of Congress in order to secure military and economic aid for the beleaguered governments of Greece Turkey. In it he called upon the United States to view the assistance within the broader context of a foreign policy to support "free peoples" against domestic subjugation or outside pressure, in substance a declaration of war against Russian expansionism and the beginning of half-century's commitment to the security of Western Europe as a vital national interest of the United States.

Mr. President, Mr. Speaker, Members of the Congress of the United States:

The gravity of the situation which confronts the world today necessitates my appearance before a joint session of the Congress. The foreign policy and the national security of this country are involved.

One aspect of the present situation, which I wish to present to you at this time for your consideration and decision, concerns Greece and Turkey.

The United States has received from the Greek Government an urgent appeal for financial and economic assistance. Preliminary reports from the American Economic Mission now in Greece and reports from the American Ambassador in Greece corroborate the statement of the Greek Government that assistance is imperative if Greece is to survive as a free nation. . . .

Greece is today without funds to finance the importation of those goods which are essential to bare subsistence. Under these circumstances the people of Greece cannot make progress in solving their problems of reconstruction. Greece is in desperate need of financial and economic assistance to enable it to resume purchases of food, clothing, fuel and seeds. These are indispensable for the subsistence of its people and are obtainable only from abroad. Greece must have help to import the goods necessary to restore internal order and security, so essential for economic and political recovery.

The Greek Government has also asked for the assistance of experienced American administrators, economists and technicians to insure that the financial and other aid given to Greece shall be used effectively in creating a stable and self-sustaining economy and in improving its public administration.

The very existence of the Greek state is today threatened by the terrorist activities of several thousand armed men, led by Communists, who defy the government's authority at a number of points, particularly along the northern boundaries. A commission appointed by the United Nations Security Council is at present investigating disturbed conditions in northern Greece and alleged border violations along the frontier between Greece on the one hand and Albania, Bulgaria, and Yugoslavia on the other. . . .

The Greek Government has been operating in an atmosphere of chaos and extremism. It has made mistakes. The extension of aid by this country does not mean that the United States condones everything that the Greek Government has done or will do. We have condemned in the past, and we condemn now, extremist measures of the right or the left. We have in the past advised tolerance, and we advise tolerance now.

Greece's neighbor, Turkey, also deserves our attention.

The future of Turkey as an independent and economically sound state is clearly no less important to the freedom-loving peoples of the world than the future of Greece. The circumstances in which Turkey finds itself today are considerably different from those of Greece. Turkey has been spared the disasters that have beset Greece. And during the war, the United States and Great Britain furnished Turkey with material aid.

Nevertheless, Turkey now needs our support. . . .

To ensure the peaceful development of nations, free from coercion, the United States has taken a leading part in establishing the United Nations, The United Nations is designed to make possible lasting freedom and independence for all its members. We shall not realize our objectives, however, unless we are willing to help free peoples to maintain their free institutions and their national integrity against aggressive movements that seek to impose upon them totalitarian regimes.

This is no more than a frank recognition that totalitarian regimes imposed on free peoples, by direct or indirect aggression, undermine the foundations of international peace and hence the security of the United States.

The peoples of a number of countries of the world have recently had totalitarian regimes forced upon them against their will. The Government of the United States has made frequent protests against coercion and intimidation, in violation of the Yalta agreement, in Poland, Rumania, and Bulgaria. I must also state that in a number of other countries there have been similar developments.

At the present moment in world history nearly every nation must choose between alternative ways of life. The choice is too often not a free one.

One way of life is based upon the will of the majority, and is distinguished by free institutions, representative government, free elections, guarantees of individual liberty, freedom of speech and religion, and freedom from political oppression.

The second way of life is based upon the will of a minority forcibly imposed upon the majority. It relies upon terror and oppression, a controlled press and radio; fixed elections, and the suppression of personal freedoms.

I believe that it must be the policy of the United States to support free peoples who are resisting attempted subjugation by armed minorities or by outside pressures. I believe that we must assist free peoples to work out their own destinies in their own way. I believe that our help should be primarily through economic and financial aid which is essential to economic stability and orderly political processes. . . .

The seeds of totalitarian regimes are nurtured by misery and want. They spread and grow in the evil soil of poverty and strife. They reach their full growth when the hope of a people for a better life has died. We must keep that hope alive.

The free peoples of the world look to us for support in maintaining their freedoms. If we falter in our leadership, we may endanger the peace of the world—and we shall surely endanger the welfare of our own nation.

Great responsibilities have been placed upon us by the swift movement of events. I am confident that the Congress will face these responsibilities squarely.

13. George Kennan, "The Sources of Soviet Conduct," Foreign Affairs, July 1947

In February 1946, George Kennan, a junior Foreign Service officer at the U.S. embassy, transmitted a "long telegram" of some 8, 000 words to the State Department in Washington. Its ideas were then condensed for an article in the journal Foreign Affairs, written under the pseudonym "X," and subsequently became the first article of the Cold War and the foundation of American policy for the next forty years.

The political personality of Soviet power as we know it today is the product of ideology and circumstances: ideology inherited by the present Soviet leaders from the movement in which they had their political origin, and circumstances of power which they now have exercised for nearly three decades in Russia. . . .

Of the original ideology, nothing has been officially junked. Belief is maintained in the basic badness of capitalism, in the inevitability of its destruction, in the obligation of the proletariat to assist in that destruction and to take power into its own hands. But stress has come to be laid primarily on those concepts which relate most specifically to the Soviet regime itself: to its position as the sole truly Socialist regime in a dark and misguided world, and to the relationships of power within it.

The first of these concepts is that of the innate antagonism between capitalism and socialism. We have seen how deeply that concept has become imbedded in foundations of Soviet power. It has profound implications for Russia's conduct as a member of international society. It means that there can never be on Moscow's side any sincere assumption of a community of aims between the Soviet Union and powers which are regarded as capitalist. It must invariably be assumed in Moscow that the aims of the capitalist world are antagonistic to the Soviet regime, and therefore to the interest of the peoples it controls. If the Soviet government occasionally sets its signature to documents which would indicate the contrary, this is to be regarded as a tactical maneuver permissible in dealing with the enemy (who is without honor) and should be taken in the spirit of caveat emptor. . . .

This means that we are going to continue for a long time to find the Russians difficult to deal with. It does not mean that they should be considered as embarked upon a do-or-die program to overthrow our society by a given date. The theory of the inevitability of the eventual fall of capitalism has the fortunate connotation that there is no hurry about it. The forces of progress can take their time in preparing the final coup de grace. Meanwhile, what is vital is that the "socialist fatherland" - that oasis of power which has been already won for Socialism in their person of the Soviet Union — should be cherished and defended by all good communists at home and abroad, its fortunes promoted, its enemies badgered and confounded. The promotion of premature, "adventuristic" revolutionary projects abroad which might embarrass Soviet power in any way would be an inexcusable, even a counter-revolutionary act. The cause of socialism is the support and promotion of Soviet power, as defined in Moscow.

This brings us to the second of the concepts important to contemporary Soviet outlook. That is the infallibility of the Kremlin. The Soviet concept of power, which permits no focal points of organization outside the party itself, requires that the party leadership remain in theory the sole repository of truth. For if truth were to be found elsewhere, there would be justification for its expression in organized activity. But it is precisely that which the Kremlin cannot and will not permit. . . .

. . . Thus the Kremlin has no compunction about retreating in the face of superior force. And being under the compulsion of no timetable, it does not get panicky under the necessity for such retreat. Its political action is a fluid stream which moves constantly, wherever it is permitted to move, toward a given goal. Its main concern is to make sure that it has filled every nook and cranny available to it in the basin of world power. But if it finds unassailable barriers in its path, it accepts these philosophically and accommodates itself to them. The main thing is that there should always be pressure, unceasing constant pressure, toward the desired goal. There is no trace of any feeling in Soviet psychology that that goal must be reached at any given time. . . .

In these circumstances it is clear that the main element of any United States policy toward the Soviet Union must be that of a long-term, patient but firm and vigilant containment of Russian expansive tendencies. It is important to note, however, that such a policy has nothing to do with outward histrionics: with threats or blustering or superfluous gestures of outward "toughness." While the Kremlin is basically flexible in its reaction to political realities, it is by no means unamenable to considerations of prestige. Like almost any other government, it can be placed by tactless and threatening gestures in a position where it cannot afford to yield even though this might be dictated by its sense of realism. The Russian leaders are keen judges of human psychology, and as such they are highly conscious that loss of temper and of self-control is never a source of strength in political affairs. They are quick to exploit such evidences of weakness. For these reasons, it is a sine qua non of successful dealing with Russia that the foreign government in question should remain at all times cool and collected and that its demands on Russian policy should be put forward in such a manner as to leave the way open for a compliance not too detrimental to Russian prestige. . . .

It would be an exaggeration to say that American behavior unassisted and alone could exercise a power of life and death over the communist movement and bring about the early fall of Soviet power in Russia. But the United States has it in its power to increase enormously the strains under which Soviet policy must operate, to force upon the Kremlin a far greater degree of moderation and circumspection than it has had to observe in recent years, and in this way to promote tendencies which must eventually find their outlet in either the break-up or the gradual mellowing of Soviet power. For no mystical, Messianic movement—and particularly not that of the Kremlin—can face frustration indefinitely without eventually adjusting itself in one way or another to the logic of that state of affairs. . . .

Surely, there was never a fairer test of national quality than this. In the light of these circumstances, the thoughtful observer of Russian-American relations will find no cause for complaint in the Kremlin's challenge to American society. He will rather experience a certain gratitude to a Providence which, by providing the American people with this implacable challenge, has made their entire security as a nation dependent on their pulling themselves together and accepting the responsibilities of moral and political leadership that history plainly intended them to bear. . . .

14. Eisenhower's Farewell Address to the Nation, January 17, 1961

Like that of George Washington, Eisenhower's farewell speech was essentially a warning, not against American involvement if European affairs—history had made Eisenhower an instrument of permanent involvement in Europe—but rather against the challenge posed to democratic self-government by the unprecedented military power of the United States.

Good evening, my fellow Americans: First, I should like to express my gratitude to the radio and television networks for the opportunity they have given me over the years to bring reports and messages to our nation. My special thanks go to them for the opportunity of addressing you this evening.

Three days from now, after a half century of service of our country, I shall lay down the responsibilities of office as, in traditional and solemn ceremony, the authority of the Presidency is vested in my successor.

This evening I come to you with a message of leave-taking and farewell, and to share a few final thoughts with you, my countrymen.

Like every other citizen, I wish the new President, and all who will labor with him, Godspeed. I pray that the coming years will be blessed with peace and prosperity for all. . . .

We now stand ten years past the midpoint of a century that has witnessed four major wars among great nations. Three of these involved our own country. Despite these holocausts America is today the strongest, the most influential and most productive nation in the world. Understandably proud of this pre-eminence, we yet realize that America's leadership and prestige depend, not merely upon our unmatched material progress, riches and military strength, but on how we use our power in the interests of world peace and human betterment.

Throughout America's adventure in free government, such basic purposes have been to keep the peace; to foster progress in human achievement, and to enhance liberty, dignity and integrity among peoples and among nations. To strive for less would be unworthy of a free and religious people. . . .

Crises there will continue to be. In meeting them, whether foreign or domestic, great or small, there is a recurring temptation to feel that some spectacular and costly action could become the miraculous solution to all current difficulties. A huge increase in the newer elements of our defenses; development of unrealistic programs to cure every ill in agriculture; a dramatic expansion in basic and applied research – these and many other possibilities, each possibly promising in itself, may be suggested as the only way to the road we wish to travel. . . .

A vital element in keeping the peace is our military establishment. Our arms must be mighty, ready for instant action, so that no potential aggressor may be tempted to risk his own destruction. . . .

Until the latest of our world conflicts, the United States had no armaments industry. American makers of plowshares could, with time and as required, make swords as well. But now we can no longer risk emergency improvisation of national defense; we have been compelled to create a permanent armaments industry of vast proportions. Added to this, three and a half million men and women are directly engaged in the defense establishment. We annually spend on military security more than the net income of all United States corporations. American makers of plowshares could, with time and as required, make swords as well. But now we can no longer risk emergency improvisation of national defense; we have been compelled to create a permanent armaments industry of vast proportions.

This conjunction of an immense military establishment and a large arms industry is new in the American experience. The total influence—economic, political, even spiritual—is felt in every city, every statehouse, every office of the Federal government. We recognize the imperative need for this development. Yet we must not fail to comprehend its grave implications. Our toil, resources and livelihood are all involved; so is the very structure of our society.

In the councils of government, we must guard against the acquisition of unwarranted influence, whether sought or unsought, by the military-industrial complex. The potential for the disastrous rise of misplaced power exists and will persist.

We must never let the weight of this combination endanger our liberties or democratic processes. We should take nothing for granted. Only an alert and knowledgeable citizenry can compel the proper meshing of the huge industrial and military machinery of defense with our peaceful methods and goals, so that security and liberty may prosper together. Akin to, and largely responsible for the sweeping changes in our industrial-military posture, has been the technological revolution during recent decades. . . .

So—in this my last good night to you as your President—I thank you for the many opportunities you have given me for public service in war and peace. I trust that in that service you find some things worthy; as for the rest of it, I know you will find ways to improve performance in the future.

You and I—my fellow citizens—need to be strong in our faith that all nations, under God, will reach the goal of peace with justice. May we be ever unswerving in devotion to principle, confident but humble with power, diligent in pursuit of the Nations' great goals.

To all the peoples of the world, I once more give expression to America's prayerful and continuing aspiration:

We pray that peoples of all faiths, all races, all nations, may have their great human needs satisfied; that those now denied opportunity shall come to enjoy it to the full; that all who yearn for freedom may experience its spiritual blessings; that those who have freedom will understand, also, its

heavy responsibilities; that all who are insensitive to the needs of others will learn charity; that the scourges of poverty, disease and ignorance will be made to disappear from the earth, and that, in the goodness of time, all peoples will come to live together in a peace guaranteed by the binding force of mutual respect and love.

Now, on Friday noon, I am to become a private citizen. I am proud to do so. I look forward to it.

Thank you, and good night.

15. John F. Kennedy's Inaugural Address, January 20, 1961

Kennedy's Inaugural Address promised to take up the Cold War struggle with more vigor and idealism, a call-to-arms that led to scientific triumph in the space race and national humiliation in Southeast Asia.

Vice President Johnson, Mr. Speaker, Mr. Chief Justice, President Eisenhower, Vice President Nixon, President Truman, reverend clergy, fellow citizens: We observe today not a victory of party, but a celebration of freedom—symbolizing an end, as well as a beginning—signifying renewal, as well as change. For I have sworn before you and Almighty God the same solemn oath our forebears prescribed nearly a century and three-quarters ago.

The world is very different now. For man holds in his mortal hands the power to abolish all forms of human poverty and all forms of human life. And yet the same revolutionary beliefs for which our forebears fought are still at issue around the globe—the belief that the rights of man come not from the generosity of the state, but from the hand of God.

We dare not forget today that we are the heirs of that first revolution. Let the word go forth from this time and place, to friend and foe alike, that the torch has been passed to a new generation of Americans—born in this century, tempered by war, disciplined by a hard and bitter peace, proud of our ancient heritage—and unwilling to witness or permit the slow undoing of those human rights to which this Nation has always been committed, and to which we are committed today at home and around the world.

Let every nation know, whether it wishes us well or ill, that we shall pay any price, bear any burden, meet any hardship, support any friend, oppose any foe, in order to assure the survival and the success of liberty. This much we pledge—and more.

To those old allies whose cultural and spiritual origins we share, we pledge the loyalty of faithful friends. United, there is little we cannot do in a host of cooperative ventures. Divided, there is little we can do—for we dare not meet a powerful challenge at odds and split asunder.

To those new States whom we welcome to the ranks of the free, we pledge our word that one form of colonial control shall not have passed away merely to be replaced by a far more iron tyranny. We shall not always expect to find them supporting our view. But we shall always hope to find them strongly supporting their own freedom—and to remember that, in the past, those who foolishly sought power by riding the back of the tiger ended up inside.

To those peoples in the huts and villages across the globe struggling to break the bonds of mass misery, we pledge our best efforts to help them help themselves, for whatever period is required—not because the Communists may be doing it, not because we seek their votes, but because it is right. If a free society cannot help the many who are poor, it cannot save the few who are rich.

To our sister republics south of our border, we offer a special pledge—to convert our good words into good deeds—in a new alliance for progress—to assist free men and free governments in casting off the chains of poverty. But this peaceful revolution of hope cannot become the prey of hostile powers. Let all our neighbors know that we shall join with them to oppose aggression or subversion anywhere in the Americas. And let every other power know that this Hemisphere intends to remain the master of its own house.

To that world assembly of sovereign states, the United Nations, our last best hope in an age where the instruments of war have far outpaced the instruments of peace, we renew our pledge of support—to prevent it from becoming merely a forum for invective—to strengthen its shield of the new and the weak—and to enlarge the area in which its writ may run.

Finally, to those nations who would make themselves our adversary, we offer not a pledge but a request: that both sides begin anew the quest for peace, before the dark powers of destruction unleashed by science engulf all humanity in planned or accidental self-destruction.

We dare not tempt them with weakness. For only when our arms are sufficient beyond doubt can we be certain beyond doubt that they will never be employed. But neither can two great and powerful groups of nations take comfort from our present course—both sides overburdened by the cost of modern weapons, both rightly alarmed by the steady spread of the deadly atom, yet both racing to alter that uncertain balance of terror that stays the hand of mankind's final war. So let us begin anew—remembering on both sides that civility is not a sign of weakness, and sincerity is always subject to proof. Let us never negotiate out of fear. But let us never fear to negotiate.

Let both sides explore what problems unite us instead of belaboring those problems which divide us.

Let both sides, for the first time, formulate serious and precise proposals for the inspection and control of arms—and

bring the absolute power to destroy other nations under the absolute control of all nations.

Let both sides seek to invoke the wonders of science instead of its terrors. Together let us explore the stars, conquer the deserts, eradicate disease, tap the ocean depths, and encourage the arts and commerce.

Let both sides unite to heed in all corners of the earth the command of Isaiah—to "undo the heavy burdens . . . [and] to let the oppressed go free."

And if a beachhead of cooperation may push back the jungle of suspicion, let both sides join in creating a new endeavor, not a new balance of power, but a new world of law, where the strong are just and the weak secure and the peace preserved. All this will not be finished in the first 100 days. Nor will it be finished in the first 1,000 days, nor in the life of this Administration, nor even perhaps in our lifetime on this planet. But let us begin.

In your hands, my fellow citizens, more than in mine, will rest the final success or failure of our course. Since this country was founded, each generation of Americans has been summoned to give testimony to its national loyalty. The graves of young Americans who answered the call to service surround the globe.

Now the trumpet summons us again—not as a call to bear arms, though arms we need; not as a call to battle, though embattled we are—but a call to bear the burden of a long twilight struggle, year in and year out, "rejoicing in hope, patient in tribulation"—a struggle against the common enemies of man: tyranny, poverty, disease, and war itself.

Can we forge against these enemies a grand and global alliance, North and South, East and West, that can assure a more fruitful life for all mankind? Will you join in that historic effort?

In the long history of the world, only a few generations have been granted the role of defending freedom in its hour of maximum danger. I do not shrink from this responsibility—I welcome it. I do not believe that any of us would exchange places with any other people or any other generation. The energy, the faith, the devotion which we bring to this endeavor will light our country and all who serve it—and the glow from that fire can truly light the world.

And so, my fellow Americans: ask not what your country can do for you—ask what you can do for your country.

My fellow citizens of the world: ask not what America will do for you, but what together we can do for the freedom of man.

Finally, whether you are citizens of America or citizens of the world, ask of us the same high standards of strength and sacrifice which we ask of you. With a good conscience our only sure reward, with history the final judge of our deeds, let us go forth to lead the land we love, asking His blessing and His help, but knowing that here on earth God's work must truly be our own.

16. Lyndon B. Johnson, Gulf of Tonkin Incident, August 4, 1964

On August 2 and 3, 1964, U.S. warships in the Gulf of Tonkin off the coast of North Vietnam reported attacks by North Vietnamese torpedo boats. On August 4, President Johnson announced to television audiences both that American forces were retaliating and that he would be seeking from Congress a resolution authorizing him to prevent further aggression against U.S. forces or against a member or protocol state of the Southeast Asia Collective Defense Treaty. The Southeast Asia Resolution, better known as the Tonkin Resolution, subsequently authorized Johnson to increase radically the U.S. military commitment to the defense of South Vietnam.

My fellow Americans: As President and Commander in Chief, it is my duty to the American people to report that renewed hostile actions against United States ships on the high seas in the Gulf of Tonkin have today required me to order the military forces of the United States to take action in reply.

The initial attack on the destroyer *Maddox*, on August 2, was repeated today by a number of hostile vessels attacking two U.S. destroyers with torpedoes. The destroyers and supporting aircraft acted at once on the orders I gave after the initial act of aggression. We believe at least two of the attacking boats were sunk. There were no U.S. losses.

The performance of commanders and crews in this engagement is in the highest tradition of the United States Navy. But repeated acts of violence against the Armed Forces of the United States must be met not only with alert defense, but with positive reply. That reply is being given as I speak to you tonight. Air action is now in execution against gunboats and certain supporting facilities in North Vietnam which have been used in these hostile operations.

In the larger sense this new act of aggression, aimed directly at our own forces, again brings home to all of us in the United States the importance of the struggle for peace and security in southeast Asia. Aggression by terror against the peaceful villagers of South Vietnam has now been joined by open aggression on the high seas against the United States of America.

The determination of all Americans to carry out our full commitment to the people and to the government of South Vietnam will be redoubled by this outrage. Yet our response, for the present, will be limited and fitting. We Americans know, although others appear to forget, the risks of spreading conflict. We still seek no wider war.

I have instructed the Secretary of State to make this position totally clear to friends and to adversaries and, indeed, to all. I have instructed Ambassador Stevenson to raise this matter immediately and urgently before the Security Council of the United Nations. Finally, I have today met with the leaders of both parties in the Congress of the United States and I have informed them that I shall immediately request the Congress to pass a resolution making it clear that our Government is united in its determination to take all necessary measures in support of freedom and in defense of peace in Southeast Asia.

I have been given encouraging assurance by these leaders of both parties that such a resolution will be promptly introduced, freely and expeditiously debated, and passed with overwhelming support. And just a few minutes ago I was able to reach Senator Goldwater and I am glad to say that he has expressed his support of the statement that I am making to you tonight.

It is a solemn responsibility to have to order even limited military action by forces whose overall strength is as vast and as awesome as those of the United States of America, but it is my considered conviction, shared throughout your Government, that firmness in the right is indispensable today for peace; that firmness will always be measured. Its mission is peace.

17. President Richard Nixon, "Vietnamization—The Great Silent Majority," November 3, 1969

A year after his election to the Oval Office, President Nixon explained to the public his policy for a graduated withdrawal from Vietnam. The speech marked the beginning of the end of the country's greatest foreign misadventure. It was also a partial refutation of the Kennedy inaugural given a decade earlier.

Good evening, my fellow Americans: Tonight I want to talk to you on a subject of deep concern to all Americans and to many people in all parts of the world—the war in Vietnam.

I believe that one of the reasons for the deep division about Vietnam is that many Americans have lost confidence in what their Government has told them about our policy. The American people cannot and should not be asked to support a policy which involves the overriding issues of war and peace unless they know the truth about that policy.

Tonight, therefore, I would like to answer some of the questions that I know are on the minds of many of you listening to me. . . .

For the United States, this first defeat in our Nation's history would result in a collapse of confidence in American leadership, not only in Asia but throughout the world.

Three American Presidents have recognized the great stakes involved in Vietnam and understood what had to be done.

In 1963, President Kennedy, with his characteristic eloquence and clarity, said: " . . . we want to see a stable government there, carrying on a struggle to maintain its national independence.

"We believe strongly in that. We are not going to withdraw from that effort. In my opinion, for us to withdraw from that effort would mean a collapse not only of South Vietnam, but Southeast Asia. So we are going to stay there."

President Eisenhower and President Johnson expressed the same conclusion during their terms of office.

For the future of peace, precipitate withdrawal would thus be a disaster of immense magnitude. . . .

In Korea and again in Vietnam, the United States furnished most of the money, most of the arms, and most of the men to help the people of those countries defend their freedom against Communist aggression.

Before any American troops were committed to Vietnam, a leader of another Asian country expressed this opinion to me when I was traveling in Asia as a private citizen. He said: "When you are trying to assist another nation defend its freedom, U.S. policy should be to help them fight the war but not to fight the war for them."

Well, in accordance with this wise counsel, I laid down in Guam three principles as guidelines for future American policy toward Asia:

First, the United States will keep all of its treaty commitments.

Second, we shall provide a shield if a nuclear power threatens the freedom of a nation allied with us or of a nation whose survival we consider vital to our security.

Third, in cases involving other types of aggression, we shall furnish military and economic assistance when requested in accordance with our treaty commitments. But we shall look to the nation directly threatened to assume the primary responsibility of providing the manpower for its defense.

After I announced this policy, I found that the leaders of the Philippines, Thailand, Vietnam, South Korea, and other nations which might be threatened by Communist aggression, welcomed this new direction in American foreign policy.

The defense of freedom is everybody's business not just America's business.

And it is particularly the responsibility of the people whose freedom is threatened.

In the previous administration, we Americanized the war in Vietnam. In this administration, we are Vietnamizing the search for peace.

The policy of the previous administration not only resulted in our assuming the primary responsibility for fighting the war, but even more significantly did not adequately stress the goal of strengthening the South Vietnamese so that they could defend themselves when we left. . . .

My fellow Americans, I am sure you can recognize from what I have said that we really only have two choices open to us if we want to end this war.

I can order an immediate, precipitate withdrawal of all Americans from Vietnam without regard to the effects of that action.

Or we can persist in our search for a just peace through a negotiated settlement if possible, or through continued implementation of our plan for Vietnamization if necessary a plan in which we will withdraw all our forces from Vietnam on a schedule in accordance with our program, as the South Vietnamese become strong enough to defend their own freedom.

I have chosen this second course.

It is not the easy way.

It is the right way.

It is a plan which will end the war and serve the cause of peace—not just in Vietnam but in the Pacific and in the world.

In speaking of the consequences of a precipitate withdrawal, I mentioned that our allies would lose confidence in America.

Far more dangerous, we would lose confidence in ourselves. Oh, the immediate reaction would be a sense of relief that our men were coming home. But as we saw the consequences of what we had done, inevitable remorse and divisive recrimination would scar our spirit as a people.

We have faced other crises in our history and have become stronger by rejecting the easy way out and taking the right way in meeting our challenges. Our greatness as a nation has been our capacity to do what had to be done when we knew our course was right. . . .

18. President Ronald Reagan's speech before the National Association of Evangelicals, March 8, 1983

Midway through his first term in office, President Reagan brought renewed vigor to American foreign policy by likening the Soviet Union to an "evil empire" and calling for a modernization of the nation's nuclear forces to meet its threat.

There is sin and evil in the world, and we're enjoined by Scripture and the Lord Jesus to oppose it with all our might. Our nation, too, has a legacy of evil with which it must deal. The glory of this land has been its capacity for transcending the moral evils of our past. For example, the long struggle of minority citizens for equal rights, once a source of disunity and civil war, is now a point of pride for all Americans. We must never go back. There is no room for racism, anti-Semitism, or other forms of ethnic and racial hatred in this country.

I know that you've been horrified, as have I, by the resurgence of some hate groups preaching bigotry and prejudice. Use the mighty voice of your pulpits and the powerful standing of your churches to denounce and isolate these hate groups in our midst. The commandment given us is clear and simple: "Thou shalt love thy neighbor as thyself."

But whatever sad episodes exist in our past, any objective observer must hold a positive view of American history, a history that has been the story of hopes fulfilled and dreams made into reality. Especially in this century, America has kept alight the torch of freedom, but not just for ourselves but for millions of others around the world.

And this brings me to my final point today. During my first press conference as president, in answer to a direct question, I pointed out that, as good Marxist-Leninists, the Soviet leaders have openly and publicly declared that the only morality they recognize is that which will further their cause, which is world revolution. I think I should point out I was only quoting Lenin, their guiding spirit, who said in 1920 that they repudiate all morality that proceeds from supernatural ideas - that's their name for religion - or ideas that are outside class conceptions. Morality is entirely subordinate to the interests of class war. And everything is moral that is necessary for the annihilation of the old, exploiting social order and for uniting the proletariat.

Well, I think the refusal of many influential people to accept this elementary fact of Soviet doctrine illustrates a historical reluctance to see totalitarian powers for what they are. We saw this phenomenon in the 1930s. We see it too often today.

This doesn't mean we should isolate ourselves and refuse to seek an understanding with them. I intend to do everything I can to persuade them of our peaceful intent, to remind them that it was the West that refused to use its nuclear monopoly in the forties and fifties for territorial gain and which now proposes a 50-percent cut in strategic ballistic missiles and the elimination of an entire class of land-based, intermediate-range nuclear missiles.

At the same time, however, they must be made to understand we will never compromise our principles and standards. We will never give away our freedom. We will never abandon our belief in God. And we will never stop searching for a genuine peace. But we can assure none of these things America stands for through the so-called nuclear freeze solutions proposed by some.

The truth is that a freeze now would be a very dangerous fraud, for that is merely the illusion of peace. The reality is that we must find peace through strength.

I would agree to freeze if only we could freeze the Soviets' global desires. A freeze at current levels of weapons would remove any incentive for the Soviets to negotiate seriously in Geneva and virtually end our chances to achieve the major arms reductions which we have proposed. Instead, they would achieve their objectives through the freeze.

A freeze would reward the Soviet Union for its enormous and unparalleled military buildup. It would prevent the essential and long overdue modernization of United States and allied defenses and would leave our aging forces increasingly vulnerable. And an honest freeze would require extensive prior negotiations on the systems and numbers to be limited and on the measures to ensure effective verification and compliance. And the kind of a freeze that has been suggested would be virtually impossible to verify. Such a major effort would divert us completely from our current negotiations on achieving substantial reductions. . . .

It was C.S. Lewis who, in his unforgettable Screwtape Letters, wrote: "The greatest evil is not done now in those sordid 'dens of crime' that Dickens loved to paint. It is not even done in concentration camps and labor camps. In those we see its final result. But it is conceived and ordered (moved, seconded, carried and minuted) in clean, carpeted, warmed, and well-lighted offices, by quiet men with white collars and cut fingernails and smooth-shaven cheeks who do no need to raise their voice."

Well, because these "quiet men" do no "raise their voices," because they sometimes speak in soothing tones of brotherhood and peace, because, like other dictators before them, they're always making "their final territorial demand," some would have us accept them at their word and accommodate ourselves to their aggressive impulses. But if history teaches anything, it teaches that simpleminded appeasement or wishful thinking about our adversaries is folly. It means the betrayal of our past, the squandering of our freedom.

So, I urge you to speak out against those who would place the United States in a position of military and moral inferiority. You know, I've always believed that old Screwtape reserved his best efforts for those of you in the church. So, in your discussions of the nuclear freeze proposals, I urge you to beware the temptation of pride—the temptation of blithely declaring yourselves above it all and label both sides equally at fault, to ignore the facts of history and the aggressive impulses of an evil empire, to simply call the arms race a giant misunderstanding and thereby remove yourself from the struggle between right and wrong and good and evil. . . .

I believe we shall rise to the challenge. I believe that communism is another sad, bizarre chapter in human history whose last pages even now are being written. I believe this because the source of our strength in the quest for human freedom is not material, but spiritual. And because it knows no limitation, it must terrify and ultimately triumph over those who would enslave their fellow man. For in the words of Isaiah: "He giveth power to the faint; and to them that have no might He increased strength . . . But they that wait upon the Lord shall renew their strength; they shall mount up with wings as eagles; they shall run, and not be weary . . ."

Yes, change your world. One of our Founding Fathers, Thomas Paine, said, "We have it within our power to begin the world over again." We can do it, doing together what no one church could do by itself.

God bless you, and thank you very much.

19. Ronald Reagan "Tear Down this Wall," remarks at the Brandenburg Gate, West Berlin, Germany, June 12, 1987

At the middle point of his second term, President Reagan challenged the leadership of the Soviet Union to remove the most potent symbol of the Cold War division of Europe.

Chancellor Kohl, Governing Mayor Diepgen, ladies and gentlemen: Twenty-four years ago, President John F. Kennedy visited Berlin, speaking to the people of this city and the world at the City Hall. Well, since then two other presidents have come, each in his turn, to Berlin. And today I, myself, make my second visit to your city.

We come to Berlin, we American presidents, because it's our duty to speak, in this place, of freedom. But I must confess, we're drawn here by other things as well: by the feeling of history in this city, more than 500 years older than our own nation; by the beauty of the Grunewald and the Tiergarten; most of all, by your courage and determination. Perhaps the composer Paul Lincke understood something about American presidents. You see, like so many presidents before me, I come here today because wherever I go, whatever I do: Ich hab noch einen Koffer in Berlin. [I still have a suitcase in Berlin.] . . .

Behind me stands a wall that encircles the free sectors of this city, part of a vast system of barriers that divides the entire continent of Europe. From the Baltic, south, those barriers cut across Germany in a gash of barbed wire, concrete, dog runs, and guard towers. Farther south, there may be no visible, no obvious wall. But there remain armed guards and checkpoints all the same—still a restriction on the right to travel, still an instrument to impose upon ordinary men and women the will of a totalitarian state. Yet it is here in Berlin where the wall emerges most clearly; here, cutting across your city, where the news photos and the television screens have imprinted this brutal division of a continent upon the mind of the world. Standing before the Brandenburg Gate, every man is a German, separated from his fellow men. Every man is a Berliner, forced to look upon a scar. . . .

In the 1950s, Khrushchev predicted: "We will bury you." But in the West today, we see a free world that has achieved a level of prosperity and well-being unprecedented in all human history. In the Communist world, we see failure, technological backwardness, declining standards of health, even want of the most basic kind—too little food. Even today, the Soviet Union still cannot feed itself. After these four decades, then, there stands before the entire world one great and inescapable conclusion: Freedom leads to prosperity. Freedom replaces the ancient hatreds among the nations with comity and peace. Freedom is the victor.

And now the Soviets themselves may, in a limited way, be coming to understand the importance of freedom. We hear much from Moscow about a new policy of reform and openness. Some political prisoners have been released. Certain foreign news broadcasts are no longer being jammed. Some economic enterprises have been permitted to operate with greater freedom from state control.

Are these the beginnings of profound changes in the Soviet state? Or are they token gestures, intended to raise false hopes in the West, or to strengthen the Soviet system without changing it? We welcome change and openness; for we believe that freedom and security go together, that the advance of human liberty can only strengthen the cause of world peace. There is one sign the Soviets can make that would be unmistakable, that would advance dramatically the cause of freedom and peace.

General Secretary Gorbachev, if you seek peace, if you seek prosperity for the Soviet Union and Eastern Europe, if you seek liberalization: Come here to this gate! Mr. Gorbachev, open this gate! Mr. Gorbachev, tear down this wall! . . .

And I invite Mr. Gorbachev: Let us work to bring the Eastern and Western parts of the city closer together, so that all the inhabitants of all Berlin can enjoy the benefits that come with life in one of the great cities of the world. . . .

As I looked out a moment ago from the Reichstag, that embodiment of German unity, I noticed words crudely spray-painted upon the wall, perhaps by a young Berliner: "This wall will fall. Beliefs become reality." Yes, across Europe, this wall will fall. For it cannot withstand faith; it cannot withstand truth. The wall cannot withstand freedom.

And I would like, before I close, to say one word. I have read, and I have been questioned since I've been here about certain demonstrations against my coming. And I would like to say just one thing, and to those who demonstrate so. I wonder if they have ever asked themselves that if they should have the kind of government they apparently seek, no one would ever be able to do what they're doing again.

Thank you and God bless you all.

20. George W. Bush, graduation speech at West Point United States Military Academy, June 1, 2002

Months after the terrorist attacks of September 11, 2001, President Bush expounded a new national security strategy based on preemption.

Thank you very much, General Lennox. Mr. Secretary, Governor Pataki, members of the United States Congress, Academy staff and faculty, distinguished guests, proud family members, and graduates: I want to thank you for your welcome. Laura and I are especially honored to visit this great institution in your bicentennial year.

In every corner of America, the words "West Point" command immediate respect. This place where the Hudson River bends is more than a fine institution of learning. The United States Military Academy is the guardian of values that have shaped the soldiers who have shaped the history of the world. . . .

History has also issued its call to your generation. In your last year, America was attacked by a ruthless and resourceful enemy. You graduate from this Academy in a time of war, taking your place in an American military that is powerful and is honorable. Our war on terror is only begun, but in Afghanistan it was begun well. . . .

For much of the last century, America's defense relied on the Cold War doctrines of deterrence and containment. In some cases, those strategies still apply. But new threats also require new thinking. Deterrence — the promise of massive retaliation against nations — means nothing against shadowy terrorist networks with no nation or citizens to defend. Containment is not possible when unbalanced dictators with weapons of mass destruction can deliver those weapons on missiles or secretly provide them to terrorist allies.

We cannot defend America and our friends by hoping for the best. We cannot put our faith in the word of tyrants, who solemnly sign non-proliferation treaties, and then systemically break them. If we wait for threats to fully materialize, we will have waited too long.

Homeland defense and missile defense are part of stronger security, and they're essential priorities for America. Yet the war on terror will not be won on the defensive. We must take the battle to the enemy, disrupt his plans, and confront the worst threats before they emerge. In the world we have entered, the only path to safety is the path of action. And this nation will act.

Our security will require the best intelligence, to reveal threats hidden in caves and growing in laboratories. Our security will require modernizing domestic agencies such as the FBI, so they're prepared to act, and act quickly, against danger. Our security will require transforming the military you will lead — a military that must be ready to strike at a moment's notice in any dark corner of the world. And our security will require all Americans to be forward-looking and resolute, to be ready for preemptive action when necessary to defend our liberty and to defend our lives. . . .

Some worry that it is somehow undiplomatic or impolite to speak the language of right and wrong. I disagree. Different circumstances require different methods, but not different moralities. Moral truth is the same in every culture, in every time, and in every place. Targeting innocent civilians for murder is always and everywhere wrong. Brutality against women is always and everywhere wrong. There can be no neutrality between justice and cruelty, between the innocent and the guilty. We are in a conflict between good and evil, and America will call evil by its name. By confronting evil and lawless regimes, we do not create a problem, we reveal a problem. And we will lead the world in opposing it. . . .

America has a greater objective than controlling threats and containing resentment. We will work for a just and peaceful world beyond the war on terror.

The bicentennial class of West Point now enters this drama. With all in the United States Army, you will stand between your fellow citizens and grave danger. You will help establish a peace that allows millions around the world to live in liberty and to grow in prosperity. You will face times of calm, and times of crisis. And every test will find you prepared— because you're the men and women of West Point. You leave here marked by the character of this Academy, carrying with you the highest ideals of our nation. . . .

Today, your last day at West Point, you begin a life of service in a career unlike any other. You've answered a calling to hardship and purpose, to risk and honor. At the end of every day you will know that you have faithfully done your duty. May you always bring to that duty the high standards of this great American institution. May you always be worthy of the long gray line that stretches two centuries behind you.

On behalf of the nation, I congratulate each one of you for the commission you've earned and for the credit you bring to the United States of America. May God bless you all.

Chronology of the Foreign Relations of the United States

1776

July 4: Continental Congress votes 12–0 in favor of a Declaration of Independence of the American colonies from Great Britain.

September 24–26: Congress approves Model Treaty for relations with Europe and appoints Benjamin Franklin, Silas Deane, and Arthur Lee to negotiate treaties with European governments.

December 26: American forces defeat British troops at Trenton.

1777

April 17: Congress establishes Committee of Foreign Affairs.

October 17: American forces victorious at Saratoga.

November 15: Articles of Confederation adopted.

December17: France recognizes American independence.

1778

February 6: Franco-American Treaty of Alliance, ratified May 4.

September 17: British and French navies clash off Brest.

1779

June 21: Spain declares war on Britain, declines alliance with American rebels, but agrees to subsidize independence forces.

September 27: Congress appoints John Adams to negotiate terms of peace with Britain, independence not negotiable.

February 28: Russia declares "armed neutrality" and is later joined by the Netherlands, the Austrian Holy Roman Empire, Prussia, Portugal, and the Kingdom of the Two Sicilies.

May 12: British troops capture Charleston, South Carolina.

May 25: General George Washington's troops mutiny at Morristown, New Jersey.

July 11: Six thousand French troops arrive at Newport, Rhode Island.

1780

December 30: The Netherlands declares war on Britain.

1781

February 3: British forces capture Dutch colony of St. Eustatius.

March 1: Articles of Confederation adopted as first Constitution of the United States.

October 19: Washington defeats Cornwallis at Yorktown; Britain seeks peace.

October 20: Robert Livingston appointed first secretary for foreign affairs.

1782

February 27: British House of Commons votes to make peace with "former colonies."

April 12: Rockingham government begins negotiations.

October 8: The United States of America signs Treaty of Friendship and Commerce with the Netherlands.

November 30: Preliminary peace terms agreed to with Britain.

1783

January 20: Articles of Peace become effective, Congress approves on April 15.

September 3: Treaty of Paris signed by Britain, France, Spain, and the United States.

December 12: Washington resigns command of American armies to Congress.

December 26: Trade with Great Britain revived.

1784

April 23: Congress approves first Northwest Ordinance.

April 30: Congress requests power to regulate trade.

June 26: Spain closes Mississippi to American navigation.

August 30: France restricts U.S. trade in West Indies.

September 21: John Jay appointed secretary for foreign affairs.

1785

February 24: John Adams appointed minister to Great Britain.

March 10: Thomas Jefferson becomes minister to France.

April 8: Britain restricts U.S. trade with Canadian maritime provinces.

May 20: Congress passes second Northwest Ordinance.

July 20: Jay begins negotiations with Spain over Mississippi.

September 20: Commercial Treaty signed with Prussia.

December 8: Adams demands British evacuation of Northwest posts.

1786

July 17: Congress approves treaty with Barbary state of Morocco.

August 29: Jay agreement with Spain in Congress.

1787

February 4: Shays's Rebellion defeated.

May 25: Philadelphia Constitutional Convention convenes.

October 27: First *Federalist Papers* published.

1788

September 13: Constitution ratified by eleven states.

December 1: Spain grants limited navigation rights on Mississippi.

Washington Presidency
1789

March 4: Senate unanimous in choosing George Washington as first president of the United States; John Adams vice president.

April 30: Washington inaugurated; establishes cabinet with Departments of State, War, and Treasury.

May 5: French Estates General convenes at Versailles.

July 4: Congress passes protective tariff.

July 14: Bastille stormed in Paris.

July 27: Congress creates Department of State.

August 27: French Assembly issues *Declaration of the Rights of Man.*

1790

April 30: Britain threatens war with Spain over Nootka Sound incident, Spain yields.

1791

June 20–25: Louis XVI attempts to flee France, is apprehended, and forced to accept constitutional monarchy.

November 4: Ohio Indians defeat American forces with help of British arms.

1792

April 20: France declares war on Austria.

August 10: Revolutionary forces storm Tuileries Palace in Paris, King's powers suspended.

September 21: First French Republic proclaimed.

December 5: Washington reelected president.

1793

January 21: Louis XVI executed.

February 1: France declares war on Britain and Netherlands.

April 1: Committee of Public Safety suspends French republic's constitution. Maximilien Robespierre institutes dictatorial Reign of Terror.

April 22: Washington declares American neutrality in European conflict.

August 1: The United States demands the recall of Edmund Genet, French minister to America, for commissioning privateers to operate against Britain.

1794

April 20: American forces defeat Indians in Ohio territory.

November 19: Jay Treaty with Britain signed.

1795

June 24: Jay Treaty with Britain approved by Congress after heated debate.

October 27: Thomas Pinckney concludes Treaty of San Lorenzo resolving Mississippi dispute with Spain.

1796

June 30: United States stops sale of French prizes of war in American ports.

July 2: France announces it will treat American and British ships alike.

August 19: Spain joins French war against Britain.

September 19: Washington's Farewell Address.

November 15: France suspends diplomatic relations with the United States.

Adams Presidency
1797

March 2: French warships directed to intercept all cargo bound for Britain.

May 31: President Adams seeks treaty of amity with France.

October 18: XYZ Affair in Paris results in an undeclared naval war with France.

1798

March 19: President Adams permits American merchant ships to arm.

March 27: Democratic-Republicans proclaim Sprigg Resolutions, opposing war with France.

April 7: Congress establishes Mississippi Territory.

April 27: Adams establishes Department of the Navy, Congress authorizes twelve warships.

May 28: Congress authorizes use of Navy to seize French ships.

June 13: United States embargos all commerce with France.

June 25: Alien Friends Act passed.

July 1: French army under Napoleon Bonaparte invades Egypt.

July 6: Alien Enemy Act passed.

July 11: United States Marine Corps established.

July 14: Sedition Act passed.

July 31: France seeks reconciliation.

August 1: British fleet wins Battle of the Nile.

December 2: Second Coalition—Austria, Britain, Naples, Portugal, Ottoman Empire, and Russia—formed against France.

December 14: Virginia legislature opposes Alien and Sedition Acts.

1799

February 9: USS *Constellation* captures French frigate *Insurgente*.

February 9: United States supports Saint Domingue revolt against France.

November 9: Napoleon made first consul, overthrowing the Directorate.

1800

June 14: Napoleon wins Battle Marengo.

September 30–October 1: Convention of Môrtefontaine restores friendly relations with France.

October 1: Second Treaty of Ildefonso gives Spanish Louisiana Territory to France.

December 3: Deadlocked presidential election decided by House of Representatives; Thomas Jefferson is president, Aaron Burr vice president.

Jefferson Presidency
1801

February 9: Franco-Austrian Treaty of Lunéville dissolves most of the Holy Roman Empire.

May 20: Jefferson orders naval force to be used against Barbary states.

August 1: American sloop *Enterprize* captures Barbary ship *Tripoli* off Malta.

1802

March 16: U.S. Military Academy established.

March 27: Anglo-French Treaty of Amiens.

November 2: France fails to suppress Saint Domingue revolt.

1803

April 30: Louisiana Purchase, the United States acquires the territory from France for $15 million.

May 12: Anglo-American Boundary Convention.

May 16: Britain declares war on France.

August 31: Lewis and Clark expedition begins.

October 31: Tripoli captures U.S. frigate *Philadelphia*.

1804

February 24: Mobil Act, Congress claims West Florida for the United States.

May 18: Napoleon proclaimed Emperor of France.

December 5: Jefferson reelected.

December 12: Spain declares war on Britain.

1805

April 11: Anglo-Russian Alliance.

May 22: British action against neutral U.S. shipping begins to increase.

June 9: Austria joins Third Coalition.

June 10: Peace with Tripoli after U.S. Marines capture Derna.

October 10: Napoleon victorious at Ulm.

October 21: Britain defeats Franco-Spanish fleet at Trafalgar.

December 2: Napoleon victorious at Austerlitz.

1806

April 10: Secretary of State James Madison protests British naval blockade and pressed service of Americans. Senate condemns "unprovoked aggression," passes First Non-Importation Act.

December 2: Congress bans all slave importation to the United States, effective January 1, 1808.

December 31: Monroe-Pinkney Treaty with Britain.

1807

June 22: Leopard-Chesapeake Affair brings Britain and the United States to the brink of war.

July 7–9: Victorious France concludes Treaties of Tilsit with Prussia and Russia.

December 22: First Embargo Act against all American overseas commerce.

1808

May 21: Canadian border incidents heighten tension with Britain.

November 22: Congress reports Embargo Act a failure.

December 7: James Madison wins presidential election.

1809

January 9: Embargo enforcement tightened.

March 1: Jefferson signs Non-Intercourse Act in response to opposition to embargo.

Madison Presidency
1809

April 19: Madison reinstates trade with Britain.

August 9: Madison revives Non-Intercourse Act.

1810

January 20: United States seeks new talks with Britain.

October 27: United States annexes West Florida.

1811

February 28: United States and Britain recall ministers.

May 16: USS *President* attacks HMS *Little Belt.*

May 16: Reinstatement of nonintercourse policy against Great Britain.

July 31: Mexico defeats Hidalgo revolt.

November 4: Congressional "War Hawks" demand action against British and Indians in Northwest.

November 8: American forces defeat Indians at Tippecanoe.

1812

April 4: Congress approves full embargo against Britain.

May 28: Britain refuses to lift commercial restrictions.

June 18: Congress declares war on Britain, War of 1812 begins.

September 14: Napoleon's army in Moscow.

October 19: Napoleon's army begins retreat.

December 2: Madison reelected.

December 26: Britain blockades U.S. ports.

December 29: U.S. and British ships duel off Brazil.

1813

February 28: Treaty of Kadish, Russian and Prussia ally against France.

March 3: Britain and Sweden ally against France.

April 17: American forces burn York, Canada.

June 15: Treaty of Reichenbach, Britain, Prussia, and Russia ally against France.

September 10: U.S. Navy wins Battle of Lake Erie.

October 5: U.S. forces win Battle of the Thames in Canada.

October 16–19: Napoleon defeated by allies in Battle of Leipzig.

December 29–30: British burn Buffalo, capture Fort Niagara.

December 30: Britain offers peace talks.

1814

March 13: Allied armies enter Paris, Napoleon exiled to Elba.

May 30: Treaty of Paris, European war ends.

August 24–25: British capture and burn Washington, D.C.

September 12–14: British attack Baltimore, bombard Fort McHenry.

December 24: Treaty of Ghent signed by American and British negotiators.

January 8: Battle of New Orleans, unaware of peace Andrew Jackson leads American soldiers to spectacular victory.

1815

March 2: Congress declares war on Algeria.

June 8: Congress of Vienna.

June 18: Resurgent Napoleon defeated at Waterloo.

June 30: Algeria accepts American terms.

November 20: Second Treaty of Paris signed.

December 22: Spain defeats Morelos rebels in Mexico.

1816

April 27: Protective tariff imposed, Second Bank of the United States established.

December 4: James Monroe elected president.

Monroe Presidency
1817

March 13: Neutrality Act limits U.S. aid to rebel Spanish colonies in Latin America.

April 29: Rush-Bagot Agreement; Great Lakes demilitarized.

1818

February 12: Chilean independence proclaimed.

April 7: U.S. forces under Andrew Jackson capture Spanish posts in Florida.

October 20: Convention of 1818 resolves commercial issues with Britain.

November 28: Secretary of State John Quincy Adams blames Spain for Florida conflict.

1819
February 22: Transcontinental Treaty with Spain; Spain cedes East Florida and renounces claim to West Florida.

February 24: House defends Jackson's Florida campaign.

1820
March 3: Missouri Compromise approved.

May 15: Congress presses Britain to liberalize trade access to West Indian colonies.

May 15: Congress declares slave trade piracy.

December 6: Monroe reelected.

1821
February 25: Mexican independence proclaimed.

June 24: Simon Bolívar victorious at Carabobo; Venezuela independent.

November 21: Terranova Incident in China.

1822
June 24: British parliament opens West Indies ports to U.S. trade.

September 7: Brazilian independence proclaimed.

1823
February 28: House seeks international agreement against slave trade.

April 28: United States supports Spanish retention of Cuba and Puerto Rico.

July 1: Central American colonies declare independence from Spain.

June 17: Britain renews duties on U.S. shipping in West Indies.

July 17: United States opposes Russian claim to Pacific Coast territory.

August 16–20: Britain seeks Anglo-American agreement against European intervention in Spanish Americas.

October 9: Britain warns France against interventions in Spanish Americas.

December 2: State of the Union address includes Monroe Doctrine opposing any European intervention in the Western Hemisphere and pledging American noninterference in European affairs.

1824
April 17: Russia accepts 54° 40' as southern boundary of its North American territory.

December 1: Presidential election yields no majority winner.

John Quincy Adams Presidency
1825
February 9: House elects John Quincy Adams president.

February 16: Russia and Britain sign treaty on 54° 40' boundary.

March 4: Erie Canal completed.

June 27: Britain bans all U.S. trade with West Indies.

August 6: Bolivia declares independence from Spain.

October 25: United States warns France not to occupy Cuba.

December 26: Adams nominates two delegates for the Panama Congress.

1826
March 14: Senate approves delegates to the Panama Congress against strong opposition.

July 15: Panama Congress adjourns with no U.S. attendance.

1827
March 27: United States closes ports to British vessels from ports in the Western hemisphere.

August 6: Anglo-American convention on Oregon Territory.

1828
January 12: Mexican-American treaty recognizes Sabine River boundary.

May 19: Congress approves "Tariff of Abominations."

December 3: Andrew Jackson elected president.

Jackson Presidency
1829
August 25: Renewed effort to purchase Texas from Mexico.

August 27: Treaty of Commerce and Navigation with Austria-Hungary.

1830
May 7: Commercial Treaty with Ottoman Empire.

May 28: Congress approves Indian removal policy.

July 5: French army captures Algiers, deposes the dey.

July 28: Revolution in Paris topples Charles X.

October 5: Jackson secures partial resolution of West Indies trade dispute.

1831

April 5: Boundary and commercial treaties with Mexico.

December 7: Jackson and Senate reject arbitrator's decision on Northeast boundary.

1832

January 26: Falkland Islands crisis with Argentina.

May 16: Treaty of Peace, Amity, Commerce and Navigation with Chile.

July 14: Tariff of 1832 passes Congress, rejected by South Carolina.

December 5: Jackson reelected.

December 15: Britain sends sloop of war to reclaim Falkland Islands.

1833

February 12: Henry Clay's Compromise Tariff resolves disputes of 1832.

1834

February 17: Van Ness Convention with Spain.

1835

November 6: United States severs relations with France over spoliation dispute.

1836

February 5: France agrees to pay spoliation claims.

March 2: Texas declares independence from Mexico.

March 6: Alamo falls to Mexican army.

April 21: Texans win Battle of San Jacinto.

May 31: Treaty of Peace, Friendship, Navigation and Commerce with Venezuela.

September 16: Treaty of Peace with Morocco.

December 7: Martin Van Buren elected president.

Van Buren Presidency
1837

March 3: Congress recognizes independence of Texas.

August 25: Van Buren rejects request to annex Texas.

December 29: Caroline incident with Canada.

1838

March 10: Revision of Neutrality Laws.

April 25: Texas-American Boundary Convention.

May 29: Sir Robert Peel Incident with Canada.

August 18: Wilkes expedition leaves for South Seas.

1839

January 14: Secretary of State John Forsyth declares United States neutral over Falklands.

February 27: "Aroostook War" along Canadian border.

September 6: Amistad incident with Spain.

November 3: Anglo-Chinese Opium War begins.

1840

December 2: William Henry Harrison elected president, John Tyler as vice president.

Harrison/Tyler Presidency
1841

March 9: U.S. Supreme Court frees *Amistad* slaves.

April 4: President Harrison dies of pneumonia, Tyler sworn in as president.

1842

March 30: Congress raises tariffs to 1832 levels.

August 9: Webster-Ashburton Treaty settles Northeast boundary issues.

August 29: Britain wins Opium War; China cedes Hong Kong in Treaty of Nanking.

October 20: Commodore Thomas Jones temporarily seizes Monterey, mistakenly claims California for the United States.

December 30: Tyler asserts U.S. interest in Hawaii.

1843

August 23: Mexico protests U.S. interest in annexing Texas.

September.23: Mexican President Santa Anna bans foreign retail business in Mexico.

December 16: U.S. Navy conducts punitive operations against African coastal villages.

1844

February 15: Texas wants annexation treaty.

April 12: Texas Treaty of Annexation.

June 8: Texas annexation treaty rejected by Senate.

July 3: Treaty of Wanghia with China.

July 18: Britain aborts efforts to keep Texas independent.

September 29: Sancola incident with Argentina.

October 31: Santa Anna overthrown in Mexico.

December 3: Tyler advocates Texas annexation to Congress.

December 4: James Polk elected president on annexation platform.

Polk Presidency
1845

March 1: Texas annexed by joint House and Senate resolution.

March 3: President John Tyler signs congressional joint resolution providing for admission of Texas to the Union.

March 4: Polk is inaugurated.

July 2: Britain rejects 49° Oregon boundary.

December 2: Polk asserts U.S. right to 54° 40' Oregon border.

1846

January 2: Mexican president Herrera overthrown in a coup.

January 13: Polk orders General Taylor to station his troops on the north bank of the Rio Grande River.

April 25: First clash between U.S. and Mexican troops.

May 13: Congress declares war on Mexico.

June 15: Oregon Treaty settles Anglo-American boundary dispute.

August 15: United States occupies New Mexico.

1847

January 13: Treaty of Cahuenga ends fighting in California.

February 23: United States wins battle of Buena Vista.

March 27: Vera Cruz surrenders to General Winfield Scott.

August 24–27: Armistice of Tacubaya.

September 14: U.S. troops capture Mexico City.

December 6: Nicholas Trist refuses Polk's order to return home.

1848

February 2: Trist completes the Treaty of Guadalupe Hidalgo, which satisfies all of Polk's war objectives in return for $15 million in compensation to Mexico.

February 22: Revolution in France, Louis Philippe abdicates.

March 10: Senate ratifies the Treaty of Guadalupe Hidalgo.

March 13: Republican uprising in Vienna.

May 18: Frankfurt National Assembly.

August 14: The Territory of Oregon is organized by an act of the U.S. Congress.

November 7: Zachary Taylor elected president, Millard Fillmore is vice president.

Taylor/Fillmore Presidency
1849

June 12: Panama Railroad Company secures authority to build across Panamanian Isthmus.

December 4: Taylor recommends annexation of California.

1850

April 19: Clayton-Bulwer Treaty on Central American Canal.

July 9: Taylor dies of acute gastroenteritis; Fillmore sworn in as president.

September 9: Compromise of 1850: California a free state; New Mexico and Utah territories.

1851

December 2: Louis Napoleon seizes power in France; Second Republic falls.

1852

April 30: Webster-Crampton Convention refines Clayton-Bulwer Treaty.

November 2: Franklin Pierce elected president.

Pierce Presidency
1853

January 20: British forces capture Rangoon and Pegu, Anglo-Burmese war ends.

July 8–13: Admiral Perry's fleet anchors in the Bay of Edo, Tokyo.

September 7: Taiping rebels capture Shanghai.

December 30: Gadsden Treaty with Mexico.

1854

February 28: Black Warrior incident in Havana, crisis in U.S.-Spanish relations.

March 28: Crimean War begins.

March 31: Perry signs Treaty of Kanagawa with Japanese officials.

April 3: Secretary of State William Marcy offers U.S. purchase of Cuba.

May 30: Kansas-Nebraska Bill passes Congress.

October 18: Ostend Manifesto favors U.S. purchase of Cuba.

December 18: Spanish Cortes rejects sale of Cuba.

1855

January 28: Panama Railroad Company of New York begins service across Isthmus of Panama.

October 15: Accessory Transit Company uses mercenaries to topple Nicaraguan government.

1856

April 16: Declaration of Paris ends Crimean War.

November 4: James Buchanan elected president.

November 16: U.S. gunboats attack Chinese Barrier forts.

Buchanan Presidency

1857

February 5: Liberal government of Benito Juárez established in Veracruz, Mexico.

March 3: Tariff of 1857 reduces tariffs and enlarges tariff-free list.

May 1: ATC regime in Nicaragua overthrown.

June 17: United States and Japan sign commercial agreement.

1858

May 28: Russian and China sign Treaty of Aigun.

June 18: Treaty of Tientsin with China.

July 29: Second commercial treaty with Japan.

August 2: India Act brings India under British political control.

August 8: Transatlantic cable completed.

November 8: United States signs commercial treaty with China.

1859

April 7: United States recognizes Juárez government in Mexico.

May 19: Vicksburg Convention demands an end to all measures against the slave trade.

June 25: Taku incident in China, followed by Anglo-French military intervention.

July 30: United States fails in its attempt to purchase more Mexican territory.

October 19: John Brown's raid on the federal arsenal at Harper's Ferry.

December 19: Congress denies Buchanan authority to intervene in Mexican civil war.

1860

August 31: United States warns France not to intervene in Mexico.

October 12: Peking occupied by Anglo-French troops.

November 6: Abraham Lincoln elected president.

December 20: South Carolina adopts Ordinance of Secession.

Lincoln Presidency

1861

January 9–26: Mississippi, Florida, Alabama, Georgia, and Louisiana, secede from the Union.

February 1: Texas secedes from the Union.

February 4: Six Southern states form the Confederate States of America (CSA).

February 19: Alexander II, of Russia, emancipates the serfs.

March 2: Morrill Tariff raises duties on manufactured imports.

March 4: Lincoln takes oath of office.

April 13: Fort Sumter taken by Confederate forces.

July 21: CSA wins First Battle of Bull Run (First Manassas).

October 31: Convention of London between Britain, France, Spain, and Mexico.

November–December: Trent Affair.

December 17: Veracruz occupied by British, French, and Spanish troops.

1862

April 6–7: Grant wins Battle of Shiloh.

July 31: Confederate commerce raider *Alabama* permitted to leave Britain.

September 17: Battle of Antietam: tactical draw but political victory for Lincoln.

September 22: Otto von Bismarck appointed prime minister of Prussia.

September 23: Lincoln issues preliminary Emancipation Proclamation.

November 1: Napoleon III proposes Britain, France, and Russia mediate U.S. Civil War.

December 13–15: CSA wins Battle of Fredericksburg.

1863

January 1: Lincoln issues full Emancipation Proclamation.

January 22: Russian troops put down Polish uprising.

February 6: Secretary of State Seward rejects French mediation offers.

May 1–3: CSA wins Battle of Chancellorsville.

June 7: French troops occupy Mexico City.

July 1–3: Meade wins three-day Battle of Gettysburg.

July 4: Vicksburg surrenders to Grant after sustained siege.

September 5: Britain agrees cease ship sales to the CSA.

September 18–20: CSA wins Battle of Chickamauga.

August 11: Cambodia becomes French protectorate.

November: 23–25: Union wins Battle of Chattanooga.

1864

April 4: House protests French actions in Mexico.

May 5: Sherman begins march to Atlanta and on to Savannah.

September 5–8: U.S., British, Dutch, and French warships fire upon Japanese fortress of Shimonoseki.

September 23: Bakufu opens Yokohama and Inland Sea to foreign trade.

October 19: United States protests Confederate raids launched from Canadian (British) territory.

November 8: Lincoln is reelected president.

September–December: Union armies besiege Richmond and Petersburg, Virginia.

1865

January–March: Union armies press siege of Richmond and Petersburg.

April 9: Lee surrenders to Grant at Appomattox Court House.

April 15: President Lincoln dies after assasination; Andrew Johnson sworn in as president.

May: Final Confederate surrender in the Trans-Mississippi Region; Civil War ends.

Andrew Johnson Presidency

1865

May 1: Uprising in Santo Domingo defeats Spanish forces.

November 6: United States refuses to recognize Maximilian as Emperor of Mexico.

December 5: United States pressures France to remove troops from Mexico.

1866

March 17: United States terminates Marcy-Elgin Treaty of 1854.

April 15: France announces withdrawal from Mexico.

May 31: The French begin their phased withdrawal from Mexico.

May 31: Irish Fenian Brotherhood conducts unsuccessful raids in Canada.

June 25: United States signs joint tariff convention with Japan.

June 27: Seven Weeks' War between Austria and Prussia begins.

July 3: Prussia wins Battle of Königgrätz.

1867

March 30: Russia sells Alaska to U.S.

June 13: U.S. warships conduct punitive actions in Formosa.

June 19: Maximilian executed by firing squad.

June 21: Dickenson-Ayon Treaty with Nicaragua provides for free transit between oceans.

July 1: British North America Act creates The Dominion of Canada under British rule.

August 28: United States takes possession of Midway Island.

October 24: Denmark agrees to sell Virgin Islands to United States.

1868

January 3: Emperor takes direct control of Japan, Tokugawa Shogunate ends, Meiji Restoration begins.

March 5: Impeachment hearings against Andrew Johnson begin.

July 28: Burlingame Treaty with China is signed.

October 10: Civil war breaks out in Cuba.

November 3: Ulysses S. Grant elected president.

1869

January 14: Johnson-Clarendon Convention signed with Britain.

Grant Presidency

1869

January 14: Senate rejects Panamanian canal rights treaty with Colombia.

April 13: Senate rejects Clarendon-Johnson Treaty.

November 17: Suez Canal opens.

1870

January 20: Senate rejects amended Panamanian canal rights treaty with Colombia.

July 19: France declares war on Prussia.

September 2: Prussian and German armies win Battle of Sedan.

September 4: French Third Republic proclaimed.

1871

January 18: Under Prussian leadership German states unite to form German Empire.

January 18: Wilhelm II proclaimed German Emperor, Bismarck is chancellor.

April 30: U.S. Army begins campaign against Apache in Arizona.

May 8: Anglo-American Treaty of Washington over *Alabama* claims.

May 10: Treaty of Frankfurt ends Franco-Prussian War.

1872

May 22: Senate rejects treaty with Samoa.

October 21: Germany arbitrates Northwest border dispute in favor of United States.

November 5: Japan obtains control of Ryukyu Islands.

November 5: Grant is reelected president.

1873
February 12: First Spanish republic proclaimed.

August 27: United States urges Spain to reform colonial regime in Cuba.

November 29: Virginius incident in Cuba.

December 31: Military coup topples Spanish republic, Alfonso XII is King.

1875
January 30: Hawaii becomes U.S. protectorate.

July 5: Insurrection against Ottoman rule in Bosnia-Herzogovina.

November 25: Britain buys controlling interest in Suez Canal.

1876
February 26: Sino-Japanese treaty on Korean independence.

March 1: U.S. attempt to mediate Cuban insurrection fails.

June 25: U.S. Army defeated by Sioux at Battle of Little Big Horn.

June 30: Serbia declares war on Turkey.

October 31: U.S. forces capture Crazy Horse and Sitting Bull, Sioux Wars end.

November 7: Presidential election produces Hayes-Tilden deadlock.

November 20: Porfirio Diaz overthrows President Tejada in Mexico.

Hayes Presidency
1877
March 2: Rutherford Hayes declared president by Congress; William Wheeler is vice president.

April 24: Russia declares war on Turkey.

June 1: U.S. troops ordered to patrol Mexican border.

1878
January 17: United States signs treaty with Samoa, establishing naval base at Pago Pago.

February 8: British fleet protects Istanbul from Russian capture.

February 10: Convention of El Zanjon, Cuban insurrection ends.

March 23: United States recognizes Diaz regime in Mexico.

May 18: Colombia grants French company exclusive Panama Canal rights.

1879
October 7: Germany and Austria sign Dual Alliance.

1880
February 24: Mexican border tension ends.

March 8: House protests French Panama Canal project.

October 27: United States fails to mediate war between Chile and Bolivia/Peru.

November 2: James Garfield elected president; Chester Arthur vice president.

November 17: Treaty with China permits immigration restrictions.

Garfield Presidency
1881
May 12: France establishes protectorate in Tunisia.

June 2: Britain pays an indemnity to U.S. fishermen for 1878 Newfoundland fisheries quarrel.

June 18: Austria, Germany, and Russia form Three Emperors League.

June 24: Secretary of State Blaine seeks revision of the Clayton-Bulwer Treaty.

July 2: President Garfield shot.

September 19: President Garfield dies; Chester Arthur sworn in as president.

Arthur Presidency
1882
January 26: Release of confidential documents thwart U.S. mediation efforts in Chile-Bolivian dispute.

May 6: Congress suspends Chinese immigration for ten years.

May 20: Austria, Germany, and Italy form Triple Alliance.

May 22: U.S. commercial treaty with Korea.

September 15: British troops occupy Cairo.

1883
February 22: Congress votes to repay Japan 1864 Shimonoseki indemnity.

March 3: Tariff of 1883 retains high duties.

March 3: Congress authorizes construction of a modern U.S. Navy.

October 20: Treaty of Ancon ends war between Chile and Peru.

1884

April 4: Truce of Valparaiso ends war between Chile and Bolovia.

June 6: Treaty of Hue gives France control of northern Vietnam.

July 5: Congress further tightens Chinese immigration.

November 4: Grover Cleveland elected president; Thomas Hendricks vice-president.

December 6: United States secures naval base at Pearl Harbor, Hawaii.

Cleveland Presidency I
1885

February 26: U.S. delegation sent to Berlin conference on Congo.

March 27: Anglo-German entente on East Africa, Samoa, and Egypt.

March 30: Russian attack on Afghan forces in Penjdeh, Britain threatens war.

April 18: Sino-Japanese agreement to withdraw forces from Korea.

May 2: Leopold II of Belgium becomes ruler of Congo Free State.

November 13: Serbia declares war on Bulgaria.

1886

January 1: Britain annexes Upper Burma.

August 3: Congress provides for construction of twenty-two steel ships for U.S. Navy.

1887

January 9: Anglo-American/Canadian seal dispute.

February 12: Britain seeks Mediterranean agreements with Austria, Italy, and Spain.

February 20: Austria, Germany, and Italy renew Triple Alliance.

March 3: United States bars Canadian fishing/shipping vessels from American ports.

June 18: Germany and Russia sign Reinsurance Treaty.

June 25: Washington conference over Samoan dispute convenes.

August 19: German marines seize control of Samoa.

October 11: United States declares neutrality on Samoan issue.

1888

February 15: Bayard-Chamberlain Treaty ends U.S.-Canadian fishing/shipping.

March 12: Treaty with China excludes Chinese laborer immigration for twenty years.

October 21: Murchison letter damages Cleveland's reelection hopes.

October 29: European powers sign Suez Canal Convention.

November 6: Benjamin Harrison elected president.

Harrison Presidency
1889

March 2: United States claims jurisdiction over Bering Sea.

May 31: British Parliament passes Naval Defense Act, applying two-power naval standard.

June 14: General Act of Berlin ends Samoan crisis.

October 2: First Pan-American Conference convenes in Washington.

1890

March 18: Bismarck resigns as chancellor of Germany.

July 2: Sherman Anti-Trust Law enacted.

October 1: McKinley Tariff hikes import duties as high as 49.5 percent.

1891

March 3: Civil war breaks out in Chile.

June 15: United States and Britain settle Bering Strait fishing dispute.

July 4: U.S. Navy captures Chilean rebel ship *Itata*.

October 16: Chilean mob attacks U.S. seamen in Valparaiso.

1892

January 25: Chile agrees to reparations for Valparaiso incident.

November 8: Grover Cleveland elected president.

Cleveland Presidency II
1893

January 17: Queen Liliuokalani of Hawaii overthrown, provisional government requests U.S. annexation.

April 23: Onset of 1893 stock market crash.

1894

January 4: France and Russia.

January 29: U.S. Navy assists republicans in Brazil.

May 31: United States recognizes new Hawaiian government but refuses annexation.

July 4: Republic of Hawaii proclaimed.

August 1: War breaks out between China and Japan over Korea.

August 28: Cleveland lowers U.S. trade tariffs.

1895

February 20: Congress recommends arbitration of Anglo-Venezuelan boundary dispute.

February 23: Renewed rebellion against Spanish rule in Cuba.

April 17: Treaty of Shimonoseki ends Sino-Japanese War, Japan triumphant.

April 27: British marines seize Corinto, Nicaragua.

June 28: United States officially neutral in Cuban rebellion.

June 25: Joseph Chamberlain becomes British colonial secretary.

July 20: United States demands arbitration in Anglo-Venezuelan dispute.

December 17: Britain refuses Venezuelan arbitration, Cleveland threatens action under Monroe Doctrine.

1896

January 3: Anglo-German Kruger Telegram incident.

January 15: Britain and France agree on Siamese independence.

March 1: Battle of Adowa, Ethiopians defeat Italian army.

April 4: United States offers Cuban mediation.

April 6: Congress calls for Cuban independence.

June 3: China and Russia sign Manchurian Treaty.

November 3: William McKinley elected president.

November 12: Anglo-American agreement on Venezuelan arbitration.

December 30: Spain executes Philippine rebel leader José Rizal y Mercado.

McKinley Presidency

1897

April 17: War breaks out between Turkey and Greece.

April 30: Austro-Russian Agreement about maintaining the status quo in the Balkans.

May 5: Japan demands end to immigration discrimination in Hawaii, sends warship.

June 16: United States signs annexation treaty with Hawaii.

July 7: Dingley Tariff raises duty rates to 57 percent.

September 18: United States demands Spain bring peace to Cuba.

November 14: German troops occupy Kiaochow and Tsingtao, China.

December 14: Russian fleet ordered to proceed to Port Arthur.

December: Diplomatic conflict between Russia and Britain over China.

1898

January 12: Rioting in Havana, United States sends USS *Maine.*

January 25: Salisbury's note to Russia offering a compromise over Asia.

February 15: Maine destroyed by explosion in Havana harbor.

February 25: U.S. Navy Asia Squadron on alert.

March 27: China leases Port Arthur and Talienwan to Russia.

March 27: China leases Weihaiwei to Britain.

March 28: First Naval Bill funds expansion of German Navy.

April 10: China leases Kuangchowwan to France.

April 11: McKinley asks congressional authority for military action in Cuba.

April 19–20: Congress approves military action to support Cuban independence.

April 25: United States declares war on Spain.

April 25: Nishi-Rosen Agreement between Russia and Japan over Manchuria and Korea.

May 1: U.S. Navy defeats Spanish fleet in Manila Bay.

May 25: U.S Army expeditionary force departs for the Philippines.

May 29: U.S. Navy blockades Spanish fleet in Cuba.

June 29: U.S. Navy captures Guam.

July 3: U.S. Navy destroys Spanish fleet in Cuba.

July 4: U.S. occupies Wake Island.

July 6: U.S. annexes Hawaii.

August 12: Spain requests armistice, Spanish-American War ends.

August 30: Britain-German Agreement about the Portuguese colonies.

September 9: Filipinos declare independent republic.

September 18: Fashoda incident between Britain and France.

November 21: Commercial treaty signed between France and Italy.

December 10: Treaty of Paris signed by United States and Spain.

1899

February 4: Fighting breaks out between U.S. and Filipino troops in Manila.

February 6: United States annexes Guam, Puerto Rico, and the Philippines.

March 11: United States, Britain, and Germany in dispute over Samoa.

May 18: First Hague Conference on Disarmament convenes.

August 9: The Franco-Russian Alliance is extended.

September 6: United States asks European power and Japan to reaffirm Open Door policy in China.

October 9: Boer Republics of Transvaal and Orange Free State issue ultimatum to Britain.

October 11: Boer ultimatum expires; Second Anglo-Boer War begins.

October 14: Windsor Treaty between Britain and Portugal renews previously established treaties between the two countries.

November 25: Baghdad Railway concession granted to Germany.

December 2: Anglo-American-German treaty partitions Samoa.

1900

February 5: First Hay-Pauncefote Treaty is established between the United States and Britain about an interoceanic canal project.

May 17: Boxer Rebellion in China increases attacks of foreigners.

May 31: U.S. Marines arrive in China to help suppress the Boxer Rebellion.

June 12: German Reichstag authorizes second major naval expansion.

August 14: Boxer siege of Peking lifted.

September 4: Russian deploys 100,000 troops to Manchuria.

October 16: British-German Yangtze Agreement supports the Open Door policy in China.

November 6: McKinley reelected president.

December 14: Franco-Italian Agreement about Morocco and Tripoli is signed.

1901

March 2: Congress passes Platt Amendment to Army appropriations bill.

September 6–14: President McKinley is shot and dies eight days later; Theodore Roosevelt sworn in as president.

December 16: Senate approves Hay-Pauncefote Treaty.

Theodore Roosevelt Presidency
1902

January 18: Walker Commission recommends Panama Canal scheme to Congress.

January 30: Britain and Japan form an alliance.

June 26: Congress approves Panama Canal project.

June 28: Austria, Germany, and Italy renew Triple Alliance for six years.

July 4: Roosevelt proclaims Philippine Government Act.

December 8: Roosevelt issues ultimatum to Germany over Venezuelan intervention.

1903

January 22: United States and Colombia sign Hay-Herran Treaty to facilitate Panama Canal construction.

February 13: Venezuelan crisis ends

July 16: Roosevelt criticizes Russian persecution of Jews.

August 12: Colombian Senate rejects Hay-Herran Treaty.

August 12: Japan denounces Russian presence in Manchuria.

October 20: U.S.-Canada Alaskan boundary dispute settled.

November 3: Panamanian revolt against Colombian rule breaks out.

November 6: United States recognizes Panamanian government.

1904

February 8: Russo-Japanese War breaks out.

February 23: Senate approves Hay-Bunau-Varilla Treaty for construction of the Panama Canal.

April 8: Anglo-French entente established.

September 7: Britain establishes protectorate in Tibet.

November 8: Roosevelt reelected.

December 6: Roosevelt announces Corollary to Monroe Doctrine.

1905

February 7: United States intervenes in Dominican Republic's debt crisis.

March 31: First Franco-German Morocco crisis.

May 25: Japanese Navy defeats Russian fleet in Battle of Tsushima Strait.

June 10: Roosevelt convinces Russia and Japan to negotiate.

July 8: Roosevelt secures Franco-German Algeciras Conference on Morocco.

July 24: Germany and Russia agree to Björkö Treaty.

July 29: United States and Japan sign secret Taft-Katsura Agreement.

August 9: Roosevelt chairs Russo-Japanese peace conference.

August 12: Britain and Japan renew alliance.

September 2: Russia and Japan sign Treaty of Portsmouth.

October 20–30: General strike in Russia.

1906

February 10: Britain launches HMS *Dreadnought*.

April 7: France and Germany conclude Algeciras Treaty.

December 4: Roosevelt advocates naturalization rights for Japanese immigrants.

1907

January 15: United States advocates reforms in Belgian Congo.

January 21: Anglo-American Jamaica incident.

August 31: Britain and Russia agree to an entente.

October 18: Second Hague Conference adjourns.

December 12: U.S. Navy begins round the world cruise.

1908

April 11: Root-Bryce Treaty signed for U.S.-Canada boundary settlement.

July 5: Young Turk revolt in Turkey.

October 6: Austria annexes Bosnia-Herzogovina.

November 3: William Howard Taft elected president, James Sherman is vice president.

November 30: Root-Takahira Executive Agreement with Japan.

December 4: London Naval Conference.

Taft Presidency
1909

February 8: Franco-German agreement on Morocco.

April 9: Payne-Aldrich Tariff lowers some duties.

November 6: United States proposes international neutrality for Manchuria.

December 16: United States assists Nicaraguan rebellion against Zelaya regime.

1910

August 22: Japan annexes Korea.

October 5: Portuguese republic proclaimed.

1911

May 21: French troops occupy Fez; Second Moroccan Crisis.

May 25: Revolutionary government of Francisco Madero takes power in Mexico.

July 26: United States offers trade reciprocity to Canada, Canada rejects offer.

September 28: Tripolitan War breaks out between Italy and Turkey.

November 29: Russia invades northern Persia.

December 30: Sun Yat-Sen elected president of the United Provinces of China.

1912

January 9: Insurrection in Honduras, U.S. Marines protect American property.

August 2: Lodge Corollary extends Monroe Doctrine to Japan and commercial ventures.

August 14: Unrest in Nicaragua, Taft sends U.S. Marines.

August 24: U.S. coastal shipping exempt from Panama Canal tolls.

October 8: Montenegro attacks Turkey, First Balkan War begins.

November 5: Woodrow Wilson elected president, Thomas Marshall is vice president.

Wilson Presidency
1913

February 9: General Victoriano Huerta overthrows Madero government in Mexico.

March 4: Wilson inaugurated as president.

May 2: Wilson recognizes republican government of Yüan Shi-K'ai in China.

1914

April 21: United States occupies and blockades Veracruz, Mexico.

June 15: Congress repeals Panama Canal toll exemptions.

July 15: Huerta flees Mexico; Constitutionalist government in Mexico City.

August 2–4: World War I begins in Europe.

August 6: Ellen Wilson dies.

August 18: Wilson's appeal to Americans to be neutral "in thought as well as in action."

December 8: Annual message rejects calls for military and naval "preparedness."

December 28: U.S. note of protest to Britain over blockade practices.

1915

February 4: German declaration of war zone around British Isles in which submarine warfare will be conducted.

February 10: Strict Accountability Note to Germany.

March 28: Sinking of *Falaba*—one American (Leon C. Thrasher) killed.

May 7: Sinking of *Lusitania*—1,200 deaths, including 128 Americans.

May 13: First *Lusitania* note.

June 7: W. J. Bryan resigns as secretary of state rather than sign second *Lusitania* note—succeeded by Robert Lansing.

July 21: Third *Lusitania* note: Wilson asks secretaries of war and the Navy to draw up programs for "adequate national defense."

July 28: U.S. military intervention in Haiti.

August 19: Sinking of *Arabic*—forty-eight deaths, including two Americans.

August 29: Wilson agrees to allow Britain and France to raise loans on U.S. market.

September 8: Arabic pledge—Germany promises no more liners will be sunk.

October 6: De facto recognition of Carranza government in Mexico.

November 4: Wilson publicly calls for preparedness.

December 18: Wilson's marriage to Edith Bolling Galt.

1916

February 22: House-Grey memorandum signed.

February 24: Wilson letter to Senator Stone calling for defeat of congressional resolutions warning Americans not to travel on armed belligerent ships.

March 9: Pancho Villa raid on Columbus, New Mexico.

March 15: Punitive military expedition under Pershing enters Mexico.

March 24: Sinking of *Sussex*—about eighty killed or injured, four Americans injured.

May 4: Sussex pledge—conditional German undertaking to follow rules of cruiser warfare against merchant ships.

May 15: Military intervention in Dominican Republic.

May 27: Addressing the League to Enforce Peace, Wilson declares U.S. willingness to join a postwar league of nations.

August 29: Navy Act, authorizing large building program, signed.

September 8: Revenue Act including provision for retaliatory action against nations infringing U.S. neutral rights.

November 7: Wilson reelected as president.

November 27: Wilson strengthens Federal Reserve Board warning against purchase of foreign Treasury bills.

November 29: U.S. occupies Santo Domingo.

December 18: Wilson sends note asking European belligerents to state peace terms.

1917

January 22: In address to Senate, Wilson calls for "a peace without victory."

January 31: German announcement of unrestricted submarine warfare.

February 3: Breaking of diplomatic relations with Germany.

February 26: Wilson requests congressional authority to arm merchant ships.

February 28: Zimmermann Telegram.

March 15: Abdication of Tsar in first Russian Revolution.

March 18: News reaches Washington of sinking of three American ships by German submarines.

April 2: Wilson's War Address to Congress.

April 6: U.S. declaration of war on Germany.

May 18: Selective Service Act signed.

August 27: Wilson's reply to Pope Benedict XV's call for peace.

November 5: Bolshevik Revolution in Russia.

1918

January 8: Wilson's Fourteen Points Address to Congress.

March 3: Treaty of Brest-Litovsk taking Russia out of the war.

March 21: Launching of German offensive on western front.

April 6: Wilson's speech calling for "Force without stint or limit."

July 17: U.S. forces sent to North Russia.

August 3: U.S. forces sent to Vladivostok, Siberia.

September 27: Wilson speech in New York insisting that League of Nations must be incorporated in peace treaty.

October 6: German note to Wilson asking for peace on basis of Fourteen Points.

November 5: In congressional elections, Republicans win control of both houses.

November 11: Signing of Armistice ending World War I.

December 4: Wilson sails from New York for Europe.

1919

January 18: Paris Peace Conference convenes.

February 14: Wilson presents draft of League of Nations Covenant to Conference.

February 14: Wilson sails for the United States.

March 3: Lodge's Round Robin signed by more than one-third of Senate.

March 13: Wilson returns to France.

May 7: Draft peace treaty presented to Germans.

June 28: Treaty of Versailles signed.

July 8: Wilson arrives back in the United States.

July 10: Wilson's speech to Senate presenting Versailles treaty.

August 19: Wilson's meeting with Senate Foreign Relations Committee.

September 2–28: Wilson's speaking trip in support of treaty cut short after collapse following speech in Pueblo, Colorado.

October 2: Wilson suffers paralytic stroke.

November 6: Lodge's Fourteen Reservations proposed.

November 19: In Senate votes, Treaty of Versailles defeated both with and without Lodge reservations.

1920

January 8: Wilson calls for 1920 election to be "a great and solemn referendum" on membership the League of Nations.

February 13: Lansing resigns as secretary of state; Bainbridge Colby appointed.

March 19: Treaty including Lodge Reservations fails to obtain necessary two-thirds majority in the Senate after Wilson had asked his followers to vote against it.

August 10: Colby note declaring policy of nonrecognition of Soviet government.

November 2: Republican Warren G. Harding elected president in a landslide.

Harding Presidency
1921

January 7: U.S. Navy's Orange War Plan approved.

March 4: Harding inauguration; Wilson leaves White House.

April 27: Allied Reparations Committee demands $33B from Germany.

June 7: Romania and Yugoslavia form Little Entente.

November 12: Washington Naval Conference convenes.

1922

February 6: Washington Naval Conference ends.

February 11: United States and Japan settle Yap Island dispute.

February 22: Britain terminates protectorate of Egypt.

March 3: Fascist coup topples Fiume government in Italy.

April 10: Genoa Conference convenes.

April 16: Germany and Russia sign Treaty of Rapallo.

September 21: Congress passes Fordney-McCumber Tariff.

October 27: Fascist March on Rome.

October 31: Benito Mussolini forms a cabinet of Fascists and Nationalists in Italy.

December 6: Irish Free State proclaimed.

December 30: Union of Soviet Socialist Republics (USSR) established.

1923

January 11: French and Belgian troops occupy the Ruhr.

June 19: Britain accepts plan to repay U.S. loans.

July 14: Treaty of Lausanne establishes Allied peace with Turkey.

August 2: President Harding dies; Calvin Coolidge sworn in as president.

Coolidge Presidency
1923

August 3: Coolidge sworn-in as president.

September 27: Britain thwarts Italian invasion of Corfu.

October 29: Turkey becomes a republic.

1924

September 1: Dawes Plan established for payment of German reparations.

October 25: Zinoviev letter incident damages Anglo-Russian relations.

November 4: President Coolidge reelected.

November 9: Nazi beer hall putsch in Munich defeated.

1925

June 27: Geneva Protocol signed.

October 5–16: Locarno Conference; Treaty of Locarno signed.

1926

September 8: Germany admitted to League of Nations.

November 11: Coolidge announces that United States will not join the World Court.

December 25: Taishō Emperor dies in Japan, Shōwa regime under Hirohito begins.

1927

April 12: Nationalist forces in China begin purge of Communists.

April 25: Coolidge Doctrine announced.

May 11: Henry L. Stimson concludes Treaty of Tipitata ending fighting in Nicaragua.

June 20: Geneva Naval Limitations Conference convenes.

July 31: Anglo-French Naval Agreement signed.

November 11: France and Yugoslavia sign Treaty of Understanding.

1928

May 3: Japanese and Chinese forces clash in Shantung.

July 25: United States recognizes Nationalist government of Chiang Kaishek.

August 27: United States signs Kellogg-Briand Pact with thirteen other nations.

November 6: Herbert Hoover is elected president, Charles Curtis is vice president.

Hoover Presidency
1929
February 28: United States revokes Roosevelt Corollary to the Monroe Doctrine.

August 31: Hague Economic Conference ratifies Young Plan for German reparations.

October 29: U.S. stock market crashes, onset of the Great Depression.

December 2: United States invokes Kellogg-Briand Pact to prevent Sino-Soviet war.

1930
February 6: Austrian and Italy sign friendship treaty.

April 22: London Naval Conference decides Naval Limitation Treaty.

November 14: Japanese prime minister Yuko Hamaguchi is assassinated.

1931
June 17: Congress approves Smoot-Hawley Tariff.

June 20: Hoover offers to postpone all debt owed to the United States.

September 18: Mukden incident, Japan occupies Manchuria.

December 9: Spain declares a republic, dissolves monarchy.

December 10: League of Nations approves Lytton Commission.

1932
January 7: United States declares Hoover-Stimson Doctrine against Japanese Manchurian occupation.

January 28: Japanese troops land in Shanghai.

February 2: Disarmament conference convenes at Geneva.

February 29: Britain imposes protective tariffs.

May 15: Japanese premier Ki Inukai assassinated, *de facto* military government established.

November 8: Franklin Roosevelt is elected president, John Garner is vice president.

Franklin Roosevelt Presidency
1933
January 30: Adolf Hitler becomes Chancellor of Germany.

February 24: Japan quits League of Nations.

April 19: United States abandons gold standard.

July 15: Britain, France, Germany, and Italy agree on Four Power Pact.

October 14: Germany quits League and Geneva Disarmament Conference.

November 17: United States and Soviet Union normalize relations.

1934
February 2: Export-Import Bank established.

March 27: Vinson Naval Act authorizes new ship and plane construction.

July 25: Attempted Nazi coup in Vienna fails.

December 29: Japan announces it will abandon 1922 Washington Naval Treaty.

1935
March 16: Hitler announces increase in size of German armed forces.

May 2: France and Soviet Union form defensive alliance.

May 16: Czechoslovakia and Soviet Union form defensive alliance.

June 18: Anglo-German Naval Agreement signed.

August 31: First Neutrality Act passes Congress.

October 3: Italy invades Ethiopia.

October 5: United States embargoes arms to Italy.

October 11: League of Nations sanctions Italy.

1936
January 15: Japan withdraws from London Naval Conference.

February 29: Second Neutrality Act passes Congress.

March 2: United States abolishes protectorate in Panama.

March 7: Germany denounces Treaty of Locarno, occupies Rhineland.

May 5: Italian conquest of Ethiopia completed.

June 5: Popular Front government elected in France.

July 17: Spanish Civil War begins.

September 25: United States, Britain, and France agree on currency stabilization.

October 25: Germany and Italy sign Anti-Comintern Pact.

November 3: Roosevelt reelected.

November 18: Germany and Italy recognize Franco regime in Spain.

November 25: Germany and Japan sign Anti-Comintern Pact.

December 23: Pan-American Peace Conference concludes.

1937
May 1: Third Neutrality Act passes Congress.

May 28: Neville Chamberlain becomes British prime minister, diplomacy of appeasement begins.

July 7: Japanese and Chinese troops clash at Marco Polo Bridge.

October 5: Roosevelt gives Quarantine Speech.

October 6: League of Nations condemns Japan for aggression in China.

December 12: U.S. gunboat *Panay* is sunk by Japanese aircraft; HMS *Ladybird* is also fired on.

December 23: Roosevelt orders naval staff talks with Britain.

1938

January 10: Ludlow Resolution passed by House.

March 13: Germany annexes Austria.

March 28: Japanese install puppet Chinese government in Nanjing.

April 16: Anglo-Italian Pact agreed.

May 17: Congress approves 20 percent increase in naval construction.

May 20: Britain and France back Czech government against Nazi secessionists.

September 12: Czech Crisis breaks out.

September 29: Anglo-French appeasement diplomacy at Munich Conference resolves Czech Crisis.

October 28: French Popular Front government collapses.

October 11: Roosevelt calls for production of 20,000 aircraft per year.

November 15: "Crystal Night" brings violent attacks on Jews all over Germany.

November 17: United States, Britain, and Canada sign Reciprocal Trade Agreements Pact.

1939

March 15: Germany declares protectorate over Bohemia, Moravia, and Slovakia.

March 28: Spanish Civil War ends with Franco victorious.

March 31: Britain and France pledge aid to Poland.

April 3: United States recognizes Nationalist Spain.

April 7: Italy invades Albania.

April 28: Germany denounces Anglo-German Naval Pact of 1935.

May 17: Britain announces proposal for independent Palestine.

August 23: Germany and Russia sign Non-Aggression Pact.

September 1: Germany invades Poland.

September 3: Britain and France declare war on Germany; World War II begins.

September 5: Roosevelt declares U.S. neutrality.

September 17: Soviet forces invade Eastern Poland.

November 4: Roosevelt signs Fourth Neutrality Act.

November 29: Soviet forces invade Finland.

1940

March 12: Finland accepts Soviet peace terms.

April 9: Germany invades Norway, occupies Denmark.

May 10: Germany invades Belgium, Luxemburg, and Netherlands.

May 10: Winston Churchill becomes British prime minister.

May 12: Germany invades France.

June 3: United States begins sale of surplus equipment to Allies.

June 17: France surrenders to Germany.

June 28: Alien Registration Act passed.

July 20: Roosevelt signs $4 billion Navy appropriation.

August 8: Battle of Britain begins.

August 18: United States and Canada sign Ogdensburg Agreement.

September 16: Roosevelt signs Selective Service and Training Act.

September 27: Japan signs tripartite pact with Germany and Italy.

November 5: Roosevelt is reelected a second time.

December 29: Roosevelt delivers "Arsenal of Democracy" speech.

1941

January 6: Roosevelt cites Four Freedoms in State of the Union speech.

March 11: Congress approves Lend-Lease Act.

April 9: United States and Denmark agree to U.S. bases in Greenland.

April 13: Japan and Soviet Union sign nonaggression pact.

May 6: Lend-Lease is extended to China.

May 27: Roosevelt announces unlimited national emergency.

June 22: Operation Barbarossa: Germany invades the Soviet Union.

July 26: United States freezes Japanese assets

August 12: Roosevelt and Churchill sign Atlantic Charter.

August 17: United States warns Japan against further aggression in Asia.

October 17: German U-boat attacks USS *Kearny*.

October 30: German U-boat attacks USS *Reuben James*.

November 6: Lend-Lease Program is extended to Soviet Union.

November 17: Neutrality Acts are repealed.

November 27: War warning is sent to U.S. forces in Pacific and Asia.

December 7: Japanese aircraft attack U.S. facilities at Pearl Harbor.

December 8: United States declares war on Japan.

December 10–25: Japanese forces attack the Philippines and occupy Guam, Wake Island, Hong Kong.

December 11: Germany and Italy declare war on United States.

1942

January 1: United Nations Declaration signed.

February 19: Roosevelt authorizes relocation and internment of Japanese Americans on the West Coast.

April 18: U.S. bombers attack Tokyo.

May 7: U.S. Navy wins Battle of the Coral Sea.

June 1: Roosevelt promises Moscow a second front by the end of 1942.

June 6: U.S. Navy wins Battle of Midway.

June 13: Office of Strategic Services (OSS) is established.

August 7: U.S. forces land at Guadalcanal.

September 13: Battle of Stalingrad begins.

November 8: Operation Torch: Anglo-American invasion of North Africa begins.

November 19: Soviet counteroffensive against Germany begins.

1943

January 24: Churchill, Roosevelt, Charles de Gaulle, and Henri Giraud meet at Casablanca Conference.

January 31: German forces surrender at Stalingrad.

May 13: Axis armies in North Africa surrender.

July 10: Anglo-American forces invade Sicily.

August 11–24: First Quebec Conference.

September 3–9: Anglo-American forces land in Italy.

November 7: Soviet forces retake Kiev.

November 22–26: Churchill, Roosevelt, and Chiang Kai-shek (Jiang Jieshi) meet at First Cairo Conference.

December 2–7: Tehran Conference of Churchill, Roosevelt, and Stalin.

December 6: Cairo Declaration.

1944

January 11: Anglo-American strategic bombing of Germany begins.

January 22: U.S. forces land at Anzio, Italy.

March 26: Soviet forces invade Romania.

June 6: Operation Overlord: U.S., British, and Canadian armies invade France in Normandy.

July 11: United States recognizes de Gaulle as leader of Free French.

July 2: Bretton Woods Conference establishes International Monetary Fund and World Bank.

August 15: Allied forces land in southern France.

September 12: U.S. forces enter Germany.

September 16: Second Quebec Conference.

October 7: Dumbarton Oaks Conference founds the United Nations Organization.

October 18: Second Moscow Conference ends.

October 20: U.S. forces invade the Philippines at Leyte Gulf.

November 7: Roosevelt reelected for a fourth term.

December 16–26: German army defeated in Battle of the Bulge.

1945

January 17: Soviet army captures Warsaw.

February 4–11: Churchill, Roosevelt, and Stalin meet at Yalta Conference.

February 14: RAF and USAF bomb Dresden.

March 9–10: USAF firebombs Tokyo.

March 17: U.S. Marines capture Iwo Jima.

April 12: President Roosevelt dies; Harry S. Truman sworn in as president.

Truman Presidency
1945

April 25: San Francisco Conference of the United Nations convenes.

May 7: German Army signs unconditional surrender.

June 5: European Advisory Commission determines the division of Germany.

June 26: United Nations Charter is signed.

July 16–August 2: Churchill (then Attlee), Stalin, and Truman meet at Potsdam Conference.

August 6: United States drops atomic bomb on Hiroshima.

August 8: Soviet Union declares war on Japan.

August 9: United States drops atomic bomb on Nagasaki.

August 15: Japan surrenders unconditionally.

September 2: Ho Chi Minh declares Vietnam's independence from France.

November 14: The International Military Tribunal at Nuremberg begins.

November 17: U.S. efforts to mediate between Chinese Nationalists and Communists fail.

November 27: George Marshall begins mission to China.

1946

January 10: First session of UN convenes in London.

January 27: Local elections held in U.S. zone of Germany.

February 24: Juan Perón elected president of Argentina.

March 5: Churchill delivers "iron curtain" speech in Fulton, Missouri.

April 14: Chinese civil war reignites.

May 3: Gen. Clay stops Soviet reparations pillage of Western occupations zone of Germany.

June 3: Japanese war crimes trials begin.

July 1: United States conducts nuclear tests at Bikini Atoll.

July 4: Philippine's are given independence.

August 31: Britain and France agree to evacuate Syria.

October 1: Nuremberg Tribunal hands down verdicts.

October 13: French Fourth Republic established.

November 19: Soviet puppet government confirmed in Romania.

December 2: Britain and United States fuse occupation zones in Germany.

1947

January 29: United States abandons Chinese mediations.

March 12: President Truman declares Truman Doctrine in Congress.

May 25: George Kennan appointed Director of State Department's Policy Planning.

June 5: Secretary of State Marshall proposes economic aid for Europe.

July 26: National Security Act passes Congress.

August 15: India and Pakistan gain independence from Britain.

November 29: UN General Assembly approves plan to partition Palestine.

1948

February 25: Communist coup topples Beneš government in Czechoslovakia.

March 17: Treaty of Brussels signed, West European defense alliance formed.

March 20: Four-Power Council in Germany breaks up.

March 28: General Agreement on Tariffs and Trade (GATT) signed; International Trade Organization (ITO) created.

April 16: Organization for European Economic Cooperation (OEEC) formed.

May 2: Organization of American States (OAS) formed.

May 7: Congress of Europe convenes at The Hague.

May 14: The state of Israel is established.

June 24: Soviet Union blockades Berlin, United States Berlin airlift begins.

November 2: Truman reelected president.

December 9–10: UN adopts the Universal Declaration of Human Rights.

1949

April 4: North Atlantic Treaty Organization (NATO) is formed.

May 8: Federal Republic of Germany is constituted in Western zones of occupation.

May 11: Berlin blockade lifted by four-power accord.

May 15: Communists gain control of Hungarian government.

June 14: France installs Emperor Bao Dai in Vietnam.

July 16: Chinese Nationalist forces retreat to Formosa.

August 10: Department of Defense established.

August 22: Joint Chiefs of Staff sanction first-use of nuclear weapons.

August 29: Soviet Union tests its first nuclear weapon.

October 1: Mao Tse-tung proclaims the People's Republic of China.

October 7: German Democratic Republic established in Soviet occupation zone.

December 28: NSC48/1 cites Southeast Asia as a vital interest of the United States.

1950

January 12: Secretary of State Dean Acheson outlines perimeter strategy for Asia.

January 21: Alger Hiss convicted of perjury.

January 24: Klaus Fuchs confesses to espionage for the Soviet Union.

February 7: United States recognizes Bao Dai government in Vietnam.

February 9: Senator Joseph McCarthy charges that 205 Communists hold State Department positions.

April 14: NSC-68 recommends increased defense spending.

May 9: Schuman Plan proposes six-nation single market for European coal and steel.

June 5: Truman approves $3 billion for European Recovery Program.

June 25: North Korea invades South Korea.

September 15: U.S. forces land at Inchon, North Koreans thrown back.

October 7: UN passes resolution for unity of the Koreas.

November 26: Chinese Communist forces launch counteroffensive.

1951

April 5: Julius and Ethel Rosenberg sentenced to death.

April 10: President Truman dismisses General MacArthur.

May 2: West Germany joins Council of Europe.

May 4: United States and Iceland agree to NATO bases in Iceland.

July 8: Korean truce negotiations begin.

August 30: United States and Philippines sign mutual defense treaty.

September 8: United States and Japan sign mutual security treaty.

September 20: Greece and Turkey join NATO.

1952

February 2: Great Britain tests a nuclear weapon.

February 6: Elizabeth II is coronated Queen of the United Kingdom.

March 10: Batista military coup in Cuba.

May 27: European Defense Community (EDC) created.

July 1: Schuman Plan goes into effect.

November 5: Dwight D. Eisenhower is elected president, Richard M. Nixon is vice president.

Eisenhower Presidency
1953

March 5: Death of Stalin.

June 17–18: Soviet troops crush anti-Communist riots by workers in East Berlin.

July 27: Korean War armistice signed.

August 8: Soviet Union tests hydrogen bomb.

August 19: Government of Mohammed Mossadegh in Iran is toppled in Ango-American aided coup.

October 30: NSC-162 outlines Eisenhower's "New Look" defense policy.

September 15: Soviet Union provides massive economic aid to China.

1954

January 12: Secretary of State John Foster Dulles outlines doctrine of "massive retaliation."

January 26: Senate ratifies mutual security treaty with South Korea.

March 1: United States tests 15 megaton hydrogen weapon at Bikini Atoll.

March 14: Vietminh forces attack French garrison at Dien Bien Phu.

April 26: Geneva Conference on Korea and Vietnam convenes.

May 7: French garrison at Dien Bien Phu falls.

May 19: United States and Pakistan sign mutual defense pact.

June 9: Arbenz-Guzmán regime in Guatemala overthrown in CIA-aided coup.

June 15: Ngo Dinh Diem becomes premier of French-sponsored Vietnamese government.

July 20: Geneva Conference approves settlement of Indochina conflict.

August 30: French parliament rejects EDC.

September 8: Southeast Asia Treaty Organization (SEATO) established.

October 23: United States offers aid to Diem government in Vietnam.

December 1: United States and Nationalist China sign mutual defense pact.

December 2: U.S. Senate censures Joseph McCarthy.

1955

January 25: Congress authorizes U.S. defense of Formosa and the Pescadores.

February 12: United States agrees to train South Vietnamese army.

February 18: Turkey and Iraq sign Baghdad Pact.

April 18–27: Bandung Conference of twenty-nine African and Asian nations held.

May 9: West Germany admitted to NATO.

May 14: Eight East European nations form Warsaw Pact under Soviet leadership.

July 18–24: Geneva four-power summit conference.

July 22: West German parliament approves rearmament.

September 16: Military coup topples Perón government in Argentina.

1956

January 28: Eisenhower rejects Soviet friendship proposal.

February 14: Soviet Premier Nikita Khrushchev attacks Stalin's crimes, advocates peaceful coexistence.

April 17: Khrushchev claims Soviet leadership in nuclear weapons.

May 9: United States refuses to supply Israel with arms.

July 19: United States cancels aid to Egypt for Aswân High Dam.

July 26: Egypt nationalizes Suez Canal Company.

October 23–November 4: Hungarian uprising crushed by Soviet tanks and troops.

October 29–November 6: Suez Crisis.

November 6: Eisenhower reelected president.

1957

January 5: President explains Eisenhower Doctrine to Congress.

March 13: Jordan gains independence from Britain.

March 24: Anglo-American meeting at Bermuda.

March 25: Treaty of Rome is signed, European Common Market founded.

May 15: Britain tests its first hydrogen bomb.

August 26: Soviet Union announces successful test of intercontinental ballistic missile.

October 5: Soviet Union orbits Sputnik, the first artificial earth satellite, with a live dog.

November 7: Gaither Report is presented to the National Security Council.

December 5: Sukarno government of Indonesia expels all Dutch nationals.

December 17: First U.S. intercontinental ballistic missile, Atlas, successfully tested.

December 19: NATO Paris summit meeting.

1958

January 23: Venezuelan government overthrown by junta.

January 31: First U.S. earth satellite launched.

February 1: Egypt and Syria form United Arab Republic.

March 27: Khrushchev consolidates power in Soviet Union.

April 28–May 14: Vice President Nixon met with anti-American sentiment in Latin American tour.

May 31: General Charles de Gaulle heads emergency government in France.

June 1: Charles de Gaulle becomes French premier amid turmoil centered on Algerian crisis.

July 14: Army coup ousts King Faisal II in Iraq.

July 15: U.S. Marines go ashore in Lebanon to quell unrest allegedly connected to Islamic rebels backed by USSR.

August 3: USS *Nautilus* completes crossing of North Pole.

August 23: China bombards Quemoy and Matsu.

September 28: French Fifth Republic established.

October 7: Coup in Pakistan establishes military control.

October 23: Soviet Union finances Aswân High Dam.

October 29: Start of reign of Pope John XXIII.

October 31: Geneva Nuclear Test Ban Conference.

November 10-December 14: 1958 Berlin Crisis.

November 27: Khrushchev vows to give East German authorities control of communication lines to West Berlin, precipitating a new Berlin crisis.

1959

January 1: Cuban Batista government falls to forces led by Fidel Castro.

January 3: Alaska becomes forty-ninth state.

March 5: United States signs defense pacts with Iran, Pakistan, and Turkey.

March 13–31: China invades and annexes Tibet.

June 29: Canadian-American St. Lawrence Seaway opens.

July 12: United States protests Castro's Cuban land reform.

July 24: Nixon-Khrushchev kitchen debate.

August 21: Hawaii becomes fiftieth state.

September 15: Khrushchev tours United States.

1960

February 13: Soviet Union and Cuba sign economic agreement.

February 13: France tests its first nuclear weapon.

May 5: U-2 Affair—U.S. spy plane shot down over Soviet Union.

May 27: Military coup in Turkey.

June 27: Communist countries withdraw from Geneva disarmament talks.

June 30: Belgium gives independence to Congo.

July 1: Soviet Union shoots down U.S. plane over Barents Sea.

July 6: Castro nationalizes all U.S. property in Cuba.

July 20: First Polaris missile launch.

September 10: Organization for Petroleum Exporting Countries (OPEC) is formed.

October 19: United States embargoes all exports to China.

November 8: John F. Kennedy is elected president, Lyndon Johnson is vice president.

December 20: National Liberation Front (NLF) formed in South Vietnam.

Kennedy Presidency
1961

January 3: United States cuts diplomatic relations with Cuba.

January 6: Soviet Union announces support for wars of national liberation.

January 17: Eisenhower's farewell speech warns of "military industrial complex."

1961

January 20: President Kennedy's inaugural pledges that the United States will "bear any burden."

March 1: Kennedy creates the Peace Corps by executive order.

March 13: Alliance for Progress with Latin America initiated.

April 17: Bay of Pigs Invasion, U.S.-backed Cuban rebels defeated.

May 25: Kennedy sets national goal of a manned moon mission by the end of the decade.

June 4: U.S.-Soviet summit conference in Vienna, Khrushchev confrontational over Berlin.

August 13: Soviets begin construction of the Berlin Wall; Berlin Crisis begins.

August 31: Moscow announces resumption of nuclear testing.

October 22–28: Berlin crisis climaxes and ends with agreement on access to the city.

November 22: United States sends first combat-support troops to South Vietnam.

Dece18mber 2: Castro announces official goal of a communist Cuba.

1962

February 20: Lt. Col. John Glenn launched into earth orbit.

April 25: United States resumes nuclear testing.

July 4: Kennedy offers multilateral nuclear defense for European allies.

July 23: Geneva Conference guarantees independence and neutrality of Laos.

October 20: Chinese and Indian border forces clash.

October 22: Kennedy informs nation of Soviet missiles in Cuba; Cuban Missile Crisis begins.

October 24–28: Cuban Missile Crisis climaxes and ends with personal letters between Kennedy and Khrushchev.

December 17: United States gives aid to UN to fight Katanga secessionists.

1963

January 14: De Gaulle announces French veto of Britain's application to join the EEC.

May 8: Buddhist monks begin demonstrations and self-immolations to protest Diem government in Saigon.

May 22: NATO foreign ministers approve a multilateral nuclear strike force.

June 14: Beijing denounces Moscow's "revisionist" communism.

June 20: United States and Soviet Union agree to establish a diplomatic "hot line."

June 26: Kennedy visits West Berlin and pledges U.S. support.

August 5: United States, Soviet Union, and Britain sign Limited Nuclear Test Ban Treaty.

November 1–2: Military coup ousts Diem government in South Vietnam.

November 22: President Kennedy assassinated, Lyndon Baines Johnson sworn in as president.

Lyndon Johnson Presidency
1963

December 12: Kenya gains independence from Britain.

December 26: Secretary McNamara calls South Vietnam unstable.

1964

February 11: Fighting breaks out between Greeks and Turks on Cyprus.

March 31: Military coup in Brazil.

April 28: France withdraws from NATO's integrated command.

August 2–7: Gulf of Tonkin incidents, Congress passes Southeast Asia Resolution.

October 14: Soviet Presidium ousts Khrushchev, Alexei Kosygin is premier.

1965

February 6: Vietcong attacks U.S. forces at Pleiku.

March 19: Operation Rolling Thunder begins.

April 28: Johnson sends U.S. marines to the Dominican Republic.

June 12: Nguyen Van Thieu and Nguyen Cao Ky take control of South Vietnamese government.

October 14: Defense Department announces major draft call-up.

1966

January 19: Indira Gandhi becomes prime minister of India.

January 28: Congressional hearings on Tonkin resolution begin.

August 18: Cultural Revolution in China begins.

October 25: Manila Conference.

November 13: Israeli reprisal attacks against Jordan for Palestinian raids.

1967

January 26: Defense Secretary McNamara brief Congress on nuclear doctrine of Mutual Assured Destruction.

February 14: British attempt to reconvene Geneva Conference on Vietnam fails.

May 23: Johnson protests Egyptian blockade of Gulf of Aqaba.

June 5: Israel attacks Egypt, Iraq, Syria, and Jordan: Six Day War begins.

June 17: China tests first hydrogen bomb.

June 25: Johnson meets Soviet Premier Kosygin at Glassboro, Pennsylvania.

November 28: Defense Secretary McNamara resigns.

November 30: Senator Eugene McCarthy announces candidacy for presidency on peace platform.

1968

January 16: Britain withdraws its forces from Persian Gulf region.

January 26: General Westmorland issues favorable report on Vietnam.

January 30: North Vietnam's Tet Offensive begins.

March 12: Johnson barely wins New Hampshire Democratic primary.

March 16: Senator Robert Kennedy announces presidential candidacy.

March 31: Johnson announces bombing halt, offer to negotiate with Hanoi, decision not to run for reelection.

April 4: Martin Luther King, Jr. assassinated.

June 5: Robert F. Kennedy assassinated.

July 1: Nuclear Non-Proliferation Treaty signed with Britain, Soviet Union and fifty other countries.

August 20: Warsaw Pact forces invade Czechoslovakia and topple Dubček government.

October 31: U.S. and North Vietnam agree to conduct peace negotiations.

November 5: Richard Nixon elected president. Spiro Agnew is vice president.

Nixon Presidency
1969

March 14: Nixon asks Congress for antiballistic (ABM) missile system.

May 14: Nixon makes first peace offer to Hanoi.

June 8: Announcement of first Vietnam troop withdrawals.

July 20: U.S. astronauts make first moon landing.

August 4: Paris peace negotiations begin.

October 21: Willy Brandt elected West German chancellor.

November 17: SALT negotiations begin.

November 25: Nuclear Non-Proliferation Treaty ratified.

1970

February 18: Nixon Doctrine unveiled to Congress.

April 29: U.S.-ARVN forces invade Cambodia.

May 4: Kent State demonstration, shooting death of four students.

June 22: Senate repeals Tonkin Resolution.

August 7: United States brokers Middle East cease-fire.

September 6–22: Jordanian crisis.

December 7: West Germany and Poland sign reconciliation treaty.

1971

March 16: United States proposes Middle East peace plan.

May 3: Massive antiwar demonstration in Washington, D.C.

June 13: New York Times begins to publish Pentagon Papers.

July 9: National Security Advisor Henry Kissinger consults with Chinese Foreign Minister, Chou En-Lai.

August 12: West Germany and Soviet Union sign borders treaty.

August 15: Nixon announces new economic policy.

September 3: Quadripartite agreement on Berlin.

December 3–17: India-Pakistan war.

1972

February 17–28: Nixon visits China.

March 30: North Vietnam launches offensive in South Vietnam.

April 4: United States renews B-52 bombing of North Vietnam.

May 8: Nixon orders mining of Haiphong Harbor, renews large-scale B-52 attacks.

May 22–30: Nixon and Brezhnev sign SALT I and ABM treaties.

June 17: Watergate burglary of Democratic National Headquarters.

September 5: Palestinian terrorists take hostages at Munich Olympic Games.

November 7: Nixon reelected.

December 16: Kissinger announces peace talk impasse.

December 18: United States begins "Christmas bombing" raids on North Vietnam.

1973

January 27: Vietnamese truce agreements signed in Paris.

March 29: Last U.S. combat troops leave Vietnam.

May 17: Senate Watergate hearings begin.

June 16: Soviet leader Leonid Brezhnev begins summit meeting with Nixon.

June 30: Selective Service expires.

September 11: Military coup in Chile ousts President Salvatore Allende.

September 21: Henry Kissinger becomes secretary of state.

October 6: Yom Kippur War begins.

October 16: Arab states announce oil embargo.

October 25: Middle East cease-fire, Nixon puts U.S. forces on alert.

1974

March 17: End of Arab oil embargo.

May 18: India explodes nuclear device.

June 27–July 3: Nixon visits Moscow.

July 20: Turkey invades Cyprus.

July 30: House Judiciary Committee votes articles of impeachment against President Nixon.

Ford Presidency
1974

August 8: Nixon announces resignation, effective August 9, Gerald R. Ford Jr. sworn in as president.

October 18: President Ford signs legislation threatening to cut off aid to Turkey.

November 24: Ford and Brezhnev meet in Vladivostock and agree to place a ceiling on offensive nuclear weapons.

December 20: Congress refuses Soviet Union most favored nation status and restricts trade pending change in Soviet Jewish emigration policy.

1975

January 8: Twenty nations agree to recycle petrodollars to avoid a global recession.

January 22: Ford approves the Geneva Protocol of 1925 and the 1972 Biological Weapons Convention.

April 12: Fighting erupts in Lebanon between Christians and Muslims.

April 13: Fighting erupts between the Christian militia and Palestinians in Lebanon.

April 17: Cambodia falls to the forces of the Khmer Rouge.

April 25: Portugal holds its first free elections in fifty years.

April 29: Saigon falls to North Vietnamese forces, last U.S. helicopter evacuates U.S. embassy.

May 12–15: Mayaguez Incident, U.S. cargo ship seized by Cambodia and recovered by U.S. marines.

June 5: Egypt reopens Suez Canal, closed since 1967 to international shipping.

June 10: Rockefeller Commission recommends reform of CIA.

July 1: Vietnam officially is reunified.

July 24: House rejects Ford's request to lift Turkish arms embargo.

August 1: Thirty-five nations sign Helsinki Accords.

September 1: Egypt and Israel sign an agreement on buffer zones in the Sinai.

November 10: UN General Assembly condemns Zionism as a form of racism.

November 21: Senate Church Committee reports on CIA efforts to assassinate foreign leaders.

December 1–5: Ford makes a five-day visit to China.

1976

January 27: Congress rejects Ford's request for aid to anti-communist forces in Angola.

March 1: Ford announces he will no longer use the word *détente.*

March 18: India Prime accuses the CIA of trying to undermine its government, U.S. stops aid.

May 28: United States and the Soviet Union sign a treaty limiting the size of underground nuclear tests.

June 16: U.S. ambassador to Lebanon, Francis E. Meloy, Jr. is assassinated.

July 4: Israeli commandos free Jewish hostages in Entebbe, Uganda.

August 18: Two U.S. Army officers killed in Panmunjon, Korea.

September 9: Mao Zedong dies.

November 2: James Earl Carter is elected president, Walter F. Mondale is vice president.

November 11: United States vetoes UN membership for Vietnam.

December 1: United States abstains as Angola joins the UN.

Carter Presidency
1977

February 17: President Carter sends a personal letter of support to Soviet dissident Andrey Sakharov.

May 17: Likud leader, Menachem Begin, is elected prime minister of Israel.

June 15: Spain conducts its first democratic election in forty years; Adolfo Suarez is prime minister.

July 1: Carter cancels the B-1 bomber program.

August 8: War breaks out between Ethiopia and Somalia.

September 7: United States and Panama sign treaties governing the future of the Panama Canal.

November 15: Israeli Prime Minister Menachem Begin invites Egyptian President Anwar Sadat to visit Israel.

December 2: Radical Arab leaders oppose Egypt's peace diplomacy with Israel.

December 14: In Cairo, U.S., Egyptian, and Israeli representatives discuss peace.

1978

March 10: Palestinian terrorists launch an amphibious raid on Israel.

March 14: Israel attacks Palestinian bases in southern Lebanon.

April 7: President Carter postpones production of the neutron bomb.

April 27: Military coup ousts Daoud regime in Afghanistan.

May 16: Ethiopia invades Eritrea.

June 16: United States and Panama exchange ratification of Panama Canal treaties.

July 18: Soviet Union sentences dissident Anatoly Sharansky to thirteen years in prison; United States protests.

September 17: Egypt and Israel sign Camp David Accords brokered by Carter.

September 23: Radical Arab states denounce Camp David Accords.

November 26–27: A twenty-four-hour strike protests the rule of the Shah of Iran.

December 3: Vietnam invades Cambodia.

December 15: United States and China establish normal diplomatic relations; United States terminates Mutual Defense Treaty with Taiwan.

1979

January 7: Vietnamese and Kampuchean forces capture Phnom Penh.

January 16: Forced from power, the Shah of Iran flees to Egypt.

February 1: The Ayatollah Khomeini forms a provisional Iranian government.

February 17: China launches punitive invasion of Vietnam.

March 26: Begin and Sadat sign Israeli-Egyptian peace treaty.

April 10: Carter signs the Taiwan Relations Act.

May 3: Margaret Thatcher is elected prime minister of Britain.

June 18: Carter and Brezhnev sign SALT II.

July 17: Nicaraguan dictator Anastasio Somoza is forced from power.

July 20: UN resolution calls on Israel to end West Bank settlement construction.

August 6: United States offers to deploy Pershing II and Cruise missiles in NATO countries.

November 4: U.S. embassy in Iran is stormed by radical students; 52 hostages are taken.

November 20: Guerrillas hostile to the Saudi government storm the Grand Mosque in Mecca.

December 28: Soviet forces invade Afghanistan.

1980

January 2: Carter asks Senate to delay ratification of SALT II.

January 4: Carter announces sanctions against the Soviet Union.

January 14: UN demands Soviet withdrawal from Afghanistan.

January 23: Carter cites the Persian Gulf a vital interest of the United States, the Carter Doctrine.

February 23: UN commission arrives in Iran to settle hostage crisis.

April 7: United States severs diplomatic relations with Iran.

April 25: Mission to rescue hostages in Teheran is aborted.

June 16: United States warns West Germany about Soviet attempt to freeze U.S. missile deployments.

June 25: Congress approves Carter's request to revive selective service system.

July 1: West German Chancellor Helmut Schmidt visits Moscow to discuss détente.

July 19: United States and fifty-eight other states boycott Moscow Olympics.

August 13: Polish dock workers strike in the Gdansk shipyard.

September 4: Iraq invades Iran; Iran-Iraq war begins.

November 8: Ronald Regan is elected president; George H.W. Bush is vice president.

Reagan Presidency
1981

January 20: American hostages in Iran freed hours after President Reagan takes oath of office.

February 18: President Reagan promotes lower taxes, welfare cuts, increased defense spending.

February 24: Military coup attempt in Spain fails.

February 25: United States vetoes UN human rights report critical of American allies.

March 2: United States increases aid to El Salvadoran government.

March 3: United States announces it will honor SALT I and SALT II treaties.

March 9: Reagan rejects Soviet proposal to freeze medium-range missile deployments in Europe.

March 30: Reagan wounded in failed assassination attempt.

April 1: United States suspends aid to Nicaragua.

April 12: Columbia, first space shuttle, is launched.

April 24: United States ends grain embargo against Soviet Union.

April 24: United States announces creation of a Persian Gulf Command to implement the Carter Doctrine.

May 10: François Mitterrand elected president of France.

June 7: Israeli jets destroy Iraqi nuclear reactor.

July 29: Iranian president Bani-Sadr ousted, Muslim radicals monopolize power.

August 9: United States resumes production of neutron bomb.

August 19: U.S. Navy jets shoot down two Libyan jets.

October 2: Reagan announces MX missile and B-1 bomber programs.

October 24: Large-scale antinuclear rallies in Western Europe.

November 18: Reagan advocates "zero option" for long-range nuclear forces.

November 23: Reagan authorizes CIA to aid antigovernment Contras in Nicaragua.

November 30: Geneva missile talks begin.

December 13: Polish government declares martial law.

December 14: Israel annexes Golan Heights.

December 23: United States imposes sanctions on Soviet Union to protest Polish martial law.

1982

January 19: Japan and European allies reject economic sanctions against Poland and Soviet Union.

January 26: United States links superpower arms negotiations to resolution of Polish crisis.

March 10: United States embargoes trade with Libya.

March 25: Argentine commandos seize South Georgia Island.

April 2: Argentina invades British-owned Falkland Islands, Falkland Islands War begins.

April 30: United States announces support for Britain in Falklands War.

April 25: Israel returns Sinai to Egypt.

April 28: UN General Assembly condemns Israel and U.S. support for Israel.

May 5: Hungary joins the International Monetary Fund (IMF).

May 9: Reagan proposes Strategic Arms Reduction Talks (START) with the Soviet Union.

June 6: Israel invades Southern Lebanon.

June 14: Argentine forces on Falklands surrender, Falkland Islands War ends.

June 27–August 6: U.S. diplomat Philip Habib negotiates cease-fire in Lebanon.

June 29: START talks begin in Geneva.

August 20: United States orchestrates debt payment plan for Mexico.

September 1: Reagan sends U.S. Marines to Lebanon to join French and Italian peacekeepers.

October 8: Polish government bans trade unions.

November 10: Soviet president Leonid Brezhnev dies, Yuri Andropov succeeds him.

December 21: Reagan signs the Boland Amendment, barring funds for the overthrow of the Nicaraguan government.

1983

January 20: France and West Germany reaffirm support for NATO and INF deployments.

March 6: West German Chancellor Helmut Kohl reelected.

March 8: President Reagan delivers "Evil Empire" speech.

March 23: Reagan unveils his Strategic Defense Initiative (SDI).

March 30: United States proposes INF limitations, Moscow rejects proposals.

April 18: Terrorists bomb U.S. embassy in Beirut, 63 killed.

May 3: Congress bans covert aid to Nicaraguan contras.

July 5: United States imposes tariffs on specialty steels.

July 21: Polish government ends martial law.

July 28: House votes to cut off covert aid to Contras.

August 21: Philippine opposition leader Benigno Aquino assassinated.

August 26: Soviet Union offers to destroy SS-20 missiles withdrawn from Europe.

September 1: Soviet aircraft shoots down South Korean passenger jet.

September 26: Reagan makes new INF proposal, Soviet Union rejects it.

October 23: Suicide truck bomb destroys U.S. Marine barrack in Beirut, 241 killed.

October 25: U.S. forces invade Grenada, Thatcher government in Britain outraged.

November 23: U.S.-Soviet arms control talks collapse.

December 4: U.S. and Syrian forces clash in Lebanon.

1984

January 13: EEC retaliates against U.S. steel tariffs.

January 16: Reagan offers new flexibility in arms control talks.

February 9: Soviet President Andropov dies, Konstantin Chernenko replaces him.

February 15: U.S. General Leamon Hunt assassinated in Rome.

April 3: Secretary of State George Schultz advocates preemptive action against terrorists.

April 4: U.S. mining of Nicaraguan ports revealed.

April 26–May 1: Reagan makes five day visit to China.

May 7: Soviet Union boycotts Los Angeles Olympic games.

May 10: Danish parliament refuses deployment of NATO INF missiles.

June 20: Nunn Amendment to reduce American troops in Europe is defeated.

June 25: United States and Nicaragua conduct peace talks in Mexico.

September 1: Nicaragua shoots down Contra helicopter, two Americans killed.

September 20: Bomb attack on U.S. embassy annex in Aukur, northeast of Beirut, twenty-four killed.

September 24: Reagan urges new superpower arms talks.

October 12: IRA bomb attack attempts assassination of British Prime Minister Thatcher.

October 12: Boland Amendment II prohibits U.S. aid to Contras.

October 23: Philippine government officials accused of Aquino assassination.

October 31: Indian Prime Minister Indira Gandhi assassinated by Sikh bodyguards.

November 6: President Reagan reelected.

November 22: United States and Soviet Union announce new arms to begin January 7.

November 26: United States and Iraq reestablish diplomatic relations.

1985

January 2: Reagan urges Japan to open markets.

January 10: United States and EEC set quotas for steel pipes and tubes.

March 10: Soviet chairman Chernenko dies, Mikhail S. Gorbachev succeeds him.

April 7: Gorbachev announces moratorium on intermediate-range missile deployments.

April 24: House rejects aid request for Contras.

May 1: Reagan slaps trade embargo on Nicaragua.

May 5: Reagan visits Bitburg military cemetery in Germany.

June 11: Gorbachev advocates reform of the Soviet economy.

July 8: Reagan charges Iran, Libya, North Korea, Cuba, and Nicaragua with supporting terrorism.

August 30: Polish Solidarity leader, Lech Walesa calls for negotiations with government.

September 9: United States imposes limited trade sanctions on South Africa.

October 1: Israeli jet destroy PLO headquarters in Tunis.

October 7: Palestinian terrorists hijack cruise ship Achille Lauro, kill one American.

October 10: U.S. Navy jet intercept plane carrying Achille Lauro hijackers.

November 1: Netherlands announces it will accept U.S. medium-range missiles.

1986

January 28: Space shuttle *Challenger* explodes.

February 25: Widespread protests of election fraud forces President Ferdinand Marcos to flee the Philippines, Corazon Aquino becomes president.

March 27: West Germany agrees to cooperate in SDI research.

April 5: Terrorist bomb explodes in West Berlin night club, Reagan blames Libya.

April 14: U.S. planes bomb five targets in Libya.

April 26: Chernobyl power plant in Ukraine has worst nuclear accident in history.

August 30: American correspondent Nicholas Daniloff arrested in Moscow.

October 4: Nicaragua shoots down U.S. plane.

October 5: London *Times* reports that Israel possesses nuclear weapons.

October 11–12: Reagan and Gorbachev discuss massive arms reductions at Reykjavík but conclude nothing.

November 3: Lebanese magazine reveals that U.S. had arms-for-hostages deal with Iran, Iran-Contra scandal begins.

1987

January 25: Chancellor Kohl reelected in West Germany.

February 2: Filipinos approve new constitution.

February 19: United States lifts sanctions on Poland.

February 26: Tower Commission Report blames Iran-Contra on Reagan's casual leadership style.

February 28: Gorbachev offers to eliminate INF forces in Europe.

March 3: Secretary of State Schultz visits China and discusses economic reform.

April 1: British Prime Minister Thatcher visits Moscow.

April 13: Schultz and Soviet Foreign Minister Eduard Shevardnadze discuss INF reductions.

May 19: U.S. flags Kuwaiti oil tankers in Persian Gulf.

May 29: Young West German, Mathias Rust, lands Cessna in Red Square, Soviet air defense fails.

June 11: Thatcher elected to third term.

August 23: Baltic Soviet republics have demonstrations for independence.

August 28: Failed coup against Aquino government in Philippines.

September 7: East German leader Eric Honecker visits West Germany.

October 3: United States and Canada sign historic Free Trade Agreement, eliminating tariffs.

October 19: Iranian missile strikes U.S.-flagged tanker, U.S. warships shell Iranian oil rig.

December 2: Contras begin peace talks with Nicaraguan government.

December 8: At Washington summit Reagan and Gorbachev sign INF Treaty.

December 9: Palestinian Intifada begins in West Bank and Gaza Strip.

December 14: United States and Israel sign ten-year alliance agreement.

1988

February 4: United States indicts Panamanian General Manuel Noriega for drug trafficking.

February 17: U.S. Army Lt.Col. in Lebanon is kidnapped by pro-Iranian Shiites.

March 23: Contras and Nicaraguan government sign truce agreement.

April 14: Soviet Union signs Geneva accord for withdrawal from Afghanistan.

April 18: U.S. and Iranian navies tangle in Persian Gulf.

May 8: French President François Mitterrand reelected.

July 3: Cruiser USS *Vincennes* shoots down Iranian passenger jet in Persian Gulf.

July 11: Nicaragua expels U.S. ambassador.

August 14: Soviet Union completes withdrawal of 100,000 troops from Afghanistan.

October 5: Chilean dictator Augusto Pinochet ousted in plebiscite.

November 8: George H. W. Bush elected president; J. Danforth Quayle is vice president.

November 8: Protests in Serb province of Kosovo oppose policies of Belgrade government.

December 6: In UN address Gorbachev pledges to reduce Soviet forces by 500,000 men.

1989

January 15: The last Soviet troops leave Afghanistan.

George H.W. Bush Presidency
1989

February 6: Polish government agrees to talks with opposition.

March 26: Multiparty elections in the Soviet Union end over seven decades of Communist Party monopoly.

April 15: In China student pro-democracy demonstrations begin.

April 25: Soviet Union begins withdrawal of troops from Eastern Europe.

May 4: Hungary opens its border with Austria, thousands of East Germans flee West.

May 25: Soviet Congress of People's Deputies elects Gorbachev president of the Supreme Soviet.

June 3–4: Chinese army attacks student demonstrators in Tiananmen Square, hundreds are killed.

June 5: President Bush protests repression in China, imposes sanctions.

July 13–19: G-7 summit leaders offer financial aid to Poland and Hungary.

August 17: Gorbachev proposes autonomy for Soviet republics.

October 6: Gorbachev advises East Germany to reform its government.

October 18: Hungarian National Assembly ends Communist Party monopoly.

November 9: East German border with West Germany opens, destruction of Berlin Wall begins.

November 28: Mass demonstrations in Prague; Communist Party agrees to share power with oppostition Civic Forum.

December 1–3: Bush and Gorbachev discuss trade and arms control in Malta.

December 19: East and West Germany agree to plan for reunification.

December 20: United States invades Panama toppling Noriega regime.

December 20: Gorbachev opposes Lithuanian independence.

December 22–25: Romanian President Nicolae Ceauşescu is overthrown and summarily shot.

December 28: Elections in Czechoslovakia end Communist rule.

1990

January 23: Yugoslavia dissolves League of Communists.

February 2: South African government legalizes the African National Congress (ANC).

February 12: 2+4 Plan for German reunification is established.

February 25: Violeta Chamorro wins Nicaraguan elections, ousting Sandinista regime.

February 25–27: United States urges European Community to cope with Yugoslav crisis.

March 18: East German elections endorse speedy reunification.

May 29: Boris Yeltsin is elected president of the Russian Federation.

June 9: Reformers win Czechoslovakian parliamentary elections.

July 5: In Yugoslavia the Serb Republic assumes direct control over the province of Kosovo.

August 2: Iraq invades Kuwait; United States and Soviet Union condemn Iraq's aggression.

August 6: Bush deploys U.S. forces to Saudi Arabia in Operation Desert Shield.

August 25: UN Security Council authorizes naval and air blockades of Iraq.

September 12: 2+4 talks adopt a treaty, Settlement with Respect to Germany, for German reunification.

September 20: East and West Germany are officially reunified.

November 29: UN Security Council authorizes "all necessary means" to end Iraqi occupation of Kuwait.

December 2: Germany hold first elections since reunification; Chancellor Kohl's Christian Democrats win.

1991

January 12: Congress authorizes military force against Iraq.

January 16: Operation Desert Storm begins; twenty-eight-nation coalition begins the liberation of Kuwait.

February 23–28: One hundred-hour ground offensive against Iraqi forces in Kuwait ends in Iraqi defeat.

March 3: Iraqi military signs UN cease-fire terms.

March 6: In a speech to Congress Bush heralds "new world order."

March 6: Uprisings by Shiites and Kurds in Iraq are crushed.

April 18: Iraq accepts cease-fire terms of UNSC Resolution 687.

May 29: Bush vows to ban all weapons of mass destruction (WMD) from the Middle East.

July 31: Bush and Gorbachev sign START I Treaty.

August 16: Baghdad rejects UN oil-for-food program.

August 19: Attempted coup against Soviet President Gorbachev is defeated.

August 20: Three Soviet Baltic republics declare independence.

September 7: Croatia and Slovenia declare independence from Yugoslavia.

September 25: UN Security Council embargoes arms sales to Yugoslavia.

November 8: NATO approves post–Cold War strategic concepts.

December 8: Three former Soviet republics form the Commonwealth of Independent States (CIS).

December 23: Germany recognizes independence of Croatia and Slovenia.

1992

January 31: UN Security Council plans higher profile in preventive diplomacy and peacekeeping.

February 5: UN Security Council reinstates economic sanctions against Iraq.

March 17: UN fails to stop fighting between Armenia and Azerbaijan.

March 26: Germany suspends all arms deliveries to Turkey.

April 6: United States and European Community recognize Bosnia-Herzogovina.

April 24: UN sends observers to Somalia to monitor cease-fire.

May: France and Germany agree to 35,000 member joint military force under NATO.

May 23: United States agrees with Russia, Belarus, Kazakhstan, and Ukraine to abide by START I.

June 2: UN sends peacekeeping force to Sarajevo.

July 3: Croats in Bosnia proclaim an independent state.

July 16: Germany's central bank raises interest rates.

August 6: United States seeks humanitarian aid for Sarajevo, rejects military action.

August 27: EC-UN conference fails to end fighting in Bosnia.

September: Britain withdraws from EMS due to Sterling's crash against the Deutschmark.

October 3: United States airlifts food and medicine to Sarajevo.

November 3: William Clinton is elected president; Albert Gore Jr. is vice president.

November 25: Czechoslovakian assembly votes for separate Czech and Slovak republics.

December 3: UN approves U.S.-led humanitarian mission to Somalia.

December 17: United States, Canada, and Mexico sign North American Free Trade Agreement (NAFTA).

December 17: Germany provides Russia with debt-relief and housing finance.

1993

January 3: United States and Russia sign START II Treaty.

Clinton Presidency
1993

January 27: Haiti refuses UN human rights observers.

February 27: Radical Islamist terrorists bomb the World Trade Center in New York.

February 28: United States drops food and medical supplies to Bosnian Muslims.

April 19: Fighting breaks out between Muslims and Croats in Bosnia.

May 1: UN and NATO reject President Clinton's lift-and-strike proposal for Bosnia.

May 28: United States renews Chinese most favored nation status.

June 16: Rival Bosnian factions reject Vance-Owen Peace Plan.

June 21: U.S. Supreme Court authorizes forcible return of Haitian refugees.

June 26: United States launches missile attack against Iraqi intelligence headquarters.

August 18: U.S. State Department designates Sudan a terrorist state.

August 25: United States imposes trade sanctions on Pakistan and China.

September 13: Israel and the Palestinian Liberation Organization sign the Oslo Accords.

September 27: Clinton asks UN to limit peacekeeping but to promote free trade.

October 3: U.S. Delta and Army Ranger troops attacked by Somali guerillas.

October 6: Clinton orders U.S. troops out of Somalia.

October 22: NATO adopts Partnership for Peace program.

November 1: The Maastricht Treaty on European Union comes into effect.

1994

January 1: Mexican rebels seize towns in the state of Chiapas.

February 3: United States ends trade embargo against Vietnam.

February 28: NATO jets shoot down Serb aircraft over Bosnia.

March 29–April 11: NATO aircraft bomb Serb artillery positions in Bosnia.

April 30: United States ends restrictions on arms sales to Taiwan.

May 13: Five-nation Contact Group issues peace plan for Bosnia.

June 8: United States agrees to help humanitarian mission in Rwanda.

July 31: UN approves U.S.-led intervention in Haiti.

August 10: United States and North Korea agree to inspections of North Korean nuclear facilities.

October 4: Clinton attempts to revive Northern Ireland peace talks.

October 26: Israel and Jordan sign a peace treaty.

November 21–28: Lack of NATO unity permits Serbs to continue aggression in Bosnia.

December 1: Senate approves World Trade Treaty, World Trade Organization (WTO) is created.

December 9: Russian forces seal the border of Chechnya.

December 27: Russia uses massive force against rebels in Chechnya.

1995

January 20: Russia prematurely declares victory in Chechnya.

January 31: U.S. Treasury intervenes in Mexico's financial crisis.

March 20: Bosnian cease-fire is broken.

March 20: Japanese terrorist cult releases nerve agent in Tokyo subway: 8 die and 4,700 are injured.

April 18: Fighting in Rwanda intensifies.

May 1: United States imposes trade embargo on Iran for assisting terrorism and seeking nuclear weapons.

June 16: China recalls its ambassador from Washington.

July 11: Serb atrocities in Srebrenica provoke international outrage.

July 30: Russian signs peace accord with Chechen rebels.

September 5–28: NATO conducts air raids against Serb military installations.

September 5: French nuclear tests at Mururoa Atoll provoke international protest.

September 5: NATO develops plans to admit new members.

September 24: Israel and Palestinian representatives sign Oslo II Accord.

November 4: Israeli Prime Minister Yitzhak Rabin is assassinated.

November 14: Terrorist bomb kills five Americans in Riyadh, Saudi Arabia.

November 21: Clinton signs Dayton Peace Accord with Serb, Croat, and Bosnian leaders.

1996

January 28: Russian forces launch new offensive in Chechnya.

March 7–25: China conducts missile tests in Taiwan Strait; Clinton reinforces U.S. naval forces in the region.

March 12: Clinton signs Helms-Burton Act restricting third nation trade with Cuba.

March 13: President Yeltsin orders an end to Russian war in Chechnya.

April 3: U.S. Secretary of Commerce Ron Brown dies in a plane crash in Croatia.

April 24: Clinton signs antiterrorist legislation.

May 6: New constitution ends apartheid in South Africa, establishes electoral democracy.

June 25: Terrorist bomb destroys apartment block in Dhahran, Saudi Arabia; nineteen Americans killed.

June 29: Refah Party heads new coalition in Turkey.

July 3: Yeltsin reelected president of Russia.

August 9: Rebels recapture Grozny, capital of Chechnya.

September 14: Elections in Bosnia confirm ethnic divisions.

September 24: Opening of Jerusalem tunnel provokes fighting between Israel and Palestinians.

September 27: Taliban extremists capture Kabul and impose Draconian version of Islamic law in Afghanistan.

October 17: Rwandan crisis erupts anew.

November 6: President Clinton is reelected.

November 25: UN Security Council approves oil-for-food program for Iraq.

December 11: NATO approves plan to admit Poland, Hungary, and Czech Republic.

1997

February 19: Deng Xiaoping dies; Ziang Zemin becomes leader of China.

March 7: United States vetoes UN condemnation of Israel's settlements east of Jerusalem.

May 1: Tony Blair is elected prime minister of Great Britain.

May 18: Rebel forces oust regime of Mobuto Sese Seko in Zaire (Congo).

May 23: Moderate cleric Muhammad Khatami is elected president of Iran.

May 27: NATO and Russia sign *Founding Act.*

May 31: Russia and Ukraine sign friendship treaty.

June 22: Russia is admitted to the G-7 group, which becomes the G-8.

July 8: Poland, Hungary, and the Czech Republic are invited to join NATO.

August 7: United States, China, North Korea, and South Korea hold talks.

September 17: United States refuses to sign international landmine treaty.

September 26: NATO-Russia Joint Council begins operations.

October 24: Onset of Asian financial crisis.

October 27–November 10: Iraq orders UNSCOM inspectors to leave, Clinton threatens bombing.

December 11: Kyoto Protocol on greenhouse gases is signed by 150 nations; United States, among others, declines to sign.

December 18: Clinton cautions that U.S. troops will stay in Bosnia indefinitely.

1998

January 21: Clinton affair with White House intern Monica Lewinsky; affair revealed to public.

February 13: UN Secretary General Kofi Annan reaches weapons inspection compromise with Iraq.

February 28–March 10: Serb police and paramilitaries slaughter Kosovar civilians.

March 5: United States imposes sanctions on Yugoslavia (Serbia).

March 23: Clinton makes eleven-day visit to Africa, announces "African renaissance" is underway.

April 10: Britain and the Republic of Ireland reach agreement on Northern Ireland.

April 19: Thirty-four nations agree to negotiate free trade in the Western Hemisphere.

April 30: Defense Department approves a plan to develop a national missile defense system.

May 21: Indonesian President Suharto is forced to resign.

May 11–13: India conducts five underground nuclear tests; Pakistan reciprocates with five nuclear test explosions. United States imposes sanctions on both countries.

July 14: Congress eases sanctions on India and Pakistan.

August 7: Terrorist bombs explode at U.S. embassies in Kenya and Tanzania.

August 17: Clinton admits affair with Monica Lewinsky.

August 20: In retaliation for African bombings, Clinton fires cruise missiles into terrorist training camps in Afghanistan; separate cruise missile attack destroys pharmacuetical plant in Khartoum, Sudan.

August 31: North Korea successfully tests long-range ballistic missile.

September 27: Gerhard Schröder is elected chancellor of Germany.

October 8: House of Representatives votes to hold impeachment hearings about President Clinton.

October 23: Clinton brokers Israel-Palestinian Wye River Accords.

October 31: Iraq ends UNSCOM inspections.

December 16: Anglo-American aircraft launch punitive raids in Iraq.

December 18: House of Representatives approves two articles of impeachment against President Clinton.

December 21: Israeli coalition collapses without approval of Wye River Accords.

December 22: U.S.-EU trade dispute erupts over banana exports.

1999

January 1: The EU's Euro currency goes into effect on stock and bond markets.

February 12: Senate acquits Clinton of impeachment charges.

March 1: Serb forces begin "ethnic cleansing" of Muslims in Kosovo.

March 21: U.S.-EU trade dispute widens.

March 23: NATO authorizes air strikes against Yugoslavia (Serbia).

May 7: U.S. aircraft accidentally bomb Chinese embassy in Belgrade, based on outdated CIA map.

June 10: Belgrade accepts NATO's terms after seventy-eight days of bombing, culminating in a shift to targeting of civilian infrastructure inside Serbia.

July 22: China outlaws Falun Gong religious sect.

September 4: Israel and Palestinians agree on tentative peace plan.

September 11: Clinton and Ziang agree on China's membership in the World Trade Organization (WTO).

October 12: Coup ousts Pakistani Prime Minister Nawaz Sharif, General Pervez Musharraf assumes power.

October 13: U.S. Senate rejects Comprehensive Test Ban Treaty.

December 1: Antiglobalization demonstrations and riots mar WTO meeting in Seattle.

December 31: Vladimir Putin named acting president of Russia.

2000

January 1: Panama gains full control of the Panama Canal.

February 21: Russian troops recapture Grozny.

March 13: United States eases sanctions on Iran.

March 15: U.S. troops stop Albanian raids into Serbia.

March 26: Vladimir Putin is elected president of Russia.

April 14–21: Russia ratifies SALT II and CTBT treaties.

May 24: House approves Normal Trade Relations (NTR) with China.

May 24: Israel precipitously withdraws from Southern Lebanon; Lebanese Christian militias collapse; Hezbollah siezes border territory.

June 3: Clinton visits Moscow, urges Putin to negotiate revised ABM treaty.

July 2: Vicente Fox is elected president of Mexico, breaking seventy-one years of PRI rule.

July 11–25: Israeli and Palestinian leader fail to reach peace agreement at Camp David.

August 12: Russian nuclear submarine *Kursk* sinks, 116 lives are lost.

September 1: Clinton postpones development of missile defense system.

September 24: Vojislav Kostunica wins Yugoslav presidential election.

September 28: Violence erupts in Jerusalem after Ariel Sharon visits the Temple Mount.

October 6: Protests in Belgrade force Milos̆evic to concede Yugoslav election.

October 12: USS *Cole* is damaged by a suicide boat while visiting Yemen.

November 7: U.S. presidential election results in disputed vote in Florida.

December 12: U.S. Supreme Court orders end to selective election recount in four Florida counties, George W. Bush is president-elect; Richard Cheney is vice president-elect.

December 18: National Intelligence Report cites increasing terrorist threat until 2015.

2001

January 20: Clinton leaves office; George W. Bush is president; Richard Cheney is vice president.

George W. Bush Presidency
2001

February 6: Likud-led coalition elected in Israel, Ariel Sharon is prime minister.

February 16: United States and British aircraft strike Iraqi air defense installations.

February 18: FBI agent Robert Hanssen arrested for spying for the Soviet Union and Russia.

April 1–3: Mid-air collision between U.S. and Chinese aircraft over Hainan brings diplomatic crisis.

April 20–22: Leaders of western hemisphere nations discuss a Free Trade Area of the Americas (FTAA).

June 7: British Prime Minister Tony Blair reelected.

August 25–September 4: U.S. and British aircraft strike Iraqi air defenses.

September 11: Terrorist attacks in New York and Washington kill over 3,500 people.

September 12: President Bush calls terrorist attacks "act of war"; NATO invokes Article V of North Atlantic Treaty.

September 20: British Prime Minister Blair pledges British support to joint session of Congress.

September 22: United States lifts sanctions against India.

September 26: U.S. embassy in Afghanistan stormed and burned.

October 7–18: U.S. and British air and missile strikes target Taliban regime and al Qaeda terrorists in Afghanistan.

October 19–20: U.S. troops conduct raids in Afghanistan.

November 1–13: Anglo-American and Northern Alliance forces advance to and capture Kabul, Afghanistan.

November 27–December 22: In Bonn, Germany, Afghan factions discuss a provisional post-Taliban government.

December 12: Bush announces that United States will abrogate the 1972 ABM Treaty.

2002

January 28: Afghan leader Hamid Karzai meets with President Bush in Washington.

February 20–21: Israeli forces conduct strikes terrorist bases in the West Bank and Gaza Strip.

March 2: U.S. and Afghan forces begin mop-up operations against Taliban and al Qaeda.

March 11–15: Twenty thousand Israeli troops sweep West Bank and Gaza.

March 29: Israeli forces enter Ramallah and surround headquarters of Yasser Arafat.

April 4: All large towns under Palestinian Authority, except Jericho, reoccupied by Israel.

April 8: Iraq announces halt to oil exports to protest Israeli operations.

May 5: President Jacques Chirac reelected in France.

May 6: United States announces that it will not cooperate with the International Criminal Court.

May 24: Bush and Russian Prime Minister Vladimir Putin sign the Treaty of Moscow.

June 1: Bush unveils preemptive strategic doctrine in West Point graduation speech.

June 14: U.S. and British aircraft strike Iraqi air defenses.

June 24: Bush calls for new Palestinian leadership, issues "road map" for Middle East peace.

August 25–26: U.S. aircraft strike Iraqi radar sites.

September 3: Blair announces Britain ready to join U.S. attack on Iraq.

September 10: Blair declares UN diplomacy vital.

September 12: Bush tells UN that Security Council resolutions will be enforced.

September 16: Iraq agrees to weapons inspections.

September 17: United States issues 2002 National Security Strategy of the United States.

October 10–11: Congress approves military force to disarm Iraq.

October 22: Bush declares regime change in Iraq "the stated policy of our government."

November 8: UN Security Council approves Resolution 1441, calling on Iraq to disarm.

November 21: NATO invites Bulgaria, Estonia, Latvia, Lithuania, Romania, Slovakia, and Slovenia to join.

November 25: Bush signs legislation creating the Department of Homeland Security.

December 10: EU invites ten East European states to join.

2003

January 9: UN Iraq weapons inspections return mixed results.

January 21: United States warns Iraq that "time is running out."

January 28: Britain declares Iraq in material breach of UNSCR 1441.

January 29: Seven European states support United States on Iraq.

February 5: Secretary of State Powell presents Iraq WMD evidence to UN.

February 10: France, Germany, and Russia issue joint declaration for continued weapons inspections.

February 17: EU calls on Iraq to disarm; France, Germany, and Russia refuse support for military action.

February 18: Canada rejects military action without UN support.

March 1: Iraq begins destroying 120 *al Samoud* missiles.

March 7: Weapons inspections reveal no revival of Iraqi nuclear program.

March 18: Australia pledges forces for Iraq war.

March 19: U.S. aircraft and missiles strike Baghdad.

March 20: Major air strikes begin; coalition grounds forces begin invasion of Iraq.

April 4: U.S. forces capture Saddam International Airport.

April 9: U.S. forces control Baghdad; British forces occupy Najaf.

April 11: Iraqi forces in North surrender; U.S. and Kurdish forces capture Mosul and Kirkuk.

May 22: UN lifts sanctions on Iraq.

May 23: United States and Japan warn North Korea against nuclear weapons development.

May 25: Israel backs U.S. Middle East "road map."

June 4: Bush meets Israeli and Palestinian leaders in Jordan.

June 18: United States presses Iran over nuclear weapons program.

July 17: In Britain, former weapons inspector David Kelly commits suicide.

July 21: Bush cites Iran and Syria for assisting terrorism.

July 22: Uday and Qusay Hussein killed by U.S. forces.

August 1: Hutton Inquiry into Kelly suicide begins.

August 7: Sporadic attacks on U.S. troops continue.

October 2: U.S.-led weapons inspections find no WMD in Iraq.

December 14: U.S. forces capture Saddam Hussein.

December 19: Libya pledges to scrap its WMD programs.

2004

January 19: One hundred thousand Iraqis demonstrate in support of Ayatollah Ali al-Sistani.

January 28: Hutton Inquiry Report clears Blair government of wrongdoing in Kelly suicide.

February 29–March 3: Rebels oust Aristide government in Haiti; U.S. and French troops intervene.

March 2: Terror bombs target Shiites in Baghdad and Kerbala.

March 11: Bomb attacks on commuter trains in Spain kill 191 people.

March 14: Socialist leader Jose Zapatero elected prime minister of Spain, pledges to withdraw Spanish troops from Iraq.

April 4–12: Bombings and insurgency on the rise in Iraq.

April 14: Bush endorses Israel's claim to part of the West Bank, rejects Palestinian "right of return."

April 19: U.S. forces surround insurgents in Falluja and Najaf.

April 29: U.S. soldiers accused of abusing Iraqi prisoners in Abu Ghraib prison.

May 22: Fahrenheit 9/11, a film critical of Bush Iraq policy, wins Palme d'Or at Cannes.

October 9: Afghanistan holds first democratic election.

November 3: Bush wins reelection with 51.6 percent of the vote.

Contributors

Adrian U-jin Ang is a doctoral candidate in the Department of Political Science at the University of Missouri-Columbia. His primary research focuses on voting behavior and party systems and his secondary research interest is in international political economy and coercion.

David Atkinson is a PhD candidate in history at Boston University. He is currently working on his dissertation on the influence of racial Anglo-Saxonism on relations among Great Britain, its Dominions, and the United States. He is also writing a history of Harvard University's Center for International Affairs, which will be published to commemorate the Center's fiftieth anniversary in 2008.

Patrick Belton is a doctoral candidate in Politics and International Relations at Oxford University, where his dissertation deals with the foreign policy influence of United States congressmen. He is also president of the Foreign Policy Society, a foreign policy research and professional association for young national security professionals; director for the Ibn Khaldun Project for Internet Political Media; and co-director of Hands Across Our City, a non-profit organization encouraging cross-community friendship in ethnically divided cities. His publications include numerous articles in both commercial and scholarly publications, dealing with issues ranging from Middle Eastern politics to the influence of the media in elections. He is currently working on two book projects, *In the Way of the Prophet* on Muslim communities in Britain, France, and America, and *Freedom You Shall Seek,* dealing with human rights and democracy in countries making democratic transitions.

Edward M. Bennett is professor emeritus at Washington State University. He is the contributor, author, coauthor, or coeditor of ten books dealing with American foreign relations including five specifically focused on Franklin D. Roosevelt's foreign policy. He was one of ten American scholars chosen to participate in the first two of five programs in the USSR and United States on Soviet-American relations in World War II.

Zbysek Brezina is assistant professor of history at Bethany College in Lindsborg, Kansas. His research specialization is U.S. foreign policy and Eastern European exile movements. His dissertation deals with Czech politics and diplomacy during the international crisis of the 1930s.

Laura Cameron is a student of history at the University of Victoria. She specializes in international history and American foreign policy.

Dane J. Cash is an advanced doctoral candidate in the Department of History at Boston University, where he is completing his dissertation under the supervision of William R. Keylor. His main areas of research are U.S. diplomatic history and foreign policy studies in the early Cold War. The subject of his dissertation is the public and intellectual debate during and about the Korean War in the United States.

David Clinton is a professor of political science at Baylor University. His teaching and research interests include international relations theory, American foreign policy, and the art and practice of diplomacy. Professor Clinton is the author of four books and numerous scholarly articles. His major works include *Presidential Transitions and American Foreign Policy,* co-authored with Frederick Mosher and Daniel Lang (LSU, 1987); *The Two Faces of National Interest* (LSU, 1994); and *Tocqueville, Lieber, Bagehot: Liberalism Confronts the World* (Palgrave, 2003). He has also edited and contributed a chapter to *Realism in the Post-Cold War World* (LSU, forthcoming). Currently, he is working on a book entitled *International Responsibilities and American Diplomacy.*

Craig Cobane is associate professor of political science and director of the honors program at Western Kentucky University, Bowling Green, Kentucky. He earned his BA in political science from the University of Wisconsin–Green Bay and his MA and PhD in political science from the University of Cincinnati. His major areas of research include international terrorism, national security policy, and European security architecture. He has published over sixty articles/essays and is the editor of the forthcoming two-volume *NATO: An Encyclopedia of International Security* (ABC-CLIO). During the 2004–2005 academic year, Cobane was a science and technology fellow through the American Association for the Advancement of Science (AAAS). Cobane was assigned to the Office of the Under Secretary of Defense for Stability Operations (OSD/P Stab/Ops) at the Pentagon. His major responsibilities included nonkinetic counterinsurgency policy in Afghanistan and issues related to the GWOT (Global War on Terrorism).

Charles-Philippe David is professor of political science, director of the Centre for United States Studies, and Raoul Dandurand Chair of Strategic and Diplomatic Studies at the University of Québec at Montréal. Professor David is a specialist in American foreign policy, conflict analysis, and peace missions. He has also taught at Duke University as well as UCLA. He has published a dozen books in French, including *Au sein de la Maison-Blanche: La formulation de la politique étrangère américaine* (Presses de l'Université Laval, 2004), and in English, including *Foreign Policy Failure in the White House* (University Press of America, 1993) and *The Future of NATO* (McGill-Queen's University Press, 1999). He has also published articles in *Security Dialogue, The Journal of Crisis Management, International Journal, Diplomacy and Statecraft, The American Journal of Canadian Studies, European Security,* and in *Contemporary Security* among others.

R. S. Deese earned his BA in American history at the University of California, Berkeley, and his MA in East Asian history at the University of Oregon. He is currently completing his doctorate at Boston University, where he teaches courses in American history and international relations. His dissertation concerns the role of Julian and Aldous Huxley in fomenting the rise of global environmentalism in the Cold War era.

Hans Eicholz is a senior fellow of Liberty Fund, Inc., an educational foundation based in Indianapolis, Indiana. He obtained his doctorate in U.S. history in 1993 from UCLA and has taught courses in both American and world history for the California State University at Los Angeles and UCLA. He is the author of *Harmonizing Sentiments: The Declaration of Independence and the Jeffersonian Idea of Self-Government* (Peter Lang, 2001).

Murney Gerlach was educated at Lake Forest College, (BA) in government and international relations; San Diego State University, (MA) European history; and New College, Oxford University, (PhD/DPhil) in British and American history. He has served as a librarian and archivist, taught at such institutions as University of San Diego, San Diego State University, Oxford, Brown University, Roger Williams University, and University of Rhode Island. He has been a senior administrator at the University of San Diego and Brown University and a corporation secretary at Brown. He has published extensively in the areas of eighteenth and nineteenth-century American political, intellectual, and cultural history, and twentieth-century public history and museums. He has worked closely with such entities as the American Association of Museums, American Association for State and Local History, National Council on Public History, and was a consultant for museums and history entities on governance and leadership. His most recent major publication is *British Liberalism in the United States: Political and Social Thought in the Late-Victorian Age* (2001), as well as others on the presidency, elections, and foreign policy. In addition, he has been

the CEO of the Rhode Island Historical Society, the Hayes Presidential Center in Fremont, Ohio, and currently is the president of the Significance Foundation in San Diego, a public foundation helping in the areas of health, education, social welfare, and philanthropy.

Carl Cavanagh Hodge is an associate professor of political science and director of the International Relations Program at the University of British Columbia-Okanagan. He holds BA and MA degrees from Carleton University and a PhD from the London School of Economics. His is a former senior Volkswagen Research Fellow with the American Institute of Contemporary German Studies at the Johns Hopkins University and a former NATO-EAPC fellow. His books include *Atlanticism for a New Century: The Rise, Triumph and Decline of NATO* (Prentice-Hall, 2004); *Politics in North America: Canada, Mexico and the United States,* with Robert J. Jackson, Gregory Mahler, and Holly Reynolds (Prentice-Hall, 2003); *NATO for a New Century: Expansion and Intervention in the Atlantic Alliance* (Praeger, 2002);*Redefining European Security* (Garland, 1999); *All of the People, All of the Time: American Government at the End of the Century* (Peter Lang,1998); *The Trammels of Tradition: Social Democracy in Britain, France, and Germany* (Greenwood,1994); and *Shepherd of Democracy? America and Germany in the Twentieth Century,* coedited with Cathal J. Nolan (Greenwood,1992). He is presently at work on *The Age of Imperialism, 1800–1914* and *Wither Expeditionary Operations? Military Conflict from Belgrade to Baghdad.*

Arthur Holst received his PhD in political science from Temple University. He is government affairs manager for the City of Philadelphia and teaches in the MPA program at Widener University. He has written extensively on politics, public administration, history, and the environment.

Michael Kort is professor of social science at Boston University. He is the author of *The Soviet Colossus: History and Aftermath,* 6th ed., 2005 (originally published in 1985 as *The Soviet Colossus, A History of the USSR*) and *The Columbia Guide to the Cold War* (1998), and coauthor of *Modernization and Revolution in China,* 3rd ed., 2004). He has just completed *The Columbia Guide to Hiroshima and the Bomb,* which will be published in 2007.

Thomas Langston is professor and chair of political science at Tulane University. He has authored several books on the presidency, including *Ideologues and Presidents,* and *With Reverence and Contempt.* He is at work on a book about "bad presidents."

Thomas M. Leonard is distinguished professor and director of the international studies program at the University of North Florida. He has been a Fulbright Lecturer at Instituto Juan XXIII Argentina and the Institute for Advanced Studies in Mexico. His most recent publications include *Fidel Castro: A Biography* (Greenwood Press, 2004); *Encyclopedia of*

Cuban-United States Relations (McFarland, 2004); *James K. Polk: A Clear and Unquestionable Destiny* (Scholarly Resources, 2001); *United States and Latin America, 1850–1903: Establishing a Relationship* (University of Alabama Press, 2000); and *Castro and the Cuban Revolution* (Greenwood Press, 1999). In addition to a Fulbright research grant, he received other research awards from the National Endowment for the Humanities, United States Department of Education, the Andrew Mellon and Ford Foundations, and the Roosevelt, Truman, Kennedy, and Johnson presidential libraries.

John G. Martin is a graduate of the Master of Science program in Defense and Strategic Studies at Missouri State University. He performs historical and defense policy research from his home in rural Missouri. Mr. Martin is currently searching for an opportunity to work with the United States Intelligence Community as a researcher and analyst.

David Mayers holds a joint appointment in the History and Political Science departments at Boston University. His area of teaching/research specialty is U.S. diplomatic history. Among his books are *George Kennan and the Dilemmas of U.S. Foreign Policy* (Oxford University Press, 1988); *The Ambassadors and America's Soviet Policy* (Oxford University Press, 1995); *Wars and Peace: The Future Americans Envisioned, 1861-1991* (St. Martin's Press, 1998); and *Dissenting Voices in America's Rise to Power* (Cambridge University Press, 2007).

Richard Melanson is professor of national security strategy at the National War College, National Defense University in Washington, D.C. He is the author of several books on presidents and foreign policy, including *American Foreign Policy since Vietnam: The Search for Consensus from Richard Nixon to George W. Bush,* 4th edition (ME: Sharpe, 2005).

Alexander Moens is a professor of political science at Simon Fraser University in Vancouver. He teaches American foreign policy and the political and security relations between Europe and North America. He is the author of *The Foreign Policy of George W. Bush: Values, Strategy, Loyalty* (Aldershot, Hampshire: Ashgate, 2004) as well as *Foreign Policy Under Carter* (Boulder, CO: Westview, 1990). His work on European security issues includes one edited and two coedited books: *Disconcerted Europe: The Search for a New Security Architecture* (Boulder, CO: Westview, 1994); *NATO and European Security: Alliance Politics from the Cold War's End to the Age of Terrorism* (Westport, CT: Praeger, 2003); and *Foreign Policy Realignment in the Age of Terror* (Toronto: Canadian Institute of Strategic Studies, 2003). In addition, Moens has published in numerous Canadian, American, and European journals, including in *Survival,* the publication of the London-based International Institutes of Strategic Studies. He periodically contributes to U.S., Canadian, and Dutch newspapers. In 1992, Moens served in the policy

planning staff of Canada's Foreign Affairs Department and in the spring of 1999 he was a visiting fellow at the National Defense University in Washington, D.C. He is also a researcher with the Council for Canadian Security in the 21st Century, and a Fellow of the Canadian Defence and Foreign Affairs Institute. In 2002, he was appointed senior fellow in American policy at the Fraser Institute in Vancouver, BC.

Cathal J. Nolan (BA, University of Alberta; MA, PhD, University of Toronto) is an award-winning teacher of international history, American diplomatic history, and military history. He is currently associate professor of history and executive director of the International History Institute at Boston University. He is the author of *Principled Diplomacy: Security and Rights in U.S. Foreign Policy* (Greenwood,1993); *The Longman Guide to World Affairs* (Longman,1995); the *Greenwood Encyclopedia of International Relations,* 4 vols. (Greenwood, 2002); and *Age of Wars of Religions,* 1000–1650, 2 vols. (Greenwood, 2006), the first of ten planned volumes of a comprehensive encyclopedia of war. He is the coeditor of *Shepherd of Democracy? America and Germany in the 20th Century* (Greenwood, 1992) and editor of *Ethics and Statecraft: The Moral Dimensions of International Affairs* (Praeger, 1995; 2nd rev. ed. 2004); *Notable U.S. Ambassadors Since 1775* (Greenwood, 1997); and *Great Power Responsibility in World Affairs* (Praeger, 2004).

Lynn Parsons is professor emeritus in the Department of History, SUNY College at Brockport. He holds degrees from Grinnell College, Iowa, and The Johns Hopkins University. He has taught at the University College, Dublin; Grinnell College; Wayne State University; and the SUNY College at Brockport. He chaired the Department of History at Brockport from 1983 to 1988, and again from 2003 to 2004. He is the author of *John Quincy Adams* (Madison House, 1998) and coeditor of *The Home-Front War* (Garland, 1992), as well as several articles on the Adams family. He currently lives in Castine, Maine, and is at work on *Jackson vs. Adams: The Election of 1828,* part of the Oxford University Press series *Pivotal Moments in American History,* edited by James M. McPherson and David Hackett Fischer.

Sherrow Pinder is an assistant professor of political science and multicultural and gender studies at California State University, Chico. She teaches in the area of American politics. Her present research focuses on social welfare policy in Canada and the United States.

William Ruger is a fellow at Liberty Fund, Inc. Before joining Liberty Fund, he taught political science at Wesleyan University and Brigham Young University. He earned his PhD in politics from Brandeis University and holds an AB from the College of William and Mary. His areas of interest include international relations, U.S. foreign policy, and civil-military relations.

John A. Thompson is a reader in American history in the University of Cambridge and a fellow of St Catharine's College, Cambridge. His research interest is twentieth-century U.S. foreign policy, particularly the internal debates about that policy. His publications include *Reformers and War: American Progressive Publicists and the First World War* (Cambridge, 1987); *Woodrow Wilson* (Longman, 2002); and many articles in scholarly journals. His current project is a historical analysis of the dynamics of twentieth-century U.S. foreign policy.

William N. Tilchin teaches U.S. diplomatic history and other subjects at Boston University. He is the author of *Theodore Roosevelt and the British Empire: A Study in Presidential Statecraft* (St. Martin's,1997) and many essays on Roosevelt's foreign policy and related topics. He is co-editor, with Charles E. Neu, of *Artists of Power: Theodore Roosevelt, Woodrow Wilson, and Their Enduring Impact on U.S. Foreign Policy* (Praeger Security International, 2006).

Ben Zyla obtained a BA in social sciences from Uppsala University in Sweden and the University of Göttingen in Germany. His MA was in political science at Carleton University. Currently, he is a PhD candidate in the War Studies Program at the Royal Military College of Canada (RMC) in Kingston, Ontario. His research interests include U.S. foreign policy, Canadian national security policy, and European politics. He also lectures at Carleton University and RMC.

Index